CHRISTIAN SOLDIER'S BATTLE NOTES

JOHN DAVIS

© 2020 JOHN DAVIS / TIME FOR TRUTH
ALL RIGHTS RESERVED
FIRST EDITION - NOVEMBER 2016
SECOND EDITION - DECEMBER 2017
THIRD EDITION - APRIL 2019
FOURTH EDITION - 2020

WWW.TIMEFORTRUTH.CO.UK
SHOP.TIMEFORTRUTH.CO.UK

INFORMATION
ABOUT CHRISTAIN SOLDIER'S BATTLE NOTES IN ENGLAND AND THE USA

John Davis and his wife Donna

John and Donna Davis have been married for 27 years and have been serving the Lord together since they were 18. They run 'The Oaks Church' (Kidderminster, England), a ministry TfT! (Time for Truth!), and a commercial business.

WWW.TIMEFORTRUTH.CO.UK
john@timefortruth.co.uk

INFORMATION
ABOUT THE USA CONNECTION TfT!

Close friends of John and Donna Davis TfT! in the USA:
Jacob and Mary Elizabeth Phillips

Jacob and Mary Elizabeth Phillips of TfT! USA are working toward making all of the TfT! tracts and book titles available in the United States. They live in Mississippi, have been married for 10 years and have three children: Abigail, William Tyndale, and Charles Wesley. Jacob is a professional voice actor by vocation, and in his spare time is working to record the entire King James Bible in audiobook form.

jacob@timefortruth.co.uk

WELCOME TO THE CHRISTIAN SOLDIER'S 'BATTLE NOTES'

I have produced this book because it is *very much needed* in this Laodicean church age in which we are living. Generally speaking, *the church* is in a terrible state, and most Christians haven't a clue as to what is happening in these *last days* preceding the Rapture. Long gone are the days when real men, *instead of the effeminate ones we so often see in pulpits today*, got hold of God's Book and *preached, taught and lived it!* We are living in very *strange* times. (Luke 5v26)

The style and format of the book is that similar to a manual, as it is to be used frequently. *You should wear it out!*

It's a book that you need to get to know your way around, know where the relevant subjects are, so you can quickly turn to the specific pages for answers. It covers a lot of ground doctrinally, and if you **look up every Scripture**, you will increase your knowledge hugely. You will also become more *skilful* in the word of God (Heb 5v12-14). This book should become your companion, and you are encouraged to make your own notes throughout, adding to the information already there.

This book is packed with Scriptures for you to look up and get to know. I have taken much of the information from Ruckman's commentaries, among other sources. If I haven't given you the relevant credit for your work, I apologise now. I am only interested in getting the truth (ammo) out to those who need it, especially those on frontline ministry. I believe this book will be a valuable tool for you to use when dealing with all the heretics that *life* throws your way. I want to help all those **Christian soldiers** on the frontline, who are doing all they can in reaching lost sinners for Jesus Christ, while in combat with the enemy. Because of the work you are doing, the Devil will certainly send you some *false preachers, teachers and heretics* at times, trying to slow you down, and stop you from what you *should* be doing. These will come in the form of Calvinists, Post-Tribbers (aka 'Posties'), Hyper-Dispensationalists (aka 'Hyper-Diapers'), 'Tongue-speaking-fake-healing-Charismaniacs', Bible 'correctors' and rejectors, along with the usual atheists, agnostics & evolutionists etc. This is where these 'Battle Notes' will come into their own. *They* will give you the ammo you need to send these **heretics** on their way immediately. Don't get drawn into their debates, *or cross-fire*, give them a copy of *this book, or use it on them*, or even send them *my way* and I'll deal with them for you, **so you can focus on the ministry of reaching lost souls with the Gospel, as this is the most important work** (Prov 11v30). I'm doing what I can to save you time, so you don't get distracted. If you would like me to *add* sections to this book, just let me know, and I'll try to include them on the next print run. If you have other Scriptures you think would be good to add to a chapter, again, just let me know. You can email me (**john@timefortruth.co.uk**). *Every Christian ought to have a copy of this manual!*

We are fighting some of the last battles *before* the Rapture. Don't quit, keep on fighting... the Lord Jesus Christ is coming again **very soon** to rescue us. Hold on no matter what, **stand your ground** and keep looking up. Make the most out of every day, and get something out of it for the Lord. Some of our family members and friends aren't saved, we need to earnestly pray for them, trying to reach them with the Gospel. Let's do it today, while we still have some time. **Hell is real folks!**

CHRISTIAN SOLDIER'S BATTLE NOTES

This is a much needed book, especially as there are so many Christians who don't even know *where or what* the word of God is today. *Do you? Does your Bible have mistakes in it?* If it does, it certainly didn't come from God and you might as well discard it, throw it away. **I have a perfect Bible that I can trust 100%**, it's my Final Authority on all matters of faith and practice.

If you are reading the NIV, ESV, NKJV, ASV, RSV or one of the other 200+ 'bibles' that are available today, then you have been deceived, *ultimately by the Devil*, as all of those *bibles* have mistakes in them. So the first thing you want to do is get a **King James Bible** (KJV), also known as the **Authorized Version Bible**, don't get confused with the corrupt 'New King James' which is only a Satanic counterfeit. Once you have got yourself a KJV Bible, you have the perfectly preserved word of God (Psalm 12v6+7) in your hands (1 Thes 2v13), *your very own two-edged sword!* (Heb 4v12, Eph 6v17, Rev 19v15+21).

To explain my comments, let me give you a couple of examples regarding 'bibles' that have mistakes in them. Look up these verses and see the evidence for yourself.

NIV (New International Version) – Omissions (*they're not there!*) – Col 1v14 (Cf. with the KJV - *what's missing in this verse?*), Mat 17v21, 18v11, 23v14, Mark 7v16, 9v44+46, 11v26, 15v28, Luke 17v36, 23v17, John 5v4, Acts 8v37, 15v34, 28v29, Rom 16v24. **Errors** – Luke 2v33, Micah 5v2, 1 John 4v3, Luke 9v56, 11v2-4, Isa 9v3 (Num 11v25), Gal 2v20, Mark 1v1+2 (Mal 3v1), Dan 3v25, Eph 3v14, James 1v10, Mark 10v24, Acts 17v29. **Who killed Goliath?** – 2 Sam 21v19, 1 Sam 17v51, 1 Chron 20v5. **Who is the 'morning star?'** – 2 Pet 1v19 cf. Isa 14v12. **The NIV has 64,098 less words than the KJV**.

If you haven't been lazy, and you've looked up every verse listed here, you should be in total shock and ready to throw the NIV away. **Now compare the KJV with the NIV and see the total opposites**... Ps 10v4+5, Ecc 8v10, Col 2v18, Isa 9v1+3, Prov 26v22, Hos 11v12, Prov 25v23, Ps 55v18. Note also, **did Jesus sin?** – Mat 5v22. **Should you confess your sins to another sinner?** – James 5v16. Now have a look how the NIV has perverted 1 Cor 6v9. One last bow shot... **is it hard to enter the Kingdom of God?** – Mark 10v24. The NIV is based upon corrupt and perverted Greek texts. **The NIV is a Satanic counterfeit 'bible'**. If you haven't got a KJV / AV Bible then you *don't* have the perfectly preserved words of God, you've been duped. Every other version falls into the same category as the NIV, in other words, they are counterfeit 'bibles'.

NKJV (New King James Version) – This one is no better, look up the following verses in comparison with the KJV... Gen 22v8, Acts 12v4, Isa 9v3, 2 Tim 2v15, 2 Cor 2v17, 1 Tim 6v10+20, 1 Thes 5v22, Ezek 23v6, James 5v16, Rom 1v18, Col 3v1-3, Ecc 12v11, Ecc 5v8, Zech 13v6. The NKJV misses out the following words... Lord x66 times, God x51, Heaven x50, Repent x44, Blood x23, Hell x22.

For further study follow these links...

> http://www.timefortruth.co.uk/content/pages/documents/1300137286.pdf - pages 2-8

> http://www.timefortruth.co.uk/content/pages/documents/1338668238.pdf - page 17

I've given you just two examples, yet *every* 'bible' other than the **King James Bible** has errors throughout them.

Now you can see from the start that this book is going to be very *hard-hitting* and controversial. It will certainly stir up a *hornets nest* in the so-called 'modern day lukewarm church', *and this is exactly what it is intended to do!* Every leader of every church should have a copy, and so should everyone in the congregation.

I shall be covering a lot of different subjects throughout this book, but due to space, I can't go into any of them in much depth, however, I shall be giving you lots of Scriptures to look up and lots of links to follow. Our **Time for Truth!** website is packed full of information.

Time for Truth! is renowned in the UK and overseas, for standing upon the word of God (KJV) as perfect, and for *shooting from the hip*. We don't mince words, we pull no punches, *we just tell it like it is!* You may be offended by what you read in this book, *but that doesn't concern me in the slightest to be honest*, as **I am only interested in getting the truth out to the masses**. We are a frontline ministry which focuses on getting the Gospel out to sinners, unlike our Calvinistic, Hyper-Dispensational and Post-Tribulation 'friends' (enemies!) Up and down our land, churches know about us and the stand we take, we make no apology for that. I love the Lord Jesus Christ with all my heart and I am only interested in serving Him, no matter who that upsets, including my own family, friends, colleagues etc. I make mistakes like everyone, but I do the best I can with what the Lord gives me. Very soon, I shall be standing before Him... and that is a very sobering thought. He is my life, my everything, and He saved me from Hell. I love and worship Him, and I am so thankful for the opportunities He gives me.

Time for Truth! produces and distributes hundreds of thousands of Gospel tracts, booklets, books, sermon CD's and Bibles all over the world. We are concerned that **156,000+ people die daily**, with most of them going to Hell. We are doing what we can to reach those lost sinners with the Gospel. *What are you doing?* You may want to request our sample *tract pack*. We also produce a *very direct, straight-down-the-line*, newsletter called **'Time for Truth! NEWS'** – you can sign up to our *free mailing list* and receive it bi-monthly. http://www.timefortruth.co.uk/tft-news/ (If you are *easily offended* please don't bother).

We also lead a small **Bible believing church** called **The Oaks Church in Harvington** (http://www.timefortruth.co.uk/the-oaks-church/) where we focus upon preaching and teaching the word of God. Most of our sermons are recorded and can be found on YouTube...

https://www.youtube.com/channel/UCPrCgH2QTa0WRZUFBV3qriQ/videos

The **Time for Truth! Team** also run a business which helps finance all of what we do. We are a dedicated team of committed Christians living for the Lord Jesus Christ. We are expecting His return anytime now, hence why we have such an urgency about us.

This book has been designed for the **Christian soldier** who is out there on the frontline needing answers (*ammunition*), to combat his enemy. It is therefore not intended to be read like a novel, but as it is stated, 'battle notes', **giving strategic answers** to questions raised, with information available at your fingertips. (1 Pet 3v15, Col 4v6, Ps 119v46, Acts 26v2, Mat 10v18+19, Acts 4v8, Acts 17v2, Acts 16v13, Acts 13v15+16). If you **look up every Scripture in this book,** you will find them a great encouragement, help and challenge to you I'm sure. You will also find that your faith will certainly be strengthened. Study this manual of *battle notes* and get to know it. Get to know your enemy too - 2 Cor 2v11, 1 Pet 5v8.

To get the *full benefit* of this book of 'battle notes', **you *must* look up *every* Scripture**. Each time you do, you are *reloading your gun,* or *unsheathing your two-edged sword... you are now ready for battle!*

Enough said, let's get to it, brace yourself, as you're in for quite a ride...

I would like to dedicate this book to **Peter S Ruckman** (1921-2016), **a true soldier of Jesus Christ** (2 Tim 2v3+4), who taught me so much... *and still does* (Heb 11v4). In my opinion, he was the greatest Bible teacher this world has ever known.

Don't forget to visit our website:

www.timefortruth.co.uk

CONTENTS

The Holy Bible	1
Understanding the Scriptures	9
Miscellaneous	25
Knowing God's will for your life	47
Living as a Christian	51
A challenge	55
Hello Pastor	59
Eternal security	65
Jesus Christ is God	71
Evolution	79
Errors of Calvinism	93
Biblical numerics / Numbers in Scripture	107
Islam	123
Cults and false religions	143
God's not finished with Israel	159
Matthew 24	165
The Rapture and Second Coming	181
Errors of the Post-Tribulation Rapture	209
Should a Christian drink alcohol?	227
Signs and wonders, tongues and healings	237
Women in the ministry	263
Marriage, divorce and re-marriage	271
Errors of Hyper-Dispensationalism	283
The Gospel	329
A few tips that may help you	335
List of 'errors' in the KJV Bible	341
Old Testament Prophecies Fulfilled in Jesus Christ	343
Jesus Christ is NOT the Father	350

MISCELLANEOUS SUB-HEADINGS

Title	Page	Title	Page
The family of God	25	Four spirits	38
Forsaken by your family	25	The love of money	38
Culture	25	Time wasters	38
CT Studd	25	Study on 'tongues'	38
Who wrote Isaiah?	26	The brevity of life	38
Rudiments of world vs Christianity	26	Love not	38
Sow a thought – reap an action	26	Sin	38
777 – The Book of the Lord	27	Four sins you should flee from	38
The threefold nature of man	27	Your survival kit	39
Communist rules for revolution	28	The apostle Peter	39
Sodomy	28	Apostles didn't even understand	39
Lust	28	That Prophet	39
The seven stages of growth	28	You know you are saved	39
Vanity of vanities	29	How much fruit?	39
Historical proofs for Jesus	29	Five Judgments / Five Crowns	40
No need to go to Bible College	30	False teachers and preachers	40
What are you?	30	The Golden Rule of Interpretation	40
Satan is cast out five times	37	OT saints after death…	40
Time periods separated by a comma	37	It's an evil perverted world	40
Interesting	37	Cock crowing	40
List of evils in Scripture	38	Who is the Antichrist to come?	41
Three types of men	38		

THE HOLY BIBLE

Let's start with the Christian's only offensive weapon, the word of God. Now either you have a perfect Bible or you have one with *errors* in it, *as I've already mentioned in the introduction*. If *your* God *can't* give you a perfect Bible, then He *isn't* worth serving. My God can, and did, by preserving His words in the **Authorized Version**, aka the **King James Bible** (KJV). How can **God's Book**, the Holy Bible, have *mistakes* in it? How can you say things like '*The original manuscripts were perfect*', when you don't *know* that, and certainly *can't prove it!* There are *no* original manuscripts existing today. God wrote one Book and He promised to preserve every word of it - Ps 12v6+7 (cf. with NIV) I have a copy of that Book in my hands right now, it's called the **King James Bible** and it has every single word perfectly preserved as God intended. Any other *translation or version* is inferior. If you haven't got a KJV Bible, make sure you get one.

Regarding the word of God, here's a great little study. **Look up every Scripture reference**. Get to know them, underline them in your Bible with a **005** pen (http://www.timefortruth.co.uk/catalogue.php?item=37)

Read Heb 4v12, Mat 4v1-11 and note verse 4

What does the Bible say about itself? – Prov 30v5+6, 1 Pet 1v23, Ps 119v89

Who wrote the Bible? – 2 Pet 1v21, 2 Tim 3v16+17

What has God promised to do with His words? – Ps 12v6+7, 1 Pet 1v25, Isa 40v8, Mat 5v18, Ps 119v160, Isa 30v8, Ps 119v152, Mat 24v35

Answer the following questions...

Is there a miracle too hard for God?

Was the creation too hard for God?

Was the worldwide flood too hard for God?

Was the parting of the Red Sea too hard for God?

Was the 40 years of manna too hard for God?

Was the virgin birth of Christ too hard for God?

Was the collection of 66 Books of the Bible, written over a period of 1,700 years too hard for God?

Was overcoming the *human nature* of the sinful writers too hard for God?

Is preserving those words too hard for God?

Is giving us a perfect Bible for today too hard for God?

CHRISTIAN SOLDIER'S BATTLE NOTES

Inspiration is far harder to believe in than *preservation*, yet the majority of Christians today do not believe that the word of God is perfect, without error. Who taught them that I wonder?

Can God lie? – Titus 1v2, Num 23v19

God has promised to magnify His word above what? – Ps 138v2

What has Satan been trying to do with the word of God? – 2 Cor 2v17, 2 Cor 4v2, Gen 2v16+17, Gen 3v1-4, Jer 36v21+32

Satan is against God and Christians in every way possible, especially when it comes to deceiving the church into believing that all 'bibles' are the same… *they are not!*

There is one true God yet there are many 'gods' today!

One true Christ yet many 'christs' today!

One true Gospel yet many 'gospels' today!

One true 'religion', (Christianity), yet many false religions and cults today!

One true Bible yet many 'bibles' today!

What does God say about His word? – Deut 4v2, Prov 30v5+6, Rev 22v18+19, Ecc 3v14

What should we do with the word of God? – Phil 2v16, Luke 4v4

Who are you trying to please? – Gal 1v10, Acts 5v29, Acts 4v18-20, Rom 3v4, Mat 23v2-7, Heb 11v25-27

How about these two very interesting verses regarding the word of God – Job 23v12, Deut 30v10-14

Questions for Bible 'correctors and rejectors'…

Since you're smart enough to find 'mistakes' in the KJV, why don't you correct them all and give us a perfect Bible?

To you, *where* is the perfect, preserved word of God today? (*The 'originals' don't exist, therefore you've never seen them!*)

If God could overshadow sinful men to produce the perfect inspired *originals*, why couldn't He do it for the perfect preserved copies? Where does it say He can't?

I would also suggest you have a look at our tab on the **Time for Truth!** website called 'Why the AV (KJV) only?'

History of the Bible

Old Testament - 4000 BC – 400 BC

New Testament - 4 BC – 90 AD

THE HOLY BIBLE

If you are a Bible 'corrector/rejector' and you don't believe the Authorized Version Bible is perfect, perhaps you would answer the following questions...

1) Do you believe in the special providential preservation of the Holy Scriptures?
2) If not, how can you believe in infallible inspiration?
3) Would God give verbal inspiration if He did not intend to preserve them?
4) If you do believe in preservation — how? In popish monasteries or through usage of believers?
5) If preserved by believers, did preservation end with the invention of printing?
6) Did God preserve Scriptures at some times and not others?
7) If preservation did not cease with printing, was the Textus Receptus providentially guided?
8) If not, which New Testament text was providentially provided?

The Answer Book - Question Number 7 by Sam Gipp

Question – If there is a perfect Bible in English, doesn't there also have to be a perfect Bible in French, German, and Japanese etc?

Answer – No. God has always given His word to *one* people in *one* language to do *one* job; convert the world. The supposition that there must be a perfect translation in every language is erroneous and inconsistent with God's proven practice.

Explanation – This explanation comes in three parts: the OT, the NT and the entire Bible.

One – The OT – It is an accepted fact that, with the exception of some portions of Ezra and Daniel, the OT was written in Hebrew. It is also accepted that it was divinely given to the Jews. Thus God initiates His pattern of operation. He gave His words to *one* people in only *one* language. God apparently un-intimidated by modern scholarship did not feel obligated to supply His words in Egyptian, Chaldian, Syrian, Ethiopian, or any other of the languages in use on the earth at the time the OT was written. The OT was given exclusively to the Jews. Anyone desiring the word of God would have to convert to Judaism. Ample provision was made for such occurrences.

Two – The NT – It is also an accepted fact that the NT was written in Greek. Koine Greek to be exact. Again, the Lord apparently saw no reason to inspire a perfect original in all the languages of the world extant at that time. Only this time, instead of giving His Book to a nation, such as Israel, He simply gave it to Christians who were told to go out and convert the world - Mat 28v19. His choice of Greek as the language of the NT was obvious in that it was the predominant language of the world at that time.

Three – The entire Bible – It is obvious that God now needed to get both His OT and His NT welded together in a language that was common to the world. Only English can be considered such a language. The English language had been developing for many centuries until the late sixteenth century. About that time it finally reached a state of excellence that no language on earth has ever attained. It would seem that God did the rest. He chose this perfect language for the consummation of His perfect Book. First England and later on the USA swept the globe as the most powerful nations on earth, establishing English in all the corners of the globe as either a primary or secondary language. Today nations who do not speak English must still teach English to many of their citizens. Even nations antagonistic to the West such as Russia and China must teach English to their business and military personnel. Thus in choosing English in which to combine His two Testaments, God chose the only language which the world would know. Just as He has shown in His choosing only *one* language for the OT and only *one* language for the NT, He continued that practice

CHRISTIAN SOLDIER'S BATTLE NOTES

by combining those two testaments in only *one* language.

Proof that the Bible is the word of God.

The Bible is unlike *all* other 'sacred books' in that it bases its 'authenticity' and 'authority' on *prophecy.* All other 'sacred books' contain *no* predictions as to the future. If their authors had attempted to foretell future events, their non-fulfillment would discredit their writings and they would be classed as *liars and fraudsters.* Fulfilled prophecy is stronger evidence for the *inspiration* and 'authenticity' of the Scriptures than miracles. Prophecy is *not* a 'haphazard guess,' nor a 'probability' made up on uncertain data, *prophecy* is *history written in advance.* Two-thirds of the Scriptures are prophetic, either in type, symbol, or direct statement; and more than one-half of the OT prophecies, and nearly all of the NT, points to events that are future. It was because the religious leaders of Christ's day were *not* students of the prophetic Scriptures that they failed to recognize Him when He came. This is also true of Christians today who do not study prophecy – they too, will *not* be ready for the Lord's return at the Rapture. The 'requirements' for a *genuine prediction* i.e. prophecy are *five* in number...

1) It must have been made known *prior* to its fulfillment
2) It must be beyond all human foresight
3) It must give 'details' – *specific*
4) A sufficient time must elapse between its publication and fulfillment to exclude the prophet, or any interested party, from fulfilling it
5) There must be a clear and evident fulfillment of the prophecy

There were many specific predictions made by the OT prophets regarding the betrayal, trial, death and burial of the Lord Jesus. These were uttered by different prophets during the period from 1000 BC to 500 BC, yet they were all literally fulfilled in 24 hours in *one* person. Like I say, there is *no* book like the Bible. It has been said that there were 109 predictions *literally* fulfilled at Christ's *first* Advent in the flesh. One verse in every 30 in the NT refers to Christ's Second Coming. There are 20 times as many references in the OT to Christ's Second Coming as there are to His first Coming.

Prophecies Fulfilled by the Lord Jesus Christ...See page 343

There are **31,102** verses in the King James Bible. Therefore there is no single middle verse. You cannot have a middle verse with an even number of verses. However there are *two* middle verses. These would be verses 15,551 and 15,552 (Psalms 103v1+2)
Ps 103v1 **Bless the LORD, O my soul: and all that is within me, bless his holy name**.
2 **Bless the LORD, O my soul, and forget not all his benefits**:
These are the middle *two* verses of the King James Bible. Both verses start with '**Bless the LORD, O my soul**'. v1 continues - and all that is within me, *bless* **his holy name.** v2 concludes with - and forget not all his benefits. These are powerful words coming from the two center verses of the Book.
Now let's count the words in these two middle verses. There are 28 (7x4).
Now let's see if we can find some middle words in the center of God's middle verses. Yes, I see four (***bless*** **his holy name.**) There are 12 words on one side of this phrase and 12 words on the other side. So the King James Bible has ***bless*** **his holy name** right in the center of the two middle verses. This phrase also has exactly 12 words on each side of it.

What else would you expect in the center of God's Holy Bible? *Bless* **his holy name.**

THE HOLY BIBLE

Total Books in the King James Bible	66
Total chapters in the King James Bible	1,189
Total verses in the King James Bible	31,102
Total books in the Old Testament	39
Total chapters in the Old Testament	929
Total verses in the Old Testament	23,145
Total books in the New Testament	27
Total chapters in the New Testament	260
Total verses in the New Testament	7,957
Middle book in the King James Bible	None – There are 2 – Micah and Nahum
Longest book in the King James Bible	Psalms
Shortest book in the King James Bible	2 John (verses) and 3 John (words)
Middle chapter in the King James Bible	Psalm 117
Longest chapter in the King James Bible	Psalm 119
Shortest chapter in the King James Bible	Psalm 117
Middle verse in the King James Bible	None – There are 2 – Psalm 103v1 and Psalm 103v2
Longest verse in the King James Bible	Esther 8v9
Shortest verse in the King James Bible	John 11v35

Total verses - 31,102. (3+1+1+0+2 = 7)
Total words in the 31,102 verses - 788,258
(Not including the Hebrew Alphabet in Psalm 119 or the superscriptions listed in some of the Psalms)
(Information taken from an article by Nic Kizziah)

Rejecting the word of God – Isa 5v24, Num 15v31, 2 Chron 36v16, Amos 2v4, 1 Sam 15v23, 2 Kings 17v15, Jer 6v19, 2 Kings 22v8+11+13 (2 Kings 23v1-3), (Ps 12v6+7), Ps 107v11, Jer 13v10, Jer 16v12.

NOTES

NOTES

NOTES

UNDERSTANDING THE SCRIPTURES

You will never understand the Bible unless you read it dispensationally, that's a fact, no matter who tells you otherwise. Unless you rightly *divide* the Scriptures (2 Tim 2v15) you won't understand God's Book. Calvinists, Post-Tribulation-Christians, Hyper-Dispensationalists, Pentecostals etc. are as *blind as bats* when it comes to understanding and rightly dividing the word of God. That may sound harsh, but that's the truth.

God deals with three different classes/types of people... **Jews, Gentiles and Christians** (1 Cor 10v32) and He directs the Scriptures at all of them in different ways at different times. If you take Scriptures that are aimed at the Jew and try to *apply them* to the Christian, then you'll mess up on your doctrine, e.g. 'Tongues' are *not* for today, as they are a sign for Israel (1 Cor 1v22, 1 Cor 14v22). There is a difference between gifts for the church and *sign*-gifts for Israel, if you don't understand that, you're going to mess up on your doctrine just like the Pentecostals do. If you think *healing and signs and wonders* are the same today as they were back in the apostolic era, then you are a very shallow student of the word of God. If you think that Acts 2v38 is the Gospel we should be preaching today, *you are so far off the radar it's frightening*. Acts 28v8 – this is the last miraculous healing ever performed in the NT. It's the end of the apostolic signs. Paul does not perform them at the end of his ministry – 1 Tim 5v23, 2 Tim 4v20. They are *not* in operation today.

There are **differences**, and there are **divisions** in the Scriptures, and you'd better get hold of these before preaching and teaching, otherwise you'll be led astray in error, and those you are speaking to.

What is Dispensationalism? In essence, it is God dealing with different people in different ways at different times. There are different Gospels in the Scriptures (1 Cor 15v3+4, Acts 2v38, Gal 3v8, Rev 14v6+7, Mat 4v23), they are *not* the same. The Kingdom of God *is not the same as* the Kingdom of Heaven. The Sabbath is not for the church *and never has been* – Num 15v32-36, John 1v17, Rom 10v4, Ezek 20v12+20. You are *not* saved *by grace through faith* (Eph 2v8+9) *under the law*, it was by faith **plus** works (Hab 2v4, Ezek 18v5-9+18+22+24), and you are *not* saved *by grace through faith* during Daniel's 70th week, aka the Tribulation, Jacob's Trouble – Rev 12v17, Rev 14v12. If you don't understand the *differences*, you'll never understand the Scriptures and you'll try to apply verses to yourself that are *not* directed to you. **Heresy is truth misplaced!** (Remember that). Not being able to *rightly* divide the word of truth is where Calvinists, Post-Tribbers, Hyper-Dispensationalists, Pentecostals etc. and all the cults go wrong. JW's are trying to bring in 'the kingdom' now. They have taken a truth and *misplaced* it, therefore they teach heresy. Mormons teach 'faith plus works' for *now*. They have taken Scriptures from James (notice to whom this book is written - James 1v1) and *put them* on the Christian in the Church Age, and they're not for us. One Scripture taken out of context can change everything.

There are *roughly* 8 dispensations (D)... (Some Bible teachers say *seven* & some say *nine*)

Creation to the fall – D of innocence – Gen 1v1 - Gen 3v22	Edenic dispensation – innocence
The fall of Noah – D of conscience – Gen 3v23 – Gen 8v19	Antediluvian dispensation – conscience
Noah to Abraham – D of human government – Gen 8v20 – Gen 11v32	Post-diluvian dispensation – human government
Abraham to the law of Moses – D of patriarchs – Gen 12v1 – Exo 19v7	Patriarchal dispensation – family / promise
The law of Moses to Christ – D of the Law – Exo 19v8 – Acts 9	Legal dispensation – Law
Christ to the Tribulation – D of grace	Ecclesiastical dispensation – Grace / Church Age
The Tribulation aka Jacob's Trouble, Daniel's 70th Week	The Tribulation / Daniel's 70th Week / Jacob's Trouble - Judgment
The Millennium to the eternal state – D of the fullness of times	Kingdom

Dispensations can overlap one another, with two different dispensations applying to two different groups of people. **Acts 21v20+21** – during this time the Jews *in* Israel were still under the Law... but in **Eph 3v2-5** – the Gentiles and Jews living *outside* of the land of Israel were already under grace, the dispensation committed to Paul.

Adam wasn't saved the same way as Moses, and Moses wasn't saved the same way as Paul. God dealt with them *differently*, at *different* times. No-one in the OT understood that the Son of God would leave Heaven, take the body of a human being and die on a cross, rising from the dead on the third day. **No-one in the OT was looking *forward* to the cross**, no matter what your pastor, teacher or preacher tells you. No-one in the OT was placed into the Body of Christ, or *spiritually circumcised* as they are today at conversion. You get *imputed righteousness* and *justification* as soon as you put your faith and trust in Jesus Christ for your sins forgiven, back then they received them at separate times e.g. Abraham got *imputed righteousness* in **Gen 15** and *justification* in **Gen 22**. The differences are in the dispensations, understand that.

To help locate these *time periods* you need to look at the different **covenants** in Scripture...

Edenic covenant – Gen 2-3	Edenic – 4000 BC – 3065 BC
Adamic covenant – Gen 3	Adamic – 3065 BC – 3000 AD
Noahic covenant – Gen 8-9	Noahic – 2450 BC – 3000 AD
Abramic covenant – Gen 12, 15, 17, 22	Abramic – 2000 BC – 3000 AD
Mosaic covenant – Exo 19-34	Mosaic – 1500 BC – 33½ AD (but returning for Israel in the T)
Davidic covenant – 2 Sam 7	Davidic – 1100 BC – 3000 AD (perhaps going into eternity)
Christian covenant – Mat 26 (Heb 9v15-17)	The NEW Covenant – 33½ AD off into eternity
Eternal covenant – Rev 21-22	The Eternal covenant – 3000 AD off into infinity

Covenants also overlap and some go right through other covenants while still in effect.

This next section will really help to break it down for you... No-one from Gen – Mal had anything more for a blood atonement and redemption, than the blood of bulls and goats (Heb 10v4). No-one in the OT was *cleared* of their sins, even *after* their sins were forgiven (Exo 34v7) and righteousness was imputed to them (Rom 4v1-6). No-one in the OT was placed into the Body of Christ. No-one in the OT was spiritually circumcised; none of them were born again, and none of them went to the third Heaven when they died (2 Cor 12v1-4). OT and NT salvation are certainly *not* identical. Not one man in the OT had his sins paid for permanently, or was redeemed (Rom 3v24, Heb 9v24), until *after* Mat 27. Up until Mat 27v50 everything is standing *doctrinally* in the OT. The NT is not even instituted until Mat 26v28, and even then, it was not in effect, for it cannot come into effect until the death of the testator (Heb 9v15-17). ***Technically,* Mat 1-27, Mark 1-15, Luke 1-23, John 1-19 are in the OT**. Note... everyone in those passages is under the OT Jewish Law and commandments, as given to Moses. Not one 'Christian' is anywhere to be found in the above verses/chapters of the Gospels. Not one 'Christian' was found on earth during Christ's lifetime or even in the first 10 chapters of Acts. The first early Christians in the Scriptures are nowhere in evidence *until* Acts 11v26 and then none of them are like any **disciple of Christ** before Acts 2. Christians are converted Gentiles who do not attend the temple (Acts 3v1), are not circumcised (all the apostles were), and they do not observe the Jewish Sabbath. (Rom 10v4). **Be very careful quoting Scripture, and building your doctrine on Pre-Crucifixion verses, as things changed *after* the Cross.**

Any man in any dispensation is saved by doing what God tells him to do – John 5v24, Acts 16v30+31, Acts 8v37, Gen 15v1-6, Gen 6v14 etc. God tells men *different* things, on *different* occasions.

The Lord Jesus Christ initially came *only* to Israel – Mat 15v24, but *knowing all that would happen*, He came to save Gentiles also – Luke 2v25-32.

The OT saint under the law must perform the works (Deut 28v14) as an evidence of his faith (James 2v21). These works do not justify him (Gal 3v11) unless faith accompanies them (Heb 11v39+40). He lives by *doing* (Ezek 18), and when he quits *doing* (Ps 51v11), *he has had it!* (Judg 16v20). God can take the Spirit from him permanently (Saul), or temporarily (Samson), or not at all (David), but even under the law exceptions are made (2 Sam 12v13). Grace is everywhere manifest in the life of Samson who never repents, confesses, or restores anything one time in a lifetime of continued transgression. But eternal security is unknown in the OT apart from the Psalms of David (Ps 91v14-16), who was given *sure mercies* (Acts 13v34) that other men were not given (2 Sam 7v14). Even in the OT 'the just' lives by faith, but it is **his** faith (Hab 2v4), whereas the NT believer is living by **the faith of the Son of God** (Gal 2v20). *The differences are in the dispensations.* You need to understand that. *Another example would be regarding forgiveness...* Read Mat 6v14+15 – here you are only forgiven *if* you forgive others, yet the Christian has already *been* forgiven of *all* his sins – Eph 4v32, Col 2v13. **Our salvation does not depend upon any form of works.** The key to understanding the Scriptures is to *rightly* divide them – 2 Tim 2v15.

You will get things wrong regarding doctrine if you...

1) *Add* words to a verse that are not in the verse.

2) *Subtract* words from a verse that are in the verse.

3) **Take a verse *out of context* in which it appears.**

4) *Confine* the words in a verse to the context *only*, so it will have no application to anyone or anything, outside of its context e.g. *the Hyper-Dispensationalists do this, as they don't understand **dual-application**.*

5) Interpret a passage *allegorically* or *spiritually* to get rid of the doctrinal teaching found in the verse. *Calvinists do this all the time, along with Roman Catholics.*

6) Run to the 'original Greek' (*there isn't one*) or the 'original Hebrew' (*there isn't one*) to get rid of words or distort them.

The Book of Acts – a very *dangerous* Book to build your doctrine upon!

Now if you get this, it will really help you in understanding the Bible... The Book of Acts (Note - **Acts of the Apostles**) is a book of *transition*, from Law to Grace; the Old Covenant to the New Covenant; from Nations to Individuals; from Israel to the Church. God begins to turn from the Jews in Acts 7, saved a Gentile in Acts 8, called the Apostle to the Gentiles in Acts 9, and in Acts 10, sent Peter into a Gentile household, although he was still clinging to a Jewish message. Acts is a Book that deals with 'signs and wonders' - 2 Cor 12v12. Did you get that, *signs of an apostle!* The Jews require a *sign* (1 Cor 1v22) and 'Tongues' are for a *sign* (1 Cor 14v22). Now this book of *transition* deals with **progressive revelation** in regard to the *new way* that God is dealing with people now, instead of under the law. His 'Body' has now been revealed and every person that gets saved is *baptised into it* and that has nothing to do with *water*, (1 Cor 12v13) yet Acts 2v38 is where every shallow Christian loses the plot. Now there are *no* 'healers' today and no-one speaks in tongues today, no matter what they say. Don't get me wrong, there are many deceived and deluded Christians who *think* they do, *but they don't!* Times have changed. *The differences are in the dispensations!*

The *difference* between OT and NT righteousness

Eze 3v20 **Again, When a righteous man doth turn from his righteousness, and commit iniquity, and I lay a stumblingblock before him, he shall die: because thou hast not given him warning, he shall die in his sin, and his righteousness which he hath done shall not be remembered; but his blood will I require at thine hand.** Salvation in the Old Testament is a combination of *faith and works*. The *righteousness* of a *righteous man* here in Ezekiel is *personal righteousness which he has done,* not imputed righteousness which he has been *given* (Rom 4v1-8). There is a huge difference here and you need to understand it. (See the difference between these verses to help – Hab 2v4, Rom 1v17) In the NT there is no such thing as a 'righteous man' (Rom 3v10) apart from the imputed righteousness of Jesus Christ (1 Cor 1v30). In the OT a man can forsake 'his righteousness' and 'die in his sins'. In the NT, a man dies *in his sins* when he does *not* trust Jesus Christ (John 8v24), and if he *has* trusted Jesus Christ, he *can't* die *in his sins* (Rom 8v29-39) because he has been regenerated and placed *into* Jesus Christ (Col 2v11+13). Now if you can get that you'd be way ahead of 95% of Christians who haven't a clue about *rightly dividing* the Scriptures. Have a look at these two verses also, and see the difference... Ezek 18v20, Deut 6v25.

Tribulation Salvation is NOT Salvation by Grace Alone which Paul preached, which WE preach today.

You should all know the difference between the Gospel of the 'Kingdom' & the Gospel of the 'Grace of God'. Salvation IN the Tribulation is NOT 1 Cor 15v1-4. Read Mat 24v45-51 – none of these verses are aimed at the Christian, you & me. These verses deal with 'SERVANTS'. After the resurrection, the Lord called His disciples 'FRIENDS' not 'servants' – John 15v13-15. Christ makes sure His 'friends' end up in Heaven (Gal 4v7) just like Him (Rom 8v29-39). The servants in Mat 24v45-51 have to 'endure unto the end' (v13) or they will end up in Hell (v51). That is NOT the way of salvation today! Salvation is certainly NOT the same in every dispensation, & the sooner you get that the more you'll understand the Bible. In the Tribulation, salvation is 'faith plus works' (Rev 12v17, 14v12), today salvation is faith ALONE (Eph 2v8+9).

UNDERSTANDING THE SCRIPTURES

This chart is dealing with the Kingdom of God and the Kingdom of Heaven, and when they were present.

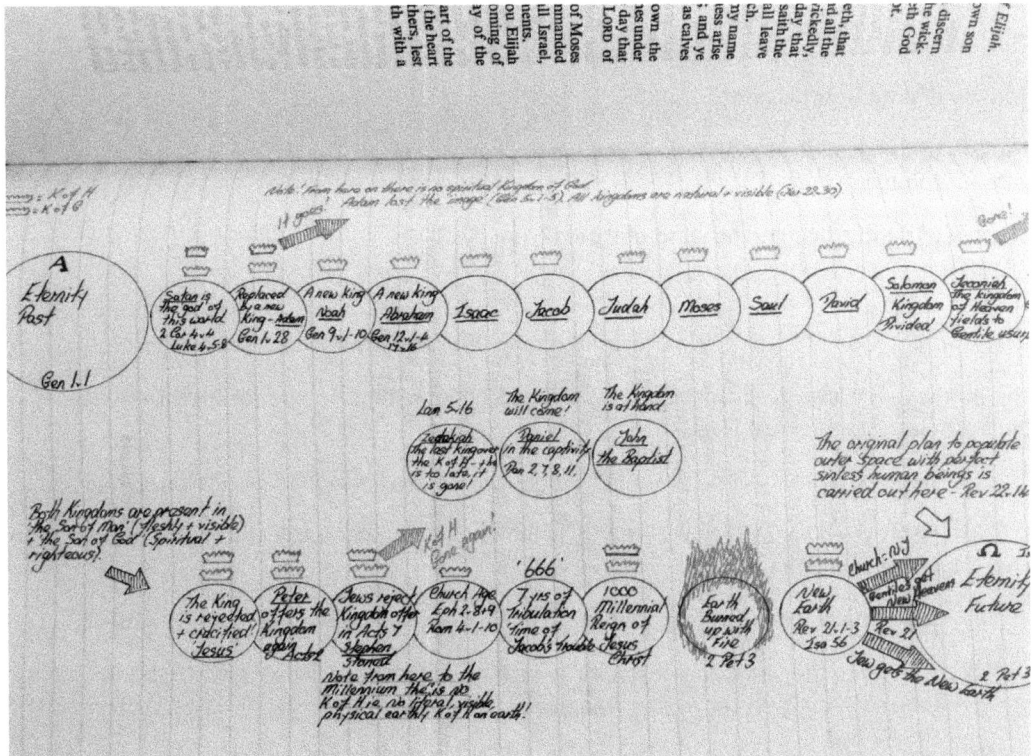

(Request a free copy of this sermon)

Biblical Hermeneutics (Laws of Biblical Interpretation) By P.S. Ruckman

This list shows you different ways of studying the Scriptures, and if put into practice, will really help you to rightly divide them.

The law of first mention

The law of literal interpretation

The law of application (fix the doctrinal meaning before any other meaning)

The law of **progressive revelation**

The law of *complete mention* (The Bible, without any reference to tradition or 'the Church', is God's complete revelation on anything important to your spiritual life)

The law of context

The law of negative discrimination

The law of agreement (never use one verse to contradict another)

The law of repetition (God repeats material for emphasis)

The law of triple reference (**historical, doctrinal, devotional**)

The law of types

The law of **double application**

The law of 'the gap' (*'yes' to those of you who are wondering!*) The Bible 'skips' periods of time without comment.

The law of rightly dividing the word of truth (2 Tim 2v15)

The Causes of *wrong* Interpretations

The hermeneutic laws given above can be violated by four simple operations which all educated Bible scholars, saved or lost, use…

1) To prove a theory or proposition, you *add* words to a verse that are not found there

2) To prove *you* are the final authority in interpretation, you *subtract* words from a verse to prove your point

3) You *remove* a verse from its *context* to make it mean *anything* you want it to mean

4) You run to the 'original autographs' (which do *not* exist) to prove that 'THE' Greek (there is no such thing on earth) says whatever you want a verse to say. As long as you get rid of the AV *text*.

(I would recommend purchasing 'The Bible Believer's Guide to Dispensationalism' by David E Walker and 'How to Teach Dispensational Truth' by Peter S Ruckman)

Application of Scripture

You can apply each verse of Scripture **historically, doctrinally or devotionally**.

1) **Historical** – it happened in history as it said it happened, where it happened, like it said it would happen.

2) **Doctrinal** – every verse in the Bible is aimed at a specific person, for a specific reason, to teach a specific truth.

3) **Inspirational** (devotional) – Since all Scripture is profitable for doctrine, reproof, correction, for instruction in righteousness, every verse of Scripture has a spiritual application which can be used to correct or instruct people.

UNDERSTANDING THE SCRIPTURES

The Old Testament (OT) and the New Testament (NT) compared

The Holy Spirit

OT – Holy Spirit could leave a person and did not perform His sealing work – 1 Sam 10v5+6, 16v14, 18v10, 19v9, Ps 51v11

NT – Holy Spirit abides with the believer forever and seals him – Eph 1v13, 4v30, John 14v16+26, 15v26, 16v7

Content of message

OT – Adam (don't eat), Noah (build an ark), Abraham (believe and offer your son), Moses (keep the Law). 'Works' are an integral part of the OT sacrificial system – Deut 6v25, Exo 19v8, Ezek 3v20, Ezek 18, Num 5v3.

NT – Believe on the sacrificial atoning death of Jesus Christ and His resurrection for complete redemption. Justified by faith. The 'works' of the law *cannot justify* in this age (dispensation) – Rom 3v21+22, Gal 3v11-13, Eph 2v8+9, 1 Cor 15v1-4, Rom 10v4, Rom 7v4, Gal 5v4, Gal 2v16, Titus 3v5, 2 Tim 1v9.

Day, place and manner of worship

OT – Sabbath a sign for the Jewish nation (Exo 31). Jerusalem chosen for the place of worship, and the temple is the habitation of God – 1 Kings 8v12+18+29, Deut 15v20, 2 Chron 7v12.

NT – The first day of the week for believers. The temple of the Christian is the body – John 20v1+19, Acts 20v7+18, 1 Cor 16v2, 1 Cor 3v16, 6v19.

After death

OT – saints went to Abraham's Bosom – Luke 16, Eph 4, Job 3v17+18, Ezek 31v15, Isa 14v11, Gen 44v31, Job 17v13, Isa 38v10

NT – saints go directly into the presence of their Saviour Jesus Christ in Heaven – 2 Cor 5v1-8, Phil 1v23

The NT covenant between God and His people was not set forth until Mat 26 and was not put into effect until Christ died at Calvary. This means that everything in Mat 1-25 has to do with the culmination of God's dealings with man under the OT covenant, not the new. Heb 9v16+17 – the NT is in effect at Mat 27v50, but it is not fully understood until Acts 15v11, where an official meeting of the leaders in the Body of Christ finally establishes what is meant by the Gospel – Acts 15v22+25+28.

Salvation by faith and works

Read Mat 19v17 and note that entering into life is based upon keeping the commandments. Now compare that verse with Gal 2v16, Eph 2v8+9, Rom 6v23. See the difference? Salvation is different in different dispensations. Under the OT, men were commanded to keep the law and many of them did – Deut 7v9, Exo 34v7, Josh 22v2, Judg 2v17, 1 Kings 11v34, 2 Kings 8v6, 1 Kings 3v3, 2 Chron 34v2. Keeping the law was never equated with sinlessness, but was the order that determined a man's personal righteousness – Deut 6v25.

Here are some verses that teach a faith and works salvation in the Tribulation – Rev 12v17, Rev 14v12, James 1v12+27, 2v24, 4v4+11, 5v7-9+12+19+20, 1 Pet 1v5+7+9+13+20, 2v3+8+12, 4v5+7+13+17+19, 5v1+4+10, 2 Pet 2v20, 1 John 2v3-9+13+14+17+18+24+28.

Note on Mat 25 – Not one member of the Body of Christ is in this entire chapter. These virgins do not go to *marry* the bridegroom, they go to *meet* Him, because He is *already married* – Luke 12v36. The Bride of Christ is never referred to as 'virgins' plural (Eph 4v4). She is one chaste virgin espoused to Christ (2 Cor 11v2). These 'virgins' are mentioned in Ps 45v14 and S of S 1v3, 6v8 as 'separate from' the Bride. In the comparison passage – Luke 12v35-37, these 'virgins' are 'men' who are servants. They are Jews. These Jewish male virgins show up in the Tribulation (aka Daniel's 70th Week, Jacob's Trouble) Rev 14v1-4 cf. Rev 7v4-8. Their salvation is connected with 'works' (Rev 12v17) which is why some of them *can lose it* (like they could in the OT – Judg 16v20, Ps 51v11).

The literal earthly throne of David where Christ shall sit – It is a literal, visible throne on Mount Zion in Jerusalem – Luke 1v32, Mat 19v28, Isa 9v7, 2 Sam 7v12-16, Ezek 37v24+25, 2 Sam 3v10, 1 Kings 1v35, 1 Kings 2v12, Ps 59v13, Ps 122v5, Ps 132v11, Isa 12v6, 24v23, Jer 3v17, Rom 15v12, Mat 25v31, Zech 14v9.

The first man saved the *same way* as you – Acts 8v26-39. It is Philip who first applies Calvary to the sins of the individual (Isa 53), this making the Ethiopian eunuch the first man in the NT who is saved exactly as every Christian has been saved since then. He also goes to Heaven when he dies, unlike the thief on the cross.

Acts 14v48 – The people who are ordained to eternal life in this verse, are ordained on the basis of 'works'. Read Acts 13v42-48. The Gentiles responded correctly to the light they had, and God rewarded that response by allowing them to believe the Gospel for salvation. The Jews responded with envy and blasphemy to Paul's preaching in Acts 13v45. *See the differences?*

Words can have different meanings...

Whenever you see the word '**saved**' in Scripture, it does not *always* mean saved from Hell. Here are some examples of different meanings for the words ***save*** and ***saved***...

1) Mat 10v22, 24v13 – relating to the preservation of life (Mark 13v20) and eternal salvation by endurance and refusal of the mark of the beast – Rev 22v14, 12v17, 14v12

2) Mat 27v42 – physical salvation and deliverance from death
3) Luke 1v71 – relating to deliverance from enemies
4) Luke 18v42 – physical healing
5) 1 Pet 3v20, 2 Pet 2v5, Acts 27v20+31 – natural disasters
6) Rom 11v26 – natural salvation/deliverance of Israel from the Antichrist
7) 1 Tim 2v15 – saved from deception
8) Jude 5 – deliverance of Israel from Egypt
9) Rev 21v24 – relating to the corporate nations that followed Christ during the Millennium

Here's another example regarding the word 'elect' – this is where the Calvinists go wrong.

The word **elect** in the Scriptures can mean the following…

1) Jesus Christ – Isa 42v1, 1 Pet 2v6
2) Jews / Israel – Isa 45v4, 2 Tim 2v10
3) Angels – 1 Tim 5v21
4) Individuals – Col 3v12, 2 John 1v1+13
5) Church – 1 Pet 1v1+2

Seven resurrections

1) Resurrection of Jesus – Mat 28v1-6
2) Resurrection of OT saints – Mat 27v52+53
3) Spiritual resurrection of the believer – Eph 2v1-6
4) Physical resurrection of believers at the Rapture – 1 Cor 15v49-55
5) Resurrection of OT saints physically – Ezek 37
6) Resurrection of Tribulation saints – Rev 11v12, Rev 7v9
7) Resurrection of unsaved dead – Rev 20v11-15

Seven baptisms

1) Baptism unto Moses in the cloud and sea – 1 Cor 10v1-3
2) Water baptism of John to Israel – Mat 3v11, John 1v31
3) Baptism of physical suffering – Mat 20v22

4) Peter's water baptism for Israel in the name of Jesus – Acts 2v38

5) Apostles water baptism for Gentiles in the name of the Trinity – Mat 28v19

6) Baptism of the lost in 'fire' – Mat 3v11

7) Saving baptism of the Holy Spirit – Eph 4v5, 1 Cor 12v13

The Church is *both* the Body and the Bride of Christ and therefore a mystery – Eph 5v32, Mat 19v4, Gen 2v23+24, 1 Cor 12v27, 2 Cor 11v2, Gal 4v26, Eph 5v23-32. There are two brides. **Israel** is God the Father's wife – Isa 54v5-8, and **the Church** is the Lamb's wife – Rev 21v2+9, Rev 22v17, Gal 4v26. Israel has been out of fellowship with God since rejecting her Messiah (Acts 7v55-60) but that fellowship will be restored at the Second Advent. Isa 2v1-4, Rom 11v25-27 referring to the nation of Israel.

Spiritual circumcision study

Col 2v11+12, Luke 16v23+24, Lev 5v2+4, Lev 7v18, Lev 23v30, Isa 51v23

OT – Rom 6v6+12+13 – Ezek 18v4+20, Ezek 3v20, John 8v24, Rev 21v8

NT – Rom 6v15, 7v17-25, Rom 6v2-7+18+22, Rev 21v8

Phil 3v21, 1 Cor 15v50-54, Rom 8v23-29

Soul touching – Lev 5v2, 7v21, 22v6 – 1 Kings 17v21+22

Soul departing – Gen 35v18, 2 Tim 4v6-8, Phil 1v23

Seven mysteries

1) The incarnation, God in the flesh – 1 Tim 3v16

2) Christ indwelling – Col 1v27

3) Body of Christ – Eph 5v32, 3v1-5

4) Blindness of Israel – Rom 11v25

5) Mystery of iniquity – 2 Thes 2v7

6) Rapture 1 Cor 15v51

7) Babylon the Great – Rev 17v5

A few notes regarding the Book of Revelation (Rev)

Written 91AD-96AD *after* the destruction of Jerusalem (70AD)

The Book of Rev is *not* a continual, progressive, historical description of the Tribulation (Jacob's Trouble aka Daniel's 70th Week), from chapter 4-19, but it contains *four* accounts of the Tribulation and Second Coming, just like Matthew, Mark, Luke and John contain *four* accounts of His First

Coming. John is told to write the Book in *three* parts (Rev 1v19), 1) **Past** – Rev 1-3, 2) **Present** Rev 4-19, 3) **Future** – Rev 20-22.

Reading chapters 1-3 we note the following...

Historically – Rev 1, 2+3 is addressed to local churches in 90AD in Asia Minor at the time John was held prisoner on the Isle of Patmos.

Spiritually – the passages can apply to local churches, and they can be taught as giving a history of the **Church Age** from the First Coming to the Second Coming.

Doctrinally – Rev 1, 2 +3 have a Tribulation application. Note Rev 1v9 and the reference to the kingdom is a literal earthly kingdom – Rev 1v7 'kindred's of the earth', Rev 1v6 'kings and priests', 'glory and dominion' – an earthly kingdom – Rev 1v10.

In the Book of Rev, Heaven is opened *twice* – 1) Rev 4v1+2 – when somebody goes up, 2) Rev 19v11 when somebody comes down.

John writing the Book of Rev is standing ahead of the present time. He has been taken by the Holy Spirit up into a future age – his 'present' is a 'future' (Rev 1v10). The Holy Spirit has carried him ahead of the 'Day of the Lord' (Second Advent). John is standing with the Church Age behind him, Tribulation 'beneath' him, and the Millennium ahead of him.

Seven Judgments

1) Judgment against sin at Calvary – Gal 3v13, 2 Cor 5v21

2) The believers daily judgment of self – 1 Cor 11v31

3) Judgment of Israel in the Tribulation – Hos 2v6-15, Ezek 20v38

4) Judgment of nations at the Second Advent – Mat 25v30-42

5) Judgment of Satan at Calvary – John 12v31

6) Judgment of the world at the Great White Throne – Rev 20v11-15

7) Judgment of angels – 1 Cor 6v3

Kingdom of God (K of G)	Kingdom of Heaven (K of H)
It is the sovereignty (supreme authority) of God, which is moral and universal. It existed from the beginning and will know no end. It is over all and embraces all.	It is a dispensational term, and is used of Messiah's Kingdom on earth, but sometimes the heavenly sovereignty over the earth. It is not from or out of this world. This sovereignty comes from Heaven, because the King is to come from hence (John 18v36). It was to this end He was born and this was the first subject of His ministry – Mat 4v17. That Kingdom was rejected, as was also the further proclamation of it in Acts 3v19-26 (according to the prophetic parable of Mat 22v2-7). Thenceforth, the earthly realization of this Kingdom was postponed and is now in abeyance (suspension, temporarily inaction) until the King shall be sent from Heaven (Acts 3v20). The secrets of this Kingdom (Mat 13v11) pertained (to have reference, relate) to the postponement of its earthly realisation, on account of it being rejected.
Has God for its ruler	
It is in Heaven over the earth	
It is unlimited in its scope	
It is moral and spiritual in its sphere	
It is inclusive in its character (embracing the natural and spiritual seeds of Abraham, the heavenly calling and the church of the mystery)	
It is universal in its aspect	
It is (in its wider aspect) the subject of NT revelation	
It is eternal in its duration	It has the Messiah for its King
Scripture calls it the mystery	It is from Heaven, and under the heavens upon the earth
Luke 17v20+21, Rom 14v17, 1 Cor 15v50	
The K of G is the reign of God in the universe over all His created creatures and includes time and eternity, heaven and earth. It is spiritual, and cometh not with observation. It is entered by the new birth (John 3v5), and is not meat and drink, but righteousness, peace and joy in the Holy Ghost.	It is limited in its scope
	It is political in its sphere
	It is Jewish and exclusive in its character
	It is national in its aspect
	It is the special subject of OT prophecy
	It is dispensational in its duration
See also TfT! NEWS issue 41 pg 4	Scripture calls it 'the mysteries' – Mat 19v28
See also The Ministry Years Volume 2 pg 434	The K of H is mentioned 32 times in Matthew.
	The K of H merges into the K of G when Christ, having put all enemies under His feet, shall have delivered up the K of G, even to the Father – 1 Cor 15v24-28
	See also TfT! NEWS issue 41 pg 5

The King shall come through the line of Judah – Gen 49v8-10. The King (the Lord Jesus Christ) shall reign and rule in the Kingdom seated on David's Throne. 2 Sam 7 (v16). God promised this to David – Ps 89v3+4+35-37. Jer 23v5+6, Isa 11v1+2, Luke 2v40, Isa 9v6+7, Luke 1v26-33. The Throne of David was on earth; it is now vacant and has been for 2500 years, but when the 'times of the Gentiles' have run their course, and the time has come to set up again the 'Tabernacle (house) of David', which has fallen down (Acts 15v13-18), the 'Throne of David' will be re-established and given to Jesus Christ.

The OT Scriptures teach that there is to be an earthly and visible Kingdom over which the Son of Man is to rule – Dan 7v13+14, Dan 2v34+35+44+45, Jer 23v5, Zech 14v9.

There are 13 places in the Gospels where the K of G matches the K of H i.e. places where Matthew will say K of H and Mark and Luke will say K of G. John uses the K of G and *never* coincides with Matthew's K of H. The reason that **both** Kingdoms would be mentioned *interchangeably* in some cases, although they are *not* synonymous (word having same or almost same meaning), would be the fact that the King of both physical and spiritual Kingdoms, was present in the Person of the Lord Jesus Christ.

The K of G is at hand – Mark 14v42, during the earthly ministry of Christ, and the Lord Jesus even gives instructions to Nicodemus on how to enter it. This Kingdom will continue throughout the Church Age, and will be realised in full when the two Kingdoms merge during the Millennial reign of Christ.

The K of H is at hand – when Jesus Christ is on earth because He is the promised King, the Messiah that is to rule the nation of Israel, and the world in a literal Kingdom. This Kingdom is **not** at hand again until the 'time of Jacob's Trouble' (Jer 30v7), when the Messiah comes to her the *second* time (Gen 41v5, 43v10, Isa 11v11, Acts 7v13) to rescue believing Israel and fulfil the promises she thought was the program of the First Coming.

The term 'Son of Man' occurs nowhere in the Pauline Epistles. It is specifically used in regard to the earthly, Jewish title connected with Christ's earthly ministry to Israel (Ezek 1-6).

NOTES

NOTES

NOTES

MISCELLANEOUS

Interesting information that you may need at some point...

The Family of God

Eph 3v15 **Of whom the whole family in heaven and earth is named.** There are *eight* groups in God's family. **1) Saved Gentiles before the Law** (e.g. Adam and Noah), **2) Saved Hebrews before the Law** (e.g. Abraham, Isaac and Jacob), **3) Jewish believers under the Law** (Moses to John the Baptist), **4) Gentile believers under the Law** (Rom 2v13-15 – These verses give insight into Gentile salvation in the OT. 'Thousands' of Gentiles were saved in the OT, even though they had no Ten Commandments in writing (Deut 5v10, Acts 14v16+17). The story of Abimelech in Gen 20v4-9 shows you that the heathen understood God's moral code perfectly (Gen 20v9 – a pagan heathen without a Bible or the Ten Commandments *knows* that adultery is a great sin) and when they followed their conscience, God honoured their actions and showed them 'mercy' – see also Jer 40v1-4, Gen 31v24-29), **5) Church Age believers** (from Acts 2 to the Rapture), **6) Jewish believers in the Tribulation** (Rev 14v1-4 cf. Rev 7v3-8), **7) Gentile believers in the Tribulation** (Rev 7v9-14), **8) Millennial saints** (Rev 20v9).

Forsaken by your family? – Ps 27v10, Ps 68v5+6, Job 19v14, Rom 7v4, Isa 40v11, Prov 18v24, Heb 2v11

We have a culture marked by *four* things...

1) **Depravity** – Promiscuity, divorce, single-parent families.

2) **Distraction** – TV, video games, iPods, iPhones, iPads etc. – Constant distractions.

3) **Despair** – Most 'living' a pointless life. No purpose or meaning to it.

4) **Death** – Massive increase in abortion, suicide, euthanasia etc. Prov 8v36.

CT Studd said...

If Jesus Christ be God and died for me, no sacrifice can be too great for me to make for him.

What sacrifices have you made for the Lord?

CHRISTIAN SOLDIER'S BATTLE NOTES

Who wrote Isaiah? – Some say that Isaiah was written by two different people (Isaiah and somebody else, saying that Isaiah didn't write chapters 40-66), but Jesus quoted Isaiah in Mark 7v6, Luke 4v17, Mat 12v17+18, Mark 8v17, and quoted him *later than* chapter 40.

The Rudiments of the world (Col 2v8)	The Rudiments of Biblical Christianity.
(Rudiments = basic 1st principles of the world)	These rules will help your decision making.
This is the philosophy of the world.	
These are alibis that the world uses to sin.	Who do you want to please? – Gal 1v10
Christians have also used these excuses to sin.	Is it right?
We've always done it that way!	Will it please God?
Everyone else is doing it!	Does it edify?
It depends on how you look at it!	Will it bring glory to God?
A little bit doesn't hurt!	Can I thank God for it?
I know when to stop!	How will it appear at the Judgment Seat of Christ?
I have to make a living!	Can God bless it?
My conscience doesn't convict me! (1 Tim 4v2)	Would I like to be doing it when the Lord returns?
Every sin you've ever committed, you committed on one of these grounds. Man has *not* progressed in 6000 years of history, because man *never* learns from history. You sin and get 'spoilt' through the rudiments of the world, and you still choose to sin.	The rudiments of Biblical Christianity are diametrically (completely, absolutely) opposed to the rudiments of the world.
Which set of rules do you use to make decisions? 99% of people, including many Christians, want to know *'How can I justify what I want to do?'* (Read Prov 18v1+2)	

Sow a thought – *reap an action!*

Sow an action – *reap a habit!*

Sow a habit – *reap a character!*

Sow a character – *reap a destiny!*

If you can bring your imaginations into subjection to Jesus Christ, you have taken the first step to victory over sin.

Casting down imaginations, and every high thing that exalteth itself against the knowledge of God, and bringing into captivity every thought to the obedience of Christ;

2 Cor 10v5

MISCELLANEOUS

777 and 'The Book of the Lord' – perfection three times.

Isa 34v16 **Seek ye out of the book of the LORD, and read**...

'**The Book of the Lord** occurs only once in Scripture'. In Isaiah **34** (3+4=7) verse **16** (1+6=7) and the words '**Seek ye out of the book of the LORD, and read**' has **34** letters (3+4=7), which makes the third seven i.e. '**777**'

Now that is found in the English only.

The Threefold Nature of man

BODY	SOUL	SPIRIT
Carnal - 1 Cor 3v1-3	Natural - 1 Cor 2v14	Spiritual - 1 Cor 2v15, 3v1
Sight	Imagination	
Smell	Conscience	
Hearing	Memory	Spiritual insight
Taste	Reason	
Touch	Affections	

And the very God of peace sanctify you wholly; and I pray God your whole spirit and soul and body be preserved blameless unto the coming of our Lord Jesus Christ.

1 Thes 5v23

For the word of God is quick, and powerful, and sharper than any twoedged sword, piercing even to the dividing asunder of soul and spirit, and of the joints and marrow (body), and is a discerner of the thoughts and intents of the heart.

Heb 4v12

(**Tripartite** - consisting of three parts)

CHRISTIAN SOLDIER'S BATTLE NOTES

Can you see the similarities of what is happening today?

Communist Rules for Revolution	Communist Manifesto 1848
Corrupt the young: get them away from religion	Abolition of private property
Break down the old moral virtues	Heavy progressive income tax
Encourage civil disorders... and a soft government attitude toward crime	Abolition of rights inheritance
	Confiscation of property rights
Divide the people into hostile groups (race, religion etc.)	Central bank
Get the people's minds off their government by focusing their attention on sport, sex, entertainment, business etc.	Government ownership of communication and transportation
	Government ownership of factories and agriculture
Get control of the media	Government control of labour
Destroy people's faith in their leaders	Corporate farms, regional planning
Cause the registration of all firearms... to eventually confiscate them	Government control of education

Sodomy – Rom 1v24-28, Lev 18v22, Lev 20v13, Gen 19, 1 Cor 6v9-11, Gen 18, Gen 2v24, 2 Pet 2v6+7, Gen 13v13, 1 Kings 15v9-12, Ezek 16v46+47, 2 Kings 23v7, Jude 7+8.

Lust - Mat 5v27+28 - What man hasn't committed this sin? **The cure** - Ps 119v9, John 17v17, Gal 5v16, John 15v3, 2 Tim 2v22, 1 Cor 6v18, Gen 39, Prov 7, 2 Pet 2v14. The only way a man is going to stay clean in this filthy life, is by getting into, staying there, and *living in the Scriptures*. Every time you are tempted to sin, grab that Book and cry out to God to help you. We're still in this body of death (Rom 7) fighting daily against the flesh (Gal 5v17) all the way until the Rapture. It doesn't get easier in this sinful world, so we must become more disciplined, just like a Christian soldier should. If you're wandering off track, you need to get some discipline into your life. Get involved with some Christian work, physical exercise, and get busy for the Lord. Have you tracted the village, town, city where you live? That will get you started!

The *seven* stages of growth for the Christian...

'**Babes**' – 1 Cor 3v1

'**Little Children**' – 1 John 2v12

'**Children**' – Gal 3v26

'**Young Men**' – 1 John 2v13

'**Fathers**' – 1 John 2v13

'**Elders**' – 1 Pet 5v1

'**Aged**' – Philemon 9

(1 Cor 13v11, Eph 4v13, 1 Cor 14v20, Eph 4v14, Ps 90v10)

MISCELLANEOUS

Vanity of vanities, saith the preacher; all is vanity. (Ecc 12v8)

Life is vanity / futile *without* God. Everything is futile *without* God.

Here is a list of Solomon's vanities...

Works done under the sun (Ecc 1v4)

The enjoyment of pleasure (Ecc 2v1)

Wisdom (Ecc 2v15)

Leaving your goods to someone else (Ecc 2v21)

The labour of wicked people who will have to be passed to those who are 'good' (Ecc 2v26)

A man's physical life (Ecc 3v19)

A man being envied for doing right (Ecc 4v4)

A man who lives for himself (Ecc 4v7)

The failure of a leader to be appreciated (Ecc 4v16)

The love of money (Ecc 5v10)

The inability to enjoy wealth (Ecc 6v2)

Coveting – by letting your desires wander all over the place to lust after various things (Ecc 6v9)

The unsatisfied appetite (Ecc 6v7)

The laughter of the fool (Ecc 7v6)

No wonder that at the conclusion of Solomon's sermon, he cries out 'Vanity of vanities; all is vanity!' He begins and ends his sermon with the same text (Ecc 1v2 – Ecc 12v8)

Without God *everything is vanity, futile!*

Historical *proofs* for the Life of Jesus

Josephus, A.D. 93 Antiquities of the Jews, Book 18, chapter 3, section 3 (verses 63-64); Book 20, chapter 9, section 1, verse 200.

Babylonian Talmud, (A.D. 500) Sanhedrin Tractus, Folio 43a, 'Eve of the Passover'.

Tacitus, A.D. 115-117: Annals, Book 15, section 44.

Mara Bar-Serapion, a Syrian philosopher whose written manuscript has been dated between A.D. 73 and 200.

Suetonius, A.D. 120: Life of Claudius, 25.4; Life of Nero, 16.2.

CHRISTIAN SOLDIER'S BATTLE NOTES

No need to go to Bible College

John 14v26, John 16v13+14, Acts 4v13, 1 Cor 2v7-11+13, 1 John 2v27, Job 32v8, Mat 16v17, John 7v15 (Isa 50v4), Ps 25v8+9, Ps 94v10-12, Ps 119v18+97-104, Luke 12v12, Rom 8v14, Job 35v11, Job 38v36, Prov 2v6, Ecc 2v26, Dan 1v17, Dan 2v21, Mat 11v25, James 1v5, Ps 119v99+100+102+105+171.

What are you? (Shortened article) *You really do need to look up every verse.*

What is man? You are a BODY, a SOUL and a SPIRIT. Look at 1 Thes 5v23, Heb 4v12, Ecc 12v7, Ecc 3v21. Your spirit (spirit of man) is *dead* until you get born again (Read John 3). Gen 35v18, 2 Tim 4v6-8, Phil 1v23. Unlike JW's and other cults, us Bible Believers understand that we are made up of *three* parts (a picture of the Trinity). Very soon I shall step out of my *body of death*, which is corrupt, and perishing day by day, and receive a *new* resurrected perfect body.

What are you? (Full article)

1 Thes 5v23+24 **And the very God of peace sanctify you wholly; and I pray God your whole spirit and soul and body be preserved blameless unto the coming of our Lord Jesus Christ. Faithful is he that calleth you, who also will do it.** Man IS a BODY, SOUL and SPIRIT. Man was made in the image of God - Gen 1v27 **So God created man in his own image, in the image of God created he him; male and female created he them.** Man was originally made out of the ground - Gen 2v7 **And the LORD God formed man of the dust of the ground, and breathed into his nostrils the breath of life; and man became a living soul.** MAN has a BODY, MAN has a SOUL and MAN has a SPIRIT. GOD has a BODY – Jesus Christ; GOD has a SOUL - God the Father; and GOD has a SPIRIT – The HOLY SPIRIT. MAN is made in the image of GOD therefore he is a tripartite being. Most things in this world can be broken down in three's... (For a breakdown of this please see our booklet 'Jesus Christ IS God' page 5+6 and see the *imprint* of God in the universe). Most people today don't even know *what* they are. Imagine going through life and hitting your 70's and 80's and still not knowing *what* you are, and *what* the meaning of life is – *tragic isn't it!* Yet that is what you are dealing with today, people who don't care and people who are just not interested; they think that it is unimportant, yet denying *what* they are (sinful) and denying that they need their sins *forgiven,* will cost them an eternity in Hell.

The AV Bible gives us absolute truth on everything.

Note the following two verses... Eze 37v9 **Then said he unto me, Prophesy unto the wind, prophesy, son of man, and say to the wind, Thus saith the Lord GOD; Come from the four winds, O breath, and breathe upon these slain, that they may live.** v14 **And shall put my spirit in you, and ye shall live, and I shall place you in your own land: then shall ye know that I the LORD have spoken it, and performed it, saith the LORD.** God tells Ezekiel to prophesy, and He says to prophesy to the four *winds* and tell those four *winds* to come and *breathe* upon the slain. So, he prophesies to the *wind*. It is interpreted in v14... **And shall put my spirit in you** – the SPIRIT is like *wind*. Man has a spirit *in* him and everyone in the world has the same spirit. 1 Cor 2v11 **For what man knoweth the things of a man, save the spirit of man which is in him? even so the things of God knoweth no man, but the Spirit of God.** Everyone has the same spirit – the spirit of MAN. Every animal has the same spirit – the spirit of a BEAST. Ecc 3v21 **Who knoweth the spirit of man that goeth upward, and the spirit of the beast that goeth downward to the earth?** So that means there are *four* spirits. There is the Spirit of God – the Holy Spirit. There is the spirit of the Devil – an *unclean* spirit. There is the spirit of MAN – the human spirit. There is the spirit of the animal – the spirit of the beast. Man has a spirit and it is like *wind*. Now if you are *not* born again you have a spirit in you, the spirit of man, but it is a *dead* spirit. John 3v5-7 **Jesus answered, Verily, verily, I say unto thee, Except a man be born of water and of the Spirit, he cannot enter into the kingdom of God.**

MISCELLANEOUS

That which is born of the flesh is flesh; and that which is born of the Spirit is spirit. Marvel not that I said unto thee, Ye must be born again. So if a man is *unsaved* he has a *dead* spirit within him. Eph 2v1 **And you hath he quickened, who were dead in trespasses and sins**; An *unsaved* man has a *live soul* but a *dead spirit.*

Now the SOUL, what is that like? Read Luke 16v19-31. Note verses 23+24. **In Hell the rich man lifted up his eyes**; That SOUL has eyes and a tongue etc. That SOUL has a *bodily shape*. Read Rev 6v9 **And when he had opened the fifth seal, I saw under the altar the souls of them that were slain for the word of God, and for the testimony which they held**: Now look at Rev 6 verses 10+11... **And they cried with a loud voice, saying, How long, O Lord, holy and true, dost thou not judge and avenge our blood on them that dwell on the earth? And white robes were given unto every one of them; and it was said unto them, that they should rest yet for a little season, until their fellow servants also and their brethren, that should be killed as they were, should be fulfilled.** See that? A SOUL can wear a robe. If a SOUL with a robe on, walked into the room you were in and then took off the robe, you would see nothing underneath it. People call that a 'ghost!' That is why 'Casper' (the so-called friendly ghost) always wears white linen, because of Rev 19v8 **And to her was granted that she should be arrayed in fine linen, clean and white: for the fine linen is the righteousness of saints**. So when folks draw a ghost, they put a white sheet on him. See how advanced THE BOOK is! So the SOUL has a bodily shape. Let's illustrate this using a football... The outer casing is leather (which represents your BODY, flesh) and inside that leather is an inner-tube. The inner-tube is *shaped* just like the football. That inner-tube represents your SOUL. Inside the inner-tube is AIR i.e. representing your SPIRIT. Three separate parts, BODY, SOUL and SPIRIT. GOD has a SOUL, a BODY and a SPIRIT – the FATHER, the SON and the HOLY SPIRIT. Now take that football, if there was no air inside that football it would be flat (dead). That is what an unsaved man is, a *dead corpse*. He needs to be born again. Note this very profound Scripture... Mat 8v22 **But Jesus said unto him, Follow me; and let the dead bury their dead**. Did you get that? An unsaved man can eat, drink, sleep and reproduce, but he is spiritually DEAD! ... **Ye must be born again.** John 3v7

Now let's go back to Gen 2v7 **And the LORD God formed man of the dust of the ground, and breathed into his nostrils the breath of life; and man became a living soul**. God made man out of the dust of the ground – there's the BODY. He breathed into him the breath of life, that's the SPIRIT; and man became a living SOUL. In Gen 2v18 we read **And the LORD God said, It is not good that the man should be alone; I will make him an help meet for him**. So God then made woman. Look what He said in v23 **And Adam said, This is now bone of my bones, and flesh of my flesh: she shall be called Woman, because she was taken out of Man.**

But what about the blood? There is NO blood there! They are only FLESH and BONES. If there had been 'blood' God would have *said* 'blood' as He does in other places in Scripture e.g. Mat 16v17, 1 Cor 15v50, Gal 1v16, Eph 6v12, Heb 2v14. In 1 Cor 15v49+50 Paul is talking about the Rapture; verse 50 says... **Now this I say, brethren, that flesh and blood cannot inherit the kingdom of God;** The reason why the kingdom cannot come on this earth until Christ comes back is because **flesh and blood cannot inherit the kingdom of God.** There is something *wrong* with *our* blood. Now look at Luke 24v39 after Jesus was risen from the dead... **Behold my hands and my feet, that it is I myself: handle me, and see; for a spirit hath not flesh and bones, as ye see me have.** Notice *no blood* in Him. His blood was shed at Calvary. Now if Christ is the *last* Adam (1 Cor 15v45) then that means the *first* Adam didn't have any blood in him either. Adam *probably* had water running through his veins before he had blood. It is very interesting to note that the first *public* miracle that Moses did in the OT was turning *water* into *blood*. The first *public* miracle in the NT (John 2) was turning *water* into *wine* (in type, 'blood' – see Deut 32v14 **Butter of kine, and milk of sheep,** with fat of lambs, and rams of the breed of Bashan, and goats, with the fat of kidneys of wheat; and thou didst drink the pure blood of the grape.**) Note also 1 John 5v8 for another *interesting* verse. When Eve ate the forbidden fruit i.e. the *grape*, it did something to her circulatory system and probably turned her water into *blood*. There is only one tree in the Book that has a *forbidden fruit* on it – it's found in Num 6, the *vine tree*. (Num 6v4). There is only one tree that is forbidden in the Garden of Eden and that is found in Gen 2v17 **But of the tree of the knowledge of good and evil, thou shalt not eat of it: for in the day that thou eatest thereof thou shalt surely die**. Did you know that there is only one thing that you are forbidden to eat *before* the Law, *during* the Law and *after* the Law? It is blood. (Out goes 'black pudding' Christian!) See Gen 9v4 – *before*; Lev 17v12 – *during*; Acts 15v20 *after* i.e. NT. The first woman took something she shouldn't have and put it in her mouth – it messed up something *inside* of her, her blood. From then on your blood is corrupt hence why it had to be a virgin birth when Christ came i.e. He could *not* partake of *our* bloodline – He had God's *Blood* pumping through His veins (Acts 20v28). So Adam's blood got corrupted and it passed on from generation to generation right up until *you* – *death* entered the bloodstream. Rom 5v12 **Wherefore, as by one man sin entered into the world, and death by sin; and so death passed upon all men, for that all have sinned**: Read all of Romans chapter 5. Because Adam sinned, his blood got messed up and he *died* inside. From that day on Adam had a live body and a live soul but a *dead* spirit. From that day on there is not a man in the Bible that was 'born-again' *until after* the death of Jesus Christ. When Jesus Christ shows up, a man can be born-again – there is *no* new birth in the Old Testament (OT), yet Abraham was saved by grace through faith with *no new birth*; David was saved by grace through faith yet *no new birth*. In the OT you find salvation *before* the law by grace through faith and *under the law* you find salvation by *faith plus works*, but *no new birth*.

Adam loses the *image* and everyone born *after* Adam is born with his image (Adam's) *not* God's – cf. these verses - Gen 1v26 **And God said, Let us make man in our image, after our likeness:** Gen 1v27 **So God created man in his own image, in the image of God created he him; male and female created he them. Gen 5v1 This is the book of the generations of Adam. In the day that God created man, in the likeness of God made he him;** Gen 5v3 **And Adam lived an hundred and thirty years, and begat a son in his own likeness, after his image; and called his name Seth:** Note the 'son' is *not* made in the likeness of God but in the likeness of Adam (i.e. *man*). He had a *dead* spirit. No *man* is made in the image of God *until* he is *born-again*. When a man is born-again, the Bible says that he is... Col 3v10 **And have put on the new man, which is renewed in knowledge after the image of him that created him**: Make sense?

Let's look at Abraham – Abraham is '**dead in trespasses and sins**' just like everyone else in the OT. No one in the OT was saved *the same way* as they were in the NT; they *don't* even go to the same place when they die. OT saints went to Abraham's Bosom *not* Heaven when they died. (This is why Calvinism is such an idiotic ridiculous man-made doctrine – How can you go to Hell for something you are *not* responsible for, if you can't go to Heaven for something you are *not* responsible for? That's their so-called *irresistible* grace which is spelt T.O.S.H. 'Intellectual' Calvinists just can't read or understand the Scriptures, they are very shallow Bible students - Heb 5v12-14). John Calvin was a 'precious, shining light *in his day'* – but I thank God that we have moved onwards, upwards and much *deeper* in the Scriptures than dear old Johnny. Calvinists think that *doctrine stopped* at Johnny Calvin – it didn't.

Now look at Exodus 35 and note we are *in* the OT; we are under the Law *in* the days of Moses. We are in a time when there is *no* new birth, and *no one* is born-again. No one is quickened by the Holy Spirit. Look at Exo 35v10+21+22+25...

Exo 35v10 **And every wise hearted among you shall come, and make all that the LORD hath commanded;**

MISCELLANEOUS

Exo 35v21+22 **And they came, every one whose heart stirred him up, and every one whom his spirit made willing, and they brought the LORD'S offering to the work of the tabernacle of the congregation, and for all his service, and for the holy garments. And they came, both men and women, as many as were willing hearted, and brought bracelets, and earrings, and rings, and tablets, all jewels of gold: and every man that offered offered an offering of gold unto the LORD.**

Exo 35v25 **And all the women that were wise hearted did spin with their hands, and brought that which they had spun, both of blue, and of purple, and of scarlet, and of fine linen.** Now what is happening here? These people are *doing* what the Lord *told them to do.* They are obeying the Lord. Now the Holy Spirit is *not* 'stirring' them up or 'moving them' or 'touching them' – There isn't one person here that the Lord is 'stirring up' – *they stir themselves up.* (Goodnight Calvinist!) Their *own heart* stirs them up. Those are hearts of people who have never been born-again – unregenerate sinners. They are *doing* what God *tells them to* with no 'coercion' from the Holy Spirit. (Get it Mr Calvinist?) You have a ***freewill*** remember - Lev 22v18+21+23, Lev 23v38, Num 15v3, Num 29v39, Deut 12v6+17, Deut 16v10, Deut 23v23, 2 Chron 31v14, Ezra 1v4, Ezra 3v5, Ezra 7v13+16, Ezra 8v28, Ps 119v108.

Now read Gen 15 where God tells Abraham that he will have as many children as there are stars - (Gen 15v4-6). Because Abraham *believed* God for this future promise, God gave him His *righteousness.* Rom 4v3 **For what saith the scripture? Abraham believed God, and it was counted unto him for righteousness.** Gen 15v6 **And he believed in the LORD; and he counted it to him for righteousness.**

Now God told me to *believe* in His Son and what He has done for me i.e. He took my sins and died in my place and was judged and went to Hell *in my place* (Isa 53, Acts 2v27+31+32, Ps 16v10) – I believe what He *said* and what He *did* therefore I have received *his righteousness* (2 Cor 5v21).

The Lord told Abraham in Gen 17 to get circumcised. Heb 9v22 **And almost all things are by the law purged with blood; and without shedding of blood is no remission.** Abraham was being *cut* in the *right* place because his seed was bad; his seed was no good. Remember what Peter said in regard to the 'seed'? 1 Pet 1v23+24 **Being born again, not of corruptible seed, but of incorruptible, by the word of God, which liveth and abideth for ever. For all flesh is as grass, and all the glory of man as the flower of grass. The grass withereth, and the flower thereof falleth away:** We die because there is something wrong with our seed, we have been affected with sin (Rom 5v12 **Wherefore, as by one man sin entered into the world, and death by sin; and so death passed upon all men, for that all have sinned:** Rom 6v23 **For the wages of sin is death**...) We have corrupt *seed* and corrupt *blood.*

In the OT there was *no* 'spiritual' circumcision; *nobody* in the OT was born-again. (Read Colossians 2 regarding *spiritual* circumcision). Note Col 2v11-13 **In whom also ye are circumcised with the circumcision made without hands, in putting off the body of the sins of the flesh by the circumcision of Christ: Buried with him in baptism, wherein also ye are risen with him through the faith of the operation of God, who hath raised him from the dead. And you, being dead in your sins and the uncircumcision of your flesh, hath he quickened together with him, having forgiven you all trespasses;** NOTE **the circumcision made without hands,** *in putting off*... what? Nothing to do with the *'foreskin!'* '**Putting off the body of the sins of the flesh by the circumcision of Christ: ...through the faith of the operation of God'.** Note the word 'operation'.

Remember what the Scripture said in Gen 3v15 **And I will put enmity between thee and the woman, and between thy seed and her seed; it shall bruise thy head, and thou shalt bruise his heel.** The seed of the woman would bruise its head. That is what God said to the Devil.

CHRISTIAN SOLDIER'S BATTLE NOTES

Now we are *this side* of Calvary in the NT; the Chosen Seed of Israel's race has shown up and the *perfect* sacrifice has been made. You have to *beware* of those 'Christians' who try to get you back on the *other side* of Calvary under the Law. Salvation *wasn't* complete on *that side* of Calvary i.e. the OT; but it *is complete this side* of Calvary. John 19v30 **When Jesus therefore had received the vinegar, he said, It is finished: and he bowed his head, and gave up the ghost**. All cults and false religions, plus those who can't *divide* that Book, try to *put something extra on you* e.g. 'keep the Sabbath' etc.

The moment you get saved the Holy Spirit comes into you and cuts your soul loose from your body (Heb 4v12, Col 2), therefore your body is no longer joined to your flesh. Rom 7v1-4 **Know ye not, brethren, (for I speak to them that know the law,) how that the law hath dominion over a man as long as he liveth? For the woman which hath an husband is bound by the law to her husband so long as he liveth; but if the husband be dead, she is loosed from the law of her husband. So then if, while her husband liveth, she be married to another man, she shall be called an adulteress: but if her husband be dead, she is free from that law; so that she is no adulteress, though she be married to another man. Wherefore, my brethren, ye also are become dead to the law by the body of Christ; that ye should be married to another, even to him who is raised from the dead, that we should bring forth fruit unto God**. This is a good illustration about a man *cleaving* to his wife. Now that the husband is no longer there, the wife is no longer *stuck* to him. So when you get saved the Holy Spirit does a *spiritual operation* in you. It's like an ice tray, the ice cubes are in the tray that has had water poured on them and now they each float in their own cubical, but they don't touch the sides. The tray is the *body* but the Christian is no longer stuck to the body.

In the OT a man's SOUL was *stuck* to his FLESH (BODY) and his SOUL could *touch* as well as his BODY - Lev 22v11 **But if the priest buy any soul with his money, he shall eat of it, and he that is born in his house: they shall eat of his meat**. Lev 22v6 **The soul which hath touched any such shall be unclean until even, and shall not eat of the holy things, unless he wash his flesh with water**. Note the SOUL is used as the *person*. In the OT, when a man touched anything, his SOUL touched it. That is *why* he needed *cleansing*. That is one reason why those people in the OT never knew from one day to the next whether or not they were saved. They were defiled every time they picked up something that wasn't right.

When you are saved this side of Calvary, the Holy Spirit comes in and *cuts* your SOUL loose from your FLESH (BODY). *What happens next?* The Holy Spirit *regenerates* your dead spirit, so that you have a *new living* spirit. John 3v6 **That which is born of the flesh is flesh; and that which is born of the Spirit is spirit**. The Trinity lives within me. *How about that!* I am IN Christ and Christ is IN me, hence I have *eternal life.* (Col 2v9+10)

Now practically speaking I am **dying** day by day until finally this old body will give up and shut down and life will end for me here on earth. As far as God is concerned, I'm in the grave, *dead* and buried – Gal 2v20 **I am crucified with Christ: nevertheless I live; yet not I, but Christ liveth in me: and the life which I now live in the flesh I live by the faith of the Son of God, who loved me, and gave himself for me**. When I was baptised it was a picture of *my death.* Spiritually speaking, I am *risen* with Christ and seated in Heaven - Eph 2v6 **And hath raised us up together, and made us sit together in heavenly places in Christ Jesus**: So now we don't serve the *corpse* (the old man) any longer we serve the *new man.* Eph 4v22-24 **That ye put off concerning the former conversation the old man, which is corrupt according to the deceitful lusts; And be renewed in the spirit of your mind; And that ye put on the new man, which after God is created in righteousness and true holiness**.

An unsaved man has a *live* body, a *live* soul but a *dead* spirit. A Christian has a *live* spirit, a *live* soul

MISCELLANEOUS

but a *dead* body. *Do you get that?* Your *body* is a corpse. All the trouble you have is with the *flesh*. Rom 7v18 **For I know that in me (that is, in my flesh,) dwelleth no good thing: for to will is present with me; but how to perform that which is good I find not**. Yet we also read... Rom 6v11 **Likewise reckon ye also yourselves to be dead indeed unto sin, but alive unto God through Jesus Christ our Lord**. Dead men can't *want* things, neither can they sin. You can't get into trouble if you're dead! No one in a graveyard has any trouble with the temptations of the world e.g. *sex, drugs and rock n' roll* do they – they are dead. The person you look at in the mirror is the one who gives you all the problems i.e. *the flesh*. If you could get rid of him you wouldn't have any! It's the *flesh* that causes you all the problems. Thank God we shall soon have a *saved body* at the Rapture (Rom 8v23) – as yet, our BODY has *not* been redeemed. The problem with a lot of Christians is that they still want to serve the *flesh*, the old man, the *corpse*, rather than live and walk in the *new man* and Spirit of God. Rom 6v16 **Know ye not, that to whom ye yield yourselves servants to obey, his servants ye are to whom ye obey; whether of sin unto death, or of obedience unto righteousness?** Rom 8v5-8 **For they that are after the flesh do mind the things of the flesh; but they that are after the Spirit the things of the Spirit. For to be carnally minded is death; but to be spiritually minded is life and peace. Because the carnal mind is enmity against God: for it is not subject to the law of God, neither indeed can be. So then they that are in the flesh cannot please God**. Gal 5v16 **This I say then, Walk in the Spirit, and ye shall not fulfil the lust of the flesh**. You're wasting your time glorying in the *flesh*, for the flesh will fade and *die* - 1 Pet 1v24 **For all flesh is as grass, and all the glory of man as the flower of grass. The grass withereth, and the flower thereof falleth away**: Imagine spending all your time and money on building up, promoting and glorying in the flesh, when it will age and die and there is *nothing* you can do about it. *What a waste of time!* When you get saved, you have a *dead body* but a *live spirit* – you're a walking 'zombie' i.e. you are a *living* 'dead man'.

If you're not saved, you are not 'IN' Christ and you are lost and on the road to an eternity in Hell (whether you believe that or not is of no consequence; that is the truth because that is what the word of God says. Gal 4v16 **Am I therefore become your enemy, because I tell you the truth?**) You may be religious (Roman Catholic or Muslim etc.) but you are still lost and on the road to an everlasting Hell where you will be punished for rejecting Jesus Christ as your Saviour – I am doing all I can to warn you of the consequences of going your own way instead of God's – believe you me, He knows best therefore trust Him. Eph 4v21 **If so be that ye have heard him, and have been taught by him, as <u>the truth is in Jesus</u>**: Religion and 'good works' does *not* put you IN Christ and if you are *not in Christ* you will never get to Heaven no matter what other road you take. John 14v6 **Jesus saith unto him, I am the way, the truth, and the life: no man cometh unto the Father, but by me**. 1 Tim 2v5 **For there is one God, and one mediator between God and men, the man Christ Jesus;** You either come God's way through Jesus Christ, and go to Heaven when you die, or, you go your own way (*whatever way* you choose) and go to Hell when you die. Now you can call this *unfair, bigoted, a 'dictatorship', brutal, arrogant, dogmatic, opinionated, intolerant, narrow-minded, blinkered*, (plus a million other things) but that doesn't change the *fact* that there is *only one way* of having your sins forgiven and *one way* of getting into Heaven and that is *only through* the Lord Jesus Christ – you have a choice, you can choose (no matter what the Calvinist tells you). It is God's way or your own way, but only God's way is *right*, no matter what you think or believe. God is God, and you are His creation. God *without* you is still God: You *without* God are *nothing...* absolutely *nothing*. Do you understand *who and what* you are yet? Have you found out that you *need* God yet? If you haven't, you are risking your life with every second you live! You can call that *scaremongering, creating fear, bullying, causing alarm and anxiety; you can call me a 'doomsayer', or troublemaker*, but again that does *not* alter the *fact* that *truth is truth* and I am doing everything I can to keep you out of Hell, even though you may hate me for doing so. Being baptised does *not* put you *into* Christ, so if you are trusting in baptism to get you to Heaven you are *doomed* and

CHRISTIAN SOLDIER'S BATTLE NOTES

will land up in Hell. That includes of course whether you were sprinkled as a baby as that means nothing.

According to Scripture... John 3v3 **Jesus answered and said unto him, Verily, verily, I say unto thee, Except a man be born again, he cannot see the kingdom of God.** John 3v7 **Marvel not that I said unto thee, Ye must be born again.** So have you been *born again*? When you are born again, the Holy Spirit comes into you and cuts you loose from your flesh, adopting you into the family of God; redeeming you, applying the Blood of Christ to your SOUL, saving your SOUL, regenerating your SPIRIT and putting you *into* Christ's Body. *How about that!* All of that because you *trusted* Jesus Christ for your sins forgiven. If you are *unsaved* you are in a terrible condition – 1 John 5v12, John 3v36, John 3v18, Eph 2v1-3. An unsaved man/woman is alone, *outside* of Christ, *dead* in trespasses and sins, lost and walking the road to Hell. What happens to an *unsaved* man/woman when they die? *Ruckman writes...* John 3v14 **And as Moses lifted up the serpent in the wilderness, even so must the Son of man be lifted up**: When Christ died on the cross He likened Himself to a serpent – the one who messed up the *seed* back in Gen 3. Now sperm looks like a 'worm' (see picture) Ps 22v6 **But I am a worm, and no man; a reproach of men, and despised of the people.** Now this IS Christ ON the Cross. (Look at Ps 22v1+14+15+18) Note the serpent is in the 'reptilian' class. Mark 9v48 **Where their worm dieth not, and the fire is not quenched.** 'Their worm' is a possessive pronoun. It is not THE worm, but it is THEIR worm. The word is also *likened* to a *red maggot.*  Rev 9v7-11 **And the shapes of the locusts were like unto horses prepared unto battle; and on their heads were as it were crowns like gold, and their faces were as the faces of men. And they had hair as the hair of women, and their teeth were as the teeth of lions. And they had breastplates, as it were breastplates of iron; and the sound of their wings was as the sound of chariots of many horses running to battle. And they had tails like unto scorpions, and there were stings in their tails: and their power was to hurt men five months. And they had a king over them, which is the angel of the bottomless pit, whose name in the Hebrew tongue is Abaddon, but in the Greek tongue hath his name Apollyon.** In Rev 9 the bottomless pit opens and something comes up and out of it. Smoke and locusts come out. Verses 7-11 describe *what* comes up and out of that pit. Whatever comes out are 'mutations, monsters' – Faces of men, hair like women, teeth like lions and tails like scorpions. These are mutant-monsters. These 'mutations' are *not* human; they are 'people' in some form of decomposition or something. *Very interesting don't you think!*

When Christ comes back, us *saved* people are going to be like Him - 1 John 3v2. Now read John Chapter 8 and note what Jesus Christ said... v44 **Ye are of your father the devil, and the lusts of your father ye will do. He was a murderer from the beginning, and abode not in the truth, because there is no truth in him. When he speaketh a lie, he speaketh of his own: for he is a liar, and the father of it.** Now Ruckman *guesses* (but it does seem feasible to me) that at the Great White Throne Judgment, when a man loses his soul, he assumes the *shape* of his father. Do you know what an *unsaved* man's father is or looks like?... A *red serpent!* (Read Rev 12 and Gen 3 again). *He goes back to that!* If that is correct, Hell will be a big pile of red maggots crawling in a lake of fire. Now like Ruckman said, he is 'guessing', but in some ways I can see the *mercy* of God in that, can you?

Mark 8v36 **For what shall it profit a man, if he shall gain the whole world, and lose his own soul?** Remember what we said the SOUL was, a *bodily shape*. An unsaved man will lose his own soul, *his bodily shape*.

Like I said, it sounds feasible. John 3v16 **For God so loved the world, that he gave his only begotten Son, that whosoever believeth in him should not perish, but have everlasting life.** Note 'perish'.

MISCELLANEOUS

2 Pet 3v9 **The Lord is not slack concerning his promise, as some men count slackness; but is longsuffering to us-ward, not willing that any should perish, but that all should come to repentance**.

Well at least this study got you thinking. It should also stir you up to get out there and reach the lost souls of this world with the Gospel while we still have the time. Have you given a Gospel tract to everyone in your own family? Have you posted one through every letterbox down your street? *What is stopping you?*

For further study on the SOUL read...

Gen 35v18 **And it came to pass, as her soul was in departing,** (from what? Her BODY) **(for she died) that she called his name Benoni: but his father called him Benjamin**.

Lev 5v2 **Or if a soul touch** (the SOUL is STUCK to the BODY in the OT! The SOUL can touch!) **any unclean thing, whether it be a carcase of an unclean beast, or a carcase of unclean cattle, or the carcase of unclean creeping things, and if it be hidden from him; he also shall be unclean, and guilty**. (See also Num 19v11-16+22, Lev 7v21, Lev 22v6, Job 6v7, Heb 4v12 etc.)

Satan has five 'casting outs'

(Five being the number of death – see chapter on Biblical Numerics)

1. From the third Heaven to the second heaven – Gen 1v2
2. From the second heaven to the first heaven – Luke 10v18
3. From the first heaven to the earth – Rev 12v9
4. From the earth to the pit – Rev 20v1+2
5. From the pit to the Lake of Fire – Rev 20v10

Lucifer means 'bearer of light' (2 Cor 11v14). New 'bibles' say he is the 'morning star' (NIV in Isa 14v12), yet the Morning Star is Jesus Christ (Rev 22v16). The NIV (among other perverted 'bibles') *kicks* Jesus Christ out of Heaven in Isa 14v12.

Time periods separated by a single comma (,) – Isa 61v2 has the First Advent and Second Advent separated by a comma. See also Jer 23v5+6, Luke 4v17-21 (in Luke 4 Jesus is quoting from Isa 61v1+2, but He stopped at the comma (,) in Isa 61v2 (see Luke 4v19) showing that the balance of Isa 61v2 *was still future*).

Other places in Scripture where the two Advents are divided by a verse or punctuation mark are... Gen 49v11+24 (cf. Rev 19v13, Isa 63v1-6, Rev 14v20), Hos 2v13+14, Hos 3v4+5, Ps 118v22-25, Lam 4v20-22, Isa 53v10, Amos 9v10+11, Zech 9v9+10, Luke 21v24, 1 Pet 1v11, Hab 2v13+14, Mic 5v2+3, Zeph 3v7+8.

Interesting (follow it through) – John 20v17 (Acts 1v3) Luke 24v39, John 20v19-21 (John 20v26-28), Mat 28v9. The 'ascension' didn't happen for another 37 days *after* this 'ascension' – why? Acts 1v3.

CHRISTIAN SOLDIER'S BATTLE NOTES

Lists of evils in Scripture – Rom 1v29-32, Gal 5v19-21, 2 Tim 3v1-7, Eph 4v29-32, Mark 7v21-23, Mark 8v38.

Three types of men in Corinthians - 1) **Natural man** (1 Cor 2v14) who is dead to all spiritual things. 2) **Carnal Christian** (1 Cor 3v1-3) 3) **Spiritual Christian** (1 Cor 2v15, Gal 6v1, Col 1v9).

Four spirits – 1) Spirit of God, the Holy Spirit. 2) Spirit of man, the human spirit. 3) Animal spirit – Ecc 3v21 4) Spirit of Satan, unclean spirit.

The love of money – 1 Tim 6v5-12, Ps 52v7, Phil 4v11, Prov 16v8, 18v11, 1 Sam 8v1-3, Mat 6v19-21, Prov 10v15, Prov 11v4+28, Ecc 5v10+12, Titus 1v11, Ps 49v6-11.

Time wasters - Avoid getting draw into arguments with Calvinists, Hyper-Diapers, Post-Tribbers, and all those who are not willing to listen or reason, including those *egotistical-arrogant-stubborn-atheistic-evolutionists* who will not look at the truth presented – 1 Tim 6v20, Col 2v4+8, 2 Tim 2v16+23, 1 Tim 1v4+7, 1 Tim 6v3-5, Titus 3v9-11, Eph 5v6. There is a time to speak and a time to keep silent and walk away (Ecc 3v7). You need to discern between the time wasters and those who are really seeking the truth. The Devil loves wasting *your* time.

Great little study on the tongue – James 3, Mat 15v11, Mat 23v25-28, 1 Thes 4v4, Eph 4v22-27, 1 Tim 4v12+13, Ps 10v7, 36v3, 55v21, Mat 12v33-37, Eph 4v31, Titus 3v2, 1 Pet 2v1, Ps 101v5, Prov 25v23, 15v1, 2 Cor 12v20, Lev 19v16-18, Prov 11v13, 17v9, 20v19, 26v20, 2 Tim 2v16+17, Ps 34v13, Prov 21v23, 10v20, 15v2+4, 31v26, Phil 2v11, Ps 119v172, Eph 5v19+20, Col 3v16+17, Ps 141v3, Gal 5v15. *Feel convicted?*

The brevity of life – Ps 90v10 - James 4v14, 1 Chron 29v15, Job 7v6+7+9+25, Ps 39v5, Isa 38v12, Ps 103v15, Prov 27v1, Hos 13v3. Don't waste one single day of life, get something out of every day for the Lord (Ps 90v12). Your wedding lasts a day, your funeral an hour… then there's eternity – Heb 9v27. Now break down your day… sleep, work, eat, recreation, travel, personal etc. 70 years = 25,550 days, 613,200 hours. Now work out how long you sleep and work for… *frightening isn't it!*

Love not - The Scriptures tell us *two* things that we are to 'love not', do you know what they are? – 1) 1 John 2v15-17 (James 4v4, Mat 6v24), 2) Prov 20v13. Do you love both? If so, it's time to change.

Sin – 1 John 3v4, James 4v17, Rom 14v23, John 16v8+9, 1 John 5v17, Ps 90v8, Mat 5v27+28, Prov 21v4, Rom 13.

***Four* sins the Scriptures tell you to *flee* are…** 1 Cor 6v18, 1 Cor 10v14, 2 Tim 2v22, 1 Tim 6v6-11 – But do you?

MISCELLANEOUS

The *word of God* is your *survival kit* – this is all you need.

Water – Eph 5v26	Bread – Mat 4v4
Meat – 1 Cor 3v2	Honey – Ps 19v10
Milk – 1 Pet 2v2	Apples – Prov 25v11
Seed – 1 Pet 1v23	Hammer – Jer 23v29
Nails – Ecc 12v11	Fire – Jer 23v29, Jer 20v9
Lamp – Ps 119v105	Mirror – James 1v22-25
Sword – Eph 6v17, Heb 4v12	*Think of anything else?*

If you only had this list of items you could survive in life!

The apostle Peter – Mat 16v18 Peter *never* went to Rome. He was married – Mat 8v14, Mark 1v29-31 (Deut 32v31). He was never a pope. Peter is a *stone* – John 1v42, (Jesus is *the* Rock – Rom 9v33, 1 Cor 10v4, 1 Cor 3v11), 1 Pet 2v5-8, Mat 21v42+44, Eph 2v20. See how the Roman Catholics have twisted the Scriptures?

Not even the apostles fully understood the Lord's coming, none of them were waiting for the Lord outside His tomb – Mark 9v31+32, Mark 8v29-33 (Mark 9v9+10, 10v32-34), Luke 18v31-34 (Luke 9v22, 24v13-27), Mat 16v21-23 (Mat 20v17-19), 1 Pet 1v10-12, Luke 9v43-45, Mat 17v22+23.

That Prophet – John 1v21+25, John 6v14, John 7v40. Israel had been waiting for 'That Prophet' – Deut 18v15+19, Acts 3v19-26 (v22+23), Acts 7v37. They would recognise Him by His signs and wonders – Acts 2v22+43, Acts 4v30, Heb 2v3+4, Isa 35v1-10, John 12v11, John 6v14, Acts 10v38.

You can *know* you are saved, you don't have to *hope* – 1 John 5v4+10-13, John 3v3+7+8, Rom 8v14+16, 1 John 3v24, 1 John 3v14, 2 Cor 5v17, 1 Pet 1v14-16, Gal 5v22-26, 2 Cor 13v5, Col 2v6+9+10, Col 1v27, Eph 3v17, Eph 4v30.

How much fruit? - What fruit are bearing in your life for the Lord, if any? If you're not, why not? *You should be!* John 15v1-5 and note the wording... ***fruit, more fruit, much fruit***. This ought to be you as you mature as a Christian, but is it? There is a reason why so many Christians aren't *bearing fruit* for the Lord. Do you know what it is? Is it time to *relook at your own life* and see where, and what you are doing? Don't waste time.

CHRISTIAN SOLDIER'S BATTLE NOTES

Five Judgments	Five Crowns
Judgment of Sin at Calvary – Rom 10v4, Rom 8v1+2, John 5v24, 2 Cor 5v21	**Obtainable at the Judgment Seat of Christ**
	Crown of Life – James 1v12, Rev 2v10
Judgment of 'works' at the Judgment Seat of Christ – 2 Cor 5v10, 1 Cor 3v11-15	Crown of Glory – 1 Pet 5v2-4
	Crown of Rejoicing – 1 Thes 2v19+20, Phil 4v1
Judgment of the Jews in the Tribulation aka 'Jacob's Trouble', Daniel's 70th Week (Rev 5-18)	Crown of Righteousness – 2 Tim 4v8
Judgment of the Gentile Nations before the Millennium – Mat 25v31-46	Crown Incorruptible – 1 Cor 9v25-27
Judgment of the wicked dead at the Great White Throne – Rev 20v11-15	

False prophets and false teachers – Mat 7v15-23, Mat 23, Mat 24v5+11+24, (Luke 6v26), 2 Cor 11v12-14, Jude 4-18, 1 Tim 4, 2 Pet 2, Jer 14v14, Deut 18, Jer 23. False teachers minimise sin, they 'humanise' God, they 'deify' man, they teach self-atonement, self-righteousness and works for salvation. They avoid preaching on Hell, judgment, sin, holiness etc. Most pastors today are not qualified to be pastors, as hardly any of them can teach the word of God (1 Tim 2, Titus 1v5-10). I would also include in this list of **false** teachers and preachers – Hyper-Dispensationalists, Calvinists and Post-Tribbers.

The Golden Rule of Interpretation – When the plain sense of Scripture makes common sense, seek no other sense. Therefore, take every word at its primary, ordinary, usual, literal meaning; unless the facts of the immediate context, *studied in the light of related passages* and axiomatic (*self-evident or obvious*) and fundamental truths, indicate clearly otherwise. God, in revealing His word, neither intends, nor permits the reader to be confused. He wants His children to understand.

What were the OT saints looking forward to *after* death? – Gen 3v22, Job 19v25, Ps 23v6, 17v15, 21v4, Dan 12v2, Isa 26v19.

It's an evil, perverted world – Gal 1v4, Phil 2v15, Acts 2v40, Mark 8v38, Luke 9v41, 1 John 5v19, John 17v14-17, 1 John 2v16, Jer 5v23, Deut 32v5, Gen 6v5+6 (imagination – Gen 8v21, Jer 7v24, 11v8, 13v10, 16v12, 18v12).

The cock crowing – a contradiction?

Mark 14v30 **And Jesus saith unto him, Verily I say unto thee, That this day, even in this night, before the cock crow twice, thou shalt deny me thrice.** The apparent contradiction between this verse and Mat 26v34 **Jesus said unto him, Verily I say unto thee, That this night, before the cock crow, thou shalt deny me thrice.** Luke 22v34 **And he said, I tell thee, Peter, the cock shall not crow this day, before that thou shalt thrice deny that thou knowest me.** John 13v38 **Jesus answered him, Wilt thou lay down thy life for my sake? Verily, verily, I say unto thee, The cock shall not crow, till thou hast denied me thrice.** ...is still used by many to cast doubt on the accuracy of the AV Bible. The passage gave Bullinger such a terrible time that he had the cock 'sounding-off' six times. The real explanation is much simpler. Jesus was warning about a period of *time* as well as an actual cock crowing in the other three passages. The *third* watch of the night (12am to 3am) was known as 'the cockcrowing' (Mark 13v35 **Watch ye therefore: for ye know not when the master of the house cometh, at even, or at midnight, or at the cockcrowing, or in the morning:**) That watch would not end *before* Peter had denied the Lord three times. Mark is the more complete passage when it comes to the number of times the cock actually crowed. **Mat 26v75 And Peter remembered the word of Jesus, which said unto him, Before the cock crow, thou shalt deny me thrice. And he went out, and wept bitterly. Luke 22v60 And Peter said, Man, I know not what thou sayest. And immediately, while he yet spake, the cock crew. John 18v27 Peter then denied again: and immediately the cock crew.** ...refer to the *second* crowing of Mark 14v72 **And the second time the cock crew. And Peter called to mind the word that Jesus said unto him, Before the cock crow twice, thou shalt deny me thrice. And when he thought thereon, he wept**.

Who is the Antichrist to come?

With so much speculation regarding WHO is going to be the Antichrist (all prophecy YouTube channels make money because they preach 'newspapers' instead of the Scriptures), let us look at what the Scriptures say in regard to this fascinating topic, rather than the newspapers.

John 17v12 **While I was with them in the world, I kept them in thy name: those that thou gavest me I have kept, and none of them is lost, but the son of perdition; that the scripture might be fulfilled.**

2 Thes 2v3 **Let no man deceive you by any means: for that day shall not come, except there come a falling away first, and that man of sin be revealed, the son of perdition**; Note 'son of perdition' S.O.P (SOP) & John 13v26 **Jesus answered, He it is, to whom I shall give a sop, when I have dipped it. And when he had dipped the sop, he gave it to Judas Iscariot, the son of Simon.** Note also the number 13 i.e. John 13v26 (2x13) & Judas Iscariot has 13 letters! John 13v27 **And after the sop Satan entered into him. Then said Jesus unto him, That thou doest, do quickly.**

The Antichrist is the Devil incarnate (incarnate = of a deity or spirit embodied in human form) – Luke 22v3 **Then entered Satan into Judas surnamed Iscariot, being of the number of the twelve.**

Who fits the verse in John 17v12 – **ONLY** Judas Iscariot does!

John 6v70+71 **Jesus answered them, Have not I chosen you twelve, and one of you is a devil? He spake of Judas Iscariot the son of Simon: for he it was that should betray him, being one of the twelve.** Judas is NOT a human being like you & I, he's 'a' devil, not 'The' Devil, but 'a' devil.

John 13v18 **I speak not of you all: I know whom I have chosen: but that the scripture may be fulfilled, He that eateth bread with me hath lifted up his heel against me.** Read also Ps 109 as this is talking about Judas Iscariot & the son of perdition (see also Rev 17v8+11, Job 15v20)

The word 'Iscariot' is a Hebrew word & the word 'Judas' is a Greek word. Judas is the Greek spelling of Judah. Iscariot is a man of **Kerioth**... **Kerioth** is in the land of **Moab**. Judas is the only disciple from outside the land of Canaan, i.e. he's from Moab & Moab is a part of Syria. **So Judas is a Syrian Jew.**

Jer 48v24 **And upon Kerioth, and upon Bozrah, and upon all the cities of the land of Moab, far or near.**

Jer 48v25 **The horn of Moab is cut off, and his arm is broken, saith the LORD.**

Jer 48v28 **O ye that dwell in Moab, leave the cities, and dwell in the rock, and be like the dove that maketh her nest in the sides of the hole's mouth.**

Jer 48v41 **Kerioth is taken, and the strong holds are surprised, and the mighty men's hearts in Moab at that day shall be as the heart of a woman in her pangs.**

CHRISTIAN SOLDIER'S BATTLE NOTES

Jer 48 is all about the judgments of Moab. So we have a Syrian Jew from Moab who has trouble with his arm!

Zech 11v16 **For, lo, I will raise up a shepherd in the land, which shall not visit those that be cut off, neither shall seek the young one, nor heal that that is broken, nor feed that that standeth still: but he shall eat the flesh of the fat, and tear their claws in pieces.**

v17 **Woe to the idol shepherd that leaveth the flock! the sword shall be upon his arm, and upon his right eye: his arm shall be clean dried up, and his right eye shall be utterly darkened.**

So he will have trouble with his arm & with his right eye!

Who is it?

Zech 11v12 **And I said unto them, If ye think good, give me my price; and if not, forbear. So they weighed for my price thirty pieces of silver.**

v13 **And the LORD said unto me, Cast it unto the potter: a goodly price that I was prised at of them. And I took the thirty pieces of silver, and cast them to the potter in the house of the LORD.** It's Judas Iscariot! Mat 26v15.

Judas is an unusual kind of character because he doesn't technically go to Hell, because he's not an 'unsaved man' who goes to Hell, he's 'a devil' remember, therefore he goes to his own place in the bottomless pit!

Acts 1v25 **That he may take part of this ministry and apostleship, from which Judas by transgression fell, that he might go to his own place.**

So Judas is a Syrian Jew, & a devil with two names, a Greek name & a Hebrew name - Rev 9v11 **And they had a king over them, which is the angel of the bottomless pit, whose name in the Hebrew tongue is Abaddon, but in the Greek tongue hath his name Apollyon.**

Rev 17v8 **The beast that thou sawest was** (he was man who WAS before John wrote Revelation), **and is not** (He wasn't around when John wrote the Book of Revelation); **and shall ascend out of the bottomless pit, and go into perdition: and they that dwell on the earth shall wonder, whose names were not written in the book of life from the foundation of the world, when they behold the beast that was, and is not, and yet is.**

Rev 13v18 **Here is wisdom. Let him that hath understanding count the number of the beast: for it is the number of a man; and his number is Six hundred threescore and six.** So the beast is a man (Judas Iscariot).

So Judas Iscariot was a spiritual being (a devil) walking around in a human body, who came UP from the bottomless pit.

You have the second coming of Christ, the second coming of Moses & Elijah (in the Tribulation) & also the second coming of Judas Iscariot in the Tribulation.

Judas had no salvation to lose as he wasn't a 'normal' human, he was a devil, so he couldn't have been 'saved'. He was a king over the bottomless pit before coming up.

Next time Judas comes back he will be the Devil manifest in the flesh, a counterfeit of the TRUE, the Lord Jesus Christ manifest in the flesh (1 Tim 3v16 – note in the Tribulation when Judas comes 'in the flesh' he'll counterfeit Jesus Christ – 1 John 4v2+3, 2 John 1v7).

MISCELLANEOUS

Gen 3v15 **And I will put enmity between <u>thee</u> (the Serpent) and the woman, and between <u>thy seed</u> (the Serpent's SEED) and her seed; it shall bruise thy head, and thou shalt bruise his heel.** The Devil therefore has a 'son'. Back to 2 Thes 2v3 **Let no man deceive you by any means: for that day shall not come, except there come a falling away first, and that man of sin be revealed, the <u>son</u> of perdition;** Note 'son', the Devil has a son.

In Acts 4v26 **The kings of the earth stood up, and the rulers were gathered together against the Lord, and against <u>his</u> <u>Christ</u>.**

Luke 2v26 **And it was revealed unto him by the Holy Ghost, that he should not see death, before he had seen the <u>Lord's</u> <u>Christ</u>.**

Antichrist is the 'man of sin' who is an egomaniac & probably a sodomite (see Dan 11v37 below) – he is associated with the animal the leopard (note a leopard is **yellow**, with **black** spots & a **white** belly – covering all the bases of race).

Dan 11v36 **And the king shall do according to his will; and he shall exalt himself, and magnify himself above every god, and shall speak marvellous things against the God of gods, and shall prosper till the indignation be accomplished: for that that is determined shall be done.**

v37 **Neither shall he regard the God of his fathers, <u>nor the desire of women</u>, nor regard any god: for he shall magnify himself above all.** (See also - Dan 7v8+11+24-25, 9v27+11v16, 2 Thes 2v4, Rev 13v5-6, Isa 14v12+13, 2 Thes 2v4, 1 Tim 4v3)

The Lord's Christ vs the Antichrist…

The Lord Jesus Christ	**Antichrist**
Christ came from above – John 6v38	Antichrist ascends from The Pit – Rev 11v7
Christ came in His Father's name – John 5v43	Antichrist comes in his own name – John 5v43
Christ humbled Himself – Phil 2v8	Antichrist exalts himself – 2 Thes 2v4
Christ is despised – Isa 53v3, Luke 23v18	Antichrist is admired – Rev 13v3+4
Christ is exalted – Phil 2v9	Antichrist is cast down to Hell – Isa 14v14+15, Rev 19v20
Christ came to do His Father's will – John 6v38	Antichrist comes to do his own will – Dan 11v36
Christ came to save – Luke 19v10	Antichrist comes to destroy – Dan 8v24
Christ is the Good Shepherd – John 10v4-15	Antichrist is the Idol Shepherd – Zech 11v16+17
Christ is the True Vine – John 15v1	Antichrist is the Vine of the Earth – Rev 14v18
Christ is the Truth – John 14v6	Antichrist is the Lie – 2 Thes 2v11
Christ is the Holy One – Mark 1v24	Antichrist is the Lawless One – 2 Thes 2v8
Christ is the Man of Sorrows – Isa 53v3	Antichrist is the Man of Sin – 2 Thes 2v3
Christ is the Son of God – Luke 1v35	Antichrist is the Son of Perdition – 2 Thes 2v3
Christ is the Mystery of Godliness – 1 Tim 3v16	Antichrist is the Mystery of Iniquity – 2 Thes 2v7

CHRISTIAN SOLDIER'S BATTLE NOTES

The Antichrist - taken from Brian Donovan's article in BBB...
When the Antichrist (a Syrian-Jew) enters the world scene, the Roman Catholic False Prophet will cause ...the earth and them which dwell therein to worship the first beast... (Rev 13v12), until no man might buy or sell, save he that had the mark, or the name of the beast, or the number of his name. (Rev 13v17). This world leader will place his mark as a black 'spot' (Rev 13v2) in the right hand or foreheads of his followers (Rev 13v16). It is interesting to note that in the Syriac language (originating about 3500 BC in Aramea, or modern-day Syria), the name Nimrod translates to mean 'spotted'. So, the Bible traces the kingdom of Syria as coming out of Babel (Gen 10), with a Syrian ruler whose name means 'spotted', to finally rule over Israel in the last days, even coming from outside the land. The implication is that he will be bold enough to 'come in his own name' (John 5v43), & that name is Judas Iscariot, being the only apostle chosen from outside the land (the literal meaning of his name is 'a man of Kerioth'). Judas was the only apostle chosen who was 'a devil' (John 6v70), & as he went out to betray the Lord, 'Satan entered into him' (John 13v27). The Muslims will be ready to receive this part Syrian Antichrist as their coming 'Mahdi', or messiah who will set himself up as ruler in the Temple Mount, while the Jews will be ready to receive this part Jewish Antichrist possessing the 'signs & wonders', that they require (1 Cor 1v22, 2 Thes 2v9).

NOTES

NOTES

NOTES

KNOWING GOD'S WILL FOR YOUR LIFE

To know the will of God is the greatest knowledge; to find the will of God is the greatest discovery; to do the will of God is the greatest achievement!

'How do I know God's will for my life?' is a question that I have been asked many times. Living for the Lord Jesus Christ is the whole meaning of life. It would be terrible to stand before Him on Judgment Day, knowing that you hadn't lived for Him and served Him while you were on earth. We should all question ourselves whether we are in the will of God. Here are a few helpful notes to see *if you are…*

Read Prov 3v5-7 (Josh 9v14)

1) You really need to pray and pour out your heart and soul to the Lord, asking Him for help and guidance in every decision you make, **get serious with the Lord** – Ps 62v8

2) Be prepared to go and do what He calls you to, it's His will *not yours* that's important.

3) Are you 100% open and honest with the Lord?

4) Are you living a holy life? If not, why would God use you? – Col 3v17, 1 Pet 1v15

5) Are you involved in soul-winning and reaching lost sinners with the Gospel? – Prov 11v30, 1 Pet 3v15

6) **Don't try to be somebody you're not!** – Rom 12v1-3, Gal 6v3

7) Are you working, do you have a job earning money? If not, get one, and get out there *where sinners are* and start being a testimony *in the workplace*, make sure you shine your light for the Lord everywhere you go (Mat 5v14, John 1v7, Rom 13v12, 2 Cor 4v4, Eph 5v8, 1 Thes 5v5, 1 Pet 2v9). This will certainly help you regarding *life-experiences* if you are ever called to pastor a church – 1 Tim 2v7. You need to be able to deal with people and situations, and you *need* experience, knowledge, wisdom and discernment – Rom 5v1-5. Usually God will call you to a work *when you are already working* – Elisha was called *while ploughing* (1 Kings 19v19). Too many Christians waste time just sitting, waiting for God to call them. Instead, they should be out there working and winning souls for the Lord, *then*, God may call them to something else. If you are not trying to reach sinners with the Gospel, you are rebelling against God. Every Christian should at least tract his own neighbourhood.

8) If you are moving from one place to another, or from one work to another, ask yourself why? Is it really *of the Lord* or is it because *you want to?* Are you running away from your responsibility? Are you giving up on what you should be doing? Be honest with yourself? God knows your heart. Too many Christians quit when the going gets tough.

9) If in doubt, don't! This is not *always* right, but it can help and it's a good rule to help you *not to rush into things.*

10) Are you being blessed *where you are?* If so, why do you want to move on? God wants faithful

Christians working and serving Him. He is not interested in *big names*. If you're being blessed where you are, *maybe* you should stay.

11) Are you living in total surrender to the Lord, in *every area* of your life? – 2 Tim 2v19, Ps 66v18. Have you any secret sins you know you need to depart from? **Do you need to have a *clean-up* in your life?** (Ps 119v9, John 17v17)

12) Are you really available and willing to go wherever the Lord sends you? – Isa 6v8

13) **Are you living in the Scriptures?** What saith the Scripture? (Rom 4v3) God speaks through His word. You should be reading the Scriptures daily, seeking the Lord through His word for answers. If you're not, I doubt He'll call you to anything.

14) Be honest in *everything* – 1 Cor 5v8, Heb 13v18, 1 Tim 2v2, 2 Cor 8v21

15) Get to know the Lord Jesus Christ the best you can, asking Him to open and close doors according to His plan and purpose. Don't try to work things out on your own.

16) Living and serving the Lord Jesus Christ brings the greatest satisfaction, peace and joy you could possibly find in life. Is it time for you to make some changes?

17) We should all check ourselves whether we are in the will of God or not. Sometimes we get too complacent, too comfortable and stuck in a rut. Keep close to the Lord, asking Him to guide you in everything you do.

18) A very challenging question to ask yourself is this… '*How much of the Lord do I want in my life?*' Are you totally *sold out* to the Lord, or are you just a lukewarm part-time Christian going nowhere?

Paul *stepped out* of the will of God – which means we can too if we're not careful. As Paul wrote Romans, he knew that Peter, James and John were the apostles called to minister to the Jews, and especially the Jews in Jerusalem (Gal 2v9). He knew that he was the apostle of the Gentiles (Rom 11v13, 15v16 *****), and should be headed to Rome and then to Spain (Rom 15v24+28). Nevertheless, he headed for Jerusalem to take an offering from the Gentiles to the Jewish people, the believers there. God warned him of what was going to happen throughout Greece, Macedonia and Asia Minor (Acts 20v22+23). *How did Paul respond?* – Acts 20v24. He was warned a number of times – Acts 21v4+10+11, Acts 22v18. By going, Paul lost two years in his ministry stuck in a Roman jail. *How many years of ministry have you lost by making the wrong decision?*

(*Paul also ministered to Jews – Acts 13v14, 14v1, 17v1, 9v15, 13v46+47, 18v6)

NOTES

NOTES

LIVING AS A CHRISTIAN

1) Get as much Scripture *into you* as you can. Read the Bible daily no matter how busy you are, *daily*, **no excuses.** Ask God to help you understand the Scriptures - Luke 24v45, Ps 1, Jer 17v5-8

2) Pray *from your heart*, asking the Lord to help you in *every* decision you make. Ask Him to open and close doors, and to guide you through all opportunities and situations. Ask Him to help you with every job and task; ask Him to help you *change,* to be the person *He wants you to be*. Ask Him to bless you in every area of your life so that you can be the best ambassador for Him as possible (2 Cor 5v20). Ask for help in your relationships i.e. wife, husband, family, friends, colleagues, employer etc.

3) Seek the Lord *with all your heart*, that He will use you in your life to reach the lost souls of this world. **Get serious with God** especially in regard to reaching lost sinners with the Gospel. Ask Him to give you the sincerity and compassion you *ought to have*. Are you *really* prepared to change?

4) Be a true *testimony and witness* for the Lord Jesus Christ, not just at church, but at work and in the home. Let others see Jesus Christ in you. Col 3v17+23, 1 Cor 10v31

5) Seize every opportunity to testify for the Lord – Don't let one pass you by, and ask the Lord to give you the strength and courage you need to take a stand. You may have to stand against your own friends and family for the Lord. Don't even *think* about it, *do it*, **always put the Lord first**. (Gal 1v10, Mat 23v2+3+7, Acts 5v9, Rom 3v4, Acts 4v18-20, 1 Thes 2v4, James 4v4)

6) Please Him in every area of your life, even if it means losing friends because of Him. I tell you this… *you won't be sorry in the long run!* Acts 17v2+17 (Ps 27v10, Ps 68v5+6, Job 19v14, Rom 7v4, Isa 40v11, Prov 18v24, Heb 2v11)

7) **Don't compromise!** Ask God to help you not to compromise. If you start to, you will find yourself doing it more and more, and you'll backslide, and this will lead into a downward spiral. You will end up not taking a stand for the Lord, and you will lose your voice as a Christian witness for Him. **Fight 'compromise' with every ounce of strength in your being!** Col 1v18, 1 Cor 10v31, Col 3v17+23, Rom 14v8, 1 Pet 4v11, Ecc 9v10

8) Live a holy life walking in the Spirit – Gal 5v16, James 1v12-15, Col 1v18, Gal 5v25, Rom 8v1+4, Rom 13v14, 1 Cor 10v13

9) **Get active in the Lord's work!** Sow tracts *everywhere* you can from *junk-mail-envelopes* that are prepaid, to leaving them in telephone boxes, pushing them through letterboxes, leaving them in libraries, doctor's surgeries, cafes etc. This is just one example. There is so much to do.

10) Get involved in *church work* – offer to help your pastor, support all the meetings, get involved in outreach. Get committed to the work of the Lord. Acts 13v2 (When did you last fast? How serious are you regarding the Lord Jesus Christ?)

11) Don't worry about losing *friends* along the way. If you really do live like a Christian should i.e. you love the Lord with all your heart, mind, soul and strength (Mat 12v30), you will find other Christians are envious, jealous and feel bitter towards you, because you are *convicting them* and putting them to shame. In this case, do just two things… 1) Extend an offer for them to get involved and come and help. *If they refuse*, go to point two… 2) Dump them.

12) Talk to the Lord about absolutely *everything*, from the most vital and sensitive, to the mundane. He wants every part of you, and wants to help you in every area of your life. Pour out (Ps 62v8) your deepest emotions; cry, 'shout' if need be, but get the deepest relationship you can with the Lord, and ask Him to lead and guide you throughout your life. If you have *marriage* problems, relationship problems, work problems, habitual sins you're finding hard to stop, struggle with laziness, *anything and everything*, pour out your deepest and most inner emotions to the Lord. We as human beings are too quick to judge, and we lack compassion and understanding. He doesn't, He understands, therefore talk to Him - Ps 62v8

13) Love him with every fibre of your being - Read Rom 12

14) Try your hardest to treat everyone around you as the Lord would. Do every job and task *for the Lord.* If you have to clean, paint, tidy up, give someone a lift, cook a meal etc. do it without murmuring… *for the Lord.* Phil 2v14.

15) **Thank Him continually** – 2 Cor 9v11, Phil 4v6, 1 Thes 5v18

16) Beware of bad women (Prov 1+5+7) and bad men (Prov 1+2+3)

17) Pay attention to your inner thought life – Ps 19v14

18) Keep your sins judged and confessed – 1 Cor 10 + 11

19) Watch your temper – James 1v19

20) Forgive quickly, and don't harbour grudges – James 5v9, Eph 4v32

21) Abstain from **all appearance** of evil – 1 Thes 5v22

22) Do not try to compete with other Christians, God gives us all a work to do.

23) Don't try to be somebody you're not – Gal 6v3

24) Be on your guard at all times – 1 Pet 5v8

25) Keep your armour on – Eph 6

26) Make each day count for the Lord. Get something out of *every* day.

These are just a few thoughts to help you in your own Christian walk.

NOTES

NOTES

A CHALLENGE...

What do you do in church?

Do you take responsibility for any of the following jobs? (*Not in any order*)

Open/lock up the church	Set the chairs and tables out	Prepare what hymns to sing
Give out necessary literature	Welcome people	Clean and clear up afterwards
Take and count the offering	Prepare the Communion bread and wine	Lead the service
Pray and read	Make the tea and coffee	Do the necessary shopping
Pay the bills	Preach/Sunday School etc.	Give a lift to folks that need one
Prepare the food	Do the banking	Prepare and give out the notices
Serve the Communion	Wash, dry and pack away	Prepare sermons
Clean the church	Music	Visitation

If you don't, who does all the work? How about offering some help to ease the work load?

Are you involved in your church outreach programme? If there isn't one, start one!

How many tracts have you given out over the last month?

If you're not distributing tracts at present, I would certainly make a start today.

Tracting challenge...

On average there are 31 days in a month. Why not photocopy this chart each month and write in how many tracts you distributed each day. Each tract is a *little missionary*, and you never know where they may land up. Post them through letterboxes, leave them in cafés, doctors surgeries, hospitals, waiting rooms, on trains and buses, in taxis, post them in 'free paid' envelopes (junk mail), leave them in phone boxes, bus shelters, at the gym, etc. (Got any more ideas?)

1st	9th	17th	25th
2nd	10th	18th	26th
3rd	11th	19th	27th
4th	12th	20th	28th
5th	13th	21st	29th
6th	14th	22nd	30th
7th	15th	23rd	31st
8th	16th	24th	**Total**

You'll be amazed who finds and reads them.

Another challenge I'd like to present to you, would be to **read the Bible within a year**. Every Christian ought to read the Bible once a year, if you're really serious about your Christian faith.

NOTES

NOTES

HELLO PASTOR

This is mainly for those who have a leadership role in the local church. There is some excellent advice here that you would do well to take heed to.

James Knox has written a great little leaflet called 'Hello Pastor'. If you are in any kind of a leadership role you ought to take on board what is being said here... (I've added/changed a few things to make it personal)

1) If a man who disagrees with your doctrine, standards and practices, feels compelled to express his disagreement, no amount of time will change his mind. Many join our churches that do not see everything as we do, but they have come to learn and to grow. Where they differ they ponder and pray. Others have enough charity and spiritual maturity to accept diversity of operations (1 Cor 12v1-10) and rejoice in all that they agree with and choose not to dwell upon their points of disagreement. But a man who *must* vocalize his areas of contention – not once or twice, but consistently – is *not* listening, is *not* learning and will *not* change his view. Often a pastor accommodates such a one in hope that 'if he just keeps attending and hearing the word he will come around.' Ah, but my brother, he is *not* hearing, he is critiquing! Do *not* give this man *any* opportunity to gain a single follower that he can take with him when he goes... **he will go!**

2) Beware of the man who grumbles about 'a one man ministry'. He is only annoyed because 'he' is not the 'one man!' Should you grant his wish and establish 'elder rule', he will grumble if he is not chosen to be one of the elders. Eventually this man **will leave** because *you* are 'a one man ministry', and will establish 'a one man ministry **in his living room**'.

3) If someone comes to your church and says things like... '*We've been looking for a church like this for years!*' OR '*How wonderful, a KJV only church, just what we want, we shall be coming to this from now on!*' or '*This is just what we've been looking for!*' or '*Now that we have found a church such as this, we shall be totally supportive and you're going to see us every week!*' etc. *Blah Blah Blah...* and on it goes. Know this, **they will be gone within months!** This is so true and it has happened at The Oaks Church a number of times. In fact, the more people who come and 'speak well of us' (Luke 6v26) the more I see through it all and my conscience *pricks* me, and the alarm bells start ringing. We've had all kinds of Christians come through our doors, from Calvinists to those that swear their loyalty to the KJV, the church and to *me! All have left! I trust none of them.* I preach and teach the word of God. Most people who attend are half-hearted Christians who will bow out at any time and *cannot* be counted on at all. I have given them so many opportunities to get involved, I've encouraged them, we've fed them and looked after them the best we can, and they still leave or turn up as and when. You know what, we are better off without them. *I kid you not!* They are just a 'pathetic effort' and best gone. I would rather just teach and preach to the *faithful few* than grow a church of *lukewarm-half-hearted-waste-of-space-Christians*, that's a fact. Most Christians are like babies, very childish and can't handle the meat of God's word. *(I have included all of that to help you if you are in the ministry and have a leadership position, or if you are contemplating going into leadership. You can count on very few people in life! If you can get one or two around you, who you can*

trust, they're worth their weight in gold).

4) The individual who comes with a catalogue of horror tales about all the other preachers in the churches he used to go to, must be rebuked for such tale-bearing and gossip. If the first rebuke does not stop him, he will be saying the same things about you to his *next pastor.*

5) One would think that grace, the fruit of the Spirit, and humility, would abound among those who have laboured long for the Lord. Such should be the case. The retired missionary, evangelist, preacher etc. who will step in and be a friend, helper and trusted advisor is more rare than platinum. If God sends one your way, praise Him for it. But, if a man comes in bragging about himself and making sure the whole congregation knows of his wondrous works, **beware**.

6) A person whose loyalty and commitment is to *anything and everything* other than the Lord, His word or His church, will cause you trouble every time.

7) A family who exalts themselves above their brethren because they believe their standards and morals to be superior to those of others in the church, will not hurt your church *only themselves.* They will seek to convince others of their piety, but when others are not convinced they will say "They just don't like us because they are so worldly". Those with high visible standards who are also kind and loving are such a blessing. Those with high visible standards, who lack the ability to make friends, fellowship with the saints and love others, are a drag. But, they will never gain a following and will not harm the church.

8) If someone is not content and they want to leave the church, **let them leave!** Persuading someone who does not want to be there will only make you wish a hundred times, they were not there. Everybody is not going to like your preaching, standards, organisational style etc. *Accept that.* **Departure, does *not* mean that you are not right with God**, or the one left, is not right with God. *But let them go!* **Devote your time to those who *are* walking in agreement**.

9) The parent who can and will graciously receive and appreciate your correction of their children is rare but a blessing. You can't be nice enough, sincere enough, concerned enough, or right enough, to get through this unscathed. The older the child, the worse the reaction will be. However, when you must speak to the parent about a disorderly child and the response is one of anger or resentment, or accusation or excuse making, know that the problem is *not* the child, *but* the parents. I have commented in previous TfT! NEWS that *when a child is ruling the parents and running their lives*, then there is a huge problem here. If you *cannot* control your child in church, then I suggest you get some help, or leave. I have met very few parents who can control their children as the Lord wants them to according to Scripture. Most let their children get away with anything, including running around in church, shouting out, and being such a nuisance. Every parent ought to bring up their children IN the Scriptures, *but hardly any do. Why?*

10) Should there be those come in among you who consider themselves above the 'little rules', **they have a *rebellious* and *proud* heart.** For example, if you say 'Everyone meet at 5.00pm at Joe's and we will go from there to the restaurant' and you get to the restaurant and 'brother A' is already waiting there... *mark that man!* He will consistently act in such a way as to show contempt for anyone in leadership. His children will be disrespectful toward those in authority. If you give this man *any part* in leadership you will live to regret having done so. (Now this is such an important point here, that most won't truly understand *unless* you are in some kind of leadership role).

11) Generally speaking, those who 'give the least', complain *the most* in the church, and I'm not

just talking about 'money'.

12) The people who sigh and say "Well, you know there's no perfect church" actually think they would not defile it if they found it! (So true!)

13) Beware of the individual who constantly pulls idiotic stunts in order to get attention. You can never give such people enough attention. Ignore them long enough and they will give up. Humour their self-centred misdeeds and the lunacy will never end.

Now there are plenty more points we could add here, but these should be enough to warn and help those of you who are in leadership. Acts 20v28-31.

Christians leave the church for lots of different reasons, but I have found that the main one is down to pride. They think they know better than the pastor, elder or leader. **They will not come under any kind of authority**, because they think they know best. The word of God, when it is faithfully preached each week, will convict and convince you of your sins and failings. **You will either come in line with it, or, you will leave and seek another church that is *lukewarm* and more *comfortable***. Many Christians leave church because they are very immature, will not join in the fight, and only want to be entertained. Some Christians would rather go to the cinema on a Bible study night, or take their children dancing instead of going to church. These kinds of Christians amount to *nothing* in life and your church is better off without them. They will never be happy in a Bible Believing Church where the truth of God's word is preached. *They can't handle it!*

NOTES

NOTES

NOTES

ETERNALLY SECURE – ONCE SAVED ALWAYS SAVED

Once you are saved you *cannot* lose your salvation... *no matter who says you can!*

A Christian in *this dispensation*, as one preacher put it, *'couldn't go to hell even if he wanted to!'* People confuse 'breaking fellowship' with the Lord, with *losing* your salvation, they are not the same. If you have a child and that child *wrongs* you, no matter what they have done against you, they are *still* your son or daughter. Once you are a child of God and adopted into His family (Gal 4v5, Eph 1v5) you are His son forever. If you could *work or earn* your salvation, then yes you could lose it; but you and I have done nothing *in ourselves* to gain or obtain salvation – Christ Jesus has done it all, and there is nothing we can *add* to what He has done at Calvary by shedding His incorruptible Blood to save us - Rom 5v9, Eph 1v7, 1 John 1v6+7. Now because we are saved eternally, doesn't mean that we have a licence to sin. A Christian will try his utmost to live a life of holiness and purity, and walk in the Spirit of God (Gal 5v16) obeying the will of God.

Yet Christians *do* mess up, and can even go as far as *losing their testimony* and turning their back upon God, yet they are still *saved*, and will go to the Heavenly Jerusalem when they die. By *still* sinning (deliberately or ignorantly) God may punish us here on earth (Heb 12v5-7). A Christian *can lose* the following... **a)** his testimony – Lot **b)** his health – 1 Cor 11 **c)** rewards – 1 Cor 3v11-15 **d)** his inheritance – Col 3v24+25 **e)** his joy – Ps 51v12 **f)** his assurance – 1 John 3v20-22 **g)** even his life – 1 Cor 10v10+11.

So the *backslider* may suffer loss *but he is still saved* because it is the Lord Jesus Christ who has *saved* him through His Blood; we have done nothing to *earn* our salvation or *work* for it. Eph 2v8-10. (*Note... should walk in them,* but not all Christians do, some backslide and live for themselves rather than the Lord). Christians who teach that you can lose your salvation often live in bondage, constantly worrying about it e.g. *'Have I lost it yet? When did I lose it? How can I get it back? Have I got it back?'* It becomes 'salvation' based upon *works!* There is no liberty in this kind of a relationship – Gal 2v4, Gal 5v1, 2 Cor 3v17. Those that say you *can* lose your salvation are getting their *dispensations* mixed up and *cannot* rightly divide the word of truth - 2 Tim 2v15.

Some excellent verses from the Scriptures that *prove* once we are saved we are saved for eternity, and *cannot* lose our salvation (note *not* fellowship) are as follows... John 10v27-30 - Once you are a 'sheep' you cannot perish. You are saved forever and *cannot* lose your salvation. Eternal life means *eternal* life. John 5v24 - You *are passed from* death unto life – no going back. Eph 4v30 - The Christian is *sealed* and God's seal *cannot* be broken. John 14v16 – the Comforter abides with you, the Christian, forever. 1 John 5v13. We may *know* that we have eternal life. Eph 2v6 - Spiritually speaking we *are* in Heaven already. The *'lose your salvation crowd'* would have us 'in and out' of Heaven like a yoyo! Eph 5v5 - Note lose our 'inheritance *not* our salvation'.

Now don't get me wrong, the Bible *does* teach that you *can lose* your salvation but certainly *not* in this dispensation i.e. the Body of Christ up until the Rapture.

The Pentecostals like to point us to John 15v1-6 as a proof text that you *can* lose your salvation. Some Christians believe that a born again believer, someone who is IN Christ can be *cut out* of Christ and go to Hell i.e. using v6 as a proof text. Now note that **not one disciple was IN Christ at that time.** Not one of them was *abiding IN Christ* and He was *not abiding* in any of them until the Comforter was come - John 14v16+17. Now the Lord is *that* Spirit – 2 Cor 3v17. *That Spirit* IS the

Lord. Col 1v27.

Note also regarding John 15v6 – No *angels* burn anyone in the fire (as in Mat 13v39+40). 'Men' gather these 'branches' and burn them. Many Christians alive now (probably 80% plus) and for the last 20 centuries, have been 'IN Christ' with the Holy Spirit *abiding* in them (John 15v5), but they did *not* bring forth *much fruit*. Ruckman writes… 'You see, when you study the Scriptures by **comparing Scripture with Scripture**, you don't find any NT Christian since AD 70 'losing his salvation' anywhere. It is simply an 'illustration' likening His **eleven disciples** to branches extending from Him. He is the 'VINE'. This is *not* the equivalent of 'the church' being His 'Body' (read 1 Cor 12v13-27). After Pentecost, believers are 'bone of His bone and flesh of His flesh' (Eph 5), not appendages *stuck on to Him* as branches are stuck on a tree. Notice that the word 'abide' here is the one used in John 14v16. It is a reference to a permanent place of fellowship, not just someone who 'comes and goes'. Note, further, that the 'branch' is cast forth (v6) 'AS' a branch. It can be doctrinally aimed at an *unsaved* man who has never been in fellowship with Christ and so is not a *real* 'branch'. The illustration *cannot* be applied to a Christian *doctrinally*, for *two* possibilities are in the passage: if you are 'IN Christ' you are bearing fruit and abiding and getting your prayers answered (v7), and if you are *not* bearing fruit and *not* getting your prayers answered you were *never* 'In Him' in the first place. As we have said before, this does *not* match the 'IN Christ' passages in the Pauline Epistles that deal with the Body of Christ'.

So John 15v1-6 *doctrinally* is *not* aimed at the Body of Christ, it is aimed at the apostles *before* Christ was crucified and *before* the Body of Christ was 'formed' i.e. became an 'organism' in Acts 2. Ruckman again regarding Acts 2… 'When Peter preaches, the local church is present and has been present since Mat 10v1-3. This local church now becomes an organism through a life-giving, activating power in the Person of the Holy Ghost, and its entire membership is regenerated. Until v41, every one of its members were baptised 'for the remission of sins' by John the Baptist, *under the law* (Luke 16v16). No one in the group could have known anything about Christ's indwelling Gentiles (Col 1v27), or the 'one Spirit' of 1 Cor 12v13, or the Jew-Gentile body - And this is why nothing about these matters is *recorded*.

Another 'proof' text, the 'lose-it-crowd' use is 1 Cor 9v22-27. The word 'castaway' is the *Hell-fire* text they give. But again, not being able to 'rightly divide the word of truth' (2 Tim 2v15) gets you into all sorts of problems. First of all this passage has **nothing** at all to do with *salvation*. It is to do with your Christian walk and the *work* you *do*. Paul was 'free' (v1) both physically and spiritually yet regarding the Gospel he made himself a slave to both Jews and Gentiles (v19). He said in Romans 1v14 **I am debtor both to the Greeks, and to the Barbarians**. Paul made himself a 'slave' (spiritually) to reach all men for Jesus Christ. Paul often, when he entered a city, went to the Jew first (Rom 1v16). He would then go into the synagogue and preach to his 'kinsmen' i.e. Jews (Acts 13v5 + 14-44, Acts 14v1, Acts 17v1-2+10+17, Acts 18v4). Paul wanted to see the Jews saved so badly (Rom 10v1) that he once consented to go to the temple and purify himself and shave his head to show the Jews that he kept the Law (Acts 21v20-24). Paul had no problem whatsoever to go to the Gentiles, in front of the Jews, when the Jews had rejected the Gospel (Acts 13v42-48, Acts 18v4-6, Act 28v17-31.) He laid no claims of the Law upon his Gentile converts (Acts 15v1-2), except those stipulations laid down by the apostles and elders in Jerusalem (Acts 15v19-22, Acts 21v25) – that is what he is saying in 1 Cor 9v21.

1 Cor 9v22 – Without 'compromising' your faith/belief, act/become like the person you're trying to reach i.e. if you are dealing with someone with some class/culture, act like a gentleman. Be sympathetic towards the Jew, the Roman Catholic, JW etc. 'Bend' but *don't* compromise to sin or *not* stand your ground when you know you should. **And this I do for the gospel's sake, that I might be partaker thereof with you.** (v23)

1 Cor 9v24 – Paul likens the Christian life to a race (compare Phil 3v13+14, Heb 12v1+2). You are to run to win, not to show off to the spectators or 'entertain' them – *run to win*. Many Christians today, in regard to the 'crucified life' (Gal 2v20) and 'self-denial/sanctification', are *not* running to win. Track athletes run to win; they do not get in each other's way or in each other's lane. They run in their own lane looking towards the finishing line (Heb 12v2) not towards the ground or the crowd. Many Christians seem to get in each other's lane. *You have your lane and I have mine!* Run *your* race and keep looking unto Jesus - Ecc 11v4.

1 Cor 9v25 – *Don't* drink, smoke or do/participate in anything where it will hinder (Gal 5v7) your walk with the Lord. If you are going to master the thing, you have to be temperate in your habits (*Temperate - Moderate; not excessive; as temperate heat; a temperate climate; temperate air. Moderate in the indulgence of the appetites and passions; as temperate in eating and drinking; temperate in pleasures; temperate in speech. Be sober and temperate, and you will be healthy. Cool; calm; not marked with passion; not violent; as a temperate discourse or address; temperate language. Free from ardent passion*).

The reward for the 'temperate' athlete is a corruptible crown, but in the Christian 'race' it is an incorruptible crown – 1 Pet 1v4. 1 Cor 9v26 – In running you have to be certain of the course. You don't weave all over the track. We read in Phil 3v14 **I press toward the mark for the prize of the high calling of God in Christ Jesus.** A boxer doesn't enter the ring and start throwing punches everywhere and anywhere, he aims his blows towards the target. 1 Cor 9v27 – We should die to the flesh daily and walk in the Spirit (Gal 5v16) keeping our body under control and in subjection. Do not fulfil the lusts of the flesh.

Finally to 1 Cor 9v27 – (Castaway - Rejected; useless; of no value worthless) In other words, if you haven't kept your body, your flesh under control, if you have fulfilled your own desires rather than the Lord's, if you have followed your own will rather than do the will of Jesus Christ you are good for nothing. Ps 127v1 **Except the LORD build the house, they labour in vain that build it**... This says nothing of being cast into Hell fire or losing your salvation. It is talking about the Christian walk/life. Regarding v27 – The idea is that the body can get out of hand i.e. lust, fornication, laziness, compromise, etc. What is your relationship like with the Lord Jesus Christ? Are you living for Him or for yourself? *Are you a castaway?*

By now you should be convinced **by Scripture** that you *cannot* lose your salvation. If not, you are not a Bible believer! A great passage on eternal security is Rom 8v35-39. Dr Ruckman writes Verse 35 '**Who shall separate us from the love of Christ?**...' Paul then lists seven possibilities... **shall tribulation, or distress, or persecution, or famine, or nakedness, or peril, or sword?** No! If anyone could have been separated 'from the love of Christ' by those things, Paul was a prime candidate. He went through all of those things and more. '**For I am persuaded**...' (v38). Paul has been convinced of what he is about to say. He is certain of it. Concerning the subject of eternal security, the companion verse to this passage is 2 Tim 1v12. His persuasion is that nothing and no one is '**able to separate us from the love of God**...'. As he did in verse 35, he listed seven things. Here in verses 38-39, he lists *ten* things, some of them natural and some of them supernatural. If you are IN God's love, you are saved. The '**love of God**' is '**IN Christ Jesus our Lord**'. If you aren't IN Jesus Christ, then you aren't IN '**the love of God**'. If you aren't IN '**the love of God**' you are lost. Since eternal security is one of the main themes of Romans 8, I want to give *seven* reasons why the salvation of the believer is secure...

1) The believer is eternally secure because of the *election of the Father*. The Lord elected anyone who was **IN Christ** to get home to Heaven. Once a sinner gets IN Christ, his journey IS complete. There is no doctrine of 'un-election' or 'dis-election!' Election IN Christ happens *in time* not in

eternity as the Calvinist teaches.

2) *The union of the believer with Jesus Christ* guarantees his salvation. If you're IN Christ, you *can't* go to Hell, because you are part of Jesus Christ, and no part of Christ will ever go to Hell 'again'.

3) *Eternal life is a free gift.* You did nothing to *earn it*, and *you can do nothing to lose it*.

4) *The intercession of Jesus Christ for us means* we can never lose our salvation. You have the greatest Prayer Warrior in the universe praying for you.

5) You are eternally secure because you are '**kept by the power of God**' (1 Pet 1v5). You are kept by the same power that raised Jesus Christ from the dead.

6) *Your security is based on the righteousness of a sinless man*, not on your goodness. You have the imputed righteousness of Jesus Christ. It isn't yours to lose. You could make the biggest mess you ever saw, and it wouldn't affect the righteousness of Christ at all. Like David, you might have to have the joy of your salvation restored (Ps 51v12), but your *salvation* went nowhere.

7) Finally, God's eternal purpose means that when everything men think could ever take your salvation away has been forgotten in eternity (Isa 65v17, Rev 21v4), God will gather everything in Christ to Himself (Eph 1v10). Jesus Christ and the Father keep us to fulfil the purpose of God the Son when He prayed... '**And now I am no more in the world, but these are in the world, and I come to thee. Holy Father, keep through thine own name those whom thou hast given me, that they may be one, as we are. While I was with them in the world, I kept them in thy name: those that thou gavest me I have kept, and none of them is lost, but the son of perdition; that the scripture might be fulfilled. Father, I will that they also, whom thou hast given me, be with me where I am; that they may behold my glory, which thou hast given me: for thou lovedst me before the foundation of the world.**' John 17v11-12+24

Now the only way you are going to *miss* Heaven is if you are *not* saved; that's the only way. As Christians we should never worry about going to Hell; it *can't* happen if we are saved by the Blood of Christ and IN His Body.

NOTES

NOTES

JESUS CHRIST IS GOD

When you are dealing with the cults such as the JW's, they will always challenge you regarding the Deity of the Lord Jesus Christ. Here are some of the best Scriptures to use against these heretics...

1 John 5v7 (Phil 2v5-11), John 10v30-33

The word **Godhead** occurs 3x in the Scriptures – Acts 17v29, Rom 1v20, Col 2v9. It is also very interesting that the words **Almighty God** appear 3x in Scripture – Gen 17v1, Ezek 10v5, Rev 19v15

Who raised Jesus from the dead? – The Father did (Gal 1v1), Jesus raised Himself (John 2v19-21) and the Holy Spirit raised Him (Rom 8v11)

John 1v1+14 (note capital 'W') cf. 1 John 1v1, Rev 19v11-13

1 Tim 3v16 – Jesus Christ **IS** God in the flesh.

Jesus Christ IS Jehovah God – note the word LORD in capitals... Zech 12v7-10, note too the words 'I' and 'ME', incredible! Cf. Rev 1v5-7

Isa 44v6 – Note the LORD for Father and Son. Cf. Rev 1v17+18

Compare these verses regarding the Father and Son as God... Isa 8v13-15, Isa 28v16 – 1 Pet 2v8, Rom 9v33

Deut 32v3+4 – 1 Cor 10v4. The LORD is the Father, and the LORD is Jesus Christ, both are God. God the Rock is also Jesus Christ.

John 20v24-28 – Jesus *accepted* what Thomas said... "My Lord and my God".

Jesus Christ had no beginning – Micah 5v2 (see how this verse is perverted in modern 'bibles' like the NIV etc.)

Jesus Christ wasn't created – John 6v62

Who is the I AM? – Exo 3v14, John 8v58 (see also John 8v24+28, John 9v9, John 13v19, John 18v5+6+8) – Jesus is the I AM.

God the Father is the first and the last – Isa 44v6, Isa 48v12 but so is God the Son – Rev 1v5-7+8+11+17, Rev 2v8, Rev 22v13

Worship *only* God. Yet Jesus Christ is to be worshipped – Exo 34v14 cf. Heb 1v6, Luke 4v8, Mat 2v11, Mat 28v9+10, Mark 5v6, Luke 24v52, John 9v38, Rev 5v11-14. Not once in Scripture do we find the Lord Jesus Christ refusing worship, yet we are told to worship God only... exactly, Jesus Christ IS God (unless you're a Bible 'rejector/corrector' that is).

Who can forgive sins but God? (Ps 32v5, Isa 43v25, Ps 130v3+4) – Yet Jesus forgives sins... Mark 2v5+7, Luke 5v20+24, Luke 7v48+49

1 John 2v22 **Who is a liar** (JW's, Mormons, Christadelphians etc.) **but he that denieth that Jesus is the Christ? He is antichrist, that denieth the Father and the Son.**

v23 **Whosoever denieth the Son,** (all the cults and false religions) **the same hath not the Father: (but) he that acknowledgeth the Son hath the Father also.** *The truth is in Jesus* – Eph 4v21

Who is the Creator? The Father (Gen 1v1, Isa 44v24) yet we read that Jesus is also the Creator – John 1v1-3, Col 1v16-20, Heb 3v4.

God the Father even calls His Son, the Lord Jesus Christ, God – Heb 1v8-10

Who is the Saviour? The Father (Isa 43v3+11, Isa 45v15+21, Isa 49v26, Isa 60v16, Hos 13v4) yet so is the Lord Jesus Christ – Luke 2v11, John 4v42, Phil 3v20, 1 Tim 2v3, 1 Tim 4v10, 2 Tim 1v10, Titus 1v3+4, Titus 2v10+13, 1 John 4v14

Who is the Holy One? God the Father is (2 Kings 19v22, Ps 89v18, Isa 31v1, Hos 11v9, Hab 1v12) yet so is Jesus Christ the Son – Mark 1v24, Acts 2v27, Acts 3v14

JESUS CHRIST IS GOD

God the Father is the husband of His people in the OT – Isa 54v5, Jer 3v14, Jer 31v32

God the Son is the husband of His people in the NT – 2 Cor 11v2, Mat 25v10, John 3v29+30, Rev 19v7+9

NAME of God or 'names' of God – Mat 28v19. One God, yet three separate Persons (Godhead/Trinity).

You can't understand God 'the Godhead/Trinity', who can? – Eph 1v20-23, Job 11v7, Rom 11v33, Isa 40v18+25, 1 Cor 2v14, it's a mystery (1 Tim 3v16)

Who created man? – Gen 1v26+27 - not in the image of angels - Gen 5v1, Gen 3v22, Gen 11v7

Acts 20v28 – **God's Blood (Jesus' Blood).**

Jesus Christ is the true God – 1 John 5v20, John 5v23, 1 John 2v23, John 8v24

The Trinity

	Father	Son	Holy Spirit
Everlasting	Rom 16v26, Deut 33v27, Ps 90v2, Isa 40v28, 1 Tim 1v17	Mic 5v2, Rev 1v8	Heb 9v14, 1 Cor 2v14
Omnipresent (Everywhere)	Jer 23v24	Mat 18v20, Mat 28v20, Eph 1v23, 2 Cor 13v5	Ps 139v7-10
Omnipotent (All powerful)	Jer 32v17, 1 Chron 29v11, Mat 19v26, Luke 1v37, 1 Pet 1v5	Mat 28v18, Heb 1v3, John 5v21-23, 2 Cor 12v9, Mat 8v26+27, Mat 9v23-26, Luke 7v11-16, John 11v43+44, Eph 1v21, Phil 3v20+21	Rom 15v13+19, Luke 1v35
Omniscient (All knowing)	Job 42v2, Ps 139v1-4, Ps 147v5, Ps 102v24, Acts 15v18, Heb 4v13, Rom 11v33, Jer 17v10	John 16v30, Mat 12v25, John 2v24+25, Col 2v3, Rev 2v23, Mat 9v4, John 21v17, John 1v47-49, John 4v17-19	Isa 40v13+14, 1 Cor 2v10+11, John 16v12+13
Called God	Gen 1v1, John 17v3	John 20v28, 1 John 5v20, Mat 1v23	Acts 5v3+4
The Creator	Gen 1v1, Mal 2v10, Isa 44v24	John 1v3+10, Col 1v16, Heb 1v10	Job 26v13, Job 33v4, Ps 104v30
Raised Jesus	Gal 1v1, Rom 10v9, Rom 6v4, 1 Cor 6v14, Eph 1v20, Rom 4v24	John 2v19-21, John 10v17+18	Rom 8v11, 1 Pet 3v18
Lives in the Believer	1 John 4v12	John 14v20	John 14v17

JESUS CHRIST IS GOD

Jesus Christ IS God		God The Trinity (1 John 5v7)
2 Pet 2v1	Mark 2v5-7, Col 3v13	**The Trinity** (Father, Son and Holy Spirit) were present in the…
Col 2v9	Mat 26v63-65	
Acts 20v28	Num 21v5+6, 1 Cor 10v9	**Incarnation** – Mat 1v20-25, Luke 2v13+14
John 1v1-3 (Gen 1v1)		**Death** – John 3v16, John 10v18, Rom 8v32, Heb 9v14
2 Cor 8v9	Ps 102v24-27, Heb 1v10-12	
John 16v28	Isa 6v1-10, John 12v39-41	**Resurrection** – Acts 2v24, John 2v19, John 10v18, 1 Pet 3v18
John 8v42		
John 3v13	Isa 8v13+14, Rom 9v33, 1 Cor 1v23	**As believers we know the reality of the Trinity in our lives** – Eph 4v6, Col 1v27, 1 Cor 6v19
John 6v62		**Godhead – 'plural'** – Acts 17v29, Rom 1v20, Col 2v9, Gen 1v26, Gen 3v22, Gen 11v7, Isa 6v8, Gen 18v1+2
John 17v5	1 John 5v20, John 17v3	
John 8v58 (Exo 3v14)	Isa 44v6, Rev 22v13	**Trinity in the Old Testament (OT)** – Isa 59v19+20, Isa 63v7-10, Isa 60v16, 2 Sam 23v2+3, Isa 48v16
John 1v14+15+29+30	Mal 3v6, Heb 13v8	**Trinity Scriptures** – Mat 28v19, Mat 3v16+17, 2 Cor 13v14, John 14v16+17, Eph 2v18, 1 Cor 12v4-6, Eph 4v4-6, 1 John 5v7, 1 Pet 1v2, Gal 4v6
John 5v23+24+28+29	Mat 18v20	
(2 Cor 5v10)	John 2v24+25, John 6v70+71, John 13v10+11	**Trinity, ONE yet separate** – 1 John 4v14, John 16v7, John 5v22+27, John 10v30+38, John 15v26, John 14v23+26, John 3v16+35, 2 Pet 1v17+18, John 8v17+18, Luke 10v16, Rev 3v21+22, 1 Cor 6v14
John 10v28		
John 16v7		
Rev 1v8, Rev 22v13-16	Isa 45v23, Phil 2v10+11	
Prov 8	Col 1v15-18, John 1v3+10, Eph 3v9	**Father and Son are Saviour** – Titus 1v3, Acts 5v31, Hos 13v4, 1 John 4v14, Luke 2v11
Isa 43v11, Acts 4v12	Acts 7v59+60	**Father and Son are coming again** – John 14v3, Rev 4v8,
Isa 45v15	John 20v24-28	Acts 1v11, 1 Thes 4v14, Rev 1v7+8, Rev 22v20
Heb 1v2+6+8	Gen 1v26	**Father and Son – First and Last** – Isa 44v6, Rev 1v17+18,
Titus 1v3+4, Titus 2v10+13	1 Tim 4v10	
	1 Tim 3v16	Rev 22v12+13
Titus 3v4+6	Ps 98v9	**Father and Son – Mighty God** – Jer 32v18, Isa 9v6
1 Tim 2v3	1 Tim 6v15+16	**Couple of 'extra' Scriptures** - John 5v23, 1 John 2v23
Rom 9v5	Isa 9v6	

NOTES

NOTES

NOTES

EVOLUTION

ATHEISM
The belief that there was nothing and nothing happened to nothing and then nothing magically exploded for no reason, creating everything and then a bunch of everything magically rearranged itself for no reason whatsoever into self-replicating bits which then turned into dinosaurs.

Makes perfect sense.

To the IDIOT!

Question to ask the *deceived* evolutionist

Animals don't have to wear clothes because they have fur or hair; therefore, why would a human (who you say came from monkeys / apes) over billions of years shed his hair / fur, to grow skin that then... needs to be covered? **See how stupid that is?** When did the monkey start shedding his fur/hair and grow skin? Seen any transitional fossils lately? Of course you haven't, neither have they, guess why? You got it, because there aren't any! Like I say, 'evolution' is for idiots. No rational, sensible, honest person would believe that tosh. Darwin was totally deceived and just couldn't understand truth so he spent his life guessing, assuming, speculating and pretending, just like all his followers do today. You've never seen a dog changing into another animal a day in your life. You have never seen one single animal (kind) changing into anything else one day in your life. The only time an evolutionist will actually experience 'evolution' is in his imagination or dreams. When it comes to hard facts and truth, 'evolution' is a myth that people want to believe in order to get rid of God, so they can live in their sin happily ever after. They forget that once

Definition of Stupid: *Knowing the truth, seeing the truth, but still believing the lies.*

they have been put to bed with a shovel in a six foot hole, **their soul has *already* left their body** & now they have found themselves in a place they never believed existed, **Hell**. Boy is Dawkins and Hawking in for the shock of their lives. A lifetime full of arrogance, ignorance & stupidity... for what? An eternity in the Lake of Fire! Is it worth it?

Adaptation

Charles Darwin observed that animals adapt to their environment. We see this in nature and in selective breeding by humans, but plants and animals *only ever* reproduce within 'kinds' or families, e.g. the dog 'kind' or the potato 'kind'. Despite all the experiments done on peppered moths, fruit flies and bacteria, **no scientist has ever *observed* a species changing into a *new* species.** Darwin admitted that his wider theory would fail if numerous transitional fossils were *not* found. 150

CHRISTIAN SOLDIER'S BATTLE NOTES

years of intensive research has *totally failed* to produce one single convincing transitional life form. Fossils appear and disappear abruptly throughout the geological record. (Taken from the leaflet 'Not by chance')

Irreducible Complexity

Then there are the animals which defy evolution because of what biologists call 'irreducible complexity'. Sea slugs have the ability to eat sea anemones without bursting the poisonous barbs. When these barbs reach the sea slug's stomach, there are tubes lined with moving hairs which lead to the *fronds* on the sea slug's back. The poisonous barbs from the sea anemone are taken along these tubes to the tips of the *fronds* – where they are used as ammunition against the sea slug's enemies. *Gradual evolution* is impossible and could *never* produce this – it must have worked perfectly from the beginning. (Taken from the leaflet 'Not by chance')

'Survival of the fittest' cannot create new forms

'Natural Selection' or the 'Survival of the Fittest' has *no power* actually to create anything new because it **does not increase genetic information**. It *cannot* build new organs or functions which are not there already. It loses information and tends to 'weed out' mutational forms. Evolutionists say one species *evolves* into another through mutations, but no mutation leading to a new species **has ever been found** or been demonstrated in a laboratory. In practice, mutations are either neutral or damaging to the plants and animals in which they occur. **Darwin knew nothing about DNA.** DNA tells a cell how to behave and grow. It has two strands twisted together in a double helix. Between the strands are four types of molecules called nucleotides and the order they are in tells the DNA what to do. This is information just like that on a computer – it *cannot* be produced by 'chance' – *not even in billions of years!* (Taken from the leaflet 'Not by chance')

Evolution presents *conjecture* as certainty.

Evolution is for idiots! Have you been deceived?

(www.dissentfromdarwin.org)

The claims for the ability of random mutation and natural selection to account for the complexity of life…

is totally, utterly, ridiculous and preposterous!

Why doesn't the giraffe get a headache?

With a long neck and massive heart generating twice our blood pressure, why does the giraffe not get a brain haemorrhage when it bends down to drink? Because of special valves in its jugular vein and spongy tissue at the base of its brain which limit the pressure and the flow. Giraffes couldn't survive without this special 'plumbing', so they must always have had it. It *couldn't* have 'evolved' gradually, and no fossils show intermediate forms with half-as-long a neck. This clever and effective design points to a wise, all-powerful Creator God. (Taken from the leaflet 'Not by chance')

www.soldiersofchrist.org.uk (Have a look at their website for further details)

EVOLUTION

If a fair maiden kisses a frog which instantly changes into a handsome prince we would call it a *fairy tale*.

But if the frog takes 40 million years to turn into a prince we call it 'evolution.'

Evolution is a fairy tale for *grown-ups!*

Evolution my left foot!

Please don't be so dumb to 'believe' that the human eye and ear *evolved*, I mean, no one is that stupid are they?

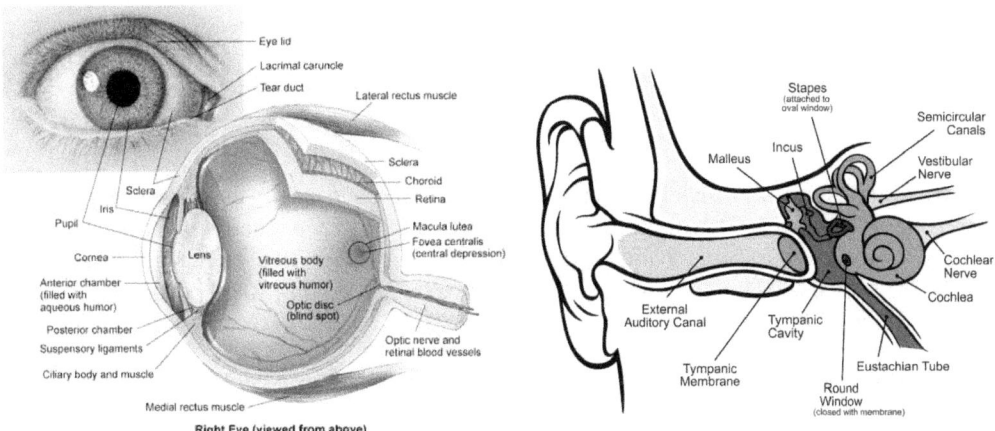

Surely not one *moron* on earth has enough **faith** to believe that the eye and ear e*volved* by themselves due to random chance, multiple mutations (*copying mistakes that **never** produce 'increased' information*) *and a lot of time!* You can see that they have been **designed** of course. Imagine someone having enough *faith* to believe that they evolved by themselves without a designer, let alone *evolving together* alongside the brain, heart, kidneys, liver, stomach, and every other organ you have in your body... *plus all the other 'bits and pieces'*. Come on folks, if you're not *designed* then I'm the tooth-fairy. (I wonder why Richard Dawkins doesn't attack the *tooth-fairy* by the way, seeing as he doesn't believe in her as well as not believing in God? Perhaps he thinks there is a chance of God being *real*? Do you think that is why his advertising campaign on the London buses read... 'There's **probably** no God!')

CHRISTIAN SOLDIER'S BATTLE NOTES

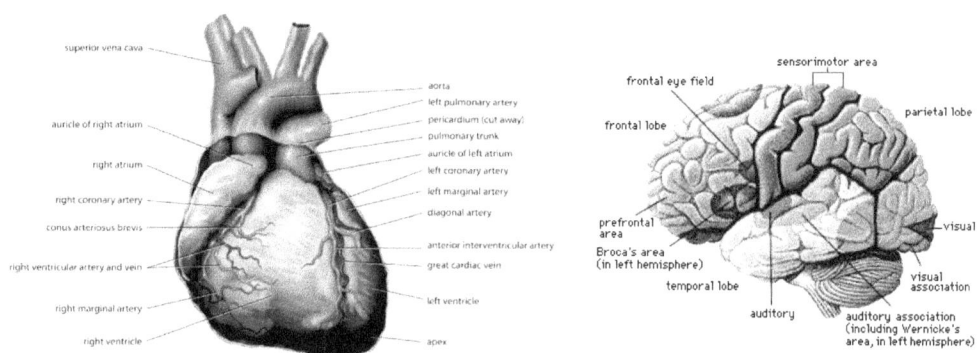

Now any honest, rational, intelligent human being can see that just by these four diagrams (eye, ear, brain and heart), it is *absolutely impossible* that these four organs could evolve by accident, random chance and billions of years (give or take a few). There is just no way on earth, that your eye, ear, brain and heart just started from nothing, then *something* formed after an explosion, and then, *little by little*, it evolved into these amazing, intricate, specifically detailed, *incomprehensible* organs all functioning together with the rest of your body parts in perfect harmony. There is just *no way on earth man*, that anyone who is in his right mind could *believe* something *so stupid*!

Evolution is a religious faith/belief. It takes *so much faith* to believe in it, as there is certainly **no evidence** for macro-evolution at all, *not one single shred of evidence*, no matter what Dawkins and Hawking's say – *everyone should 'baulk' at Dawk and Hawk*, because **they have made their living** (1 Tim 6v10) at *guesswork* backed up with *no proof or scientific evidence* whatsoever; and millions of suckers have *bought* into their *religion!* (1 Tim 6v20)

Evolution is a *religion* - it takes so much faith to believe in something so ridiculous.

I am not religious, I trust in God the Creator, the Designer of everything. I trust in the Authorized Version Bible 100% - it is without error and tells us everything we need to know about ourselves and the universe.

So called 'atheists' deny God exists because they want to live their lives *their own way* and *not be held accountable* to anyone. That's like saying I do not believe in electricity but daily I use appliances that use electricity. Atheists are just God denying people who *think* they are clever, yet really they are the biggest fools of them all – Ps 14v1, 1 Cor 2v14.

Well of course the heads of these presidents in the mountainside evolved **over billions of years!**

EVOLUTION

Evolution is impossible! Evolution is biologically impossible. Evolution is mathematically impossible. Here are some reasons. **The Earth's Magnetic Field** - The strength of the earth's magnetic field has been measured for well over a century. This provides scientists with exceptionally good records. In an important recent study, Dr. Thomas G. Barnew has shown that the strength of the earth's magnetic field is decaying exponentially at a rate corresponding to a half-life of 1,400 years. That is to say, 1,400 years ago the magnetic field of the earth was twice as strong as it is now. If we extrapolate back as far as 10,000 years, we find that the earth would have had a magnetic field as strong as that of a magnetic star. This is, of course, **impossible**. Thus, based on the present decay of the earth's magnetic field, 10,000 years appears to be an upper limit for the age of the earth. Finally, evolutionists believe that the earth's magnetic field is due to circulating electric currents in its core. If we extrapolate backward about 20,000 years, we find that the estimated heat produced by the currents would have melted the earth. Clearly, the testimony of the earth's magnetic field is strongly in favour of a relatively young earth, not an ancient one.

Memorable Quotes '*Everyone who is seriously involved in the pursuit of science becomes convinced that a **spirit** is manifest in the laws of the universe - a **spirit vastly superior to that of man**, and one in the face of which we with modest powers must feel humble.*' - Albert Einstein, towards the end of his life.

'*Once we see, however, that the probability of life origination at random is so utterly minuscule as to make it **absurd**, it becomes sensible to think that the favourable properties of physics, on which life depends, are in every respect deliberate. It is, therefore almost inevitable that our own measure of intelligence must reflect **higher intelligence** . . . even to the limit of **God**.*' - Sir Fred Hoyle, British mathematician and astrophysicist, an atheist for much of his life, until he finally admitted the truth.

The chance of evolution ever occurring is so remote as to be mathematically *impossible*. The theory of evolution is like placing a monkey at a keyboard and having him start typing. Assume the monkey never dies and give him 5 billion years to type. What are the chances the monkey will type out the entire works of the Encyclopaedia Britannica volumes A-Z in the exact order with no spelling or grammar errors? The chances of that happening are actually *better* than the theory of evolution ever happening!

The *nonsense* of Evolution
It takes a lot of *faith* to believe in Evolution.
Imagine believing in the following, *how absurd*...
Nothing produces *everything*
Non-Life produces *life*
Randomness produces *fine-tuning*
Chaos produces *information*
Unconsciousness produces *consciousness*
Non-reason produces reason
Only a *monkey* would believe something so stupid!

Creation declares God exists - Ecc 1v6+7, Isa 55v10+11, Job 28v24-26, Job 36v26-29, Ps 135v6+7, Rom 1v18-22, Psa 19v1

CHRISTIAN SOLDIER'S BATTLE NOTES

The *nonsense* of Evolution - Regarding Evolution, which is **the greatest *hoax* of all time**, which *evolved* first and how long did it work without the others...?

The digestive system, the food to be digested, the appetite, the ability to find and eat the food, the digestive juices, or the body's resistance to its own digestive juice (e.g. stomach, intestines etc.)

The *drive* to reproduce or the ability to reproduce?

The lungs, the mucus lining to protect them, the throat, or the perfect mixture of gases to be breathed into the lungs?

How about this one... The plants or the insects that live on and pollinate the plants? *See how ridiculous evolution is!*

Which evolved first, the bones, ligaments, tendons, blood supply, or muscles to move the bones?

What about the nervous system, repair system, or hormone system, *which evolved first?*

How can love, mercy, guilt, satisfaction, anger, sympathy, revenge etc. *evolve?*

The *theory* of evolution...

'Hydrogen is a colourless, odourless gas which given enough time, turns into people'

The evolutionary formula for making the universe...

Nothing + nothing = two elements + time = 94 natural elements + time = all physical laws and a completely structured universe of galaxies, systems, stars, planets and moons orbiting in perfect balance and order

This is the evolutionary formula for making life...

Dirt + water = living creatures

Evolutionists theorise that the above two formulas can enable everything about us to make itself – with the exception of man-made things, such as cars or buildings. Complicated things, such as wooden boxes with nails in them, require thought, intelligence and careful workmanship. But everything else about us in nature (such as hummingbirds and the human eye) is declared to be the result of accidental mishaps, random confusion and time. You will not even need raw materials to begin with, they make themselves too!

44 reasons why evolution is just a fairy tale for adults – by Michael Snyder

1) If the theory of evolution was true, we should have discovered millions upon millions of transitional fossils that show the development of one species into another species. Instead, we have zero!

2) When Charles Darwin came up with his theory, he admitted that no transitional forms had

EVOLUTION

been found at that time, but he believed that huge numbers certainly existed and would eventually be discovered... *'Lastly, looking not to any one time, but to all time, if my theory be true, numberless intermediate varieties, linking closely together all the species of the same group, must assuredly have existed. But, as by this theory, innumerable transitional forms must have existed, why do we not find them embedded in countless numbers in the crust of the earth?'*

3) Even some of the most famous evolutionists in the world acknowledge the complete absence of transitional fossils in the fossil record. For example, Dr. Colin Patterson, former senior palaeontologist of the British Museum of Natural History and author of 'Evolution' once wrote the following... *'I fully agree with your comments about the lack of direct illustration of evolutionary transitions in my book. If I knew of any, fossil or living, I would certainly have included them .... I will lay it on the line – there is not one such fossil for which one could make a watertight argument.'*

4) Stephen Jay Gould, Professor of Geology and Palaeontology at Harvard University, once wrote the following about the lack of transitional forms... *'The absence of fossil evidence for intermediary stages between major transitions in organic design, indeed our inability, even in our imagination, to construct functional intermediates in many cases, has been a persistent and nagging problem for gradualistic accounts of evolution.'*

5) Evolutionist Stephen M. Stanley of Johns Hopkins University has also commented on the stunning lack of transitional forms in the fossil record... *'In fact, the fossil record **does not convincingly document a single transition from one species to another**.'*

6) If 'evolution' was happening right now, there would be millions of creatures out there with partially developed features and organs. **But instead there are none**.

7) If the theory of evolution was true, we should not see a sudden explosion of fully formed complex life in the fossil record. Instead, that is precisely what we find.

8) Palaeontologist Mark Czarnecki, an evolutionist, once commented on the fact that complex life appears very suddenly in the fossil record... *'A major problem in proving the theory has been the fossil record; the imprints of vanished species preserved in the Earth's geological formations. This record has never revealed traces of Darwin's hypothetical intermediate variants – instead **species appear and disappear abruptly**, and this anomaly has fuelled the creationist argument that each species was created by God.'*

9) The sudden appearance of complex life in the fossil record is so undeniable that even Richard Dawkins has been forced to admit it... *'It is as though they [fossils] were just planted there, without any evolutionary history. Needless to say this appearance of sudden planting has delighted creationists. Both schools of thought (Punctuationists and Gradualists) despise so-called scientific creationists equally, and both agree that the major gaps are real, that they are true imperfections in the fossil record. The only alternative explanation of the sudden appearance of so many complex animal types in the Cambrian era is divine creation and both reject this alternative.'*

10) **Nobody has ever observed macroevolution take place in the laboratory or in nature**. In other words, nobody has ever observed one kind of creature turn into another kind of creature. **The entire theory of evolution is based on blind faith.**

11) Evolutionist Jeffrey Schwartz, a professor of anthropology at the University of Pittsburgh, openly

admits that 'the formation of a new species, by any mechanism, **has never been observed.'**

12) Even evolutionist Stephen J. Gould of Harvard University has admitted that the record shows that **species do not change**. The following is how he put it during a lecture at Hobart and William Smith College... *'Every palaeontologist knows that most species **don't change**. That's bothersome....brings terrible distress. ....They may get a little bigger or bumpier but **they remain the same species** and that's not due to imperfection and gaps but stasis. And yet this remarkable stasis has generally been ignored as no data. **If they don't change, it's not evolution so you don't talk about it.**'

13) Anyone that believes the theory of evolution has 'scientific origins' is fooling themselves. It is actually a deeply pagan religious philosophy that can be traced back for thousands of years.

14) Anything that we dig up that is supposedly more than 250,000 years old should have absolutely no radiocarbon in it whatsoever. But instead, we find it in everything that we dig up – even dinosaur bones. This is clear evidence that **the 'millions of years' theory is simply a bunch of nonsense**... *It's long been known that radiocarbon (which should disappear in only a few tens of thousands of years at the most) keeps popping up reliably in samples (like coal, oil, gas, etc.) which are supposed to be 'millions of years' old. For instance, CMI has over the years commissioned and funded the radiocarbon testing of a number of wood samples from 'old' sites (e.g. with Jurassic fossils, inside Triassic sandstone, burnt by Tertiary basalt) and these were published (by then staff geologist Dr Andrew Snelling) in Creation magazine and Journal of Creation. In each case, with contamination eliminated, the result has been in the thousands of years, i.e. C-14 was present when it 'shouldn't have been'. These results encouraged the rest of the RATE team to investigate C-14 further, building on the literature reviews of creationist M.D. Dr Paul Giem. In another very important paper presented at this year's ICC, scientists from the RATE group summarized the pertinent facts and presented further experimental data. **The bottom line is that virtually all biological specimens, no matter how 'old' they are supposed to be, show measurable C-14 levels. This effectively limits the age of all buried biota to less than (at most) 250,000 years.**

15) The odds of even a single sell 'assembling itself' by chance are so low that they aren't even worth talking about. The following is an excerpt from Jonathan Gray's book entitled 'The Forbidden Secret'... *Even the simplest cell you can conceive of would require no less than 100,000 DNA base pairs and a minimum of about 10,000 amino acids, to form the essential protein chain. Not to mention the other things that would also be necessary for the first cell. Bear in mind that every single base pair in the DNA chain has to have the same molecular orientation ('left-hand' or 'right hand')? As well as that, virtually all the amino acids must have the opposite orientation. And every one must be without error. 'To put it another way, if you attempted a trillion, trillion, trillion combinations every second for 15 billion years, the odds you would achieve all the correct orientations would still only be one chance in a trillion, trillion, trillion, trillion ... and the trillions would continue 2755 times!'* '**It would be like winning more than 4700 state lotteries in a row with a single ticket purchased for each. In other words... impossible.'**

16) **How did life learn to reproduce itself? This is a question that evolutionists *do not have an answer for.***

17) In 2007, fishermen caught a very rare creature known as a Coelacanth. Evolutionists originally told us that this 'living fossil' had gone extinct 70 million years ago. It turns out that they were only off by 70 million years.

EVOLUTION

18) According to evolutionists, the Ancient Greenling Damselfly last showed up in the fossil record about 300 million years ago. But it still exists today. So why hasn't it evolved at all over the time frame?

19) *Darwinists believe that the human brain developed without the assistance of any designer.* **This is so laughable it is amazing that there are any people out there that still believe this stuff**. *The truth is that the human brain is amazingly complex. The following is how a PBS documentary described the complexity of the human brain: 'It contains over 100 billion cells, each with over 50,000 neuron connections to other brain cells.'*

20) The following is how one evolutionist pessimistically assessed the lack of evidence for the evolution of humanity… *'Even with DNA sequence data, we have no direct access to the processes of evolution, so objective reconstruction of the vanished past can be achieved only by creative imagination.'*

21) The most famous fossil in the history of the theory of evolution, '**Piltdown Man**', turned out to be **a giant hoax.**

22) If the neutron were not about 1.001 times the mass of the proton, all protons would have decayed into neutrons or all neutrons would have decayed into protons, and therefore life would not be possible. How can we account for this?

23) If gravity was stronger or weaker by the slimmest of margins, then life sustaining stars like the sun could not exist. This would also make life impossible. How can we account for this?

24) Why did evolutionist Dr. Lyall Watson make the following statement?… *'The fossils that decorate our family tree are so scarce that there are still more scientists than specimens. The remarkable fact is that **all of the physical evidence we have for human evolution can still be placed, with room to spare, inside a single coffin!'***

25) Apes and humans are very different genetically. As DarwinConspiracy.com explains, 'the human Y chromosome has twice as many genes as the chimpanzee Y chromosome and the chromosome structures are not at all similar.'

26) How can we explain the creation of new information that is required for one animal to turn into another animal? No evolutionary process has ever been shown to be able to create new biological information. One scientist described the incredible amount of new information that would be required to transform microbes into men this way… *'The key issue is the type of change required — to change microbes into men requires changes that increase the genetic information content, from over half a million DNA 'letters' of even the 'simplest' self-reproducing organism to three billion 'letters' (stored in each human cell nucleus).'*

27) Evolutionists would have us believe that there are nice, neat fossil layers with older fossils being found in the deepest layers and newer fossils being found in the newest layers. This simply is not true at all… **The fossil layers are not found in the ground in the nice neat clean order that evolutionists illustrate them to be in their textbooks. There is not one place on the surface of the earth where you may dig straight down and pass through the fossil layers in the order shown in the textbooks. The neat order of one layer upon another does not exist in nature.** The fossil bearing layers are actually found out of order, upside down (backwards according to evolutionary theory), missing (from where evolutionists would expect them to be) or interlaced ('younger' and 'older' layers found in repeating sequences). 'Out of place' fossils are the rule and not the exception throughout the fossil record.

28) Evolutionists believe that the ancestors of birds developed hollow bones over thousands of generations so that they would eventually be light enough to fly. This makes absolutely no sense and is beyond ridiculous.

29) **If dinosaurs really are tens of millions of years old, why have scientists found dinosaur bones with soft tissue still in them?** The following is from an NBC News report about one of these discoveries… *For more than a century, the study of dinosaurs has been limited to fossilized bones. Now, researchers have recovered 70 million-year-old soft tissue, including what may be blood vessels and cells, from a Tyrannosaurus Rex.*

30) **Which evolved first**: blood, the heart, or the blood vessels for the blood to travel through?

31) **Which evolved first**: the mouth, the stomach, the digestive fluids, or the ability to poop?

32) **Which evolved first**: the windpipe, the lungs, or the ability of the body to use oxygen?

33) **Which evolved first**: the bones, ligaments, tendons, blood supply, or the muscles to move the bones?

34) In order for blood to clot, more than 20 complex steps need to successfully be completed. How in the world did that process possibly evolve?

35) DNA is so incredibly complex that it is absolutely absurd to suggest that such a language system could have 'evolved' all by itself by accident… *When it comes to storing massive amounts of information, nothing comes close to the efficiency of DNA. A single strand of DNA is thousands of times thinner than a strand of human hair. One pinhead of DNA could hold enough information to fill a stack of books stretching from the earth to the moon 500 times.* Although DNA is wound into tight coils, your cells can quickly access, copy, and translate the information stored in DNA. DNA even has a built-in proof-reader and spell-checker that ensure precise copying. Only about one mistake slips through for every 10 billion nucleotides that are copied.

36) **Can you solve the following riddle by Perry Marshall?…** 1) DNA is not merely a molecule with a pattern; it is a code, a language, and an information storage mechanism. 2) All codes are created by a conscious mind; there is no natural process known to science that creates coded information. 3) Therefore DNA was designed by a mind. If you can provide an empirical example of a code or language that occurs naturally, you've toppled my proof. ***All you need is one.***

37) Evolutionists simply cannot explain why our planet is so perfectly suited to support life.

38) Shells from living snails have been 'carbon dated' to be 27,000 years old.

39) **If humans have been around for so long, where are all of the bones and all of the graves?** The following is an excerpt from an article by Don Batten… Evolutionists also claim there was a 'Stone Age' of about 100,000 years when between one million and 10 million people lived on Earth. Fossil evidence shows that people buried their dead, often with artefacts—cremation was not practised until relatively recent times (in evolutionary thinking). If there were just one million people alive during that time, with an average generation time of 25 years, they should have buried 4 billion bodies, and many artefacts. If there were 10 million people, it would mean 40 billion bodies buried in the earth. If the evolutionary timescale were correct, then we would expect the skeletons of the buried bodies to be largely still present after 100,000 years, because many ordinary bones claimed to be much older have been found. However, even if the bodies had disintegrated, lots of artefacts should still be found.

40) Evolutionists claim that just because it looks like we were designed that does not mean that we actually were. They often speak of the 'illusion of design', but that is kind of like saying that it is an 'illusion' that a 747 airplane or an Apple iPhone were designed. And of course the human body is far more complex than a 747 or an iPhone.

41) **If you want to be part of the 'scientific community' today, you must accept the theory of evolution no matter how absurd it may seem to you.** Richard Lewontin of Harvard once made the following comment regarding this harsh reality... *We take the side of science in spite of the patent absurdity of some of its constructs, . . . in spite of the tolerance of the scientific community for unsubstantiated commitment to materialism. . . . we are forced by our a priori adherence to material causes to create an apparatus of investigation and set of concepts that produce material explanations, no matter how counterintuitive, no matter how mystifying to the uninitiated. Moreover, that materialism is absolute,* **for we cannot allow a Divine Foot in the door.**

42) Time Magazine once made the following statement about the lack of evidence for the theory of evolution... *'Yet despite more than a century of digging, the fossil record remains maddeningly sparse. With so few clues, even a single bone that doesn't fit into the picture can upset everything. Virtually every major discovery has put deep cracks in the conventional wisdom and* **forced scientists to concoct new theories***, amid furious debate.'*

43) Malcolm Muggeridge, the world famous journalist and philosopher, once made the following statement about the absurdity of the theory of evolution... *'I myself am convinced that the theory of evolution, especially the extent to which it's been applied, will be one of the great jokes in the history books of the future. Posterity will marvel that so very flimsy and dubious an hypothesis could be accepted with the incredible credulity that it has.'*

44) **In order to believe the *theory* of evolution**, you must have enough blind faith to believe that life just popped into existence from nonlife, and that such life just happened to have the ability to take in the nourishment it needed, to expel waste, and to reproduce itself, all the while having everything it needed to survive in the environment in which it suddenly found itself. Do you have that much blind faith?

For years, I have been looking for someone that can explain to me the very best evidence for the theory of evolution in a systematic way. My challenge has been for someone to lay out for me a basic outline of the facts that 'prove' that evolution is true. Perhaps you believe that you are up to the challenge?

My comment... Evolution is definitely the dumbest *religion* ever invented by mankind. It's not only dumb, but totally impossible! **Evolution is indeed a fairy tale for grown-ups.** If you believe it, you have been sucked in and deluded by the Devil, as the evidence for evolution is non-existent. May I suggest that you leave your pride behind, and do some proper research into this false *religious claptrap!*

In the beginning God created the heaven and the earth. Gen 1v1

(Fact)

If *evolution* is true... Why are the planets 'round?' ...and how come some of them spin in the opposite direction to the others?

When was the last time an explosion produced something round?

CHRISTIAN SOLDIER'S BATTLE NOTES

If you think this picture is science, then you are a NUT!

Evolution is the greatest HOAX of all time, it is a blatant LIE sucked in by billions of people who do NOT think! It is IMPOSSIBLE for time & chance over billions of years to produce YOU, absolutely, unequivocally IMPOSSIBLE, no matter if fools like Dawkins, Hawking, 'Aron Ra' & such like believe & promote it, they haven't a clue when it comes to TRUE SCIENCE in-regard-to macro-evolution, not a clue. Evolution is NOT science, it is a 'belief' system, a 'religion' that billions follow because they do NOT want to submit to God for the way they live their lives, therefore they ignore Him & make pretend He isn't there. The problem with that is, these people will one day stand before Him once they have died. Stephen Hawking believes in God NOW, although it is sadly too late

for him, he had ample chances of becoming a Christian, but chose not to, preferring his own belief system rather than God's. Just for a moment 'STOP & THINK'... look at your own DESIGN, your hands, your head, your eyes. Have a look in the mirror & start 'thinking', do you really *think* that all this DESIGN, all the bones, veins, nerves, ligaments, hair, saliva, your kidneys, heart, liver, eyebrows, ears, nails, fingerprints, plus a thousand other things happened by chance over time? Your DNA, the way your joints move, your eyes & brain (so intricately complicated), your reproduction system, your 'repair' system... **COME ON... THINK!!!** You were CREATED & DESIGNED by God, end of story. There is a GOD, & you will stand before Him one day, you'd better find out what He wants before it's too late! (Gen 1v1 – Heb 9v27)

How the eye works – info taken from RNIB

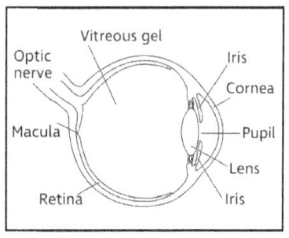
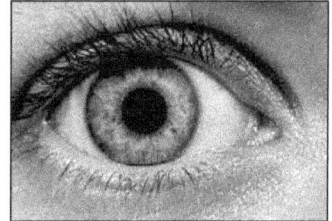
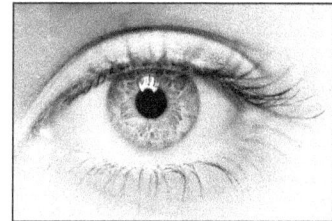

A diagram showing cross section of the eye with different parts The picture can't be displayed. labelled. We need light to see what is around us and to see colour.

Light bounces off the objects we look at and different objects reflect different amounts of light, which we see as different colours. The different parts of the eye work together to turn these light rays into images.

<u>Front of the eye</u> - Light rays enter the front of our eye through the clear **cornea** and **lens**. It is very important that both the **cornea** and **lens** are clear as this allows the light to pass directly through the front of the eye to the **retina**. The **cornea** and **lens** bends light so that it can focus on the **retina**

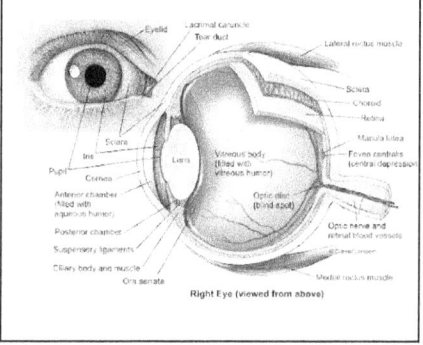

at the back of our eye. This gives us a clear, precise image. The cornea focuses the light towards our retina. The lens fine tunes the focusing of this light. Our tears form a protective layer at the front of the eye and also help to direct the light coming into our eye. The iris, the coloured circle at the front of our eye, changes the of the pupil which allows different amounts of light into our eye. The pupil is the dark

EVOLUTION

hole in the middle of the coloured part of our eye. The **pupil** gets smaller in bright conditions to let less light in. The **pupil** gets bigger in dark conditions to let more light in.

<u>Middle eye</u> - The middle of our eye is filled with a jelly-like substance called the **vitreous**. The **vitreous** is clear and allows light to pass directly from the front to the back of our eye.

<u>Back of the eye</u> - The **retina** at the back of the eye is a light-sensitive layer which consists of **rod** and **cone** cells. These cells collect the light signals directed onto them and send them as electrical signals to the **optic nerve** at the back of our eye.

Rod cells are concentrated around the edge of the **retina**. They help us to see things that aren't directly in front of us, giving us a rough idea of what is around us. They help us with our mobility and getting around by stopping us from bumping into things. They also enable us to see things in dim light and to see movement.

Cone cells are concentrated in the centre of our **retina** where the light is focused by the **cornea** and **lens**. This area is called the **macula**. **Cone** cells give us our detailed vision which we use when reading, watching TV, sewing and looking at people's faces. They are also responsible for most of our colour vision.

The **optic nerve** is made up of thousands of nerve **fibres**. These **fibres** pass the electrical signals along to our **brain** where they are processed into the image we are looking at.

<u>How we see</u> - Seeing can be likened to the process of taking pictures on a film with a camera which you then get developed. The **retina** is like a camera film which stores an image of what we are looking at. The image directed onto the retina is then sent along to the **brain** where it is processed, like developing a camera film. Therefore we actually "see" in our brain with the light information sent to it from our eyes. This whole process happens very quickly so that everything we see is in focus. *Now after reading that, how on earth can anyone who is sensible, rational, and honest, believe that the human eye evolved over millions of years... it's just impossible.*

NOTES

THE ERRORS OF CALVINISM

Calvinists are not TULIPS, they're MUPPETS!

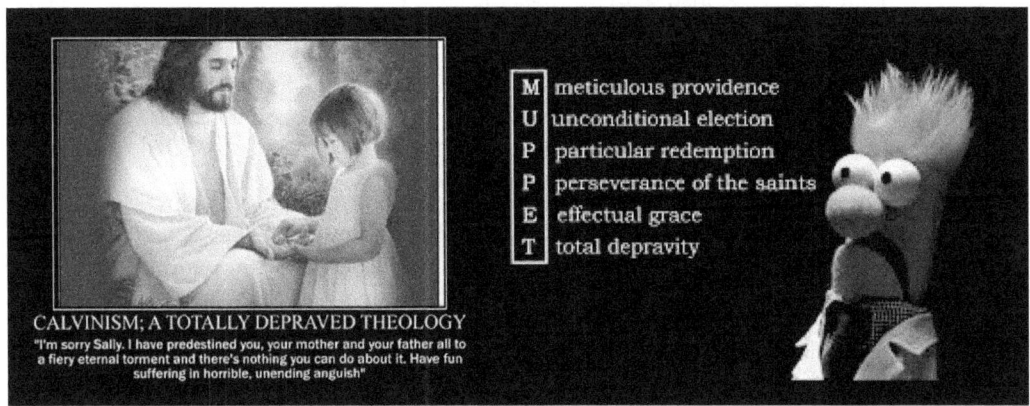

Questions to ask the *Tulip Sniffing* Calvinists

1. How do you know you are one of the elect?

2. How do you know your 'salvation experience' was genuine?

3. How do you know you were regenerated and given the gift of faith?

4. How do you know that your faith is genuine, that it came as a gift from God and not from yourself?

5. How do you know you have the right kind of faith or enough faith?

6. How do you know you are truly saved, one of the *elect*, and will persevere in good works and godliness till the end of your life?

7. How can anyone know? (Yet **1 John 5v13** says we can know we have eternal life).

8. If the faith to believe in Jesus Christ is given through irresistible grace as a gift, why does the Bible command and exhort us to believe in Jesus Christ? Why give commands that are impossible to obey?

9. No one is perfect and we all sin. How can one know he is truly elect and is persevering to the end if there is still sin in his or her life?

10. How many sins indicate one is not persevering and therefore not truly elect?

11. Which sins would indicate one is not persevering?

12. Where can these answers be found in the Bible?

13. Calvinists believe the elect must be regenerated before they are given the faith to believe the Gospel. But how can they be regenerated through the Gospel when they can't understand the Gospel until regenerated?

14. Why are there so many warnings in the Bible to believers not to drift away, **Heb 2v1**, not to fall away **Heb 4v11**, not to come short of the grace of God, **Heb 12v15**, not to shrink back, **Heb 10v28**, not to be carried away by unprincipled men and fall from their steadfastness, **2 Peter 3v17**, and not to desert Christ, **Gal 1v6**? If all the elect are assured of persevering to the end, then why are there all of these warnings?

15. **1 Cor 9v24-27** speaks of running a race for a prize. The Apostle Paul said he disciplined himself so he would not be disqualified. Certainly Paul was one of the elect, so how was it possible for him to be disqualified if all the elect persevere to the end?

16. If Jesus Christ died only for the elect, then the un-elect must be judged at the Great White Throne for their sins because Christ was not judged for them. Why does **Rev 20v12+13** say they will be judged according to their works/deeds? If they are to be judged for their sins as Calvinists say, why are their sins never mentioned at this Judgment?

17. How can God withhold grace and Christ's atonement from some of His creatures and then condemn them to the Lake of Fire for all eternity for not accepting what was never offered to them?

18. How can Christ be just, loving, compassionate, and merciful if He chose to die on the cross for some when He could have easily died on the cross for everyone?

19. Why preach 'repent or perish' when the non-elect can't repent and the elect can't perish?

20. How can God hold the non-elect responsible for 'not believing' and damn them for it, when He deliberately did not give them the faith to enable them to believe in the first place?

21. If Christ has already made an efficacious atonement for the sins of an elect person, is that elect person actually lost during the period prior to their being saved?

22. During the period before an elect person gets saved, how are they condemned already (for not believing) when their unbelief (which is a sin) has already been paid for by Christ on the cross?

23. If repentance is a gift only given to the elect, what did Jesus mean when He said that some of the people in Hell would have repented if they had had the same opportunity as the people to whom He preached?

24. Why does the Spirit of God strive and convict some sinners who later prove, by dying and going to hell, that they were non-elect? What is the purpose of such moving's of the Spirit?

If the following is true…

John Smith is deliberately foreordained to commit sin

Is hated by God before he is born

Is predestined to go to Hell before he is born

Cannot repent because God deliberately refuses to give him the gift of repentance

THE ERRORS OF CALVINISM

Cannot believe because God deliberately refuses to give him the gift of faith

Was not, is not and never will be loved by God in the slightest degree

Was deliberately excluded from the group of people Jesus died for on the cross so that salvation was intentionally and for ever put completely out of his reach:

Then, how is it John Smith's fault that he will end up burning forever in the Lake of Fire?

As you can see Calvinism is a wicked and unscriptural idiotic doctrine.

You're a total moron if you believe in it!

The Forgotten Five Points of Calvinism as Stated by John Calvin.

1) **Amillennialism** - "But a little later there followed the Chiliasts, who limited the reign of Christ to a 1000 years. Now their fiction is too childish either to need or to be worth a refutation. And the Apocalypse, from which they undoubtedly drew a pretext for their error, does not support them. For the number 1000 does not apply to the eternal blessedness of the church but only to the various disturbances that awaited the church, while still toiling on the earth."

2) **Religious persecution** - "Servetus lately wrote to me, and coupled with his letter a long volume of his delirious fancies, with the Thrasonic boast, that I should see something astonishing and unheard of. He takes it upon him to come hither, if it be agreeable to me. But I am unwilling to pledge my word for his safety, for if he shall come, I shall never permit him to depart alive, provided my authority be of any avail."

3) **Predestination to Hell** - "We call predestination God's eternal decree, by which he compacted with himself what he willed to become of each man. For all are not created in equal condition; rather, eternal life is foreordained for some, eternal damnation for others. Therefore, as any man has been created to one or the other of these ends, we speak of him as predestinated to life or death."

4) **Infant baptism** - "Now, if we choose to investigate whether it is right to administer baptism to infants, shall we not say that a man is talking nonsense or indeed raving who would halt with the mere element of water and outward observance, but cannot bear to turn his mind to the spiritual mystery? If any account of this is made, it will be evident that baptism is properly administered to infants as something owed to them."

5) **Sacraments** - "Therefore, let it be regarded as a settled principle that the sacraments have the same office as the word of God; to offer and set forth Christ to us, and in him the treasures of heavenly grace."

Taken from the internet – submitted by Jeffrey D. Nachimson

Job 9v29 **If I be wicked, why then labour I in vain?** If you are *not* one of the *elect*, you are wasting your time trying to be good, because you're going to Hell anyway!

Why I am *not* a Calvinistic TULIP Sniffer...

TULIP	TULIP	FOR	AGAINST	Comments
T	Total Depravity	Eph 2v1-4 Has NOTHING to do with the 'will'	Ezra 7v13+15+16 Mat 23v37 Exo 35v5+21+29	Total depravity doesn't affect responsibility – John 3v36, Isa 45v19, Luke 17v1
U	Unconditional Election	Eph 1v4 Rom 9v15+21	1 Pet 1v2 Rom 8v29 Eph 1v4 'in him'	Election is conditioned on *foreknowledge*.
L	Limited Atonement	John 10v11	Luke 10v42 1 Tim 2v4+6 2 Pet 3v9 2 Pet 2v1	Did Christ die for the 'elect' against their *will*?
I	Irresistible Grace	Acts 13v48 Eph 2v1-4	Heb 10 Acts 7v51 Mat 23 Mat 12	Tosh!
P	Perseverance or Predestination of the saints	Eph 1v5	Gen 6 + Rom 9 God predestines a *saved* person to be conformed to the image of His Son, *not* to become a Son.	Predestination is *only* applicable to someone **who has received Christ** i.e. *after* he has been 'born again!'

How about this for a great verse *against* Calvin's 'Limited Atonement'

2 Pet 2v1 **But there were FALSE PROPHETS also among the people, even as there shall be FALSE TEACHERS among you, who privily shall bring in DAMNABLE HERESIES, even denying the Lord THAT BOUGHT THEM, and bring upon themselves swift destruction**. That what? **That bought them!** *Get it?* How clear do you want it? Christ paid the way for the false lost teachers and false lost prophets. In fact He paid the way for *everyone* including all the lost souls who have ever lived. But from their own *free-will* they *chose* not to ask the Lord Jesus Christ to forgive them of their sins. Calvin's 'TULIP' is as unscriptural as the Jehovah's Witness 'annihilation' - 1 Tim 4v10, 1 Tim 2v4, Exo 12v3.

Mat 20v28 **Even as the Son of man came not to be ministered unto, but to minister, and to give his life a ransom for *many***. Of course the anti-Scriptural-Calvinist loves this verse i.e. *his life a ransom for many*. But can 'many' mean ALL? Look at Rom 5v19 **For as by one man's disobedience *many***

were made sinners...I thought *everyone* was a sinner? Rom 3v23 **For all have sinned, and come short of the glory of God**; Therefore *many* in the Scriptures can mean *all!*

2 Pet 3v9 **The Lord is not slack concerning his promise, as some men count slackness; but is longsuffering to us-ward, not willing that any should perish, but that all should come to repentance**. This verse states that if you go to Hell you are going against the will of God. Not only that, but the Lord doesn't want you there; He didn't create it for you - **Then shall he say also unto them on the left hand, Depart from me, ye cursed, into everlasting fire, prepared for the devil and his angels**: Mat 25v41. God did everything He could to keep you out of Hell, the decision is now yours - **For whosoever shall call upon the name of the Lord shall be saved**. Rom 10v13. Now of course the foolish Calvinist (who is *not* a Bible believer) reads the 'us-ward' of the verse (v9) as 'us-elect!' Now just stop and think for a second about that. How can God be longsuffering to the elect...*he knows they're going to get saved*. 'Longsuffering' implies that God gives you so much time before His patience runs out. God's patience doesn't run out at all with the 'elect' under Calvin's system. He *knows* they are going to repent, and they can't repent until he regenerates them. Surely he knows when he is going to regenerate them. And when He regenerates them, according to Johnny Calvin, they can't resist his will. So how can 'longsuffering' have anything to do with that load of foolishness?

More questions to ask a Calvinist...

1. Is the 'world' of John 1v29, 3v26 the 'world' of John 17v9, 16v8-11?

2. Why aren't 'the ungodly' the 'elect' when they're the ones for whom Christ died (Rom 5v6)?

3. The 'ungodly' go to Hell in Jude 15; are they the 'elect' since Christ died for them?

4. Who commits the unpardonable sin in Mark 3v29 when *all* the sins of the non-elect are unpardonable in Calvin's system?

5. If the 'elect' were dead in sins before they were saved (Eph 2v17), were their names 'written in the book of life from the foundation of the world?' (Rev 17v8)

6. Why are the non-elect in Isa 1v10 commanded to listen and challenged to 'reason' with the Lord about salvation when they can't listen and can't be saved?

7. Since the 'wicked' are commanded to forsake their way in order to live (Isa 55v5-7), are the 'wicked' the elect?

8. Why preach the Gospel (Acts 15v7, 26v18) if the 'elect' are saved anyway and the lost are damned no matter what? (2 Pet 2v2)

9. Why are the non-elect commanded to repent in Acts 17v30 (note '*all* men everywhere'; see also Acts 3v19); if they can't repent?

10. *Why follow a MAN rather than the Scriptures?*

Facts Calvinists won't face

- Heb 2v9 says Christ tasted death 'for every man', *not* just for the 'elect' – 'Every man' is 'IN Adam' at birth (1 Cor 15v22); not one of them *was* 'IN Christ', including the 'elect'.

- The 'elect' were *unknown* by God until salvation (Gal 4v9). They were 'chosen' IN Christ

(Rom 16v4) which means they had to be IN Him for them to be 'chosen...IN HIM' (Eph 1v4)

- **You were NOT 'IN Christ' before Gen 1v1.** *If you were*, you then got OUT of Him at birth and INTO Adam ...and then got back INTO Christ *again* at salvation? The Lord is saying in Eph 1v4 that God decided, before Gen 1v1, to choose you IF you 'wound up' IN His Son. If you 'wind up' there, you got there by obeying John 1v12 and ***not*** a moment before.

- Rom 9v11 is *not* an 'election' to salvation at all. Thousands of Jacob's descendants went to Hell and weren't 'elect' at all. What you have in Rom 9-11 is an 'election' *within* an 'election' (Rom 11v5-7). Israel was 'elected' as a nation with 'elect' and NON-elect individuals in it. If you are really interested in reading about the ERRORS of Calvinism, you need to get the book 'The Other Side of Calvinism' by Lawrence Vance (1991)

Calvin wrote '*We were as much ordained to faith in Christ before the foundation of the world as we were chosen to the inheritance of life in Christ!*' Scripture back up Johnny? No one in the Church Age 'inherits life in Christ!' Your heavenly inheritance is IN the New Jerusalem (1 Pet 1v4), and your Millennial inheritance is earned *by works* (Col 3v24, Luke 19v17). Calvin and 'Calvinists' don't know what they are talking about regarding this inheritance.

God *striving* with man! Aren't you glad He does?

Job 33v29 **Lo, all these things worketh God oftentimes with man, To bring back his soul from the pit, to be enlightened with the light of the living**. These verses imply that God *strives and struggles* with unsaved men to try to get them to receive the Truth. Read Rom 2v4, 1 Tim 2v4, 2 Pet 3v9 etc. Calvin and his followers haven't a clue about God's love and compassion for the lost when it comes to seeking out lost souls. Luke 19v10 **For the Son of man is come to seek and to save that which was lost**. I thank God that His love extends to the whole world, to *every* sinner and not just to the ridiculous notion *of just the 'elect'.*

Jesus Christ died for *everyone*, that's *all* of humanity *not* 'just' for the elect.

Heb 2v9, 1 John 2v2, 2 Cor 5v14+15, Rom 5v6-8, 2 Pet 3v9, 1 Tim 2v4-6, 1 Tim 4v10

Read also – 2 Pet 2v1, 1 John 4v14, Rom 10v13, John 12v47, Rom 11v32 and John 6v52 to quote but a few.

Calvinism is heresy! It's a man-made doctrine unfounded in Scripture.

- **T = Total Depravity** – this is the teaching that the unregenerate man is totally dead in sin, to the extent that he has the inability to freely accept Jesus Christ. (Heresy!)

- **U = Unconditional Election** – this is the teaching that God, by a sovereign, eternal decree, unconditionally elected a certain number of men to salvation. (Heresy!)

- **L = Limited Atonement** – this is the teaching that Jesus Christ, by His death on the cross, only made an atonement for the group of men previously elected to salvation. (Heresy!)

- **I = Irresistible Grace** – this is the teaching that God irresistibly overpowers the will of the elect sinner with his grace and regenerates him, granting him faith and repentance to believe on

THE ERRORS OF CALVINISM

Jesus Christ. (Heresy!)

- **P = Perseverance of the Saints** – this is the teaching that all of the elect who have been regenerated by God will persevere in the faith and ultimately die in a state of grace. (I believe in Eternal Security *because* it is Scriptural *not* because John Calvin believed it. Some Calvinists say the 'P' stands for Predestination of the Saints *before* Gen 1v1 – which is heresy!

Rom 5v18 - Now either ALL means ALL in *both* cases or it doesn't. Judgment and condemnation came upon **ALL** men because of the *first* Adam. The righteousness of Christ (the last Adam – 1 Cor 15v45) is *offered* to **ALL** men. Now the Calvinist will wrest that Scripture (2 Pet 3v16) (read also 2 Pet 2v1 for another enlightening Scripture that ***destroys*** Calvinism dead), and *distort* that Scripture, and try to bend that Scripture to fit his idiotic doctrine. If you *stay* with the Scriptures you can see how ridiculous Calvinism *really* is. Like I have said many times, Calvinists are *not* Bible Believers, they are Bible *twisters, distorters*, and finally they *all* end up as Bible 'correctors'.

Mat 23v37 - This verse completely ***destroys*** Calvin's entire system. Here the will of God was *rejected* by the 'sovereignty of man', and *irresistible grace* failed to accomplish its purpose. God was willing to save the Jews, and they would have none of it. It was *their will* that 'left' their 'house'... *desolate* (see v38) When it comes to *freewill*, Calvin's system has no understanding or comprehension. Calvin's T.U.L.I.P. is just a five petal (*five being the number of death*) flower that is very poisonous indeed to those who sniff it. Nothing kills a church *deader* or *quicker* than Calvinism, avoid it like the plague.

The word 'elect' in Mat 24v22

Mat 24v22 - Most Christians assume the term 'elect' here is a reference to Calvin's 'election' in Eph 1v3-11 (See Appendix 109 in RRB). But long before any Christian showed up in the Bible (Acts 11v26), ISRAEL was God's ELECT. See Isa 45v4, 65v9+22 etc. The context here has been talking about the Jews (vs15+16+20); there is *no* reference to the Body of Christ anywhere in the chapter. The word 'elect' has at least *five* different meanings in Scripture. Calvinism is for dummies, Bible illiterates and those that are willingly ignorant; it is not for Bible believers.

Calvinists like to avoid these Scriptures - Acts 7v51, 2 Pet 2v1, 1 Tim 4v10, 1 Tim 2v4 (Rom 5v18), Exo 12v3, Mat 20v28 (Rom 5v19, Rom 3v23) - ***Calvin's TULIP always wilts and dies under Biblical scrutiny!***

Ps 119v30 **I have chosen the way of truth: thy judgments have I laid before me**. Who has chosen?

John 6v44 **No man can come to me, except the Father which hath sent me draw him: and I will raise him up at the last day.** This is the great Calvinistic passage used by Calvinists and Reformed 'theologians' to prove that if 'Irresistible Grace' does not 'draw you' according to the doctrines of 'Unconditional Election' and 'Limited Atonement,' you cannot come to Jesus Christ. If you take this verse literally, then *all unsaved sinners* are 'the elect,' because Jesus is careful to tell you that He'll 'draw **ALL** men' to Him (John 12v32 – the elect and *non*-elect) The apostles in Acts are very careful to tell you that ALL of the Gentiles can repent and be saved, whether they are elect or *not* (Acts 11v18 **When they heard these things, they held their peace, and glorified God, saying, Then hath God also to the Gentiles granted repentance unto life.** All any 'non-elect-sinner' on earth would have to do to become 'elect' would be to ask the Father to 'draw him' (S of S 1v4, Mat 7v7, Luke 11v9). Note also regarding John 6v44 that the reference is *not* to *any* Christian who showed up on this earth *after* Acts 2: **'I will raise him up at the last day'** (as in John 6v39+40). Calvinists misapply these verses to A.D. 33 – A.D. 2016 onwards, *not realising that after* Christ was crucified (John 12v32), He drew *'all men'* to Him. When God 'granted repentance to the Gentiles,' He certainly did not grant it just to the 'predestinated elect *among* the Gentiles' (Acts 11v18). Any unsaved man in *this* dispensation, who is mentally 'responsible,' will be held accountable for *not* accepting Christ. Note – Jer 31v3 **The LORD hath appeared of old unto me, saying, Yea, I have loved thee with an everlasting love: therefore with lovingkindness have I drawn thee.** Here the 'loved ones' whom God 'drew to Him' were *cast out of his sight* (Jer 14v16, 7v15, 15v1) for over 2000 years and burned, a million at a time, dying alone, *without* Him or Christ (Eph 2v1-4, 1 Thes 2v15+16), and then pitched into outer darkness (Mat 8v12). No Calvinist gets that.

Eph 1v4 **According as he hath chosen us in him before the foundation of the world, that we should be holy and without blame before him in love**: Note the phrase **IN** Him i.e. **IN** Christ! (vs 1+3+10+12+20) 'Election' here and 'predestination' (vs 5+11) and 'adoption' (v5) and the Christian's 'inheritance' (v11) are all **conditioned** on being **IN** Christ. This verse is the root and source of all Calvin's *hogwash*. It is linked with Rom 9v22+23 to 'prove' that you were saved *before* Adam showed up, even though you were damned *after* Adam sinned. Calvinists read the verse as though you were actually **IN** Jesus Christ '*before* the foundation of the world' which is nonsense. No one was **IN** Christ 'before' Gen 1v1 because He had *no* 'Body' to be **IN**. If any man was, then in Gen 3v6 he got IN Adam (Rom 5v12, 1 Cor 15v21+22). This means that he was **IN** Christ, 'then' *fell out into Adam*, and then *fell out* of Adam *back into* Christ. No man is **IN** Christ until He *trusts* Christ (v13)

More on John 6v44 for the mor-on Calvinist – that's funny!

John 6v44 **No man can come to me, except the Father which hath sent me draw him: and I will raise him up at the last day.** John 12v32 **And I, if I be lifted up from the earth, will draw all men unto me.** Calvinists, who are heretics, always like to jump upon John 6v44 to 'prove' their heresy. Now in order to get this right (2 Tim 2v15) we need to go back to John 6v40 **And this is the will of him that sent me, that every one which seeth the Son, and believeth on him, may have everlasting life: and I will raise him up at the last day.** This verse has *no* connection with anyone who didn't *see* Jesus Christ with their *eyes* between Mat 1 and Acts 2. The 'last day' is a reference to John 5v28+29 **Marvel not at this: for the hour is coming, in the which all that are in the graves shall hear his voice, And shall come forth; they that have done good, unto the resurrection of life; and they that have done evil, unto the resurrection of damnation.** This is where there is a judgement based on *works* (Rev 20v12 **And I saw the dead, small and great, stand before God; and the books were opened: and another book was opened, which is the book of life: and the dead were judged out of those things which were written in the books, according to their works.**) No one since Acts 9 (Paul) has actually *seen* Jesus Christ. Therefore *no one* between A.D. 33 and A.D. 2015 could meet the *requirements* of the text for 'everlasting life' (John 6v40). To get raised 'at the

THE ERRORS OF CALVINISM

last day' (John 6v39+40) is to *come up* at Rev 20v12 and Rev 11v18 *after* the Millennium. Not one saved child of God from Acts 2 to Rev 20 *comes up* or is *raised up* at *that* resurrection. (Did you get that?) When the resurrection on the 'last day' takes place, *every* Christian who got saved from Acts 2 to the Rapture will have *already* been reigning with Christ on earth for 1000 years (Rev 20v1-6), having been 'conformed to His image' (sinless perfection) *before* the Millennial reign begins. Now back to John 6v44... **No man can come to me, except the Father which hath sent me draw him: and I will raise him up at the last day.** Note again that the reference is *not* to any Christian who showed up on this earth *after* Acts 2 'I will raise him up at the last day' (as in v39+40) Calvin and his bunch of merry heretics all *misapplied* the passage to A.D. 33 – A.D. 2017, *not realising* that *after* Christ was crucified (John 12v32) He drew **'ALL MEN'** to Him! (Get that!) Any *unsaved* man can *ask* God to 'draw him' (Song of Sol 1v4, James 1v14) When God 'granted repentance to the Gentiles,' He certainly did *not* grant it just to 'the predestinated elect *among* the Gentiles' (Acts 11v18). You have a ***free will*** (Lev 22v18, 22v21, 22v23, 23v38, Num 15v3, 29v39, Deut 12v6, 12v17, 16v10, 23v23, 2 Chron 31v14, Ezra 1v4, 3v5, 7v13, 7v16, 8v28, Ps 119v108) Any *unsaved* man in this dispensation, who is mentally *responsible*, will be held to account; not only for not accepting Christ, but accountable for not knowing the contents of the Bible, if he could read! You see the policeman gives you the speeding ticket for not *seeing* the speed warning sign. He takes it for granted that you could/should have seen it. Either way, you are *guilty* and get punished. If the work of the Holy Spirit in the Church Age doesn't involve 'drawing men to Christ,' then what is John 16v7-11 doing in your Bible? Not coming to Christ, in belief, is the one outstanding sin that the Holy Spirit uses when 'reproving' men of sin! If the work of the Holy Spirit (John 14v26 + John 16v13) in this age among *lost* people, is not meant to *draw* them to Christ, why is it that in John 16v9 the *one sin* for which He reproves mankind is their *not coming* to Christ.

Now onto John 12v32 **And, if I be lifted up from the earth, will draw all men unto me.** Now realise here that Calvin's idiotic heresy is blown clean out of the English Channel as this verse says *all men* are drawn to Christ, and 'they are' *after* the crucifixion. Now Calvin and his band of merry heretics also jump on John 6v65 to prove their nonsense, so we might as well destroy their 'theology' here also! John 6v65 **And he said, Therefore said I unto you, that no man can come unto me, except it were given unto him of my Father.** (Note just in passing that in v64 it says *from* the beginning and *not* 'before'. Calvinists can't seem to read English for some reason!?) In John 6v64 naturally Jesus *knew* 'who should betray Him'. This is why He talked about the Father 'drawing' sinners, back in John 6v44. It had *nothing* to do with the 'unconditional election' by passing the 'decree of reprobation' (Calvinism) '**Therefore said I unto you**' has to refer to something He had *just said*. What it was is found in v39+44, which we have already covered.

Great little email from Alan O'Reilly regarding the nonsense of Calvinism...

Hi John, Re: Errors of Calvinism http://www.timefortruth.co.uk/errors-of-calvinism/: I get the impression that a Calvinist professes to believe, by means of Ephesians 1v4, that he was placed in Christ before the foundation of the world. If so, he was only half-saved at best, which is unsaved, even though in Christ, supposedly. The reason is as follows. You rightly refer to Revelation 17v8 in the above link. It states: **The beast that thou sawest was, and is not; and shall ascend out of the bottomless pit, and go into perdition: and they that dwell on the earth shall wonder, whose names were not written in the book of life from the foundation of the world, when they behold the beast that was, and is not, and yet is.** Your name has to be in the book of life for you to be saved, Revelation 20v15. For a Calvinist though, his name would therefore have to be in the book of life before the foundation of the world but names are entered into the book of life from the foundation of the world Revelation 17v8, not before it. Nowhere does the scripture refer to names being entered into the book of life before the foundation of the world. That seems to splinter one of the main planks of Calvinism.

See also - The AV1611 verses TULIP - http://www.timefortruth.co.uk/why-av-only/why-the-av-only-7434.php

Calvinistic 'Sovereign Grace' tosh…

This totally unbiblical term of 'sovereign grace' is *hogwash*, as grace is never sovereign. Titus 2v11 **For the grace of God that bringeth salvation hath appeared to all men**, Rom 10v8 **But what saith it? The word is nigh thee** (an *unsaved* Roman), **even in thy mouth, and in thy heart: that is, the word of faith, which we preach;** Acts 11v18 **When they heard these things, they held their peace, and glorified God, saying, Then hath God also to the Gentiles** (not the elect) **granted repentance unto life**. All Gentiles *can* repent, and all of them *can* believe, *but*, according to Johnny Calvin there isn't enough of Christ's Blood to go around.

Calvin's 'Eternal Decrees' Overruled!

Johnny Calvin (The Protestant Pope of a Pope hating people) taught that all of God's decrees are 'eternal' (i.e. made *before* Gen 1v1) and unconditional. Here are seven of God's decrees that were *not* 'eternal' at all, and they were all conditioned on **free will**… (Oh dear Johnny!)

Jer 38v17 **Then said Jeremiah unto Zedekiah, Thus saith the LORD, the God of hosts, the God of Israel; If thou wilt assuredly go forth unto the king of Babylon's princes, then thy soul shall live, and this city shall not be burned with fire; and thou shalt live, and thine house**: (Oh dear Johnny!)

2 Kings 13v19 **And the man of God was wroth with him, and said, Thou shouldest have smitten five or six times; then hadst thou smitten Syria till thou hadst consumed it: whereas now thou shalt smite Syria but thrice**. (Oh dear Johnny!)

Deut 25v19 **Therefore it shall be, when the LORD thy God hath given thee rest from all thine enemies round about, in the land which the LORD thy God giveth thee for an inheritance to possess it, that thou shalt blot out the remembrance of Amalek from under heaven; thou shalt not forget it**. (Oh dear Johnny!)

Jon 3v4 **And Jonah began to enter into the city a day's journey, and he cried, and said, Yet forty days, and Nineveh shall be overthrown**. (Oh dear Johnny!)

1 Sam 2v30 **Wherefore the LORD God of Israel saith, I said indeed that thy house, and the house of thy father, should walk before me for ever: but now the LORD saith, Be it far from me; for them that honour me I will honour, and they that despise me shall be lightly esteemed**. (Oh dear Johnny!)

1 Kings 20v42 **And he said unto him, Thus saith the LORD, Because thou hast let go out of thy hand a man whom I appointed to utter destruction, therefore thy life shall go for his life, and thy people for his people**. (Oh dear Johnny!)

2 Kings 8v10 **And Elisha said unto him, Go, say unto him, Thou mayest certainly recover: howbeit the LORD hath shewed me that he shall surely die**. (Oh dear Johnny!)

THE ERRORS OF CALVINISM

Rom 9v22 – 'The vessels of wrath...' are *clay* (v21). There was *no clay* before Gen 1v1. The 'decree of reprobation' (Calvinistic jargon) takes place '**in time**' based on what a *man does* with what God told him to do. The two examples given in Rom 9 are Esau (v13) and Pharaoh (v17). Esau found no place of repentance (Heb 12v17) because he sold his birth right (Heb 12v16), *not* because God damned him *before* Gen 1v1. God hardened Pharaoh's heart (Exo 7v13+14) *after* Pharaoh rejected God's words (Exo 5v1-9). *Eternal election and eternal reprobation is just Calvinistic claptrap and hogwash!*

Why Calvinists don't preach 1 Cor 9v22

1 Cor 9v22 **To the weak became I as weak, that I might gain the weak: I am made all things to all men, that I might by all means save some**. This kind of verse drives Calvinists stir crazy. It is such an anti-Calvinistic verse isn't it. If you are elected to be saved 'before' the foundation of the world, then this verse is pointless. Think about it.

Calvinists are NOT Bible Believers

Eph 1v4 **According as he hath chosen us in him before the foundation of the world, that we should be holy and without blame before him in love**: Calvin, Berkoff, Pink, Shelton, along with every other 'Calvinist', can't handle this verse, it's too deep for their shallow minds. They all think that 'foreknowledge' means 'fore-ORDAINED', I kid you not. That's the start of their *man-made* logic. Calvinists are trying to get you IN Christ BEFORE the foundation of the world, which is what us English Bible Believers call TOSH. They think you were IN Christ BEFORE you were IN Adam (1 Cor 15v22), see how mad they are? Calvinists are novices (1 Tim 3v6) when it comes to rightly dividing the word of God (2 Tim 2v15). NO man was ever IN Christ until he was BORN AGAIN, and that happens IN time, not IN eternity. Every man comes into this world IN Adam (Gen 2 and Gen 5v1-3). The 'elect' (remember there are FIVE meanings of the word 'elect') were NOT 'in' Christ – they were 'aliens' (Eph 2v12), alone in the world, 'children of wrath' (Eph 2v3), 'dead in trespasses and sins' (Eph 2v1), 'having no hope' (Eph 2v12), 'without God' (Eph 2v12), and 'unknown' (Gal 4v7-9, Eph 2v1+3+12). Neither Jacob nor Israel were 'chosen... BEFORE the foundation of the world'; neither was Paul or Abraham according to Scripture, it's just the Calvinistic CULT that think they were. The 'believer' was 'chosen' **FROM** (get that?), **FROM** the 'beginning' (2 Thes 2v13), NOT 'before' the beginning. Perhaps our Calvinistic friends could answer this question... 'If election is eternal, how were you sanctified in eternity (1 Pet 1v2), when Eph 2v12+13 clearly states that you were anything BUT sanctified'? Note also, in Mat 22v14 the CALL precedes the 'election!' All we are doing here is *playing* with the Calvinists, let Ruckman and all us Bible BELIEVERS finally DESTROY their *man-made* doctrine... If you were IN Christ BEFORE the foundation of the world, then you plainly FELL OUT OF CHRIST in Gen 2 and got INTO Adam, whereupon, you FELL OUT of Adam at your conversion and got back INTO Christ... why can't you FALL OUT OF CHRIST AGAIN if this is the case? Like I have said on numerous occasions, the dumbest CULT that has ever 'graced' (excuse the pun) planet earth is the Hyper-Dispensationalists (Moore, Stam, Pfenniger etc.) but in *second* place is the Calvinists. BEFORE the foundation of the world, God declared that He would 'choose' NO ONE in this age to become 'holy and without blame' (Eph 1v4) UNLESS they were IN Christ, and you ONLY get INTO Christ IN TIME never IN eternity! You were never IN the beloved (Eph 1v6) BEFORE Gen 1v1, no one was. You were never IN Christ BEFORE Gen 1v1, no one was. Christ has NO 'Body' UNTIL Acts 2, into which you could enter (John 17v23, 1 Cor 12v13). This is Scriptural PROOF that Calvin's TULIP is TOSH and all those who promote it are following a man-made-Satanic-spawned-HELLISH doctrine. Predestination (Eph 1v5) always follows FOREKNOWLEDGE (Rom 8v29), and election always follows FOREKNOWLEDGE (1 Pet 1v2) – this is something Calvinists just can't understand because they read the Bible through Johnny Calvin's dirty glasses, and you will never get your doctrine right if you are *starting off* IN ERROR. Like I shall keep saying all the way to the Rapture, DUMP CALVINISM it's a terminal disease and will KILL your spiritual life. God does NOT *choose* some to be saved and some to burn in the Lake of Fire forever, without giving them the opportunity of repenting and coming to Christ. That is a blasphemous doctrine started by the Devil himself and the Devil's disciples promote it.

Limited Atonement is TOSH – 2 Pet 2v1. The whole issue of accepting or rejecting salvation is to do with your WILL, your FREEWILL – Isa 14v13+14, John 5v40, Mat 23v37, Rev 22v17, Acts 7v51. (FREEWILL is a Biblical term - Ezra 1v6, 3v5, 7v13, Lev 22v21, Ps 119v108). Of course, God KNOWS who will *Receive* Him and who will not (Rom 8v29, 1 Pet 1v2). Those who will receive the Lord as Saviour are 'elected' and 'predestined' to be 'conformed to the image of his Son' (Rom 8v29) and 'unto the adoption of children' (Eph 1v5). Calvinists just can't handle 'freewill'. They can't understand that a sinner can *accept or reject* Jesus Christ on his own freewill. Calvinists believe that if a sinner is 'elected', he is 'overpowered' and quickened by the Holy Spirit without the consent of his will, and if he was NOT one of the elect, he was dead anyway and could NOT *will* to accept Christ if he had decided to. It's quite amazing isn't it, Calvin's 'corpse' is held responsible for 'rejecting' Christ but is NOT responsible for 'accepting' Him. Without a doubt, Calvinism is a Satanic doctrine and any Christian who believes in it and promotes it, is a Bible illiterate. No system in the world has more contradictions in it than Calvinism, taught by Berkhof, Dabney, Mauro, Gill, Hodge, Shelton, Pink, James White etc.

The difference between these shallow men and what the Bible actually teaches is as follows...
God knew who WOULD and who WOULD NOT accept His Son BEFORE they did.
On the basis of 'foreknowledge', God predestined those who WOULD accept Him, to be 'conformed to the image of his Son' at a future date.
No human merit was involved, no matter what any Calvinist may tell you.
To uphold the doctrine of 'Total Depravity', and the deadness of the sinner, Calvin eradicated man's freewill, never noticing that the WILL was NOT subject to depravity.
The fact that a man can 'accept or reject' anything (including the Holy Spirit – Acts 7v51), shows 'depravity' extends ONLY to man's mental, emotional, and spiritual makeup. The 'Will' is a function of the mind; it is not a thought, feeling, or inspiration that passes through the mind. God foreknew who WOULD and who WOULD NOT accept His Son, but that in no way affects their responsibility. You either have or you haven't.

Eph 1v6 **To the praise of the glory of his grace, wherein he hath made us accepted in the beloved**. You are only accepted in the beloved when you are IN Christ and that is IN time, NEVER IN eternity and it is by your own FREEWILL.

Here are just a few basic questions that Calvinists can't answer, because they are NOT dispensational...

How was Adam saved and where did he go when he died... before the Law?
How did someone get saved during the Law?
How does one get saved AFTER the Law?
How does one get saved during the Tribulation?
How does one get saved during the Millennium?
Where did OT saints go when they died?
Why didn't they go to Heaven?
Do you have to endure to the end to be saved? (Matthew) OR be baptised (Acts 2), or is it by Faith ALONE (Eph 2) or is it by faith PLUS works Rev 12 + 14?
How did they get imputed righteousness and justification in the OT compared to the NT? If they are the same, he needs to back that up in the Scriptures.
What are the differences between the Kingdom of Heaven and Kingdom of God - one is physical and can be seen and one is spiritual plus 'what?'
Why do James and Paul contradict each other - James 2 vs Rom 4 - THEY DO regarding Abraham.
Is Acts 2v38 the Gospel for today? If not, why not? How many Christians were in that

chapter?
Acts 10v43 is saying something different BUT the same preacher? What has changed?
When did the Body of Christ start and who was FIRST in it?
Why is there NO 'Body' in the OT?
What baptism SAVES YOU out of the *seven* mentioned?
What is spiritual circumcision? Why didn't this happen in the OT?
Why is the Rapture a mystery but the Second Advent isn't?
Who goes up at the POST-Tribulation Rapture if it is NOT the Church?
When can you eat 'black pudding' according to the Scriptures?
When could a Jew eat an unclean animal?
When did signs start?
What is the difference between a 'sign' gift to Israel and a gift for the church?
What FOUR books in the NT are transitional books that every cult and heretic take their doctrine from?
Why should we NOT build our doctrines on THESE FOUR books?

You have enough Scripture here to refute any Calvinistic heretic!

NOTES

BIBLICAL NUMERICS
NUMBERS IN SCRIPTURE

To think that everything in the world that is man-made is 'made' by *only* 10 numbers and 26 letters…

1 2 3 4 5 6 7 8 9 0

A B C D E F G H I J K L M N O P Q R S T U V W X Y Z

Even without entering into this study on numbers, it is obvious after careful study, *man* could not have written the Holy Bible. The Scriptures were *authored* by God and *penned* via man **without mistake** i.e. the Scriptures are preserved **perfect** today in the Authorized Version aka KJV Bible. Note the following three verses… 2 Tim 3v16, 2 Pet 1v21, Ps 12v6+7

But another *proof* of God's perfect words, and giving us a Book, is by looking into the number patterns in Scripture.

Most people see the Bible as just another book, even worse, a Book that is not relevant for today as it is out of date, full of myths and is just not accurate according to science and mathematics. *They're dead wrong!*

Mat 7v13 (note 13 is the number of rebellion)
Mat 7v14 (note 7 is the number of perfection and completeness (14 = 2x7))

The Bible is so different to any other book: no other book dare do what the Bible does i.e… It accurately predicted 48 details of the Lord Jesus Christ's life *before* He was even born, and some of the predictions were given 1,000 years *beforehand.* Every one of those predictions came to pass literally as prophesied. *What book has ever done that?* **Prophecy proves the Bible!**

Regarding number patterns in Scripture…

In Hebrew and Greek, every letter, word, sentence, and passage has a definite numeric value or sum. The Hebrews and Greeks did not use figures such as 1, 2, 3 or 4 to count numeric value. Rather, they used the letters of their alphabet. For example, if a Hebrew or Greek wanted to write '1' he would write the first letter of the alphabet. If he wanted to write '2' he would write down the second letter of the alphabet etc.

Each letter in the Hebrew and Greek alphabet stands for a certain number; every letter is a number, as well as a letter.

Since each letter has a numeric value, each word, phrase, or sentence has a sum total. The numeric sum of a word is obtained by adding the values of the various letters in that particular word, phrase, or sentence.

The most important word in the Bible is the name 'Jesus'.
In Greek, Jesus is spelled - 'I-E-S-O-U-S.'

I = 10
E = 8
S = 200
O = 70
U = 400
S = 200

If we add these numbers, we find the numerical value of 'Jesus' is 888.

The number '7' is very significant in Scripture as we shall find out. In Gen 1v1 the three important nouns are... God, heaven and earth.
The numeric values of these three words are 86, 395 and 296. When we add these three numbers up we get 777 (111 x 7) If another word was used or another letter added (i.e. 'heaven**s**'), the mathematical pattern would have been broken. The numeric value of the Hebrew verb 'created' in the first verse is exactly 203 (29 x 7)

For a mere human being like Matthew, Mark, Luke or John to have purposely determined to have designed and written a single chapter to conform to an established mathematical pattern would have taken a lifetime. Dr. D.B. Turney related how he attempted to construct a passage that would show some numeric features, and he concluded, 'I gave numeric values to the English alphabet, and tried to prepare a passage which would adhere to the numerics, and make every section a multiple of *seven* (7), and present all the other features of Biblical arithmography', without letting the meaning of the passage descend to nonsense. After working thereon for days, I could get no satisfaction. Yet this feature is accomplished in every one of the thousands of Bible paragraphs without the slightest visible effort.'

The Bible must have one Author; how could 40 men living in different centuries, over a period of 1,700 years, have compiled a consistent account of creation, the fall of man into sin, and his ultimate redemption through faith in the promised Redeemer of God?

And so to numbers in Scripture... The KJV Bible has...
1,189 chapters, **31,102** verses (Incidentally 3+1+1+0+2 = **7**), and **788,258** words

It is divided into two parts: the OT and the NT. The first section has 39 books; the second section contains 27 books. In order to remember this numerically, the following has been worked out...
Old Testament – Old = 3 letters; Testament = 9 letters. 3 and 9 beside each other gives 39 books in the OT
New Testament – New = 3 letters; Testament = 9 letters. Multiply 3 x 9 =27 books in the NT

39 books in the OT and 27 books in the NT = 66 books in total. The only book that bears 66 chapters is Isaiah. Isaiah is a 'little' Bible within the Bible...

1) The first chapter of Isaiah says... **Hear, O heavens, and give ear, O earth:** (Isa 1v2). The first book in the Bible says... **In the beginning God created the heaven and the earth.** (Gen 1v1)
2) The last chapter of Isaiah says...**For as the new heavens and the new earth, which I will make, shall remain before me, saith the LORD,** (Isa 66v22). The 66th and LAST book of the Bible (Revelation) says...**And I saw a new heaven and a new earth:** (Rev 21v1)

3) Isaiah 40v3 says...**The voice of him that crieth in the wilderness, Prepare ye the way of the LORD, make straight in the desert a highway for our God.** The 40th book of the Bible is Matthew and Mat 3v3 says...**For this is he that was spoken of by the prophet Esaias, saying, The voice of one crying in the wilderness, Prepare ye the way of the Lord, make his paths straight.**

ONE (1)

The number ONE in Scripture signifies **unity**. It occurs in 1698 verses.

The word ONE occurs for the first time in the word of God in Gen 1v9...**And God said, Let the waters under the heaven be gathered together unto one place, and let the dry land appear: and it was so.**

The great statement to Israel is...**Hear, O Israel: The LORD our God is one LORD:** (Deut 6v4)

Another great case for the number ONE is found in Gen 11...

Gen 11v1 **And the whole earth was of one language, and of one speech.**

Gen 11v6 **And the LORD said, Behold, the people is one, and they have all one language; and this they begin to do: and now nothing will be restrained from them, which they have imagined to do.**

So the number ONE as it stands refers to strength of unity

Paul says he wants to have the believers to be of ONE mind, he goes on to say...

- ➢ ONE body
- ➢ ONE Lord
- ➢ ONE faith
- ➢ ONE Spirit
- ➢ ONE baptism

See also Gen 2v24, Mat 19v5, Mat 19v6, Eph 5v31.

TWO (2)

TWO occurs in 703 verses.

The number TWO in Scripture signifies **division** – Amos 3v3 **Can two walk together, except they be agreed?**

1) On the SECOND day of creation, God made a firmament that...DIVIDED the waters...from the waters (Gen 1v6-8)
2) On the FOURTH day (2x2), God made 'TWO great lights' that DIVIDED the day from the night (Gen 1v16)
3) Adam became TWO in Genesis TWO (Gen 2v22)
4) In the SECOND book of the Bible (Exodus), Israel was DIVIDED from Egypt
5) In Gen 10v25, a man named Eber had TWO sons, and in his days (Peleg) was the earth DIVIDED!
6) TWO angels SEPARATED Lot from Sodom in Gen 19
7) No man can serve TWO masters - **No man can serve two masters: for either he will hate the one, and love the other; or else he will hold to the one, and despise the other. Ye cannot serve God and mammon.** (Mat 6v24)
8) Jesus Christ is the mediator of the NT (Heb 9v25), and He caused the Temple veil to be RENT in TWAIN (Mat 27v51) and a DIVISION among the Jews (John 7v43 + John 10v19)
9) At His SECOND Advent He SPLITS the Mount of Olives (Zech 14v4)
10) Mark 10v37 **They said unto him, Grant unto us that we may sit, one on thy right hand, and the other on thy left hand, in thy glory.** DIVISION/SPLIT
11) A schizophrenic is a SPLIT personality

THREE (3)

THREE occurs in 426 verses.
Some numbers in the Bible have 'primary' and 'secondary' meanings.
THREE is such a number. Its *primary* meaning is **Godhead** (Trinity); God being first in all things.

1) Mat 28v19 Go ye therefore, and teach all nations, baptizing them in the name of the Father, and of the Son, and of the Holy Ghost:
2) In Mat 3 (verses 16+17) Jesus was baptised (1) the Spirit of God descended (2), and the Father spoke (3)
3) 1 John 5v7 **For there are three that bear record in heaven, the Father, the Word, and the Holy Ghost: and these three are one.**

The *secondary* meaning is **resurrection**.

1) The Gospel of the grace of God is the death (1), burial (2) and resurrection (3) – 1 Cor 15v1-4
2) Jesus raised THREE from the dead in His earthly ministry – the widows son, Jarius's daughter and Lazarus
3) Israel is to be raised as a nation on the THIRD day (Hos 6v2)

Something special about the number THREE is that in the *resurrection* of the Lord Jesus Christ, He was *raised* on the THIRD day (Mat 12v38-40) by the DIVINE THREE in the Godhead: God the Father *raised* Him (Gal 1v1), Jesus *raised* Himself (John 2v19-21), and the Holy Spirit *raised* Him (Rom 8v11).

In the Lord Jesus Christ dwells...all the fullness of the Godhead bodily (Col 2v9)

It is also very interesting to note that the word Godhead occurs THREE times in Scripture... Acts 17v29, Rom 1v20, Col 2v9

The number THREE also shows the...

The imprint of the Godhead in the universe.
The significance of 'THREE'...

	FATHER	**SON**	**HOLY SPIRIT**
Man	Soul	Body	Spirit
Man	Childhood	Manhood	Maturity
Family	Man	Woman	Child
Reality	Space	Matter	Time
Space	Length	Width	Depth
Time	Past	Present	Future
Matter	Liquid	Solid	Gas
Kingdoms	Animal	Vegetable	Mineral
The Americas	North	Central	South
Education	Lower	Middle	High
Location	Land	Sea	Air
Astronomy	Sun	Moon	Stars
Height	Top	Middle	Bottom
Music	Harmony	Rhythm	Melody
Musical Note	Pitch	Volume	Duration
Offices	Bishops	Elders	Deacons

Races	Japheth	Ham	Shem
Bible Languages	Hebrew	Syriac (Aramaic)	Greek
Bible Writers	Fathers	Prophets	Apostles
Old Testament	Law	Prophets	Writings (Psalms)
New Testament	Gospels	Acts	Epistles
Conditions	Hell	Earth	Heaven
Mt. of Transfiguration	Peter	James	John
Electricity	Positive	Negative	Neutral
H20	Water	Steam	Ice
Scripture Application	Historical	Doctrinal	Spiritual

FOUR (4)

FOUR occurs in 282 verses.

Some say that FOUR is the number of the **world**.

There are FOUR directions / FOUR points on a compass – North, South, East and West
There are FOUR seasons – Spring, Summer, Autumn, Winter
There are FOUR elements – Earth, Air, Fire and Water
There are FOUR kingdoms – mineral, vegetable, animal and spiritual
ON the FOURTH day the material creation was finished – Gen 1v14-19

1) FOUR Gospels record Christ's EARTHLY ministry
2) FOUR WORLD kingdoms are in Daniel 2 – Babylon, Medo-Persian, Greece and Rome
3) For the FOUR directions of the WORLD, read the following passages – Rev 7v1, Dan 7v2, Matt 24v31, Zech 2v6, Zech 6v1-5, Ezek 37v8-10
4) FOUR groups of people are redeemed from the EARTH in Rev 5v9 – nations, kindreds, tongues and peoples
5) WORLDLY religion is a system of salvation on the basis of *works*. WORKS occurs FOUR times against grace in Rom 11v6
6) The FOURTH time 'the Word' is mentioned in John 1, He is coming into the WORLD (v14)
7) FOUR occurs 282 in Scripture and FOURTH occurs 78 times – but there is a little confusion over what FOUR actually stands for. The number FOUR in the Bible is still quite a mystery.
8) In the first and second chapters of Genesis, in the record of the CREATION, the word 'creature' is found FOUR times – Gen 1v20, 1v21, 1v24 + 2v19
9) FOUR is the number that is associated with CREATION. In Rom 8v19-22 the words CREATURE and CREATION are used FOUR times.

FIVE (5)

FIVE occurs in 270 verses.

FIVE is associated with **death**.

'Mayday' is the international distress signal. It has our FIFTH month (May) in the first syllable.

1) The words 'Christ died' occur in FIVE verses – Rom 5v6+8, Rom 14v15, 1 Cor 8v11, 1 Cor 15v3
2) David takes FIVE smooth stones from the brook before he KILLS Goliath (1 Sam 17v40). Incidentally, if you have an NIV David didn't kill Goliath in 2 Sam 21v19 'Elhanan' did. Another *error* in the New International PER-version.
3) In 2 Sam 2v23, Abner KILLED Asahel by hitting him under the FIFTH rib

4) In 2 Sam 4v5+6, the sons of Rimmon hit Ishbosheth under the FIFTH rib and he DIED
5) 'Sleep' in the Bible often refers to *death* (John 11v11-13, Acts 13v36, 1 Cor 11v30, 1 Cor 15v51) Adam's FIFTH rib was taken for Eve (Gen 2v21+22) when God caused a deep *sleep* to come upon him. Both Adam and Christ were opened in the side (John 19v34) *for a bride* (Eph 5v25 note '5 and 5x5'). Jesus' side being opened was the FIFTH wound.
6) The first man that ever *died*, died in Gen 5v5 (compare Prov 5v5, Acts 5v5) (But what about Abel? Abel didn't *die* he was *killed* – Gen 4v8)
7) In Exo 27v1, the altar used for *slaying* sacrifices is FIVE cubits! i.e. 5x5
8) There are six parts to Christ's ministry (Luke 7v22) – the FIFTH mentioned is the '*dead* are raised'
9) Lucifer was the FIFTH cherub before his fall (Ezek 28v14, Ezek 1v10, Ezek 10v14 and Rev 4v6-8), the one positioned above the Throne. But when he said 'I will' FIVE times in Isaiah 14v13+14, he lost his 'seven-letter' name and became a FIVE letter name i.e. 'DEVIL' and 'SATAN'
10) The following words have FIVE letters... DEATH, DYING, SLAIN, GRAVE, SLEEP, DEVIL, CROSS, SATAN, CURSE...
11) With the opening of the FIFTH seal in Rev 6v9, the 'souls' that were 'SLAIN for the word of God' appear
12) There are FIVE offerings in Leviticus – burnt, meal, peace, sin, trespass
13) The FIFTH thing to happen to Jesus (Mark 8v31) is His *death*
14) Romans 5 is the DEATH chapter comparing Adam and Christ

The *secondary* meaning of the number FIVE is GRACE (note FIVE letters)

1) GRACE is found FIVE times in Rom 11v5+6
2) The FIFTH time Noah's name is found in the Bible he... found GRACE in the eyes of the Lord (Gen 6v8)
3) Jesus Christ has FIVE names in Isa 9v6 - **Wonderful, Counsellor, The mighty God, The everlasting Father, The Prince of Peace.**

The 'main' meaning connected with the number FIVE is *death* rather than *grace*.

SIX (6)

SIX occurs in 191 verses.

The number SIX is the number of **MAN.**

1) Man was created on the SIXTH day – Gen 1v27+31
2) Rev 13v18 says that 666 is the number of a man
3) The Bible has 66 books and it was written for MAN
4) Gen 6 has the word MAN in it SIX times
5) Gal 6 has the word MAN in it SIX times
6) 2 Chron 6 has the word MAN in it SIX times
7) The following are interesting facts about the book of **Joshua**...
    - It is the SIXTH book
    - It is the first book named after a MAN
    - Joshua has SIX letters
    - It has 24 chapters (4x6)
    - 'MEN' is found SIX times in chapter SIX
    - Israel marched around Jericho SIX days in chapter SIX
    - 'MAN' is found SIX times in chapter SIX and 30 times (5x6) in the whole book
8) The following are interesting facts about **Romans**...
    - It is the SIXTH book in the NT

BIBLICAL NUMERICS

> - Romans has SIX letters
> - The name 'RoMANs' has 'MAN' in it
> - 'MAN' is the SIXTH word in Rom 6v6
> - 'MAN' is the SIXTH word in a verse SIX times in Romans! The SIXTH time is in Rom 6v6; the others are... Romans 2v1, 2v3, 2v6, 3v28, 5v7, 6v6
> - It has 16 chapters and teaches us how a 'Gentile' (number of a Gentile is 10) MAN (man's number is 6) can be made just before God

9) The number, as it stands by itself (I.e. NOT 'sixth'), occurs for the first time in Gen 7v6 where Noah is 600 (6x100) years old when the flood comes
10) Later in the Bible we find 600 MEN a very common expression for some reason
11) Solomon, as a type of the Antichrist, has his throne with SIX steps and SIX lions on one side and SIX lions on the other side making 666
12) In Ezra 2v13 we see 666
13) In 2 Chron 9v13 we see 666
14) In Rev 13v18 we see 666
15) As it has been said, Solomon is a type of the Antichrist; so what do we read in 1 Kings 10v14 - 666

SEVEN (7)

SEVEN occurs in 395 verses.

SEVEN is the number of **PERFECTION** or **COMPLETION**.

In Ps 19v7 **The law of the LORD is perfect, converting the soul: the testimony of the LORD is sure, making wise the simple.** (Note verse SEVEN. What is the SEVENTH word? PERFECT!)

Someone has written 'The whole word of God is founded upon the number seven. It stands for the seventh day of the creation week, and speaks of the millennium rest day. It denotes completeness or perfection'.

Lev 23v15+16. The number seven and the Sabbath, which was the seventh day (Gen 2v1-3), is connected with the word 'complete'.

The word 'finished' is also connected with the number seven. In Rev 10v7 we read... **'But in the days of the voice of the seventh angel, when he shall begin to sound, the mystery of God should be finished, as he hath declared to his servants the prophets.'**

'It is done' is another expression found in connection with the number seven – Rev 16v17 **'And the seventh angel poured out his vial into the air; and there came a great voice out of the temple of heaven, from the throne, saying, It is done.'**

1) Regarding the Creation in the first 2 chapters of Genesis the word 'created' occurs seven times.
2) God appointed seven days for the week (Exo 20v11)
3) There are seven notes in the musical scale (C,D,E,F,G,A,B then it goes back to C). Man named the notes but God fixed the sounds.
4) There are seven colours (red, orange, yellow, green, blue, indigo, violet) – white is *not* a colour, it is 'colourless')
5) Light broken down (i.e. through a prism) makes up seven colours, i.e. a rainbow; also seven colours (red, orange, yellow, green, blue, indigo, violet,) This is called refraction.
6) There are SEVEN continents – Europe, Asia, Africa, North America, South America, Australia, and Antarctica
7) According to the Encyclopaedia Britannica, there are SEVEN SEAS – North Pacific, South Pacific, North Atlantic, South Atlantic, Indian Ocean, Arctic Ocean, Mediterranean Sea. The word 'good' appears SEVEN times in Gen 1 (Gen 1v4,10,12,18,21,25+31)
8) A lunar month, the time it takes for the moon to circle around the earth, is 28 days (4x7); the distance the moon is from the earth is 238,000 miles (34,000 x 7). The diameter of the moon

is 2,100 miles (300 x 7)
9) The verb 'made' is also found SEVEN times in regards to God's specific creative acts – Gen 1v7+16+25+26+31 + Gen 2v2+3
10) 'heaven' is mentioned SEVEN times in Gen 1v1+8+9+14+15+17+20
11) In Gen 1v1 the number of Hebrew words is seven
12) Revelation has seven seals, seven trumpets, seven vials etc.
13) Noah took the clean beasts into the ark by sevens (Gen 7v2). Seven days after Noah went into the ark the flood came (Gen 7v9+10)
14) Before Aaron and his sons entered their priestly work they were consecrated seven days. (Lev 8v31-36)
15) On the day of atonement the high priest sprinkled the blood upon the mercy seat and before the mercy seat seven times (Lev 16v14). This is a picture of the completeness of the redemptive work of the Lord Jesus Christ.
16) There are seven dispensations (Innocence, Conscience, Human Government, Promise or Patriarchal, Law, Grace, Kingdom)
17) The Book of Life is mentioned seven times in the book of Revelation.
18) The **seventh** time Noah's name occurs is where it is said… '…Noah was a just man and **perfect** in his generations, and Noah walked with God.'
19) Revelation mentions 'the Lamb' (Jesus Christ) 28 times i.e. 4x7
20) In John, Jesus says 'I am' and 'I will' seven times each. In chapter 4 Jesus says seven things to the Samaritan woman and the seventh saying contains seven words '**I that speak unto thee am he**' (John 4v26)
21) Jesus uttered 7 sayings from the cross… Luke 23v34+43, John 19v26+27, Mat 27v46, Mark 15v34, John 19v28,+30, Luke 23v46
22) The title Pilate wrote and hung on the cross of Jesus had eight words… **JESUS OF NAZARETH THE KING OF THE JEWS.** (John 19v19) When the Jews asked him to change it, he replied… "What I have written I have written." (John 19v22) – SEVEN words (note 19v22 = 1+9+2+2=14 i.e. 2x7)
23) Ps 12v6+7 **The words of the LORD are pure words: as silver tried in a furnace of earth, purified seven times. Thou shalt keep them, O LORD, thou shalt preserve them from this generation for ever.**

EIGHT (8)

EIGHT occurs in 80 verses.

EIGHT is the number of **NEW beginnings**.

The EIGHTH note begins a NEW scale.

The EIGHTH day starts a NEW week.

1) EIGHT persons were saved from the Flood, and they started a NEW human population on the earth – (1 Pet 3v20)
2) The EIGHTH dispensation will bring NEW heavens and a NEW earth
3) Israel observed seven feasts, the seventh being the Feast of Tabernacles which pictures the Millennial reign of Christ. The EIGHTH day after the feast was a Sabbath (Lev 23v39), typical of the NEW heavens and NEW earth which appear after the Millennium.

NINE (9)

NINE occurs in 49 verse

NINE is connected with **fruitfulness**.

NINE also may have some connection with 'covenants'

1) There are NINE fruits of the Spirit (Gal 5v22+23 – Note – Gal is the NINTH book and v22+23 added up = NINE); Galatians has NINE letters.
2) Gen 9v9 **And I, behold, I establish my covenant with you, and with your seed after you;**
3) Abraham is ninety-nine when God makes a covenant with him and he was ninety and nine when Sarah conceived Isaac (the first FRUIT of her womb!) Sarah was NINETY (Gen 17v1+17)
4) NINE is the period of gestation (the process of carrying or being carried in the womb between conception and birth.) i.e. NINE months for women in producing fruit.
5) Holy Bible has NINE letters
6) KING JAMES has NINE letters!
7) AV 1611 = NINE added up!
8) 1611 divided by NINE = 179 i.e. ONE (1) PERFECT (7) Book that bears FRUIT (9)

TEN (10)

TEN occurs in 223 verses.

The number TEN relates to the **Gentiles**. TEN is a **Gentile** number.

The TENTH man from Adam is Noah, who is the father of the Gentiles. Isn't it a strange thing that Gentiles count by TENS!

In Gen 10 you have the first Gentile kingdom started, and the last Gentile kingdom has TEN nations in it (Dan 2)

Gen 10 lists the genealogies of the Gentiles.

In Acts 10 you have the opening of the door to the Gentiles in the NT

In John 10 you have the sheep of the *other* fold

In Rom 10 you have the missionary call message to the Gentiles

In Rev 10 the Lord put His foot on the EARTH and takes possession of the Gentile kingdoms

One preacher has written... 'The first time the word TEN occurs in the Bible, it occurs in Gen 5v14. The days were 910 years in a man's life, the word TEN occurring here for the first time, which is a reference to the life of somebody before the law. They are all Gentiles before the law. Of course I know that they're divided off into Gentiles coming from Japheth, and then the Shemites and Ham under another one, but the division in the NT is Gentile, Jew and church; and before the law, Abraham is an uncircumcised Gentile'.

The last world power on this earth under the United Nations will be a TEN federated kingdom of Gentiles represented by the toes on Daniel's image, and represented by the TEN kings of Rev 17. This is Gentile world dominion when Christ Jesus returns to set up an Everlasting Kingdom. The first Gentile kingdom was set up in Gen 10 by Nimrod, the thirteenth from Adam.

ELEVEN (11)

ELEVEN appears in 24 verses.

ELEVEN is not conclusive; it's quite a tricky number to locate its meaning.

It has been said by some that ELEVEN is the number of **judgment**.

1) There were ELEVEN judgments upon the Egyptians...
    1) The plague of Blood (Exo 7v19-21)
    2) The plague of Frogs (Exo 8v1-7)
    3) The plague of Lice (Exo 8v16-17)

    4) The plague of Flies (Exo 8v21-24)
    5) The plague of Murrain (Exo 9v1-7)
    6) The plague of Boils (Exo 9v8-11)
    7) The plague of Hail (Exo 9v22-25)
    8) The plague of Locusts (Exo 10v12-15)
    9) The plague of Darkness (Exo 10v21-23)
    10) The plague of First-born (Exo 12v29-30)
    11) The overthrow at the Red Sea (Exo 14v24-28)
2) Noah pronounced judgment upon Canaan, a son of Ham, because Ham saw his father's nakedness when he was uncovered in his tent. Noah said... **And he said, Cursed be Canaan; a servant of servants shall he be unto his brethren.** Gen 9v25 In Gen 10v15-18 it says that Canaan had ELEVEN sons...
3) 1 Kings 11v11 pronounces God's judgment upon Solomon
4) In John 16v11, Jesus said... **Of judgment, because the prince of this world is judged.**
5) Divine Judgment is pronounced against Tyrus 'in the ELEVENTH year' (Ezek 26v1-8)
6) Divine Judgment is given to Egypt in the ELEVENTH year (Ezek 30v20+21)
7) There are ELEVEN things associated with the Great White Throne Judgment (Rev 20v11-15)
    1) Great White Throne
    2) Him that sat on it
    3) The dead, small and great stand before God
    4) Books were opened
    5) Another book – the Book of life
    6) The dead were judged out of those things written in the books
    7) Sea gave up the dead
    8) Death and hell delivered up the dead
    9) These were judged, every man, according to their works
    10) He saw death and hell being cast into the lake of fire
    11) And he saw those cast into the lake of fire whose names were not found written in the Book of life
8) There were ELEVEN apostles in the end because one of them fell and was judged (Judas)

TWELVE (12)

TWELVE occurs in 165 verses.

The number TWELVE is a reference to **Israel**

1) There are TWELVE saved nations in eternity - Deut 32v7+8
2) There are TWELVE children of Israel, and they have TWELVE breastplate stones that represent them – Exo 39v14
3) We find that the TWELVE stars on the woman in Rev 12 represent the TWELVE tribes
4) There are TWELVE gates for the tribes, TWELVE foundations for the apostles (all Jews) in the city, and TWELVE manner of fruits for the nations who are numbered after the number of the tribes. There are TWELVE constellations in the Zodiac which match the TWELVE months in a year, and these match the nations in the birthstones in the breastplate
5) There are TWELVE chapters in Daniel dealing with the salvation of Israel during the Tribulation
6) In Gen 12, the first Hebrew or Jew is called out. There are NO Jews before Gen 12
7) In Exo 12 you see the beginning of the Jewish nation as such.

THIRTEEN (13)

THIRTEEN is one of the most interesting of all numbers. It occurs in 15 verses.

It is clearly associated with **rebellion** - Gen 14v4 **Twelve years they served Chedorlaomer, and in the thirteenth year they rebelled.** This is the first reference to *thirteen* in the Bible!

1) Gen 13v13... **But the men of Sodom were wicked and sinners before the LORD exceedingly.** (Note 13 words)
2) In Gen 13 Lot pitched his tent towards Sodom
3) *Rebellion* is found in...Gen 13v13, Mark 13v13, Ezek 13v13 and Rev 13v13
4) Deut 13 contains the rules for a false prophet whose miracles come to pass. In Rev 13v13, the false prophet of the Tribulation period causes fire to come down out of heaven in the sight of men, a miracle that comes to pass. Since both Deut 13 and Rev 13 have 18 verses, Deut 13 is the key to interpreting Rev 13 (note 18=6+6+6)
5) Deut 13v13 contains the first reference to the 'sons of Belial'
6) 1 Kings 13 relates the story of a *rebellious* prophet. Verse 26 (2x13) gives the reason for his apostasy – Rebellion against the word of the Lord)
7) 2 Sam 13 tells the story of Amnon, son of David, who raped his sister, Tamar. The chapter has 39 verses (3x13)
8) *Rebellion* is the 26th word (2x13) in Ezra 4v19
9) Rev 17v5 has 13 words in block capitals... **MYSTERY, BABYLON THE GREAT, THE MOTHER OF HARLOTS AND ABOMINATIONS OF THE EARTH.**
10) Mark 7v21+22 lists 13 things that proceed out of an evil heart.
11) John 13v26 (13 + 2x13) says, **Jesus answered, He it is, to whom I shall give a sop, when I have dipped it. And when he had dipped the sop, he gave it to Judas Iscariot, the son of Simon.** – Judas Iscariot has 13 letters.
12) Psalm 55v13 contains a prophecy about Judas... **But it was thou, a man mine equal, my guide, and mine acquaintance.** It has 13 words.
13) Job 26v13 (2x13 +13) says... **By his spirit he hath garnished the heavens; his hand hath formed the crooked serpent.**
14) 666 is associated with the number 13 – 2 Chron 9v13, Ezra 2v13, Rev 13v18
15) Nimrod is the 13th from Adam (Gen 10v6-8)
16) Gal 3v13... (3 X 13 = 39) **Christ hath redeemed us from the curse of the law, being made a curse for us: for it is written, Cursed is every one that hangeth on a tree:** CURSE is the last word in the OT (the OT has 39 books i.e. 3x13)
17) The word 'dragon' is mentioned 13 times in Revelation.
18) Satan turns up in Mark 1v13.
19) Gen 3v13 – the woman rebels against God and then blames the serpent
20) Gen 12v13 – a prophet of God is asking his wife to lie! Note there are 26 words in this verse (2x13)
21) Leviticus 13 – This entire chapter deals with leprosy and the leper. Those who had leprosy were considered 'unclean'. They had to live 'away' from society, they were outcasts. The word leprosy occurs 39 times in Scripture (3 x 13)
22) 1 Chron 10v13 – Here is the record of the death of Saul which contains information about his rebellion against the word of the Lord and his counsel from a witch. Note it contains 39 words (3 x 13)
23) Job 24v13 – Considering that rebellion is connected to the number 13 it should be of no surprise that the word rebel is located in the 13th verse; it also just happens to be the 6th word.
24) Psalm 55v13 – This Messianic Psalm speaks of the traitor Judas Iscariot (13 letters)
25) Prov 13v13 – people who rebel / despise the word of God.
26) Ezek 23v13 – There are 13 words in this verse describing the defilement of the Holy City, Jerusalem.
27) Mat 13v19 – First time the phrase 'the wicked one' occurs! 'Wicked one' occurs a total of 6

times in Scripture.
28) Luke 13v16 – a woman bound for 18 years (6+6+6)
29) There were 12 chosen apostles. Judas is always associated as number 12 in the lists. In Heb 3v1 we are told Jesus is 'the Apostle' therefore Judas moves down to number 13
30) John 13v27 – Notice in this verse, Satan is mentioned entering a man and he does it in a sentence of 18 words (6+6+6). The phrase 'Satan entered' is *not* used anywhere else in the Bible
31) 1 Chron 21v1 – The first time the word 'Satan' appears in the Bible is in the 13th book of the Bible. The next time it occurs is in the 6th verse of the first chapter of the 18th (6+6+6) book of the Bible i.e. Job 1v6
32) Isa 13v1 – This is the first mention of 'Babylon' in the book of Isaiah, chapter 13. Note Babylon occurs 13 times in Isaiah.
33) Mat 26v6 – It is the 26th chapter (2 x 13), It is the 6th verse! The verse contains 13 words and it's about a leper! Note 'Simon the leper' contains 13 letters.
34) Rev 12v3 – Dragon, the 13th word in this verse; it also occurs 13 times in the Book of Revelation.

FOURTEEN (14)

It occurs in 23 verses.

FOURTEEN means **deliverance**

In Gen 14, Abram delivered Lot from King Chedorlaomer (in his 14th year – verse 5)
In verse 20, Melchizedek said, **And blessed be the most high God, which hath delivered thine enemies into thy hand. And he gave him tithes of all.**

1) In Christ's genealogy there were 14 generations from Abraham to David, 14 generations from David to the Babylonian captivity, and 14 generations from the captivity to Christ (the Divine Deliverer). This makes THREE 14's (Divine *deliverance*)
2) If you count back 14 books from the last book in the OT i.e. Ezekiel and look at 14v14, it lists THREE men who experienced Divine *deliverance* – Noah (delivered from the Flood), Daniel (*delivered* from the mouth of the lion) and Job (delivered from the Devil) – Note the FOURTEENTH word in the verse is *deliver*.
3) Philip is mentioned FOURTEEN times in Acts 8; he brought the message of *deliverance* to the Samaritans and the Ethiopian eunuch.
4) The FOURTH time 'Word' is mentioned in John 1 is in v14 where he comes to bring *deliverance*.
5) The Passover lamb was to deliver Israel on the 14th day of the first month (Exo 12v6+7+12+13).
6) The ONLY place the word *delivery* is found in the Scriptures is in Isa 26v17 – it is the *fourteenth* word of that verse.
7) The 14th day brought *deliverance* to Paul and the men on a ship (Acts 27v19-39).
8) 'Son of Man' appears 85 times in the NT BUT the verse in Heb 2v6 is a small 's' and is *not* in regard to THE SON of Man i.e. the Lord. Therefore 'Son of Man' in relation to the Lord appears 84 times in the NT i.e. 14x6. The Son of Man comes to *deliver* (14) MAN (6) from sin.
9) In Exodus 14, Israel was *delivered* from Pharaoh and his host in the Red Sea.

FORTY (40)

Forty occurs in 145 verses.

FORTY is the number of **probation** or a **testing** period of time

Nearly every time the number shows up in the Scriptures it is in connection with **testing**.

1) The first time the number FORTY shows up (by itself i.e. *not* eight hundred and forty Gen 5v13) is in Gen 7v4 where the flood was upon the earth FORTY days and FORTY nights (see also Gen 7v17)
2) Esau is FORTY years old when he messes up and takes the wrong kind of wife

3) Isaac is FORTY years old when he takes Rebecca to wife
4) Notice the children of Israel are tested FORTY years in the wilderness until the rebels are purged out from among them – Heb 3v9+17, Num 14v33+34, Deut 2v7, 8v2
5) Jesus Christ fasted FORTY days and nights
6) Moses was on the Mount for FORTY days and nights fasting (Exo 24v18) see also Deut 10v10
7) Elijah the prophet was in the same condition in 1 Kings 19v8. Elijah goes FORTY days and nights without anything to eat.
8) Eli judges FORTY years in 1 Sam 4v18
9) Israel was in Egypt for 400 (40 x 10) years (Gen 15v13)
10) Israel was under the judges 400 (40 x 10) years
11) Israel and Judah were under the kings for 400 (40 x 10) years
12) There were 400 (40 x 10) years from the return of Israel from Babylon to Jesus Christ
13) At the time of the flood, it rained for 40 days and nights
14) Jesus was tempted of the Devil for 40 days
15) There were 40 years from the time of the crucifixion to the destruction of Jerusalem and the end of Israel as a nation
16) FORTY days Jonah preached judgment would come to the city of Nineveh – Jonah 3v4
17) God tested Israel in periods of 40 years

FORTY is plainly a period of **testing** or **probation** (*the process of testing*) or a kind of 'interim' before God does something in a certain situation.

The relationship between SEVEN (7) and FORTY (40)

There is a strange relationship between the numbers SEVEN and FORTY…
1) Gen 7v4 – first the word SEVEN and then the word FORTY
2) Gen 25v17+20 – SEVEN and FORTY
3) Lev 12v2+4 – v2 SEVEN days unclean and v4 thirty three days continuing her purifying of her blood (i.e. 7 plus 33 = FORTY)
4) Num 13v22+25 - SEVEN and FORTY
5) 2 Kings 11v21 and 2 Kings 12v1 – SEVEN and FORTY

FIFTY (50)

Fifty occurs in 138 verses.

Fifty is the number of **Jubilee** and **redemption**. Land in Israel could be redeemed by the family that originally owned it during that year. From the end of WW1 in 1917 and the drafting of the Balfour Declaration giving Israel the right to the land to the reclaiming of Jerusalem by Israel in 1967 was FIFTY (50) years.

ONE THOUSAND (1,000)

The word THOUSAND occurs six times in Rev 20 indicating that there is a 6,000 year span of time, before the seventh day Millennial Sabbath rest of the Lord Jesus Christ, when He returns to the earth to set up His kingdom.

It has been said that the word THOUSAND, where it occurs, is the division that divides off the ages. The ages are divided off into periods of ONE THOUSAND years each, and these periods are roughly, as found in your Bible…

1st – from the time of Adam down about the year 3,000 BC
2nd – the next period would come down about the year 2,000 BC which would be right after the Flood around 2,300 BC
3rd – you could date the time of Abraham right on the 2,000 BC mark!
4th – The founding of the temple by Solomon would be right on the mark at 1,000 BC

5th – The middle of the Dark Ages at the Crusades would be at 1,000 AD
6th – the Second Advent in the fall (September or October) at the Feast of Tabernacles when the Lord Jesus is coming to set up His Millennial kingdom on this earth.

2 Pet 3v8, 1 Chron 29v21. In Rev 20v2-7 we see the word thousand SIX times. The Millennium is ONE THOUSAND YEARS (1,000) no matter what the A-Millennialist tells you. If this wasn't enough, the night God appeared to Solomon, Solomon offered **1,000** burning offerings on the altar (2 Chron 1v6).

Biblical numerics is a fascinating subject to study!

NOTES

NOTES

ISLAM

Jesus vs Mohammed

(Is there a difference between them? You decide!)

Jesus	Mohammed
IS God – 1 Tim 3v16, John 20v28, John 10v30-33, Zech 12v7-10	NOT God
Everlasting, had NO beginning – Mic 5v2	NOT from everlasting, just a 'man!'
Part of the Godhead / Trinity – 1 John 5v7, Col 2v9	NOT part of the Godhead / Trinity!
Called 'The Lord' – 1 Cor 12v3	NOT called 'The Lord!'
Could forgive sins – Mat 9v2	Could NOT forgive sins!
Accepted worship – Mat 28v9	NOT to be worshipped as he is NOT God!
Created the world / everything – Col 1v14-17	Created NOTHING!
The **only** way to Heaven – John 14v6	Can't get you to Heaven!
Omnipresent – Mat 18v20	Could only be in ONE place at a time due to being JUST human!
Omniscient – Mark 11v2-6, John 2v25	NOT omniscient!
Omnipotent, had ALL power - Mat 28v18	NOT omnipotent!
Virgin born – Mat 1v23	NOT born of a virgin!
Saviour of the world – Luke 2v11, John 4v42, 2 Tim 1v10	Can't save 'anyone' NOT even himself!
Could control nature – Mark 4v39	Had NO power over nature!
Could walk on water – Mat 14v25	Could NOT walk on water!
Could heal and raise the dead – Mat 8v16, John 11v43+44	Could NOT heal or raise the dead!
Is coming back in the clouds – Acts 1v9-11	Will NOT 'come again!'
Think how many miracles Jesus did!	Mohammed did none!
Jesus will judge everyone – John 5v22	Mohammed will judge no one!

So why do Muslims get all upset over *just* a human being claiming to be a 'prophet,' compared to Jesus Christ who IS GOD! Imagine if Christians cut off the heads of all those who blasphemed the name of the Lord Jesus Christ; there would be rivers of blood in your neighbourhood!

Why do Islamic terrorists blow themselves up while trying to kill other people?

Why do Islamic terrorists want to kill other people?

What is their goal, purpose, and aim in regard to killing people?

Where do they get their ideas from? Who or *what* says that they *should* be killing people?

Where did all this originate from? Who started the idea of killing for religious beliefs?

Is it the Quran/Koran that teaches this?

If they are obeying the Koran, then *why* are we allowing children to be taught the Koran in England? Why are we allowing Muslims to build mosques over here when the Koran condones killing of non-Muslims? Isn't that fuelling the fire?

Shouldn't we be banning the teaching of the Koran and not allowing Islam to grow here in the UK?

If the above is right, why is the Government allowing all this?

How can it all be stopped? If it can't, what is next on the horizon?

What are you doing to change things? How about writing to MP's everywhere, asking them these questions?

Islam a religion of peace?

Islam and its enemies - 'If you do not go out and fight, god will punish you severely...' Sura 9:39. 'You who believe, fight the disbelievers near you...' Sura 9:123. 'Fight in god's cause against those who fight you, but do not overstep the limits... Kill them wherever you encounter them and drive them out from where they drove you out, for persecution is more serious than killing... Fight them until there is no more persecution and worship is devoted to god (Allah).' Sura 2:190-193. Those who will not fight: '...we expect god to inflict punishment on you, either from himself or at our hands...' Sura 9:52. ...and 'they are cowardly' Sura 9:56. 'He who fights so that Allah's word (Islam) should be superior, then he fights in Allah's cause.' Hadith Vol 1, Book 3, Number 125.

If you convert *from* Islam - 'Whoever changes his religion, **kill him**.' (Hadith 9:57)

Does a Muslim believe he has assurance of Heaven? - No assurance **unless you die fighting**. 'Let those of you who are willing to trade the life of this world for the life to come, fight in god's way. To anyone who fights in god's way, whether killed or victorious, we shall give a great reward.' (Sura 4:74) Suicide bombers believe that because of their murderous act, their sins (and those of their relatives) will be forgiven and that they will go straight to Paradise. In fact, if they die in the act of murder, **they go straight to Hell.** How sad for Muslims who sacrifice their precious lives for *nothing*. How tragic when, the second after they die, they find themselves burning in Hell and realize they have believed a lie. Even Mohammed was not sure he would get to Heaven. He taught that the righteous would get to Heaven if their good deeds outweighed their bad deeds. At the end of his life Mohammed said: 'By Allah, though I am the apostle of Allah, yet I do not know what Allah will do to me.' (Vol 5:266 Hadith).

Islam and women - 'If you fear high-handedness from your wives ... when you go to bed, **then hit them**.' Sura 4:34

Ever wondered why Muslims don't have dogs as pets? - Penalty for keeping a dog as a pet - 'Allah's apostle (Mohammed) said, "If somebody keeps a dog, he loses one Qirat (of the reward) of his good deeds every day, except if he keeps it for the purpose of agriculture or for the protection of livestock."' Hadith Vol 4, Book 54, Number 541.

Islam - the books - The books of Islam are the Koran, which has 114 chapters or Suras, and the Hadith, which is in several volumes. Mohammed was illiterate. He could not read or write. He began having visions of a terrifying being which he claimed to be the angel Gabriel. Mohammed told other people about the visions, and after he died of poison, they wrote down what he said. Those writings are the 114 chapters of the Koran. After Mohammed died many people related things they had heard him say in his lifetime, and these were all written down. These sayings of Mohammed make up the various volumes of the Hadith. The entire religion of Islam rests on the word of one illiterate Arab man who lived in the 7th century in the desert (modern day Saudi Arabia). Muslims are gambling their eternal destiny on the word of one illiterate 7th century Arab man! (Article taken from The Free Press)

Islamic Sharia Law - Government according to the strict rules of the Quran/Koran

The Islamic pattern for conquest is... **INFILTRATE** (Move in), **POPULATE** (Grow large families and recruit others), **LEGISLATE** (Make laws that are PRO Muslims), **DECIMATE** (Take over the country little by little, one city at a time), **ELIMINATE** (Destroy those who do not submit to Sharia law) Here are *just a few* of the Sharia laws...

1) A Muslim can lie as and when if it is to fulfil Allah's commandments such as Jihad.

2) Jihad, defined as 'to war against non-Muslims to establish the religion,' **is the duty of every Muslim** and Muslim head of state (Caliph). Muslim Caliphs who refuse Jihad are in violation of Sharia and unfit to rule.

3) A Caliph can hold office through seizure of power, meaning through force.

4) A Caliph is exempt from being charged with serious crimes such as murder, adultery, robbery, theft, drinking, and in some cases of rape.

5) A percentage of alms must go to Jihad.

6) **A Muslim who leaves Islam must be killed immediately**.

7) A Muslim will be forgiven for murder of an apostate, adulterer, highway robber etc. thus making vigilante street justice and **honour killings acceptable**.

8) A Muslim will not get the death penalty if he kills a non-Muslim but he will get it for killing a Muslim.

9) Blasphemy of Islam, Muslims, Sharia, Quran, or Hadith is punishable by fines, imprisonment, flogging, **amputation, or beheading**. Use of derogatory remarks about Mohammed is **punished by death**.

10) Sharia *never* abolished slavery or **sexual slavery** and highly regulates it. A master will not be punished for killing his slave.

11) Non-Muslims are not equal to Muslims under the law. They are given three choices... convert, live as a debased third-class citizen **or be killed**.

12) Non-Muslims are to comply to Islamic law if they are to remain safe. They are forbidden to

marry Muslim women, publicly display wine or pork, recite their Scriptures, or openly celebrate their religious holidays or funerals. They are forbidden from building new churches or building them higher than mosques. They may not enter a mosque without permission.

13) Banks must be Sharia compliant, and interest is not allowed.

14) Homosexuality is **punishable by death**.

15) **There is no age limit for marriage of girls.** The marriage contract can take place any time after birth and **consummated at age eight or nine**.

16) Rebelliousness on the part of the wife nullifies the husband's obligation to support her and **gives him permission to beat her** and keep her from leaving the home.

17) Divorce is only in the hands of the husband and is as easy as saying "I divorce you", and it becomes effective even if the husband did not intend it.

18) A man has the right to have up to four wives, and she has no right to divorce him even if he is polygamous.

19) Marriage is a buyer/seller contract whereby **the dowry is given in exchange for the woman's sexual organs**.

20) A man is allowed to have sex with slave women and women captured in battle, and if the enslaved woman is married, her marriage is annulled.

21) **To prove rape, a woman must have four male witnesses**.

22) **A Muslim woman must cover every inch of her body which is considered 'awrah', a sexual organ.**

23) Sharia severely punishes free speech when it comes to any criticism of Mohammed, the Quran, Hadith and Sharia itself. Free speech is unprotected in the Islamic State.

These are just a few of the laws of Sharia – taken from a leaflet by Nonie Darwish (the author of Cruel and Unusual Punishment; the Terrifying Global Implications of Islamic Law.) He is also the founder of Former Muslims United.

All of the above deprives people of freedom of speech, freedom of conscience, equality of all people before the law, and equality of the rights of women with men.

Rev 20v15 **And whosoever was not found written in the book of life was cast into the lake of fire**.

This is where *every* Muslim is headed who does *not convert* to Christianity.

This is what the Koran says... (Taken from Ruckman's RRB)

Jesus Christ never created anything (Sura 16v21)

Jesus Christ lived to be 120 years old and was buried in Kashmir, India (M. M. Ali's note 1753 on Sura 23v50)

Jesus Christ didn't die on the cross (Sura 3v54)

Jesus Christ was made of dust, just like Adam (Sura 3v59)

If you don't believe in 'Allah' instead of Christ's Father, Jehovah, you'll be thrown in Hell (Sura 17v39)

The Moslems are the chosen people of God who replaced Israel (Sura 7v10)

Peter, James, John, Matthew et al. are all in Hell (Sura 21v98)

Every word in the Koran came from a 600-winged angel (Sura 19v19, note 1537, cf. Hadith, Bukhari, Vol VI no 380)

The Kingdom of Islam is to rule all of the nations on earth (Sura 24v55, footnote 1763)

Jesus Christ was not the prophet likened to Moses – Mohammed was (Sura 28v44, footnotes 1884, 1885)

God created the Heaven and the Earth in two days (Sura 41v9)

God never begat any son (Sura 112v3)

Angels are females (Sura 53v27)

There are other creators beside Allah (Sura 37v125) although all Moslems claim to be monotheists (which they're not according to the verse!)

Jesus Christ asked his disciples to help promote Allah (Sura 61v14, 17v81, footnote 1461)

Mohammed fulfilled all the prophecies for both advents of Christ (Sura 2v253)

Islam is the only true religion (Sura 5v13, 48v28, 9v29, 62v1, 29v48) because it replaced Israel (Sura 5v13 note 406, 3v18, 110)

Ishmael was just as much a prophet as Jesus Christ (Sura 19v54, note 1552)

The Scriptures declare in John 8v44 **Ye are of your father the devil, and the lusts of your father ye will do. He was a murderer from the beginning, and abode not in the truth, because there is no truth in him. When he speaketh a lie, he speaketh of his own: for he is a liar, and the father of it**. Islam is a religion created by the Devil which has deceived millions and taken millions to Hell when they thought they were going to Heaven.

Just one reason why the Bible is different to every other book in the world...

In all of the 114 Suras of the Koran/Quran how many prophecies did the 'prophet' prophesy? Mohammed was not a prophet. He didn't predict one single prophecy during his lifetime or after he was dead. Mohammed could not prophesy when he would die, where he would die or how he would die! Moses knew when and where. Elijah knew when he was going up to glory (2 Kings 2), Jesus Christ listed 10 details of His coming death, Mohammed didn't. All of the 'prophecies' in the Koran that turn out to be 'historical' were *stolen* from a Book, 'THE Book' (i.e. THE BIBLE) that was complete (and in circulation) more than 900 years *before* Mohammed was born. Have you ever stopped to think that not one of the world's major religions (Mormons, Buddhists, Moslems, Hindus, Confucians, Jews and Christian Scientists) were able to put on paper one historical prophecy dealing with anything that would happen in actual history after their founders were dead. All genuine prophecies in Judaism are taken from 'THE LAW' and 'THE PROPHETS' (i.e. THE BIBLE) – Luke 24v44. The Scripture of truth (Dan 10v21) does not fail to predict histories that deal with weather conditions, nations, military engagements, alliances, religions, apostasy, churches, and individuals, anywhere from 10-2000 years ahead of time! *For example...*

> Gen 3v15 – That was 1,500 years ahead of time.
>
> Gen 49v10-11 – That was 1,500 years ahead of time.
>
> Zeph 3v8 – That was 2,600 years ahead of time.
>
> Isa 11v1-8 – That was 2,700 years ahead of time.
>
> Mic 7v14 – That was 3,319 years ahead of time.
>
> Dan 2v34-35 – That was 2,500 years ahead of time.
>
> Isa 2v1-7 – That was 2,630 years ahead of time.
>
> Josh 10v12 – That was 3,439 years ahead of time.
>
> Zech 14 – that was 2,430 years ahead of time.
>
> Isa 14v1-3 – That was 3,800 years ahead of time.
>
> Ps 22v1+18 – That was 990 years ahead of time.

The majority of the information below is taken from Dr Robert Morey's book 'Islamic Invasion'.

Muhammad

1) Muhammad was born in A.D. 570 in Mecca.

2) Parents were Abdullah and Aminah.

3) Born into the Quraysh tribe - this tribe was custodian of the Kabah.

4) He was distantly related to the Arab royal family of Hashim.

5) Muhammad's father died before he was born, and his mother died when he was young.

6) He was then sent to live with his grandparents.

7) Then he was sent to live with a wealthy uncle who then sent him to live with a poor uncle.

8) **It is interesting to note that many of his family members never accepted Muhammad's claim to be a prophet, and never did embrace Islam**.

9) Muhammad at a young age began to experience religious so called visitations.

10) Tradition has it that Muhammad experienced miraculous visions.

11) He claimed that a heavenly being had split open his stomach, stirred his insides around, and then sewed him back up. It is referred to in the Quran Sura 94v1 'Did we not open

ISLAM

thy breast for thee?'

12) We are not told why this thing happened? (Try finding that in the Quran).

13) Muhammad's mother, Aminah, was involved with the occult.

Interesting to note, the Quraysh tribe in which Muhammad was raised was particularly addicted to the cult of the moon god. As Muhammad grew up near Kabah, the 360 idols, and the sacred magical black stone which was considered the 'good luck charm' for the Quraysh tribe, he witnessed pilgrims coming to Mecca every year. He watched them worship at the Kabah by running around it seven times, kissing the black stone, and then running down to a nearby Wadi to throw stones at the devil.

Therefore it is no surprise then to find that most of the elements of his religious upbringing were transferred into the religion of Islam and did not come from a 'new' revelation from Allah as Islam claims.

14) Muhammad married his first wife at the age of 25, she was 10 years older.

15) They had two sons who both died when they were young. They also had four daughters.

16) One of the daughters married Uthman, who became the caliph who later standardised the text of the Quran.

17) At the age of 40 Muhammad experienced another visitation.

18) He claimed that Allah had called him to be a prophet and an apostle.

But now we have four conflicting versions of this in the Quran

In the Quran, we are told that Allah called Muhammad to be a prophet and an apostle, but unfortunately, there are several alternative versions of these events...

Either one is right or they are all wrong?

- Sura 53v2-18 and Sura 81v19-24 says that Allah personally appeared to Muhammad in the form of a man and that Muhammad saw and heard him.

- This is later abandoned because we see in Sura 16v102 and Sura 26v192-194 we are told that Muhammad's call was issued by the 'holy spirit?' We are not told who or what this *holy spirit* is!

- The third different account of his original call is given in Sura 15v8 where we are told that the angels were the ones who came down to Muhammad and announced that Allah had called him to be a prophet.

- But yet again this is later amended in Sura 2v97 so that it is only the angel Gabriel who issues the call to Muhammad and hands down the Quran to him.

And this last point is *only* used because it was Gabriel who played a significant role in the birth of guess who? The Lord Jesus Christ.

19) The Quran is supposedly to have been handed down from Allah to Muhammad. There were no human writers involved.

20) Some believe Muhammad suffered from epilepsy.

21) At one time because of his fears that he was demon possessed, he became terribly depressed that he decided to commit suicide.

22) Yet just before doing so he believed he had another vision that said he was not to.

23) His message and his preaching stirred up unrest against him, even among the members of his own family.

24) At one point the hostility against Muhammad was such that people in Mecca laid siege to the section of the city where Muhammad lived. He then faced a very difficult situation.

25) In order to appease his pagan family members and the members of the Quraysh tribe, he decided that the best thing he could do was to admit that it was perfectly proper to pray to and worship the 3 daughters of Allah, Al-Lat, Al-Uzza, and Manat.

26) This led to the famous 'satanic verses' in which Muhammad in a moment of weakness and supposedly under the inspiration of Satan (according to the early Muslim authorities) succumbed to the temptation to appease the pagan mobs in Mecca (Sura 53v19)

27) This *fact* is supported in every general and Islamic reference work, Muslim or Western. It is also included in all the biographies of Muhammad. *This account cannot be denied! Muhammad sinned!*

28) When Muhammad's disciples at Medina heard of his fall into polytheism, they rushed to him with rebukes and counsel.

29) Muhammad would later claim that even the angel Gabriel himself came down from heaven and rebuked him for allowing Satan to inspire him to worship other gods.

30) He then reverted back to just worshipping Allah, and stated that Allah had cancelled his past revelation.

31) After Muhammad's death, the satanic verses were not included in the Quran.

32) **In the Quran it is a sin to have more than four wives.**

33) **Muhammad had at least 16 therefore sinned again**. Khadija, Swada, Aesha, Omm Salama, Hafsa, Zaynab (of Jahsh), Jowayriya, Omm Habiba, Safiya, Maymuna (of Hareth), Fatema, Hend, Asma (of Saba), Zaynab (of Khozayma), Habla, Asma (of Norman), Mary (the Christian), Rayhana, Omm Sharik, Maymuna, Zaynab (a third one), Khawla.

34) Muhammad married Aesha who was only 8/9 years old at the time.

35) Muhammad died in A.D. 632.

36) Islam claims that Muhammad and Jesus of Nazareth were both Muslims and both prophets sent by Allah, therefore the message they both bring must be the same otherwise Allah would be contradicting himself.

ISLAM

37) The Quran uses the Biblical Gospels for information about Jesus, thus the Bible cannot be corrupt otherwise the Quran would be corrupt.

Let us look at a comparison of Jesus Christ and Muhammad, and the Bible and the Quran...

Prophecy

First, the birth, life, death, and resurrection of Jesus were clearly prophesied in the Old Testament according to the New Testament.

Several examples will suffice. Micah 5v2 gives us the very name of the town in which the Messiah would be born. On the day Christ died, no less than 33 OT prophesies were fulfilled. The coming of Christ was preceded by the preaching of John the Baptist, in the spirit and power of Elijah, according to the prophecy in Isa 40 and Mal 4.

This is in stark contrast to the coming of Muhammad, which was not predicted by pagan soothsayers, Old Testament prophets, or New Testament apostles.

Birth

The birth of Jesus Christ was miraculous in that He was conceived by the Holy Spirit in the womb of the virgin Mary.

The Quran and orthodox Islam fully accept the virgin birth of Jesus.

There is nothing miraculous or supernatural about the birth of Muhammad. He was the natural product of the sexual union of his father and mother.

Sinlessness

According to the NT, Jesus Christ lived a perfect and sinless life (2 Cor 5v21, 1 John 3v5, Heb 4v15, Heb 9v14, 1 Pet 1v19). When His enemies came to accuse Jesus before Pilate and Herod, they had to invent charges because no one could find anything against Him.

But when we turn to the life of Muhammad, we find that he was a normal human being engaged in the same sins which affect all of us. He lied, cheated, lusted after women, failed to keep his word etc. He was neither perfect nor sinless.

Where in the Quran does it state that Muhammad was sinless?

In the Quran - Sura 18v110 Muhammad is commanded by Allah 'Say, I am but a man like yourselves.

Nowhere in the Quran is Muhammad said to be sinless. Instead, Allah tells Muhammad that he is no different than any other man.

Muslims who claim that Muhammad was sinless have failed to note Sura 40v55, where Allah told Muhammad to repent of his sins. Not only was Muhammad commanded to repent of his sins and to seek forgiveness, but he was also reminded of his past sins that Allah had already forgiven and of future sins which would need future forgiveness.

Muhammad was not sinless according to the Quran. He was just one more poor sinner in need of forgiveness and redemption.

Miracles

During his lifetime, Jesus did many great and mighty miracles. He healed the sick, raised the dead, cast out demons, and even ruled the wind and the waves.

But according to the Quran in dozens of places such as Sura 17v91-95, Muhammad never performed a single miracle. According to the Quran (not tradition or testimonies) Muhammad never did a miracle.

The Love of God

Jesus Christ preached the love of God, but nowhere in the Quran does Muhammad preach the love of God.

As a matter of fact, neither God's love for man, nor man's love for God, plays any significant role in the preaching of Muhammad, the Quran, or the religion of Islam.

Christianity points to the coming of Christ as the greatest proof and example that God loves mankind, Islam cannot point to anything that reveals the love of God.

Human and Divine nature

According to the Bible, Jesus Christ was perfect man and perfect God, but Muhammad was only a man.

Jesus Christ our perfect example

The way Jesus lived and the way He was willing to die for sinners has given us a high moral example to follow. But when you turn to the example of Muhammad, you do not find a high moral example; you find him involved in many acts which must be deemed as immoral and unjust.

Killing or robbing

Jesus never killed or robbed anyone. According to the Quran Muhammad killed and robbed people in the name of Allah.

Winning people to Himself

Jesus never used physical violence to force people to believe His message or to accept Him. When Peter took out his sword to fight, Jesus told him to put it back in its sheath. But when we turn to Muhammad we find that he frequently used physical violence to force people to give up their idols and to accept Islam.

Directing disciples to kill

Jesus never instructed His followers by the way of command, example, or precept to kill in His name, to rob in His name, or to subdue enemies in His name.

Muhammad did. He taught his disciples by example, command, and precept that they could and should rob in Allah's name and force people to submit to Islam.

On taking another man's wife

Jesus did not take any man's wife to be his wife. Muhammad did. This is one of the most distressing aspects of Muhammad's life. Muhammad's adopted son, Zaid, had married a beautiful young woman with whom he was deeply in love. Then one day, according to Muslim traditions, Muhammad saw

Zaid's wife without her veil and lusted after her.

Faced with the refusal of Zaid and his wife to dissolve their marriage, Muhammad had a 'convenient' revelation from Allah, which not only commanded Zaid to give up his wife to Muhammad but also decreed that there was no evil in a father-in-law taking his daughter-in-law away from his adopted son.

Zaid and his wife were told that they did not have any choice in the matter. They had to submit to the will of Allah.

Sura 33v36-38 *'It is not for any believer, man or woman, when God and his messenger have decreed a matter, to have the choice in the affair. Whosoever disobeys Allah and his messenger has gone astray into manifest error. When you said to him whom Allah had blessed and you had favoured, 'Keep your wife to yourself, and fear Allah,' and you were concealing within yourself what Allah should reveal, fearing other men; and Allah has better right for you to fear him. So when Zaid had accomplished what he would of her, then we gave her in marriage to you, so that there should not be any fault in the believers, touching the wives of their adopted sons, when they have accomplished what they would of them; and Allah's commandment must be performed. There is no fault in the prophet, touching what Allah had ordained for him.'*

It is no wonder that this passage in the Quran has led many Muslims to renounce Islam!

Dying for others

When Christ died He died for others. When Muhammad died, he died for his own sins. He did *not* die for anyone.

Resurrection

Jesus did not remain dead. He conquered sin, Hell and death by rising on the third day. (Rom 4v25) But when Muhammad died, he stayed dead. He did not rise from the dead. Muhammad is dead! Jesus Christ is alive!

Ascension

Jesus ascended bodily into heaven. This was witnessed by the disciples in Acts 1v9-11, Muhammad did not ascend into heaven, the Quran never states that he did.

Heavenly intercession

Jesus is now in heaven as our intercessor and Saviour, the only mediator between God and man (1 Tim 2v5)

Muhammad is not an intercessor nor a saviour. The Quran states that there is no intercessor or saviour. (Sura 6v51,70+10v3) You have to save yourself.

Worship

In the NT, Jesus was worshipped as a living Saviour – Mat 2v11, Mat 8v2, Mat 9v18, Mat 14v33, Mat 15v25, Mat 18v26, Mat 28v9+17, Mark 5v6, Mark 15v19, Luke 24v52, John 9v38, Acts 10v25, Rev 5v14.

But the Quran *never* speaks of worshipping Muhammad. That would be blasphemous, because he was only a man!

Personal relationship

According to the NT, people can have a personal relationship with Jesus Christ as He enters into their hearts through His Spirit at conversion. This is why we so often talk about the love of God.

How can you have a personal relationship with Muhammad, he is dead?

The Lord's Return

Jesus Christ is coming back again soon to collect His Church and judge all men. Muhammad isn't coming back again, Muhammad is dead.

So by comparing the life of the Lord Jesus Christ with the life of Muhammad, we can see a huge difference, Muhammad is *definitely inferior* to the Lord Jesus Christ.

They came with different messages and did not represent the same God. They did not live or preach like each other. On all the essential issues they were totally different. Jesus Christ is Lord, God and King, Muhammad was a sinful man.

The structure of the Quran

The Muslim scholar 'Ali Dashti' comments on the defects of the Quran... *'Unfortunately the Qur'an was badly edited and its contents are very obtusely arranged. All students of the Qur'an wonder why the editors did not use the natural and logical method of ordering by date of revelation as in Ali b. Abi Taleb's lost copy of the text'*

The standard Islamic reference work, 'The Concise Encyclopaedia of Islam' refers to the *'disjointed and irregular character'* of the text of the Quran.

38) Muhammad, although a prophet so-called, did not foresee his own death.

There are no original manuscripts of the Quran. Due to Muhammad's unexpected and sudden death, there was made no preparation for his writings to be taken down. Instead this was taken up by his followers. They wrote down what they could remember what he said. These recordings were written down on whatever was available at the time.

The Concise Encyclopaedia of Islam comments... *'The Koran was collected from the chance surfaces on which it had been inscribed: 'from pieces of papyrus, flat stones, palm leaves, shoulder blades and ribs of animals, pieces of leather, wooden boards, and the hearts of men."*

Even the internationally known Muslim scholar Mandudi admits that the Quran was originally recorded 'on leaves of date-palms, bark of trees, bones, etc.'

The strange materials on which the Quran was written are verified by all general reference works such as encyclopaedias and by the standard reference works of Islam.

When there was nothing around which could be written on, the attempt was made to memorise Muhammad's revelations as closely as possible. According to Mandudi, the task that confronted the followers of Muhammad after his unexpected death was to gather together the scattered sermons of Muhammad, some of which were written on biodegradable articles, and others which were not written down but committed only to memory.

This, of course, created great difficulties. Some of the tree bark crumbled or broke and some of the stones were lost. Worse yet, Ali Dashti notes that animals at times ate the palm leaves or mats on which the Suras had been recorded.

ISLAM

Some of those who were the only ones who remembered certain Suras died in battle before they had the opportunity to commit in writing what they had heard. The gathering together of material for the Quran lasted several years. Much confusion remained as the memory of one person did not match up or correspond with that of another.

The Order of the Suras

39) There are 114 Suras, or revelations given by Muhammad.

40) They are not arranged in chronological order in which Muhammad received them.

41) Instead they are laid out from the largest Sura to the smallest, irrespective of any kind of order.

42) **There are 'many' mistakes and contradictions in the Quran**

43) Due to reconstruct the life and teaching of Muhammad in a chronological order, one must jump all over the Quran from one Sura to another. (There is no natural order)

44) Muslims claim that the Quran is always written in the first person i.e. that Allah himself is always speaking to man.

45) Such a claim, however, does not fit the text of the Quran. There are 'many' sections in which it is clear that Allah is *not* speaking, but Muhammad.

When you pick up the Bible, you learn in chronological order about creation, the fall of man into sin, the great flood, the tower of Babel, the calling of Abraham, the patriarchs, the calling of Moses, the Exodus, the building up of the nation of Israel, the ultimate captivity of the nation, the people going into exile, their return under Cyrus, the rebuilding of Israel, the prediction of the coming of the Messiah, the coming of the Messiah and His life, death, and resurrection, and the beginning of the Church Age. Then you come to the last book of the Bible, and you read about the end of the universe. The Bible gives us a complete picture, the Book is complete and perfect.

But when you turn to the Quran, because of its disjointed and disordered condition, you are left with the feeling of incompleteness.

You are, as it were, left hanging after each Sura because there is no longer connection from one to the other. For example... one Sura will deal with some pedestrian matter such as Allah wanting Muhammad's wives to stop arguing and bickering in his presence while the next Sura attacks the idols of the Arabians.

If you were to contrast the 66 books of the Bible (The word of God) written over a period of 1700 years by at least 40 different writers, with the Quran which only came through one man, Muhammad, during only his own lifetime, there would be no contest as to which was the superior literature.

Since Muslims claim that the Quran was 'handed down' from heaven, and that Muhammad cannnot be viewed as its human author, it is interesting to point out that, according to the 'Concise Encyclopaedia of Islam', the Arabic of the Quran is in the dialect and vocabulary of someone who was a member of the Quraysh tribe living in the city of Mecca. Thus Muhammad's fingerprints can be found all over the Quran.

If the Quran were written in some kind of heavenly, perfect Arabic, why then does it clearly reveal that it was spoken by someone who was a member of the Quraysh tribe residing in Mecca?

The Quran, in its dialect, vocabulary, and content, reflects the style of its author, Muhammad - not some heavenly Allah.

To go from the Bible to the Quran is to go from the superior to the inferior, from the greater to the lesser, from the real to the counterfeit, from the perfect, inerrant word of God to a book written by a sinful man!

46) The Quran is not written in perfect Arabic. It contains many grammatical errors, such as the Suras 2v177, 192 / 3v59 / 4v162 / 5v69 / 7v160 / 13v28 / 20v66 / 63v10 etc.

Ali Dashti comments... *'The Quran contains sentences which are incomplete and not fully intelligible without the aid of commentaries; foreign words, unfamiliar Arabic words, and words used with other than normal meaning; adjectives and verbs inflected without observance of the concords of gender and number; illogically and ungrammatically applied pronouns which sometimes have no referent; and predicates which in rhymed passages are often remote from the subjects. To sum up, more than 100 Quranic aberrations from the normal rules and structure of Arabic have been noted'*

47) There are over 100 words of the Quran that are not even in the Arabic language.

48) There are Egyptian, Hebrew, Greek, Syriac, Akkadian, Ethiopian, and Persian words and phrases in the Quran.

49) Some of the original verses of the Quran were lost. For example, one Sura originally had 200 verses in the days of Ayesha. But by the time Uthman standardised the text of the Quran, it had only 73 verses. A total of 127 verses had been lost, and they have never been recovered.

50) John Burton's book, 'The Collection of the Quran, states, concerning the Muslim claim that the Quran is perfect... *'The Muslim accounts of the history of the Quran texts are a mass of confusion, contradiction and inconsistencies.'*

51) One interesting way that some of the original verses of the Quran were lost is that a follower of Muhammad named Abdollah Sarh would make suggestions to Muhammad about rephrasing, adding to, or subtracting from the Suras. Muhammad often did as Sarh suggested.

Ali Dashti explains what happened... *'Abdollah renounced Islam on the ground that the revelations, if from God, could not be changed at the prompting of a scribe such as he. After his apostasy he went to Mecca and joined the Qorayshites.'*

It is no wonder that when Muhammad conquered Mecca one of the first people he killed was Abdollah, for he knew too much and opened his mouth too often.

52) Not only have parts of the Quran been lost, but entire verses and chapters have been added to it. For example, Ubai had several Suras in his manuscript of the Quran which Uthman omitted from his standardised text.

Thus were Quarans in circulation before Uthman's text which had additional revelations from Muhammad that Uthman did not find or approve of, and thus he failed to place them in his text.

53) There *never* was a single 'manuscript' of the Quran.

54) When Muhammad died there existed no singular codex of the sacred text - writes Caesar Farah in his book on Islam.

ISLAM

55) Older copies of the Quran differed much with Caliph Uthman's later copy, he ordered the older ones to be destroyed. Some had many more Suras than the others.

56) Some of the older materials have survived and have been recovered by such scholars as Arthur Jeffrey. Western scholars have shown beyond all reasonable doubt that Uthman's text did not contain all of the Quran. Neither was what it did contain correct in all its wording.

57) As to the Muslim claim that the Quran cannot be translated, it is amazing to us that the English Muslim Mohammed Pickthal could state, *'The Koran cannot be translated'* (p vii) in the very introduction to his translation.

58) The claim that the Quran cannot be translated is clearly refuted by the existence of many such translations.

59) The Quran was written by a man, Muhammad, fact.

60) **Since the Quran claims to be free from all error as proof of its inspiration in (Sura 85v21-22), the presence of just one error in the Quran is enough to cast serious doubt on that claim.**

61) Muhammad came 600 years *after* The Lord Jesus Christ. The Quran thus comes *after* the completion of the NT.

62) The Quran itself claims that it is a continuation of the Bible and it will not contradict it (Sura 2v136).

What this means in logic is that whenever the Bible and the Quran have a conflict or contradiction, the Quran is to give way, *not* the Bible. This is particularly true when the text of the Quran contradicts the text of the Bible. The Muslim position is that the 'same' God (Allah) revealed the Bible and the Quran. Thus the Quran will *never* contradict the Bible, otherwise Allah would be contradicting himself. It is obvious that if Allah contradicted himself, he is not perfect. And if he is not perfect, then he cannot be God.

63) If the Quran does not correspond to the text and teachings of the Bible, then the Quran contradicts the Bible. If it contradicts the Bible, then the Quran must yield. *Why?*

Since the Bible was *before* the Quran and the Quran itself appeals to the Bible for verification, then whenever there is conflict between the two, the newer and the lesser (the Quran) must give way to the older and greater (THE BIBLE).

64) The Quran contradicts the Bible in that it denies that Jesus was crucified.

65) If the Muslim rejects the Bible, he must also reject the Quran because it appeals to the Bible. On the other hand, if he accepts the Bible, he still must reject the Quran because it contradicts the Bible. Either way, the Quran loses. The Bible wins.

Errors in the Quran

How many days of creation?

When you add up all the days mentioned in Sura 41v9+10+12 the Quran says that it took God eight days to create the world (4 days + 2 days + 2 days = 8 days).

But according to the Bible it only took God 6 days.

Thus the Quran begins its contradiction of the Bible.

Also, in Sura 7v51 and 10v3 the Quran agrees with the Biblical account of only 6 days.

If 6 days is wrong, then the Quran in Suras 7 and 10 are wrong. If 8 days is wrong, then the Quran in Sura 41 is wrong. *This is a mistake!*

Noah, the Flood, and His Sons

According to the Bible, all 3 of Noah's sons went onto the Ark with him and were saved from the flood. (Gen 7v1+7+13)

Yet, the Quran in Sura 11v32-48 says that one of the sons refused to go into the ark and was drowned in the flood. Sura 11v44 also claims that the ark came to rest on top of Mount Judi while the Bible says Mount Ararat.

These contradictions cannot be clearer.

Mistakes about Abraham

The Quran makes many errors concerning Abraham...

The Quran says that Abraham's father's name was Azar, but the Bible says his name was Terah (Sura 6v74 / Gen 11v26)

He did not live and worship in the valley of Mecca (Sura 14v37) but in Hebron according to the Bible (Gen 13v18)

It was Isaac he went to sacrifice according to the Bible *not* Ismael which the Quran states. (Sura 37v100-112 / Gen 22)

Abraham had 8 sons *not* 2 as the Quran says.

He had 3 wives and *not* 2 as the Quran says.

He did not build the Kabah, even the Quran says so in Sura 2v125-127.

He was not thrown into a fire by Nimrod as the Quran claims in Suras 21v68-69 and 9v69 - This last error is serious because Nimrod lived many centuries before Abraham. How then did Nimrod manage to throw Abraham into the fire when Nimrod had been dead for centuries?

Mistakes about Joseph

The Quran makes the mistake of saying that the man who bought Joseph, Jacob's son, was named Aziz (Sura 12v21ff) when his name was really Potiphar (Gen 37v36)

Note other mistakes of names...

Instead of Goliath the Quran says Jalut

Instead of Saul the Quran says Talut

Instead of Enoch the Quran says Idris

Instead of Ezekiel the Quran says Dhu'l-Khifl

Instead of John the Baptist the Quran says Yahya

ISLAM

Instead of Jonah the Quran says Yunus etc.

Mistakes about Moses

It was not Pharoah's wife who adopted Moses as the Quran claims in Sura 28v8-9. It was actually Pharaoh's daughter (Exo 2v5)

Noah's flood did not take place in Moses' day (Sura 7v136 cf. 7v59)

The Quran says that Haman lived in Egypt during the time of Moses and worked for Pharoah building the tower of Babel (Suras 27v4-6, 28v38, 29v39, 40v23+24+36+37). But Haman actually lived in Persia and was in the service of King Ahasuerus. See the book of Esther for details.

Crucifixion was not used in the time of Pharoah although the Quran says so in Sura 7v124

Mistakes about Mary

Her father's name was not Imran (Sura 66v12)

She did not give birth to Jesus under a palm tree but in a stable - Sura 19v22 / Luke 2v1-20

Muhammad clearly made up fraudulent speeches and miracles for her (Sura 19v23-26)

Zacharias could not speak the entire time until his son was born, not just 3 days as the Quran claims. (Sura 19v10 / Luke 1v20)

The Quran's Self-Contradictions...

The Quran contradicts itself in many ways. Since the Quran claims in Sura 39v23+28 to be free from all contradictions, just one contradiction is sufficient to show that it is not God's word.

The Quran differs on whether a day is a 100 years or 50,000 years in God's sight (Sura 32v5, 70v4)

At first Muhammad told his followers to face Jerusalem in prayer. Then he told them since God was everywhere they could face any way they wanted. Then he changed his mind yet again and directed them to pray toward Mecca. (Sura 2v115, 2v144)

Who was the first to believe? Abraham or Moses (Sura 6v14 or 7v143?) you can't have two firsts!

Questions to ask a Muslim

1) How can I as a sinner get right with God?

2) What is love?

3) How did Muhammad show God's love to the people?

4) What message does the Muslim bring to today's people?

5) When you die where will you go?

6) What is your FINAL AUTHORITY?

7) What happened to Jesus Christ?

8) How can I get saved?

9) What am I saved from?

10) How do I know the Muslim faith is the right one?

11) What is your main aim in life?

12) What has Allah ever done for me?

13) What is Allah's message to mankind?

14) Where is Muhammad right now, and how do you know?

Islam a Religion of Peace?

The Koran's 164 Jihad Verses		
Chapter	Verse	Running Count
002	178-179, 190-191, 193-194, 216-218, 244	10
003	121-126, 140-143, 146, 152-158, 165-167, 169, 172-173, 195	35
004	071-072, 074-077, 084, 089-091, 094-095, 100-104, 144	53
005	033, 035, 082	56
008	001, 005, 007, 009-010, 012, 015-017, 039-048, 057-060, 065-075	90
009	005, 012-014, 016, 019-020, 024-026, 029, 036, 038-039, 041, 044, 052, 073, 081, 083, 086, 088, 092, 111, 120, 122-123	117
016	110	118
022	039, 058, 078	121
024	053, 055	123
025	052	124
029	006, 069	126
033	015, 018, 020, 023, 025-027, 050	134
042	039	135
047	004, 020, 035	138
048	015-024	148
049	015	149
059	002, 005-008, 014	155
060	009	156
061	004, 011, 013	159
063	004	160
064	014	161
066	009	162
073	020	163
076	008	164

Extra verses from the Hadiths...

Hadith Bukhari (1:35) - "The person who participates in (Holy Battles) in Allah's cause and nothing compels him do so except belief in Allah and His Apostle, will be recompensed by Allah either with a reward, or booty (if he survives) or will be admitted to Paradise (if he is killed)."

Hadith Bukhari (8:387) - Allah's Apostle said, "I have been ordered to fight the people till they say: 'None has the right to be worshipped but Allah'. And if they say so, pray like our prayers, face our Qibla and slaughter as we slaughter, then their blood and property will be sacred to us and we will not interfere with them except legally."

Hadith Bukhari (11:626) - [Muhammad said:] "I decided to order a man to lead the prayer and then take a flame to burn all those, who had not left their houses for the prayer, burning them alive inside their homes."

Hadith Bukhari (52:73) - "Allah's Apostle said, 'Know that Paradise is under the shades of swords'."
Hadith Bukhari (52:177) - Allah's Apostle said, "The Hour will not be established until you fight with the Jews, and the stone behind which a Jew will be hiding will say. "O Muslim! There is a Jew hiding behind me, so kill him."
Hadith Bukhari (52:256) - The Prophet... was asked whether it was permissible to attack the pagan warriors at night with the probability of exposing their women and children to danger. The Prophet replied, "They (i.e. women and children) are from them (i.e. pagans)." [In this command, Muhammad establishes that it is permissible to kill non-combatants in the process of killing a perceived enemy. This provides justification for the many Islamic terror bombings.
Hadith Muslim (1:30) - "The Messenger of Allah said: I have been commanded to fight against people so long as they do not declare that there is no god but Allah."
Hadith Muslim (1:33) - the Messenger of Allah said: I have been commanded to fight against people till they testify that there is no god but Allah, that Muhammad is the messenger of Allah.
Hadith Muslim (1:149) - "Abu Dharr reported: I said: Messenger of Allah, which of the deeds is the best? He (the Holy Prophet) replied: Belief in Allah and Jihad in His cause..."
Hadith Muslim (19:4294) - "When the Messenger of Allah (may peace be upon him) appointed anyone as leader of an army or detachment he would especially exhort him... He would say: Fight in the name of Allah and in the way of Allah. Fight against those who dis-

believe in Allah. Make a holy war... When you meet your enemies who are polytheists, invite them to three courses of action. If they respond to any one of these, you also accept it and withhold yourself from doing them any harm. Invite them to (accept) Islam; if they respond to you, accept it from them and desist from fighting against them... If they refuse to accept Islam, demand from them the Jizya. If they agree to pay, accept it from them and hold off your hands. If they refuse to pay the tax, seek Allah's help and fight them."
Hadith Tabari (7:97)* - The morning after the murder of Ashraf, the Prophet declared, "Kill any Jew who falls under your power."
Hadith Tabari (9:69)* - QUOTING MUHAMMAD: "Killing Unbelievers is a small matter to us".
Hadith Tabari (17:187)* - "'By God, our religion (din) from which we have departed is better and more correct than that which these people follow. Their religion does not stop them from shedding blood, terrifying the roads, and seizing properties.' And they returned to their former religion." The words of a group of Christians who had converted to Islam, but realized their error after being shocked by the violence and looting committed in the name of Allah. The price of their decision to return to a religion of peace was that the men were beheaded and the woman and children enslaved by the caliph Ali.

The difference between The Lord Jesus Christ & Muhammad

Death	Jesus died and rose from the dead.	Muhammad died and stayed dead.
Fighting	Jesus never fought.	Muhammad fought many times.
Hearing from God	When Jesus heard from God, he went to the desert to be tempted and began his ministry with boldness. (Mark 1v14+15).	When Muhammad heard from God (supposedly through an angel), he cowered, was uncertain, and wanted to commit suicide. (Quran 74:1-5)
Identity	Jesus claimed to be God (John 8v24, 8v58) as well as a man. Jesus claimed to be the way, the truth, and the life. (John14v6).	Muhammad claimed to be a man.
Instructions Received	From God the Father (John 5v19)	Allegedly from an angel.
Killing	Jesus never killed anyone.	Muhammad killed many.
Life	Jesus had the power to take life but never did. He restored it.	Muhammad had the power to take it, but he never restored it.
	No one ever died in Jesus' presence.	Many people died in Muhammad's presence--he killed them.
Marriage	Jesus never married.	Muhammad had over 20 wives and even married a nine-year-old girl.
Ministry	Jesus received his calling from God directly. (Matt 3v17). Jesus received his commission in the daylight.	Muhammad allegedly received it from an angel (Gabriel). Muhammad received his words in the darkness of a cave.
Ministry Length	Jesus taught for 3½ years.	Muhammad taught for more than 20 years.
Miracles	Jesus performed many miracles including healing people, calming a storm with a command, and raising people from the dead.	Muhammad's only alleged miracle was the Quran.
Prophecy	Jesus fulfilled biblical prophecy about being the Messiah.	Muhammad did not fulfil any biblical prophecy except the ones about false teachers (Matt 24v24).
Sacrifice	Jesus voluntarily laid his life down for others.	Muhammad saved his own life many times and had others killed.
Sin	Jesus never sinned. (1 Pet 2v22)	Muhammad was a sinner. (Quran 40:55; 48:1-2)
Slaves	Jesus owned no slaves.	Muhammad owned slaves.
Virgin Birth	Jesus was virgin born.	Muhammad was not virgin born.
Voice of God	Jesus received and heard the direct voice of God. (Mark 1v10+11)	Muhammad did not receive or hear the direct voice of God. It was an angel instead.
Women	Jesus spoke well of women.	Muhammad said women were ½ as smart as men (Hadith 3:826; 2:541), that the majority in hell will be women (Hadith 1:28,301; 2:161; 7:124), and that women could be mortgaged.

NOTES

CULTS AND FALSE RELIGIONS

Roman Catholicism - Revelation chapter 17 'The Great Whore' is Rome! (Read it). Note v5 **And upon her forehead was a name written, MYSTERY, BABYLON THE GREAT, THE MOTHER OF HARLOTS AND ABOMINATIONS OF THE EARTH.** The 'Babylon' of chapter 17 is the same as that of chapter 18 (v2 cf. 18v3, v5 cf. 18v2, v6 cf. 18v24). It is a specific 'city' (v18), not a nation. It is a city with a religious aspect (here) and a political/economic aspect (chapter 18), so it is a 'church-state'. The 'city' is undoubtedly Rome (v9), since no other city (including Jerusalem) can fit the description of verse 6 and Rev 18v24. Jesus Christ may have been crucified at Jerusalem (Rev 11v8), but no Jew beat Him, nailed Him to the cross, or shoved a spear in His side; it was Rome that was responsible for that (John 19). Rome killed the Apostle James (Acts 12v2) and the Apostle Paul (2 Tim 1v6+17, 4v6), and Rome was responsible for exiling the apostle John (Rev 1v9). *If you want to see the full extent to which Rome fulfils these murders etc. read 'Foxe's Book of Martyrs', Ruckman's two volumes on 'The History of the New Testament Church', 'The Secret History of the Jesuits' by Edmond Paris, 'Hitler's Pope – The Secret History of Pius XII' by John Cornwell, 'The Vatican's Holocaust' by Avro Manhatten and 'Smokescreens' by Jack Chick.*

Although the colours of *the woman* (purple and scarlet) match pagan Rome (See Mark 15v17+20, John 19v2+5, Mat 27v28), she cannot be merely a reference to that, because the symbol of imperial Rome was an eagle. This woman's symbol is a golden cup. The Roman Catholic Church is more than just a church; it is its own political state (v 18). It has its own bank and its own army. It has diplomatic relations with the governments of other nations. It signs treaties with the heads of other States (e.g. Hitler and Mussolini during WWII). Not only is this Church-State filthy (Rev 18v2), drunken (Rev 18v3), pagan (Rev 18v4 cf. 2v20-22), proud (Rev 18v7), popular (Rev 18v9 – it boasts of nearly one billion members), mighty (Rev 18v10); it is also commercial (Rev 18v11) and rich (Rev 17v4, 18v12). Roman Catholicism is a dirty, godless, depraved, false counterfeit of Biblical Christianity. It is damned (Rev 18v5) and absolutely doomed by God (Rev 18v21). It is destined to burn (Rev 17v16, 18v8+9) and keep on burning after it is destroyed here on earth (Rev 19v3) just like Sodom and Gomorrah (2 Pet 2v6, Jude 7). The response of Heaven to this is 'AMEN' and 'HALLELUJAH' (Rev 19v1-4). If you are a Roman Catholic get out while you can. If you know of others in this false religion, do all you can to get them out. Roman Catholicism is **not** Christian; it will lead you to an eternity in the Lake of Fire.

The ERRORS of Roman Catholicism

The Catholic Church, from its first private interpretations (2 Peter 1v20) by Augustine, Cyprian and Iranaeus, to those of the Council of Trent (A.D. 1546), has been consistent in one thing... wresting and perverting the word of God (2 Peter 3v16, 2 Cor 2v17, 2 Cor 4v2, Jer 23v36) in an effort to force it to approve of her own heresies and traditions. Catholics are taught that anything written or preached contrary to the teachings and traditions of the Vatican State is a lie, even if Paul, Jesus or Moses said it.

Peter was *not* the first Pope as the Roman Catholics teach – Mat 16v17+18 – This passage is given before the resurrection, by a Jew, to a Jewish audience, as the minister of circumcision (Rom 15v8).

So straight away the Roman Catholics (RC's from now on) have overlooked the epistles written to the church by the Apostle to the Gentiles, who preached in Rome i.e. Paul. Instead of starting with Ephesians, Colossians and Timothy, the RC's begin in a pre-crucifixion passage addressed to Jews. Like we have said so often, **nearly all heresies come from the books of the Bible that are directed at the Jew** e.g. Matthew, Hebrews, James and Acts (which is a book *in transit* i.e. *moving from* the Nation of Israel to individual believers; *from* the Law to grace; *from* Jews to Gentiles; *from* the apostle to the circumcision - Peter, to the apostle to the Gentiles - Paul; *from* the old covenant to the new covenant etc. – so why is it that Pentecostal and CharisMANIAC Christians, claim Scriptures for themselves that are *directed* at the Jew e.g. the **sign-gifts are for the Jews**...tongues, healings, Sabbath keeping etc. – read and re-read 1 Cor 14v22 and 1 Cor 1v22. To understand the Scriptures correctly we need to be able to *rightly divide* them – 2 Tim 2v15, and you must compare Scripture with Scripture to get the meaning and context – 1 Cor 2v13. Scripture is not to be interpreted *privately* - 2 Pet 1v20, and notice who said that, Peter. Notice who does interpret the Scriptures in their own private way, Rome. And the RC's say that Peter was the first Pope. What do the Scriptures tell us about Peter? (Rom 4v3, Gal 4v30)

Read **Mat 8v14** - His what? I thought RC's said Pope's can't marry. The Scriptures teach that Peter was married. See also **Mark 1v29-31. Mat 16v23** - What about that, Peter the first Pope being called Satan by the Lord Himself. See also the *first pope* swearing in **Mat 26v74. Acts 10v25+26** – how about these verses for a contrast between Peter and the pope. So far, we have the *first* pope who is a **married, cursing, mistaken, satanic believer, who would not let men bow down to him!** Not very good qualifications for a pope are they. By the way, **Peter *never* went to Rome according to the Scriptures**.

Also, when Peter wrote to Christians and defined the Rock (**Mat 16v17+18**), he said that the Rock was Christ and not himself. **1 Peter 2v4-9.** Christ is the Rock – **1 Cor 10v4, Rom 9v33** (The rock of the RC is not the Rock of the Bible – **Deut 32v31**) – In the Scriptures, Peter is a 'stone' not a rock – **John 1v42.** The Lord Jesus Christ will build His church *not* Peter... **Mat 16v18 Eph 1v22+23, Col 1v24**. The Church is His Church, it is His Body, He builds it, it is certainly not the Roman Catholic satanic *counterfeit* church.

What does Rome say about Peter (the so-called *first* Pope) and the 'church?'... (Taken from the Canons and Dogmatic Decrees of The council of Trent) – *'I acknowledge the holy, Catholic, and Apostolic Roman Church as the mother and teacher of all churches; and I promise and swear true obedience to the Roman Pontiff, the vicar of Christ and successor of Blessed Peter, Prince* ('Prince' Scripture back up?) *of the Apostles' 'The Roman Pontiff is the true Vicar of Christ, and the head of the whole Church, and the Father and teacher of all Christians'. 'The Roman Pontiff, speaks ex-cathedra* (ex-cathedra means, with the full authority of office especially that of the Pope, implying infallibility as defined in Roman Catholic doctrine). Origin - Latin, 'from the (teacher's chair') *are irreformable of themselves...!'* Where Jesus is the Christian's invisible Head, no longer in the flesh, the Pope claims to be the Christian's head, still in the flesh. Without a doubt, RC's don't follow Scripture in context (if at all at times), they have their own *private* interpretations, and we know what Scripture says about that – **2 Pet 1v20 + 2 Pet 3v16** - *To think that the 'pope' penned both of those Scriptures, how about that!*

The Bible – with *no* interpretation	Rome – with her *own* interpretation
Peter is a Jew who confesses Christ and is promised keys to a 'kingdom.' Paul is the God-called and God-commissioned Apostle to the Gentiles, to whom alone was revealed the mystery of the church in this age and who straightened Peter out on his false doctrine in Galatians 2. **The 'church'** – is Christ's church and is a living body into which a man has to be born again by the baptism of the Holy Spirit (1 Cor 12v13). **The Rock** – is Jesus Christ (see Scriptures above) **The Bible** – Nine-tenths of the NT is written in Asia Minor not Rome; and Paul never mentions Peter *directly* or *indirectly* when writing to the Roman church.	**Peter** is a Catholic who is promised the keys to Heaven. Peter is the 'Prince' of Apostles and therefore, infallible in matters of Church doctrine for the Roman Catholic. **The 'Church'** - is the Roman See (*See - The place in which a cathedral church stands, identified as the seat of authority of a bishop or archbishop*) at the Vatican – the head of all Catholics who are baptized by water into the Universal Roman Church. The RC can lose his salvation at any time, therefore he must continue to *work* for it. **The 'Rock'** – is Peter the first Pope. **The Bible** – They add, subtract, change and distort the Scriptures to suit themselves. RC tradition is put on a par with the Scriptures and oftentimes overrules the Scriptures.

The RC's ERRONEOUS interpretation of Matthew 16v19

The Kingdom of Heaven in Scripture is always Jewish (*never* Roman), always Davidic (*never* Popish), always in a mystery form until the Second Advent (*never* in a visible, political form), always is earthly and literal (*never* spiritual or heavenly).

Peter OR Paul?

Peter had no authority whatsoever over Paul anywhere in the NT at any time, and Paul was the Apostle to the Romans (Rom 15).

The ERRORS of Roman Catholicism
(RCC = Roman Catholic Church)

What is the Mass?

RCC – The Mass is the unbloody sacrifice of the body and blood of Christ.

Is the Mass the same sacrifice as that of the Cross?

RCC – The Mass is the same sacrifice as that of the Cross.
This is anti-Scriptural - **Heb 7v27, Heb 9v11-15+26+28, Heb 10v10-12+14+18, 1 Pet 1v18+19**
The Scriptures are perfectly clear that the Lord Jesus Christ was offered *once*, it was a perfect sacrifice and shall never be repeated. The Mass is not only a *mess*, it is Satanic ritual.

What is Baptism in water?

RCC – Baptism is a Sacrament which cleanses us from original sin, makes us Christians, children of God, and heirs of Heaven!

This is anti-Scriptural.

The thief on the cross knew nothing about baptism, yet the Lord took him to paradise...*without* baptism. We are *only* saved by the Blood of the Lord Jesus Christ – Eph 2v13 **But now in Christ Jesus ye who sometimes were far off are made nigh by the blood of Christ**. Read these verses... Heb 9v22, 1 John 1v7, Eph 1v7, Col 1v14, Heb 10v10-19, Rom 5v9, Heb 13v12, Rev 1v5, Eph 2v13, 1 Pet 3v21, Eph 2v8+9 etc. *Water* has *nothing* to do with your salvation.

Idolatry

Exod 20v4 - The RCC fills its churches and homes with images and idols – this is against the clear teaching of Scripture. 1 Sam 15v23, Acts 17v16, 1 Cor 10v14, 1 Cor 6v9, 1 Cor 10v7, Rev 21v8, Rev 22v15, Lev 19v4, Lev 26v1, 1 Kings 21v26, 2 Kings 17v12.

Prayers to Mary and the Saints

RCC – The saints will help us because both they and we are members of the same Church, and they love us as their brethren. This is anti-Scriptural - 1 Tim 2v5. It is only the Lord Jesus Christ who is the Mediator. Mary and the saints are not everywhere like God is, like Jesus Christ is, and like the Holy Spirit is, so how can they hear all the people's prayers from around the world? It's not about church tradition, that counts for nothing, it's what the Scriptures say that matters. (Rom 4v3, Gal 4v30) Dump all this false teaching and **believe what the Bible says**. Read **Mat 12v46-50** - Jesus never called Mary His mother. He called her woman - John 19v26.

What does Justification mean and when are you Justified?

Justification means - absolution (*formal release from guilt, obligation, or punishment; declaration of forgiveness of sins*), remission of sin and absolution from guilt and punishment; or an act of free grace by which God pardons the sinner and accepts him as righteous, on account of the atonement of Christ; to pardon and clear from guilt; to absolve or acquit from guilt and merited punishment, and to accept as righteous on account of the merits of the Saviour, or by the application of Christ's atonement to the offender.

So when are you Justified?

Acts 13v39, Rom 3v28, Rom 5v1+9, Gal 2v16, Gal 3v11+24, Gal 5v4, Titus 3v7, Rom 4v25.

We are justified by faith, by the Blood of Jesus Christ and by His resurrection. The moment you trust Christ for your sins forgiven you receive imputed righteousness and justification; it all happens at the new birth. *Works* has nothing to do with your justification in this dispensation, absolutely nothing.

The RCC claims she *never* changes

The following list of events *proves* the opposite, and shows also its degradation (Degrade - cause to suffer a severe loss of dignity or respect; demean; lower the character or quality of; reduce to a lower rank, especially as a punishment; cause to break down or deteriorate).

Prayers for the dead instituted – AD 330

Making the sign of the cross – AD 330

The worship of Mary, and the use of the words 'Mother of God' – AD 431

Worship in the Latin language – AD 600

The Papacy is of pagan origin – The title of pope, or 'Universal Bishop', was first given to the Bishop of Rome by the wicked emperor Phocas in the year 610. This he did to spite Bishop Circiacus of

Constantinople, who had justly excommunicated him for having caused the assassination of his predecessor, Emperor Mauitius. Gregory the 1st, then Bishop of Rome, refused the title, but his successor Boniface III, first assumed the title of POPE – AD 610

Kissing the Pope's feet – AD 709 – It had been a pagan custom to kiss the feet of emperors. The word of God forbids such practices – Acts 10v25+26, Rev 22v9, Ps 2v12

Adoration of Mary and the Saints – AD 788

Adoration of the cross, images and relics – AD 788

Fasting, lent, advent and Fridays – AD 998

Fabrication of Holy Water – AD 1009

Marriage of Priests forbidden – AD 1079

Rosary beads invented – AD 1090

Sale of indulgences – AD 1190

Sacrifice of Mass – AD 1215

Transubstantiation of bread – AD 1215

Adoration of the wafer – AD 1220

Confession of sins to a priest – AD 1215

Purgatory proclaimed – AD 1438

Tradition held equal to Bible – AD 1545 (The Council of Trent, held in 1545. By tradition is meant *human* teachings. The Pharisees believed the same way, and Jesus bitterly condemned them, for by *human* tradition, they annulled the commandments of God – Mark 7v7-13, Col 2v8 etc.)

Apocryphal books *added* to the Bible – AD 1546

Immaculate Conception of Mary – AD 1845

Infallibility of the Pope – AD 1870

It amazes me how normal, average, *intellectual* individuals, can fall for and believe such man-made drivel...*kissing the Pope's feet indeed!*

Christianity and Roman Catholicism are different

The two 'basic' differences between a **Bible Believing Christian** and a Roman Catholic is on the question of authority...M**at 21v23+24+27** etc. Bible Believers accept the 66 books of the Bible as their final authority on all matters of faith and practice. The Church of Rome also accepts the Bible as God's revelation **but** accepts it as only **part** of God's 'word' i.e. they believe the Bible **plus** the Apocryphal books, **plus** tradition, **plus** decisions of church councils, **plus** the decrees of the Pope when he speaks ex-cathedra (i.e. from his throne as the 'head of the church'). As a result of this, the majority of **Roman Catholic doctrine is nowhere to be found in the Scriptures**, but are *additions* made centuries later by accepting traditions, actions of church councils, and the 'infallible' edicts (an official order or proclamation) and decisions of a *mortal* pope. When the Church declares a new dogma (a principle or set of principles laid down by an authority as incontrovertible) by official action or papal-bull (papal edict), every Catholic is commanded to believe it and accept it without question, upon pain of discipline. The Roman Catholic Church also claims *it alone* is the true church with the pope as its head. This church also speaks with infallibility through councils and the pope. **This church is entered into by sprinkling water on a person in baptism**. There is no salvation possible outside the Church of Rome – only Roman Catholics can be saved. The Church of Rome is an *organisation* rather than an *organism*. Christians believe that the true church is an organism, a body of living members of which **the Lord Jesus Christ is the Head**. The members consist of people from all walks of life who by personal faith in Jesus Christ, have been born again and thus baptised into the Body of Christ by the Spirit of God. (1 Cor 12v13, Col 1v18+24). It is interesting to note that Cardinal Newman (one of the most respected authorities in the Roman Church), says on page 359 of his book 'The Development of the Christian Religion'... "Temples, incense, candles, votive offerings, holy water, holidays, and seasons of devotions, processions, blessing of fields, sacerdotal vestments, priests, monks and nuns, images etc. *are all of pagan origin!*" How about that!

Reasons why I am not a Roman Catholic

- The Papacy is a HOAX – Peter never claimed to be pope'. He was *never* in Rome - Mat 23v9

- Maryolatry is a HOAX – Acts 4v12

- Purgatory is a HOAX – it is a money-making 'racket' - 1 John 1v7

- The Mass is a HOAX – the 'wafer-god' is a blasphemous fraud – Heb 10v12

- The Rosary is a HOAX – Mat 7v6

- The Confessional is a HOAX – It is unchristian, indecent and immoral! – 1 Tim 2v5

- Miraculous 'medals' are a HOAX including images, crucifixes, bleeding hearts, holy water and other heathen inventions. - Exod 20v4

- Forbidding to eat meat or forbidding the marriage of priests is a HOAX – 1 Tim 4v1-3

Why water baptism *cannot* save you

Water baptism is *never* connected with redemption – (Col 1v14); it cannot affect a dead spirit (Eph 2v5); it is never connected with justification (Rom 5v9); it is never connected with adoption (Rom 8v15). Water-baptism is administrated by a sinner, while saving-baptism is done without hands by God (Col 2v11+12, 1 Cor 12v13, Gal 3v27)

Why water baptism is not part of your salvation

You are not a Jew of the dispersion (Acts 2v38+39)

You are not under the ministry of John the Baptist (Acts 13v24)

No one baptises anyone in water till *after* that person is saved (Acts 10v47, Acts 8v36-38)

CULTS AND FALSE RELIGIONS

Paul never mentions water within fifty verses of 'baptism' in any passage in the Pauline epistles

Water baptism occurs nowhere in any passage that deals with the New Birth (John 3v1-16)

Now you either believe **THE BOOK** that **GOD** has written, or you believe a lie that some man has made up.

Christians cannot pray to Mary

The Roman Catholic Church worships and prays to Mary the mother of Jesus more than it does to either God or Christ. Since God chose Mary to be the mother of our Lord, we cannot but esteem her highly, honouring her as a pattern for all motherhood, but, Jesus said in Mat 4v10 '**…Thou shalt worship the Lord thy God, and him only shalt thou serve.**' Therefore the worship of Mary is wrong and anti-Scriptural.

- Nowhere in the Bible is there recorded *any* worship of Mary.

- The wise men worshipped the Babe; they did not worship Mary – Mat 2v11

- In referring to Jesus and Mary together, the Bible *always* puts Jesus first – Mat 2v11+13+14+20+21

- Mary herself confessed that she was a sinner, for she *needed* a Saviour – Luke 1v46+47

- Mary cannot save anyone – Acts 4v12, Heb 7v25 etc.

- Mary is not the 'Mother of God' but the mother of *the man* Jesus Christ – Luke 1v43

- Mary is not a mediator – 1 Tim 2v5

The ERRORS of Roman Catholicism

By the way since the number 13 is associated with rebellion it is very interesting to read in Rev 17v5 regarding the Roman Catholic Church the words **And upon her forehead was a name written, MYSTERY, BABYLON THE GREAT, THE MOTHER OF HARLOTS AND ABOMINATIONS OF THE EARTH.** (How many words in capitals? *Thirteen!*)

Another *private interpretation* of the Roman Catholic Church is what they say regarding the priest being able to 'forgive' sins…when he **certainly cannot**. Let's look at a few Scriptures regarding this erroneous doctrine of a priest *forgiving sins* when only God can - **Heb 9v22, Heb 10v10-12+18, Acts 13v38+39, Mat 26v28, Rom 3v24+25.** So by reading these Scriptures we conclude that 'remission' is by shed blood. Priests have never been able to remit anyone's sins. Remission or forgiveness of sins lies in the atonement of Jesus Christ (Heb 10v1-12 – it is never to be 'repeated') God forgave all through the Old Testament (Exod 34v7) but could not clear the guilty until Mat 26v28 (Heb 10v4). Therefore **no Roman Catholic priest can forgive your sins** and he certainly is *not* a mediator between God and man – 1 Tim 2v5. Anyway, all Christians *are* priests – **Heb 3v1, 13v15, 1 Pet 2v1-5** – Since there is not one verse in the Bible indicating that there is any priesthood in the New Testament, except a priesthood of born-again believers (1 Pet 2) – therefore the entire system of two million priests in the Roman Catholic church is utterly non-Biblical, non-Christian, and non-New Testament. There are no priests ordained in the NT – married 'bishops and elders' *(did you get that,* *'married'*) are 'ordained' but there is no 'ordination', spiritual or ceremonial, for a 'priest' **(Titus 1, Acts 14, 1 Pet 5, 1 Tim 3).**

You would be better off visiting the gym than visiting a Roman Catholic priest; it would be more profitable. No more can a Roman Catholic priest forgive your sins than a Pentecostal can 'Rightly Divide the word of truth'. Luke 24v45 **Then opened he their understanding, that they might understand the scriptures,**

The Lord Jesus Christ and the Pope Contrasted

Christ wore a crown of thorns	The Pope wears a crown of jewels
Christ carried on His shoulders the Cross	The Pope is carried on the shoulders of his servants in splendour
Christ declared the laws of His kingdom and urged His followers to do the same	The Pope tramples them under-foot and substitutes his own in their stead
Christ sent the Holy Spirit to be His Vicar on earth	The Pope claims to be the Vicar of Christ on earth
Christ is the Head of the Church	The Pope claims to be the Head of the Church
Christ taught that sin should be confessed to God	The Pope teaches that sin should be confessed to the priests
Christ taught that He alone is the Saviour	The Pope teaches that the Church is the Saviour
Christ taught that there was but one Mediator between God and man. (1 Tim 2v5)	The Pope teaches that there are many mediators between God and man.
Christ taught that salvation was by grace	The Pope teaches that salvation is by works
Christ claimed infallibility for Himself and the Word of God alone	The Pope claims infallibility for himself in matters of faith and morals
Christ had no place to lay His head	The Pope lives in a magnificent palace surrounded by wealth
Christ gave his Gospel free to all	The Pope sells his masses and other favours
Christ said: "Call no man your father upon the earth: for one is your Father, which is in heaven" (Matt 23v9)	The Pope commands all to call him 'Holy Father', and his priests feel insulted if persons do not address them as 'Father'
Christ was poor and lowly	The Pope's wealth is immense
Christ washed His disciples' feet, thus manifesting a spirit of humility worthy of emulation by His followers	The Pope presents his foot to be kissed and requires genuflections and kneeling from those who have audiences with him
Christ taught His followers to pray to God through Him	The Pope teaches his followers to pray to the Virgin Mary

The Hypocrisy of the Seventh Day Adventists (SDA)

In Exodus 20, God gave the 10 Commandments *to the Jews* (not the church). The Law clearly described what punishment to give each sin. The Law required not only the punishment of an eye for an eye but also a 'life for a life'. The death penalty was also imposed for many other infractions (a violation or infringement of a law) under the Law. One could be stoned to death under the Law for the following...

Gathering sticks on the Sabbath – Num 15v32-36

Blasphemy – Lev 24v11-14

Serving other gods – Deut 13v6-10

Being a disobedient, unrepentant child – Deut 21v18-21

When was the last time you heard a SDA cult member carry out the penalty for the above sins? (Yet they say we should *keep* the Law today, especially the Sabbath). You can imagine the sharp decline in the *average life expectancy* in England and around the world, if God imposed the same penalties for the same infractions on everyone today. The Lord Jesus Christ put an end to many of the punishments required under the Law. He clearly restates God's position in the following texts... **Mat 5v38+39, Rom 10v4, Rom 7v4, Gal 5v4, Gal 2v16, Gal 3v11, John 1v17**.

The biggest difference between the Seventh Day Adventists (SDA) and a Bible Believing Christian (BBC), is that a BBC can *rightly* divide the word of Truth and a SDA can't (2 Tim 2v15). *What do I mean?*

There is a difference between Israel and the Church. The Church has certainly not 'replaced' Israel – that is a heresy. (Rom 9 and 11) God has laid aside Israel and will pick them up again during 'Jacob's' Trouble aka The Tribulation. There is a difference between the Great White Throne Judgement and the Judgment Seat of Christ. There is a difference between the Kingdom of God and the Kingdom of Heaven. They are *not* the same. There are *at least* seven dispensations and at least four Gospels taught in the Scriptures. The word 'saved' itself, has at least five different meanings – saved *from what to what*. Noah was saved a different way to you and I. How was Peter saved seeing Christ hadn't died yet? He didn't even understand the full reason why Christ came. A SDA will divide the law up, but *can't divide the dispensations*. All of the Scriptures are written *for us* but not all of them are written *to us*. The Sermon on the Mount is certainly *not doctrinally* written *to us!* My salvation is based on no works at all. If I don't forgive someone, it certainly does not mean that God does not forgive me in regard to salvation. The church requires no signs, Jews do. Their nation started with signs – Exod 4. Signs are to do with Israel not the church. 1 Cor 1v22. The SDA's will always mess up on doctrine e.g. the Sabbath etc. because they base their doctrines on books that are predominately *directed at the Jew*, including *transitional* books such as Acts or James. Matthew and Hebrews are also books you have to watch out for in regard to *whom* they are written/directed to *doctrinally*. The Sabbath has no hold whatsoever on, or over, a Christian in *this* dispensation – those who say it has cannot rightly divide the word of truth.

A few questions for a SDA

Were the 10 Commandments associated and attached to the old Covenant?

Has Israel a future (as a nation) in your eyes? Or has God replaced Israel with the church?

Can you lose your salvation?

Jesus said 'Keep my commandments' – but which ones?

Show me just one verse of Scripture in any of Paul's letters that states categorically that the church and the Christian are to obey and keep the Saturday Sabbath... just one?

Do you preach the Kingdom of Heaven today?

What is *your* Gospel i.e. what Gospel do you preach in regard to salvation?

Paul mentions the Sabbath in just **one** of all his books, and his books are the ones that the church today take their doctrine from... Col 2v16. The Sabbath is not for the Christian at all.

What the SDA does, is *wrongly divides* the word of God and takes *Jewish Scriptures* and tries to apply them to the church. It will never work. In the end you will do what Peter warned about in 2 Pet 3v16. This is what all cults do e.g. JW's, Mormons, Christadelphians etc.

The Sabbath has nothing to do with the Christian in today's dispensation. It is a **sign** for ISRAEL – 1 Cor 1v22, Exo 31v13-17. Now 'Mr SDA' if you want to keep it fine, but if you preach it as compulsory, you are in error. It doesn't really matter what day you keep as holy, as Paul stated in Colossians - Col 2v16. The Sabbath has nothing to do with sin or salvation for a BBC hence it has no hold on a BBC whatsoever. Nine out of the Ten Commandments were reaffirmed in the NT but have nothing to do with salvation. The law is our schoolmaster, but once saved, we are no longer bound by it... **Rom 10v4-6, Rom 7v4-6**. I don't have to eat, dress, wash, worship or keep the Sabbath like a Jew does – I am not under the law. If you don't get the Jew in his rightful position in Scripture, you will mess up on doctrine every time. That is why Pentecostals and Charismatics *think* they speak in *tongues* when *they don't!* **1 Cor 14v22** – tongues, like the keeping of the Sabbath are **signs** to the Jew. If salvation was by keeping the Sabbath, every time you worked on it, you would lose your salvation. According to a SDA... when are you **saved**? Water baptism, tongues and Sabbath keeping have nothing to do with salvation and eternal life in the Heavenly Jerusalem. The SDA is just another cult like the JW's, Morons etc.

The Sabbath – The Sabbath was created for the Jews (Exod 31v16+17, Ezek 20v12). The only time you find apostles going to worship on the Sabbath was when they entered synagogues (not churches) to preach to Jews (not Christians) – Mat 28v1, John 20v19, Acts 20v17, 1 Cor 16v2.

Mormons

The Book of Mormon	The Scriptures (KJV)
Salvation by grace and works – 2 Nephi 25v23	Salvation by grace alone – Eph 2v8+9
Jesus born at Jerusalem – Alma 7v10	Jesus born at Bethlehem – Matt 2v1
Three days of darkness at the Crucifixion – Helaman 14v27	Three hours of darkness at the Crucifixion – Luke 23v44
God has flesh and bones like a man – D&C 130v22	God is a Spirit – John 4v24
Believers were called 'Christians' before Christ (70BC) – Alma 46v15	First called Christians at Antioch – Acts 11v26
Mormonism teaches a 2nd chance after death – D&C 76v106-112 and v88-99	After death is judgment – Heb 9v27 Hell is everlasting – Rev 21v8, Matt 13v24-43

CULTS AND FALSE RELIGIONS

A few contradictions *in their own* Mormon literature...

Book of Mormon	Doctrines and Covenants (D&C) / Pearl of Great Price (PofGP)
One God – Alma 11v28+29+44, Nephi 31v21, Mormon 7v7, 3 Nephi 11v27, Mosiah 15v3-5	**Plural Gods** – D&C 121v32, 132v18-20+37
God is Unchangeable – Mormon 9v9+19, Moroni 8v12+18, 2 Nephi 27v23, Alma 31v17	**God has progressed** – D&C 132v18-20
God is a Spirit – Alma 34v36	**God has a body i.e. flesh** – D&C 130v22
God dwells in the heart – Alma 34v36	**God doesn't dwell in the heart** – D&C 130v3
Creation – One God – 2 Nephi 2v14, Jacob 4v9	**Creation – Plural gods** – PofGP Abraham 4-5
God cannot lie – Ether 3v12, 2 Nephi 9v34	**God commands lying** – PofGP Abraham 2v22-25
God's word is unchangeable – Alma 41v8	**God's word can change** – D&C 56v4-5
No pre-existence of Man – Jacob 4v9, Alma 18v28+34-36	**Man pre-existed** – D&C 93v23+29-33, PofGP Abraham 3v18+21-23
Death seals man's fate – Mosiah 2v36-39, Alma 34v32-35	**Chance after death** – D&C 76v106 -112+88-99
Saved without baptism – Moroni 8v22+23 2 Nephi 9v25+26, Mosiah 15v24-27	**Baptism for the dead** – D&C 128v5+17+18
Murder can be forgiven – 3 Nephi 30v2	**Murder cannot be forgiven** – D&C 42v18
Polygamy condemned – Jacob 1v15, 2v24, 3v5, Mosiah 11v2	**Polygamy commanded** – D&C 132v1+37-39+61

Other interesting information regarding the Mormons

1) The Book of Mormon contains at least 25,000 words from the Authorized Version. In fact, **verbatim quotations**, some of considerable length, have caused the Mormons no end of embarrassment for many years. Check out the following (*you'll be amazed!*) – The comparison of Moroni chapter 10 with **1 Cor 12v1-11**, 2 Nephi 14 with **Isaiah 4**, 2 Nephi 12 with **Isaiah 2**. The book of Mosiah chapter 14 is a reproduction of **Isaiah 53**. 3 Nephi 13v1-18 copies **Mat 6v1-23**.

2) From the 1830 edition of the Book of Mormon up until the present day, this so-called *'most correct of any book on earth'* has undergone **over 3000 changes** – *that's wild man!*

3) No Book of Mormon cities have *ever* been located.

4) No Book of Mormon names have been found in new world inscriptions.

5) No genuine inscriptions have been found in Hebrew in America.

6) No genuine inscriptions have been found in America, in Egyptian, or anything similar to Egyptian, which could correspond to Joseph Smith's 'reformed Egyptian'.

7) No **ancient copies** of the Book of Mormon 'scriptures' have been found.

8) No ancient inscriptions of any kind in America which indicate that the ancient inhabitants had Hebrew or Christian beliefs have been found – **see the video/DVD - 'DNA vs the Book of Mormon'**.

9) No mention in the Book of Mormon - persons, nations, or places have been found.

10) No artefact of any kind which demonstrates the Book of Mormon is true, has been found.

The Mormons – By Nathan Young

The Mormon beliefs are similar to the beliefs of the Jehovah's Witnesses which I showed in last month's newsletter, therefore please excuse any duplicates from last months which you will see below. There are different off-shoots/denominations with Mormons, so not every Mormon would hold to the below, however the majority will. Joseph Smith, the founder of the Mormon Church, testified one day that he would have his own Judgement Seat, like that of Christ's, where he would judge people once they entered Heaven. He, as well as Brigham Young, taught that men lived on the moon, and their ambition was to preach to the inhabitants there.

#	**Mormon Errors**	**Biblical Refutation**
1	Baptism for the Dead to save souls in Hell.	1 Cor 1v17, Acts 16v30-31
2	Must be married to get in Heaven	1 Cor 7v8, Col 1v5
3	Jesus Christ is not God, rather a separate god	John 1v1, 1 Tim 3v16, Heb 1v8-10
4	Wearing Holy garments will protect from evil	Eph 6v10-18, 2 Sam 22v3
5	Jesus Christ was created	Micah 5v2, Heb 1v8, Rev 22v12-13
6	God was once a man, like we are	Psalm 41v13, Ps 90v2, Hab 1v12
7	Jesus Christ is not Almighty	Rev 1v7-8, Rev 11v17
8	Salvation by works	Eph 2v8-9, Titus 3v5, Gal 2v16, Phil 3v19
9	Baptism is vital for Salvation	1 Cor 1v17, 2 Tim 1v9, Rom 4v1-5
10	You can lose your salvation, if not faithful	Eph 1v13, Eph 4v30, Rom 8v38-39
11	We all once lived as spirits in heaven	Gen 2v7, Job 33v6, Jer 1v5
12	Teach a universal salvation, that everyone will one day be saved, even those in Hell.	Heb 9v27, Rev 20v10
13	God has a Prophet on earth today	Heb 1v1-2
14	We can become as God	Rev 11v15, 1 Thes 4v17
15	Don't use God's word alone for teaching	2 Tim 2v15, 2 Tim 3v15-16, 1 Cor 2v5,
16	They believe there are errors in God's word	1 Pet 1v23, Ps 12v6-7, Prov 30v6
17	God comes from the Planet Kolob	1 Kings 8v39, Ps 93v1-2, 1 Kings 22v19, Acts 7v49
18	Must enter and endure the tribulation	1Thes 1v10, 1 Thes 4v14-18, 1 Thes 5v9
19	Believed that Mary had sexual intercourse with the Father to create the Lord Jesus	Isa 7v14, Mat 1v23

CULTS AND FALSE RELIGIONS

20	Joseph Smith was visited by the Angel Moroni to preach a gospel.	Gal 1v8
21	Satan and Jesus are spiritual brothers	Col 1v14-17
22	There are many Gods like God the Father	Isa 43v11,
23	God the Father has flesh and bones	John 4v24, Luke 24v39
24	Joseph Smith met/saw God the Father	John 1v18, John 6v46, 1 John 4v12, 1 John 4v20
25	Adam the first man, was God the Father	God cannot sin (Titus 1v2, Heb 6v18, Jam 1v13)

Jehovah's Witnesses

Some verses to use when confronted by the JW Cult.

(Verses in brackets are connected with the *previous* verse)

1 Pet 3v15

1) **The Deity of Jesus Christ** – John 1v1, John 5v18, John 5v23, John 8v58 (Exo 3v14), John 10v30-33, John 17v5, John 20v28, Heb 1v8, Matt 1v23, Col 2v9 etc.

2) **Only Jehovah God is to be worshipped** – Matt 4v10, yet we see Jesus being worshipped and accepting it – Matt 8v2, Matt 9v18, Matt 14v33, Matt 15v25, Matt 28v9+17, Heb 1v6.

3) **Jehovah God alone created the world** – Isa 44v24, yet we see that Jesus created all things – John 1v3+10, Col 1v16+17

4) **We were told that Jehovah God would come Himself to be our Saviour** – Isa 35v4 (Isa 45v21) – yet the Apostles who wrote the NT always spoke of Jesus Christ as being the Saviour – Luke 2v11, John 4v42, Titus 1v4

5) **The Doctrine of the Trinity** – Luke 1v35, Matt 3v16+17, Acts 3v26 (John 2v19-21, Rom 8v11), Ps 100v3 (Neh 9v6, John 1v3, Col 1v16+17, Job 33v4, Job 26v13, Gen 1v2), Ps 93v2 (Mic 5v2, Isa 9v6, Heb 9v14), 2 Tim 3v16 (1 Pet 1v10, 2 Pet 1v21), 1 Cor 8v6 (John 6v27, John 1v1, John 20v28, Heb 1v8, Acts 5v3+4)

6) **Bodily resurrection of Jesus Christ** – John 2v19-21, John 20v27, Luke 24v36-40

7) **Existence of Hell** – Matt 5v22, Matt 10v28, Matt 13v42, Matt 25v46, Matt 26v24, Rev 20v15, Isa 66v24, Luke 16v20-25 (Parables *never* use 'proper' names)

8) **Existence of the soul** – 1 Cor 6v20, Matt 10v28, Acts 7v59, John 19v30, Matt 26v38, Gen 2v7

9) **Infinite atonement of Christ** – Eph 2v8+9, Titus 3v4-6, Acts 4v12, John 3v16-18, 2 Cor 5v21, Heb 9v28

New World Translation (NWT) 'bible' Contradiction

Q – Did Abraham, Isaac, and Jacob know God by His first name?

A – According to the NWT they did. **Gen 28v13** "I am Jehovah the God of Abraham your father and the God of Isaac.

Yet Jehovah was *not* known as 'Jehovah' until the time of Moses over 300 years **after** Abraham had died.

Exo 6v3 And I appeared unto Abraham, unto Isaac, and unto Jacob, by the name of God Almighty, but by my name JEHOVAH was I not known to them. (AV/KJV) Now look at this verse in the NWT - And I used to appear to Abraham, Isaac, and Jacob as God Almighty, but with regard to my name Jehovah I did not make myself known to them. (Exo 6v3)

How about that! That shows you what a *corrupt* and *false* Satanic counterfeit 'bible' the JW's use.

Now check out **Gen 28v13** in the AV - **And, behold, the LORD stood above it, and said, I am the LORD God of Abraham thy father, and the God of Isaac: the land whereon thou liest, to thee will I give it, and to thy seed**; See how accurate that is.

Just 25 ERRORS of the JW's – By Nathan Young

Here are some of the Jehovah's Witness errors relating to what they have been spoon fed by false teaching.

For further answers on how to refute their beliefs, please go to **www.JWanswers.co.uk**

#	**Jehovah's Witness Errors**	**Biblical Refutation**
1	Holy Spirit is God's active force, not a person	John 14v16, John 16v13, Acts 8v29, Acts 10v19-20
2	God is one person, trinity is not in the bible	1 John 5v7, 1 John 5v20, John 10v30, Isa 44v6
3	Jesus Christ is not God	John 1v1, 1 Tim 3v16, Heb 1v8-10
4	Jesus Christ is not LORD	Acts 10v36, Heb 1v10, Rom 10v9,
5	Jesus Christ was created	Micah 5v2, Heb 1v8, Rev 22v12-13
6	Jesus Christ is an Angel (Michael)	Heb 1v5, Heb 1v13, Jude 1v9
7	Jesus Christ is not Almighty	Rev 1v7-8, Rev 11v17
8	Salvation by works	Eph 2v8-9, Titus 3v5, Gal 2v16, Phil 3v19
9	Baptism is vital for Salvation	1 Cor 1v17, 2 Tim 1v9, Rom 4v1-5
10	You can lose your salvation, if not faithful	Eph 1v13, Eph 4v30, Rom 8v38-39
11	Salvation is only through the Father	John 10v9, John 14v6, John 3v16, Acts 16v30-31
12	Salvation not outside the Watchtower	Mat 11v28, John 6v37, 2 Thes 2v13, 2 Pet 3v9

13	The Gospel message is the Kingdom message	1 Cor 15v1-4, Rom 2v6, Rom 16v25
14	Jesus never rose again bodily	Luke 24v37-39, Ps 16v10, 1 Cor 15v17
15	Only 144,000 can enter into Heaven	Col 1v5, Rev 7v9
16	There is no Hell	Mat 7v21-23, Luke 16v19-31, Mat 25v41
17	There is no everlasting punishment	Rev 19v20, Rev 20v13-15, Mat 25v46, 2 Thes 1v8-9
18	Must enter and endure the tribulation	1 Thes 1v10, 1 Thes 4v14-18, 1 Thes 5v9
19	The Father (Not Jesus) is the creator only	John 1v1-3, Col 1v15-17, Eph 3v9
20	Jesus should not be worshipped	Mat 2v2, Mat 28v9, Luke 24v52, John 9v38, Heb 1v6
21	When we die, we cease to exist	2 Cor 5v3-8, Phil 1v21-23, Rev 6v9-11
22	God is not Omni-present	Ps 139v7, Jer 23v23-24
23	Jesus is not the mediator of men	Rom 8v34, 1 Tim 2v5, Heb 7v25, Heb 12v24
24	Being Born again is not essential	John 3v3-8, 1 Pet 1v22-23
25	A person does not possess a soul or spirit	Rom 8v16, 1 Thes 5v23, Heb 4v12, Heb 10v39

NOTES

ISRAEL

GOD'S NOT FINISHED WITH ISRAEL

There are many false teachers and preachers today that say Israel has no future, God has finished with the Jews. This is heresy. Anti-Semitism is just another sign that we are living in the *last of the last days* preceding the Rapture of the church.

The Land God gave to Israel…

God gave the land of Palestine to *the children of Israel* – Lev 25v3, Deut 32v52, 4v1, 5v31, 9v23, 12v9+10, Josh 1v2+3+6+11+13+15

He gave it to them as an *unconditional promise* – Lev 26v25+26+21 cf. 26v44+45

God said it was *His land* and that He dwells there with His people Israel – Num 35v34, Deut 32v43, Lev 25v23

God swore to give the Jews that land – Deut 1v8, 6v10+23, 10v11, 11v9, 31v7

God gave the Jews Transjordan – the *East Bank* – Deut 3v20

God's *name* is there in that land – Deut 12v5+11+21, 14v23+24, 16v2+6

The Jews are a special people to God – Deut 14v2

The Lord plans on giving them *all the land* He swore to give them – Deut 19v8 cf. Gen 15v18

'Jacob' is God's 'inheritance' – Deut 32v9

God gave the land to Jacob's *seed* – Deut 34v4

The *Gaza Strip* belongs to Israel – Josh 15v20+45-47

Only Moab, Edom, and Ammon were promised any land – Deut 2v4-9+19 and *not one* promise to any of them was *everlasting* – Ps 105v10+11

When it comes to the 'Palestinians', God said to Israel… "I… gave you *their* land" – Judg 6v9. That's *all the land* – Josh 21v43 on both sides of Jordon.

Here are the number of times in one Book of the Bible, where it is stated that Palestine was given to the Jews by God – Deut 1v8+21+25+35-39, 2v12+24, 3v2+20, 4v1+21+38+40, 5v16+31+33, 6v10+18+23, 7v13, 8v1+7-10, 9v5+6, 10v11, 11v9+17+21+31, 12v1+10, 15v4+7, 16v20, 17v2+14, 18v9, 19v1-3+8+10+14, 20v16, 21v1+13, 24v4, 25v15+19, 26v1-3+9+10+15, 27v2+3, 28v8+11+52, 30v20, 31v7+20+21+23, 32v52, 34v4.

God's message to the United Nations…

God's HOUSE is in JERUSALEM – 1 Kings 8v48, 9v3 NOT Rome or Mecca

God's CITY is JERUSALEM – 1 Kings 8v44+48, 11v13 – NOT Rome or Mecca

God's LAND is PALESTINE, THE LAND OF CANAAN – Deut 32v43, Hos 9v3

God's NAME is in JERUSALEM – Deut 12v5+11, 1 Kings 11v36

God's MOUNTAIN is ZION in JERUSALEM – Isa 2v2+3, Ps 2v6

No Catholic, Greek Orthodox, Mohammedan, African, or Arabian has any business in Bethlehem, Hebron, the Gaza Strip, the Golan Heights, Sinai, Jaffa, Tel Aviv or Jerusalem. You will occupy those cities and that land at the peril of your *life*, your *family*, and your *nation* – Zech 14v1-3.

Rom 11v1-36 – **The preservation of Israel is the miracle of history!**

Facts concerning God's dealing with Israel – 1) Israel is blind spiritually, as a nation, but only in part as there are some Jews receiving Jesus Christ today. 2) The 'fullness' of the Gentiles is about to come to an end. The Rapture will fulfil the Body of Christ and then Jews and Gentiles will be saved separately. 3) At the end of Jacob's Trouble, when Jesus returns, all surviving Jews will look upon the glorified body of their Messiah and accept Christ Jesus as their Lord and Saviour 4) God will establish a NEW Covenant with Israel (Heb 8v8-12). After the apostles, Israel has no more prophets until Rev 7 + 11 in Jacob's Trouble.

To say that Israel has no future and the Church has replaced Israel is to be a Biblical illiterate and one who cannot rightly divide the Scriptures. I am noticing more and more 'Christians' *attacking* Israel, all because they are following *men* rather than the Scriptures. Anti-Semitism is Satanic, so you'd better be sure you get your doctrine right. Israel's survival is a miracle and they will get *the land* God promised... all of it!

Amos 9v15 – Israel shall get 'the land' forever...

This is the permanent restoration of Israel as a nation and government at the Second Advent (Isa 60v21, Isa 11v11+12, Rom 11v12, Rom 15v26) God intends to do this by destroying all seven major world religions and all 191+ Gentile nations (Isa 60v12, Isa 11v4) The Lord is going to preserve Israel as the leading government over every other nation on earth, on the grounds that the entire world has called Him a liar to His face (John 8v47, 1 John 5v10). He is going to repay them for it, with *interest!* (Deut 7v10, 32v41+43, Ps 149v7, Isa 35v4, Isa 47v3, Isa 61v2, Isa 63v4, Mic 5v15, Nah 1v2 etc.)

The 'whole piece of dirt' is laid out in Genesis 15v18-21, Gen 13v14-17, Gen 17v8, Gen 22v16-18, Gen 24v7

Israel is God's *chosen* land and the Jews are His *chosen* people and there is *nothing* that is going to change that!

Take a look at this map. Israel is surrounded by Muslim countries and they all want to wipe Israel off

the face of the earth. Look how tiny Israel is, yet the Lord Jesus Christ shall deliver Israel and save Israel and set up His Kingdom, with Jerusalem as the Capital, as He sits upon His throne and rules with a rod of iron – Rev 19v15. God gave the Oracles to the Jews (Acts 7v38, Rom 3v2) and promised to preserve His words, which He did through the Authorized Version Bible which He gave to England to produce. Two small countries God used to fulfil His will. Islam and Roman Catholicism headed up by their god Satan, is against the Jew and against the AV Bible. Time is running out and we as Christians have a job to do, take

ISRAEL

the Gospel message to all four corners of the world. Jesus Christ is coming again very soon indeed. He will then deal with Israel and ultimately deliver her from all her enemies: He will then set up His Kingdom of Heaven *on earth*. The church has *not* replaced Israel, and those Christians who think it has, are as shallow in the Scriptures as you can get. (Read Romans 9-11) Israel has an amazing future ahead of her, yet a very tough one too. Scripture teaches a literal *regathering, rebirth, and restoration* of the twelve tribes of Israel, to the Land as specified in the Holy Bible. Their Messiah, Christ Jesus, will bring salvation and restoration to Israel in fulfilment of the Covenant promise. During the Tribulation, 144,000 Jews will offer to the Jews and Gentiles alike, the final invitation for entrance into the Kingdom, sins forgiven and eternal life assured – read the following Scriptures in regard to a study on Israel – Deut 7v6, Isa 43v10+11, Ps 24v1, Deut 32v8+9, Ezek 5v5, Ps 132v13, Gen 12v7, Gen 17v7+8+18+19, Gen 28v13, Gen 35v12, Gen 15v18, Exo 23v31, Ps 105v8-11, Luke 21v24, Lev 26v45, Deut 30v4+5, Isa 16v14+15, Ezek 37v12, Ezek 36v1-15, Zech 12v2+3, Jer 30v7, Zech 14v9. It's been said in regard to Israel's *boundaries*... 'In present day terms these boundaries of Israel are from Egypt to Iraq and from the Gulf of Aqabah to the Mediterranean, *including* Gaza, West Bank, Golan Heights and ALL Jerusalem'.

Who is a Jew?

Est 2v5 **Now in Shushan the palace there was a certain Jew, whose name was Mordecai, the son of Jair, the son of Shimei, the son of Kish, a Benjamite;** Notice that a 'Benjamite' is a 'Jew', just like Paul (Gal 2v15 cf. Phil 3v5). In fact, a 'Jew' does not have to be from the southern tribes (Benjamin and Judah) at all. Paul called Peter a Jew in Gal 2v14, and Peter was from one of the ten northern tribes (Mat 4v13-18). The term Jew is *not* limited to Judean Jews or Pharisees at all (John 4v22). Understand this and you will never be deceived by the British Israelite cult.

The last verse in the Bible for the Jew

2 Chron 36v23 **Thus saith Cyrus king of Persia, All the kingdoms of the earth hath the LORD God of heaven given me; and he hath charged me to build him an house in Jerusalem, which is in Judah. Who is there among you of all his people? The LORD his God be with him, and let him go up.** This is the last thing every unsaved Jew sees in his Bible, if he is 'orthodox' and attends the synagogue. This is the last verse in the Hebrew Bible. If the Jew got saved, he would get a Bible that had the OT plus the NT in it. Then when he got to the end of the OT, he would not see an admonition to go back to Jerusalem (2 Chron 36v23), he would be reading Malachi 4. He would be looking for the 2nd Coming of Jesus Christ heralded in by Moses and Elijah. Rom 11v25. Aren't you pleased that we're going *up* at the Rapture, rather than back to Jerusalem, to await the Great Tribulation?

Listen to our two part study on Israel...

Israel Part one - http://www.timefortruth.co.uk/media/forcedown.php?file=1783-1416931899.mp3

Israel Part two - http://www.timefortruth.co.uk/media/forcedown.php?file=1783-1417136797.mp3

The Bible facts as to the Jewish nation are as follows... 1) God specifically called out a people from Abram (Gen 12) to be separated unto Himself. 2) He gave them national status with physical and spiritual blessings. 3) He gave them His Law and spiritual revelation through *signs and wonders* – Exo 7v3, Deut 4v34, Dan 6v27, John 4v48, Acts 2v22, Acts 4v30, Rom 15v19. 4) God even chose to bless the entire earth through this one group. He even chose to send His seed through this pedigree, by which He would redeem the world – Gen 12v3, John 4v9. Though oppressed, downtrodden, carried captive to other lands, and scattered throughout the world, the Jews *haven't* lost their identity. **Their preservation is the miracle of history!**

After the apostles, Israel has no more prophets till Rev 7+11 in the Tribulation. The fullness of the Gentiles is about to come to an end. The Rapture will fulfil the Body of Christ and then Jews and Gentiles will be saved separately. At the end of the Tribulation (Jacob's Trouble), when Jesus returns, all the surviving Jews will look on the glorified body of their Messiah and accept Christ as their Lord and Saviour - Rom 11v26. God will establish a new covenant with Israel - Rom 11v2, Heb 8v8-12.

More than 1400 years before Jesus showed up, the Scriptures said the Jews would be dispersed – Jer 16v13-16, 30v11+12, Hos 3v4, Ezek 36v20-23, Ezek 6v8, 11v16, 22v15, 12v15-18, Mic 4v11, Joel 2v17-19, Jer 48v37. Isa 11v11 – The dispersion and return took place in 606 BC – 538 BC (see Dan, Ezek, Ezra, Hag, Neh + Esther). It also happened again (Isa 11v11) in AD 135-1948.

NOTES

NOTES

MATTHEW 24

Matthew 24... *that confusing chapter!*

So many Christian denominations and cults cannot rightly divide this chapter. It is where all the A-Millennial and Post-Millennial Christians break their spiritual necks doctrinally. Many Christians think that this passage applies to either this present age or to the years preceding the destruction of Jerusalem in 70 A.D. – it doesn't.

Mat 24v1-5. Note the words in our first passage... '**And Jesus went out.**' The words are to be *connected* with what has just taken place – '**your house is left unto you desolate**'. (Mat 23v38) This is very interesting. It is left desolate because the Builder and Maker of the House is *deserting* it (Heb 3v1-6), and He will *not* return until the restoration and conversion of Israel in the future, when they shall say, '**Blessed is he that cometh in the name of the Lord**' (Mat 23v39 + Mat 21v9). Now all of you who know something about dispensationalism, will know that the word *dispensation* means '**the laws by which a household is operated, or the way the master of the house arranges his household.**' Yet since 1700 the word 'dispensation' has been used to mean '*a period of time*' – this of course is due to the master of the house (Heb 3v2 + Eph 2v19), God, setting up *different* ways of running His 'family' at **different times**, according to His own wisdom. Dispensationalism can also mean *stewardship and administration.* Now folks, this is *critical* for you to understand if you are to make sense of Mat 24.

So back to our first portion of Scripture, read it again – Mat 24v1-5... '**And his disciples came to him.**' The speaker is undoubtedly Judas, in the questioning that follows, and a careful reading of the passage will produce some excruciating insight into the nature and character of the *type of people* who are hypnotized by beautiful buildings, and cannot take their eyes off the visible long enough to behold the invisible (Read Heb 11v27 + 2 Cor 4v18). In Mark 13v1 it is '**Master, see what manner...**' and the Holy Spirit calls to your attention that this question is asked by *only one* of His disciples (Mark 13v1). There is *only one* person who habitually calls Him 'Master.' This of course, is Judas (Mat 26v22+25, Mat 26v49, John 13v13). Furthermore, when Jesus begins the 'Olivet discourse' (Sermon on the Mount), He waits until the one who asked Him this question is gone. Notice that in Mark 13v3 it says '**Peter and James and John and Andrew asked him privately.**' In plainer words, Judas is *left out* of the explanations which deal with the Second Coming of Christ. **Like the A-Millennial and Post-Millennial bunglers of Mat 13, who are *blinded* so they cannot discern the course of the age from 70 A.D. to the Advent, so Judas represents that class of expositors who remain *in the dark* concerning the great prophetic events of the end-time.** Judas is interested in the time and money gone into the building of the Temple (Hos 8v14) and this is because money is involved in the work, and he (being treasurer) holds the money bag. (John 12v6). Judas *never* did get the answer to the question... '**Tell us, when shall these things be? and what shall be the sign when all these things shall be fulfilled?**' (Mark 13v4), the answer was given to four fisherman instead. **And Jesus answering them...** (Mark 13v5) What Jesus says has already had a *past* fulfilment in Jeremiah 52 and Lamentations. It has a ***present*** fulfilment at the time He says it, since it involves the life of the disciples (70 AD) when Titus destroyed the Temple, and it has a ***future*** fulfilment in Rev 11v1-4 and 2 Thes 2v3-8, where the Anti-Christ appears.

Mat 24v2 ...**There shall not be left here one stone**... The fulfilment of this prophecy would be most unlikely, for some of the 'stones' were 65 feet by 8 feet by 10 feet. Not only this, but since the temple was built by Romans, why would they destroy it? Yet it *did* come to pass because Jesus said it would. The soldiers not only took the stones apart, they ploughed up the ground underneath, looking for gold supposedly buried beneath the temple (Jer 26v18). This passage is not only true of the literal temple, but it is true of the Church (1 Cor 3v10-16), the Universe (Heb 1v10-12), and the Human Body (1 Cor 6v13).

Mat 24v3 **And as he sat upon the mount of Olives, the disciples came unto him privately, saying, Tell us, when shall these things be? and what shall be the sign of thy coming, and of the end of the world?** The standard way of handling v3 is to point out that 3 questions are asked, and then, to find out the answer to these 3 questions. The *first* question being answered in vs 4-14; the *second* in vs 15-22, and the *third* in vs 23-25. This however, is very improbable as we shall see upon examining the verses. The attempt is made by fundamentalists to preserve this three-fold distinction, in an effort to prove that *some of the chapter* must refer to something other than the past destruction of Jerusalem under Titus in 70 A.D. But this is a needless and wasteful compromise to make. If the believer will stick to the insistence that vs 14+21+29+30 say what they mean and mean what they say, there is no danger at all that anyone can apply the chapter to the destruction of 70 A.D. The trouble is that the Bible believer, assailed with science on the left, and beset with A-millennial scholarship on the right, is afraid to insist anymore that the book says what it means and means what it says.

Applying this rule however, the analysis would be that the first question is '**When shall these things be?**' (i.e. the throwing of one stone off another) This question would be answered in vs 4-14. Immediately the rule breaks all to pieces, for sitting right in the middle of the 'answer', is '**He that shall endure to the end, the same shall be saved.**' The end of what? It cannot be the end of Jerusalem for nearly 300 brethren *die* before Titus ever showed up (1 Cor 15v6-9), and the verse will *not* match any way with v14.

So without bothering to trace the other two questions, let us assume that the three questions of v3 are only 2 questions (*which they are*, as the question marks are found), and that the answer to the first question *is the answer to the second question*. The event will take place once (locally and historically), at the destruction of Jerusalem – but the detailed doctrinal fulfilment will by no means take place **until** the Second Advent. Since up till here, *both* Advents appear together, the two destructions appear simultaneously.

Read Mat 24v3+4 – The first sign of the coming is *deception.* (Read also 2 Pet 2v1-4, 1 Tim 4v1-5, 2 Tim 3v1-6) Notice the verse said '**Take heed that NO MAN deceive you. For many shall come in MY NAME...**' There are so many wolves in sheep's clothing, who make out they belong to Jesus Christ (some even claiming to BE Christ). Deception *in* the church is everywhere. There are many leaders of Churches who are not even Christians; the Anglican Church is a prime example. ...**and shall deceive MANY**. (Mat 7v13+22, 2 Tim 4v1-8) Did you get that, *many*. Many shall be deceived; many are deceived today. If there was one sound Bible Believing Church in Kidderminster we would be in it. We pass seven churches on the way to Oaks Church every Friday and Sunday; not one of them is sound and not one of them has a single 'watchman' in them (1 Cor 14v8, Ps 127v1). Read Mat 24v5+11+24, 2 Pet 2v1+2.

Now read Mat 24v6-11 – 'wars and rumours of wars' cannot be applied to that immediate time; there is no mention of 'wars or rumours of wars' in the Book of Acts, which runs right up to 62 A.D. Thus it is seen immediately how vs 6-11 do *not* answer the first question as it applies to Titus' destruction. Note also '**the end is not yet.**' The 'end' here, is (as it is in most places) a reference

MATTHEW 24

to the end of the Tribulation (Mat 24v21-29), and *not* 'the end' of the apostolic age. '**For nation shall rise against nation**...' – again it is impossible to force the passage into the 33-70 A.D. setting. Nation does *not* rise against nation until there are some nations to do the 'rising'. The passage, then, undoubtedly begins with discussing the events of the *end* time (Dan 7 + 9 + 11), and only by desperate *mishandling and misapplication* can the chapter be applied to 70 A.D.

90% of the events that are described in Mat 24 *did not happen in* 70 A.D. *and have to be future.* The A-millennialists and Post-millennialists have to *pervert* the word of God to teach otherwise... and this is exactly what they do. This is why the Reformed Christian who lives in the **error of Calvinism**, treats the Book of Revelation, as apocalyptic, figurative and symbolic rather than literal. *They spiritualise anything they don't understand and don't believe to be literally true.* (It's interesting that John Calvin *never* produced a commentary on the Book of Revelation. It was obviously too deep for a shallow student such as him).

In 70 A.D. nation did *not* rise against nation, and kingdom against kingdom. Nor were there 'pestilences and earthquakes' (Mat 24v7). Furthermore, *none* of the apostles here addressed were 'delivered up and hated of all nations' after 70 A.D. because *none of them were alive*, except John. (Mat 24v9) So with a little bit of common sense and enough faith to equal that of a mustard seed, you can see very clearly that Mat 24 is *not* a discourse on the fall of Jerusalem in 70 A.D. Those who 'believe' it is, are just arrogant, irreverent, Bible-denying heretics, who think their own interpretations are superior to the words of Scripture.

The word 'many' is found applied to 6 kinds of people in the remaining verses 9-12.

1) MANY shall be offended 2) MANY shall betray one another 3) MANY shall hate one another 4) MANY false prophets shall rise 5) MANY shall be deceived by them 6) MANY shall lose their love for each other.

The only difficult part of the passage so far is v9. It has some application in the Book of Acts (See James - Acts 12, Peter – Acts 12, Paul – Acts 28) and yet the final application cannot have reference to the audience *then* present, unless those apostles are resurrected at the Rapture for a return ministry to Israel. (Man alive, that's too much! So much so that we will drop it... but notice, the identical type of statement in Mat 10v23. In both statements He is telling half-truths, unless those addressed have a *future ministry* in Palestine).

'**Many false prophets... shall deceive many.**' – *Then and now*, there are *many false* 'prophets, teachers, pastors, elders, deacons, bishops, 'Christians' etc.' – note many. 2 Pet 2v1 **But there were false prophets also among the people, even as there shall be false teachers among you, who privily shall bring in damnable heresies, even denying the Lord that bought them, and bring upon themselves swift destruction**. Every dispensation has a shed-load of *false* teachers and preachers; there's more on earth today than ever before. Ever counted how many cults and 'religions' there are in the world today; ever counted how many false teachers and preachers there are *in the church* today, in *every* denomination. Man alive, you'd be counting all the way up until the Rapture! You want to cross reference these verses with Mat 24v11... Deut 13 and Deut 18, Acts 20v30, 1 Cor 11v19, Phil 3v19, 1 Tim 4v1+2, 2 Tim 3v1-5, Heb 10v29, 1 John 4v1, Jude 1v4+18.

Read Mat 24v12-20 – Now this is a passage that is often misapplied, misinterpreted and misunderstood. '**But he that shall endure unto the end**...' Now the Christian who does not read, study or understand the Scriptures, will lift this verse *from its context* and teach that a Christian can lose his salvation if he does not 'hold-out' till the end. This of course is what we English call 'tommy-rot!' A-millennial and Post-millennial Christians who believed in apprehending the promises to Israel for the church would teach such nonsense also; this is where it probably originated from, i.e.

the Roman Catholics. Read Mat 24v13+14 again and notice the following...

1) No one's life is being discussed (Mat 24v14)

2) It is the end of a period of time, *not* an individual's life (Mat 24v14)

3) There are *no* Christians present (Mat 24v3)

4) The land being discussed is Palestine (Mat 24v16)

5) The audience addressed are Jews (Mat 24v1-3)

6) They are observing the OT Law (Mat 24v15-20)

7) They are worshipping in a temple in Jerusalem (Mat 24v15 and 2 Thes 2)

8) They are *not* 'spiritual-Jews', and no one but a Bible *pervert* would distort the context to get the meaning (Rom 2v29)

9) The Christian *already* has a promise that he *will endure to the end* if that was under discussion (1 Cor 1v7+8, Phil 1v6)

10) The 2nd Coming follows the 'END', in this passage, and *not the death* of the believer (Mat 24v14+21+29).

It is therefore apparent that Mat 24v13 has *nothing* to do, directly or indirectly, with the salvation of *anyone* in the age of grace, and it was *never* intended to be used by *anyone*, under any condition, for any purpose in that manner. Like Heb 3v6+14, a period of time is being discussed, and this period of time is defined in the immediate context; *the context defines* how the verse is *applied* and it is *not* applied to anyone in this dispensation.

The very next verse (v14) *defines* 'THE END!' Verse 14 *locates* 'THE END' as that period of time, wherein the 'Gospel of the Kingdom' (Not the Gospel we preach today) is preached. Since *this* Gospel is *not* the Gospel of the 'Grace of God' (1 Cor 15v1-6) given to the Christian (Gal 1v11-13), by the Apostle to the Gentiles (Rom 2v16), it most certainly would have *no bearing* on the life of any Christian from Pentecost to the Rapture.

'**He that shall endure unto the end**', is *plainly* a reference to a law-abiding Jew in Palestine, immediately preceding the Advent of the Lord Jesus Christ, and no amount of distortion could ever make it apply to anything else, unless you are a Bible 'corrector'.

'**And this gospel of the kingdom**' – The different Gospels are...

1) The Gospel of the Kingdom – 2 Sam 7v16, Dan 2, Mat 4v23, 9v35, 24v14 etc.

2) The Gospel of the Grace of God – 1 Cor 15v1-5 ('Paul's' Gospel – Rom 2v16, Eph 3v1-7)

3) The Gospel preached to the Jews – Acts 2v38 which included water baptism (This is not the Gospel we preach today)

4) The Gospel preached to Abraham – Gal 3v8 (Think about it; it obviously couldn't be the death, burial and resurrection of Jesus Christ)

5) The Everlasting Gospel – Rev 14v6

This '**Gospel of the kingdom**' (v14) – Matthew *defines* it in a score of passages – Mat 3v2, 4v17+23,

8v12, 9v35, 10v7 etc. In every case, it is a *literal, physical, visible, messianic, Davidic* kingdom promised to the Son of David, who will reign **on** David's throne at Jerusalem – Ezek 37v25. (JW's cannot differentiate the difference between the *two* kingdoms, but then again, neither can most Christians... Pentecostal, Reformed and Calvinistic, Baptist, Brethren etc.) The Kingdom of Heaven is *not* the Kingdom of God.

v14 -'**For a witness unto all nations**' – Notice that the word 'nations' as in Mat 28v18+19 is set over against the word 'kingdom.' The Kingdom is the Lord's and it is Jewish (Acts 3v19-26) and this message is to be preached to the Gentiles *in the Tribulation* as a witness. There is nothing in the passage remotely connected with missionaries spreading the Gospel to all nations in *this age*. If you were preaching *that* Gospel in *this age* you would be cursed according to Gal 1v7-10.

So as you can see Mat 24v13+14 is the parting of the ways for the Bible Believer and every other cult and religion. The JW thinks that this refers to him and he must *endure to the end to be saved*; he's trying to endure in an age that has *not even begun yet.* The A-Millennialist grabs it and pretends that the Jewish Gospel of the Kingdom is the plan of salvation in *this age*. See what a mess Christians get into when they *wrongly* divide the word of truth.

There are many preachers, teachers, pastors etc. who do *not* know what 'The End' is, what the 'Kingdom' is, what the 'Gospel of the Kingdom' is, who 'The Nations' are, nor to whom the message is addressed.

Mat 24v15 **When ye therefore shall see the abomination of desolation, spoken of by Daniel the prophet, stand in the holy place, (whoso readeth, let him understand:)** Here's another corker of a verse '...**the abomination of desolation, spoken of by Daniel the prophet...**' is found in Dan 11v31 and Dan 8v13. Note that in Dan 8v13+14 *the time* is given for the desolation and it is not a time that any scholar has ever found connected with 'Antiochus Epiphanes'. Furthermore, the sanctuary was *not cleansed* (Dan 8v14) when Antiochus was through.

'...**the abomination that maketh desolate**.' Dan 11v31, Dan 12v11 – clearly marks the taking away of a *literal* sacrifice, which is being made in a *literal* temple (Rev 11v1-4) in the real future (2 Thes 2v1-6). It is *not* Antiochus and it is *not* Titus. All passages point to a *literal* fulfilment in the middle of Daniel's 70th week (The End-Time). To take place *after* the Rapture. You will arrive at this interpretation if you read 'desolate' where it says 'desolate', and 'abomination' where it says 'abomination', and 'temple' where it says 'temple'.

'...**the abomination of desolation, spoken of by Daniel the prophet, stand in the holy place**' – The Holy Place, of course, refers to that part of the Temple at Jerusalem where the shewbread, candlestick, and altar of burnt incense were kept (Heb 9v1-5). It says plainly that there is a *literal temple standing* at the time these events take place. Rev 11v1-4, in the Tribulation, confirms this and 2 Thes 2v1-6 states just as plainly that when the Man of Sin comes that he will sit down in the '**temple of God, shewing himself that he is God**' (2 Thes 2v4 cf. Dan 11) Note...

1) The Anti-Christ will profess to be God in the flesh – 2 Thes 2

2) As such, he will install himself as the object of worship – Rev 13

3) As an object of worship, he will demand sacrifice to replace the authorised sacrifices of the Jews (Dan 8, 11, Lev 1-7)

4) These sacrifices will be *human beings*, who are decapitated at the altar on the court of the temple, and the flesh and blood *eaten* by the black robed priests of the mass (John 6v40-71, Rev 20v4, Lev 1, Rev 6v9-11, Isa 6v13, Ps 16v4, Ps 14v4 etc.)

Since the 'Man of Sin' is the *fifth* cherub (now vacant from the third Heaven – Rev 4v7, Eze 1v10+28), and since the cherubim have the privilege of surrounding the throne, *this* cherub will resume his place in the Temple as the 'anointed' cherub that covereth the throne (Eze 28v14) and will seat himself on the 'Mercy Seat' and dictate to the entire world - Mat 24v15.

Mat 24v16 **Then let them which be in Judaea**... Notice how the Holy Spirit keeps driving home the fact that the setting is Jewish, *not* Gentile; it is under the Law, *not* under Grace; it is a period of time *in the future, not the past*; and this period is terminated by the Advent (Mat 24v29). It is absolutely ridiculous to think that Mat 24 was 70 A.D. when you are told that the Lord Jesus Christ *returned at the end of that period of time*. He could *not* have returned, for John writes of His coming as *future*, in the Gospel, and John's Gospel is written 20 years after the destruction of Jerusalem.

'**flee into the mountains**:' – The details of this are found in Rev 12v1-15, Micah 7v14-16, Jer 50v19+20, Hosea 2 etc. For those Christians who do *wrongly* divide the word of truth and cling to the 70 A.D. heresy please note...

1) Christians do *not* observe the Sabbath (Mat 24v20)

2) *Nowhere* did Jesus warn Christians *not* to have children (Mat 24v19)

3) *Nowhere* are any Christians addressed in the passage

This does *not* mean that 'certain' events that took place in 70 A.D. *cannot* 'foreshadow' what is to take place later – for Jer 52 'foreshadows' 70 A.D. and the future destruction under the Antichrist. But it does mean that we do not have the liberty to relegate *future passages* to the *past* simply because we are too *stupid* to adopt the Pre-millennial position.

Mat 24v19 ...**woe unto them that are with child**, ...**in those days**. Again the 'days' are exactly located, for we find the same expression in Luke 23v28-31, and here, also, it is addressed to *Jews only*, and the quotation is from the Tribulation. It thus appears that the Gospels are 'shot through' with references which can only be interpreted by the Book of Revelation. Revelation opens the Old Testament (OT), and the OT opens the New Testament (NT). This is why A-Millennial and Post-Millennial Christians cannot tackle the Book of Revelation e.g. John Calvin.

Only one man in the Bible was forbidden to marry or have children. It was not a priest. It was Jeremiah (Jer 16v2) Jeremiah was living at the time that Nebuchadnezzar, king of Babylon (Rev 17!) destroyed Jerusalem. When this is done *again*, it will be by a man who is typified by Nebuchadnezzar (i.e. the Antichrist), and who is connected with Babylon (Rev 17v1-9). Jeremiah, therefore, would perfectly typify the Jewish remnant in the Tribulation at the time the Anti-Christ takes over. This remnant is called '**the virgin of Israel**', and '**the virgin daughter of Jerusalem**' and is addressed by Jesus in Luke, '**Daughters of Jerusalem, weep not for me, but weep for yourselves, and for your children**' (Luke 23v28) Notice that this expression, as it occurs also in Mat 2v17+18, is connected with Jeremiah and speaks of *a nation in mourning at a time when men are calling, "Mountains, fall on us, Rocks cover us!"* (Rev 6v16) The 'green tree' of Luke 23v31 is Israel in her own land in peace with the Messiah present. The 'dry tree' is Israel in bondage under religious Rome, and with the *false* 'messiah' in the 'driver's seat' – Ezek 17v22-24.

Mat 24v20 **But pray ye that your flight be not in the winter, neither on the sabbath day**: The route of this flight will be found in the OT prophets, and it is clear that it is to Southern Palestine (Petra), by crossing the Jordon and fleeing down the King's highway through Moab and Ammon. Another danger is that there will be no time to get adequate *clothing* for the trip – Mat 24v18. We see it today don't we, in the example of a tsunami, there is no time for preparation. '...**on the sabbath**

day' – This causes 'scholars' a problem. It is argued that if it was the Sabbath they would violate it by going more than a Sabbath's day journey, which would get them no further than the Mount of Olives (Acts 1v2). But this interpretation is strained to say the least. If the Sabbath is '**made for man**' (Mark 2v27) and the '**Son of man is Lord also of the sabbath**' (Mark 2v28), why would it be 'breaking the Sabbath' to run from the Antichrist till you were out of breath?

Read Mat 24v21-25 – '**Then shall be great tribulation**' – This *period of time* is *never* to be confused with *routine tribulations* that all of God's people, in any age, are to expect – Acts 14v22, 2 Thes 1v5, etc. This period of time is called 'The Great Tribulation' – Rev 7v14 (note also Rev 1v9) It is called this to indicate that peculiar *period of time* in which a nation is *born in a day*, exactly as a woman is in 'tribulation' with her *birth pangs* (Deut 4v30, Isa 54v1, 66v7+8, Mic 5v3, Jer 30v6, 49v24, 50v43, Hos 13v13, 1 Thes 5v3 etc.) You cannot compare this Tribulation, called 'The Time of Jacob's Trouble' (Jer 30v7), and the Time of 'Trouble' (Dan 12v1), and *affliction* (Mark 13v19), with *anything* that this world has ever seen, including WW1 and WW2 combined). '...**such as was not since the beginning of the world to this time,**' Now if you think this passage is referring to 70 A.D. *you are a nut-bar, jam-packed with peanuts, Brazils and pecans!* Reformed Calvinistic 'Baptists' are just mad-hatters, when it comes to rightly dividing *that Book*. I don't know of a Calvinist who understands Mat 24.

'**No, nor ever shall be.**' Do you get the tense? Jesus says that *this Tribulation* will be *worse* than *anything* since Genesis 1 and will be *worse* than *anything* to ever *come in the future*. This passage of Scripture in Mat 24v21 certainly has no reference whatsoever to Titus in 70 A.D.

Mat 24v22 ...**there should no flesh be saved: but for the elect's sake**... In this passage, the word 'elect' is the Jew, as in v31. Confirmation of this lies not only in the fact that the passage is a Jew talking to Jews about a Jewish period of time when the Jews are in the Jewish homeland (and the passage occurs in Matthew's Gospel, which presents Jesus as the King of the Jews), but it lies also in a careful examination of Isa 45v14, 27v13, 65v9-12, 28v4, Zech 2v5+6, Dan 7v21, Isa 45v4 etc. The '**his elect**' of v31 is *forced* to apply to Christians in the Church Age by over-zealous advocates of the Rapture, who fail to see the Rapture of the *Tribulation saints* mentioned in Isa 26, S of S 2, Ps 50 etc. There is more than one 'Rapture' in the Scriptures. (Actually there are *seven* – Acts 1v9-11, Gen 5v21-24, 2 Kings 2v8-12, 1 Thes 4v16-18, Rev 11v3-12, Rev 14v1-5, Rev 7v9-17)

'**Except those days should be shortened**' – is an expression full of mystery and dormant information. The Tribulation is said to be an even week of years – *seven years* (Dan 9v25, Gen 29v27) in *two periods* of 3½ years each (Rev 11v2+3, 12v6, 13v5). Yet these measurements are flexible and undefined. As God worked out history to Acts 7 so that it could *swing either way* on man's *free will* (and still preserve His own 'sovereign' plan), so here the Lord has a situation set where the 'END' can be lengthened or shortened, according to the flow of events. Notice four different measurements given for this period in Daniel and Revelation.

1) 1260 days – Dan 7v25, Rev 13v5

2) 1290 days – Dan 12v11

3) 1335 days – Dan 12v12

4) 2300 days – Dan 8v14

Mat 24v48-50 describes the condition of a man in this Great Tribulation who fails to reckon on this divine 'time-table!'

Read Mat 24v25-31 – '**Go not forth... believe it not**...' The Tribulation Jew is warned against anyone deceiving him about the 2nd Coming. The actual *coming* will be so climatic, catastrophic and 'apocalyptic', that the Roman Catholic Gentile system will be *utterly destroyed* - Dan 2.

'For as the lightning...' The 2nd Coming, then, is to be *visible*, thunderous, appalling, terrifying and *brilliant*. It is going to be the exact opposite of everything taught by the Post-Millennialist. The 2nd Coming of Christ therefore is the *literal, physical, visible* event that will transpire in *power*, wrath and glory when the crucified, risen Saviour returns to this sin-cursed earth to take that which rightfully belongs to Him, as the Kingly-Last-Adam. (Ezek 21v26+27, 1 Cor 15v45, Rev 11v15)

'For wheresoever the carcase is...' The exact passage is found in Luke 17v37 and again, there is not the slightest reference to the destruction of Jerusalem in 70 A.D. The 'carcases' are the carcases of 200,000,000 horses and riders who came from the East in a UN army to help Roman Catholics wipe out Jerusalem. (Rev 16v14, 14v20, 9v16, 19v15-20, Ezek 38 and 39 etc.)

'Immediately after the tribulation of those days...' If there is a shred of doubt left as to the *time* that the verses in Mat 24 describe, *this verse* (v29) *should end it!* Where is there room for the Church and the Church Age if Mat 24v1-28 applies to 70 A.D.? For if it did, the Lord would have returned 1890 *years ago* and there would have been no Church Age. Where is the 'conversion of the world' found, about which the Post-Millennialists talk so much? If the Lord returns '**Immediately AFTER the Tribulation of those days...**', and *those* 'DAYS' are 70 A.D., *where* is the 'conversion of the world?'

You may as well face it – the A-Millennial and Post-Millennial systems of Bible interpretation are a total waste of time and do *not* make sense at all. Those that follow these systems have certainly perverted the Scriptures to get to their conclusions, or, they have just followed their favourite 'heretics' regarding this doctrine e.g. Origen, Augustine, Jerome, Calvin, Strong, Berkhof etc. None of the events in vs 29-31 have taken place! Note, '**The sun, the moon, the stars, the powers, the sign, the tribes, the clouds, the power, great glory, his angels, a trumpet, his elect**' – here we have the completed elements of the Second Advent listed together. Phenomena in the heavens, demoniac powers thrown to the earth, a *sign* in heaven, the repentance of the Jews who are left, the Advent with the heavenly hosts, and the Rapture of the Tribulation saints immediately *preceding* the Battle of Armageddon. The companion passages are as follows...

1) '**The sun... the moon... the stars...**' – Rev 6v12+13, 8v12, Joel 2v10, 3v15, Rev 16v8, Amos 8v9, Hab 3v11, Isa 13v10, Jer 15v9, Acts 2v20 – Notice in regard to Acts 2v20 the Bible 'corrector/rejector/perverter' will have to 'spiritualise' this verse to make it 'literally' apply to Pentecost, even though it did *not* take place at Pentecost. – Isa 13v10, Joel 3v15 etc.

2) '**The powers of the heavens**' – (Eph 6v10-13, Isa 24v21, Rev 12v1-4, 12v7-9) Notice that a 'star' in the Bible is defined as an 'angel' – Rev 1v20, 9v1.

3) **The conversion of the 'tribes of Israel'** – Notice in all references that they are *literal tribes* (where it says 'tribes', *read* 'tribes') - Rev 1v7, Zech 12v9+10, Amos 8v10, Jer 6v26, Rev 7v1-11, Ps 105v37, Zech 9v1, Ezek 37-48 etc.

4) **The clouds... with power and great glory** – Gen 49v9-11+18+23+24, Num 23v23+24, 24v9+17+20-24, Deut 32+33, Judges 5, Ps 110, 128, 129, Jude 14, Isa 26+27, Dan 7v13-15, Hab 3, Mal 4, Rev 14v14, Zech 1+14 etc. Many Christians have 'cut Israel off' from her promises, and have stolen the promises and tried to claim them for the 'church', which they are not.

5) '**The sign of the Son of man**' – The *sign* has been left till last, as it is the most difficult

to locate. A-Millennial and Post-Millennial 'expositors' will place *it first and identify it* because... a) All heretics like to begin with an obscure passage about which there is difficulty, like, Heb 6, 10 or Rev 7, or Mat 5, 6, 7 etc. 2) All heretics like to line up with Roman tradition. 3) All heretics like to state 'dogmatically' what an obscure thing is, like, Mat 16v18 or Acts 2v38 or 1 John 3v9, so people will think they 'know something' about the Scriptures. '*My, isn't he amazing!!!*' (Luke 6v26) For an in-depth study on the *sign* of the 'Cross' you need to read 'The Mark of the Beast' by Dr Ruckman.

6) **'The sign of the Son of man in heaven'** – The statement seems to be nearly beyond exposition. It is the '**Son of man**' here referred to, *not* the '**Son of God**', as we find it in the Pauline Epistles and in the writings of John (who had all of Paul's revelation on his table in front of him while he wrote). But '**the sign of the Son of man**', if traced back Scripturally would wind up in the following places... 1) The planets, sun and moon, are themselves for *signs* (By this token, phenomena on the sun could be the sign, for the sun is said to be a type of Christ – Mal 4v2) 2) The *sign* of the 'rainbow' (Noah) or 'circumcision' (Abraham) is given to bring to remembrance a covenant (Gen 9 and 17v13) 3) The *sign* of the Sabbath, which is *strictly* for Israel in application, as no Gentile was ever commanded to observe it in either Testament *until* the Millennium (Ex 31v13-17, Col 2v16) 4) The *sign* of the Virgin Birth (Isa 7v14), which would be signified in the constellations by 'Virgo' (the Virgin) 5) The *sign* of Christ (which was the *only sign* that He gave a wicked generation, and is said to be a *sign* 'which shall be spoken against' – Mat 12v39+40, Luke 2v30-35). This *sign* is the *sign* of Jonah the prophet, who strangely enough, fits the requirements of a Jewish remnant who will be in the Tribulation, *preaching* to Gentiles. But how this *sign* can be seen in heaven is a problem that has yet to be worked out. Simeon mentions '**a sword**' in connection with the *sign* in Luke 2v34+35, and since this sword is a *soul-piercing sword* (Heb 4v12), it may have reference to the word of God at Armageddon (Rev 19v13+15) – Very interesting! '**The sign of the Son of man in heaven**' has yet to be found.

'**And he shall send his angels with a great sound of a trumpet**' (v31) *This* trumpet will be the 7th in Rev 11v15, and since it occurs *immediately after the Tribulation* (in the passage in Revelation as well as here), then the *angels* present are those coming *with* Christ, who have already been transformed at the Rapture *preceding* the Tribulation. Notice the teaching – 1 Thes 4v13-17 shows that Christians will be **caught out before** the Tribulation (1 Thes 5). 1 John 3 + Phil 3v20+21 show that they will be like Christ when this takes place. Christ IS 'the Angel of the Lord' (Gal 4v14), therefore, the members of the Body of Christ at His return are '**as the angels of God in heaven**' (Mat 22v30). Reinforcement of this teaching is found in 2 Thes 1v7-10, Jude 14, Deut 33v2, Ps 68v17, Mat 22v30 etc.

'**Gather together his elect**' – This passage has been mistakenly applied to the church on numerous occasions and the occasions have been multiplied till non-studious 'preachers/teachers' (Anderson, Hovind et al.) are now teaching that the Church will go *through* the Tribulation because of v29. The erroneous preacher will even run to Heb 9v28 (which also *applies* to the end of the Tribulation) and teach a 'partial' Rapture in the age of grace. (*Not all the clowns are in the circus! Many of them (clowns) are IN pulpits!*) Now the interpretation of the text is found in Zech 2v5+6, Isa 45v4 +27v13 (65v9-12) + 28v4, there is no need to 'botch' the thing up running around in 1 Thes 4 and 1 Cor 15. Remember, **the Book of Revelation opens the OT and the OT opens Mat 24.** Mat 24 is *not* connected *doctrinally* with the Pauline Epistles dealing with the Rapture of the Church. The *doctrine* is Israel's.

'**From one end of heaven to the other**' – Note, there are *three* Heavens in Scripture. (One where the birds fly, one where the stars shine and one where God sits – 2 Cor 12v2) Note also, that the 'heavens' in Mat 24v29 is *different* from the 'heaven' of Mat 24v31. Furthermore, the expression **'four winds'** is used as it is found in Rev 7v1, and here the *context* is *the earth*, *not* the solar system or the moon. The summation of the teaching found in Mat 24v29-31 is that there will be a Rapture at THE END of the Tribulation (Rev 11v11+12). This Rapture is of Jewish saints (Ps 50v2-5) occurring at the undetermined interval (see notes on Mat 24v22) *before* the Battle of Armageddon (Isa 26v20+21). It is comparable with the Feast of Tabernacles in the OT (Lev 23) and *completes* the *third* and *final* part of the *first* resurrection: the other *two parts* being OT saints at the Feast of Unleavened Bread (Deut 16v16), and NT saints at Pentecost, the Feast of Weeks (Deut 16v16).

Indications are that this *Post-Tribulation* Rapture of dead and living saints (typified by Moses and Elijah), will occur 40 days to 6 months *before* the actual Advent itself – '**but the end is not yet**' (Mat 24v6).

We now approach a parable that deals with Israel in the END TIME. **Read Mat 24v32-35** – '**Now learn a parable**' – that is, 'get it!' Don't say it is '*figurative, obscure or teaches a general truth*' – Get it! There is not one parable in the Bible given to illustrate a '*general truth*' – this is pure scholastic *hogwash* taught by Bible 'correctors and rejectors'. Every parable interpreted (Jesus interprets two in Mat 13) has an *exact, specific* meaning to *every detail* - e.g. '**The sower is the Son of Man**', '**The good seed are the children of the kingdom**', '**The seed is the word of God**', '**The field is the world**', '**These are they by the wayside**' etc.

Any 'system' of interpretation other than a PRE-Millennial system will so handicap the 'scholar' that when he gets to the Kingdom parables in Mat 13, 20, 22+25, he *cannot* find a meaning to every detail; therefore he hobbles out with one leg shorter than the other (Prov 26v7). '**Now learn a parable**' – *learn it!* Don't run back to 'THE Greek' (there isn't one) to try to *prove* your ignorance.

'**The fig tree**' – Again, no need to run back to 'THE Greek' *again* (there isn't one), since the Bible is self-interpreting, we just have to seek the Holy Spirit to reveal the truth to us – 1 John 2v26+27. The 'fig tree' is the tree of self-righteousness (Luke 18v9, Luke 16v15, 1 Sam 16v7, Phil 3v9, Isa 64v6, Rom 10v3, 2 Pet 2v10+12-18 etc.) It is the only tree that God ever cursed. (Gen 3, Mat 21v19+20). It stands for *religious* Israel without the fruit (Jer 24v2+5+8), exactly as it stood in Eden for man's attempt to cover *his righteousness* with *dead works* and no fruit (Luke 13v6-9). Where Jesus says '**the fig tree, and all the trees**' (Luke 21v29) the reference is to all nations. The parable, then, speaks of the revival of national Israel. The first part of the parable is to observe the sign of 'nationalism', and in particular, the *beginning* of Israel as one of the nations yet unable to put forth *fruit* that will please God (John 15v1-6). '**When his branch is yet tender**'. We must find some place in history where Israel *begins as a nation*. This cannot be Exod 15, 20, or 40, as this is *past*. It cannot be Joshua 24, Judges 13, 1 Sam 15, or 2 Sam 1-3, for this is *past*, and it cannot be the restoration under Ezra, Zerubbabel or Nehemiah for this is *past*. It will have to be a **second restoration after** 70 A.D. This amazing prophecy is found in Isa 11v11 and Jer 3v18 and 16v14. It was fulfilled *in our generation*, 1948, with both A-Millennialists and Post-Millennialists, watching and neither believing what was taking place right in front of their eyes. The branch is tender now. '**Now learn a parable of the fig tree**' – *learn it!*

Trees in the OT are likened to 'Kings and Kingdoms' (Jud 9v7-14, Ezek 15, 17, 19, 31, Dan 4) The 'Fig Tree' is Israel, and the 'trees' are the other *nations* non-designated, exactly as outside of Christ or Israel, there are *only Gentiles* (heathen, not saved).

'**...and putteth forth leaves, ye know that summer is nigh**' (v32) The audience could not miss the illustration, for not a day earlier they had seen a fig tree with leaves, and the time that they saw it was the Jewish first month (March-April). They knew that summer was only two months away. The

Song of Solomon has an interesting addition to these facts in Chapter 2 (S of S 2v10-13). Notice the appearance of the *fig tree*, and this time it is bearing fruit. The Rapture is found in the passage – S of S 2v10+11.

'So likewise ye, when ye shall see all these things, know that it is near, even at the doors.' (v33) The **'THESE THINGS'** will have to refer to the events in vs 15+19+21+24+27+29+31. **'know that it is near, even at the doors.'** 'IT' in **'that IT is near'** can *only* refer to the Second Advent. That is, 'When you see the events taking place that I have just described, you can be *certain* that the end of the age and *my* coming (Mat 24v3) are *just around the corner* – They are *right at the doors'*.

'Verily I say unto you, This generation shall not pass, till all these things be fulfilled.' (v34) – Now we are in a tight spot again... 'WHICH generation?' (Key – '**this generation**' *never* refers to Israel as a race anywhere in the Bible) Here we go... **'This generation'** means **'THIS generation!'** (How's that for *deep!*) **'THIS generation'** (that sees all these things, v33) **'shall not pass till all these things'** (v29-31) **'BE FULFILLED!'** The implication is thrilling! The unbelieving Jew who goes back to Palestine and sees the establishment of Israel as a nation (1948) will be *in the generation that sees the Advent!* **The Believing Christian who lives to see it (1948) will be *in the generation that is caught out before the Advent!***

How long is a generation? According to the standard set down in Gen 15v13, a generation is an even 100 years. According to Moses, in Ps 90, it is 70 years. According to the passage in Mat 1v17, it is about 42 years. By this system of figuring, a man *born* in 1948 would certainly live to *see* the Rapture and the Advent! *The exact date cannot be fixed, since there is no way to ascertain the reliability of the calendar since Pope Gregory fooled with it.* At any rate, it is clear that the generation that sees the events described in v14-28 will undoubtedly live to see the Advent of Jesus. This generation is described as the generation that is alive and sees the budding of the fig tree, the leaf-blossoming of National Israel. This date can be fixed with certainty – 1948 A.D. So there are certain 'signs' we are to look for preceding the Rapture – read 1 Thes 5v1-7 + Luke 12v54-57.

'Heaven and earth shall pass away, but my words shall not pass away.' (v35) – Did you get that Bible 'corrector and rejector'; His words will *never* pass away. (Read Ps 12v6+7) The word is settled in Heaven (Ps 119v89). Now we could spend our lifetime discussing this subject, but suffice to say, we believe God when He said that He would *preserve* them and we know 'where' they are i.e. in the Authorized Version Bible (aka KJV). Now that my friend is the end of the argument; you believe what you want, we know. (For more details see our website)

Read Mat 24v36-41 – **'Knoweth no man, no, not the angels of heaven'** – The thing that is *unknown* is the **'day and hour'** of the Advent.

'The days of Noe' – It has already been mentioned that Mat 24 deals primarily with the future Tribulation, in a Jewish setting, and the *proof* of this lies also in the constant use of the expression **'Son of man'** (which is *not* the designation for the Saviour in relation to the Christian, awaiting the Rapture. Paul doesn't use it in any of his Epistles, with the exception of 'Hebrews' – get it...? Jewish!) However, in this passage between the paragraphs (v26+41), there may be some reference to the Church Age. If this seems to be 'heresy', remember that there is a knowledge of a *Gentile conversion period before* the Tribulation – Mat 12v18-21. The Tribulation passages do not occur until v22-45 in Mat 12. Another thing that adds weight to the application is the fact that Enoch, a Gentile, is 'caught out' *before* the flood (Gen 5), and since he is the *only* man in the Bible who has *never* died and will *never* die, he *cannot* represent a Tribulation saint, either Jew or Gentile – he will have to represent the Body of Christ caught out. (John 11v26 + 1 Cor 15v50-53)

That isn't all – Noah preserves 'animals' through the flood and animals are stated to be 'Gentiles' (see Acts 10v12+15+16+19, Mat 15v26) The passage in Mat 24v37 *may have* some reference to the end of the Church Age. It is certain that the '**one shall be taken, and the other left**' in Luke 17v34-37 *cannot* be the Church Age, for the '**days of Lot**' are said to be '**in the day when the Son of Man is REVEALED**' (Luke 17v30) Luke 17v37 further identifies the place and time of the passage as the END of the Tribulation. But the '**days of Noe**' are said merely to be '**the DAYS of the Son of man**' (Luke 17v26); there can be an *overlapping* into the Church Age, and there probably is. (We are *not* Hyper-dispensational as some are – Eve is a type of the Church in Gen 2+3 before Paul's mother knew she was going to have a baby) The passage, then, in Mat 24v37-41 can have some application to the Rapture, by virtue of the other things involved in the rest of the Bible. If Noah's flood is a 'type' of the Tribulation, then the '**days of Noe**' are found in Gen 4-6; so if we are on the eve of the Rapture (and I believe we are) we should be paying heed to Gen 4-6. If there is application, then the ones *taken* are those *saved*, while those *left* are left to judgment. In the days of Lot, the reverse is true; *those taken* are *killed*, those *left* are as Lot. Thus the Lord gives a picture of *both ends of the Tribulation* – Noah at the END of the Church Age; Lot at the END of Daniel's 70th week.

Read Mat 24v42-44 – The exhortation again is for the *hour* (v36+42+44) and the DAY (v50). Mark cuts it further to *watches* (Mark 13v34+35, 13v22). The context is still Jewish at THE END of the Tribulation, and is confirmed by Luke's statement in Luke 12v36, where the Lord is said to be *returning from a wedding* (Mat 25v11). Since the marriage of the Lamb (2 Cor 11v1-4, Ps 45, S of S 6, Rev 19v6-10) takes place *after* the Rapture and *before* the Advent, then it is certain that the expression '**return from the wedding**' (Luke 12v36) is a reference to the servant waiting for his Lord to return at the Advent, *not* the Rapture. (Many Christians mess up their doctrine regarding the 'virgins' in Mat 25, making out that this is the Church waiting for the Rapture to get married; yet *none* of these virgins *are* Christians, *none* are getting married, *none* are the bride, *none* marry the bridegroom, and *none* get the oil *free by grace*). In Mat 24v42-44, the Son of Man is likened to a 'thief' (He is crucified between two thieves) and His coming is a *night-time* coming, to a *house* where the *goodman* of the house is sleeping instead of watching (1 Thes 5v1-5). The applications therefore are numerous. Historically, the Advent could have occurred before Acts 7, and therefore the day and hour are unknown to Christ until *after* His ascension (Acts 1). Spiritually speaking, the Lord can come **anytime**, therefore we should *watch* and not get sleepy (1 Thes 5v1-10). Doctrinally, we find *four* watches in a Jewish night, representing 500 years apiece in the Church Age; Christ's departure being as the sun going down (John 11v9+10) and His return as the Sun coming up (Mal 4v2). The first watch ends at 9pm with Pope Gregory the Great; the second watch ends at midnight with the Crusades; the third ends at 1500 with Martin Luther; the Christian is *now* in the *fourth* watch – knowing the times and seasons perfectly, and is awaiting the *rise* of the DAY STAR (2 Pet 1v19). He *knows* in what watch his Lord is coming, although he does *not* know the *day* or the *hour* (Mat 14v25). This of course, all lies hidden until the writing of the Pauline Epistles and could have remained dormant and unfulfilled if the Jews had received Stephen's message (Acts 7) and brought on the deliverance of Israel from Rome by a bloody and vengeful Advent from Heaven.

Read Mat 24v45-51 – The man discussed here is a servant, *not* a 'friend' (John 15v15). He is waiting for the Lord to return at the Advent *not* the Rapture. He has the possibility of losing 'salvation' and he *loses it*. (You *can* lose your salvation *in* the Tribulation). Facing Mat 24v45-51, the Lord is 'his lord', and 'My Lord' and the man is *in* the household, and the Lord is 'the Lord of *that* servant', and the servant *does* go to Hell at the Second Advent, *not* the Rapture. (Notice the same excuses in Mat 25v20-30). The man *loses* it. Let us consider a few facts here before moving on...

1) No man from Adam to Christ is *born again*.

2) The *new birth* begins with the regenerating work of the Holy Spirit (John 3v3-6, Titus 3v5,

Rom 8v14-17)

3) John the Baptist ends a line '**born of women**' – Mat 11, Luke 16v16

4) The *new birth* brings in a *dispensation* in which the believer is made an *organic part* of Jesus Christ (1 Cor 12, Gal 3, Eph 5)

5) As being IN Christ (2 Cor 5v17, Col 2v10, Rom 7v1-4), the believer is part of the *body* that is *eternally* secure – John 14v16+17, 1 Cor 1v8+9 etc.

6) There is no indication, whatsoever, that under the Law (Exo 20 – Acts 2) *any believer* apart from David (!) had this *security*, nor is there any indication that *any believer will have it 'after'* the Body of Christ is raptured.

7) To the contrary, every verse which deals with the Jewish *dispensation*, that follows the Church Age, indicates that *faith* and *works* justify, and that *works* are not only a part of the fruit of salvation, but part of the *operation* that *justifies the man.* – Read the following verses *in context without any preconceived ideas...* Rev 12v17, Rev 14v12, James 1v1, 2v24, 5v19+20, Mat 25v1-9, 25v26+30, Heb 3v6+14, 6v4-6, 10v26-31!

8) Notice that in the last reference (Heb 10v25-31), **there is not one reference to a born-again Believer!** The name of the *book* gives the clue. Right in front of your eyes (v30) is the quotation from Deut 32v35+36, with *his people defined* as it is defined anywhere in the Bible – **Israel**, not the Body of Christ.

9) There is *not* a verse in the Bible that teaches that a man *can lose it* (salvation), which does not fit perfectly into Daniel's 70th Week, without anyone distorting anything in the verse.

A man who believes the Book, understands that the *servant* of Mat 24v46-51 *had it, and lost it* (salvation). He did *not* 'endure to the end' as instructed – See Mat 24v13 *in the context*. His oil *ran out*. The *servant* in Mat 24v51 *had it* in the Tribulation, and missed the calculation on the end of the *seven years* (see notes on Mat 24v6+22), and *lost it* (i.e. salvation), and *went to hell.* Not being IN Christ (and unable to get IN Christ, because the Body of Christ has *left* at the Rapture), the Believer in the Tribulation (see Rev 6+7) **is saved by faith and works**, and his *works* must hold up till the END of the Tribulation, even unto death. This period, then, is *not today*, '**the day of salvation**', it is *not* '**the day of grace**', and it is *not* '**the dispensation of the Gospel of the grace of God**'. It is an OT, legal, Jewish *dispensation* in Daniel's 70th Week, where the Archangel Michael stands up for Israel (Dan 12). *More than 50* verses in the NT refer to this *losing of salvation*, by a man who does *not* 'hold out faithful' – **none of them** are targeted at the Christian **IN** Christ.

Helpful note – **The ENTIRE Bible is NOT written to be *taught as Church-doctrine* to NT Believers between Pentecost and the Rapture!** (Get that and you have learnt a great deal!) The *entire* Bible is for comfort, learning and *examples* TO the Christian – Rom 15v4, 1 Cor 10v8-14 etc. The Bible Believing Christian IS PRE-Millennial, PRE-Wrath and PRE-Tribulation; He understands that the *only* way to truly understand the Scriptures is to read them **dispensationally** and *rightly divide* them. The Calvinist along with all other sects and cults, change, distort, pervert, add, subtract, *run to the Greek* etc. to try to get the Bible to line up with their man-made heresies. We will *never* do that. Like I said, there is a massive difference between a Bible *believer* and a 'Christian' today. We are living in the very last days before the Rapture and the majority of Christians don't realise it, and *couldn't care less!* **Amos 8v11+12.**

Prophecy

Isaiah's prophecies have mainly to do with the Messiah and Israel. **Jeremiah** is the Prophet of Israel's return to their own land. **Ezekiel** has to do with the Restoration of Israel to their own land, and with the Millennial Land, Restored Temple, and the form of worship. **Daniel** is the Prophet of the Gentiles and their final great leader – Antichrist. **Zechariah** is most concerned about the events that shall happen at the Second Coming of Christ, as…

1) Antichrist – The Idol Shepherd – Zech 11v15-17
2) Armageddon – Zech 14v1-3
3) Conversion of Israel – Zech 12v9-14
4) Christ's return to Olivet – Zech 14v4-11
5) Old Age in Jerusalem – Zech 8v3-8
6) Feast of Tabernacles – Zech 14v16-21

Scriptures telling us that Jesus Christ is coming AGAIN – Mat 16v27, Mat 25v13+31+32, John 14v2+3, John 21v22, Acts 1v10+11, Phil 3v20+21, Titus 2v13, Heb 9v28, James 5v7, 2 Pet 1v16, Jude 14+15, 1 John 2v28, Rev 1v7, 1 Cor 11v26, John 21v21-23, Luke 21v24-28 etc.

NOTES

NOTES

THE RAPTURE AND SECOND COMING OF JESUS CHRIST

First and Second Advents

In Mark 11v9+10, a promise of the Second Advent is being fulfilled (Zech 9v8-10). The Son of David' (Mat 22v42) is coming 'in the name of the Lord' (cf. Mat 23v39) to offer the *earthly, visible, literal, physical, Davidic kingdom*. The first and second Advents are spoken of together in the OT and the Gospels, and *the gap between them* is *not* revealed until *after* Acts 7 (See Eph 3v1-6).

The Second Advent – 'variable'

Mark 12v33 - At this point in time, the date of the Second Advent was variable because it was dependent on the decisions of the Sanhedrin (Acts 7v55+56 - Jesus is *standing* here, *ready to return if accepted* (cf. Mark 14v62) Stephen's statement about Christ's standing (v56) is what finally set the Pharisees off, after already being enraged enough to kill him, for Stephen was quoting what Jesus said when the Jews 'slapped' and mocked Him (Mark 14v62-65)).

The Rapture and the 2ⁿᵈ Advent are *not* the same

If it says in one place that it is a mystery, a moment, in the twinkling of an eye (1 Cor 15v51+52), and in *another place* that it is a visible coming with clouds to the unsaved people (Rev 1v7), then the **two** are **not** the same, *because* they are **not** the same, *did you get that?* The first time Jesus Christ came He appeared privately, secretly, alone at night to His chosen disciples, in a manger. He appeared to the shepherds, His mother and stepfather or foster father - *not* His real Father (Luke 2v33 KJV cf. NIV). He appeared to Joseph, Mary, and the shepherds. The *second* time He comes He will appear privately, in a mystery, in the twinkling of an eye, and catch out *saved* people only. The first time He came He appeared *publicly*, *thirty years after* His birth, at the ministry of John the Baptist, to His *enemies*. At the 2ⁿᵈ Coming He will appear publicly, openly to His enemies, seven years *after* the Rapture, seven years *after* His private appearance. Things *different* are *not* equal. When Jesus Christ arose from the dead, He appeared *only* to saved people. There isn't one unsaved person who ever saw His birth or His resurrection. *Did you get that?* Now I am expecting the Lord Jesus Christ to return anytime and I mean *anytime*. It could be this moment and if it isn't today, it is only because of the grace of God i.e. 2 Pet 3v9 **The Lord is not slack concerning his promise, as some men count slackness; but is longsuffering to us-ward, not willing that any should perish, but that all should come to repentance.** I wonder who will be the last one saved before the Lord returns?

The Path of the Second Advent

Isa 19v1 **The burden of Egypt. Behold, the LORD rideth upon a swift cloud, and shall come into Egypt: and the idols of Egypt shall be moved at his presence, and the heart of Egypt shall melt in the midst of it**. The order of God's judgments at the Second Advent seem to be arranged with God coming 'from the north' (Isa 14v31) to Damascus (Isa 17v1) in Syria (Amos 1v5) then down to Tyre (Amos 1v10). From Tyre He goes down and hits Armageddon (Zech 12v11). Then He travels down the 'Gaza Strip' where the original 'Palestinians' (Philistines) lived and wipes out the modern Palestinians. From there, He goes into Egypt (here in the verse) and makes a 'U-turn' at Sinai (Deut 33v2). Then He goes up into Edom (Amos 1v11); through Moab (Jer 48); across the Jordan where the ark of the covenant, Joshua, David, Elijah, and Elisha crossed, and where Christ was baptized; and then lands on the Mount of Olives at Jerusalem (Zech 14v4) in Judah (Amos 2v4). This is our Saviour coming back... *and we are with Him!*

50 Evidences for the Pre-Trib Rapture

(Article from the Internet)

Historical Doctrine of Imminency

1. The early church believed in the imminency of the Lord's return. While it can be debated which church father said what, there is a consistency in the early church on imminency which is essential to the Pre-Trib position and in opposition to some other positions.

2. The Pre-Trib position is the *only* one which truly teaches imminency.

3. The fact that there is a greater development of the doctrine in recent centuries does not preclude it from the early centuries. In the very early years of the church you see the development of great fundamental doctrines of Trinity, Deity, God-Man, canon of Scripture, etc. Following those early church councils is a time of decline of the corporate church into great apostasy. The teachings of that time are built on many of the heresies of Augustine. When the Reformation comes, there is a period of re-establishing the foundational doctrine of salvation. Now, in these last days there is both an ability and a need in the church to better understand the doctrines of eschatology and the Spirit is continuing His ministry of guiding the church into all truth.

4. The exhortation to be comforted by the 'coming of the Lord' (1 Thes 4v18) is valid only in the context of the Pre-Trib view. It could even be a fearsome thing in a Post-Trib view.

5. We are exhorted to look for the 'Glorious Appearing of our Lord and Saviour Jesus Christ' (Titus 2v13). If there are any prophetic events (i.e., Tribulation) to come first, then this passage is nonsensical.

6. Again, we are to 'purify ourselves' in view of his coming (1 John 3v2-3). If His coming is not imminent then the passage is meaningless.

7. The church is told 'only' to look for the Coming of Christ. It is Israel and the tribulation saints that are told to look for signs.

Nature of the Church

(Those who do not understand the nature of the church as unique in the program of God will continually be confused about the nature of His coming for the church.)

8. The translation of the church is never mentioned in any context dealing with the Second Coming of Christ at the end of the Tribulation.

9. The church is 'not appointed to wrath' (Rom 5v9, 1 Thes 1v9-10). The church cannot enter into the 'great day of their wrath.'

10. The church will not be 'overtaken by the Day of the Lord' (1 Thes 5v1-9). Day of the Lord is another term for the Great Tribulation.

11. The church will be 'kept from the hour of testing that shall come upon all the world' (Rev 3v10).

12. The believer will escape the Tribulation (Luke 21v36).

13. It is in the character of God to deliver His own from the greatest times of trial (Lot, Rahab, Israel, Noah, etc.).

14. It is clear that there is a time interval between the translation of the church and the Return of Christ (John 14v3).

15. Only the Pre-Trib position does not divide the Body of Christ on a works principle as does partial Rapture so clearly and others to a lesser extent. It becomes a climactic finale to the grand plan of salvation by grace alone.

16. The Scriptures are adamant that the church is undivided. In this age the church is divided by the continuing old nature in the believers. When we are glorified at the coming of Christ, the church is no more divided.

17. The godly remnant of the Tribulation has the attributes seen in OT Israel and not the church. The church is not present in the prophecies of Revelation.

18. The Pre-Trib view, unlike the Post-Trib view, does not confuse terms like *elect* and *saints* which apply to believers of all ages, as opposed to terms like church and *in Christ*, which apply only to those who are the Body of Christ in this age.

The Work of the Holy Spirit

19. The Holy Spirit is the Restrainer of evil in the world. He cannot be taken out as prophesied unless the church which is indwelt by the Holy Spirit is taken out.

20. The Holy Spirit will be taken out before the 'lawless one' is revealed. That lawless one will certainly be revealed in the tribulation. In fact, the tribulation begins with the signing of the covenant between that lawless one and Israel. That act will reveal him.

21. The 'falling away' in 2 Thes 2v3 would better be understood in its context as 'the departure.' This is a reference to the departure of the Holy Spirit as He indwells the church.

22. The work of the Holy Spirit making the church like Christ where they submit to death and persecution, whereas the OT saints (see many of the Psalms) and the Tribulation saints cry out for vengeance (Rev 6v10).

The Hermeneutical Argument

23. Only the Pre-Trib view allows for a truly literal interpretation in all of the OT and NT passages regarding the Great Tribulation.

24. Only the Pre-Trib position clearly distinguishes the church and Israel and God's dealing with each, and the necessity of an interval of time between the Rapture and the Second Coming.

25. All believers must appear before the Judgment Seat of Christ (2 Cor 5v10). This event is never mentioned in the account of events surrounding the Second Coming.

26. The 'four and twenty elders' in Rev 4v1 - 5v14 are representative of the church. Therefore it is necessary that the church, undivided, be brought to glory before those events of the tribulation.

27. There is clearly a coming of Christ for his bride before the Second Coming to earth (Rev 19v7-10).

28. Tribulation saints are not translated at the Second Coming of Christ but carry on ordinary activities. These specifically include farming, construction, and giving birth (Isa 65v20-25).

29. The Judgment of the Gentile nations following the Second Coming (Mat 25v31-46) indicates that both the saved and the lost are in a natural body which would be impossible if the translation had taken place at the Second Coming.

30. If the translation took place at the same time as the Second Coming, there would be no need to separate the sheep from the goats at the subsequent judgment. The act of the translation would be the separation.

31. The Judgment of Israel (Ezek 20v34-38) occurs after the Second Coming and requires a regathered Israel. Again, the separation of the saved and the lost would be unnecessary if all the saved had previously been separated by a translation at the Second Coming.

Differences between the Rapture and the Second Coming

32. At the Rapture, the church meets Christ in the air. At the Second Coming, Christ returns to the Mt. of Olives.

33. At the time of the Rapture, the Mt. of Olives is unchanged. At the Second Coming it is divided, forming a valley east of Jerusalem.

34. At the time of the Rapture, saints are translated. No saints are translated at the time of the Second Coming.

35. At the time of the Rapture, the world is not judged for sin, but descends deeper into sin. At the Second Coming, the world is judged by the King of kings.

36. The translation of the church is pictured as a deliverance from the day of wrath, whereas the coming of Christ is a deliverance for those who have suffered under severe tribulation.

37. The Rapture is imminent whereas there are specific signs which precede the Second Coming.

38. The translation of living believers is a truth revealed only in the NT. The Second Coming with the events surrounding it is prominent in both the OT and NT.

39. The Rapture is only for the saved, while the tribulation and Second Coming deals with the entire world.

40. No unfulfilled prophecy stands between the church and the Rapture. Many signs must be fulfilled before the Second Coming of Christ.

41. No passage in either OT or NT deals with the resurrection of the saints at the Second Coming nor mentions the translation of living saints at that same time.

The Nature of the Tribulation

42. Only the Pre-Trib view maintains the distinction between the 'Great Tribulation' and the tribulations in general which we all experience.

43. The Great Tribulation is properly understood in the Pre-Trib view as a preparation for the

RAPTURE

restoration of Israel (Deut 4v29+30, Jer 30v4-11, Dan 9v24-27, Dan 12v1-2).

44. Not one single passage in the OT which discusses the Tribulation, mentions the church.

45. Not one single passage in the NT which discusses the Tribulation, mentions the church.

46. In contrast to Mid-Trib or Pre-Wrath views, the Pre-Trib view offers an adequate explanation for the beginning of the Great Tribulation in Rev 6. These others are clearly refuted by the plain teaching of Scripture that the Great Tribulation begins long before the 7th trumpet of Rev 11.

47. There is no proper groundwork providing that the 7th trumpet of Rev is the last trumpet of 1 Cor 15. It is accepted only on the basis of assumption. The Pre-Trib view maintains the proper distinction between the prophetic trumpets of the church and the trumpets of the Tribulation.

48. The unity of Daniel's 70th week is maintained by the Pre-Trib view. By contrast, the Mid-Trib view destroys the unity and confuses the program for Israel and the church. The Post-Trib view usually denies the clear teaching of the 70 weeks by subverting it into some form or another of allegory.

49. The gathering of saints after the Tribulation is done by angels whereas the gathering of the church is done by 'The Lord Himself.'

50. Rev 22v17-20 And the Spirit and the Bride say, Come. And let him that heareth say, Come ... He which testifieth these things saith:

'Surely, I come quickly. AMEN. Even so, come, LORD JESUS.

Separation by a comma or semicolon

Gen 3v15 **And I will put enmity between thee and the woman, and between thy seed and her seed; it shall bruise thy head, and thou shalt bruise his heel.** The man has the 'seed'. This is a prophecy regarding the virgin birth, where a man's seed is *not* involved. All Bible 'correctors' make Christ 'bruise' the serpent's head on Calvary, but this is error. It doesn't take place until the Second Advent (Ps 68v21, Jer 23v19, Hab 3v13). Here in Gen 3v15 we have *both* Advents prophesied: everything down to 'her seed' is the *first* Advent. Everything after that is the *Second* Advent.

Gen 49v11 **Binding his foal unto the vine, and his ass's colt unto the choice vine; he washed his garments in wine, and his clothes in the blood of grapes:** - This is the second time that the First and Second Advent of Jesus Christ in the OT are separated by a comma or semicolon, including a two-thousand year interval.

Gen 49v24 **But his bow abode in strength, and the arms of his hands were made strong by the hands of the mighty God of Jacob; (from thence is the shepherd, the stone of Israel:)** The two Advents are separated by a comma. First Advent – 'the shepherd', Second Advent – 'the smiting, crushing stone of Dan 2.' Here are some more places in the Scriptures where the two Advents are divided by a verse or by punctuation – Hosea 2v13+14, 3v4+5, Ps 118v22-25, Lam 4v20-22, Isa 53v10, Amos 9v10+11, Zech 9v9+10, Luke 21v24, 1 Pet 1v11, Hab 2v13+14, Mic 5v2+3, Zeph 3v7+8.

The Second Coming of Christ

You can tell what state the church is *really* in today by the lack of emphasis it puts on the return of Jesus Christ; hardly any church these days preaches on the imminent return of Jesus Christ. When was the last time you heard a sermon on the Rapture? *Why do you think this is?* John 14v3 **And if I go and prepare a place for you, I will come again, and receive you unto myself; that where I am,**

there ye may be also. The church is so comfortable down here that it doesn't want the Lord Jesus Christ to come back and take it to Heaven to be with Him forever… does it? *Don't kid me!* I talk to Christians, correspond with Christians… I know Christians. The majority of Christians I have met, *do not want* the Lord to return just yet.

1) Without the 2nd Advent the Lord's Supper is meaningless - 1 Cor 11v26

2) Without the 2nd Advent your redemption is incomplete (Rom 8v29) because your body has not been 'saved' yet. It is *saved* at the Advent – Phil 3v20+21, 1 John 3v1-3

3) Without the 2nd Advent, none of the covenants with Israel are valid – Gen 15v18, Exo 19v3-8, 2 Sam 7v12-16 etc.

4) Without the 2nd Advent, no Christian will 'inherit' any Kingdom – Eph 5v5, 2 Tim 2v12, Col 3v24

5) Without the 2nd Advent there will *never* be any lasting peace on this earth – Ps 2v6-12, Ps 72v1-20, Ps 110v1-4, Isa 2v2-4, Isa 9v6+7, Isa 11v1-20, Dan 7v22-27

6) Without the 2nd Advent, 'nature' will never be delivered from the 'bondage of corruption' (Rom 8v19-22), that includes all vegetation and animals - Isa 11v4-9

Here are a few SIGNS for the 2nd Advent…

The return of the Jews to their land – Ezek 20v34, Isa 11v10-12

The rebirth of Israel – Isa 66v8

The appearance of a pure language – Hebrew - Zeph 3v8+9

The restoration of the Shekel as the standard Israeli currency by the Knesset in 1980

The cities of ancient Israel (Cana, Nazareth, Jericho etc.) being rebuilt – Ezek 36v10+22+25+38

The productivity of the land – Isa 27v6

Perfect irrigation – Isa 58v11+12

Trees are now growing in forests – Isa 41v19+20

The internet problem – the whole world is caught up in the 'net' - Ecc 9v12. via TV and computers

The rebuilding of the temple – 2 Thes 2v4, Rev 11v1+2

Fake peace treaties with the 'Palestinians' and Arabs – Dan 11v27

Unbelief and apostasy within the Body of Christ – 1 Tim 4v1-3, 2 Tim 3v1-9+13, 4v3+4, 1 Pet 2v1-3 etc.

Satanic Bible Per-versions – Jer 23v1-40, 2 Pet 3v16, 2 Cor 2v17 etc.

What will the 2nd Advent Accomplish?

The renovation of nature – Isa 35v1+2

The taming of wild animals – Isa 11v6-9

The resolution of the 'Jewish problem' – Zech 14v1-21

RAPTURE

The establishment of world peace – Isa 9v6+7, Mic 4v3+4

The abolition of *all* religions and 'sacred-scriptures/holy books' – Isa 2v2+3

The obliteration of the Roman Catholic Church – Rev 17-19

The fulfilment of 500 prophecies written 400-1,500 years before Christ

> Yet there is a work to be done now *before* the Lord returns
>
> Are you *involved* in the work?

The Lord is not slack concerning his promise, as some men count slackness; but is longsuffering to us-ward, not willing that any should perish, but that all should come to repentance. 2 Pet 3v9

By the way, when was the last time you heard a Roman Catholic talk about the return of Jesus Christ?

That's the last thing they want to happen!

Behold, he cometh with clouds; and every eye shall see him, and they also which pierced him: and all kindreds of the earth shall wail because of him. Even so, Amen.

Mathew, Acts and Hebrews are probably the most difficult books to understand *doctrinally* in the NT because they are 'transition-books'...

1) **Mathew** – Doctrinally you are moving from the OT (Mat 1-26) to the NT (Mat 27, Heb 9v15-17)

2) **Acts** – You are moving from Israel to the Church

3) **Hebrews** – You are moving from the Church Age into Daniel's 70th Week (aka Jacob's Trouble)

Read - 1 Thes 4v13-18

This is the 2nd greatest passage in the NT regarding the Rapture, the first is found in 1 Cor 15v51-54.

Other passages that speak of the Rapture are...

- 1 John 3v1-3
- Phil 3v20-21
- Rom 8v21-24
- John 11v24-26
- Rev 4v1+2

The word 'Rapture' does *not* occur in the English Bible but the dictionary definition certainly 'qualifies' it as to what will happen when the Lord returns.

Rapture - Websters 1828 Dictionary. 1) A seizing by violence. 2) Transport; ecstasy; violence of a pleasing passion; extreme joy or pleasure.

Rapture – Concise Oxford Dictionary. 1) A feeling of intense pleasure or joy. 2) (The Rapture) North American (according to some millenarian teaching) the transporting of believers to heaven at the Second Coming of Christ.

Origin - C16 (in the sense 'seizing and carrying off'): from obsolete French, or from Medieval Latin raptura 'seizing', partly influenced by rapt.

The word 'Rapture' means the state of being *carried away* or *carried off* – that is what is going to happen when the Lord Jesus Christ returns.

Many Christians do *not* understand the Rapture and therefore deny its teaching in the Scriptures. They believe in the Second Coming of Christ but not in the Rapture, yet the Rapture is connected with the Second Coming, but it's *different*.

1) Neither the resurrection of the dead or the Second Advent are 'mysteries' in the Bible. They are both clearly mentioned centuries *before* Christ shows up – Job 19v25-27 **For I know that my redeemer liveth, and that he shall stand at the latter day upon the earth: And though after my skin worms destroy this body, yet in my flesh shall I see God: Whom I shall see for myself, and mine eyes shall behold, and not another; though my reins be consumed within me.** Ecc 12v14 **For God shall bring every work into judgment, with every secret thing, whether it be good, or whether it be evil.** Also Ezek 37.

2) The Rapture is a *mystery* – 1 Cor 15v51 **Behold, I shew you a mystery; We shall not all sleep, but we shall all be changed,** unrevealed till *after* Pentecost.

3) The local churches and the Body of Christ are lukewarm at the end of the Church Age preceding the Rapture; they are *not* lukewarm at the end of the Tribulation – the Body of Christ is *not even there* – Rev 7v9 **After this I beheld, and, lo, a great multitude, which no man could number, of all nations, and kindreds, and people, and tongues, stood before the throne, and before the Lamb, clothed with white robes, and palms in their hands**; also Rev 3v10 **Because thou hast kept the word of my patience, I also will keep thee from the hour of temptation, which shall come upon all the world, to try them that dwell upon the earth.**

4) At the Advent, Christ lands *on the ground* - Zec 14v4 **And his feet shall stand in that day upon the mount of Olives, which is before Jerusalem on the east, and the mount of Olives shall cleave in the midst thereof toward the east and toward the west, and there shall be a very great valley; and half of the mountain shall remove toward the north, and half of it toward the south.** At the Rapture He comes in the AIR and does *not touch the ground* – 1 Thes 4v17 **Then we which are alive and remain shall be caught up together with them in the clouds, to meet the Lord in the air: and so shall we ever be with the Lord.**

5) At the Rapture there is no change in Satan's position: he doesn't get locked up in any 'pit' as he does at the Advent. There are no changes in nature at the Rapture. By the time of the Second Advent, nearly two-thirds of the world has been destroyed on both land and sea (Revelation chapters 6-18).

6) At the Rapture, Christ doesn't judge any Jews or any nations (as in Joel 2, Hosea 2, Jer 25, Mat 25). At the Advent, He judges the entire world... Mat 25v31+32, Ps 47v8, Ps 96v10-13, Isa 60v12.

7) None of His enemies are killed at the Rapture; more than 200,000,000 are killed at His 2nd Advent – Isa 63, Rev 9, Luke 19v27.

RAPTURE

So as you can see, there are *differences* between the Rapture and the Second Coming.

It has been said by some Christians (i.e. the 'Reformed' lot who follow the teachings of Luther, Calvin, Dabney, Hodge, Gill etc.) that the Rapture was 'invented' or 'started' by Darby, Scofield or Bullinger; It has also been alleged by some who oppose dispensational truth that J.N. Darby received (the truth of) the Pre-Tribulation Rapture from a demon-inspired Irvingite 'prophetess about 1832'. **There is not the slightest foundation in fact for this allegation!**

In 1830 J.N. Darby *understood* the Pre-Tribulation Rapture; he *understood* the **differences** between Israel and the Church – the Church has *not* 'replaced' Israel and God has *not* 'finished' with the Jews.

R.A. Huebner writes... In the 1800's E. Irving, at that time a Presbyterian clergyman, translated from the Spanish a long work by the Jesuit, Lacunza. This was printed in English in 1827. In March 1829, what we may call the Irvingite organ, 'The Morning Watch' (a magazine) was begun, putting forth the views of Irving and his followers concerning prophecy and their ideas on the restoration of gifts to the church. Demon possession and tongue-speaking began to take place in Irving's congregation, which was alleged to be the power of the Spirit. While under the power of demons certain persons in his congregation gave forth teachings on prophecy. It is alleged that these demon-inspired utterances are the source of the Pre-Tribulation Rapture. The charge was first made by S.P. Tregelles in 1864, he alleging the incident to have occurred about 1832 in E. Irving's church. The 'tongues' broke out first, not in Irving's congregation but in Scotland; and recently it was alleged that Miss M. MacDonald of Scotland put forth the Pre-Tribulation Rapture in 1830 while under the power of a demon.

Yet the Rapture of the Body of Christ was taught more than 1,500 years ago. It appears in the writings of Ephraem the Syrian... *'For all the saints and the elect of God are gathered **prior** to the Tribulation that is to come and are taken to the lord lest they see the confusion that is to overwhelm the world because of our sins'*.

Now how about that! That was a 'Premillennial Baptist Pre-Tribulation Rapture' letter from the **6th century AD** ascribed to Ephraem Syrus (306 to 373 AD). It was from a sermon on 'The Last Times, the Antichrist, and the End of the World' and it is cited in a footnote in Alexander's Byzantine Tradition, 1985, page 210.

The NT doctrine of the Rapture...

1) Stimulates (excites, creates enthusiasm / interest) loyalty – Luke 12v42 **And the Lord said, Who then is that faithful and wise steward, whom his lord shall make ruler over his household, to give them their portion of meat in due season?**

2) Stimulates a godly walk – Titus 2v11-13 **For the grace of God that bringeth salvation hath appeared to all men, Teaching us that, denying ungodliness and worldly lusts, we should live soberly, righteously, and godly, in this present world; Looking for that blessed hope, and the glorious appearing of the great God and our Saviour Jesus Christ;**

3) It is an antidote (something that counteracts an unpleasant feeling or situation) for worry – Phil 4v5+6 **Let your moderation be known unto all men. The Lord is at hand. Be careful for nothing; but in every thing by prayer and supplication with thanksgiving let your requests be made known unto God.**

4) Stimulates brotherly love – 1 Thes 3v12-13 **And the Lord make you to increase and abound in love one toward another, and toward all men, even as we do toward you: To the end he may**

stablish your hearts unblameable in holiness before God, even our Father, at the coming of our Lord Jesus Christ with all his saints.

5) Comforts the bereaved – 1 Thes 4v18 **Wherefore comfort one another with these words.**

6) Purifies the inner life – 1 John 3v1-3 **Behold, what manner of love the Father hath bestowed upon us, that we should be called the sons of God: therefore the world knoweth us not, because it knew him not. Beloved, now are we the sons of God, and it doth not yet appear what we shall be: but we know that, when he shall appear, we shall be like him; for we shall see him as he is. And every man that hath this hope in him purifieth himself, even as he is pure.**

7) Brings rewards – 2 Tim 4v8 **Henceforth there is laid up for me a crown of righteousness, which the Lord, the righteous judge, shall give me at that day: and not to me only, but unto all them also that love his appearing.**

8) Develops patience – James 5v7 **Be patient therefore, brethren, unto the coming of the Lord. Behold, the husbandman waiteth for the precious fruit of the earth, and hath long patience for it, until he receive the early and latter rain.**

It is *not* a comforting thought (1 Thes 4v18) to...

1) Think that you have got to go through the Tribulation

2) Or you must not take the mark of the beast (Rev 13)

3) Or you *must* endure to the end (Mat 24v13)

4) Or that 'works' will determine your salvation (Mat 25)

5) Or that more world wars are to take place – Rev 9v16, Rev 6v8, Joel 2, Isa 63 etc. That is *not* 'comfort'

Therefore it is another proof that the Christian is *not* going to go through the Tribulation (It is Jacob's Trouble – Jews not ours – Jer 30v7)

The Christian will *not* go through Rev 6 – 18.

1 Thes 1v10 **And to wait for his Son from heaven, whom he raised from the dead, even Jesus, which delivered us from the wrath to come.** I'm waiting for His Son *not* the Tribulation or a 'peace treaty' etc.

1 Thes 4v13 **But I would not have you to be ignorant, brethren, concerning them which are asleep, that ye sorrow not, even as others which have no hope.**

...that ye sorrow not, even as others which have no hope...

No hope! – Someone has drawn a picture of Hell and put a sign on the entrance saying *'Abandon all hope, ye who enter in!'* There is *no hope* in Hell.

All unsaved people have that one great tragic 'trait' (a distinguishing quality or characteristic) in common... *no hope*, but they don't realise it. Eph 2v12 **That at that time ye were without Christ, being aliens from the commonwealth of Israel, and strangers from the covenants of promise,**

RAPTURE

having no hope, and without God in the world: That is why all unsaved, highly educated people are 'positive thinkers'. They try to manufacture a hope while in a *hopeless* condition. Then they offer it to depraved sinners as a 'real' hope yet it is a *false* hope – 2 Pet 2v19 **While they promise them liberty, they themselves are the servants of corruption: for of whom a man is overcome, of the same is he brought in bondage.**

You see as a Christian we have all the hope in the world. 1 Thes 4v13 is talking about our dead loved ones. If they were saved, we shall see them again. Now what a great hope that is.

You have so much hope. No matter what happens, if you're a Christian, you are going to spend *eternity* with the Lord Jesus Christ in Heaven. 2 Cor 5v1-8 - What a hope friends.

1 Thes 4v14 - ...**even so them also which sleep in Jesus will God bring with him**. Now notice the *dead* Christian comes *with* Christ at the Rapture. This *cannot* refer to their bodies, for their bodies have rotted in the grave. Then it is their *souls* that come to get glorified bodies just like you will get if you are alive at that time (v15 **that we which are alive and remain unto the coming of the Lord**).

Now whenever the NT talks about the Christian 'sleeping' in regard to *death* (Mat 9v24, Mark 5v39, Luke 8v52, John 11v11, 1 Thes 4v14, Mat 27v52, 1 Cor 15v20 - The word 'slept' (e.g. slept with his fathers) occurs in 44 verses in the OT and 5 in the NT, it is *always* talking about his *body* never his *soul*. There is no such thing as soul-*sleep*. Notice in Mat 27v52... **many bodies of the saints which slept arose**,

Now the word 'bring' in 1 Thes 4v14 must imply a resurrection in order for God to *bring* them back *with* Jesus at His coming...

➢ The passage wasn't on His coming back to earth – 1 Thes 4v17

➢ The saints He brought *with* Him never *landed* on earth – Song of Sol 2v10

➢ They were up there *with* Him before any resurrection – 1 Thes 5v10

➢ All saints are *present with* the Lord after death – Phil 1v2+23

We will *not* go up to meet the Lord in the air *before* the dead bodies that 'slept' (v15) come out of the graveyards (i.e. battlefields, bottom of the ocean etc.)

1 Thes 4v16 - Note the word 'prevent' – meaning *pre-event* – *before* an event takes place as well as to *stop* an event from taking place.

For the Lord himself... not the Holy Spirit. This is the same Lord that went up in Acts 1... **shall descend from heaven with a SHOUT... the VOICE... and with the TRUMP of God**... Here we have three *noises*...

1. a voice
2. a shout
3. a trump

The 'trump' is the sound that a trumpet makes – 1 Cor 15v52 - It is *not* a 'trumpet' like the Angel's trumpet in Rev 8v6 (**And the seven angels which had the seven trumpets prepared themselves to sound.**)

Rev 11v15 is at *the end* of the Tribulation - **And the seventh angel sounded; and there were great voices in heaven, saying, The kingdoms of this world are become the kingdoms of our Lord, and of his Christ; and he shall reign for ever and ever**.

In 1 Thes 4v16 *no* angel blows *this* trump; it is called **the trump of God**.

Note how so many Christians confuse the trumpet in Rev 11v15 (**And the seventh angel sounded; and there were great voices in heaven, saying, The kingdoms of this world are become the kingdoms of our Lord, and of his Christ; and he shall reign for ever and ever.**) and Mat 24v31 (**And he shall send his angels with a great sound of a trumpet, and they shall gather together his elect from the four winds, from one end of heaven to the other.**) with the trumpet of 1 Cor 15v52 (**In a moment, in the twinkling of an eye, at the last trump: for the trumpet shall sound, and the dead shall be raised incorruptible, and we shall be changed.**) which is *the* trumpet, not one trumpet out of seven (Rev 8v6 - **And the seven angels which had the seven trumpets prepared themselves to sound.**)

The trump in 1 Thes 4v16 is God Himself *speaking* (the voice of the archangel). Look at what John said in Rev 4v1 - **After this I looked, and, behold, a door was opened in heaven: and the first voice which I heard was as it were of a trumpet talking with me; which said, Come up hither, and I will shew thee things which must be hereafter**. Also Rev 1v10 - **I was in the Spirit on the Lord's day, and heard behind me a great voice, as of a trumpet**,

It was a trumpet *talking*. Do you know what the trumpet *said*?

...come up hither!

I'm *listening* for a *sound*...

Rev 4v1 **After this I looked, and, behold, a door was opened in heaven: and the first voice which I heard was as it were of a trumpet talking with me; which said, Come up hither, and I will shew thee things which must be hereafter.** The words 'Come up hither' occur 3 times in Scripture; the other 2 being in Prov 25v7 + Rev 11v12.

This is interesting because there are three *main* Raptures in the Scriptures.

When we get to Revelation chapter 4 we have reached the end of the Church Age, typified by the seven messages to the seven churches in Asia Minor. Although these messages apply *historically* to seven local churches in 90 A.D. and *doctrinally* to local churches IN the 'Tribulation', they represent, in type, the history of the Church Age, which can be seen by comparison of the first church (Ephesus), with the last church (Laodicea).

The word 'church' disappears in Rev 3v22, and is *not* mentioned again from chapter 4 to chapter 19, then we see her in Heaven at the marriage supper of the Lamb.

Note also, the Holy Spirit is spoken of as being *in the midst* of the churches **on earth** in Rev 2 and 3. Yet, the Spirit (spoken of as seven Spirits) is found *up in the third Heaven* in Rev 4v5, indicating there has been both a change in the churches' position, and in the position of the Spirit.

Note also in Rev 4v1 a door opens – Heaven only opens *two* times in the Book of Revelation – once when somebody goes up, and in Rev 19 where somebody comes down. Notice that when the door is opened (Rev 4v1) there is a voice and a trumpet. If you will compare this passage with 1 Thes 4v15-18, there will be no doubt in your mind what the voice is, or what the trumpet is. This is the Lord calling somebody (in both passages), and they respond by ascending through the clouds.

RAPTURE

The Bible teaches 3 main 'Raptures'...

1) The Rapture of the **OT saints** at the resurrection of Christ (Mat 27v50-54, Eph 4v8-12)

2) The Rapture of the **NT saints** of the Church Age (1 Cor 15v49-53, 1 Thes 4v13-18)

3) The Rapture of **Tribulation saints** at the end of the Tribulation (Mat 24 and Rev 11v12)

This means that the 'first resurrection' is the first resurrection of *saved* people, and has *three* parts to it.

This corresponds to a *harvest* as that too has three parts to it... Paul illustrates this in 1 Cor 15 i.e. the chapter on the *resurrection* – 1 Cor 15v22-24 (**For as in Adam all die, even so in Christ shall all be made alive. But every man in his own order: Christ the firstfruits; afterward they that are Christ's at his coming. Then cometh the end, when he shall have delivered up the kingdom to God, even the Father; when he shall have put down all rule and all authority and power**) – the first resurrection has *three* parts to it just like a crop has three parts to it...

Every crop has...

1) **Firstfruits** – the first part which you pick when it gets ripe

2) **Harvest** – the main part that ripens later

3) **Gleanings** – the part that ripens at the end

Anyone who has grown tomatoes will understand this!

1 Cor 15v22 **For as in Adam all die, even so in Christ shall all be made alive.**

v23 **But every man in his own order: Christ the firstfruits** (plus the OT saints)**; afterward they that are Christ's at his coming.** (Rapture of the Church)

Firstfruits *then* the 'main' harvest – NT saints. (Firstfruits - **But now is Christ risen from the dead, and become the firstfruits of them that slept.** 1 Cor 15v20 – So of all the people back in the OT that all died and all passed away, HE was the first one of them to get out of the grave *permanently*. He is the firstfruit, 'the first begotten of the dead' (Rev 1v5), in that HE is the first man that ever came up from the dead *never to die again*.

Lazarus came up and died.

Jonah came up and died.

Eutychus came up and died.

Dorcas came up and died.

But Christ is the first man that came up *never to die again.*

Moses died and will come back and die again.

Elijah went up alive one time, but he will die later.

Enoch went up *without* dying. (The perfect example of a Raptured saint)

The *only* man that died and came up and will *never die again* is Jesus Christ! He is the *firstfruits!*)

24 **Then cometh the end** (*after you harvest you always have some gleanings left*)**, when he shall have delivered up the kingdom to God, even the Father; when he shall have put down all rule and all authority and power.**

25 **For he must reign** (Millennium)**, till he hath put all enemies under his feet.**

26 **The last enemy that shall be destroyed is death.** (i.e. Rev 20 at the end of the Millennium).

Remember '**Come up hither**' occurs *three* times in Scripture. These three references mark the *three* 'Raptures'.

1) Prov 25v7 would refer to the OT saints

2) Rev 4v1 – John being caught up – a type of the Bride of Christ i.e. the Rapture of the Church

3) Rev 11v12 – regarding Moses and Elijah, would refer to a Post-Tribulation Rapture of the Tribulation saints

The signal for the Rapture is a 'shout' from Heaven; up come the dead. (1 Cor 15v51-55 & John 11v25+26)

This signals the end of the church age – Dan 12v1+2 **And at that time shall Michael stand up, the great prince which standeth for the children of thy people: and there shall be a time of trouble, such as never was since there was a nation even to that same time: and at that time thy people shall be delivered, every one that shall be found written in the book. And many of them that sleep in the dust of the earth shall awake, some to everlasting life, and some to shame and everlasting contempt.** Michael is 'the Prince who stands for Israel'. He was the one who got the body of Moses (Jude 9), so Moses could show up on this earth immediately following the Rapture of the Body of Christ (Rev 4v1+2).

So at the Rapture up go the *bodies*. They are not like our bodies now, they are glorified bodies just like the one the Lord Jesus Christ had when he arose from the dead. Phil 3v20+21, Rom 8v29.

God's voice sounds like a trumpet (Rev 4v1+2). Zechariah is the one who tells us that this is *not* the seventh trumpet of Rev 11v15. Zech 9v14 ...**and the Lord GOD shall blow the trumpet...** *not* some angel.

Look at these interesting verses in Exo 19v16-19 regarding the *voice* of the trumpet.

What the unsaved hear is *thunder* - Job 37v1-4, John 12v28+29. We as Christians shall hear, *instead of thunder*, His voice calling His sheep... *John Edric Davis*, come up hither. John 10v3, John 10v14.

Moving on to 1 Thes 4v17 - This cannot be the Second Advent, for the Judgment Seat of Christ and the Marriage of the Lamb (2 Cor 5, 1 Cor 3, Rom 14, Rev 19) have to take place *before* the Second Advent. Here in 1 Thes 4v17 no one is coming down but everyone's going *up*. No Bible Believing Christian is waiting for 'thy kingdom come' we are waiting for His church *to go.* We are *not* looking for a *sign*, we are *listening for a sound*... **to meet the Lord *in the air*** not on the ground at the Mount of Olives (Acts 1) or on Mount Zion (Isa 2, Ps 2). The Rapture is *not* the Advent.

At the Rapture, Jesus Christ has come to call his espoused bride - 2 Cor 11v1-3. Espoused - Betrothed; affianced; promised in marriage by contract; married; united intimately; embraced, archaic marry. (Be espoused to) be engaged to. Song of Sol 2v8+10+13. Eternal security – perfect everlasting safety... Rom 8v29, Phil 3v20, 1 John 3v1-3. Nothing shall ever separate us from Him again. 2 Cor 5v1-10.

RAPTURE

Back to 1 Thes 4v18 - **Wherefore comfort one another with these words.** When a loved one dies, their *body* 'sleeps' in the grave. They are *not in their body*; they are... 2 Cor 5v6+8. Note in 1 Thes 5v10 **Who died for us, that, whether we wake or sleep, we should live together with him**. It says live *together* with Him. So those *'sleeping saints'* are already up there *living* with Him. **...whether we *wake* or *sleep*** - The expression obviously refers to being alive or dead, so the blessing in the verse is the word *'live... with him'*.

This settles the matter of absolute difference between the *body* that 'sleeps' (Acts 7v60 **And he kneeled down, and cried with a loud voice, Lord, lay not this sin to their charge. And when he had said this, he fell asleep**. Mat 27v52 **And the graves were opened; and many bodies of the saints which slept arose,**) and the *soul* that *doesn't.* No such thing as *soul*-sleep. We are said to be *alive* 'with Him' after death. This takes place when the soul *departs* from the body. Gen 35v18, 2 Tim 4v6, 2 Cor 5v1-7.

Now we come to the number one passage regarding the Rapture – 1 Cor 15v51-58. Paul *expected* the Rapture *in* his lifetime; note – 1 Thes 4v17. Also... 1 Cor 15v51 - Are you *really* expecting the Rapture *in* your lifetime; tomorrow, *today*? Because Paul was expecting the Rapture in his lifetime, we say the Rapture is imminent (meaning - about to happen).

Now the Bible does *not* tell us exactly when the Rapture will happen but it does give some indicators... Song of Sol 2v8-13 seems to indicate it *could* be in the springtime. But it could be *today*.

We are to work right up until the Rapture, winning souls for Jesus Christ. In Luke 19v13 it says... **Occupy till I come**. Whatever God calls you to, do it until He comes.

Now notice in v51 of 1 Cor 15 it says... **Behold, I shew you a mystery**; Paul is going to show you something that has *not* been revealed before. Now this is a good verse to use in regard to *proof* for a Pre-Tribulation Rapture. Throughout the OT the Second Advent was clearly seen, it was *not* a mystery i.e. verses like... Ps 50v4+5, Isa 26v16+17, Isa 26v19+21.

So 1 Cor 15 i.e. 'the Rapture' is a *mystery* – it wasn't *revealed* in the OT. It's like the Church Age – the Church may be found in the OT but it wasn't revealed until it was *revealed* to Paul. So what is this 'mystery?' – First, '**We shall not all sleep**' i.e. not every Christian will have to *die*. That was a mystery. The next part of the 'mystery' is '**we shall all be changed,**' – that's part of the mystery. The corruptible body of the Christian will be changed into an incorruptible body like Christ's. Living Christians at the time of the Rapture shall be 'transformed'. 1 Cor 15v52 **In a moment, in the twinkling of an eye** – the thing will be quicker than the blink of an eye. Note '**at the last trump**'...

It is *not* 'trumpet', but '**at the last trump**'. The 'trump' is the *sound* that a trumpet makes. Notice it *doesn't* say the *seventh* trumpet as in the book of Revelation. Notice it *doesn't* say an 'angel's' trumpet. It just says '**at the last trump: for the trumpet shall sound**'.

People who teach one Post-Tribulation Rapture of *all* saints, teach that the Christian will go into the Tribulation i.e. Daniel's 70th Week. In Revelation chapters 8 + 9 and 11v15, we read about a series of seven trumpet judgments. That seventh trumpet goes off and people say that it is the last trumpet of 1 Thes 4 and 1 Cor 15 *but it's not* – The last *trumpet*, that seventh *trumpet*, is blown by an *angel*. The seventh trumpet of Rev 11v15 is ***not*** '**the last trump**' of 1 Cor 15v52.

In Rev 11v15, there is the seventh angel blowing the seventh trumpet '**And the seventh angel sounded; and there were great voices in heaven, saying, The kingdoms of this world are become the kingdoms of our Lord, and of his Christ; and he shall reign for ever and ever.**' The seventh trumpet of Rev 11v15 *ends* the Tribulation and *begins* the Millennium. *It doesn't 'catch up' anybody.*

Note further, the seventh trumpet comes *after* a 'Rapture'... Rev 11v12... **And they heard a great voice from heaven saying unto them, Come up hither. And they ascended up to heaven in a cloud; and their enemies beheld them**. Moses and Elijah are Raptured *before* the last trumpet. So the seventh trumpet has *nothing* to do with any Rapture. There is another way we can know this, in 1 Thes 4 notice that the trumpet which calls you is not a trumpet blown by an *angel*.

Note - If we were going to go through the Tribulation (which we are *not*), we should be *looking for* the Tribulation and *not* Christ. Paul *never* mentioned or told us to *look for* the Tribulation, he told us to look for the Lord.

1 Thes 4v16 - There was *no* 'angel' in the passage; it was *the archangel*. In the Bible there is only *one* archangel, and that is Michael. And besides that, '**the last trump**' of 1 Cor 15v52 is '**the trump of God**'.

So when the Lord comes back, He will give a shout which will sound like a trumpet – Rev 4v1. The world will *not* hear it that way. To the unsaved world it is like thunder – Job 37v2-5. When this 'thunder' happens notice verse 4 '**he will not stay them when his voice is heard**' – somebody is going to 'take off'. Look at John 12v29 when the Father spoke to Jesus **The people therefore, that stood by, and heard it, said that it thundered: others said, An angel spake to him**. So as we hear a trumpet call in the shout, everyone *left behind* hears thunder, so loud, like never before.

When the Lord calls you *up*, He also calls you by *name* - John 10v3 – We hear the 'Good Shepherd's' voice and He leads us *out, out* of this world.

At the same time, Michael the archangel accompanies the Lord down to this earth; why? Because the Rapture of the church signals the beginning of Daniel's 70th Week – Dan 12v1... **And at that time shall Michael stand up, the great prince which standeth for the children of thy people: and there shall be a time of trouble, such as never was since there was a nation even to that same time: and at that time thy people shall be delivered, every one that shall be found written in the book**. This verse indicates that when that *trump* goes off and you are caught up, Michael the archangel shows up and God begins to renew His dealings with Israel.

There are other ways we know that the Rapture of the church is Pre-Tribulation...

1) The seventh trumpet of Rev 11v15 is *not* connected with '**the last trump**' of 1 Cor 15v52.

2) In the Tribulation, there is a 'FAITH and WORKS' system of salvation – Rev 12v17, Rev 14v12. A Christian has eternal security under 'grace-through-faith' but in the Tribulation, a person *can* lose their salvation. The foolish virgins of Mat 25 'run out' of the Holy Spirit. The slothful servant of Mat 25 is cast into '**outer darkness**'.

3) In the Church-Age, all believers are in *one* 'body' – the body of Christ. A saved Jew is no longer a Jew, he is a member of the '**church of God**'. A saved Gentile is no longer a Gentile, he is a member of the '**church of God**' – Gal 3v28 **There is neither Jew nor Greek, there is neither bond nor free, there is neither male nor female: for ye are all one in Christ Jesus**. But, IN the Tribulation there is *one* body of Jewish believers and another *separate* body of Gentile believers (Rev 7) – Therefore NO Christian goes through the Tribulation.

In 1 Cor 15v52, the order of the Rapture is the same as that of 1 Thes 4, it is dead believers (from Acts 2 to the present day) come up in their new resurrection *bodies*, and then the living Christians are changed and caught up. We don't *know* the interval between the two, but 1 Thes 4 indicates

RAPTURE

that it won't be very long.

As we have looked at beforehand, the word Rapture (although *not* in the Bible, but neither is the word 'Bible' or 'Trinity') is from a Latin word *'rapere'* which means *to seize by force*, and that is exactly what the Lord does at the Rapture. He enters the strong man's house and binds him and *steals the best thing in the house.*

Both Peter and Paul said **'the day of the Lord'** was like a **'thief in the night'** (1 Thes 5v2 and 2 Pet 3v10). Christ said to those who came to take Him in the garden... **'Are ye come out, as against a thief...'** (Mark 14v48). Note the Lord was crucified between two *thieves*. Paul (His main disciple in the NT) said **'I robbed other churches,'** (2 Cor 11v8)

Of course we know that He is 'stealing' what is *His own*. But it is the Devil's too because the Devil is the god of this world (2 Cor 4v4). The Lord comes down to the Devil's 'house' and takes the 'valuables' out by force; He 'kidnaps' you.

There are two classes of Christians in 1 Cor 15v53+54 based on their order in the Rapture

1) The first is **'corruptible'**. It is the *dead* Christians whose *bodies* are rotting in the ground. They come up with a *body* that *cannot* decay.

2) The second class is the **'mortal'**. That is the Christian who is still alive but is *subject to death*. When Christ returns at the Rapture, those Christians who are still alive will be given a *body* that cannot die.

There are *two* Scripture quotations Paul uses in verse 54+55

1) The first is **'DEATH is swallowed up in victory'** (v54). It is a quote from Isa 25v8 **He will swallow up death in victory; and the Lord GOD will wipe away tears from off all faces; and the rebuke of his people shall he take away from off all the earth: for the LORD hath spoken it.** But note a division in this verse, after the first semicolon **'the Lord GOD will wipe away tears from off all faces'** – this isn't fulfilled until Rev 21v4 **And God shall wipe away all tears from their eyes; and there shall be no more death, neither sorrow, nor crying, neither shall there be any more pain: for the former things are passed away.** What the Holy Spirit has done here is He has led Paul to a verse in Isa 25 that has a 'general application' to his subject (i.e. 'victory over death'), yet He will then lead Paul to apply that verse to the church, so that he will have Scriptural authority for what he is saying. Don't forget the Rapture was a *mystery* in the OT. If the Holy Spirit hadn't revealed that application to Paul, we would never see it. Notice, one semicolon can indicate years of division.

2) Look at 1 Cor 15v55 **O death, where is thy sting? O grave, where is thy victory?** That is a quote from Hosea 13v14 **I will ransom them from the power of the grave; I will redeem them from death: O death, I will be thy plagues; O grave, I will be thy destruction: repentance shall be hid from mine eyes.** Now this quote from Hosea is what you could call a 'free-quote'; in other words, it is the Holy Spirit, as Author, who is quoting the verse in the way He wants in order to make His own application. The verse in Hosea is not even a question and it has *nothing* to do with the church. **I will ransom them from the power of the grave**; the 'them' in this verse is the children of Ephraim, the northern kingdom of Israel, in the context of Hosea (Hos 13v12-13).

There are some wonderful 'spiritual applications' which you can make in the OT, especially in 'typology', but you *can't* press some of those things *doctrinally*. The first purpose of Scripture is for *doctrine*. (2 Tim 3v16).

Now 1 Cor 15v55 is a tremendous verse... **O death, where is thy sting? O grave, where is thy victory?** This verse says that if Jesus came this minute I would never know the sting of death. I wouldn't know what it would be like to die, because this mortal would '**put on immortality**'.

In John 11v25+26 we have the promise of Jesus Himself that we don't have to wait until the Great White Throne Judgment to come up... Jesus said unto her, **I am the resurrection, and the life: he that believeth in me, though he were dead, yet shall he live**: We have the word of someone who has already come up from the grave *never* to die again - **he that believeth in me, though he were dead, yet shall he live**: If you have a dead loved one who was *saved*, you *shall* see them again... **And whosoever liveth and believeth in me shall never die. Believest thou this?** This is a reference to the Church Age Rapture. So *death* is *not* going to 'sting' every Christian (v55). And *death* will *not* be victorious over the dead Christian.

1 Cor 15v56 **The sting of death is sin; and the strength of sin is the law.** The thing that hurts about dying is sin. Dying wouldn't be so bad if it wasn't for sin. Sin is the thing that makes a man die; it is sin that makes death painful. '**...and the strength of sin is the law**' – The law is what makes sin operate and shows you what sin is. Paul says in Rom 7v7 **I had not known sin, but by the law:** When you know what is wrong, the condemnation of the wrong is greater than when you don't.

1 Cor 15v57 **But thanks be to God, which giveth us the victory through our Lord Jesus Christ**. The Christian is able to have victory over sin and death because the Lord Jesus Christ has fought the battle for us and won. As we yield ourselves more to Him and identify ourselves more with Him in His death and resurrection, we can have victory over sin (Rom 6). Victory over death is freely given to us because of our position *in* Christ (Rom 8).

We may not know the actual date or time of the Rapture but we can *know* '**the times and the seasons**'... 1 Thes 5v1-11

Extra notes regarding the Rapture and 'end-times'...

Cars were prophesied in the Scriptures 2,500 years before they showed up – Nahum 2v4 - Tanks also – Isa 9v5

Israel's return to the land of Palestine (1917-1949) was clearly written in the Scriptures at least 2,000 years before it took place – Ezek 34v13, Ezek 37v25 – The return of the Jews to their native homeland after centuries of dispersion among the nations is one of the most obvious proofs of Biblical authority and the providence of God. No other ancient nation has survived to our present day with the same religion, practices, language, and sacred literature, but the Hebrew people have been set apart by the Lord as an example and a warning to the nations. God controls history, and when He so desires He changes politics to fulfil His prophecies. Jesus promised that this warning would come just before the Second Coming – Luke 21v29-32

The generation was born in 1949 (when the UN recognized the existence of the nation of Israel), this is the last generation before '**the kingdom of God**' appears at the Second Coming of Christ, which makes the re-emergence of Israel the most important and surprising event since the resurrection of Jesus Christ.

At the Rapture there will be an amazing flash of light – Mat 24v27, Ps 50v1-5

At the Rapture there will be a tremendous sound like a huge thunder storm – Job 37v1-4, John 12v28+29

The sound of a trumpet shall accompany this thunder – 1 Thes 4v16, 1 Cor 15v52

RAPTURE

At this trump every born again Christian on earth will *hear his name called* - John 10v3, followed by the words *come up hither* – Rev 4v1+2, Rev 11v12

The dead in Christ rise *first*... '**and the dead in Christ shall rise first**:' 1 Thes 4v16 – Out of the graveyards, and from the ocean and the battlefields of this world the bodies of saved sinners will come back together, atom to atom, molecule to molecule, as glorified bodies of 'flesh and bones' with NO blood in them - **Behold my hands and my feet, that it is I myself: handle me, and see; for a spirit hath not flesh and bones, as ye see me have.** Luke 24v39 **Now this I say, brethren, that flesh and blood cannot inherit the kingdom of God; neither doth corruption inherit incorruption.** 1 Cor 15v50

1 Thes 4v17 - The living saved sinners shall be transformed and their bodies will be made like unto Christ's heavenly body – 1 Cor 15v42-49, 1 John 3v2. In your new glorified body you shall be able to pass through solid objects - Luke 24v31, John 20v19. You will be able to travel faster than the speed of light - John 20v17, Mat 28v9 – Jesus ascended to the *third* Heaven and back to earth again in less than a few hours.

At the Rapture all Christians with their glorified bodies will leave the Solar System faster than the speed of light and be carried up straight **North** into the Throne Room – Ps 75v6+7, Ps 48v1-3, Ezek 1v1-4, 2 Cor 12v1-4, Rev 4v1-5, Isa 57v15

There the Christian will face the Judgment Seat of Christ to be rewarded for their good works as Christians and to suffer loss of rewards for their bad deeds – 1 Cor 3v11-15, 2 Cor 5v10. At the Judgment Seat of Christ the saved sinner is dealt with about his *service* for the Lord; it has *nothing* to do with his salvation. The Rapture, therefore, has no connection with 'Judgment Day' or 'The Last Judgment'.

How can we know the *time* of the Rapture – We can't, but, we can guess pretty closely

There is a Biblical system in which the Holy Spirit Himself established His own rules for interpretation. This system is called 'The Thousand Year-Day system' – 2 Pet 3v8.

2 Pet 3v8 is a key Scripture to understanding Lev 23 in more depth... Lev 23v3. If you follow the pattern given here and apply the 'Thousand Year-Day System' you see that man has to be here 6000 years, and then the last period of 1000 years has to be a Sabbath of rest (Gen 2v1-3). This Sabbath of rest, lasting a 'thousand' years (i.e. Millennium), is mentioned six times in Rev 20v1-8. The whole earth is at *rest* after Satan is done away with in Isa 14v7... **The whole earth is at rest, and is quiet: they break forth into singing.**

According to the figures, dates, and ages given in Genesis through 1 Kings, the period of time that extends from Gen 2 (the creation of man) to the birth of Christ (Mat 1) is four thousand years, or very near it. (Most calendars would indicate that Adam's creation should be dated 4004 B.C. making the birth of Christ actually 4 years early, in other words 4 B.C.)

The first coming was in Bethlehem four thousand years after Adam was created, and nearly two thousand years have elapsed since the birth of Christ. That places us virtually at the six thousand year mark, and on the threshold of the Millennium, or the seventh and *final* one thousand year period.

The Bible also declares that in the last days '**But thou, O Daniel, shut up the words, and seal the book, even to the time of the end: many shall run to and fro, and knowledge shall be increased.**' (Dan 12v4). Now just dwell on that statement for a while...

'**many shall run to and fro**' – travel, the speed of it and the places you can go now, even to the Moon (maybe!)

'**knowledge shall be increased**' – think of all the technology now available, the computers, radar, lasers, weapons, TV, radio, Bluetooth, mobiles, robots, drones, social media etc.

2 Tim 3v1-4 describes our society perfectly today - We *cannot* determine the actual day nor hour of the Rapture (Mat 24v36) but we can identify '**times and the seasons**,' (1 Thes 5v1) and be prepared for it.

The Scriptures that deal with the Rapture place it in the 'springtime' – Song of Sol 2v11-13. Some have said that the Rapture is most likely to happen on the Jewish feast day of Pentecost, for that is the day the Holy Spirit initially put the believers into one Body as part of the Lord Jesus Christ; who had gone back to heaven about seven days earlier. The Jewish feast day comes fifty days after the Passover, which would put it in May or early June.

When the Rapture occurs, you will either leave this planet bodily, going straight up in the air faster than the speed of light, or you will be left exactly as you are now – a human being stuck in a material world that is heading for the greatest disaster in history. Read about what will happen on earth in Rev 6 through to Rev 19 for the full picture.

It will be a world that is controlled by one dictator, whom the Bible calls 'the Man of Sin, the Son of Perdition and the Antichrist'. In that world you *cannot* buy or sell without taking the number 666 – why do you think the number 666 is everywhere *now* i.e. barcodes on groceries, international banking code, Health Service (NHS), internet etc. You are being *groomed* for this number at present. *Beware!*

Now if you *miss* the Rapture your only chance to 'make-it' will be to stay on the earth and try to endure to the end - Mat 24v13. Every Christian has gone. If you had a baby that baby has gone. Sin is not imputed when there is no law (Rom 5v13). Sin is *not* charged when the baby or child is 'innocent'.

If you miss the Rapture, you will have entered 'The Great Tribulation' – start *working* your way to Heaven because you are going to *have to!* The plan of salvation in the Great Tribulation is *faith* in Jesus Christ **plus** your own *good works*. Rev 12v11, Rev 6v9, Rev 14v12, Rev 22v14, Rev 7v14.

You *must* keep the Ten Commandments (all of them – Ecc 12v13), *keep* the Golden Rule (Mat 7v12, 1 John 3v10), give your money to the poor, get baptized, take up your cross, hold out to the end of the Tribulation, wait for Jesus Christ to show up at the Battle of Armageddon and be prepared to die for what you believe. In the Tribulation you *cannot* be saved by grace *alone*, like you could before the Rapture.

And remember *don't* take any *mark* or *number* – if you *do*, you will go to Hell forever – Rev 14v9-11, Rev 13v16-18.

In the Tribulation become a religious fanatic and die as a martyr for Jesus Christ - **And they overcame him by the blood of the Lamb, and by the word of their testimony; and they loved not their lives unto the death.** Rev 12v11, Rev 20v4.

It will take faith in Christ's shed Blood, plus works – exactly as in the OT, it took faith in shed blood and works... Isa 1v16+17, Prov 28v13, Ps 51v1+2, Rev 14v12+13.

If you go through the Tribulation make sure you *support* the Jewish people. When Jesus returns at the Second Coming, all will face 'The Judgment of Nations' - Mat 25v31+32.

The test for a Gentile is how he treated Jesus' brethren – the Jews. The Antichrist will be 1000 times worse than Hitler ever was in regard to the Jews. At first he will negotiate a peace treaty with the nation of Israel (Isa 28v15) *but* three and a half years later he will break the covenant and try to destroy them (Dan 9v27, Mark 13v13-25, Mat 24v4-51). So if you are a Gentile in the Tribulation do *not* assist the tracking down and killing of the Jews. The Lord will judge anyone who stops the Jew from escaping – Obad 14+15. Always help the Jewish people. Go against *everybody* (including your own family) to *help* the Jew, because they are God's chosen people; even sacrifice your own life for the Jew in the Tribulation. Gen 12v3. Later, God said to the nation of Israel - Isa 41v11. So no matter how much pressure you are put under, *never* hurt a Jew; your own soul depends upon it.

The sad fact is that the majority of people on earth will reject the Lord Jesus Christ as their Saviour and go to Hell forever. Jesus said - Mat 7v13+14.

The world population presently stands around 7 billion. Over 2 billion are in China and India alone. Most of these people are lost in their sins and vain religions. Over 1 billion people are Muslims who don't even believe that Jesus is God's Son. Another billion are Roman Catholics who believe in praying to Mary and bowing down to idols. That's 4 billion already and we haven't even mentioned the atheists, the agnostics, the cult members, the new-ager's, the Jews, the religious but lost, and the millions of 'good' people who are working their way to heaven. Probably 95%-99% of people on this earth are *not* saved. *Broad is the road!*

Once the Rapture happens, *all* these people will enter the Great Tribulation and they will start facing tragedy after tragedy. The book of Revelation talks about this period of time. Here are a few things that are going to happen once the Rapture has taken place and the Christians have *gone*...

      Rev 6v4 – war

      Rev 6v5+6 – famine

      Rev 6v7-8 – 25% of the population destroyed

      Rev 6v9 – martyrdom

      Rev6v12 – earthquakes, sun darkened, moon as blood

      Rev 6v13 – stars fall

      Rev 8v7 – a third of trees burned, all grass burned

      Rev 8v8 – a third of the sea becomes blood

      Rev 8v9 – a third of all sea life dies, a third of all ships destroyed

      Rev8v10+11 – a third of the water poisoned

      Rev 9 v1-21 – army of 200,000,000 monster locusts

      Rev 12v9-12 – Satan and his angels cast into the earth

      Rev 13v1-18 – world worships the beast and takes his mark

      Rev 16v12-16 – Armageddon occurs – a massive world war

      Rev 16v18 – greatest earthquake ever

Rev 16v21 – giant hailstones fall

Rev 18v1-24 – Babylon destroyed

Rev 19v11-21 – armies of the beast destroyed at the 2nd Coming of Christ

More notes... (*some of which will be duplication*)

In the Song of Solomon, Jesus Christ is calling for His Bride to... Song of Sol 2v10.

The setting is May (Pentecost) which is not within 4 months of the Feasts of Trumpets or Feast of Tabernacles.

The 'beloved' in the Song of Sol 2v10 is a *Gentile* Bride, *not* a Jewish Bride - Song of Sol 1v5.

Many Christians confuse the angel's trumpet (Mat 24v31, Rev 11v15) with God's trump (1 Thes 4v16, Rev 4v1+2). By confusing these 'trumpets and trumps', many Christians place the Rapture at the Feast of Trumpets in September-October.

The 'Last *trump*' is *not* a trumpet; it is the last *sound* made by a trumpet, but in this case it was God's *voice* (the *trump* of God) speaking *as* a trumpet.

John is careful to tell you that the 'trump of God' is *not* an actual trumpet but a *voice* (John 12v29, Job 37v1-5, Rev 4v1+2). The *voice* sounds like two things... 'Thunder' and a 'Trumpet'. When the 'trump' is heard, a voice is heard (Song of Sol 2v10), calling *sheep* home (John 10v3-4).

No *voice* is heard after the 7th trumpet of Rev 11, which was blown by an *angel*, not God. It is *voices* (plural) that are heard *after* the 7th trumpet, and they do *not* call anyone up anywhere, they announce that Jesus Christ is going to land *on earth* (Job 19v25) to take over the 'Kingdoms of the world' (Dan 2v35+44+45)

However, there is a voice (a 'great voice') which does call someone *up* just *before* the 7th angel blows his trumpet. This voice says *'Come up hither'* – that is what John heard in Rev 4v1. But this time, the same voice (speaking the *same* words) is calling someone up at the *end* of Daniel's 70th Week. The two men who are addressed directly are both Jews; Moses and Elijah. They are caught up in a *Post*-Tribulation Rapture.

Now here are *two* 'Raptures' – a 'PRE' and a 'POST' Tribulation Rapture.

The 'POST' is said to be 'POST' in Mat 24v29. Now many 'PRE-Millennialists' will break their theological necks in Mathew's Gospel. They do what Calvin did and mistake the 'elect' in Mat 24v24, for the 'elect' of Eph 1v5.

In Mat 24v24 they overlooked the 'elect' to whom the passage was aimed... Isa 45v4, Isa 65v9+22. Dan 7v18+21+25+27.

They pretended the *elect* were Christians in the Body of Christ.

With Mat 25v1 following Mat 24, they insist that a bunch of 'virgins' are going to marry Christ. This is after being told His Bride was *one* 'chaste virgin' (2 Cor 11v2), the *only one* of her 'mother' (Song of Sol 6v9).

If that weren't enough, the Holy Spirit told them in Mat 25 that *none* of the virgins in the chapter married *anybody*. They were called out to *meet* somebody (Mat 25v1).

RAPTURE

And if that weren't enough, the Lord finished the entire chapter (Mat 25) with a *works* salvation set up (Mat 25v35-40) where the Gospel Paul preached (Gal 1) was not even a factor in keeping sinners out of 'everlasting fire' (Mat 25v41).

Look at the following verses – Rev 6v16, Rev 14v14, Mat 24v30, Rev 1v7, and see that not one of them matches with the Second Advent as described in these verses – Rev 19v11-15, Isa 63v1-6, Joel 2v1-3, Judg 5v1-20, Hab 3v3-14.

Somebody sees Jesus Christ at the end of the Tribulation *before* He arrives at Armageddon with His divine *cavalry* – Rev 19.

The requirements for the 'elect' *seeing* this POST-Tribulation 'appearance' are…

1) Purity of Heart – **Blessed are the pure in heart: for they shall see God**. Mat 5v8

2) Holiness - **Follow peace with all men, and holiness, without which no man shall see the Lord**: Heb 12v14

3) And watchful and waiting - **So Christ was once offered to bear the sins of many; and unto them that look for him shall he appear the second time without sin unto salvation**. Heb 9v28

There is a 'split' Rapture (Mat 25v7-13) at that time. This is the Rapture that Pentecostals and Charismatics mistake for the Rapture of the Church. Oftentimes the confusion comes when the 'Day of the Lord' is said to be *only* a reference to the Second Advent at the end of the Tribulation. 'That day' in the Prophets, is applied to…

The birth of Christ – Isa 2v12, Isa 4v2, Isa 7v14+18

The attack of Sennacherib – Isa 10v5-20

The defeat of Babylon by Persia – Jer 50 + 51

The Millennium - 2 Pet 3v8

The Great White Throne Judgment – 2 Pet 3v10

'The day of the Lord' is *not* just limited to refer to the events of Revelation chapters 16-19.

It is also interesting to note that Moses and Elijah were caught up (Rev 11v12) and they were *not* in the Bride. Also, the 144,000 Jews show up in the third Heaven around the throne in Rev 14v1-4 who were on earth before the Tribulation started (Rev 7v3-4) and *they* weren't in the Bride. They were raptured and none of them were IN Christ's Body. They sang the song of Moses. (Rev 15v3) That song is Deut 32, the one that is quoted (Deut 32v36) in Heb 10v30.

The harvest of Rev 14v15 precedes the harvest of Rev 14v18-20. The Post-Tribulation appearance of Jesus Christ to His enemies, as a Lamb *seated* on a throne, cannot match His appearance as seated on a horse (Rev 19v11-16).

His enemies see Him long enough, before He comes, to gather troops to fight against Him, at the place where they saw Him (Rev 19v19).

Jesus Christ is *seated* on a cloud in Rev 14 when the *Post*-Tribulation Rapture takes place. Those caught up at that time do *not* face the Judgment Seat of Christ, and they marry *no one.* They are *guests* at a wedding, and we were told this in Mat 22v10+11.

Thus when we say '*Post*-Tribulation', the terminology is not 100% accurate. It would be more accurate to say 'somewhere right near the END of the Tribulation' this Rapture will occur. '**Immediately after the tribulation of THOSE DAYS**' is the wording in Mat 24v29, but '*those days*' can be 'shortened' or they can be delayed – Mat 24v22.

So here we have *one* '**chaste virgin**' (2 Cor 11v2) being caught up *before* the 'Mark of the Beast' starts damning men (Rev 14v9+10, and she is caught up in the Spring (Song of Sol 2v10-13) by a voice that sounds like a trumpet (1 Thes 4v16) to the child of God, but sounds to the *unsaved* like thunder (John 12v28-30, Job 37v1-5). Every saint in the Bride is called by *name* (John 10v1-7) and is first 'led *out*' i.e. an 'Exodus' out of the world system (John 10v3) and then brought back to earth behind their Shepherd (John 10v4).

Here we have a number of virgins (Song of Sol 6v8) in *two separate groups* (Rev 7v4+9) unlike the *one body* (Gal 3v28, Eph 3v1-8). They are being caught up after the Mark of the Beast is required worldwide (Rev 13). These groups are caught up sometime around the Feast of Trumpets, when the Angel blows the Seventh Trumpet, called 'a great sound of a trumpet' in Mat 24v31. This 'sister' marries *no one* when she is called to 'Come up hither', and she has to stand before the Great White Throne Judgment (Rev 11v18, Rev 20v11-14) for the Judgment Seat of Christ is *past*. She comes out of a *faith and works* situation (Rev 12v17, Rev 14v12).

No member of the Body of Jesus Christ will ever be alive in a situation where saved Jews and saved Gentiles make up two separate bodies of saints (Rev 7), and no member of the Body of Christ will be alive when a man can lose his salvation by taking the mark, number or name – Rev 13v1-18, Rev 14v9+10. No member of the Body of Christ will be present when an angel preaches *another* Gospel that Paul did *not* preach (Gal 1v6-8) and is blessed for doing it (Rev 14v6+7) - and no member of the Body of Christ will ever be told that his 'enduring to the end' (Mat 24v13) depends upon keeping the *commandments of God, and the faith of Jesus Christ*' – Rev 12v17, Rev 14v12.

As stated previously, I am waiting for the Lord Jesus Christ to *return*, I'm not looking for a *sign*, I am waiting for a *sound*.

I am *not* looking for any of the following *before* Christ returns...

1) A great revival

2) Daniel's 70th Week to show up

3) The temple to be rebuilt

4) Regathering of the Jews

5) The Son of Perdition to show up

6) The rise of the ten-federated Kingdom (Rev 13 + 17)

7) Russia to invade Palestine

8) A Peace Treaty etc.

The church today has been led astray into looking for *anything* other than what they should be looking for, i.e. the Lord Jesus Christ to return - Mat 24v42+44, Luke 12v35-37, Phil 3v20.

I am waiting for the Lord to come back anytime now... 1 Thes 1v10.

Many Christians use Mat 24v31 to *drag* the Church into some part of the Tribulation. Most

RAPTURE

Christians teach that you are saved in the Tribulation the *same way* as you are saved in the Church Age. This is heresy.

Once you try to put the following verses into the Church Age and the 'Gospel of Grace' (Acts 20v24) you will 'wrest the Scriptures to your own destruction' (2 Pet 3v16). *For example* - Rev 12v17, Rev 14v12, Heb 3v14.

The Raptures' that are described in the following verses are *not* connected with the NT Body of Christ that is *now* on earth... Ps 50v1-6, Isa 26v20+21, Rev 14v14-16, Heb 9v28, 2 Sam 22v17-20, Ps 18v6-19, Mat 24v40-42.

Even so come Lord Jesus!

The Lord Jesus Christ COULD return today... You're IN the generation that COULD see it happen!

Mat 24v34 **Verily I say unto you, This generation shall not pass, till all these things be fulfilled.** 'THIS generation' is the 'generation' that is alive at the time of Israel becoming a nation again (1948). If the length of a 'generation' is 42 years (figuring the time of the 'generations' in Mat 1v17), then Christ would have come back in 1990. If a 'generation' is 70 years (as in Ps 90v10), then the Second Advent would be no later than 2018. If a 'generation' is 100 years long (as figured by Gen 15v13), then the Lord would return NO LATER than 2048. If the Lord has a particular person in that 'generation' in mind (see notes on Gen 5v21 in RRB), then the Second Coming will occur sometime within the lifetime of THAT person. That means that any unbelieving Jew born in 1948 WILL BE IN the 'generation' that sees the Second Advent, & any believing Christian WILL BE IN the 'generation' that is CAUGHT OUT at the Rapture BEFORE the Second Advent! Man alive folks!!! Are you ready for the Rapture? Makes you think doesn't it! What are you doing with your life FOR THE LORD?

The Rapture
1 Thes 4v16 **For the Lord himself shall descend from heaven with a shout, with the voice of the archangel, and with the trump of God: and the dead in Christ shall rise first**: Note three noises – a shout, a voice and a trump. The 'trump' is a sound that a trumpet makes (1 Cor 15v52). It is NOT a 'trumpet' like the angel's trumpet in Rev 8v6. Rev 11v15 is at THE END of the Tribulation. No angel blows this trumpet in verse 16, it is called 'the trump of God'. Note how all of the POST-Trib Rapture HERETICS and ALL the PRE-Wrath Rapture HERETICS can't understand this and mess up the 'trumpets' with the 'trumps'. They think the trumpets of Rev 11v15 + Mat 24v31 are the same as 1 Cor 15v52... they are NOT. There is a difference between 'THE' trumpet and 'one trumpet out of seven' (Rev 8v6). The 'trump' is God Himself SPEAKING ('the voice of the archangel') - Rev 4v1 **After this I looked, and, behold, a door was opened in heaven: and the first voice which I heard was as it were of a trumpet talking with me; which said, Come up hither, and I will shew thee things which must be hereafter.** Rev 1v10 **I was in the Spirit on the Lord's day, and heard behind me a great voice, as of a trumpet,** Note the trumpet in these verses were 'talking', and saying 'Come up hither'. His voice sounds like a trumpet. Zechariah is the one who tells you that this trumpet is NOT the seventh trumpet of Rev 11v15. **And the LORD shall be seen over them, and his arrow shall go forth as the lightning: and the Lord GOD shall blow the trumpet, and shall go with whirlwinds of the south.** Zech 9v14. The Lord God shall blow the trumpet NOT some angel. (Note also Exod 19v16-19) What the unsaved hear is thunder (Job 37v1-4, John 12v28+29), see also John 10v3+14. The signal for the Rapture is a SHOUT from Heaven... up come the dead (1 Cor 15v51-55, John

11v25+26). This signals the end of the Church Age, for Michael is 'the Prince who stands for Israel' (Dan 12v1+2). He was the one who got the Body of Moses (Jude 9) so Moses could show up on this earth immediately following the Rapture of the Body of Christ (Rev 4v1+2 cf. Rev 11v3-6).

1 Thes 4v17 – This cannot be the Second Advent because the Judgement Seat of Christ and the Marriage Supper of the Lamb (2 Cor 5, 1 Cor 3, Rom 14, Rev 19) must take place BEFORE the Second Advent. In 1 Thes 4v17 no one is coming down as in Rev 19, millions are going up, to meet the Lord in the air, not on the ground at the Mount of Olives (Acts 1, Zech 14) or on Mount Zion (Isa 2, Ps 2). The Rapture is NOT the Advent. At the Rapture the Lord Jesus Christ will come to call His espoused bride 'away' – 2 Cor 11v1-3, S of S 2v8+10+13.

(No Calvinist has ever understood this and none of them ever will until it happens. What a blessing they miss by following Johnny Calvin).

Differences between the Rapture and the Second Advent

1) Neither the resurrection of the dead or the Second Advent are 'mysteries' in the Bible. They are both clearly mentioned centuries BEFORE Christ showed up – Job 19v25-27, Ezek 37, Ecc 12v14
2) The Rapture IS a 'mystery' (1 Cor 15v51), unrevealed till AFTER Pentecost.
3) The local churches and the Body of Christ are lukewarm at the end of the Church Age preceding the Rapture. They are NOT lukewarm at the end of the Tribulation; the Body of Christ is NOT EVEN THERE!
4) At the Advent, Christ 'lands' on the ground (Joel 2, Isa 2, Rev 5v10+14+19); at the Rapture, He comes in the Air (1 Thes 4v16) and does NOT touch the ground (1 Thes 4v17)
5) At the Rapture, there is no change in Satan's position, he doesn't get locked up in any 'pit' as he DOES at the Advent. There are no changes in Nature at the Rapture. By the time of the Advent, two-thirds of the world has been destroyed on both land and sea (Rev 6-18)
6) At the Rapture, Christ doesn't judge any Jews or any nations (as in Joel 2, Hos 2, Jer 25, Mat 25). At the Advent, He judges the entire world (Mat 25v31+32, Ps 47v8, 96v10-13, Isa 60v12). None of His enemies are killed at the Rapture, more than 200,000,000 are killed at the Advent (Isa 63, Rev 9, Luke 19v27)

NOTES

NOTES

ERRORS OF THE POST-TRIBULATION RAPTURE
POST-TRIBBERS AKA 'POSTIES'

If the church, which is His Body (Col 1v24, Eph 1v22+23, Eph 5v29+30), was to go through the Tribulation, that would mean God is pouring out His wrath (Eph 5v6, 1 Thes 1v10, Rev 6v16, Rev 16v1) upon His own Body. *How mad is that!* The Church, which is His Body will *not* go through any part of the Tribulation. We are raptured *out* before it starts (1 Thes 4v13-18), hence why we can *comfort one another with these words*. Try to find the Church between chapters 4 and 21 in the Book of Revelation... It isn't there. Rev 4-20 describes the Tribulation on earth and the church is *not* there. How clear can you get?

If you are a Christian, you are part of the Body of Christ, you are part of the Bride of Christ. (1 Cor 12v27, Eph 4v12, Rom 7v4, Eph 5, Rev 19v7-9) Therefore the Lord Jesus Christ would *not* pour out His wrath upon His Bride. Therefore the Church will *not* go through the Tribulation. Also, if a Christian was going to go through the Tribulation and he took the Mark of the Beast, that means he would *lose* his salvation and a Christian *cannot* lose his salvation, as we are *sealed* by the Holy Spirit - Eph 1v13, Eph 4v30. The Christian is IN the Body of Christ and there is NO 'amputation' in the Body of Christ.

Post-Tribber *Bob-the-boob-Mitchell* calls 'his cruncher', that Jesus said to Peter the following... John 21v18 **Verily, verily, I say unto thee, When thou wast young, thou girdedst thyself, and walkedst whither thou wouldest: but when thou shalt be old, thou shalt stretch forth thy hands, and another shall gird thee, and carry thee whither thou wouldest not. This spake he, signifying by what death he should glorify God. And when he had spoken this, he saith unto him, Follow me**. Now just to show you how shallow Post-Tribbers (aka Posties) are, just follow me through here... One thing Posties don't understand is that God knows *everything*. God *knows* who will get saved and who won't, yet, He gives us a freewill to choose. Now let me break it down in bite sizes for the *Posties* as they can't cope with the *strong meat* of the word of God (Heb 5v12-14). If you played chess with the Lord, the Lord would *know* every move you would make, and therefore would win the game. You could change your mind a million times, yet the Lord would *know* every move you'd make. Now turn to Acts 7 *with this in mind.* Read Acts 7v55+56. **Question** – *Why was God standing?* If you think it was to receive Stephen, then *not all your branches go to the top of the tree!* I mean, imagine if Jesus stood for *every* Christian soul that died; *He'd be up and down like a 'yoyo'.* You see what we have here in Acts 7 is a readiness for the Second Advent that would have *triggered* Daniel's 70th Week '**IF**' the NATIONAL response would have been acceptance of Stephen's words and *repentance* (Acts 3v19) towards God. Deut 21v1-9 would have gone into action, the Rapture would have taken place (Ps 50v4, Song of Sol 2v10, Isa 26v19 etc.), Judas would have come *up* from the pit (Acts 1v25 and comments in RRB), and the *covenant* between Rome and Israel would have been signed (Dan 9v27, Dan 11v27+30). The Body may have remained an *unrevealed* mystery (something the Hyper-Diapers *don't* understand *still*), depending upon whether or not God decided to reveal it. It was *already* a Jew-Gentile Body which is apparent from Acts 2v10 and Acts 6v1 (something again the Hyper-Diapers *don't* understand!) Now sadly this is too *deep* for the Posties, hence why they teach their shallow 'POST-Trib' heresy (it's an easy cop-out like teaching

Calvinism, i.e. it doesn't take much study to confuse 'children').

Now Posties are very close to being Calvinists and following Calvin's errors regarding Acts 7, and the concept of 'eternal decrees', for some of them are *flexible* and can be adjusted to meet the situation *without contradicting one former decree or one former oath.* Go back to the game of chess. But this *blows* old Bobby's theory of Peter's 'death' clear out of the English Channel. *Why?* Because **IF** (did you get that '**IF**!') Daniel's 70th Week would have *started* because of the acceptance of Stephen's words and the *repentance* of the nation of Israel (i.e. they accepted Jesus as the Messiah) **then Paul's letters would *not* have been written and therefore *neither would the Book of John*, as this was written *after* Paul's letters, you would *not* have read John 21v18.** And that dear friends, is *Bob-the-Boob's cruncher!'* (It's as crunchy as a bowl of crunchy-nut-cornflakes and is no meal for a man!) It also means that Stam and Bullinger (the Hyper-Diaper's 'gods') are also in *error* because a Rapture *here* would *not* have affected the 'mystery of the revelation' of that Body (see comments on Eph 3v1-5 in RRB) but the time of revelation hardly matches the time of *institution* (see comments on Gen 2v13 in RRB). More than that, the great dispensational shift here is screened from the eyes of 98% of the major commentators and revisers including all the Hyper-Diapers, Calvinists and Post-Tribbers.

Post-Tribbers only see one 'general' Rapture rather than the Scriptural *three*. Remember those 'tomato' plants? i.e. Firstfruits (OT saints Mat 27), Harvest (1 Thes 4, 1 Cor 15) and Gleanings (Tribulation saints Rev 11). They confuse the Harvest with the 'Gleanings'.

The Rapture described in 1 Thes 4 differs from that which occurs at the end of the Tribulation. *This one* occurs *before* the Tribulation (Rev 4v1) since the Tribulation is *the time of Jacobs Trouble* (Jer 30v7) *not* the Church's. The *comfort* of 1 Thes 4v18 is the prospect of *missing* the wrath that accompanies 'the day of the Lord' – 1 Thes 5v1-9. Facing salvation based on your own righteousness and martyrdom (Rev 7v14 cf. Rev 1v5), and the possibility of taking the Mark of the Beast and *losing* your salvation (Rev 14v9-12) is *no comfort at all!* The Rapture in 1 Thes 4 is the Rapture of those IN Christ (v16) – the Church, the Body of Christ (Eph 1v1-23). In the Tribulation, saved people are in **two** 'bodies' (Rev 7v4+9) *not* one (Eph 4v4), and these two bodies are *not* the same as the Body of Christ *pre*-Rapture (the Hyper-Diapers mess that up too). The Rapture in 1 Thes 4 occurs at 'the *trump* of God' (v16) *not* the 'trumpet' sounded by the 7th angel in Rev 11v15. (See note on 1 Cor 15v52 in RRB) **There is *not one single* 'righteous' man in Scripture where God directly poured out His judgment upon him!** Why then would God pour out His judgments upon His Bride during the Tribulation? *He won't!* He will deliver His Bride *before* the judgments start to fall.

John Davis is looking for the Lord Jesus Christ! Posties are looking for the *Antichrist!* It's as simple as that.

Posties, in order to *try* to prove their heresy will run back to the Church 'Fathers' and 'THE Greek' (to which there ISN'T one). Of course they *don't* speak Greek, and they never tell you *which Greek text* they are referring to out of the 100+ available, but that doesn't bother these *false* teachers in the slightest. *Oh and by the way Posties...* how do you *know* 'the Greek' is correct? They'll run everywhere and anywhere, to try to prove their **heresy** because they are *unskilled* in the Scriptures themselves, as they have **no final authority**.

Another mistake Posties make is their understanding of the Day of the Lord. The Day of the Lord has different meanings. They just change the Scriptures to suit their heresy. Let me give you *seven* different time periods for '**the Day of the Lord**'...

1) The invasion of the 10 northern tribes by Assyria in Isa 10v5-16+20+21+24+27+32, Isa 7v14+17+20, Amos 5v18-20, 6v9+11+14

ERRORS OF POST TRIBULATION RAPTURE

2) The destruction of Jerusalem by Nebuchadnezzar – Joel 1v6-15, Isa 2v12+20, 3v7+16+25+26, 5v25-30, Micah 3v1+2, Jer 17v18+19+27

3) The virgin birth and the 1st Advent of Jesus Christ in 4 BC – Isa 7v14-18, 61v1+2, Zech 9v9+10+14+16

4) The millennial reign of Jesus Christ – Isa 19v18-25, 24v21-23, 26v1-4, Hosea 2v18+19, Zech 13v1-6, 14v8-21

5) The battle of Armageddon at the 2nd Advent – Joel 2v1-11, 3v9-18, Micah 5v1-15, Isa 25v7-11, Mal 4v1-3, Zech 14v1-6, Ezek 38v19

6) The last Judgment at the end of the Millennium – 2 Pet 3v10, Isa 66v22-24, Dan 7v9-11

7) The destruction of Babylon by Persia – Isa 13v6+9+17+19

So the '**Day of the Lord**' does not just apply to the 2nd Advent *exclusively*. The Day of the Lord, applied to Armageddon, does not come till the Antichrist has been revealed as 'the son of perdition'. The Rapture and Judgment Seat of Christ will not take place **till there has been a falling away first**, *which we are seeing today.*

Salvation is *different* 'before' the Tribulation, *during* the Tribulation and *after* the Tribulation. If the Church, the Bride of Christ, the Body of Christ, *entered* the Tribulation, it would mean that *members of His Body* could *lose* their salvation, something which we know is *impossible* for those who are 'IN' Christ i.e. *no one gets **out** of Christ.*

Post-Tribbers think Matthew 24 is in the New Testament. *Did you get that?* If not read Heb 9v16+17. Mat 24 is still **IN the Old Testament** *doctrinally*. Mat 24 is *directed* to Jews *not* Christians. Posties think *the elect* (i.e. Jews) in Mat 24 is the Body of Christ being 'gathered'. Now this gross misrepresentation of Scripture is beyond belief! Regarding Mat 24 where are the *dead in Christ*? They are *not* there because the two events are different. The Rapture and the Second Advent are ***not*** the same. The church has *not* replaced Israel.

Posties think that 1 Thes 4 and 1 Thes 5 are *both* talking about the Second Coming when they are not. One is talking about the Rapture and the other is the Second Coming. The Day of the Lord is *not* the Rapture.

Post-Tribbers think that Acts 14v22 is talking about Jacob's Trouble, *which is as wild as you can get!*

By taking a text out of context you get a pretext

Not **once** in the Scriptures are you ever told to *look for* the Tribulation. You are told to look for the Lord Jesus Christ.

The word *trump* is connected with the Rapture (it only appears **twice** in Scripture – 1 Cor 15v52 and 1 Thes 4v16). Note *both* the Scriptures are found in **Rapture** passages. The word 'trumpet' is connected with the Second Advent. If you confuse the two like the Posties do, you'll never understand *when* Jesus Christ is coming back.

The Post-Tribbers are *looking for* the Tribulation, the Anti-Christ, peace treaties etc. etc. Bible Believers are looking for Jesus Christ.

Another error Post-Tribbers make is that they confuse the Rapture of the Tribulation saints with the Rapture of the Body of Christ. They do this because they don't understand that there is more than one Rapture in the Scriptures; actually there are seven Raptures in the Scriptures...

1) Jesus Christ – Acts 1v9-11

2) Enoch – Gen 5v21-24

3) Elijah – 2 Kings 2v8-12

4) Body of Christ - 1 Thes 4v16-18

5) Moses and Elijah (plus Tribulation saints) – Rev 11v3-12

6) The 144,000 Jewish evangelists just after the middle of the Tribulation – Rev 14v1-5

7) The great martyred Gentiles in Rev 7v9 who came 'out' of great tribulation – Rev 7v9-17

Paul was looking for Jesus. 2 Tim 4v8. Many Post-Tribbers believe that the church has replaced Israel, they teach the Roman Catholic 'replacement' theology. They are anti-Semitic and *wrongly* divide the Scriptures.

Were the apostles and disciples looking for the Lord's return in their day? *What saith the Scriptures? Are these verses talking about the Rapture or the Second Coming? Phil 3v20, 1 Cor 1v7, Titus 2v13, 1Thes 4v15, 2 Thes 2v1.*

Questions to ask Post-Tribbers...

1. Where is the resurrection of *dead* saints mentioned in Mat 24, Mark 13, Luke 17+21?

2. Did Jesus and Paul preach the *same* Gospel?

3. Can you provide documented proof of Bible Believing Christians teaching a pre-wrath Rapture *before* 1830?

4. Please explain the prophecy Jesus gave concerning the rebirth of the fig tree in Mat 24v32-34?

5. What is the 'fullness of the Gentiles' and when will it 'come in?'

6. Who are the 'elect' mentioned in 2 Tim 2v10?

7. Could you give one reference where the words 'The Tribulation' or 'The Great Tribulation' are used as a title for this *coming* time period?

Beware when anyone runs to the Gospels and takes their *doctrine* from *pre*-Crucifixion Scriptures. **Pre-Crucifixion Scriptures are standing in the Old Testament** – *did you get that?* (Heb 9v15-17). So all the Post-Tribbers run to *pre*-Crucifixion Scriptures to teach their heresy. *Beware of that!* God does *not* pour out His wrath upon His Bride. Christians *cannot* lose their salvation, yet in Jacob's Trouble (aka 'The Tribulation' – although it is never given this title in Scripture) you *can* lose your salvation. If you do not *rightly* divide the Scriptures, you will *wrongly* 'join' them. Ask a Post-Tribber *why* the term 'Son of Man' doesn't appear in any of Paul's letters, yet it appears in 193 verses of Scripture. *Here's another question to ask a Postie...* 'What happens if a 'Christian' doesn't endure to the end of the Tribulation? – Mat 10v22' Can a Christian take the Mark of the Beast?

In the 'Tribulation', the saints have their *robes* washed (Rev 7v14), today **we** are washed (1 Cor 6v11) – *they are not the same!* Salvation is different *pre*-Crucifixion, during the Church Age and in Daniel's 70th Week.

ERRORS OF POST TRIBULATION RAPTURE

There are two *main* Raptures, one is *before* the time of Jacob's Trouble (Jer 30v7) - 1 Thes 4v15-18 aka 'The Tribulation', and one is *at the end* of the time of Jacob's Trouble - Mat 24v31.

The word Rapture means to seize something, snatch it away or transport something. The Rapture will take place before the Resurrection (John 11v25) and will include all *living* believers (John 11v26) and all *dead* believers (John 11v25). The 'living' and 'dead' are also mentioned again in the other Rapture passage 1 Cor 15v52-54.

If you were to look at verses in the OT, take Job 19v25-27, you will notice that Job is speaking of an *earthly* Redeemer standing on the *earth*, with no mention of a Heavenly King on a Heavenly throne reigning over a *spiritual* Kingdom (Eph 5v5, Ps 110v1, Dan 4v3 etc.) Throughout the OT there is a 'hint' of a *pre*-'resurrection.' – Read Ps 50v4+5, Job 37v1-5, Isa 26v19-21 – note the 'voice' (Job 37) and the 'thunder' (Job 40) which accompanies it. See also John 12v28-30 in relation to this.

Ruckman writes...

1) In the Song of Solomon, Jesus Christ is calling for His Bride to... 'Rise up... and come away' – Song of Sol 2v10. The setting is May (Pentecost) which is not within four months of the Feast of Trumpets or the Feats of Tabernacles. The 'beloved' in the Song of Sol 2v10, is a Gentile Bride, not a Jewish Bride (Song of Sol 1v5).

2) Every Bible teacher/preacher who confounded the Angel's trumpet (Mat 24v31, Rev 11v15) with God's trump (1 Thes 4v16, Rev 4v1+2) located the Rapture at the Feast of Trumpets in September – October.

3) 'The last *trump*' is **not** a trumpet! It is the last *sound* made by a trumpet, but in this case, it was God's *voice* ('the *trump of God*') speaking **as** a trumpet. John is careful to tell you that the 'trump of God' is **not** an actual 'trumpet' but a *voice* (John 12v29, Job 37v1-5, Rev 4v1+2) which sounds like *two* things – '*thunder* and a *trumpet*'.

4) When this 'trump' is heard, **a voice** is heard (S of S 2v10), calling *sheep* home (John 10v3-4). No *voice* is heard *after* the 'seventh trumpet' of Rev 11, which was blown by an *angel* **not** God.

5) It is 'voices' that are heard *after* the seventh trumpet, and *they do not call anyone up anywhere*; they announce that Jesus Christ is going to land 'on earth' (Job 19v25) to take over 'the Kingdoms of the world' (see Dan 2v35+44+45). However, there is a voice (a 'great voice') which does call someone *up* just **before** the *seventh angel blows his trumpet*. This voice says '**Come up hither**'. That is what John heard in Rev 4v1. But this time the *same voice* (speaking the *same words*) is calling someone *up* at the **end** of Daniel's 70th Week. The two men who are addressed directly are **both Jews** – Moses and Elijah (**not** Enoch). They are caught up in a **post**-Tribulation Rapture, **not** a 'pre-wrath' Rapture. So what we have above are **two** Raptures, a **pre** and a **post** Tribulation Rapture. The **post** is said to be **post** in Mat 24v29, so that is where many of the Premillennialists will break their 'theological necks' – i.e. the Book of Matthew. By doing what Calvin did, mistaking the *elect* of Mat 24v24 for the *elect* of Eph 1v5, they overlooked the *elect* to whom the passage was **aimed** – Isa 65v9+22, Dan 7v18+21+22+25+27, and *pretended* the *elect* were Christians in the Body of Christ.

By not *rightly* dividing the word of truth, many Christians mess up regarding the ten virgins in Mat 25v1 and apply this verse also to the Church when it has **nothing** to do with the Church – the ten virgins don't *marry* Christ, they *meet* Him. The Church is His Bride and a chaste **virgin** (note **not** plural 'virgins') – 2 Cor 11v2. You will also note that Mat 25 ends with a **works** salvation set up – Mat 25v35-41; *Paul's Gospel was nowhere to be seen as Paul wasn't even saved yet!*

Now look up the following verses – Rev 6v16, Rev 14v14, Mat 24v30, Rev 1v7+17. *Not one* of those passages matches the Second Advent as described in Rev 19v11-15, Isa 63v1, Joel 2v1-3, Judg 5v1-20, Hab 3v3-14.

Somebody sees Jesus Christ at the **end** of Jacob's Trouble (aka The Tribulation) **before** He arrives at Armageddon with His divine 'cavalry' (Rev 19).

The requirements for the *elect* 'seeing' this Post-Tribulation 'appearance' are… 1) Purity of heart – Mat 5v8, 2) Holiness – Heb 12v14, 3) Be watchful and waiting – Heb 9v28.

Note also, that 'The Day of the Lord' is not just confined to the Second Advent. 'That Day' in the Prophets can refer to… 1) The Birth of Christ – (Isa 2v12, 4v2, 7v14+18), 2) The attack of Sennacherib – (Isa 10v5-20), 3) The defeat of Babylon by Persia – (Jer 50+51), 4) The Millennium – (2 Pet 3v8), 5) The White Throne Judgment – (2 Pet 3v10). Post-Tribbers who follow Rosenthal, take 2 Pet 3v10 and apply it to the *beginning* of the Millennium, because it said 'The Day of the Lord', as he had already *limited* that expression to refer to the events of Rev 16-19 just before the Millennium started. Rosenthal wound up with no Millennium, he was Amillennialist, Armageddon ran right into the White Throne Judgment.

Moses and Elijah are 'caught up' in Rev 11v12. The 144,000 Jews show up in the Third Heaven around the throne in Rev 14v1-4, and they were on earth **before** the 'Tribulation' started – Rev 7v3+4. These were all *raptured* and none of them were **IN** the Bride of Christ, the Body of Christ, the Church.

The 144,000 sang 'the song of Moses' (Rev 15v3), it's the song of Deut 32. It's quoted in Deut 32v36, Heb 10v30.

The *harvest* of Rev 14v15, **precedes** the *harvest* of Rev 14v18-20.

The *post-Trib* appearance of Jesus Christ to His enemies, as a Lamb seated on a throne, cannot match His appearance as seated on a horse (Rev 19v11-16). His enemies *see* Him long enough **before** He comes, to gather troops to fight against Him, at the place where they saw Him (Rev 19v19).

Jesus Christ is *seated* on a cloud in Rev 14 when the Post-Trib Rapture takes place. Those caught up at that time do **not** face the Judgment Seat of Christ, and they *marry* no one. They are *guests* at a wedding, and you were told this in Mat 22v10+11. So when we say 'Post-Trib', the terminology is not 100% accurate. It would be more accurate to say 'somewhere right near the end of the Tribulation' this Rapture will occur. Mat 24v29 **Immediately after the tribulation of those days**…, but *those days* can be shortened, or they will be delayed (Mat 24v22).

Paul's conversion is a *type* of 'that appearance' of Christ (Acts 9v1-5), which explains his 'born out of due time' statement in 1 Cor 15v8. This 'appearance' is foreshadowed in places like Isa 60v1-3, Joel 3v16 and Ps 50v2. It is God 'shining forth brighter than the sun' (Ps 67v1, Mat 17v2, Acts 22v6). Daniel has a run in with the Lord – Dan 10v5-11, and so does Ezekiel – Ezek 8v1+2. You will notice that not once did you need to run back to 'the Greek' (there isn't one) or 'the Hebrew' (there isn't one) to find all this out, just stay with the English Authorized Version King James Bible.

Daniel, Ezekiel and Paul were all Jewish evangelists sent to preach to the **Gentiles** as well as to the Jews (Dan 2-5+7+9, Ezek 26-30, 38-39, Rom 15-16). It will be 144,000 Jews who preach to **Gentiles**

ERRORS OF POST TRIBULATION RAPTURE

in Jacob's Trouble (aka The Tribulation).

Ruckman continues... So here we have *one* 'chaste virgin' (2 Cor 11v2) being caught up **before** the Mark of the Beast starts damning men (Rev 14v9+10), and she is caught up in the Spring (Song of Sol 2v10-13) by a voice that sounds like a trumpet (1 Thes 4v16) to the child of God but sounds like thunder to the unsaved (John 12v28-30, Job 37v1-5). Every saint in that Bride is called by *name* (John 10v1-7) and is first 'led ***out***' ('Exodus') of the world system (John 10v3) and then brought back in to earth *behind* their Shepherd (John 10v4).

So we have a number of *virgins* (Song of Sol 6v8) in **two separate groups** (Rev 7v4+9) unlike the 'one Body' (Gal 3v28, Eph 3v1-8). They are being **caught up after** the Mark of the Beast is required worldwide (Rev 13). These groups are caught up sometime around the Feast of Trumpets, when an Angel blows the *seventh* Trumpet, called 'a great sound of a trumpet' (Mat 24v31). This *sister* marries *no one* when she is called to 'Come up hither' and she has to stand before the White Throne Judgment (Rev 11v8, Rev 20v11-14) for the Judgment Seat of Christ is *past*. Note again that she came out of a **faith plus works** set up (Mat 25) requiring 'commandment keeping' (Rev 12v17, 14v12) as well as faith in Jesus Christ. *Works* show up at the White Throne – Rev 20.

No member of the Body of Christ will ever be alive in a situation where saved Jews and saved Gentiles make up *two separate* bodies of saints (Rev 7), and no member of the Body of Christ will be alive when a man can *lose* his salvation by taking a mark, or a number, or a name – Rev 13v1-18, Rev 14v9+10. No member of the Body of Christ will be present when an angel preaches 'another Gospel' that Paul did *not* preach (Gal 1v6-8) and is *blessed* for doing it – Rev 14v6+7. No member of the Body of Christ will ever be told that his 'enduring to the end' (Mat 24v13) depends upon keeping the commandments - Rev 12v17, Rev 14v12.

Many Christians today have stopped looking for the Lord Jesus Christ's return, they've given up for whatever reason. Many Christians don't want to talk 'End Times' because they have been so screwed up by the Post-Tribbers that they don't know what to believe anymore. The Devil is certainly using the **Post-Trib heresy** to bring confusion to the Body of Christ, when really, if you just take the Scriptures in their context, rightly dividing them, then you won't have a problem. None of the Post-Trib heretics understand the different plans of salvation in the different dispensations.

We should be *looking* for Jesus Christ... Acts 1v11, 1 John 3v1-3, Titus 2v13, Phil 3v20 etc. **not** the Antichrist.

Bible Believing Christians who can rightly divide 'The Book' are *not* looking for... an end time revival (*there won't be one*), Daniel's 70th Week, The Temple to be rebuilt, The Son of Perdition to show up, Russia to invade Palestine etc. **We are waiting for Jesus Christ to appear at the Rapture.**

We are told to... **Occupy till I come**. (Luke 19v13) In other words, live for God in everything you do, work for the Lord, serve the Lord and do His will not your own. This is another thing most Christians aren't doing, because they're not *looking* for Him, and think they have *years* left. I am expecting the Lord Jesus Christ to come anytime now - 1 Thes 1v10, Phil 3v20.

Many a Christian who *wrongly* divides the word of truth tries to drag the church into Mat 24v31, and into the Tribulation. When a Christian tells you that sinners are saved in the Tribulation the same way they are saved in every 'dispensation' including now, that should be a *warning sign*, as you know they will try and drag you into the Tribulation e.g. the **Post-Trib heresy**. Once you try to put Rev 12v17, Rev 14v12 and Heb 3v14 into the Church Age Gospel of the Grace of God (Acts 20v24), you open up the door to heresy, and heresy *is truth misplaced*.

Now there may be a gap between the Rapture and the beginning of Jacob's Trouble, however that will need studying in greater depth, but one thing is sure... The Rapture taught in Ps 50v1-6, Isa 26v20+21, Rev 14v14-16, Heb 9v28, 2 Sam 22v17-20, Ps 18v6-19 and Mat 24v40-42 is *not* connected with the New Testament Body of Christ that is *now* on the earth.

1 Thes 5 - Everything in the **first 10 verses** of 1 Thes 5 is dealing with the Second Advent, *not* the Rapture, you want to note that down right from the start.

1 Thes 5v1 **But of the times and the seasons, brethren, ye have no need that I write unto you**. Note Acts 1v6+7 **When they therefore were come together, they asked of him, saying, Lord, wilt thou at this time restore again the kingdom to Israel? And he said unto them, It is not for you to know the times or the seasons, which the Father hath put in his own power**. Paul is telling the Christians in 1 Thes 5 that there is *no need* to know the times and seasons on the run up to the 'day of the Lord' as this is *not* for them, as they will *not* be there for it, as the Church does *not* go through Jacob's Trouble (aka The Tribulation). Just like the disciples asked the Lord in Acts 1 about the restoration of the Kingdom, and He said it's *not* for them. (Just an interesting point... 'Times' refers to YEARS (Rev 12v14). There, the first time is one year, the 'times' are 2 YEARS, and the 'half a time' makes up to **3½ YEARS** as in the time of Moses and Elijah (Rev 11v2+3), and the Antichrist's times (Rev 13v5)).

1 Thes 5v2 **For yourselves know perfectly that the day of the Lord** (Second Advent *not* the Rapture) **so cometh as a thief in the night.** (NIGHT represents The Tribulation). A Jewish 'night' had 12 hours in it (John 11v9), divided into FOUR 'watches' which is exactly as a YEAR has 12 months divided into FOUR seasons – Winter, Spring (seedtime), Summer and Autumn (harvest). The four matching 'hours' are 6-9pm (Evening), 9-12pm (Midnight), 12-3am (Cockcrowing), and 3-6am (Morning) Mark 13v35 **Watch ye therefore: for ye know not when the master of the house cometh, at even, or at midnight, or at the cockcrowing, or in the morning**:

In 1 Thes 5v4 **But ye, brethren, are not in darkness, that that day should overtake you as a thief**. We are told that the DAY (v2) is *not* going to overtake you 'as a thief in the night'. This is where a lot of Christians mistake this verse for the Rapture instead of the Second Advent. Note in v1-10 the *different people* Paul is addressing, as this will help you out to whom he is speaking to... v1 – 'brethren' and 'you' i.e. Christians. **v3** – 'they' and 'them' i.e. those IN Jacob's Trouble (The Tribulation) **v4** – 'ye brethren' i.e. Christians (the Body of Christ) Paul says that 'THAT DAY' should NOT overtake US (Christians) as a thief, why? Because WE are *not* going to go through the Tribulation i.e. Jacob's Trouble. The Church is raptured out *before* the Tribulation starts.

So back to v4 – We know the 'thief' is coming. He's coming in the *morning* watch (3-6am). Now for something *very* interesting look at Mat 14v25 and cross reference that with Hab 3v15... *mind blowing stuff eh?*

Let old 'Rucker's' take us even deeper... We can't date the Rapture of course, plus our calendar could be 'out', but notice this... Read Job 3v4+6 and also get a hold of Clarence Larkin's book Dispensational Truth and turn to pages 71+72. God is not *counting* certain years in His *figuring* of the Rapture and End Times, He's omitting some. Note too where you just read from, Job. Job means *persecuted one* and points to the Tribulation. It was Satan who persecuted Job (see Rev 12v4+13). Israel is to be persecuted for forty two months. Why there are 42 chapters in the book of JOB, *how mad is that!* But it gets deeper... When God healed Job, the Holy Spirit wrote in Job 42v10 **And the LORD turned the captivity of Job,** knowing He had used the expression 14 times for the *restoration of the nation of Israel* at the end of the Tribulation – Deut 30v3, Ps 126v1+4, Jer 29v14, 33v7+11+26, Lam 2v14, Zeph 2v7 etc.

ERRORS OF POST TRIBULATION RAPTURE

Who on earth would have used *that* expression for a man getting *healed* of several diseases? *See the depth? You can read a verse and just glaze over it not realising that it has so much more depth.*

This is why it is so important to *dump all* 'bibles' other than the Authorized Version King James Bible, because if you change *one single letter* it can change the entire meaning. (Let me give you a classic verse that has duped all prophecy teachers and preachers... 2 Thes 2v7 compare it in the KJV with the NKJV and see something incredible! *Did you get it?* Now you know *why* prophecy teachers teach the 'he' is the Holy Spirit) *Have a listen to this sermon in regard to 2 Thes 2v7...*

http://www.timefortruth.co.uk/media/forcedown.php?file=1783-1420905407.mp3

I keep saying it, but if you use any other 'bible' other than the AV/KJV you'll mess up on End Time prophecies, let me give you another example... we've just looked at Job 42v10 and the words **'turned the captivity of Job'** in regard to the 'restoration of Israel' and what do we find in the NKJV, NIV, ASV, NASV, RSV, ESV etc.? *They all omit those words.* Is it any wonder why modern day Christianity which uses modern day 'bible' *perversions,* is turning *against* Israel? Anti-Semitism is on the rise *in the church*, and one reason for this is because of *perverted* 'bibles'.

So when it comes to *time*, God may have already stopped His clock, and won't start it again until He returns at the Second Advent, I don't know, but there is that possibility. Ruckman says that there is a possibility that the 'clock' won't start *running* again until Jesus Christ *lands* on the earth in the Jewish seventh month (Tabernacles) as 'King of kings and Lord of lords' (2 Pet 1v13-18).

Now, let's go back to 1 Thes 5v3 **For when they shall say, Peace and safety; then sudden destruction cometh upon them, as travail upon a woman with child; and they shall not escape**. It is Satan who starts off peaceably in the Tribulation (Read Dan 11v21+24) so that he can *destroy many* (Dan 8v24) through 'peace'. Watch him sit down in the Holy of Holies (2 Thes 2v4) calling himself 'God' and pulling out his Roman Catholic 'bible' and quoting Luke 2v14. **He'll move from Rome to Jerusalem!**

The *sudden destruction* is Joel 2, Isa 63, Jer 25, Mat 24v16-19+29, Rev 14+19.

Remember who Paul is talking to in 1 Thes 5v5... **Ye are all the children of light, and the children of the day: we are not of the night, nor of darkness**. Note the 'YE', that's Paul's readers who are *not* in the Tribulation and will *not* be going through it, that's the Body of Christ, the Church... *you and me!* Remember 'in the night, and in the dark' is a reference to The Tribulation. WE are children of the LIGHT not of the night or darkness, hence the passage is talking about the Second Advent and *not* the Rapture. *Post-Tribbers haven't a clue!*

The SUN of Mal 4v2 is THE ADVENT. That 'SUN' comes to burn up CHAFF. Read Mal 4v1+2, Mat 13v42+43, Zeph 3v8.

So the Christian (us) is *not* of the night nor of darkness, because we have the '**light of the world**' (John 8v12) and '**walk in the light, as he is in the light**' (1 John 1v5-7)

1 Thes 5v6 – We are told *not* to sleep. (Incidentally, there are *two* things we are to 'love *not*' in the Scriptures... one is *the world* (1 John 2v15) and the other is *sleep* Prov20v13). Here in 1 Thes 5v6, we are told not to sleep but to watch. The Christian should be alert, on his guard and ready for action just like any **soldier** (2 Tim 2v1-4, 1 Tim 6v12, 1 Tim 1v18), yet Christians are half-soaked today and haven't a clue what is going on. Most Christians are just plain lazy, when it comes to reading and studying the Scriptures, and there are hardly any Bible Believing Christians who are true **soldiers** for the Lord Jesus Christ left in England. The population of the UK is just over 64 million people. I wonder how many Bible Believing Christians are among that lot. England is shot through, the sodomites and Muslims seem to be taking over, while the church just sits back not

having a clue what is going on. **COME LORD JESUS!** We need our Captain to get us out of here – Heb 2v10. Regarding v6 and being spiritually alert, most Post-Tribbers are not only spiritually blind, but **dead**.

Note also the 'others' of v6 and the 'they' of v7 are the 'they' of v3, i.e. those IN the Tribulation, *not* the Church. We are of the DAY, not the night (v8) and it goes on to say *in context* in v9 **For God hath not appointed us to wrath, but to obtain salvation by our Lord Jesus Christ**. Did you see that *'us'* that's *us!* We don't go into, or through the time of Jacob's Trouble. Now follow it through to v11 **Wherefore comfort yourselves together, and edify one another, even as also ye do**. We can comfort ourselves knowing that we are *not* going *into, or through* the Tribulation. You couldn't say that if you thought you would be facing the worst time this world has ever known i.e. 'hell on earth' where Satan is given free reign. *Thank the Lord that the church will not be going through any part of Jacob's Trouble. I'm looking for Jesus Christ not the Antichrist.*

2 Thes 2v2 – A problem for Bible 'correctors' *not* Bible believers. (See RRB page 1577)

That ye be not soon shaken in mind, or be troubled, neither by spirit, nor by word, *nor by letter as from us*, as that THE DAY OF CHRIST is at hand. 2 Thes 2v2. Most Christians, especially a lot of the prophecy 'teachers' change the 'Day of Christ' to the 'Day of the Lord'. By doing this they have so-called 'corrected' an 'error' in the Scriptures, when really they have cut their own spiritual throats when it comes to Biblical illumination/revelation. **Touch THE BOOK and you've had it!** If you don't understand something in the Scriptures you do *not* change it trying to get it to fit in with your preconceived ideas. **Never do that!** This is something the PWMI (Prophetic Witness Movement International) do. *They change the Bible!* Some of them don't even use the AV/KJV so they'll NEVER get their 'End Time' doctrine right. Without THE BOOK, and we *know* 'which' Book don't we folks, you will never be straight on your doctrine.

Now back to our text... The reason why these shallow Bible students change the 'Day of Christ' to the 'Day of the Lord' is because of what follows in verses 3-12, which is a reference to the Antichrist in the Tribulation. But the 'Day of Christ' is a reference, in the Pauline epistles, to the Rapture, *and* the Judgment Seat of Christ - 1 Cor 1v8, 1 Cor 5v5, 2 Cor 1v14, Phil 1v6+10, Phil 2v16.

The problem the Thessalonians had was that someone had written to them, pretending to be Paul, (***nor by letter as from us***) and had told them that the Rapture, about which Paul had told them in 1 Thes 4v13-18, had *already* taken place and they had *missed it*. Paul assures them in v1 that the Rapture has not *yet* occurred. He is not saying in this verse that the Rapture wasn't *'at hand'*, because in Rom 13v12 he said *that it was!* He says in v3 that something must take place *first* 'before' the Rapture. **In the Bible a thing can be 'at hand' and yet any number of events can occur *before* it shows up** (see Isa 13v6, Jer 23v23, Joel 1v15, Zeph 1v7, Mat 3v2, Mat 4v17, Mark 1v15, 1 Pet 4v7, Rev 1v3, Rev 22v10).

The *key* to understanding v1-3 is that 'the Day of Christ' *can* encompass a number of events just like 'the Day of the Lord' can. Paul told you back in 2 Thes 1v10, that *'that day'*, in reference to 'the Day of Christ' (see v3), *can* include the *Advent* as well as the Rapture (cf. 2 Tim 1v12+18).

Post-Tribulation / Pre-Wrath - Just a few more helpful notes...

Mat 24v10-14 – We do *not* preach the Gospel of the Kingdom. That is *not* for the church.

Note in Mat 24 the church and the *new* covenant were not formed, revealed or manifested. (Heb 9v15-17)

ERRORS OF POST TRIBULATION RAPTURE

Mat 24 is directed to **the Jews** not the church.

The *mid-Trib* Rapture is for the **believing Jews**.

The word *elect* is mentioned three times in Mat 24v22+24+31 and *not once is it referring to the church*. It is referring to **Israel**.

The word 'tribulation' occurs 22 times in the Bible. It has *four* meanings - 1) 'THE' Tribulation (occurs in *only* 3 out of the 22) Dan 4v30, Mat 24v29, Mat 13v24, 2) Tribulation in the Christian life – John 16v33, 3) General Tribulation in life, 4) 'GREAT' Tribulation (only occurs 3 times) - Mat 24v21, Rev 2v22, Rev 7v14.

Wrath – also has *four* meanings - 1) God's wrath - John 3v36, 2) Man's wrath – Rom 4v15, 3) Miscellaneous wrath, 4) THE wrath is always connected with the Jews.

Enoch is the perfect example of a Raptured saint who doesn't see *death* before the Judgment (Flood). Some of us will *not* see death *before* the Judgment (Tribulation).

Paul **never** tells us that we are going to go through the Tribulation or 'how' we are to get through it.

1 Cor 3v11-16, 2 Cor 4v14, Gal 6v7-9, Eph 1v13, – none of these verses talk about us going through the Tribulation, Paul **never** mentions it. It's all positive what is ahead of us. Paul only talks about the tribulation that we all face *here* in life, *not* 'THE' Tribulation which is *to come*... which the church will *not* go through. Paul would have majored on 'THE' Tribulation and let us know how we should get through it etc. but he doesn't. Paul doesn't *teach anything* about us going through 'THE' Tribulation.

It's not about 'survival' through THE Tribulation, it's about living for the Lord *now* and expecting His return *now*.

The **post-Trib heresy** is being used *by the Devil* to cause *division* among Christians and get their eyes *off* the Lord Jesus Christ.

Another proof that the church will *not* go through the Tribulation.

Here is a simple proof why the Body of Christ does *not* go through the Tribulation. The main verse that prophecy teachers use proving the SEVEN (7) year Tribulation aka 'Jacob's Trouble' aka 'Daniel's 70th Week', is Dan 9v27 **And he shall confirm the covenant with many for one week: and in the midst of the week he shall cause the sacrifice and the oblation to cease, and for the overspreading of abominations he shall make it desolate, even until the consummation, and that determined shall be poured upon the desolate.** In Dan 9v25 we read... **Know therefore and understand, that from the going forth of the commandment to restore and to build Jerusalem unto the Messiah the Prince shall be seven weeks, and threescore and two weeks: the street shall be built again, and the wall, even in troublous times.** Now ADD all the weeks up and you get what? 70 (seventy). *Now look at this beauty...* Dan 9v24 **Seventy weeks are determined UPON THY PEOPLE** (Who are 'Thy people'??? The answer of course is **ISRAEL!**) **and upon thy holy city, to finish the transgression, and to make an end of sins, and to make reconciliation for iniquity, and to bring in everlasting righteousness, and to seal up the vision and prophecy, and to anoint the most Holy.** Now HOW MANY weeks are determined and upon WHOM? The answer 70 weeks, which **INCLUDES the 70th Week aka 'The Tribulation'** and those 70 weeks are FOR ISRAEL NOT the Church, the Body of Christ. *How simple can you get?* The Church will *not* go through the Tribulation. *The 'Posties' are very shallow Bible students, who couldn't rightly divide* **THAT BOOK** *if their lives depended upon it.* Oh and by the way, do you know how these heretics try to get *around this clear teaching? They say that THEY 'are' Israel, they **replace** Israel with the church and say that THEY are now Israel. Follow me...* Dan 9v24 again **Seventy weeks are determined upon thy people and upon thy holy city, to finish the transgression, and to make an end of sins, and to make reconciliation for iniquity, and to bring in everlasting righteousness, and to seal up the vision and prophecy, and to anoint the most Holy.** *If they are Israel, that means their SINS have **not** been totally dealt with.* Note it says 'the holy city' – what on earth could this be for the Body of Christ where YOU live? Jerusalem is *not* where I live, that's in **Israel.** MY sins have already been paid for on the Cross, (1 Cor 15v1-4, Gal 1v4, Heb 9v26+28, Heb 10v10, 1 Pet 3v18, Rom 5v6+8 plus loads more...) and I have Christ's righteousness NOW, and I 'HAVE BEEN' reconciled (2 Cor 5v18). This verse is certainly NOT talking to ME, and no one IN the Body of Christ today is a 'JEW', we are Christians. (Gal 3v28). (It is such a shame that **Kent Hovind has been deceived** into *falling for the lie* that the church will go *through* the Tribulation. Be very careful who you follow, & make sure you check everything out with the Scriptures. Many of his *followers* are no longer looking for Jesus Christ). *I believe the Lord Jesus Christ could return today!*

POST-Trib vs. PRE-Trib

The confusion lies when you confuse the two. You find the Rapture of Tribulation saints in Mat 24v31, Ps 50v2-5, Isa 26v19-21 & Rev 11v15. You find the Rapture of the Body of Christ in 1 Thes 4 & 1 Cor 15. The TWO are NOT the same. This is where AnderSNAKE & Hovind mess up, they don't RIGHTLY DIVIDE the Scriptures (2 Tim 2v15), & therefore confuse the two. When you don't rightly divide the Scriptures, you'll teach that the Church will go through all or part of the Tribulation, calling this kind of Rapture a 'Pre-Wrath-Rapture', which is what us Bible Believers call 'Hogwash'. These POST-Tribbers get all in a mess when dealing with '**the Day of Christ**' & '**the Day of the Lord**'.

The term 'day of the Lord', as Paul's 'THAT day' (2 Tim 4v8 & 1v18) is a reference to SEVEN DIFFERENT periods of time in the OT which are 3,800 years apart. In the OT, 'the day of the LORD' is used to mark...

1) The invasion of the ten northern tribes by Assyria in Isaiah 10v5-16+20+21+24+27+32, 7v14+17+20, Amos 5v18-20, 6v9+11+14.

2) The destruction of Jerusalem by Nebuchadnezzar in Joel 1v6-15, Isa 2v12+20, 3v7+16+25+26, 5v25-30, Mic 3v1+2, Jer 17v18+19+27.

3) The Virgin Birth & the FIRST Advent of Christ in 4 B.C. in Isa 7v14-18, 61v1+2, Zech 9v9+10+14+16.

4) The Millennial reign of Christ (yet future) in Isa 19v18-25, 24v21-23, 26v1-4, Hos 2v18+19, Zech 13v1-6, 14v8-21.

5) The Battle of Armageddon at the SECOND Advent in Joel 2v1-11, 3v9-18, Mic 5v1-15, Isa 25v7-11, Mal 4v1-3, Zech 14v1-6, Ezek 38v19.

6) The Last Judgment at the end of the Millennium in 2 Pet 3v10, Isa 66v22-24, Dan 7v9-11.

7) The destruction of Babylon by Persia in Isa 13v6+9+17+19.

The trouble with people like AnderSNAKE, Hovind etc. is that they follow Rosenthal who used the term 'day of the LORD' exclusively for the Second Advent, again, NOT *rightly* dividing the word of truth.

How about this for ADVANCED REVELATION in the KJV Bible... notice the words in italics... 2 Thes

ERRORS OF POST TRIBULATION RAPTURE

2v3 Let no man deceive you by any means: for *that day shall not come*, **except there come a falling away first, and that man of sin be revealed, the son of perdition**; Those words in italics are not found in ANY Greek manuscript, so WHY do ALL the modern day perverted 'bibles' PUT IT IN??? Because THE STANDARD is the KJV Bible, they have to! The KJV sets the pace & the others try to keep up. Think about it, why do all the modern 'bibles' put these words (*that day shall not come*) IN the text when they were NOT in the original manuscripts? *Makes you think don't it!*

You see, 'the day of Christ' indicates that the 'day of the Lord' OVERLAPS the end of the Church Age & the BEGINNING of the Millennium as well as THE END of the Millennium – 2 Pet 3v10. This makes an 8th application of 'the day of the Lord'. The 'day of Christ' would INCLUDE the Rapture & the Judgment Seat of Christ, & the Marriage of Jesus Christ. As Ruckman continues... The thing is, it would refer to events that take place UPSTAIRS that are *simultaneous* with what is going on DOWNSTAIRS in the Tribulation. What this means is this...

1) The day of the Lord applied to Armageddon, does not come until the Antichrist has been revealed as 'the son of perdition'.

2) The Rapture & the Judgment Seat of Christ will not take place till there has been a 'falling away first'.

To test this hypothesis, pick up Clarence Larkin's book 'Dispensational Truth', published before WW2, & learn why 'THAT DAY' can refer not only to the Millennium & the Second Advent but also the Judgement Seat of Christ (2 Tim 1v18, 2 Cor 1v14, 1 Cor 5v5, 2 Tim 4v8). This explains why the Holy Spirit chose to call the 'beginning' of 'the day of the Lord' (it overlaps the White Throne Judgment – 2 Pet 3v10-12), 'the day of Christ'. Between pages 43 & 44 in 'Dispensational Truth' are 'The Prophetic DAYS of Scripture'. There you will find this note... 'The Day of Antichrist, the Day of Man, & the Day of the Lord OVERLAP, but for clearness the 'overlapping' is NOT SHOWN.' So Larkin left it up to the Bible student to search the Scriptures for themselves.

Clearly, in the drawn chart, the 'upstairs events' are shown, & the title over them is the title of 2 Thessalonians – 'THE DAY OF CHRIST'. The 'Day of Salvation' clearly ends in the drawing with THE RAPTURE, not the Second Advent, while the 'Day of Man' OVERLAPS the Tribulation, since the 'MAN of sin' is a MAN. Ruckman goes on to say that Larkin only missed one overlap, 'The day of the Lord' with the 'White Throne Judgment'. This is too deep & too confusing for Hyper-Diapers (Bullinger, O'Hair, Stam, Baker, Moron-Moore, Baby-Eli & Fake-Pfenny etc.) these Hyper-Diapers don't believe that covenants & dispensations can overlap... they can, & they DO! The covenant in Gen 3 goes right through the next FIVE DISPENSATIONS & is as applicable for saved people in the Church Age as it was BEFORE the Genesis Flood.

2 Thes 2v2 – So the Day of Christ has to INCLUDE the Advent & the Millennium, so it is not 'at hand' in that sense. Several things have to happen first. The word 'Christ' was inserted to confirm His Deity. Our 'gathering together unto him' (v1) will not take place until a 'falling away' (v3) takes place & that will precede the appearance of the Antichrist. The time bracket is not given. The problem comes when you see 'that man of sin be REVEALED' (v3). Obviously when he is 'revealed' he is revealed in his true nature which is NOT JUST 'the man of sin' BUT the SON OF DAMNATION – the 'son of perdition' (aka the 'angel of the bottomless pit' – Rev 9v11. He was a King, so it was 'his own place' - Acts 1v25). He appeared on earth as A MAN (John 6v70), & Jesus Christ called him 'the son of perdition' (John 17v12) because he goes into 'perdition' finally (Rev 17v8). We are NOT waiting for the Antichrist to be revealed like AnderSNAKE & Hovind ARE! *I'm outta here fella!* In v6 we see that he WILL be revealed at a later time... 'that he might be revealed in his time'. But that is a reference to the whole world getting to know him (Rev 13). He will then be revealed to the

sinners described in vs 10-12.

The man to be 'revealed' to the world has already been so well 'revealed' to us who read the Scriptures... he will be a Syrian-Jew with Hamitic blood in him (Jer 48v24+25); he will be an hermaphrodite (double-sexed – Dan 4v37) & reign as a 'wicked prince' (Ezek 21v25) & false 'messiah' ('anointed') on Mt. Zion in the rebuilt temple (vs 4 in our context). He will profess to be 'God... in the flesh' (v4) after denying that Jesus Christ WAS! Jerusalem will be 'Sodom & Egypt' as long as he reigns (Rev 11v8), & he will reign for 42 months (Rev 13v5) while beheading anyone who does not take his *mark* (a black spot), or his number (666), or his name ('Apollyon' in Greek, 'Abaddon' in Hebrew – Rev 9v11) – see also Rev 20v4. He will demand that all nations in the UN worship a 'living' idol (Rev 13v14+15), & that all of them agree to wipe out every JEW on earth (Zech 11v15-17, 12v3, 14v1+2). His *letter* is 'X', & his *sign* is a 'kiss of peace'. For the rest of the material get Ruckman's book 'The Mark of the Beast' – it's a definitive work on the subject.

2 Thes 2v3 – 'Be revealed'? Future? Not for anyone who has a KJV Bible! No Christian would be waiting for the Antichrist to 'be revealed'. Paul is simply telling the Thessalonians what is going to take place before 'the day of the Lord', & he calls it 'the day of Christ' because 'that day', for ***them***, will begin with the Rapture (1 Thes 4), NOT the Second Advent. For the world, 'that day' is in Rev 19, Mal 4, Isa 63, Jer 25, Judg 5 & Joel 3.

'The day of Christ IS at hand' (2 Thes 2v2) – Well it might be 'at hand' for the Christian, but 'that day' which is 'the day of the Lord' will *not come for the...* until... No *interval* is given for the time *between* his writing (Paul's) & the Rapture; it was IMMINENT in 1 Cor 15v51 & Rom 13v11+12.

The best way to handle these verses is to say that the 'man of sin' (NOW) is 'the Pope', who will later become Satan incarnate, & thus, 'the seed of the serpent' (Gen 3v15) will be the literal 'son of Satan'. It is probable that he will come up from the dead after being assassinated – Zech 11v17, Job 3v8, Ezek 31v15.

More Ruckman quality... From a Scriptural standpoint, the Tribulation temple (which 'the son of perdition' will enter & sit down on the 'mercy SEAT' – Exod 25v18-22, Rev 2v13) could be 'built' in less than 48 hours. Once you believe that the Antichrist reigns for 42 months (which he does) & Moses & Elijah witness against him for 42 months (which they do), while Israel runs to the wilderness to be fed manna (which they will – Mic 7v14, Exod 16, Rev 12v6+14), you will have to have the 'temple' PRESENT at the START of those 42 months (Rev 11v1+2).

That means that the Rapture could be delayed if the Body of Christ is NOT going to be here during those 42 months (Rev 11v1+2)... & IT'S NOT! The Rapture would be 'conditional' on the 'building' of the temple. This would mean that, at this *present* moment, there is no possibility the Rapture could take place, because to rebuild a building that took SEVEN YEARS to build in 1 Kings 6v38, & took more than FORTY YEARS to build in the First Century B.C. (John 2v20), means that no one in 2017 can throw that building up in even a week, not if it's going to match Herod's Temple, or Solomon's Temple!

But here comes a corker! Follow this closely for some real insight... The Lord has a 'tabernacle' being 'built' & NOT a 'temple!' The NIV blunders into it innocently by giving you a 'formal equivalence' in Acts 15v16 (cf. with KJV). It says 'I will REBUILD David's fallen TENT!!!' In Amos 9v11+12, where 'It is written' (Acts 15v15) in Hebrew, the word chosen was 'sukkah' connected with the 'Feast of Tabernacles'. Thus, Amos ties himself up with the Hebrew word 'mishkan' used throughout Exodus in describing the OT 'TENT' & 'TABERNACLE' which Moses erected (Exod 40) in the wilderness; it was NOT any reference to a BUILDING that could be 'built'. But James in Acts 15v13-16 IS referring to that TENT! You see, that cloth & skin TENT that was the 'tabernacle' IS CALLED a 'TEMPLE' in

ERRORS OF POST TRIBULATION RAPTURE

1 Sam 1v9, long before Solomon built anything. That 'temple' even had 'posts' (1 Sam 1v9). This makes the KJV reading 'tabernacle' superior to 'tent' (NIV), for it was separate from the tabernacle according to Exo 36v19, 40v19 & Num 3v25. **THAT IS ABSOLUTELY WILD FOLKS!!!**

The TABERNACLE was the *whole structure* that was covered by 'the tent' (Exo 40v19). That is the 'Tabernacle' that 1 Sam 1 called 'THE TEMPLE!' *Now you show me another prophecy teacher to whom God revealed that? The Lord certainly blessed Ruckman! Genius!*

A 'temple' can be 'rebuilt'. That is why the Lord said what He said in Acts 15v16. He did not say 'dwelling place' or 'tent' because David's 'tabernacle' (2 Sam 6v17) was NOT the 'real tabernacle'; it was a 'tent' he set up for the Ark of the Covenant *when there was no temple!* Till that time, God Himself said He Himself had 'walked in a TENT & in a TABERNACLE' (2 Sam 7v6). The OT 'tabernacle' could be erected in less than 'forty-eight hours' if it had to be done & the Jews had been preparing to do it. The 'tabernacle' that David pitched for (2 Sam 6v17) did NOT contain the Golden Candlestick, the Table of Shewbread, or the Altar of Incense; it contained just the ARK. It was just a tent! The 'Tabernacle' wasn't in Jerusalem, it was in the 'high place of Gibeon' (1 Chron 16v39, 21v29, 2 Chron 1v3).

I would highly recommend you buying the book 'Israel – A Deadly Piece of Dirt' by Peter Ruckman. (See Appendix THREE)

The Psalms & their placement in the KJV Bible

David's name is given as the author of 73 of the Psalms, while other names are attached to some of them... Asaph, Solomon, Ethan, Moses, & the sons of Korah. There are about 49 of the Psalms that are anonymous. Some of them were written during the Exile in Babylon, & others were 'post-Exilic' (Ps 85 +126). The most remarkable thing about the Psalms is their placement in the English Bible against the 'original' Hebrew order, for in all the Hebrew Bibles, the Psalms follow Malachi instead of Job. The KJV (aka The Authorized Version Bible, or AV Bible) order gives 2 Chronicles for the dispersion of Israel (matching A.D. 70), Ezra for the regathering of Israel (matching A.D. 1918), Nehemiah for the rebuilding of Jerusalem (matching A.D. 1948), Esther, showing the rejection of a Gentile Queen during a seven-day feast in a King's palace (matching the Marriage Supper of the Lamb in Rev 19v7), & then Job – on the ground of Uz, seven days & nights (matching the Tribulation). Job is the clearest 'type' of the Tribulation found in either Testament. He is followed by 'The Blessed Man' (Ps 1) who is to reign over 'the kings of the earth' as God's begotten Son (Ps 2). The order of the King James' books is premillennial, without a premillennialist on the committee. The order of the books in the 'original' (an Alexandrian Cult term) is NOT! It's also very interesting to note that the longest chapter in THE BOOK (Ps 119) is speaking about THE BOOK! Ps 119 is about the word of God. There is also more material on the Second Coming of Christ in the Psalms than there is in Matthew, Mark, Luke & John combined. Shallow students of the Scriptures like Andersnake, Bob-the-boob, & Kent-beg-for-money-Hovind, haven't a clue regarding this, they wouldn't even think about expounding the Psalms doctrinally & prophetically... devotionally maybe at a push. This is why their 'teaching / preaching' is very lame & more than often, spiritually dead.

NOTES

NOTES

NOTES

ALCOHOL

Should Christians drink alcohol?

I honestly *cannot* believe why Christians would even *consider* drinking alcohol, it just doesn't make any sense at all, knowing the harm it does to millions. Today, most Christians are very worldly and *want to fit in*, that is why the church is so weak and the majority of Christians haven't a clue when it comes to *living* holy lives - 2 Tim 3v12. Christians today want to keep *mixing* with the world, yet Scripture teaches us to be separate - 2 Cor 6v17, 2 Cor 6v14. So *why* do you want to *join* with the world? What *good* does that do you in your Christian walk? What kind of witness and testimony for the Lord is that? 1 Cor 10v2. Yet many Christians desire to drink alcohol and *'be one of the lads'*. Eph 5v6-8. Have you ever thought *why you are not* having more of an impact upon your family, friends and work colleagues for the Lord? *It's probably because you are too worldly!* They can't tell the difference from *your* life to *theirs*. Now have a read of the following verses regarding alcohol and let them speak to you... Isa 65v8 get that? **New wine is found in the cluster** – that's *grape juice* and *not* alcoholic wine. That's Scripture. (Look up every verse that talks about NEW wine). **Gen 40v11, Deut 32v14**.

Now for those of you who know your Scriptures and can rightly divide *that Book*, you will know that **grape juice, water and blood** are interconnected. There is a special relationship between them all. This Scripture reference is to new wine not alcoholic wine. Fermented/alcoholic wine does *not* picture the pure Blood of Christ at all. You have un-fermented... (**un**leavened) bread at the communion table because the leaven represents sin. You should therefore have **un**fermented (**un**leavened - Exod 12v15+19, Exod 13v7, Exod 34v25, Lev 2v11, Lev 6v17, Lev 10v12, Mat 13v33. Leaven is always seen in the *negative* - Mat 16v6+11, Luke 12v1, 1 Cor 5v6-8, Gal 5v9 - leaven is sin in 'type' or false doctrine - Mat 16v6-12, Gal 5v9, 1 Cor 5v6-8) ...wine at the communion table because Christ's Blood was pure and incorruptible. *Get it?* Isn't it interesting that every time Christ talks about the wine and drinking the cup He always puts it like this... Mat 26v29, Mark 14v25, Luke 22v18, **fruit of the vine**, i.e. **grape juice**. *What is the fruit of the vine?* It is a **grape**. Go on, now have a guess what the *forbidden fruit* was? *You got it!*

Water, blood and grape juice – they are all connected. Alcohol is a *poison* and no Christian should drink it. It's mad to think that for some people, including children, their *first taste of alcohol* **is in church** at the communion table. If you are a pastor, elder or deacon and you allow this to happen; *you* will be judged for this! That *poison* that you are mixing with 'blood' i.e. fermented wine – 'alcohol' will cause many problems in people's lives. *Just look around at the devastation alcohol has caused to this world, to the place where you live and the people you know.*

Jer 48v33 - *Get that?* Wine to fall from the winepresses – none shall *tread*. (Tread what? *You got it!*) What was the wine? **It was new** wine i.e. **grape juice** and *not* alcoholic wine. If you drink alcohol, you are not only going against God and His word, you are *sinning*. If you disagree with that, I suggest you read the deeper study I produced which you will find on our website (*or I can send you a hard copy upon request*) – follow this link...

http://www.timefortruth.co.uk/content/pages/documents/1300042238.pdf

If you have booze in your house, pour it down the sink and get rid of it now. If you are a Christian that likes to have a bottle of wine with your meal, grow up and stop being such an idiot just because *you want to mix with the world.* If you're a Christian that likes to have a beer with the lads, grow up and stop acting like a moron and take a stand for once in your life. It's great fun *to go out with the lads* and order an orange juice! It starts a whole conversation off and gives you a great opportunity to testify for the Lord Jesus Christ. *Be a man!*

A *worldly* Christian will try to justify all those *sins* that he wants to hold on to.

Alcohol is addictive - 1 Cor 6v12. We are told *not* to be **brought under the power** or to be controlled by anything. The only exception is the Holy Spirit - Eph 5v18. Alcohol is clearly a powerful substance (Prov 23v35). Because *alcohol is addictive*, we should choose not to drink alcoholic beverages.

There are *loads* of good reasons a believer should not drink. One should be enough!

It's interesting to note that when the Scriptures talk about the office of a bishop/elder/pastor, it mentions about wine. *Interesting!* Just by running these Scripture references you will know it is wrong to drink alcohol... Prov 31v4-7 (Neh 8v10). We don't need drink to help us through sorrows and trials. Hos 4v11, Isa 28v1+3+7, Rom 14v21, James 4v4, Prov 20v1, Gen 9v21, Isa 5v11, Hab 2v15, Prov 23v29-35, Eph 5v18, Luke 21v34+35, Gal 5v19, Prov 4v17, Isa 56v12, Hab 2v5, Prov 23v31+32, Deut 32v33, Hos 7v5, Isa 5v22-24, 1 Cor 6v10.

The Lord's Supper - Mat 26v26+27 - Having finished the Passover, the Lord 'took bread', *unleavened, unfermented* bread, and blessed it. This was done always at the Passover, and was by Christ, transferred to the Supper. He gave it to His disciples as the symbol of His body. Then He took the cup, and gave thanks. This also was done on giving the third cup at the Passover. This He also transferred, and gave it to His disciples as the symbol of His blood. We have mentioned about leaven and the representation of sin, thus the bread was *unleavened* i.e. *unfermented* and *so must the wine be unfermented*. If leaven was used in any of the Passover sacrifice they were 'cut off from Israel'.

Acts 13v37 - All admit that the bread was *unleavened* – and was therefore, the proper emblem for the Body of Christ, which saw no corruption. For the same reason, there was a necessity that the wine should be *unfermented*, that it might be the fit emblem of the great sacrifice which saw no corruption. Leaven, because it was corruption, was forbidden as an offering to God - Exo 34v25. If leaven was not allowed with the sacrifices, which were the types of the atoning Blood of Christ, how much more would it be a violation of the commandment to allow leaven, or that which was *fermented*, to be the symbol of the blood of the atonement? Ecc 7v29.

UK Statistics on Alcohol

- More than 9 million people in England drink more than the recommended daily limits
- In the UK, in 2014 there were 8,697 alcohol-related deaths
- Alcohol is 10% of the UK burden of disease and death, making alcohol one of the three biggest lifestyle risk factors for disease and death in the UK, after smoking and obesity
- An estimated 7.5 million people are unaware of the damage their drinking could be causing
- Alcohol related harm costs England around £21bn per year, with £3.5bn to the NHS, £11bn tackling alcohol-related crime and £7.3bn from lost work days and productivity costs
- Alcohol was 61% more affordable in 2013 than it was in 1980

Alcohol and Health

- Alcohol is a causal factor in more than 60 medical conditions, including: mouth, throat, stomach, liver and

ALCOHOL

breast cancers; high blood pressure, cirrhosis of the liver; and depression

- In the UK in 2012-13, there were 1,008,850 hospital admissions related to alcohol consumption where an alcohol-related disease, injury or condition was the primary reason for hospital admission or a secondary diagnosis
- However, if you include deaths where alcohol was a contributing factor (such as various cancers, falls and hypertensive diseases), the figure increases to 21,512: 13,971 for males and 7,541 for females
- Males accounted for approximately 65% of all alcohol-related deaths in the UK in 2014
- Alcohol now costs the NHS £3.5bn per year; equal to £120 for every tax payer
- In England and Wales, 63% of all alcohol-related deaths in 2012 were caused by alcoholic liver disease
- Liver disease is one of the few major causes of premature mortality that is increasing
- Deaths from liver disease have reached record levels, rising by 20% in a decade
- The number of older people between the ages of 60 and 74 admitted to hospitals in England with mental and behavioural disorders associated with alcohol use has risen by over 150% in the past ten years, while the figure for 15-59 years old has increased by 94%

Treatment

- The NHS estimates that around 9% of adult men in the UK and 4% of UK adult women show signs of alcohol dependence
- Only 1% of dependent drinkers access treatment in the UK
- The overall number of people in treatment in 2013-14 increased by 5% (5,237) from 109,863 in 2012-13

Crime

- Alcohol-related crime in the UK is estimated to cost between £8bn and £13bn per year
- A fifth (29%) of all violent incidents in 2013–14 took place in or around a pub or club. This rises to 42% for stranger violence. Over two thirds (68%) of violent offences occur in the evening or at night
- There were 8,270 casualties of drink driving accidents in the UK in 2013, including 240 fatalities and 1,100 people who suffered serious injury
- Victims believed the offender(s) to be under the influence of alcohol in over half (53%) of all violent incidents, or 704,000 offences

Young People

- In 2012, 43% of school pupils (aged 11-15) said that they had drunk alcohol at least once
- 193 males and 121 females between 15 and 34 years of age died from alcohol-related causes in 2011 in the UK
- The number of alcohol-related hospital admissions of 15 to 24 year-old male patients increased by 57%, from 18,265 to 28,747 from 2002 to 2010
- The number of hospital admissions of 15 to 24 year-old female patients increased at a faster rate [76%], from 15,233 in 2002 to 26,908 in 2010
- In a sample of over 2000 15-16-year-olds from the UK, 11% had had sex under the influence of alcohol and regretted it

- Almost one in ten boys and around one in eight girls aged 15 to 16 have unsafe sex after drinking alcohol
- Every year in the UK, more than 10,000 fines for being drunk and disorderly are issued to young people aged 16 to 19
- Almost half of young people excluded from school in the UK are regular drinkers
- Just 8% of 11 to 15-year olds said they had drunk alcohol in the previous week in 2011

Regarding the USA

- 17 million Americans are said to be alcoholics
- Americans spend $50 'billion' a year on alcohol
- Alcohol related problems cost the national economy 469 'billion' each year
- The leading cause of mental retardation is alcohol use during pregnancy
- 25,000 Americans die each year in alcohol related accidents. That's 70 a day!
- Alcohol consumption is the leading cause of death for the 15-24 age group
- 83% of all fire fatalities are alcohol related
- 68% of all drowning is alcohol related
- 80% of all suicides are alcohol related
- 86% of all murders are alcohol related
- 65% of child abuse cases are alcohol related
- At least 200,000 Americans die each year as a result of somebody else's alcohol consumption
- One out of every 18 persons who takes a drink will become an alcoholic. There is no way of knowing which one it will be. Therefore, the only way to be sure you will not live a drunkard's miserable life and die a drunkard's dreadful death is to TOTALLY ABSTAIN from wine and strong drink.
- Alcohol is addictive! We are told in 1 Cor 6v12 note – The Bible NEVER uses the word 'wine' in describing the Lord's Supper. It is always referred to as 'the fruit of the vine', which is a GRAPE. It was grape juice not fermented wine. Grape juice is a picture of the Lord's blood shed for us. (Deut 32v14, Mark 14v25, Luke 22v18).
- It is also interesting that the bread used in the Lord's Supper was 'unleavened' i.e. yeast taken out. Leaven speaks of sin in the Scriptures. Alcoholic wine needs fermentation (*i.e. ferment means a substance productive of fermentation such as yeast. Fermentation is the gradual decomposition of organic compounds induced by the action of living organisms, by enzymes, or by chemical agents; specifically, the conversion of glucose into ethyl alcohol*), which typifies sin. Therefore it would be reasonable to assume that the fruit of the vine (note – not wine) used in the Lord's Supper was unfermented i.e. it was just grape juice – i.e. no yeast, no sin.
- The priests were forbidden to use fermented wines when they entered the holy place in the OT Tabernacle - Lev 10v9. These priests, entering into the Tabernacle, were types of the Lord Jesus Christ, our Great High Priest. If those who were types of the Great High Priest were not to use wine or strong drink, it seems inconceivable (incomprehensible, impossible) to us that Jesus would drink fermented wine or strong drink before going to the crucifixion and entering into His high priestly work. Ezek 44v21. Jesus would not have drunk fermented, alcoholic wine. He knew the scriptures!
- It is interesting to read Isa 65v8 - new wine is grape juice. Deut 32v14.

ALCOHOL

- Prov 3v9+10 the firstfruits, barns and presses is in regard to the grape and the presses are pressing out new wine i.e. grape juice.

- King's and priests do not drink - Prov 31v4+5, Lev 10v8+9. We are kings and priests; therefore we should not drink. 1 Pet 2v9, Rev 5v9+10.

- It is interesting that the first mention of alcoholic drink is associated with nakedness! Gen 9v20+21.

Still think the Lord wants you to drink alcoholic beverages? If you do, you're not only a Bible *rejector*, you're an absolute nut!

For further reading I would suggest the following...

1) **BOOZE** – The Devil's Nuclear Bomb – By Pastor Perry F. Rockwood

2) **Wine and The Bible** – By Pastor Steve Harmon

3) **A searching look at the History, Chemistry, Industry and Legacy of ALCOHOL** – by T. Allan Dunlop

4) **Liquid Devil!** The BIBLE and the BOTTLE – by Hugh Pyle

5) **The Double Curse of Booze** – by John R. Rice

6) **Bible Wines**. Laws of Fermentation – by William Patton

7) **Did Jesus Drink Wine?** – By Dr. Paul E. Heaton

8) **Alcoholism or Drunkenness?** Sin or Disease? – By James M. Resh

Now to finish with I want to list 55 Bible references on the evils of drinking alcoholic drinks...

1) Gen 9v20-27 – The first 'man of distinction' and the tragic consequences of his drunkenness

2) Gen 19v30-38 – Drinking results in Lot's debauchery of his own daughters

3) Lev 10v8-11 – The Lord commanded Aaron and his sons not to drink either wine or strong drink while rendering service for God

4) Num 6v3 – The vow of the Nazarite excluded drinking wine and strong drink

5) Deut 21v20 – Drinking is one of the attributes of a stubborn, rebellious and disobedient son

6) Judg 13v4+7 – Samson's mother was expressly commanded by the angel of the Lord not to drink wine or strong drink

7) 1 Sam 25v36-38 – Nabal, a churlish, evil, drinking man was smitten by the Lord

8) 2 Sam 11v13 – By the use of strong drink David led Uriah into a fatal trap

9) 2 Sam 13v28-29 – Amnon, on a drinking spree, was murdered by the servants of his brother, Absalom

10) 1 Kings 16v8-10 – While Elah, King of Israel, was 'drinking himself drunk' one of his captains who had conspired against him, killed him

11) 1 Kings 20v13-21 – While Ben-hadad, King of Syria, and 32 other kings were drinking themselves drunk in their pavilions, a small band of Israelites fell upon the Syrians and put them to flight

12) Est 1v5-22 – After a week's feasting and drinking King Ahasuerus drunkenly tried to subject Vashti, his

queen, to the beastly gaze of the inebriated people and princes

13) Prov 20v1 – No wise person will allow himself to be deceived by wine which is a mocker or by strong drink which is raging

14) Prov 21v17 + 23v21 – Drinking leads to poverty

15) Prov 23v29-30 – Strong drink produces sorrow, woe, contentions, babbling, wounds without cause and redness of eyes

16) Prov 23v21 – An admonition to refrain from even looking upon wine

17) Prov 23v32 – At the last, alcohol bites like a serpent and stings like an adder

18) Prov 23v33 – It fills men's minds with impure and perverse thoughts

19) Prov 23v34 – It brings on danger, accidents and insecurity

20) Prov 23v35 – Insensibility follows drinking rendering man into a clod and it is habit forming so that the drinker upon awaking seeks it 'yet again'

21) Prov 31v4+5 – Officials with the responsibility of human life on their hands should not imbibe (drink, drink in, absorb)

22) Ecc 2v3 – The writer of Ecclesiastes tried strong drink but in the end admitted that this too was vanity (Ecc 2v11 + 12v8)

23) Ecc 10v17 – That nation is blessed whose leaders eat for strength and refrain from drunkenness

24) Isa 5v11+12 – Woe is pronounced on those who give themselves to strong drink

25) Isa 5v22 – Further woe is pronounced upon the drunkards

26) Isa 23v13 – Drinking often goes with carnal living

27) Isa 28v1 – A woe is pronounced upon the drunkards of Ephraim

28) Isa 28v3 – The drunkards of Ephraim to be trodden down and destroyed

29) Isa 28v7 – Prophets and priests become incapable of spiritual leadership because of their drinking

30) Isa 56v12 – Drinking accomplishes foolish optimism and the sinner's vain hope that his sins will not find him out

31) Jer 35v5-8+14+19 – Rechabites who steadfastly held to total abstinence assured of God's continued blessings

32) Dan 1v5+8+16 + 10v3 – Daniel who refused to drink the king's wine was especially blessed by the Lord

33) Dan 5v1+2 – This is the tragic example of a king who drank and who led his people to do likewise

34) Dan 5v3 – Drinking leads to profaning sacred things

35) Dan 3v25-28 – Moral degradation, of which drinking is a symptom, is ultimately punished by God

36) Hos 4v10+11 – Strong drink and immorality go hand in hand

37) Hos 7v5 – The king by his drinking was not only made sick but became scornful

38) Joel 3v3 – Young women were sold for the price of a drink

39) Amos 4v1 – Dissolute women, oppressors of the poor, call for their drink

ALCOHOL

40) Amos 6v3-6 – The evil, idle rich who were given to imbibing wine were not concerned about the afflictions of the poor

41) Hab 2v5 – Arrogance is inflamed by drink

42) Hab 2v15 – It is wrong to lead another to drink

43) Hab 2v16 – Drink leads to shame and humiliation

44) Mat 24v48-51 – Drinking is not consistent with alertness

45) Luke 1v15 – Greatness of John the Baptist linked with total abstinence

46) Luke 12v45 – Christ warns against drunkenness

47) Luke 21v34 – Drinking prevents men from being prepared for the judgement day

48) Rom 13v13 – All are admonished to walk honestly, not in rioting and drunkenness

49) Rom 14v21 – Christians are admonished not to drink lest a brother be caused to stumble

50) 1 Cor 5v11 – Christians forbidden to keep company with drunkards

51) 1 Cor 6v10 – No drunkard shall inherit the Kingdom of God

52) 1 Cor 11v21 – The Lord's Supper is no time for drunkenness

53) Gal 5v21 – Drunkenness prevents men from inheriting the Kingdom of God

54) Eph 5v18 – Christians commanded not to be drunk with wine but to be filled with the Spirit

55) 1 Tim 3v3+8 – Church leaders must be 'not given to wine'

First mention of wine and drunkenness in the Bible is Gen 9v20-24. It resulted in…

1) Nakedness

2) Sexual Perversion (i.e. Sodomy)

3) A division in the family

4) The cursing of a grandchild, and his offspring (v25)

Another early mention of wine in the Bible is Gen 19v30-38. It resulted in…

a) Nakedness

b) Sexual Perversion (Incest)

c) A destruction of God's order of the family

d) Trouble for the people of Israel in years to come

You should *not* use alcoholic wine in the communion service. Drinking alcohol is a sin.

Read Mat 26v27-29 (note v27+28 are 'figurative' just like 2 Sam 23v16+17). The Roman Catholic Church teaches that the Mass is a '*literal bloody sacrifice!*' The *only* 'sacrifices' any Christian is to offer are 'spiritual' ones – 1 Pet 2v5. The only '*drink offering*' (Num 28v7) offered in the NT is offered to the Devil (Hos 9v4, 1 Cor 10v20+21, Ps 16v4). The eating of 'blood' was forbidden before the Law (Gen 9v4), under the Law (Lev 17v14), and during the Church Age under Grace (Acts 15v28+29). The 'wine' in the Lord's Supper was *not* fermented/alcoholic. It was *new wine* (...*new wine* **is found in the cluster... Isa 65v8**) and is defined in the verse. It is called '**the fruit of the vine**', which is '**the pure blood of the grape**' (Deut 32v14 ...**and thou didst drink the pure blood of the grape**.) It is obtained by *squeezing* a bunch of **grapes** *into a cup* (Gen 40v11 **And Pharaoh's cup was in my hand: and I took the grapes, and pressed them into Pharaoh's cup, and I gave the cup into Pharaoh's hand**.) Drinking the poison of alcohol is a sin.

Prov 20v1 – *I repeat*... It is absolute madness to think that for some people, their first taste of alcohol is in a church, at the communion table – *now you just think about that for a while!*

NOTES

NOTES

SIGNS AND WONDERS – TONGUES AND HEALINGS

Signs and Wonders are associated/connected with **Israel** and the **Kingdom of Heaven** *not* for the Church today. Read Mat 10v1-10 - Read it *again* and notice the *'don't* go to the Gentiles'. Only go to lost Israelites. Preach the Kingdom of Heaven Gospel (not the Grace of God Gospel like we preach today) and *do signs and wonders* (which are connected with Israel and *not* with the Gentiles or the Church). So these first *ten* verses have *nothing* to do with *any* Gentile or Christian today. Did you get that? If you really *think/believe* you speak in tongues, or you have a *healing* ministry... *You are a self-deluded fool!* If you are a pastor/leader in a church and you think/believe you speak in tongues & believe that signs and wonders are for today, or you believe that *healing* is the same today as it was in the *apostolic* time, you ought to do one of two things...

1) Grow up and start *really* studying the Scriptures and apologise for the *tosh* you have been teaching your church, *then start* teaching that Book dispensationally.... OR...

2) Quit the ministry, grow up and get out there in the real world and work for a living. 1 Thes 4v11 **And that ye study to be quiet, and to do your own business, and to work with your own hands, as we commanded you**; Read also Acts 20v35, Eph 4v28, 2 Thes 3v7-8+11-12.

I'm sorry I can't say it any nicer than that, but there are too many 'Christian' liars and deceivers out there, who are fleecing the sheep rather than feeding them. (Mat 7v15, 2 Pet 3v16-18) I'm trying to warn you and make you aware of that fact. (Gal 4v16) Be very careful who you trust, and check everything out with the Scriptures.

Signs and Wonders – Tongues and Healings – Truth and Counterfeit – Bible Believing Christians vs. CharisMANIACS

The true gift of healing as seen by the Lord Jesus and the Apostles...

1) Healing was by word or touch. There is no deliberation or elaborate ceremony.

2) Healing was instantaneous, without delay.

3) Those who were healed were healed totally. There was not a recuperation period.

4) Its purpose was *not* to keep Christians healthy. In fact, **most cases did *not* even involve Christians**.

5) They healed organic diseases – crippling deformities, withered hands, blindness etc. *not* 'functional' problems like colds, sore joints, headaches etc.

6) The healer could also raise the dead.

7) All were healed. No one was left feeling guilty for not having enough faith.

No one today is healing the way Jesus or His Apostles did back in those days. We have *fake* healers today.

There is Scriptural support that would show that the gift of healing was NT exercised in the latter years of the apostolic age – 3 John 1+2, 2 Tim 4v20, 2 Cor 12v9, 1 Tim 5v23, Phil 2v27.

Tongues

SIGN gifts were for the purpose of confirming the words of the apostles (Mark 16v20). The gift of tongues specifically served as a **SIGN** to the *unbelieving* Jews (1 Cor 14v21+22, 1 Cor 1v22). It showed them that their Messiah has been rejected and now the Gospel is going out in *other tongues* to *all* men – Jews (Acts 2), Gentiles (Acts 10), Samaritans (Acts 8), John's disciples (Acts 19). Do we need *signs* to show that God's grace is given to all men? No. Unlike the early Church, we have His word, which tells us plainly. (No one in the Bible had the 66 Books collated into one volume like we do today).

Signs and wonders were directly linked with the Apostles

Read Acts 14v3, 2 Cor 12v12, Heb 2v3+4, Mark 16v20 etc. The apostles were present when signs and wonders occurred – Acts 2v1-36, Acts 3v2-10, Acts 5v15+16, Acts 8v14-17, Acts 10v44-47, Acts 14v8-10, Acts 19v1-7, Acts 28v8+9.

Signs and wonders are not for today

The Christian walk for the post-apostolic Church is to be a walk of *faith* and *not* by sight (2 Cor 5v7). **A wicked and adulterous generation seeketh after a sign...** Mat 16v4 (Read also Exo 32v1-6, 1 Sam 8v4-7) ***signs* are associated with Israel**; they started with Israel – See Exodus chapter 4. Look up *every* reference to 'sign' and 'signs'. The word of God is enough for the man of God (2 Tim 3v16+17). Faith comes by the word of God *not* by *signs* (Rom 10v17, Heb 4v12 etc.)

Now if you believe that **SIGN** gifts are in operation today, you are either deceived or a liar, or both. Signs and wonders are certainly not for this dispensation. You have something no one in the Bible had, a complete copy of the word of God from Genesis to Revelation – *they never did!*

Apart from the word of God, I have also taken information from the following, very helpful, books, leaflets and a DVD.

1) **Signs, Wonders and Miracles** – by James Knox (This is an excellent book and much of this study has come from this work)

2) **All about speaking in Tongues** – By Fernand Legrand

3) **'Tongues'** DVD by Dr Peter Ruckman

Most Christians do *not* study their Bibles. Many Christians will say things like '*Well I believe this...*' without studying the issue themselves.

Regarding this issue, Christians fall into three camps... - A, B and C

A) **Camp A** - In this camp are those who have already decided what they believe and search their Bibles to find some passage or verse (even a part of a verse will do) to support their *predetermined* position.

B) **Camp B** - In this camp are those who spend long hours of Bible study looking for verses and passages (even a part of a verse will do) to use in disputes with those in Camp A. Their searching of the Scriptures is motivated by a desire to point out the errors and mistakes of the Camp A group. This kind of 'Christian' will always look to find fault and critique every sermon

SIGNS AND WONDERS

and Bible study they hear.

C) **Camp C** - In this camp are those who may have strongly held beliefs and convictions but are willing to change them in a moment should they learn from the word of God that they have been in error. In camp C are those who love the Lord Jesus and His word and place the Scriptures as their *final authority* on all matters of faith and practice!

We shall be examining every reference in the Book of Acts to 'speaking in tongues', as well as all the other Biblical references to this gift i.e.

1. **Unknown tongues**
2. **Strange Tongues**
3. **Other tongues**
4. **Divers tongues**

There are two primary rules for Bible study set forth in the Bible itself - 1 Cor 2v12+13, 2 Tim 2v15.

These two Scriptures make it clear that in order to **understand the word of God**; we *cannot* remove any Bible verse from the surrounding context, but must compare Scripture with Scripture. God has placed dividing lines throughout His word to mark off time periods in which He deals with men at *different* times in *different* ways. (The Bible must be read 'dispensationally' otherwise many errors will occur when Christians try to apply verses to themselves that are *not directly* written, *doctrinally* to themselves).

Nearly all (if not all) false teaching and every Scriptural misunderstanding today is a result of either…

Private Interpretation – This is a man interpreting the Scriptures (*as opposed to teaching them*) on the basis of his experience or feelings, or on the basis of his background 'training', reading, or denominational 'tradition'.

Truth Misplaced – This is a man setting forth genuine Bible truth but seeking to apply that truth to people it was never directed to. Truth misplaced is *error* – We must *rightly divide* the word of truth. (2 Tim 2v15).

For all the prophets and the law prophesied until John – Mat 11v13. The Bible states that the law and the prophets were until John (the Baptist). So John the Baptist marks a transition (*i.e. a change*). John came, and in Mark 1v4 he preached… **John did baptize in the wilderness, and preach the baptism of repentance for the remission of sins.** Jesus said in Mark 1v15 **And saying, The time is fulfilled, and the kingdom of God is at hand: repent ye, and believe the gospel.** We find that through John the Baptist's ministry he preached 'repentance and baptism for the remission of sins.' The tradition continued through the ministry of Jesus Christ who took the OT law and expounded upon its precepts. He went beyond a strict word-for-word meaning and called upon men to go beyond quoting the law, to go beyond the letter of the law, and to live according to the life and spirit of the law. For example, the law forbade committing adultery. Jesus carried this further and said in Mat 5v27+28… The Lord *often* said things like '**Ye have heard it said… But I say unto you…**'

Read Mat 5v21+22, Mat 5v27+28, Mat 5v31-33, Mat 5v38+39, Mat 5v43+44. The law and the prophets were until John. His ministry was to prepare the way for the Messiah, the King of the Jews. When Christ Jesus, the Messiah, came, He pointed to Himself as the fulfilment of the law. Having fulfilled the law, Jesus went to the cross, died, was buried and rose again. After the resurrection of Jesus Christ we find, in the first seven chapters of the Book of Acts, that the believers continued to preach the message of John the Baptist, with the person and work of Jesus Christ **added**. Read carefully the statements and sermons of the apostles in Acts 2 – 7 and this will be perfectly clear. Prior to Acts 8, no one preached that an individual could be saved solely on the merits of the finished work of the Lord Jesus Christ. When the Ethiopian eunuch was taught from Isaiah by Philip we find an individual Gentile converted by preaching the death, burial and resurrection of Jesus Christ (Isa 53). He was saved by grace, through faith, and baptised afterwards. Saul of Tarsus is converted by believing on the Lord Jesus Christ (Acts 9) and is called to be the apostle to the Gentiles (Rom 11v13). His Gospel message, found in 1 Cor 15, is the death, burial and resurrection of Jesus Christ, according to the Scriptures.

These great Gospel truths of the suffering Saviour paying for the sins of the world with His own precious blood are found throughout the OT writings but prior to the conversion of the apostle Paul **they were hid from the hearts and minds of men.**

The Gospel message of salvation by grace, and birth into the church of God, the Body of Christ, was a *mystery* at that time - Col 1v24-28, Rom 16v25+26, Eph 3v4+6. It is interesting to note that the word *mystery* occurs 22 times in the Bible and 17 times it occurs in Paul's letters. Nearly all of the mysteries in the Bible were revealed to the apostle Paul 1 Cor 2v7-10. The salvation of the soul through faith in the finished work of Christ is taught all though the law and the prophets but was not revealed until the Holy Spirit allowed Paul to unfold such truth in his epistles. Peter writes...1 Pet 1v10-12.

Now think about this for a moment; until Paul wrote the NT epistles containing the doctrines of the NT church, there was nothing in the hands of the apostles and believers but the OT Scriptures. Throughout the Book of Acts they could *not* turn to the NT Scriptures for doctrine, reproof, correction, or instruction in righteousness, because there wasn't any NT Scriptures; there was no NT. Therefore, what these men preached was an OT of which John the Baptist marked the end, and of which Jesus Christ marked the fulfilment. Along with that, they taught a new Gospel that one can be *born again* and receive eternal life through the death, burial and resurrection of Jesus Christ without ever bringing a sacrifice, keeping a feast day or bringing offerings to a priest in Jerusalem. However, they had nothing *in writing* to justify this radical change from nearly 2,000 years of God ordained worship.

Thus to *confirm the word* of the apostles, God gave the signs and wonders given to Moses (the law), Elijah (the prophets) and Jesus Christ (grace) to *confirm the truth of this* **new** *dispensation* - Mark 16v14-20. We shall look into these verses in more depth later on, but note, the... '**Confirming the word with signs following'.**

Now in the Book of Acts we can see why this matter of tongues becomes so confusing, so controversial, and so dangerous. The doctrinal setting in which each occurrence of speaking in tongues is found is a *transitional period* during which men are preaching, teaching, living Christian lives and seeking to obey God *without any written direction* from God by which to judge their thoughts, words and actions. They had *no infallible written* NT, like we have, in which to turn to for absolute statements of what is right and wrong. This is not to say their thoughts, words and actions were wrong; it is obvious from Scripture that they were led and directed, for the most part, by the Holy Spirit. Thus, great confusion comes from making one's *doctrinal foundation* on an historic period of *transition* within the word of God when *nothing was definitely settled.*

For example, the Bible passages on tongues are found in...

1) **Mark 16** – A time after the resurrection but before the descent of the Holy Spirit

SIGNS AND WONDERS

2) **Acts 2** – After the descent of the Holy Spirit but before Israel rejects the Messiah (Acts 7) and God begins to turn to the Gentiles (Acts 8 - 10)

3) **Acts 10** – After the Lord begins to turn to the Gentiles but before the NT Scriptures are written

4) **Acts 19** – The Gospel reaching for the first time an area which knew *only* the preaching of John the Baptist

You would be foolish to build your foundational doctrines upon the Book of Acts which is a book of *transition*. This is where many Pentecostals go wrong. They spend far too long preaching and teaching from the Book of Acts rather than preaching and teaching from Paul's Epistles.

Back to Mark 16v14-18 - The eleven apostles were the ones to whom the Lord Jesus gave this word. These *signs* were divinely given signs from the Saviour **to the apostles** for *their* preaching ministry to all the world. As previously stated; these men would be preaching a NT which was instituted and made alive by the Lord Jesus Christ, but they could *not* point to any NT Scriptures yet. The context of Mark 16v14-18 clearly shows that these signs were given to establish that these men were speaking as the oracles of God - **So then after the Lord had spoken unto them, he was received up into heaven, and sat on the right hand of God. And they went forth, and preached every where, the Lord working with them, and confirming the word with signs following. Amen.** Note... **confirming the word** - *with signs following!*

So, we see in this first mention of tongues that they were given by the Lord Jesus Christ to His apostles as one aspect of a five-fold proof that they were speaking the truth of God.

Note carefully... **these** (plural) **signs** (plural) **shall** (definite) **follow them** (plural) **that believe; In my name shall** (definite) **they** (plural)...

1) **Cast out devils**
2) **Speak with new tongues**
3) **Take up serpents**
4) **Drink any deadly thing without hurt**
5) **Lay hands on the sick and heal them**

From the passage we see that Jesus Christ gave the signs to His eleven Jewish apostles to confirm that they were speaking His words. These signs given were *five* in number. Therefore, if a man was an apostle and had the apostolic signs they would be five-fold in their manifestation. To claim a 6th would be unbiblical. To say that you had the gift of 'healing' but you could not drink 'any deadly thing' would be unscriptural. To say that one had the apostolic sign of speaking in tongues, but not the other four signs, would be contrary to what the text of Mark 16 *actually says*. This fact has nothing to do with interpretation, this is what Jesus said.

Let us now look at Acts 2 - Here we find 120 believers (Acts 1v15 - **And in those days Peter stood up in the midst of the disciples, and said, (the number of names together were about an hundred and twenty,)**) gathered together in an upper room. These men and women were doing what Jesus Christ told them to do. They were waiting for the promise of the Father which is the Holy Ghost. Jesus had told His apostles they would receive power after the Holy Ghost had come upon them (Acts 1v8 - **But ye shall receive power, after that the Holy Ghost is come upon you: and ye shall be witnesses unto me both in Jerusalem,** (the city) **and in all Judaea,** (the immediate area surrounding Jerusalem) **and in Samaria,** (the region just beyond Judaea) **and unto the uttermost**

part of the earth (everywhere)), to enable them to be His witnesses.

Thus we pick up right where we left off in Mark 16. Having said this, the Lord ascended up to Heaven. What we find when we begin Acts 2 are about 120 believers waiting in an upper room for God to send power, brought by the Holy Ghost from on high, which would enable them to go into all the world and preach the Gospel with the ability which superseded that of the flesh or human will. (*Signs* **would follow to confirm the word they were preaching**). These men would be given God's power, by God's Spirit, to be God's witnesses declaring God's gift of eternal life through God's own Son.

And when the day of Pentecost was fully come, (Acts 2v1), this promise was fulfilled. This was a Jewish feast day which came 50 days after the feast of Passover. On this particular occasion the feast day marked 50 days since the Lamb of God, the Lord Jesus Christ, offered Himself as the supreme blood sacrifice for the sins of the whole world. After laying down His life at Calvary, Christ visited the underworld while His body lay in a sealed and guarded tomb for 3 days and 3 nights. Following His resurrection He walked and talked among men on earth for forty days (Acts 1v3 - **To whom also he shewed himself alive after his passion by many infallible proofs, being seen of them forty days, and speaking of the things pertaining to the kingdom of God:**). This accounted for 43 days.

So, when the day of Pentecost arrived these disciples had been waiting for the promise a full *seven* days since Jesus ascended. Acts 2v1...**they were all with one accord in one place.** – These were the 120 believers of Acts chapter one. They were simply waiting for God to do what He said He would do. Acts 2v2 - **And suddenly there came a sound from heaven as of a rushing mighty wind,** - note the sound came from Heaven.

Acts 2v2 - ...**a sound from heaven *as of* a rushing mighty wind,** - Notice the Bible says nothing of a rushing mighty wind but 'a sound' came from heaven having this likeness. It is a simile (i.e. *expressing comparison or likeness, by the use of such terms as like, as, so etc.*) There is no rushing mighty wind.

Acts 2v2 ...**and it filled all the house where they were sitting.** – *What filled the house? The sound. What were they doing in the house?* Sitting. Notice there was no dancing or crying out, no loud music, no singing repetitive choruses; *they were just sitting*.

Acts 2v3 - **And there appeared unto them cloven tongues *like as of* fire, and it sat upon each of them.** - Note again that there were no actual tongues of fire here; there was no fire. It is another simile so we can understand what happened. Pentecostals often get this mixed up with the 'Baptism of Fire' in Mat 3v11+12 - We see that this 'baptism of fire' is to be *immersed in the Lake of Fire* for rejecting the Messiah. *You certainly don't want to pray for the 'baptism of fire!'*

Acts 2v3 - ... **and it** (what appeared) **sat upon each of them.** – No one present was excluded; all obeyed and all received the promise. Note carefully that the filling with the Holy Ghost and speaking with other tongues are *two* separate statements.

Acts 2v5 – This day of Pentecost was one of the *three* great Jewish national festivals when all the males were required to go to Jerusalem - Deut 16v16 - **Three times in a year shall all thy males appear before the LORD thy God in the place which he shall choose; in the feast of unleavened bread, and in the feast of weeks, and in the feast of tabernacles: and they shall not appear before the LORD empty:**). It was also called the *feast of weeks* - Deut 16v10 - **And thou shalt keep the feast of weeks unto the LORD thy God with a tribute of a freewill offering of thine hand, which thou shalt give unto the LORD thy God, according as the LORD thy God hath blessed** thee:) because it was *seven* weeks from the Passover; **the feast of harvest** - Exo 23v16 - **And the feast of harvest, the firstfruits of thy labours, which thou hast sown in the field: and the feast of ingathering, which is in the end of the year, when thou hast gathered in thy labours out of the field.**) because it was a feast of thanksgiving for the harvest...

Deut 26v5-10. It was also called the feast of the first fruits (**Num 28v26**) because on this day the Jews offered to God the first fruits of the wheat harvest, in bread made of new grain (**Lev 23v15-20**).

The feast was also regarded as commemorating the giving of the law which was delivered from Mount Sinai on the fiftieth day after the departure from Egypt, i.e. after the institution of the Passover.

So God in His wisdom selected a day on which all the males of Israel would be present in the city of David's throne. They would be gathered to worship under the old covenant on the day the law was given. On this day the Father sent the gift of the Holy Ghost. In the manifold wisdom of God, the preaching of the new covenant began on a day when the men of His chosen people have gathered out of every nation under heaven. But how would they all hear and understand this preaching? **Acts 2v6** – Now these men were not confounded because they were hearing babbling and a stringing together of nonsensical syllables; the men who heard the believers speak with other tongues were confounded because they could understand what was being said! (*Note - it was **not** a heavenly 'prayer' language!*)

Therefore the 'other tongue' received on the day of Pentecost by those in the upper room was the ability to speak in a language *unknown* to the speaker but *known* to the hearer.

Acts 2v7-11 - So that there would never be any confusion or false doctrines about a *secret prayer language and jibber-jabber babbling* being called a work of the Holy Spirit, God told us three times in plain English that these men were speaking in a language that was **known** to their hearers.

And what audience was being addressed? Jews of the dispersion from every nation on the face of the earth. Within weeks of the day the Holy Ghost came to indwell the Body of Christ, all the world will have heard the amazing story, with **signs confirming the message** – this was from God.

Acts 2v14-21 - So who was preaching and proclaiming the Gospel to this multitude of Jews? – It was the apostles who were given the promise of **signs** to **confirm** the word as seen in Mark 16v20.

Note in this passage (Acts 2v14-21) it doesn't say that Joel 2 was being *fulfilled*, nor did it say that the events included in Joel could have their completion on this day. It is clear that God did *not* pour out His Spirit on *all flesh* by the number of conversions (i.e. only 3000), which is far short of the number of people in Jerusalem on that day. The sun was not darkened and the moon did not turn to blood. Why then did the Holy Ghost move Peter to cite Joel 2 in the sermon he delivered? Because the **latter days** spoken of throughout the old covenant prophetic writings **began** on this day.

Who were Peter and the eleven speaking to... **Ye men of Israel, hear these words; Jesus of Nazareth, a man approved of God among you by miracles and wonders and signs, which God did by him in the midst of you, as ye yourselves also know:** (Acts 2v22)

Why in Mark 16, did Jesus promise that signs would follow the apostles?

Why did signs accompany the apostles when their public preaching ministry began in Acts 2?

Simply to equate the apostles with the Lord Jesus Christ in the minds of the men that had heard and seen Jesus, and knew that the Lord worked *signs, wonders and miracles;* therefore the *signs* were given these apostles to testify that they were the true spokesmen of the Lord Jesus Christ.

Read Acts 2v23-36 - Twelve Jewish apostles, on a Jewish feast day, addressed a Jewish congregation and proclaimed the Jewish Messiah had been crucified by the Jews, and had risen from the dead.

They declared that God was calling the Jews to pay attention to a group of men that had the same *signs, wonders and miracles* that were wrought by the Lord Jesus Christ. *That was the message of Pentecost.*

They did *not* speak about tongues nor encourage anyone to receive them. They did speak of the wonderful works of God and encouraged men to receive Him.

Acts 2v37-40 **Now when they** (the reference is still to Acts 2v5) **heard this, they were pricked in their heart, and said unto Peter and to the rest of the apostles,** (*not* 120 believers) **Men and brethren,** (Jews speaking to Jewish apostles) **what shall we do? Then Peter said unto them,** (the same thing John the Baptist would have said) **Repent, and be baptized every one of you in the name of Jesus Christ for the remission of sins, and ye shall receive the gift of the Holy Ghost. For the promise is unto you, and to your children,** (verse 5 Jews) **and to all that are afar off, even as many as the Lord our God shall call.** (v6 Jews out of every nation under heaven) **And with many other words did he testify and exhort, saying, Save yourselves from this untoward generation.** (Note – *not* save yourself from Hell). Peter preached and the multitude cried out 'What shall we do?' (Note it doesn't say 'What must we do to be saved!')

Remember the Book of Acts is a book of transition…

1) From Law to Grace

2) From the old covenant to the *new* covenant

3) From nations to individuals

4) From Israel, to the calling out of the Body of Christ, the church

5) God begins to turn from the Jews in Acts 7 (the stoning of Stephen), saves an individual Gentile in Acts 8, calls the 'apostle' to the Gentiles in Acts 9 (i.e. Paul), and in Acts 10 sent Peter to a Gentile house even though Peter was still clinging to a **Jewish** message

- No one in Acts 2 was a 'Christian' – the term Christian doesn't even show up until Acts 11v26

- Every man, woman, boy and girl in Acts 2 is a Jew or Gentile proselyte to Judaism (see v1, 5 ,8-11, 14, 22, 36)

- No one in Acts 2 is asking how to get saved. The nation of Israel is asking Peter… 'In the view of the fact that we have crucified the Messiah, what shall we do?'

- Nowhere in Acts 2 does it mention about Christ dying for *anyone's sins!*

- From Acts 1 to Acts 7 the 2nd Advent (2nd Coming of Christ!) is looming, and then postponed to the end of the Church Age

Having no New Testament, no written Scriptures beyond Malachi, no doctrine of salvation by grace through faith given freely to individual believers, Peter spoke to this crowd exactly as John the Baptist had spoken when he came to mark the beginning of a transition from the Old Testament law and the prophets. His word was clear...**Then Peter said unto them, Repent, and be baptized every one of you in the name of Jesus Christ for the remission of sins, and ye shall receive the gift of the Holy Ghost.** (Acts 2v38) ...Repent, be baptized in the name of Jesus Christ for the remission of sins, and ye shall receive the gift of the Holy Ghost. **Then they that gladly received his word were baptized: and the same day there were added unto them about three thousand souls.** (Acts 2v41) These 3000 believers received the gift of the Holy Ghost as Peter promised.

This leads us to a very simple, very logical, and very Scriptural conclusion: from the day of Pentecost onward, speaking in a language *unknown* to the speaker was a gift given to some believers ***and not to others.*** The idea that the 'initial evidence' of receiving the Holy Ghost was speaking in tongues was *not* the case in the very first Pentecostal converts in Acts 2 and is therefore shown by the Bible to be a false doctrine.

That is the complete Biblical account of the first time in NT history that anyone spoke with tongues. Just as the Lord Jesus said in Mark 16, it was a *sign* wrought by Jewish apostles as a testimony to all nations that they were indeed speaking and declaring the true word of God. We see from a very careful examination of the chapter that those present, those addressed, and those converted, were all Jews. These Israelites were converted under the preaching of the doctrine of John the Baptist combined with the person and the work of Jesus Christ. A combination message was declared in a transition period and the Lord's blessing upon it was marked by ***signs and wonders.***

Before we again come across speaking in tongues there are some very important events set forth in the Book of Acts... After 5 full chapters of presenting the Messiah to Israel for a 2nd time (Acts 2 - 6) Stephen preached to the leaders of the nation and showed them *from the OT Scriptures* that Jesus was their true Messiah and declared them guilty of His murder. Rather than repent and receive this Lord Jesus Christ they confirmed the words of Stephen by stoning him.

The turning from Israel to the Gentiles, which is explained in Rom 9 – 11, began with the execution of Stephen. In Acts 8 an individual Gentile is saved by grace, through faith, upon hearing the preaching of the Cross from Isa 53. He was saved upon *believing*, with no mention of works. He was a believer before he was baptised and even though he was led into a saving faith by an apostle, he did *not* speak in tongues.

In Acts 9, Saul of Tarsus was converted by believing the words of the Lord Jesus Christ. By calling on the resurrected Jesus as the living Lord, this self-righteous murderer received salvation and received the Holy Ghost before he was baptised. There is no record that he spoke in tongues at his baptism, conversion, or at the time the Holy Ghost was given. This man was then called of God to be the apostle to the Gentiles.

This shift in God's dealing with Israel and the Gentiles must be understood or much of the NT will remain a mystery. *How many false teachings have arisen because of a failure to distinguish between the Jew, the Gentile and the church of God!* 1 Cor 10v32.

As the Lord makes this obvious turn away from Israel to the Gentiles, we must hearken back to the promise of Acts 1v8... **and ye shall be witnesses unto me both in Jerusalem, and in all Judaea, and in Samaria, and unto the uttermost part of the earth.** As we examine the 2nd Biblical case of speaking in tongues we find the Lord beginning the proclamation of the good news to the uttermost part of the earth...

Read Acts 10v1-14 - Peter is given a vision regarding Jews and Gentiles. He is about to learn that NT salvation was *not* a national matter based upon law, but an individual matter, based upon grace.

Read Acts 10v15-28 - Peter knew what God showed him but he was still not convinced. He knew what he had seen; he knew what the Lord had told him to do; but the statement of verse 17 was still the case...**Now while Peter doubted in himself what this vision which he had seen should mean, behold, the men which were sent from Cornelius had made enquiry for Simon's house, and stood before the gate**... Peter doubted in himself what the vision should mean. Peter had said... **God hath shewed me that I should not call any man common or unclean.** (Acts 10v28)

Read Acts 10v29-36 - Peter had not accepted the revelation God had shown him. He knew intellectually what the Lord had shown him and he could not deny that the Holy Spirit brought him to a Gentile household but he was still trying to cling to the gospel message as the exclusive property of the nation of Israel - Acts 10v36-43.

When Peter preached to Jews at Jerusalem he said... Acts 2v38 **Then Peter said unto them, Repent, and be baptized every one of you in the name of Jesus Christ for the remission of sins, and ye shall receive the gift of the Holy Ghost.** When Peter preached to Gentiles in Cornelius' household he said...Acts 10v43 **To him give all the prophets witness, that through his name whosoever believeth in him shall receive remission of sins.**

The Book of Acts is a book of *transition* from law to grace, from the old covenant to the new covenant, from nations to individuals. God began to turn from the Jews in Acts 7, saved a Gentile by grace in Acts 8, called the apostle to the Gentiles in Acts 9 and in Acts 10, sent Peter into a Gentile household (but he was clinging to a Jewish message) Acts 10v43-48.

So we see that Peter went to the household of Cornelius as God directed. There Peter preached what God told him to preach, though he did so in relative unbelief and with obvious reluctance. The Gentiles to whom he preached believed the words they heard and had the Holy Ghost fall on them *when they believed the words of God.* The Father sent the Spirit to save and indwell these Gentile believers and they spoke with other tongues.

Note that these tongues were **a sign to the circumcision** who were astonished because they did not believe that God was going to save the Gentiles with the same salvation wherewith He saved the Jews. God used tongues here in Acts 10 as a **sign to an 'unbelieving' Jewish apostle** to *confirm* that the Gentiles were going to be included in this new covenant.

Note also that the NT doctrines of unity in the *one Body* found in 1 Corinthians and Ephesians had *not* been written or revealed yet. God must *confirm* the word of the apostles even to the apostles in this *transition* period.

Again here in Acts 10 the tongues could be understood. Acts 10v46 **For they heard them speak with tongues, and magnify God.** If they were speaking in some 'heavenly prayer language' they wouldn't have known this. Note also in Peter's recounting of this event to those in Jerusalem, (who did not believe that the new covenant included Gentiles), Acts 11v17 **Forasmuch then as God gave them the like gift as he did unto us,** (i.e. Acts 2) **who believed on the Lord Jesus Christ; what was I, that I could withstand God?**

So in Acts 2 and Acts 10, 'Tongues' were *known* languages, *not* 'jibber jabber' or a special 'heavenly prayer language'.

So let us recap and conclude regarding the second occurrence of speaking in tongues found in the Scriptures... We find a group of Gentiles who received the Holy Ghost by believing the preaching of the death, burial and resurrection of the Lord Jesus Christ. They spoke with tongues and Jewish apostles and Jewish believers were astonished because they did not believe that God saved Gentiles

SIGNS AND WONDERS

the same way He saved the Jews. In this case (i.e. Acts 10), as in Acts 2, tongues were a *sign* to the *unbelieving* Jews and served to *confirm the word of God* and the truth of God in a *transitional* period which the doctrines which were in effect were *not* found in the *written* Scriptures.

In Acts 1 we read about the person who was going to replace Judas Iscariot...Acts 1v21 **Wherefore of these men which have companied with us all the time that the Lord Jesus went in and out among us,**

22 **Beginning from the baptism of John, unto that same day that he was taken up from us, must one be ordained to be a witness with us of his resurrection.** Now read Acts 10v39-41...Acts 10:39 **And we are witnesses of all things which he did both in the land of the Jews, and in Jerusalem; whom they slew and hanged on a tree:**

40 **Him God raised up the third day, and shewed him openly;**

41 **Not to all the people, but unto witnesses chosen before of God, even to us, who did eat and drink with him after he rose from the dead.** These passages clearly teach that in order to 'qualify' as an apostle a man must have accompanied Jesus from the time He was baptised of John until the time of His ascension. That man must have beheld the works that Jesus did and been eyewitness of the resurrected Christ.

The apostle Paul, who was one born out of due time (1 Cor 15v8), certainly 'qualified'. He was among the counsel at the stoning of Stephen, and a student of the noted leader Gamaliel. Prior to that he certainly would have beheld the works of the Lord Jesus Christ at some point during the three and one half years of the Lord's public ministry. He also met the resurrected Christ on the Damascus Road (Acts 9).

The events of Acts 10 were so outstanding and important that the Holy Spirit chose to take the 11th chapter of the Book of Acts and recount what took place in the 10th chapter.

Read Acts 11v13-18 - Knox goes on to write... It is interesting to note from these words of Peter, recorded by the Holy Spirit, that he did not remember (until God sent him to this Gentile household) that the Lord taught his disciples that NT salvation would be a matter of Spirit baptism and not water baptism. That which God gave them is said to be a gift in Acts 11v17 and you will notice that it wasn't until this time that Peter was fully convinced that the Gentiles would be saved just as the Jews. It was not until this retelling that the Jewish brethren were convinced that Peter had done the right thing and that the gospel which they were to carry to the uttermost part of the earth was to be carried to all nations, kindreds, tongues and tribes dwelling upon the face of the earth. You will note, there was still some reservation about this matter until it was finally bound on earth at the great Jerusalem meeting in Acts 15.

Acts 19 is the 3rd and final case in the Bible of someone speaking in, with other, or unknown tongues. (We shall deal with the Corinthian 'perversion' of tongues a little later).

Acts 19v1 **And it came to pass, that, while Apollos was at Corinth, Paul having passed through the upper coasts came to Ephesus: and finding certain disciples,**

Notice he was *not* in Jerusalem, Judea or Samaria. Paul had made his way into one of the 'uttermost parts of the earth' i.e. a region beyond the immediate influence of Judaism. When the Gospel was proclaimed in a NEW area i.e. Jerusalem, 'signs and wonders' accompanied. When the Gospel was proclaimed among a NEW people i.e. Gentiles, 'signs and wonders' accompanied.

In each case the gift of tongues was given as a sign to *confirm* the spoken new covenant, for there was *no written* new covenant.

Now we come to another NEW region, Ephesus - Acts 19v2 **He said unto them, Have ye received the Holy Ghost since ye believed? And they said unto him, We have not so much as heard whether there be any Holy Ghost.** (Obviously they had not heard the preaching of Acts 2 or Acts 10)

3 **And he said unto them, Unto what then were ye baptized? And they said, Unto John's baptism.**

When Paul got to the uttermost parts of the earth he found a people who were in the very same spiritual condition in which the Jews of Jerusalem found themselves in Acts 2. These people had no more understanding than Cornelius. They were disciples of God to the extent of their understanding. They were believers in all they had been given to believe. But these baptised believers were *not* saved and born again for they had *not* heard the Gospel message of the NEW covenant. This was made clear by their ignorance of the truth and the absence of the Holy Ghost.

Now Paul could *not* ask these people to turn to Matthew 26 or Luke 23 so that he could show them from the Scriptures the cross of Christ. He could *not* take them to the book of Romans and expound NT salvation. There was NO 'written' record of these things as yet. These baptised converts of John needed some strong evidence that Paul and company brought them truth.

Acts 19v4 **Then said Paul, John verily baptized with the baptism of repentance, saying unto the people, that they should believe on him which should come after him, that is, on Christ Jesus.** (That is, the law and the prophets were until John, but grace and truth came by Jesus Christ)

5 **When they heard this, they were baptized in the name of the Lord Jesus.**

These people were glad of the good news; they had already responded to the announcement of the forerunner i.e. John the Baptist, and they were just as quick to respond to the good news carried by the apostle. Once they had, they were baptised in the name of the Lord Jesus.

Acts 19v6 **And when Paul had laid his hands upon them, the Holy Ghost came on them; and they spake with tongues, and prophesied.** So when we get to the 'uttermost part of the earth', we find Jews and proselytes that are in the very same condition that Jews and proselytes were in on the day of Pentecost at Jerusalem. They had responded in faith to John's baptism but must now respond to the good news that God sent His Son into the world to die and rise again in payment for the sins of man. They then received the Holy Ghost with 'signs and wonders' accompanying the message to *confirm* that these were *true* apostles who proclaimed the words of God.

Every time we find tongues in the Bible it was a *confirmation of the word of God* to those who had not previously believed the new covenant message.

The gift of tongues is...

1) A language *not* known to the speaker

2) Given as a gift by God to believers

3) Given as a ***sign to confirm the word*** for a witness to unbelievers

4) Connected only with the apostolic ministry

The Corinthian use of Tongues - First let us look at what Corinth was like as a city - Corinth was the capital of the ancient province of Achaia. In the apostolic period, Corinth was a thriving commercial and industrial city with a population of 700,000 approx. (Isa 5v8) Greek civilisation, with its learning

SIGNS AND WONDERS

and arts flourished there. Athletic games and schools of philosophy were numerous. It was in an ideal situation for traders to come from all around the world, thus not only bringing their goods and wealth to Corinth but also their customs, religions, and their gross sins. Sin and immorality were the order of the day. The entire city was filled with drunkenness, gluttony, prostitution and paganism. The Greeks in their worship of the 'love' goddess Aphrodite had reached levels of degradation seldom seen. The moral level of the city was so low that one living a wicked life in those times was said to be *'living as a Corinthian'*. Having first preached at Athens, Paul made his way to Corinth. Acts 18 verifies that God used Paul to establish a Christian church there. He ministered in that 'hell hole' for a year and a half. Jews and Gentiles alike were saved by the preaching of the cross. Some of the leading Jews of the city were saved, including Crispus, the chief ruler of the synagogue. Most of the converts came from the lower classes of the Gentiles (1 Cor 1v26). There was also Erastus, a chamberlain, and Gaius, a wealthy man, who were converted (Rom 16v23), but these were notable exceptions.

We can of course compare the Corinthian church with the Laodicean church of today. The most carnal church in the Bible was the Corinthian church. Many of the 'members' were basing their Christian lives on their feelings and experiences rather than on the authority of Scripture – just like so many Christians do today - *'If it feels good do it!'*

In the Corinthian church we find 'clicks' and divisions, men following men rather than following the word of God and the Lord. There was incestuous fornication among them, they were suing one another in courts of law, there was idol worship, people were coming to the Lord's Table in any kind of a manner, divorce was an accepted practice etc.

Although we have listed many of the problems in the Corinthian church, their main problem was their lack of Divine authority i.e. they had no final authority. Without a *final authority* that everybody is in subjection to, there can be no union or Christian harmony but instead chaos.

1 Cor 12v1-7 - The manifestation of the Spirit is given to profit withal. Wherever a saved member of the Body of Christ goes he is to be filled, led and controlled by God's Holy Spirit so that all with whom he comes in contact with may be benefited.

1 Cor 12v8-11 - So not 'everyone' receives the same gift. Therefore not everyone receives the gift of tongues. 1 Cor 12v12 **For as the body is one, and hath many members, and all the members of that one body, being many, are one body: so also is Christ.**

1 Cor 12v13 **For by one Spirit are we all baptized into one body, whether we be Jews or Gentiles, whether we be bond or free; and have been all made to drink into one Spirit.**

Therefore...

1) We are placed into the Body of Christ by an operation of God's Holy Spirit

2) The members of the Body of Christ will be as different in their functions and abilities as the members of a human body

3) These manifestations will *differ* from person to person according to the dispensation of God in their lives

4) To say that someone is not in Christ because they do *not* speak in 'tongues' is a *false* doctrine

You cannot have Christ and *not* have the Holy Spirit - Rom 8v9, Col 2v9, 1 John 5v7.

In 1 Cor 12v14-27 we have a discussion of the unity of the body. The discussion of the gifts resumes in verse 28... **And God hath set some in the church, first apostles, secondarily prophets, thirdly teachers, after that miracles, then gifts of healings, helps, governments, diversities of tongues.** This list of gifts is not in the order they were given by God i.e. On the day of Pentecost when the baptism of the Holy Ghost took place, men spoke with other tongues *before* they prophesied. On that day men spoke in tongues *before* there was any gathering of believers to govern. On that day men spoke in tongues and there is no record of anyone being healed. Therefore the above list of gifts is not in the order they were given to the church, the Lord's Body.

This gives only one possible conclusion. The gifts set forth are listed in the order of their measure of *importance* to the establishment of the NT church. This ordering of the gifts is set forth by the inspiration of the very God who gave the gifts (1 Cor 12v5). This view is confirmed by the first clause of verse 31, **But covet earnestly the best gifts:**

Therefore the gifts are *not* all of 'equal' importance as the Lord here declares some gifts are better than others. He tells us to covet earnestly the *best* gifts and *not the least* of the gifts. Yet today in this Laodicean age the church is coveting the least of all the gifts in the body of Christ i.e. *tongues*.

Note in verse 29+30...

>Are all apostles? – NO!
>
>Are all prophets? – NO!
>
>Are all teachers? – NO!
>
>Are all workers of miracles? – NO!
>
>Have all the gifts of healing? – NO!

We have been shown throughout the course of this chapter that a body is *not* a group of ears, feet or hands. It takes many different members to make up a human body. Even so, the Lord has shown, it takes many different spiritual gifts to make up the Lord's body, the church.

But there is another question in 1 Cor 12v30 - **Do all speak with tongues?** Following on *in context* the answer is obviously NO!

So often these false 'teachers', tell the people that if you *don't* speak in tongues...

Then you have never really been saved; or

You've been saved but you don't have the Holy Ghost; or

You are saved but you lack the power of the Holy Spirit etc.

None of this is taught in the Scriptures, it is man-made and false, it is error.

So in 1 Cor 12, the Triune God is the giver of spiritual gifts. He not only gives these gifts to believers but empowers them to manifest these gifts. One of these gifts is the ability to speak in languages *not* known to the speaker i.e. tongues. Not every saved person is given this particular gift. Tongues is the *least* of the gifts listed in this chapter.

Now we move on to 1 Cor 13v1-3 - Now the standard handling of this passage by the Pentecostals and Charismatics is that since Paul spoke with the tongues of men and angels, therefore this teaches a *heavenly language*. Note – every time in our Bible that the words spoken in heaven are identified linguistically, the language is said to be **Hebrew**. Ruckman writes... *'In the Bible, the tongue of angels is Hebrew. When the Lord Jesus spoke from Heaven to Paul in Acts 9, He spoke in Hebrew. The Holy Spirit teaches us to call God 'Abba' (Rom 8v15, Gal 4v6); that's Aramaic. (Aramaic – the language of the Jews in Palestine after the captivity and that spoken by Christ and His disciples) When the citizens of Heaven rejoice over the destruction of Babylon, they cry 'Alleluia'; that's Hebrew (Rev 19v1-6). Why wouldn't Hebrew be the language of Heaven?'*

Paul did *not* say that he spoke in the tongues of angels. He is setting forth an argument so to speak...

Charity is the *greatest*. It is greater than faith and hope (1 Cor 13v13), it is greater than spiritual gifts (1 Cor 13v8), it is greater than our knowledge (1 Cor 13v9-12) and it is greater than good works in the energy of the flesh (1 Cor 13v3)

The entire statement of verses 1-3 is an argument! Did Paul...

1) Understand all mysteries?

2) Have all knowledge?

3) Have all faith?

4) Give his body to be burned?

The answer is NO of course. Therefore, in the context of the passage, did he speak with the tongues of angels? NO!

He is saying that *if he did do those things*, but did *not* do them as a genuine love offering to God for others, they would be vain works only to perish at the Judgment Seat of Christ.

If he exercised spiritual gifts including tongues and miracles but did so for self-gratification, spiritual pride or obedience to some human authority, such use of the gifts would be nothing more than an awful noise. The point of the verses is that no matter what we do for God, or in the name of God, no matter how good it looks or feels, if we do not have charity, it is of no profit. 1 Cor 13v4-6. We should always want to and seek the truth. 1 Cor 13v7+8 - So tongues *shall* cease, but when?

1 Cor 13v9+10 - One interpretation of this passage is that when Paul wrote this epistle the NT was not complete; there would yet be knowledge and prophecy given; the full and complete revelation of Scripture would then be perfect; when this perfect Bible was finished the signs and gifts would cease. Now this is quite a good interpretation but it does have some flaws.

First, the context of the remarks is *not the written Scriptures*, but charity. Second, if that which is part means the Scriptures in their part and that which is perfect means the Scriptures in their fullness, the phrase **'that which is in part shall be done away'** makes no sense at all. It's like saying *'We now have the sign gifts because we only have part of the Bible, but when we have all the Bible we will do away with the part of the Bible we had before it was complete?'*

Knox writes...1 Cor 13v11 is the picture of a child... **When I was a child, I spake as a child, I understood as a child, I thought as a child: but when I became a man, I put away childish things.** A child is a human being as much as he will ever be but there will be growth and progression to manhood. This complete maturity is the Biblical definition of *perfect* throughout the Scriptures. Perfect *never* means sinless. In verse 12 is the picture of our understanding... **For now we see through a glass, darkly; but then face to face: now I know in part; but then shall I know even as also I am known.** The believer has all of God, of salvation, of eternal life that he will ever have, but there is a growth and progression to greater apprehension of the truth. In verse 13 we have faith, hope and charity with the Lord showing by these verses a progression in spiritual life unto perfection. This is the perfect complement to the first 3 verses of the chapter. These last 3 verses conclude the teaching which has run through the chapter. Simply put, spiritual gifts are *not* to be the aim and goal of the believer's life. If we see a man occupied with prophecies or *tongues* or any other gifts of the Spirit we know that man is not yet a *perfect* man. He may have faith or he may have hope but he is yet a child lacking clear spiritual vision. The carnal Corinthians were given spiritual gifts by God to benefit the Body of Christ (1 Cor 12). They used them selfishly because they lacked charity. As a result, their occupation with the gifts of the Spirit kept them from being mature Christians (1 Cor 13).

Moving on to 1 Cor 14...v1 **Follow after charity, and desire spiritual gifts, but rather that ye may prophesy.** Here we see again that there are some gifts of the Spirit more to be desired than others.

v2 **For he that speaketh in an unknown tongue speaketh not unto men, but unto God: for no man understandeth him; howbeit in the spirit he speaketh mysteries.** In this verse there is nothing that instructs anyone to speak in an unknown tongue. Nor is there any indication that a person speaking in an unknown tongue is conversing in a Heavenly or a secret prayer language. The wording of this verse is quite plain. This is a man at Corinth misusing a gift, at worst, or using it as it was never used in all the Book of Acts. He is speaking to no man. This verse does *not* say that God understands the speech, only that the man is speaking to God. 'Tongue speakers' today often say '*I was speaking to the Lord!*'

Note also the word 'spirit' (verse 2) in lower case. It is *not* referring to the Holy Spirit.

1 Cor 14v3+4 - Charity seeketh not her own. The gifts were given to profit withal *not* one's self. Tongues cannot be linked with charity. These carnal Corinthians claimed a spiritual gift and used it contrary to the way it was used when given by the Holy Spirit in the Book of Acts. They made it a matter of carnal self-gratification. It is clear from these verses that tongues does *not* edify the church.

1 Cor 14v5+6 - Paul didn't forbid the use, exercise or manifestation of any gift of the Spirit. However, he appealed to these believers to seek after those gifts which would be most profitable to the body. It is like Paul said... '*If I'm going to come and talk to you in order that you might be built up in the faith, why would I talk to you in some gibberish that you cannot understand? What good would that do you? How would that profit you? It might be thrilling to your carnal self but it would not edify you spiritually*'. 1 Cor 14v7-9 - These words make one thing clear; *nothing* made by God gives sounds which cannot be understood by their kind. There is a gift of tongues from the Holy Spirit and there is a babbling from the human 'spirit'. There is no doubt which is which. So comparing v2 with v9 we see that when the carnal Corinthian thought he was speaking to God he was actually speaking into the air.

1 Cor 14v10-13 - We have already been told that tongues does *not* edify but prophesying does. Prophesying is greater. Tongues *must be interpreted* to be of any value. So, why not just speak to men for edification, exhortation and comfort in their own language from the start? v13 does *not* say to pray that we may speak with tongues more and more but to pray that you may interpret. Find out what you are trying to say and give it to us so we can understand it. This is the only way to benefit the church. 1 Cor 14v14 **For if I pray in an unknown tongue, my spirit prayeth, but my understanding is unfruitful.** Again a comparison is necessary with v2...**For he that speaketh in an unknown tongue speaketh not unto men, but unto God: for no man understandeth him; howbeit in the spirit he speaketh mysteries.** According to the Bible this is *not* praying in the Holy Ghost,

SIGNS AND WONDERS

but rather the *human* 'spirit'.

Every case of speaking in tongues in the Scriptures was connected to the **apostolic** ministry and the gift was manifested to *confirm the word* to unbelievers as the NT Gospel was carried into an area where its truth had not previously come. When we come to the carnal church at Corinth we find believers speaking as barbarians, speaking into the air and calling something produced by their own *human* 'spirits', a manifestation of the Holy Ghost.

v14 continues... ***my spirit* prayeth, but my understanding is unfruitful.** In other words, if you speak in an unknown tongue, *in your spirit*, you cannot understand what you are saying. So these people who say 'Well I just know I am praising God when I speak in tongues!' – How do they know? You can't go on the authority of feelings i.e. it feels good. *The heroin addict will tell you 'It feels good'.*

1 Cor 14v15-19 - These are the words of an apostle with the apostolic gift. Note Paul said that 10,000 words in an unknown tongue are *not* worth 5 words that you can understand. Why don't Christians today put the emphasis on the 5 words with understanding rather than the 10,000 without?

1 Cor 14v20 - So in other words let's grow up and face the facts of what the Bible says, rather than what your preacher, teacher or pastor says. What does the Bible teach? That is what we should really seek for... the truth – Rom 4v3, Gal 4v30.

1 Cor 14v21 - Now to whom was the law given? Beginning at Exodus 19 God gave the law to Moses. Moses read that law in the hearing of the nation of Israel. The nation of Israel accepted the law and confirmed/sanctioned it as their rules and guidelines for living as one nation under God. No other nation on the face of the earth was ever given that law. It was binding upon *no* Gentile unless he chose to become a proselyte to Judaism. And in the law it was written that God would speak to His people (i.e. Hebrews) with men of *other tongues*.

1 Cor 14v22 **Wherefore** (i.e. because of this Bible truth) **tongues are for a sign, not to them that believe, but to them that believe not: but prophesying serveth not for them that believe not, but for them which believe.**

Thus, by definition from Mark 16 - Acts 2, from Acts 10 – Acts 19, and from 1 Cor 12 – 14, *signs* were given to Jewish apostles for use in ***confirming the word***. In each case this sign gift of tongues was manifest **because there were Jews present who were in a state of unbelief**. There is no record in the Bible of tongues being used when believers were gathered as a local church. And, if an unbeliever came into a place like the carnal church at Corinth, where *human* 'spirits' were leading men to 'babble' into the air, he would think he was in a madhouse, *not* the house of God.

1 Cor 14v23-31 - When these Corinthians spoke in tongues no one learned anything and no one was comforted. If some among them did speak unto men to edification, exhortation and comfort (*i.e. the definition of prophesying* - **But he that prophesieth speaketh unto men to edification, and exhortation, and comfort**), all could learn and all could be comforted. This is why the Lord told us earlier that prophecy was a *better* gift.

1 Cor 14v33 - So, according to the word of God, if the above procedures are violated we may be dealing with the flesh seeking a 'feeling', or we may be dealing with the manifestation of unclean spirits, but we certainly are *not* seeing God's Holy Spirit at work. After the authority of the Bible and the matter of tongues, the 3rd most hated subject on the face of the earth is the role the word of God gives to women for their happiness and protection... 1 Cor 14v34+35 - *How clear can you get?* If a woman speaks in the church rather than keeping silent, as commanded in both OT and

NT by the Holy Spirit who inspired the Scriptures, we may be in the midst of a 'spirit' led church service, but it certainly is not the Holy Spirit leading the service.

God gave His word so that we would *not* be deceived and led into error by the sleight of men and cunning craftiness whereby they lie in wait to deceive.

God has laid out in His word some clear rules for this matter of speaking in tongues and how it would be manifest if it truly was a working from God. Disobeying the word of God can *never* bring any joy to the person of God. *If you put a stop to every church service where more than one person is speaking in tongues at one time, or where someone spoke a word of gibberish without an interpreter, or where a woman spoke out rather than kept her God given place of silence in the assembly, this 'modern day' tongues movement would stop overnight!* Something being conducted in a fashion so *contrary* to the plain teachings of Scripture *cannot* possibly be of God.

1 Cor 14v36+37 - The Scriptures are the word of God. No man wrote this Book; God did - 1 Thes 2v13. Now Christian, it is either your final authority or it is not. You either obey the word of God or disobey it; it's your choice. Any man or woman who thinks themselves spiritual, or Spirit filled, or Spirit led, will *submit* to the authority of the word of God.

These verses we have read are *not* suggestions or recommendations; these verses do *not* contain ideas to be debated. These Scriptural teachings are to be obeyed.

The Holy Spirit will lead us to acknowledge that...

1) If a man says he speaks in tongues but is merely babbling, he is controlled by his *own* 'spirit' or an unclean spirit, but *not* God's Holy Spirit, for *every* Bible case of speaking in tongues involves a *known* language.

2) If a man speaks in a language not known to himself, but no one in the church interprets, he is controlled by his *own* 'spirit' or an unclean spirit, but *not* God's Holy Spirit, for the Holy Spirit will not go against the commandments of the Lord and His word.

3) If more than one man speaks in tongues at the same time, or more than three men speak in tongues in the church, they are under the influence of their *own* 'spirit' or an unclean spirit, but *not* the Holy Spirit, for the Holy Spirit will not go against the word of God.

4) If a woman speaks in tongues in the church she is being provoked to do so by her *own* 'spirit', or an unclean spirit, but *not* the Holy Spirit, for the Holy Spirit will *not* go against the word of God.

Now these 4 points are Scriptural; if you disobey them you disobey God and His word.

So let us briefly review what we have talked about so far...

1) Tongues are a gift of the Holy Spirit

2) Tongues are a *sign* to unbelieving Jews, who require a *sign*

3) Tongues accompany the apostolic ministry

4) Tongues are a known language, not jumbled up nonsensical syllables, unknown to the speaker

5) Tongues were given by God throughout the course of the apostolic ministry to *confirm the word* of the apostles to the Jews

SIGNS AND WONDERS

6) Tongues, if used in the church, will *never* be used by more than one individual at a time, and *never* by more than three persons per gathering

7) Tongues, if used in the church, will be interpreted

8) Tongues, if used in the church, will *never* be used by women

These points are taken from the Scriptures, they are not opinions.

Eph 4v8-16 - Ephesians presents the church of which Jesus Christ is the Head. The book of Ephesians does not record the history of a transitional period as does the Book of Acts. There is no more question about *signs, wonders and miracles* to get things started. We are dealing with the Body of Christ, the truth of which has been revealed to and through the apostle Paul. In Ephesians we are dealing with the doctrines that concern the members of the Body described in 1 Corinthians. The purpose of the spiritual gifts as listed in the book of Ephesians is the *perfecting* of the saints. Remember *perfect* in 1 Corinthians was a reference to the ultimate aim of the individual believer as he *grows* in grace. God gave the gifts listed here for the *perfection* of the saints. Note here the *sign* gifts that are listed. There is no mention of healings, interpretations, tongues, or miracles. This confirms again that the *sign* gifts were given to the apostles to *confirm the word*.

Once the word was received and a local church established, the need was growth to *perfection*. That is the purpose for the manifestation of the gifts listed here. These gifts were given for the work of the ministry. The theme of Ephesians is the Church of which the Lord Jesus Christ is the Head. The ministry of this Church, once it grew beyond its infancy, was to become like the Lord Jesus; to be a visible manifestation on earth of the risen Lord in Heaven. Why are the *sign* gifts *not* listed here? Because they contribute nothing to this end. They do *not* assist in the Holy Spirit's work of fitly joining and compacting the members of the body into a Christ honouring unity. The verses quoted teach that these gifts were given for the edification of the Body of Christ. The proper use of *tongues* was to signify truth to the unbeliever and the improper use of *tongues* was the self-edification of a believer. Hence, when the Lord lists the gifts which *edify* the body, *tongues does not appear.*

Therefore we are told in Eph 4v14 '**That we henceforth be no more children**,' Note this links in with 1 Corinthians 13v11. A childish Christian will remain tossed about by every wind of doctrine and will be so easily deceived by the sleight of men and will be taken in by the cunning craftiness of deceivers. (Eph 4v14) As Christians we need to mature and *not* be baby Christians.

Now let us briefly look at a few verses the Pentecostals (P) and Charismatics (C) use to support their 'case' for speaking in 'babblings and gibberish' as a 'heavenly' language...

Rom 8v26+27 - The P and C standard line is that '*we don't know the words to say*', so we just continue to repeat (nonsensical) syllables (Mat 6v7) and soon the Holy Spirit will take over and pray to God for you in a 'heavenly' language! This argument is soon 'blown out of the water' by verse 26 of Rom 8... **the Spirit itself maketh intercession for us with groanings *which cannot be uttered.***

The P and C also use 2 Cor 12v1-4 - The P and C picks up on '**heard unspeakable words, which it is not lawful for a man to utter.**' Even if this passage did mention a heavenly language, *which it does not*, the words state clearly that these words were not beyond the capabilities of human speech, but that God had passed a law forbidding them to be spoken.

The P and C also use Eph 6v17+18 - The P and C tell us that praying *in the Spirit* means praying *in tongues*. Does this mean that the command to *walk in the Spirit* (Gal 5v16) means to *walk in tongues*? To pray in Jesus' name is to pray so that He may agree with us in His intercession before the Father.

The P and C also use 3 references to John being *in the spirit,* from the book of Revelation - Rev 4v2, Rev 17v3, Rev 21v10.

You've got to be desperate to try to prove from these verses a 'heavenly language'. Note also in all 3 cases the 'spirit' is all in the 'lower case!' – *Interesting!*

There IS a Heavenly language but every time the Bible identifies it, it is Hebrew.

Fifty things you should know about tongues and healing - (by James Melton)

(Note this list also includes information and Scriptures to do with 'healing' even though we are focusing on tongues).

1) The Jews, as a nation, began with SIGNS (Rom 4v11, Exo 4v8+9+17+28+30, Exo 7v3, Exo 8v23, Exo 10v1+2, Exo 13v9, Exo 31v13+17, Deut 4v34, Deut 6v22)

2) The OT Jews lived by *signs* (Deut 11v18, Jos 4v6, 1 Sam 10v7, 2 Kings 19v29, Isa 7v14, Isa 38v7+22, Ezek 4v3, Ezek 20v12+20)

3) The Jews demanded *signs* from the Lord Jesus Christ (Mat 12v38, Mat 16v1-4, Mat 24v3, John 2v18, John 6v30)

4) The Jews require a *sign,* not the Gentiles (1 Cor 1v22, John 4v48)

5) According to the Lord Jesus, the gifts of *tongues* and healing are SIGNS (Mark 16v16-20)

6) These *signs* were for the purpose of *confirming the word of God* (Acts 14v3, Heb 2v3+4

7) These *signs* were spoken of in the *past* tense in 2 Cor 12v12 and in Heb 2v3+4, *not* in the present or future tense

8) Those who still look for *signs and wonders* today are on dangerous ground, for the Antichrist will deceive the world with *signs and wonders* (Rev 13v13+14, 2 Thes 2v8-12)

9) The Lord Jesus said that an evil and adulterous generation seeks after a *sign* (Mat 12v39)

10) The Bible speaks of various spiritual gifts to believers, but tongues and healing are *never* emphasised more than the other gifts (1 Cor 12v4-11)

11) The gifts of tongues and healing were *not* considered the best gifts (1 Cor 12v28-31)

12) The gift of healing was a *sign* (Mark 16v17+18, Exo 4v6-8, 2 Kings 20v8+9)

13) It is not God's will for all Christians to be healed (2 Cor 12v5-10)

14) The apostle Paul could not heal himself (2 Cor 12v5-10)

15) Near the end of his ministry, Paul could not heal Trophimus (2 Tim 4v20)

16) Instead of healing Timothy, Paul gave him medical advice (1 Tim 5v23)

17) Contrary to the 'modern faith healers,' 'love gifts' and 'faith offerings' were *not* a part of the healing ministries of the disciples (Mat 10v8+9)

18) A Christian who hasn't confessed his sins and repented of them has no business expecting God

SIGNS AND WONDERS

to heal him of anything (Ps 6v1-4, Psa 41v4, 2 Chro 7v14, Hos 5v10-13, 1 Cor 11v29-32, Jam 5v14-16, 1 John 1v7-10)

19) If modern faith healers really have the gift of healing, then they should prove their ministry by visiting hospitals and nursing homes and healing the sick, rather than writing books, holding healing meetings, and begging for money on television (2 Tim 4v5, Mat 10v8-16, 1 Tim 6v5-10)

20) Satan has the power to heal and this will cause millions to be led astray in the coming Tribulation period (Rev 13v1-4 + 12)

21) The gift of tongues was given as a *sign* (Mark 16v17, 1 Cor 14v22)

22) The gift of tongues was the supernatural ability of some Christians to speak in foreign languages in the presence of unbelieving Jews (Acts 2v7-11)

23) God has never caused or commanded Christians to speak in *unknown* tongues (Mark 16v17, Acts 2v4, 1 Cor 12v10, 1 Cor 14)

24) The Bible *never* says once, that tongues is the initial evidence of the baptism of the Holy Ghost

25) There is *no* baptism of the Holy Ghost in 1 Cor 14

26) Paul said that all true Christians were baptised *into* the body of Christ *by* the Holy Ghost (1 Cor 12v13), and all true Christians were sealed with the Holy Ghost until the day of redemption (Eph 4v30), but all Christians did *not* speak in tongues (1 Cor 12v29-31)

27) The Bible *never* says that baptism of the Holy Ghost is a second Christian experience or blessing

28) The baptism of *fire* is the condemnation of the *wicked* in Hell (Mat 3v11+12), *not* being 'on fire for the Lord'

29) Acts 2v3 speaks of 'cloven tongues *like as* of fire', *but* the Book of Acts says *nothing* at all about tongues of *fire* or a baptism of *fire*

30) If a person does *not* have the Spirit of Christ, he has no business waiting for the baptism of the Holy Ghost, because he doesn't even belong to Christ (Rom 8v9)

31) Pentecost was never a religious movement, or a religious experience. It was a Jewish feast day which always occurred fifty days after the Passover (Lev 23v15-22)

32) Jesus said that when the Holy Ghost came, He (the Holy Ghost) would not speak of Himself, because He would glorify the Lord Jesus Christ (John 16v13-14)

33) *No* Christian in the Bible is ever told to pray, preach or praise God in tongues

34) The disciples received the Holy Ghost in John 20v22, but they did *not* speak in tongues when this happened

35) The filling of the Spirit in Acts 4v31 and Eph 5v18-20 does *not* include speaking in tongues

36) When speaking of spiritual gifts in Eph 4v8-12, Paul does *not* mention tongues

37) There were only three cases in the Book of Acts where people spoke in tongues, and these tongues were a *sign* to the Jews *each* time, because the Jews require a *sign* (Acts 2v1-11, Acts 10v44-46, Acts 19v6-8, 1 Cor 1v22, 1 Cor 14v22)

38) The former and latter rain of Joel 2 has *nothing* to do with Acts 2 or the modern-day Charismatic movement, because the rain of Joel 2 is literal wet rain from the sky in Israel (Joel 2v1-31)

39) Tongues are *not* even mentioned in the list of spiritual gifts in Rom 12v6-8

40) Although tongues were permitted in 1 Cor 14 (because there was a Jewish synagogue in Corinth – Acts 18v1-4), they were *not* encouraged because tongues did *not* edify the church (1 Cor 14v4+5+26)

41) It is better to speak five words clearly than ten thousand with an unknown tongue (1 Cor 14v19)

42) No more than three people were allowed to speak in tongues in the church assembly, and then only one could speak at a time (1 Cor 14v27)

43) No one was permitted to speak in tongues in the church without an interpreter (1 Cor 14v27+28)

44) Women were *not* allowed to speak in tongues in the church (1 Cor 14v34+35)

45) Those who did speak in tongues (foreign languages) had power over their own spirit (1 Cor 14v32)

46) A religious man who doesn't bridle his tongue is deceived and he has vain religion (James 1v26)

47) Many 'seducing spirits' are in the world and it is every Christian's duty to 'try' these spirits (1 Tim 4v1, 1 John 4v1, Rev 2v2)

48) The word of God is the standard by which we are to judge all doctrines (Isa 8v20, 2 Tim 3v16+17)

49) He that is spiritual judges all things (1 Cor 2v15)

50) Teaching the Scriptural truth about *signs*, *healing* and *tongues* is *not* a matter of being mean, prejudiced, or intolerant. It is simply a matter of obeying the command to *rightly divide* God's word (2 Tim 2v15)

Extra notes...

Tongues, wherever you find them in the Bible *are languages* – Acts 2v4+6+9-11, Acts 26v14, Ezra 4v7, Dan 1v4, Rev 9v11

Tongues were for a *sign* as prophesised... Isa 28v11-13, 1 Cor 14v21+22

Where is there *one* instance in the Bible of the use of tongues in *private* devotions? Prov 25v14

Signs and lying wonders - 2 Thes 2v8+9

Signs given for accreditation - Mark 16v20, Heb 2v3+4, Isa 35v1-10, Acts 2v22

They either accredited God's man – Exo 4v1-10, John 20v30, 2 Cor 12v12, Mark 16v20, Acts 4v29+30

Jews require a *sign* - Exo 4v30+31, Exo 31v13, Num 14v11, Judg 6v17, 1 Sam 10v7-9, Isa 7v11+14, Ezek 4v3, Mat 12v38+39, Mat 24 v3+30, Mark 8v11+12, Luke 2v12+34

The four *sign* gifts in Mark 16v17+18 - Cast out devils, speak in tongues, take up deadly serpents, healing

SIGNS AND WONDERS

All can be found in the Book of Acts – Acts 16v18, Acts 28v3-5, Acts 3v6-8

The *sign* gifts were temporary and directed to the Jews.

The *sign* of tongues was to be a specific warning of imminent judgment upon Israel at various times in their history – Deut 28v49+64, Isa 28v11, Jer 5v15, 1 Cor 14v21. In AD 70 this judgment came. Jerusalem was destroyed by the Romans and the nation dispersed. There is *no* Biblical record of any *sign* manifested *after* this date. When the *signs* were fulfilled the *signs* ceased.

2 Pet 1v19-21 teaches that the *gift* of prophecy was *replaced* by the *written* word of God.

1 John 2v20+21 emphasises that the *gift* of knowledge has been *replaced* by the *written* word of God.

The Devil can do signs and wonders - Exo 7v10-12, Exo 7v22, Exo 8v7, Mark 13v21-23, 2 Cor 11v13-15, 2 Thes 2v9, Rev 13v13+14

The Biblical usage for the word 'tongue' is *always* a *known* language - Gen 10v5+20, Deut 28v49, Ezra 4v7, Acts 21v40, Acts 22v2, Rev 5v9, Rev 7v9, Rev 13v7

Regarding signs associated with Israel also look up – Ezek 20v12+20, Exo 4v9+17+28+30, Deut 6v22, Deut 26v8, 29v3, Isa 8v18, (Mark 13v22), Mark 16v17+20, John 4v48, 20v30, Acts 2v22 (John 12v11, Heb 2v3+4, Isa 35v1-10, John 3v2, John 6v14, Acts 10v38), Acts 2v43, 4v30, 5v12, 8v13, 13v49-14v3, 2 Cor 12v12, 2 Thes 2v9, 1 Cor 1v22, 1 Cor 14v22.

NOTES

NOTES

NOTES

WOMEN IN THE MINISTRY

Should women be bishops, pastors, elders, deacons etc?

1 Tim 3v1-7, **Titus 1v1-9** - Note 'he' is told to *hold fast* the word of God *not* to ignore it, change it or go against it. He is told to *obey it*. Titus 1v10-16.

Just for interest...

Not one woman was chosen to be an apostle.

Not one woman was used to record *any book* in the Bible.

Bishops, elders, pastors and deacons are all **male** roles in Scripture i.e. not one woman.

There is no mention of one single *woman* 'preacher' in the New Testament. Not one single sermon in Scripture was ever preached by a woman.

Read **Acts 6v1-4** – how many women did the apostles choose? None.

The serpent was in the garden before Adam but he never tried to deceive Adam, he went straight for the woman. *Why?*

Male leadership in the church has never been a problem *until* this **Laodicean age**.

God established the **Messianic line** through **Kings** not Queens.

Read **1 Pet 3v7** – I never wrote that, God did.

Read **1 Tim 2v11+12** and **1 Cor 14v33-37** – I never wrote that, God did.

The list goes on and on...

Now the rise of women leaders/preachers etc. in the church has resulted in the *errors* of **Spiritualism** (The Fox Sisters), **The Seventh Day Adventists** – SDA (Ellen White), **Christian Science** (Mary Baker Eddy), **The Foursquare Gospel** (Aimee Semple McPherson) among loads of other *errors* (**Isa 3v12** – *read it! God wrote it not me*) because people followed women like Kathryn Kuhlman and now Joyce Meyer. All of these are as false as a £666 coin! You follow these women and they'll lead you *away* from Biblical truth. Men and women are *equal* in status but we have ***different*** roles to play. According to the Bible women are not to take the lead *over men*, like it or lump it, that is *not* an opinion, it is Scriptural truth.

1 Tim 2v11+12 - The reason why the woman's role in the church is *such an issue today,* is because *the world* has had such an influence on the church rather than the church influencing the world. The feminist movement along with marketing, advertising, and the rest of the media, has bombarded us 24 hours a day, brainwashing us that men ought to be more like women and women ought to be more like men; *we are the same*, **the world tells us**, there is no *difference*. Men and women in the world, having rejected Biblical truth, are confused about the most basic things. Many men are trying to be like women in dress and manner, while many women are demanding the right to be like men, to dress like men, to do the same work as men, to play the same sports as men, to fight in armies like men. They want equal pay for equal work; they are demanding a man's place in society, at home and in the church. Sadly the church is always affected by society. Thus the rebellion of women in the world is causing similar problems in the church, and we find women demanding leadership roles in many Christian groups/churches.

We do not realise how powerful the TV is when it comes to *propaganda and brainwashing* us into thinking like the Devil wants us to think. The only way to combat the enemy is by reading, studying and living the Scriptures, which most Christians *don't* do. **For 1900 years the woman's role was never an issue** but with the invention of TV and such likes, now women want equal rights on everything, *'we are all the same* and there is no difference'. But the Bible, **God's word, says there is a difference**.

The Bible speaks too clearly on this subject for there to be any confusion. The problem is that churches too often are looking to sources, *other than the Bible* for guidance. **God loves women as much as He does men**. Women are as important to the home, church and society as men are. In Jesus Christ, women enjoy the same spiritual position and blessings before God as men do. This does not mean, though, there is no *difference* in men and women in their appearance and in their roles. There is a basic truth which needs to be restated in the church and society today; ***men and women are different!*** Men and women were made for *different* roles. The NT affirms that **men** are to be the leaders in the home, church and society. Women were not created to rule these divine institutions, **men** were.

It is interesting to note the following facts from the Bible… (*Includes some reiteration*)

1) Adam was *first* formed *then* Eve 2) Christ didn't choose one woman when He chose the 12 apostles, they were *all* men 3) Not one woman was used to record any book of the Scriptures 4) Under the Law 'Priests' were restricted to males from the tribe of Levi 5) Bishops, elders, pastors and deacons are **all male roles** according to Scripture 6) There is no such thing as a 'deaconess' in the Scriptures 7) There is *not* one woman preacher mentioned in the NT church according to the Scriptures 8) Not one sermon preached in the Bible was preached by a woman 9) In **Acts 6v1-4** when the 12 apostles chose seven people to take some of the burden from them so they could continue to give themselves to prayer and to the ministry of the word, they chose seven men 10) Moses was told to gather 70 men (**Num 11v16+17**) 11) Moses was told to send out *men* to spy out the land of Canaan (**Num 13v1-3**) 12) The serpent was in the garden *before* Adam but he never tried to deceive Adam, he went straight for the woman when she came onto the scene, *why?* 13) When the Bible talks about the gathering together of the saints i.e. in the church, the assembly, it always insists upon **male leadership** and that has never been a problem *until* this Laodicean Church Age 14) God's chosen people, the nation of Israel, descended *from* Patriarchs and *not* Matriarchs – they did *not* descend from Sarah, Rebecca and Rachel, they descended from Abraham, Isaac and Jacob 15) God established the Messianic line through Kings and *not* Queens 16) When God Almighty came into this world in the flesh He came as a *man* and *not* a woman 17) The Scriptures state plainly that the woman is a weaker vessel **1 Pet 3v7**, note also in regard to the woman's *silence* as quoted in **1 Tim 2v11+12, 1 Cor 14v33-37** - The Bible commands *women* to be silent in the churches *not men*. That is a *commandment* from the Lord. The Scriptures are plain and clear that a woman should not teach, speak or usurp authority over the man in the church gathering. They should not usurp authority over the man anywhere, including the home etc.

Now that is a hard thing to take in for the carnal worldly woman, but that is what God has stated in His word.

WOMEN IN THE MINISTRY

Now some women start jumping up and down because of this, but these are *not* godly or spiritual women otherwise they would want to *obey* the Scriptures.

Question - If a woman cannot preach or teach in the church what about if someone who we work with i.e. a man asks us a question in relation to our faith, what then? Can a woman teach then?

Let us look at an example... **Acts 18v24-26**. Here a man who only knew the baptism of John was preaching in the synagogue and Aquila and Priscilla took him unto them i.e. privately, and expounded unto Apollos the way of God more perfectly. The Bible never forbids women to expound in private but they must be silent in the church. There is a difference when it comes to the gathering of the saints as a church, as the Body of Christ. I've had a number of 'dealings' i.e. talks, correspondence with so-called 'women pastors', 'deaconesses' etc. which is anti-Scriptural. **Nowhere in the NT is there a woman pastor, or Bible teacher in the church**.

I have written to a number of women 'pastors / leaders' asking them to show me from the Scriptures where it says they can occupy the office they do? Not one has ever written back, I wonder why? Because they *cannot* prove from the Scriptures that they are doing right in the occupation/role they have taken i.e. 'pastor, elder, bishop, deacon, 'deaconess' etc. Now as stated previously, we have been so influenced by the world today that church order, God's order, has been turned on its head. Women want to do men's jobs and men want to do women's jobs, yet according to Scripture we are *different* and have *different* roles to play.

When a woman heads up the household it is wrong **according to Scripture**. When a woman gets up to preach and teach in church (where men are present) it is wrong **according to Scripture**. Now, you can of course *disobey* the Scriptures, but be it on your head. God is a God of order and *not* confusion, He knows what is best for us.

Now according to 1 Cor 14 Paul said in v37 **If any man think himself to be a prophet, or spiritual, let him acknowledge that the things that I write unto you are the commandments of the Lord**. Note the commandments of the Lord. Are you spiritual? If so you will obey the commandments of the Lord.

In 1 Timothy the apostle gives the very same instructions concerning women, and this epistle was said to have been written to teach the proper order for churches in general. **But if I tarry long, that thou mayest know how thou oughtest to behave thyself in the house of God, which is the church of the living God, the pillar and ground of the truth. 1 Tim 3v15**.

The things contained in 1 Timothy are general instructions about church order to be obeyed by all churches in every century; and it is in this book, the book which contains the standards for church leaders, that God has *forbidden* women from taking authority over, or teaching, men. That is absolutely clear.

In giving instructions about women in the church, the Holy Spirit referred back to the original order of creation – Adam *first* and then Eve. The Holy Spirit, in guiding Paul's pen, used this order of creation to prove that women must not take authority over the men. Don't forget that Adam was *not* deceived, and the serpent never targeted Adam even though Adam was here *first*. **For Adam was first formed, then Eve. And Adam was not deceived, but the woman being deceived was in the transgression**. 1 Tim 2v13. The woman was deceived. See also **1 Pet 3v7**. The word of God says that the woman is the *weaker* vessel. I didn't say that, the word of God said it.

Just according to these few Scriptures we can see that the woman has a different makeup than man. She was designed for a *different* role in life – that of a wife and mother. Her emotional, psychological and rational makeup is geared up perfect for this, but **she was *not* designed for leadership**. Now again, that is hard to swallow for some women in this day and age, but it is the truth, **according to the Bible**.

In the Garden of Eden the Devil deceived the woman but this was *not* true of Adam. He sinned, but he was *not* deceived, he knew what he was doing, and is a picture of Christ regarding this i.e. Christ 'willingly' laid down His life for the church. Eve had allowed herself to be thrust into a position of decision making, which she was not supposed to occupy. She should have sought her husband regarding the situation. Why does the Bible, the Book that God has written, state that the woman is a *weaker* vessel? *Because she is.* She is oftentimes more emotional, more sensitive, more caring, more loving, more gentle and *more easily deceived.*

For the spiritual and godly woman this is *not* hard to take on board, *but* for the carnal woman this goes 'right against the grain'.

John R Rice writes… 'In the Bible several women were called prophetesses, including… 1) Miriam (Exo 15v20) 2) Deborah (Judg 4v4) 3) Huldah (2 Kings 22v14) 4) Noadiah (Neh 6v14) 5) Anna (Luke 2v36) 6) Four daughters of Philip (Acts 21v9). Some people who never studied this matter think that prophetesses were preachers. But they were not. It is never mentioned that a single one of these prophetesses preached or addressed public congregations of people in any way. Prophetesses did *not* preach, they did not do the work of a pastor or Bible teacher. To prophesy means to speak by divine revelation. A prophecy is a special revelation by the Spirit of God. A prophet is a man who receives a divine revelation. A prophetess is a woman who receives divine revelation concerning the future. Prophets (masculine) were sometimes also preachers. Isaiah, Jeremiah, Daniel and Ezekiel all preached. But they were primarily prophets, that is, they received divine revelation of what should happen to Israel. They were also preachers, though they are called prophets. But prophetesses *never* preached in the Bible. They received brief divine revelation to give to individuals, but were *never* sent to preach, to address public assemblies as expounders of the word, nor to do the work of a pastor or evangelist. The work of a prophet is indicated in **Deut 18v22**. Let us look at Deborah for a moment. **Judg 4v4-9**. Deborah arose, and went with Barak to Kedesh. Deborah, the prophetess in the OT, did *not* preach, and she took *no* authority over men. Deborah lived under a palm tree and the children of Israel came up to her for Judgement. There was no government in the land. When two neighbours had a dispute and could not come to an agreement, they said, 'We will go and ask Deborah to decide'. So they came to Deborah and she would advise, possibly by divine revelation, how to settle the difference. And those who wished would take her decision. She had no authority. Note that the prophecy of Deborah given in **Judg 4v6+7** is a divine revelation. Note that it takes less than two verses to record it, and note that it was addressed to one man, Barak. In verse 9 God gave Deborah a further revelation in this phrase, '**…for the LORD shall sell Sisera into the hand of a woman.**' and shows that Barak's insistence on taking Deborah with him displeased the Lord. Deborah was *not* a preacher, nor a leader. God did *not* want her leading the army. She did not take authority over men and did *not* teach men. She simply delivered a brief message from God to Barak.

One more case before closing… Miriam, the sister of Moses and of Aaron, is called a prophetess in **Exo 15v20+21**. There we are told that… Miriam the prophetess, the sister of Aaron, took a timbrel in her hand; and all the women went out after her with timbrels and with dances. And Miriam answered them, Sing ye to the LORD… Miriam led *women* in singing. **She *never* led men in singing nor preached to men**. But Miriam the prophetess was used of God as a *startling object lesson* to women who seek authority and leadership in religious matters, and God cursed her with leprosy for her sin. Read **Num 12v1-15**. Note that Miriam and Aaron said, '**Hath the Lord indeed spoken only by Moses? Hath he not spoken also by us?**' Miriam and Aaron were ***both*** in the *same sin* and in verse 9 the Scripture says... '**And the anger of the LORD was kindled against them...**' God was angry with Miriam and with Aaron because each of them wanted to *usurp authority*. **But only Miriam was stricken with leprosy for her sin**.

The difference was that Aaron had been appointed of God as the high priest. Aaron was a man and was given a man's place. So Miriam's sin was much more wicked than that of Aaron, and God made of her an appalling object lesson to all women who would seek to take authority or leadership over men or alongside them. Miriam was a prophetess, but even a woman who is a prophetess sins terribly against God when she seeks leadership as a preacher, teacher or leader over men.

In conclusion... The rise of women preachers has meant the rise of multiplied sects and cults. The trouble is today there is such effeminate preaching in the pulpits, churches are seen as 'effeminate' and therefore very few churches have **men** as the 'majority' in the congregation. The *'man's man'* is seldom seen today therefore *few men* are drawn into the church. Oftentimes, preachers are *milksops* rather than men who have a cutting edge and *'tell it like it is'*.

Extra notes – Titus 2v4+5, 1 Tim 2v11-14, 1 Cor 11v3+8+9, Gen 3v16, 1 Tim 3v4+5, Eph 4v22-24, Isa 3v12, Heb 13v17, 1 Cor 14v34+35, Eph 5v22-24, 1 Tim 5v14, 1 Pet 3v4+7, Prov 31v10-31, 1 Sam 1v13.

If you disagree with this article that's fine, but you'll need to *back up* your argument **with Scripture**, which I don't believe is possible.

NOTES

NOTES

NOTES

MARRIAGE, DIVORCE AND REMARRIAGE

Marriage, Divorce and Remarriage. What does Scripture say on the matter?

I'm *not* interested in what you *think* or what your *opinion* is, I want to *know* what the Scriptures say and teach on the subject - Rom 4v3, Gal 4v30. The majority of churches today have departed from the word of God and teach what they *feel* is right and will compromise in order not to offend the majority. Here at TfT! we are only concerned with what the Bible says and teaches, not what your pastor or leader *thinks is right*.

Now when it comes to sins of 'sex' i.e. adultery, 'a remarriage' etc. Christians think that these *kinds of sins* are unforgivable and unpardonable. You will understand what I mean by this if you have been divorced and notice the *stigma* that other Christians put on you. If you have been divorced and remarried, you will also notice how church members and leaders feel towards you. Most Christians have the inability to see where God has made allowances regarding *remarriage* etc. in His Book for other people, other than themselves. In other words, as long as you have a happy marriage and you haven't gone through divorce, then it is *wrong* and unscriptural for anyone else to. This is what we Bible believers call hypocrisy, and a Pharisaical spirit. Listen, I don't recommend *divorce* and would encourage anyone to try to work things out if they can, but in the real world, it happens, even with the best of intentions not to, *it happens!* If it does, are you to stay *single* for the rest of your life? Some Christians would have you to, but that's because they are illiterate and unscriptural and haven't a clue when it comes to what God allows and what God teaches through His word, as we shall see.

What is a marriage? A marriage 'ceremony' is *not* a marriage, because a marriage 'ceremony' does *not join your flesh together*.

Let us start by looking at 1 Cor 7... *read it* before going any further, and read it *only* in the Authorized Version Bible.

In v1+2 it is good for a man to stay single... **Now concerning the things whereof ye wrote unto me: It is good for a man not to touch a woman. Nevertheless, to avoid fornication, let every man have his own wife, and let every woman have her own husband.** In v7 Paul says that as far as he was concerned, it would be good for a man to stay single – **For I would that all men were even as I myself. But every man hath his proper gift of God, one after this manner, and another after that.**

There is a 'condition' in v9, if you *can't* stay single, *get married* - **But if they cannot contain, let them marry: for it is better to marry than to burn.** Don't burn with lust, and commit fornication, if you can't *contain*, get married, but make sure you involve the Lord in your choosing and that person has to be a Christian of course. (2 Cor 6v14, 1 Cor 7v39, 1 Cor 1v10, Amos 3v3, Deut 7v2-4).

Note also in v7 that certain men have a 'gift' for staying single - **For I would that all men were even as I myself. But every man hath his proper gift of God, one after this manner, and another after that.** This goes hand in hand with what Jesus said in Mat 19v11+12 **But he said unto them, All men cannot receive this saying, save they to whom it is given. For there are some eunuchs, which were so born from their mother's womb: and there are some eunuchs, which were made** eunuchs of men: and there be eunuchs, which have made themselves eunuchs for the kingdom of heaven's sake. He that is able to receive it, let him receive it**.

So the first admonition is for a person to stay *single* if possible. Paul not only gives this advice to young men who haven't been married, but he also says in 1 Cor 7v8 **I say therefore to the unmarried and widows, It is good for them if they abide even as I** and again to the widow in v40 **But she is happier if she so abide, after my judgment: and I think also that I have the Spirit of God**. That is, she is happier staying *single*. So if you *can* stay single do so, but if you *can't* get married. (There are *advantages* and *disadvantages* for both).

Now, what is not so clear about it, is that the Bible *defines* marriage as a *physical matter* in 1 Cor 7v9 **But if they cannot contain, let them marry: for it is better to marry than to burn**. The marriage has to do with a man and woman coming together lest they burn in lust. Look at the context of 1 Cor 7v5 **Defraud ye not one the other, except it be with consent for a time, that ye may give yourselves to fasting and prayer; and come together again, that Satan tempt you not for your incontinency**. Marriage is *flesh joining flesh.* Mat 19v5 **And said, For this cause shall a man leave father and mother, and shall cleave to his wife: and they twain shall be one flesh?** Moses said that a marriage is where *flesh joins flesh* - Gen 2v23+24 **And Adam said, This is now bone of my bones, and flesh of my flesh: she shall be called Woman, because she was taken out of Man. Therefore shall a man leave his father and his mother, and shall cleave unto his wife: and they shall be one flesh**. Paul said that's where *flesh joins flesh* - Eph 5v31 **For this cause shall a man leave his father and mother, and shall be joined unto his wife, and they two shall be one flesh**. Then Paul makes a very interesting remark in 1 Cor 6v16 **What? know ye not that he which is joined to an harlot is one body? for two, saith he, shall be one flesh**. According to **Scripture**, a *marriage* is where *flesh joins flesh* to make *one* body.

This explains why *fornication* is warned against in 1 Cor 6v18 **Flee fornication. Every sin that a man doeth is without the body; but he that committeth fornication sinneth against his own body** and this thoroughly explains what Jesus Christ said in Mat 19v9 **And I say unto you, Whosoever shall put away his wife, except it be for fornication, and shall marry another, committeth adultery: and whoso marrieth her which is put away doth commit adultery**.

Now this may not be to some of your liking, but this is **Bible**. We have too many 'Christian-Pharisees' going around lording it over the flock and telling them what they *can and can't do* according to them. It is very interesting that Jesus is speaking about these matters to *Pharisees*. See also in Luke 16, talking about the law and the prophets and John, Christ suddenly says in Luke 16v18 **Whosoever putteth away his wife, and marrieth another, committeth adultery: and whosoever marrieth her that is put away from her husband committeth adultery**. The context was this, Luke 16v15 **And he said unto them, Ye are they which justify yourselves before men; but God knoweth your hearts: for that which is highly esteemed among men is abomination in the sight of God**. Don't you find that significant about 'God knowing the hearts,' in view of the fact that the same Saviour who spoke to the same crowd about the same matter said in another place Mat 5v28 **But I say unto you, That whosoever looketh on a woman to lust after her hath committed adultery with her already in his heart**.

What's the *context* of that one? It's the righteousness of the Pharisees Mat 5v20 **For I say unto you, That except your righteousness shall exceed the righteousness of the scribes and Pharisees, ye shall in no case enter into the kingdom of heaven**.

So the Bible believer sees the facts thus far as...

    1) A marriage is *not* just a marriage 'ceremony'.

MARRIAGE, DIVORCE AND REMARRIAGE

2) A marriage ceremony is *not* necessarily 'marriage'.

3) Marriage in the Bible is a *physical* matter where *flesh joins flesh*.

4) Fornication with a whore constitutes *that much of a marriage*, i.e. *flesh joining flesh*.

Therefore, if a man lived a life of fornication and only had *one* marriage 'ceremony', he could pass off as only 'having one wife', whereas he had dozens; and that's what the Pharisees were doing. The Lord knew it; that is what He said, and it was said *to the Pharisees.*

This bunch got upset with Paul when he wrote that *fornication* was *flesh joining flesh.* (Read the following verses regarding fornication - Rom 1v29, 1 Cor 5v1, 1 Cor 6v13+18, 1 Cor 7v2, 1 Cor 10v8, 2 Cor 12v21, Gal 5v19, Eph 5v3, Col 3v5, 1 Thes 4v3).

In John 8 when they brought that woman to Jesus Christ stating that she had been caught in the act of adultery, they quoted John 8v5 **Now Moses in the law commanded us, that such should be stoned: but what sayest thou?** Now the idea behind this was, if He said *'Don't stone her',* He'd make a liar out of Moses, and they (the Pharisees) would get Him on that. If He said *'Do stone her,'* then the people would think *'Well, what about that! There He is, a friend of sinners, forgiving and having mercy on them, yet having this sinner killed!'* But the Lord's wisdom is *perfect* and so He stooped down and wrote on the ground, and suddenly they all left. Do you know what He wrote on the ground? It would probably have been Lev 20v10 **And the man that committeth adultery with another man's wife, even he that committeth adultery with his neighbour's wife, the adulterer and the adulteress shall surely be put to death.** *Get it?* The woman was caught in the *act,* yet *where was the man?* It was probably one of *them.* Moses wrote stone the *woman* and *the man,* not just the woman. John 8v9 **And they which heard it, being convicted by their own conscience, went out one by one, beginning at the eldest, even unto the last: and Jesus was left alone, and the woman standing in the midst.**

So in the Scriptures, *marriage* is a physical matter. The *first* marriage has *no* preacher, *no* ring, *no* ceremony, and *no* licence. Yet today, we are to *obey* the laws of the land (Rom 13v1-5) except when they go *against* Scripture.

When speaking of marriage, Christ likens it to eunuchs who cannot have children physically, and Paul likens it to joining your body to a harlot, physical.

With this in mind let us turn to Mat 19v4-6 **And he answered and said unto them, Have ye not read, that he which made them at the beginning made them male and female, And said, For this cause shall a man leave father and mother, and shall cleave to his wife: and they twain** (that's *two*) **shall be one flesh? Wherefore they are no more twain** (that's *two*), **but one flesh. What therefore God hath joined together, let not man put asunder**. Now because this passage is read at marriage *ceremonies,* some people think that when two people are standing at an altar, *God is joining them together.* Yet the context here in these verses is Adam and Eve. Think about this for a moment; are you telling me that when two *unsaved* people get married at an altar that *God is joining them together?* What about when a *saved* woman marries an *unsaved* man? Is God joining *them* together? The Lord tells us *not* to join an unsaved man to a saved woman, so why would He *join* them and see it as a marriage? Look at Mat 19v7+8 **They say unto him, Why did Moses then command to give a writing of divorcement, and to put her away? He saith unto them, Moses because of the hardness of your hearts suffered you to put away your wives: but from the beginning it was not so.** *Why* did Moses command to give a writing of divorcement? *Where* is that found? It is spoken of in Romans 7. It is found in the OT law, yet look at Rom 7v1-3 **Know ye not,** brethren, (for I speak to them that know the law,) how that the law hath dominion over a man as long as he liveth? For the woman which hath an husband is bound by the law to her husband so long as he liveth; but if the husband be dead, she is loosed from the law of her husband. So then if, while her husband liveth, she be married to another man, she shall be called an adulteress: but if her husband be dead, she is free from that law; so that she is no adulteress, though she be married to another man.** When you throw out the cross references to Mat 19v7+8 on the grounds that all that was 'Old Testament' (therefore the law was past), and you could no longer have a writing of divorcement for anything, you were told that the very place where Christ was referring to *applies to a man and a woman in a Gentile church in the Body of Christ* (Rom 7v1-3).

Deut 24v1 **When a man hath taken a wife, and married her, and it come to pass that she find no favour in his eyes, because he hath found some uncleanness in her: then let him write her a bill of divorcement, and give it in her hand, and send her out of his house**. Now *this* is what the Pharisees were referring to in Mat 19 (which Christ discusses in Mat 19, and to which Paul referred to in Rom 7). This is why this passage is *never* looked up nor referred to by '*modern day Bible rejecting Christians*'.

Let's look at Deut 24v1 briefly... Deut 24v1 **When a man hath taken a wife, and married her, and it come to pass that she find no favour in his eyes,** (because WHY?) **because he hath found some uncleanness in her: then let him write her a bill of divorcement, and give it in her hand, and send her out of his house.** There was *no* mention of her being a 'virgin' or having 'stepped-out' with another man. It said *some uncleanness*. That means *anything* he didn't like. *How do you know?* Because the New Testament passage said that's what it was... Mat 19v8 **He saith unto them, Moses because of the hardness of your hearts suffered you to put away your wives**... Mat 19v3 **The Pharisees also came unto him, tempting him, and saying unto him, Is it lawful for a man to put away his wife for every cause?** Now look at that! The bill of divorcement (spoken of in Mat 19v7 **They say unto him, Why did Moses then command to give a writing of divorcement, and to put her away?**) is the bill of divorcement in Deut 24v1 (**When a man hath taken a wife, and married her, and it come to pass that she find no favour in his eyes, because he hath found some uncleanness in her: then let him write her a bill of divorcement, and give it in her hand, and send her out of his house.**) The '**every cause**' of Mat 19v3 is the '**some uncleanness**' of Deut 24v1. Now all that is doing is comparing Scripture with Scripture. Many modern day apostate 'Christians' today teach that the only cause for a 'bill of divorcement' in the time of Moses was the fact that if a man was 'engaged' to a woman and found out that she wasn't a 'virgin', he could get rid of her! That is a load of *hogwash* and *not* what the above verses say, or mean.

In the very context you just read in Deut 24, you'll find that in v3, a man can give his wife a bill of divorcement *because he doesn't like her!* Deut 24v3 **And if the latter husband hate her, and write her a bill of divorcement, and giveth it in her hand, and sendeth her out of his house;** Those Pharisees knew that when they asked the question of Jesus Christ and said, 'Mat 19v3 ...**Is it lawful for a man to put away his wife for every cause?**' In Deut 24v1-4, it is plainly *not* fornication or adultery, because one bill of divorcement is given because the man *hates his wife* (v3). So when Christ says Mat 19v9 **And I say unto you, Whosoever shall put away his wife, except it be for fornication, and shall marry another, committeth adultery: and whoso marrieth her which is put away doth commit adultery**. He is setting up a *new* precedent that is *not* in Deut 24v1-4, and all understand Him. You say, 'How do you know they understand Him that way?' Look at Mat 19v10 **His disciples say unto him, If the case of the man be so with his wife, it is not good to marry.** Having said that the *only* reason a man can get rid of his wife is because of *fornication*, **His disciples say unto him, If the case of the man be so with his wife, it is not good to marry.** Notice they understood perfectly and exactly what Jesus Christ is talking about. They ask Mat 19v3 ...'**Is it**

lawful for a man to put away his wife for every cause?'

Now the reason why we have had to cover all this *background* is because modern day apostate 'Christians' all run to Rom 7 to prove otherwise, and you *cannot* understand Rom 7 until you understand *the Law*, because Rom 7v1 said that it was written to them *that knew the Law*. Rom 7v1 **Know ye not, brethren, (for I speak to them that know the law,) how that the law hath dominion over a man as long as he liveth?** So you had better know the Law, and what the Scriptures *actually* teach, before you start going around *judging* other Christians in regard to marriage, divorce and remarriage.

Now in Mat 19, these facts are clear...

1) Marriage is a *flesh joining flesh*, physical matter, which is found in vs 5+6+12... Mat 19v5 **And said, For this cause shall a man leave father and mother, and shall cleave to his wife: and they twain shall be one flesh?** Mat 19v6 **Wherefore they are no more twain, but one flesh. What therefore God hath joined together, let not man put asunder.** Mat 19v12 **For there are some eunuchs, which were so born from their mother's womb: and there are some eunuchs, which were made eunuchs of men: and there be eunuchs, which have made themselves eunuchs for the kingdom of heaven's sake. He that is able to receive it, let him receive it**.

2) In the Old Testament, a man could put away his wife for *any cause*. Mat 19v3 **The Pharisees also came unto him, tempting him, and saying unto him, Is it lawful for a man to put away his wife for every cause?** Deut 24v1 **When a man hath taken a wife, and married her, and it come to pass that she find no favour in his eyes, because he hath found some uncleanness in her: then let him write her a bill of divorcement, and give it in her hand, and send her out of his house.** Deut 24v3 **And if the latter husband hate her, and write her a bill of divorcement, and giveth it in her hand, and sendeth her out of his house...**

That's clear! New Testament grounds for divorce (where you can give your wife a bill of divorcement and put her away) is *fornication*. Mat 19v9 **And I say unto you, Whosoever shall put away his wife, except it be for fornication, and shall marry another, committeth adultery: and whoso marrieth her which is put away doth commit adultery.** Why did he say *fornication*? 1 Cor 6v16+18 **What? know ye not that he which is joined to an harlot is one body? for two, saith he, shall be one flesh. Flee fornication. Every sin that a man doeth is without the body; but he that committeth fornication sinneth against his own body.** If a man's wife steps out on him and joins her body to the body of another man, *flesh* has left *flesh*, and that man can give her a bill of divorcement and 'put her away' **according to Jesus Christ**.

Back to Mat 19v9 - **And I say unto you, Whosoever shall put away his wife, except it be for fornication, and shall marry another, committeth adultery: and whoso marrieth her which is put away doth commit adultery.** Notice the *remarriage* in the same context with the *legitimate* divorce. The only remarriage that is considered illegitimate is where the *grounds of divorce* are illegitimate. Where the bill of divorcement was for the right thing – *fornication* – the remarriage was allowed. Get that! It is *in the context*. It is in the middle of the verse.

Every time grounds for a *legitimate* divorce are mentioned, a *remarriage* is mentioned *in the context*.

Example, in the case of widowhood – 1 Cor 7v39 **The wife is bound by the law as long as her husband liveth; but if her husband be dead, she is at liberty to be married to whom she will; only in the Lord**. That's a *remarriage*. This is in the case of *death*.

Example – 1 Cor 7v27 **Art thou bound unto a wife? seek not to be loosed. Art thou loosed from a wife? seek not a wife**. Note 'Art thou loosed from a wife?' – notice he didn't say *what grounds*, just 'loosed'. This is a man who has been *divorced*. 1 Cor 7v28 **But and if thou marry, thou hast not sinned; and if a virgin marry, she hath not sinned. Nevertheless such shall have trouble in the flesh: but I spare you**. Notice a *remarriage* here *in context*.

Now on the basis of comparing Scripture with Scripture, let us look at Rom 7...

It is sound doctrine that the marriage bed is undefiled and honourable in all - Heb 13v4 **Marriage is honourable in all, and the bed undefiled: but whoremongers and adulterers God will judge**. Sound doctrine is also found in teaching that if an *unsaved* person wants to *stay with* a saved person, then let them *stay* and *stick together*. 1 Cor 7v12+13 **But to the rest speak I, not the Lord: If any brother hath a wife that believeth not, and she be pleased to dwell with him, let him not put her away. And the woman which hath an husband that believeth not, and if he be pleased to dwell with her, let her not leave him**. That is Scriptural teaching and *sound doctrine*.

Remember, marriage is *flesh joining flesh* and divorce is *flesh leaving flesh*, and where *flesh leaves flesh*, those are spiritual grounds for *divorce* according to Jesus Christ.

Rom 7v1 **Know ye not, brethren, (for I speak to them that know the law,) how that the law hath dominion over a man as long as he liveth?**

Rom 7v2 **For the woman which hath an husband is bound by the law to her husband so long as he liveth; but if the husband be dead, she is loosed from the law of her husband**.

Rom 7v3 **So then if, while her husband liveth, she be married to another man, she shall be called an adulteress: but if her husband be dead, she is free from that law; so that she is no adulteress, though she be married to another man**.

Note there is *no* 'divorce' in Rom 7v1-3. Remember a 'marriage' is *not* a ceremony.

The heretical teaching taught today on this passage is as follows... 'If you were ever married, you could *never* marry again as long as the person you were married to was still living'. They take this for granted by saying 'If she be married to another man, she had to get a *divorce* from her first husband'.

Note again, there is *no divorce* in Rom 7v1-3. You see that word 'loosed' in v2? That's a divorce, but that is if the man *is dead*. You never read in v3, 'So while her *former* husband lives, she got a *divorce* and got married again, she is an adulteress'. *You read*... 'While the man she is married to is *alive* and they're still *married*, then if she gets another fellow, she is an adulteress'. *That* is what you *read*.

Let's get the correct reading... **For the woman which hath an husband** (present tense, married to him now) **is bound by the law to her husband** (the man that's true to her, to whom she is married) **so long as he liveth; but if the husband** (the man she is married to legally and righteously) **be dead, she is *loosed* (divorced) from the law of her husband** (she can get married). **So then if, while her husband** (not the fellow 'she was divorced from', it is her husband – the man she is married to legally and righteously) **liveth, she be married to another man, she shall be called an adulteress** - She is guilty of what? Adultery, and that is why she is called an 'adulteress,' because *she is*!

Now, do you see that thing right there? Go back and look at Lev 20v10; I mean, he wrote to them that know the Law. Lev 20v10 **And the man that committeth adultery with another man's wife,** (*not* a divorced woman legally divorced and 'put away' – it is *another man's wife!*) **even he that**

MARRIAGE, DIVORCE AND REMARRIAGE

committeth adultery with his neighbour's wife, the adulterer and the adulteress shall surely be put to death.

So in Romans 7 the woman is *not* divorced. The man is *not* divorced. The man is true to his wife, he has *not* stepped out on her, *she has stepped out on him*, and in doing that, she has committed two things...

1) The *act* of *fornication* – which gives her husband a legal right to give her a bill of divorcement.

2) She's committed adultery, in stepping out on him – she's an adulteress.

For the time being (until her husband gives the bill of divorcement and puts her away), in the eyes of God, she has *two men at the same time.*

Christ says to the woman in John 4v18 **For thou hast had five husbands; and he whom thou now hast is not thy husband** – now this shows you the difference between speaking about it *practically* and speaking about it *legally*. You see, practically (openly), the woman has *two husbands*. She's shacking up with *both* of them. In the eyes of the Law she would be guilty of bigamy; if she had papers to go with *one* of them, she is an adulteress – stepping out on her husband. In the eyes of God, she has swapped husbands, and her husband is single – he is *loosed*. If he is *loosed*, there is a *remarriage* that we looked at in 1 Cor 7v27+28.

In 1 Cor 7 we have another *ground for divorce*, death. Death 'looses' the other party and makes him (or her) single and available for *remarriage*. 1 Cor 7v39 **The wife is bound by the law as long as her husband liveth; but if her husband be dead, she is at liberty to be married to whom she will; only in the Lord**. Then we also find *desertion*, which 'looses' one party and makes them single and available for *remarriage*. 1 Cor 7v15 **But if the unbelieving depart, let him depart. A brother or a sister is not under bondage in such cases: but God hath called us to peace**. So you can now see that death is *not only* the grounds for divorce *according to Scripture.* Romans 7 talks about a woman *stepping out* on her husband, i.e. grounds for *divorce*, i.e. **it's not just 'death' that gives grounds for divorce like is commonly taught among modern day illiterate Christians.**

Look at 1 Tim 3v1+2 **This is a true saying, If a man desire the office of a bishop, he desireth a good work. A bishop then must be blameless, the husband of one wife, vigilant, sober, of good behaviour, given to hospitality, apt to teach**; Now that *can't* mean *'only married once'*. That would disqualify 1000's of ministers straight away, as many have been married more than once, especially if their first wife had died. It has to mean he is *faithful to the one wife he's got*. If he's *Scripturally* and *legally* divorced and *remarried*, he *has only one wife*. Remember *marriage* is *not* a ceremony, it is *flesh joining flesh*.

1 Cor 7v8-10 **I say therefore to the unmarried and widows, It is good for them if they abide even as I. But if they cannot contain, let them marry: for it is better to marry than to burn. And unto the married I command, yet not I, but the Lord, Let not the wife depart from her husband:** That is a commandment. The wife is told *not* to depart from her husband. But now look at v11 **But** (this is the *permissive* will of God i.e. His second choice) **and if she depart, let her remain unmarried** (not join her body up to the body of another man), **or** (if she **is** going to join her body up to a man) **be reconciled to her husband:** (her body come back and join his body) **and let not the husband put away his wife**.

But what happens if they leave *for good?* Look at 1 Cor 7v15 **But if the unbelieving depart, let him depart. A brother** (a saved man) **or a sister** (a saved woman) **is not under bondage in such cases:**

but God hath called us to peace. Where the other party departs and *deserts* the believing party, the believing party is *not bound* to the party that *leaves*.

Now most modern day preachers preach *slop,* and just *can't* handle the subject of marriage, divorce, and remarriage from a **Scriptural** standpoint. They can only give opinion, or quote what their *tradition* says, i.e. Brethren, Pentecostal, Baptist etc. Many Christian 'ministers' have put **'heavy burdens and grievous to be borne'** (Mat 23v4) upon a young man who's marriage has failed, and told him *'That's it, no more marrying for you now!'* This is the type of *hogwash* that is preached today in modern day 'fundamental' churches. *It's claptrap!*

Paul says in 1 Cor 7v27 **Art thou bound unto a wife?** (Okay, answer...) **seek not to be loosed.** That's clear. But along comes a modern day preacher and he tells you 'Well, you've got two *living* husbands, so you ought to divorce your second and go back to your first'. Yet we started off by saying **'I speak to them that KNOW the LAW'** – Don't you know that the Law *forbade* that. Look at Deut 24v2-4 **And when she is departed out of his house, she may go and be another man's wife. And if the latter husband hate her, and write her a bill of divorcement, and giveth it in her hand, and sendeth her out of his house; or if the latter husband die, which took her to be his wife; Her former husband, which sent her away, may not take her again to be his wife, after that she is defiled; for that is abomination before the LORD: and thou shalt not cause the land to sin, which the LORD thy God giveth thee for an inheritance.** *How about that!* Go back to your *first* husband, *first* wife should you? Not according to THE LAW.

There are *three* grounds for divorce; that is, there are THREE things that LOOSE a body from another body and cause that person to be SINGLE...

        1) **Fornication** – with a *remarriage* in the context.

        2) **Desertion** – with a *remarriage* in the context.

        3) **Death** – with a *remarriage* in the context.

We're told in 1 Cor 7v27 that if we're *loosed* from a wife, we're *not* to 'seek a wife,' *but*, if we *remarry, we have not sinned.* (1 Cor 7v28).

Some modern day apostate Christians try to teach this heresy in regard to 1 Cor 7v28 – They try to tell you that the marrying in v28 is getting married for the 'first' time, and the 'first' half of the verse refers to a *male* getting married, while the 'second' half of the verse refers to a *female* getting married, and this is 'proved' by the fact that it says that if a 'virgin' marry, *she* hath not sinned. (That's called *straining at a gnat and swallowing a camel* - Mat 23v24). Tell me something; if the 'first' half of the verse is *not* a reference to v27 (a *remarriage* with a statement on a first marriage), to a person who has never been married, *why* would Paul say if a *man marries*, he hasn't sinned? What would be the point of saying that, if it was a *first marriage?* Is there anybody on planet earth who would think that the first marriage was a sin? Christ recommended it, and Paul said it was **'honourable in all'** and Paul just told them it was alright in 1 Cor 7v2+9. Now this just shows you the lengths that some modern day apostate 'ministers' will go to, to try to get around Biblical truth.

If what you read here is *true* (if a man is *loosed* from a wife for any of the reasons given before), if that man is *loosed* and *single*, then that man has a right to *remarry* if v28 *goes with* v27. 1 Cor 7v27+28 **Art thou bound unto a wife? seek not to be loosed. Art thou loosed from a wife? seek not a wife. But and if thou marry, thou hast not sinned; and if a virgin marry, she hath not sinned. Nevertheless such shall have trouble in the flesh: but I spare you.** Notice, **'seek not a wife. *But'* – *but* and if thou marry.** Why that's a reference to a man who has been *loosed from a wife.* The man

MARRIAGE, DIVORCE AND REMARRIAGE

who *needed* to be told that it was *alright* to marry (because a lot of people would be convinced it would be a sin to get married if he did get married) would obviously be the man who had been *loosed from a wife* in v27.

Summing up – There are three grounds for divorce – **death, desertion and fornication.** In all three cases, the party who is left alone is *single*, and as a *single person*, they are allowed to *remarry* **according to Scripture** (maybe *not* according to modern day apostate fundamentalists, ***but according to Scripture***)

The *remarriage* is warned against because of *trouble in the flesh*. The *remarriage* is advised against, and they are told they would be happier if they would stay single. They are told that if they get married, they will *not have sinned*, but they will have 'trouble in the flesh'.

If you disagree with it, *you are wrong!* This is the **Scriptural teaching** on the subject without bending *any* text to try to fit your man-made *opinions* or your church's standpoint on the subject. It is Biblical truth, clear as crystal, and if your pastor teaches otherwise, *he is dead wrong!* Amen and Amen.

NOTES

NOTES

NOTES

ERRORS OF HYPER-DISPENSATIONALISM

There is a cult in the USA who have recently started up that teach 'if you ask the Lord Jesus Christ to save you He won't because this is *working* for your salvation!' They are called 'Hyper or Ultra Dispensationalists.' I have nicknamed them 'Hyper-Diapers' (as a diaper in the USA is a nappy, and these are babies when it comes to understanding the Scriptures – Heb 5v12-14). They are the most arrogant bunch you'll ever come across, much worse than the JW's, Mormons or Christadelphians. I have included a section on them to make you aware of what other heresies they teach. Titus 1v9-16 describes the Hyper-Diapers! They take much of their teachings from men like Stam, Bullinger, O'Hare, Baker, Moore. This cult is only small to be honest, as they do not believe in evangelism, saving souls, reaching lost sinners with the Gospel (*because they don't know what the Gospel is*) and mainly focus on their family members, friends and associates. Most of what they do is online (e.g. blogs) *from their bedrooms*, as they are too scared to get out where the sinners are. (cf. Acts 17v17) **Their main aim is to *try* to talk weak Christians *out of their faith*, and therefore they just want to argue and *debate* all the time (2 Cor 12v20) – beware of these time wasters!** They also believe that there are three/four different 'Bodies' of Christ, and they are against water baptism (*yet Paul was baptized and he also baptized* – 1 Cor 1v13-16). As you can see, they are nuttier than a pecan pie. Why I am taking the time here to expose this cult is because of their wickedness in telling Christians that if you *ask* the Lord to save you He won't. This is an evil doctrine and has caused a few problems among young Christians in the faith. The Hyper-Diapers say that people like Ruckman, Larkin, Billy Sunday, John Wesley, Martin Luther, John Bunyan, Charles Spurgeon, plus *millions* of other Christians, are not saved because they *prayed* to God *asking* Him to forgive their sins, and according to this cult, that is a 'work'. For a deeper study on this cult I would refer you to the following TfT! Newsletters...

http://www.timefortruth.co.uk/errors-of-hyperdispensationalism/

TfT! News Issue 55 pages 3-8, Issue 72 pages 22-23, Issue 73 page 5+6+11+16, Issue 74 page 5, Issue 74 page 6+11, Issue 75 pages 14-20, Issue 75 page 33, Issue 76 page 5+8+9+13+19, Issue 77 page 6+43, Issue 78 page 6+12+13+18+19+31+36, Issue 79 page 3+6

The Hyper-Diapers also reject anything that is not of Paul in the Scriptures. They do not believe that there is doctrine for the church, the Body of Christ, in books like James, Hebrews and 1+2 Peter etc. They think the church started with Paul and no one was IN Christ before the apostle Paul, so they have a very tough time dealing with Scriptures like Rom 16v7, hence why they have to *create* another 'body'.

Here are a few bullet points of some of the errors they teach...

1. As already stated, the Hyper-Diapers get hung up on non-baptism (i.e. no water baptism for this dispensation) – yet what do the Scriptures teach... In Acts 16 we see the apostle Paul baptized converts *after* he knew about the Gospel of the grace of God. In fact, according to Acts 15, the Gospel of the grace of God was known to all the apostles, for Simon Peter in Acts 15v11 says... **But we believe that through the grace of the Lord Jesus Christ we shall be saved, even as they**. And plainly when the Philippian jailer asked '...**what must I do to be saved?**' in Acts 16, Paul does not tell him to repent and be baptized in the name of Jesus Christ for the

remission of sins. But rather he tells him… '**Believe on the Lord Jesus Christ, and thou shalt be saved**…' This is the teaching of Ephesians and Romans. So, it is perfectly apparent that in Acts 16, even though Paul knew the 'Gospel of the grace of God', he *still baptized* the convert after getting him saved by grace through faith. If it was *wrong* for Paul to baptize, don't you think there would be a chapter devoted to it? For example, did you notice the difference in Simon Peter in Acts 11 when he found out that he had been wrong in telling the people they had to be baptized in water to receive the Holy Ghost? Why, when Peter rehearses the matter he says in Acts 11v15-18… (Read it). When Simon Peter found out that a man *didn't have to be baptized in water* to receive the Holy Ghost, he explained it, made a speech on it, rehearsed it, gave it to the brethren, and then made a final declarative (*declarative = the nature of or making a declaration*) statement on it in Acts 15v11. Paul would have done the same if he found out that it was wrong to baptize his converts in water. When they quote '**For Christ sent me not to baptize, but to preach the Gospel**' the Hyper-Diapers either quote half a verse OR they quote it OUT of context like the cults do. Read 1 Cor 1v12-17. Now the context of 1 Cor 1v17 has *nothing* at all to do with the doing away of water baptism because of any *advanced revelation*. The context of verses 14-17 is plainly dealing with arguments of people about *who* baptized them, and Paul was thanking God that he hadn't been responsible for that lest they claim him against the rest – read v13. Note also that he baptized Crispus and Gaius and the household of Stephanas and some more whose names he had forgotten. Even though Paul was not sent *primarily* to baptize, he *did* baptize his converts. Paul wasn't a *pastor* of a local congregation, he was a travelling evangelist. The Hyper-Diapers are very good at giving you *part* truth rather than *all* the truth.

2. They teach that only the prison epistles written by Paul after the close of the Book of Acts could be considered as *doctrine* for the Christian. They also teach that the 'body' found in the Book of Acts is not the Body of Christ mentioned in Ephesians 2 and 3 – they have to create more than one Body. (Yet the Scriptures teach only *one* Body of Christ – Rom 12v4+5, 1 Cor 12v12+13+20, Eph 2v16, Eph 4v4, Col 3v15)

3. Their *hero* Bullinger taught that the 'mystery Body' Paul mentions in Eph 2 and 3 did not show up until *after the close of Acts 28*. Yet in 1 Cor 12 we are already dealing with the 'mystery Body' and the members in the Body… 1 Cor 12v13 **For by one Spirit are we all baptized into one body**…

4. One question the Hyper-Diapers find very difficult to answer (*many in this cult disagree with each other*) is '*When did the Body of Christ begin?*' Some say it began with Paul, yet that theory is blown out of the water by Rom 16v7.

5. Cornelius Stam and Bullinger (the idols of the Hyper-Diapers) think that something cannot be *revealed* until it is *present* and that if it isn't *revealed* it isn't *there*. They deny this but it's the truth. In the Scriptures 'something' can be *present* yet not *revealed* until its appointed time… *but it's there!*

6. Eph 3v1+2 - Stam reads this as one 'age', the 'Dispensation of Grace' but of course it is not saying that. The verses are talking about God *dispensing grace* to Paul. '**If ye have heard of the dispensation of the grace of God which is given me to you-ward**' – Read Eph 3v3-9 - Three times you are told that the dispensation was the *handing out of grace* to Paul. It had *nothing* to do with any 'period of time.' The trouble with this reading is that somebody is confusing *when* the thing *took place* with the *time* it was *revealed*. Also, Paul is writing to the Ephesians and he was dealing with the Ephesians back in Acts 19 and 20, and at this time he already *knows* the mystery. Paul *knew* about the mystery of the Body in 1 Cor 12 and this places it *before* Acts 18

in time; not like some of the Hyper-Diapers say about it having to be *after* Acts 28. You have to be very careful following men like Stam and Bullinger, Moore, Baker, O'Hare etc.

Another sign to watch out for to know if you're dealing with a Hyper-Diaper cult member is that they no longer talk about the Gospel in 1 Cor 15v1-4, it is now the *Gospel of reconciliation* – 2 Cor 5v18+19. This is one of the terms they like to use.

Ruckman writes... 'We Bible believing Baptists have taught two things for many years. We have taught that the local church did not begin at Pentecost. This is perfectly clear in the passage in Matthew 16 and 18, the calling out of the twelve, and in the commissioning of this local church in Matthew 28 and Acts 1. This group has a roll of 120 names on it in Acts 1. It had a treasurer who died and was replaced in Acts 1 and Matthew 26. It had a leader who was spokesman for the group, Simon Peter, Acts 1 and 2. It was a local, called out assembly, called out and chosen by the Lord. As such, it was a Jewish church. It certainly had Jews and Gentiles in it *after* Pentecost. This local church became a *living-organism*, and its members were placed **IN** Christ by a baptism of the Holy Spirit. When Paul says in Eph 4v4+5 **There is one body, and one Spirit, even as ye are called in one hope of your calling; One Lord, one faith, one baptism,** he can only refer to the *same* Holy Spirit and to the *same* baptism that put the Pentecostal disciples, Cornelius' family, the apostle Paul himself and the Ephesians *into* the Body of Christ... 1 Cor 12v13.

This is why it is so dangerous to build your doctrine in the Book of Acts like the Pentecostals do. In the Book of Acts one group of people *have to be baptized* to receive the Holy Ghost – Acts 2; another group receive the Holy Ghost *before* they are baptized – Acts 10; another man is born again *before* he is baptized in water – Acts 9; another group believe and are saved and are baptized *without receiving the Holy Ghost* – Acts 8; another group of people get saved and get baptized and *don't* speak in tongues until hands are laid on them – Acts 19. There is one baptism, **one Body** and one Spirit.

A question that the Hyper-Diapers dread is... **'Were** Peter, James and John IN the Body of Christ? If so, *when* did this take place?' Now read carefully the following Scriptures... John 17v6 **I have manifested thy name unto the men which thou gavest me out of the world:** (There's Peter, James and John) **thine they were, and thou gavest them me; and they have kept thy word.** (There's Peter, James and John)

7 **Now they have known that all things whatsoever thou hast given me are of thee.**

8 **For I have given unto them the words which thou gavest me; and they have received them, and have known surely that I came out from thee, and they have believed that thou didst send me.**

9 **I pray for them: I pray not for the world, but for them which thou hast given me; for they are thine.** (There's Peter, James and John)

10 **And all mine are thine, and thine are mine; and I am glorified in them.** (There's Peter, James and John)

11 **And now I am no more in the world, but these are in the world, and I come to thee. Holy Father, keep through thine own name those whom thou hast given me, that they may be one, as we are.**

12 **While I was with them in the world, I kept them in thy name: those that thou gavest me I have kept, and none of them is lost, but the son of perdition; that the scripture might be fulfilled.**

13 **And now come I to thee; and these things I speak in the world, that they might have my joy**

fulfilled in themselves.

14 **I have given them thy word; and the world hath hated them, because they are not of the world, even as I am not of the world.**

15 **I pray not that thou shouldest take them out of the world, but that thou shouldest keep them from the evil.**

16 **They are not of the world, even as I am not of the world.**

17 **Sanctify them through thy truth: thy word is truth.**

18 **As thou hast sent me into the world, even so have I also sent them into the world.**

(There's Peter, James and John, all the way through!)

19 **And for their sakes I sanctify myself, that they also might be sanctified through the truth.**

20 **Neither pray I for these alone, but for them also which shall believe on me through their word**;

21 **That they all may be one; as thou, Father, art in me, and I in thee, that they also may be one in us: that the world may believe that thou hast sent me.** (Get it?) **There is *one baptism, one Body and one Spirit.***

22 **And the glory which thou gavest me I have given them; that they may be one, even as we are one**:

23 **I in them, and thou in me, that they may be made perfect in one; and that the world may know that thou hast sent me, and hast loved them, as thou hast loved me.** So are Peter, James and John IN Christ? **Are they IN** His Body?

This is the difference between a Bible Believing Christian who can rightly divide the word (note the small 'w') of truth and a Hyper-Diaper who *wrongly* divides the word of truth.

Jesus Christ was **IN** Peter, James and John; and Peter, James and John were going to be **IN** Him and this would take place at Pentecost. How could they have gotten *into* Christ *before* then? He had no Body for them to be IN then, as He was sitting opposite them. He didn't come into them when he arose from the dead. He simply breathed upon them and said *Receive* **ye the Holy Ghost**. (John 20v22)

There is only one place where *one Spirit* could have baptized Peter, James and John into *one Body,* and this one body, that one Spirit, baptizes into, is the *same one* mentioned in Corinthians and Ephesians. One Spirit, **one Body**, one baptism.

In Ephesians (Eph 4v5 **One Lord, one faith, one baptism,**) Paul is talking about the baptism that *saves*. This baptism puts the person *into* Christ; it is the baptism of the Holy Spirit.

God used multiple means and multiple methods in manifesting things throughout the Book of Acts with the same Spirit and the same baptism; Bible Believers understand that, Hyper-Diapers don't.

If Peter, James and John were *not in* Jesus Christ, you're not either, and neither is Paul. John 17v23 **I in them, and thou in me, that they may be made perfect in one**...

Turn to Eph 2v19+20 **Now therefore ye are no more strangers and foreigners, but fellowcitizens with the saints, and of the household of God; And are built upon the foundation of the apostles**

and prophets, Jesus Christ himself being the chief corner stone; There *are* prophets in the Body of Christ... **And he gave some, apostles; and some, prophets; and some, evangelists; and some, pastors and teachers; For the perfecting of the saints, for the work of the ministry, for the edifying of the body of Christ**: Therefore the *apostles were in the Body of Christ and so were the prophets!*

Not only that, read it again and a *little further*... Eph 2v19-3v1...

19 **Now therefore ye are no more strangers and foreigners, but fellowcitizens with the saints, and of the household of God;**

20 **And are built upon the foundation of the apostles and prophets, Jesus Christ himself being the chief corner stone;**

21 **In whom all the building fitly framed together groweth unto an holy temple in the Lord:**

22 **In whom ye also are builded together for an habitation of God through the Spirit.**

Eph 3v1 **For this cause**... and Paul goes straight into the Body mystery.

Go back to Eph 2v11-15...

11 **Wherefore remember, that ye being in time past Gentiles in the flesh, who are called Uncircumcision by that which is called the Circumcision in the flesh made by hands;**

12 **That at that time ye were without Christ, being aliens from the commonwealth of Israel, and strangers from the covenants of promise, having no hope, and without God in the world:**

13 **But now in Christ Jesus ye who sometimes were far off are made nigh by** (what?) **the blood of Christ.**

14 **For he is our peace, who** (past tense - *not when* he got the Body mystery. *Not when* the mystery was 'revealed' in the late Acts period. *Past tense!*) **hath made both one, and hath broken down the middle wall of partition between us;**

15 **Having abolished in his flesh the enmity, even the law of commandments** (When did he do this? When he died on the Cross. See v16) **contained in ordinances; for to make in himself of twain one new man, so making peace;**

16 **And that he might reconcile both unto God in one body by the cross, having slain the enmity thereby:**

The fact the Gentiles didn't enter that Body until they got saved in Acts 2 and in Acts 8 (the Ethiopian eunuch), and the fact that pure-Gentiles who weren't Jewish proselytes didn't get into that Body until Acts 13, 14, 15 and 16 means nothing. *The way was made for them to get in there when Jesus Christ died on the cross* – see v16. And it was preached '**to you which were afar off, and to them that were nigh.**' It got preached first at Jerusalem to a group of Jews and then to those *afar off* i.e. the Gentiles. '**For through him we both have access by one Spirit unto the Father.**'

The dying thief on the cross, believed on Jesus as the Kingly Messiah, instead of the exact manner later revealed in the Pauline epistles, yet he was still *saved, and he was saved by grace through faith.*

Ruckman writes... 'The truth of the matter is that the Body of Christ was formed with the death of Christ, exactly as Adam had his body formed when he slept the sleep of death and Eve was taken from his side. The fact that the Body did *not begin to be built* until Pentecost means absolutely nothing. The fact that the Body, at first contained Jews only, means absolutely nothing. It was destined to have Jews and Gentiles in it and this is the mystery that was revealed to Paul after Acts 9. The fact that it was revealed to Paul after Acts 8 has no bearing upon when it *started* at all. It was three years before Paul was saved. His kinsmen were IN Christ before he was IN Christ. He persecuted Christ in the person of the saints in Acts 7 + 8 because they were part of the Body of Christ. This Body is called *the church of God* in Gal 1v13, and we are told in 1 Cor 10, 11 + 12 that the church of God is composed of *Jew and Gentile* - 1 Cor 12v13. What has this to do with water baptism? Just this. Even if John the Baptist's water baptism was to manifest Christ to Israel, which it was, even if Simon Peter's water baptism 'for repentance' was so that God could give the Holy Spirit to Israel, even though the baptism of the Ethiopian eunuch was after he was saved by grace through faith, and even though the baptism of Paul was for purification of sin, the salient *fact* remains that the Author and Finisher of our faith, the Lord Jesus Christ, was baptized in water, the eleven apostles who followed Him and wrote part of our New Testament were baptized in water, and *Paul* was baptized in water and baptized some of his converts in water. The apostle who said **Be ye followers of me, even as I also am of Christ**. (1 Cor 11v1) submitted to water baptism; and when Paul told a man how to get saved by grace through faith in Acts 16, he let him follow the Lord in baptism. And although Paul was not sent *primarily* to baptize, he *did* baptize. And although he may not have given a clear commandment in the Pauline epistles on the relation of water baptism to the Body of Christ, he certainly left the matter open and certainly set the example *himself* and certainly *never* repented of his own baptism or told anybody to repent of theirs. **All unrighteousness is sin** (1 John 5v17) and if it were *not* right to get baptized in water, because water baptism is a sin, I don't recall one place in the Pauline epistles where Paul ever confessed *that* sin. However, I can turn you to *five* other places where he confessed a dozen sins he committed before he was saved. In his great statement after he was saved he said... **Christ Jesus came into the world to save sinners; of whom I am chief**. (1 Tim 1v15) In his great confession of sin as a Christian in Rom 7, Paul never mentioned water baptism one time. Paul followed the Lord in baptism and rested in it content. He only taught that there was one *saving* baptism, that was the Holy Spirit, and that the same Spirit that put people *into* the Body of Christ in Acts 2, put them *into* the Body of Christ in Acts 8, 9, 10, 16, 18, 28 and up until the Rapture'. Baptism is only a *figure* of salvation (1 Pet 3v21).

Hyper-Diapers take Eph 4v4+5 *out of context* and pretend that it is talking about *water baptism* being replaced by Spirit baptism. The context of Eph 4v4-6 is the unity of the Body of Christ, *not* 'disunity' caused by carnal Christians who say 'I am of Christ...' (1 Cor 1v12). The same baptism that put Paul *into* Christ ('WE' – 1 Cor 12v13) put Gentile believers (Corinth, Ephesus) INTO Christ. The same baptism that put *'the twelve' into* Christ (Acts 1v5) put the Roman converts *into* Christ (Rom 6v1-3, 16v7).

By the way, there are *seven* baptisms IN Scripture - 1 Cor 10v1-5, Mat 3v11, Mat 20v22, Rom 6v1-3, Acts 2v38, Acts 10v44-48, Mat 3v11-13.

More of the Hyper-Diapers false teachings include...

1. *Peter and Paul preached 'different' Gospels!* – If they *did* then Peter was *cursed!* (Gal 1v8+9). God taught Peter the Gospel in Acts 10v43, which he publicly acknowledges in Acts 15v11, while *all are practicing water baptism.*

2. *Repentance should not be preached in this age!* – Paul preached it constantly (Acts 20v21) and asked exactly what John the Baptist asked for when he preached it (Acts 26v20). Paul did this after writing Romans 16v25+26.

3. *The 'Body' could not have been at Pentecost because no-one mentioned it.* Neither did anyone

mention the complete abolition of *the Law* (Levitical) or the fulfilling of the Law (Acts 13v38-40) though both (Col 2v14-16) were accomplished *facts* (Gal 3v13)

4. *Mat 28v19-20 is limited to the Tribulation!* – Pure conjecture (see 1 Tim 6v3 written to the saints in *the one Body*) The *'all things'* of Mat 28v20 does not include all *pre-crucifixion* instruction, which is apparent to anyone by comparing Mat 10v1-10 with Mat 28v19-20 and John 13-17. The Tribulation had *not* begun in 33AD, note 'unto the end of the world'.

5. *Paul was deceived about water baptism and the 'one body' until he wrote Eph 3-4 (After Acts 28)* – Tosh! *Every Christian leader in the NT was baptized in water and none of them repented of it!*

Romans 10 proves too tough for many *Hyper-Diapers*, especially those that follow Stam etc. Note... Rom 10 is in the middle of a 'three chapter section' that deals specifically with Israel – v1+v5 (Moses) +v19+v21. *but*, those of us who have studied 'Biblical numerics' a little, will note that the number 10 is the number of the Gentile, and this is very significant. Rom 10 is a great chapter on Gentile salvation, i.e. it has a *dual* purpose, which for some reason, the Hyper-Diapers just can't seem to grasp!? The **'thou'** of v9 is to the Romans to whom Paul is writing! You have **'man'** in v10, as in *any* individual man; **'whosoever'** in v11; **'no difference between Jew and the Greek'** in v12; **'whosoever'** in v13; **'them that are no people'** and **'a foolish nation'** (as opposed to the Jews who are provoked **'to jealousy by them'** in v19) Look at v20+21... **I was made manifest unto them that asked not after me. BUT TO ISRAEL he saith**... So the group that *didn't* ask after God was *the Gentiles*. Rom 10 is about how *the Gentiles get saved*, and Paul uses that as an example to the Jews he loves (v1).

The ERROR of teaching that *if you pray* for the Lord to save you He won't because *it is work!*

It is an obvious fact that the mere *act* of praying itself cannot save you. In Luke 18v10-14, two men go to pray at the temple, and that story ends with one man saved and the other man *lost!* Cornelius prayed on a regular basis (Acts 10v2), and God honoured his prayers (Acts 10v4). But Cornelius did not get saved *until* he heard Peter preach (Acts 10v34-43) and he believed on Christ (Acts 10v43-47). So prayer *in and of itself* doesn't *save* a man. So up pop this bunch of *heretical*-Hyper-Diapers that teach 'if a man prays to get saved (or more specifically prays the *sinner's prayer*), then he is lost'. The idea being that prayer is a 'work' and man isn't saved by works (Eph 2v8+9). So that means that 99% of Christians are *not* saved according to this cult. Now there is nothing in the Scriptures that say you have to pray to get saved. There is no evidence that the Ethiopian eunuch prayed to get saved, even though he *did* confess with his mouth (Acts 8v37). As far as we know Cornelius and his household did not pray to get saved (Acts 10v43-47). At the same time, though, you cannot say that it is wrong to pray to get saved. The so-called 'sinners prayer' finds its origin in Luke 18v13 in a parable *told* by Jesus Christ. The publican who prayed that prayer went home justified (Luke 18v14). What made the prayer efficacious (effective) to the publican was the person to whom it was addressed – Luke 18v11 cf. Luke 18v13; also, the spirit in which he prayed (humble *'repentance'*), and that for which he prayed (God's mercy to a sinner.) To that prayer Christians have added *'and save me* for Jesus' sake' – fulfilling Rom 10v9-13. If any sinner *prays that prayer, or a similar one*, expressing the belief he has in his heart on the Lord Jesus Christ and His death, burial and resurrection, do you really think that the Lord is going to reject that *act of faith* IN Jesus Christ, expressed *through prayer*, after He said ...**him that cometh to me I will in no wise cast out**. John 6v37? If you do, then my little heretic, you are a complete nut! (*Colic-Caldwell thinks that Ruckman, Wesley, Luther, Sunday, O'Reilly, Gipp, Walker, Stauffer, Larkin, plus billions of others aren't saved because they all **asked** 'in prayer' for the Lord to save them! This is what a cult does to you, it twists, distorts and perverts your mind!*)

CHRISTIAN SOLDIER'S BATTLE NOTES

A Bible Believer can spot a member of the Hyper-Diaper cult a mile off, just by asking them a couple of questions, and listening to their *warped and twisted* answers. If you are talking to a 'Christian' who is zealous to get rid of *repentance, water baptism, the Lord's Supper and says that the Gospel we preach is the Gospel of 'reconciliation', and the Body of Christ started with Paul, and 'prayer' is a work*, then my dear friend, you are dealing with a *cultish*-Hyper-Diaper who fills his nappy as soon as you ask him whether Matthew, Mark, Luke and John were IN Christ (John 17), OR, *when* could you eat 'unclean' animals (Col 2), or, 'According to Rom 16v7' were there Christians IN Christ *before* Paul's conversion? (*Note those points down!*)

Now, if prayer is a form of calling upon the name of the Lord (and it certainly IS) then if a man confesses his faith in Jesus Christ to God in prayer *then he is saved!* He might not have to do it just that way, but if he does *he isn't working his way to Heaven!* After all, it isn't his prayer that saves him anyway, **it is Jesus Christ that saves him!** But Jesus saves the sinner *when* he places his faith in Him, and the same Lord who told the sinner to believe, also told him to *confess* Him with the mouth and call upon His name. (Rom 10v13) – You can do both *in prayer*. Generally speaking, when a man receives Christ into his heart, it will come out of his mouth. (Mat 12v34) It is a similar thing with baptism e.g. Mark 16v16 – Obviously in this passage, salvation is conditioned on *belief,* not belief and 'baptism', *but*, if a man is saved by belief in the Gospel (Mark 16v15), then as a general rule, he will get baptized in water.

In John 12v42, there are a bunch of 'chief rulers' that believed on Christ. When Jesus Christ addressed these men in John 12v44-50, He addressed their *belief, not* their lack of 'confession'. He made it very clear that it was their *belief* that saved them (John 12v44-46). Were they cowards? Yes! Did they love the wrong thing? Yes! *Were they lost?* No way! Joseph of Arimathea was among that group, and eventually he came forward and confessed Jesus Christ (John 19v38). Nicodemus was in that group, and he came out for Jesus Christ too (John 19v39). In fact, in the book of Acts (6v7), we discover that... **the word of God increased; and the number of the disciples multiplied in Jerusalem greatly; and *a great company of the priests were obedient to the faith*.**

So *generally speaking*, a saved man will confess Jesus Christ to others. There is *no set format* to this though, just like there is *no set way* to 'pray'. When a baby gets hungry, he cries to let someone know. When a sinner gets saved, he will '**call upon the name of the Lord....**' (Rom 10v13). A saved sinner, who never goes to church, or gets baptized, will still one day *confess* Christ to someone. Rom 10v12 defines the 'whosoever' of v13. 'Whosoever' does *not* mean 'the elect;' it means *whatever* Jew or Gentile that has called '...**upon the name of the Lord... shall be saved!**' There is much in Scripture that has *dual application*, don't be like the Hyper-Diapers and miss it because it doesn't fit in with your cult teaching.

To say that the Body of Christ started with Paul is absolute tosh and total heresy when the apostles were IN Christ and Christ ***in them*** according to John 17v21+23. Peter wouldn't eat a bacon sandwich in Acts 10 but he *could have* back in Mat 28 (Heb 9v16+17 and Heb 8v8+13, Heb 12v24) under the NEW Covenant. These verses are great to use against the heresy of the Hyper-Diapers - Rom 16v7, Gal 1v13 - The church of God existed *before* Paul.

2 Tim 2v2 **And the things that thou hast heard of me**... Hyper Diapers say that this *excludes* Peter, James, Matthew, Mark, Luke and John. Yet the same author writes in the *same* Book... 1 Tim 6v3+4 **If any man teach otherwise, and consent not to wholesome words, even the words of our Lord Jesus Christ, and to the doctrine which is according to godliness; He is proud, knowing nothing, but doting about questions and strifes of words, whereof cometh envy, strife, railings, evil surmisings**, Do you know *where* the words of the Lord Jesus Christ are mainly found? They are found in Matthew, Mark, Luke and John! *How about that!*

ERRORS OF HYPER-DISPENSATIONALISM

Hyper-Diapers would *exclude* the four Gospels, Paul did *not!* **All Scripture is profitable** – 2 Tim 3v16+17, did you get that, *all* Scripture, that includes Matthew, Mark, Luke, John, Peter and James. If you think these Books are not relevant for us today, you are a heretic. Hyper-Diapers teach that you should just stay in the epistles of Paul excluding all the other Books for doctrine, to them they are not relevant. Hypers don't think Peter preaches 'grace' and yet we read in Acts 15v7-11 and note v11... **But we believe that through the grace of the Lord Jesus Christ we shall be saved, even as they**. Peter, James and John were IN the Body of Christ, and even if they didn't fully understand about the Body of Christ, it doesn't mean it wasn't present just because it hadn't been fully revealed. Paul explained it to them in Gal 2 (read it). Note in John 1v17 **For the law was given by Moses, but grace and truth came by Jesus Christ**. 'Grace' came *before* Paul and it was by Jesus Christ. Note also that in John 17v21-23 Jesus is praying that Peter, James and John should be IN Him and IN the Father as He is IN them. Peter, James and John were as much IN the Body of Christ as Paul was.

The Body of Christ certainly did *not* start in Acts 9. Eph 2v14-17 – the 'Body' *starts* at Calvary, even if it was *not* revealed, it was *present*.

Now read 1 Pet 1 and tell me that Peter didn't preach the same Gospel as Paul did, he did. Peter received progressive revelation from Acts 2 onwards. Read Acts 10v43 cf. Acts 2v38.

There isn't a verse in all Scripture that says that the Church, the Body of Christ 'started' with Paul, *that is just heresy*. The Blood atonement was preached in Acts 8 *before* Paul.

'The Body' was *present* in Acts 2, even though it wasn't fully 'revealed'. There are *not* two 'Bodies' of Christ. The *one* Body was made possible at the crucifixion, even if no one understood it (Eph 2v14-18). I was talking to a Christian Bible 'corrector' up in Cheshire who read the NIV, when I asked him '*Who killed Goliath according to your NIV in 2 Sam 21v19?*' He turned to it and said... 'It must have been *another* Goliath!' You see, he did what the Hyper-Diapers do when they *can't handle truth*, they make things up and create *new* things e.g. 'another body' instead of **one** Body of Christ. All cults do it!

In Acts 15 all the apostles came to the same conclusion in regard to the Gospel, up until then it was *progressive revelation*.

The church of God IS the Body of Christ (*not* two separate 'bodies') which was present *before* Paul – Gal 1v13 – get that, it existed *before* Paul. Every time Paul used the term 'church of God,' it always referred to the Body of Christ.

Remember every verse of Scripture can be applied either *doctrinally, historically or devotionally* – the Hyper-Diapers want to get rid of all the Books that Paul didn't write.

The Body of Christ – The Church - A Mystery - Eph 2v16 **And that he might reconcile both unto God in one body by the cross, having slain the enmity thereby**: This is the 'mystery' Paul discusses in Eph 3v1-6. The Body of Christ composed of both Jews and Gentiles (Eph 2v11-14) does *not* begin with Paul. It does *not* begin in Acts 9, Acts 13, Acts 18 or Acts 28, as all the Hyper-Diapers tell us. The *one Body* was made possible at Calvary. The members of the local church were placed *into* that Body at Pentecost, and *the church* was converted *into* His Body (Eph 1v22+23).

Another Hyper-Diaper heresy - Eph 3v2 **If ye have heard of the dispensation of the grace of God which is given me to you-ward**: Here the hyper-diapers pull off one of the most monstrous '*private* interpretations' (2 Pet 1v20) that ever confounded Scripture. They define **'the dispensation of the grace of God'** as just a period of time. A 'dispensation' is *never just a period of time* anywhere in the Bible (1 Cor 9v17, Eph 1v10, Col 1v25) Look at that last reference by the *same author* – '**the dispensation of God**'. Is anyone stupid enough to think that there is a period of time called 'God?' The word 'dispensation', as used in the Scriptures, means the act of *dispensing* something. '**The dispensation of the grace of God**' is '**the grace**' that was dispensed to Paul to be given to his converts. If you made this '**dispensation**' a period of time, you couldn't begin the Body of Christ with Paul anyway, since '**grace and truth came by Jesus Christ**' (John 1v17) *not* Paul.

The Hyper-Diaper-cult tell us that Acts 2 is *not* the birthday of the Body of Christ, and that it is rather, the 'rebirth' of the 'Hebrew' Church! This led Bullinger further out on the backside of the desert where he began to apply the new birth to Israel only (John 3v3-5), and consequently he taught that the new birth was not for this dispensation. Stam and Baker cannot quite hack this, however, because Paul was plainly 'born again' (1 Cor 15v8); so the modern day half-hearted 'Bullingerite' *begins* The Body of Christ with Paul. The 'Stamites' stumbling block is that a thing *cannot exist before it is revealed.* Now there are a number of reasons for believing that the organic Body of Christ *began* in Acts 2, where every member of the *local* church (already established) was a 'disciple'…

1. In Christ's high priestly prayer (John 17) He prayed for Peter, James and John to have the same position **IN Him** that Paul occupied in the Epistle to the Colossians (cf. Col 1v27 and 2v10). If Peter, James and John were not IN the 'church which is His Body,' then Christ's prayer was of no avail.

2. The Body of Christ is to leave this earth in a moment, in the 'twinkling of an eye,' according to the same Epistle that states *one baptism* put the believer into *that Body* (cf. 1 Cor 12v13 with 1 Cor 15v49-55).

3. What would lead any Christian to suppose that the Body of Christ was formed *gradually* from one man, when it disappears *suddenly* with hundreds of men?

4. Granting Pentecost was a *Jewish* Feast, and those speaking had no knowledge of any immediate message except to their Jewish audience, how does one explain 'Two wave loaves' in the Pentecostal offering (Lev 23v17), but only *one* sheaf is found in Lev 23v11, where the resurrection of Christ is typified? If the OT Hebrew saint under the Law went up with 'Christ the *first-fruits*' (cf. 1 Cor 15v23 with Mat 27v50-54), and were presented by *one* sheaf, what do you make of *two* in the Pentecostal Feast?

With *Gentile* proselytes present in Acts 2 (v10) who are you to say that this didn't constitute 'Jew and Gentile' (Gal 3v28) IN Christ, simply because God didn't tell *Simon Peter* about it *at that time*?

The 'middle wall of partition' between Jew and Gentile was broken down 50 days before the Holy Spirit descended in Acts 2. The fact that no one present is *aware* of the transaction means *nothing at all* dispensationally, for as late as Acts 3v19 Simon Peter is not *aware* of the finished Blood atonement for the salvation of the *individual*, and to say that this meant it was *not an accomplished fact* (Heb 10v8-10) would be dispensational *nonsense! (See how shallow the Hypers really are?)* Acts 2v1-4 is the beginning of an era that will end at the Rapture.

Bullinger and Stam (plus Baker and Ballinger) all confound *revelation* with *origin* and *knowledge* with *source.* They are so overwhelmed with the Jewish aspects of the scene that they absolutely refuse to admit that anything could be taking place other than what the Apostles were *aware of*. It is apparent that this dispensation *begins* with *signs and wonders* exactly as the giving of the Law was accompanied by these things. It is also apparent that the context is the *last days* (Acts 2v20) of Israel, and that no one present is *aware* of the forming of an *organic body*. But from this, the

ERRORS OF HYPER-DISPENSATIONALISM

Hyper-Diaper cult make a *wrong* deduction. Since the Church, which is His Body (Col 1v18) was not *revealed* to the prophets in the OT in their prophecies (1 Pet 1v10-12), it is taken for granted that this church could not *start* anywhere until it had been *revealed*. This is more dispensational nonsense. It is not *revealed* to the prophets in the OT that *the eating of pork and lobster would be legitimate*, but what fool would think that Col 2v14 was not in *effect* until Peter found it out in Acts 10? (It was in effect after the crucifixion).

(Note also that 'fillings' of the Holy Spirit occur many times in the book of Acts *without* any accompanying 'tongues'. Acts 4v8, 4v31, 6v3, 6v5, 7v55, 9v7, 13v52)

Just because Acts 2 doesn't mention the 'Body of Christ' doesn't mean it wasn't *there*, neither do chapters 9, 10, 11, 12, 13, 14, 15, 16, 17, 18, 19, 20, 21, 22, or 23, but Stam has the Body of Christ being formed well before Acts 23, so for him to use this argument shows what a spiritual nut he was. The 'record' of Acts 2 said *nothing* about believers being IN Christ or Christ IN *them*, but what does that mean? Neither does Acts 9, 10, 11, 12, 13, 14, 15, 16, 17, 18, 19, or 20. Are we to suppose that Christ was not IN Simon Peter after the prayer of John 17? Why would the record of Pentecost say anything about something that *nobody* knew about till God *showed it* to Paul (Eph 3v15)? Did the record of Pentecost tell them that pork was alright to eat? Well, according to Col 2v16 they could have eaten it the morning they ate fish with Christ in John 20. *Hyper-Diapers are nuts! They just don't understand 'progressive Revelation' in Scripture.* It is not until Acts 8v30-37 that anyone grasps the significance of the Blood atonement for the sins of the individual sinner, but this took place more than five years before it was *revealed*.

Those baptized in Acts 2v38-41 still received **the gift of the Holy Ghost** and were saved as anyone having salvation today, 3000 being added unto them i.e. the apostles, Acts 2v41. Hypers say that the apostles weren't actually saved until Acts 9, *which is stupid, and also a blatant lie*.

Hypers say that Paul founded the church by appealing to 1 Corinthians 3v9-11 while listing Ephesians 2v19-20 that he clearly never read. **Now therefore ye are no more strangers and foreigners, but fellowcitizens with the saints, and of the household of God;** ***And are built upon the foundation of the apostles and prophets,*** **Jesus Christ himself being the chief corner stone**. Ephesians 2v19-20 reveals that the foundation for the Body of Christ pre-dated Paul. Paul alone is *not* 'the apostles', plural, neither 'the prophets', plural in the passage.

The Bible Believers Guide to Dispensationalism – by David E. Walker (A must for all Bible students and pastors)

This is one of the best books I've come across regarding rightly dividing the word of truth. Unlike the Hyper-Diaper-Cult heroes i.e. Stam, Bullinger, O'Hair etc. this guy knows his stuff and shows them up for what they are, *heretics*. Here is an excerpt from that book...

Their Founding Fathers - As detailed previously, hyper-dispensationalism (or ultra-dispensationalism) arose primarily from the teachings of E.W. Bullinger (1837-1913), and was later Americanized by J.C. O'Hair, Charles F. Baker, and Cornelius R. Stam (1908-2003). Modern day 'Bereans' believe those men 'recovered the truth of Pauline revelation.'

'Ultra' or 'Hyper' - Whether you use the Greek prefix (hyper) or the Latin (ultra), makes no difference. Shelton Smith (editor of The Sword of the Lord) creates his own definition by differentiating between an 'ultra,' and a 'hyper' dispensationalist: 'By my definition, an ultra-dispensationalist is somewhere between a dispensationalist and a hyper dispensationalist.' Smith's label is aimed at

CHRISTIAN SOLDIER'S BATTLE NOTES

Bible believing, soul-winning Baptists, who reject the 'saved the same' scenario. Smith knows they are not 'Hypers,' but he disagrees with them; hence, the label 'ultra.'

Hyper-dispensationalism is a dead end divergence that kills any real 'Bible Study.' Articles in 'The Berean Searchlight' include such titles as: *'Are the twelve apostles in the Body of Christ,' 'No other doctrine but right division,' 'Why Paul,' 'The confession of sins,' 'Paul, the apostle of Grace,' 'At what age was Jesus Baptized,' and 'The Devil and the mystery.'*

What is 'Paul's Gospel?' - Instead of 'Paul's Gospel' including the message of salvation by 'grace through faith,' (with an emphasis on the mystery of the Body of Christ and the Rapture) Hypers attribute the doctrine of substitutionary atonement to Paul alone. Ricky Kurth of the Berean Bible Society answers the question: 'Did Philip preach 'Christ died for our sins' to the Ethiopian eunuch?' It is tempting to think that Philip preached this to the eunuch when we read that he 'preached unto him Jesus' from Isaiah 53 (Acts 8:26-35). However, this message that was later given to the Apostle Paul (1 Cor 15v3+4) had not yet been revealed. Thus we know that Philip rather preached Christ according to the kingdom program.

The 'Issue' - A person can easily be identified as a Hyper by their unorthodox view of when the Body of Christ began. In fact, this is 'the issue.'

Stam states their position - We believe, and are sure, however, that the present dispensation began, not with Peter and the eleven at Pentecost, but with Paul, to whom the risen, glorified Lord later revealed His will and program for our day.

Ryrie correctly notes that most 'Dispensationalists say that the church began at Pentecost, while ultra dispensationalists believe that it began with Paul sometime later.' Whether or not they hold to the 'Acts 28' view (Bullinger), or the Acts 18 view (O'Hair) or the so-named 'mid Acts' view (Acts 9 – Stam and Sadler) makes no difference. They all add an extra dispensation between Acts 2 and Paul. **This is done to eliminate water baptism.** [Bullinger, and his followers also did away with communion since they only held Paul's prison epistles (of which 1 Cor. 11 is not included) as doctrine for the Church Age.]

Ironside, in his classic pamphlet 'Wrongly Dividing the Word of Truth', categorizes the errors of Hypers who took Bullinger's position:

1. The 'four gospels are entirely Jewish.'

2. The church in the book of Acts 'is simply an aspect of the kingdom and is not the same as the Body of Christ.'

3. Only Paul's prison epistles are Church Age material. 'Paul did not receive his special revelation of the mystery of the body until his imprisonment in Rome.'

4. 'The entire book of Revelation has to do with the coming age and has no reference to the Church today.' [Note: The fact that some of the doctrinal verses in Rev. 1-3 teach a person can lose his salvation imposes at least a primary application to the Tribulation, with a historical and devotional relevance to the Church Age. See: Rev. 4:1- 'things which must be hereafter.']

5. The bride of Jesus Christ is NOT the body of Christ, but 'Jewish.'

6. 'The Christian ordinances . . . Have no real connection with the present economy.'

Ruckman outlines the teachings of hyper-dispensationalism as follows:

ERRORS OF HYPER-DISPENSATIONALISM

1. There is a period of time called 'The Grace of God' which began in Acts 9 (Stam, Baker, Moore, Watkins) or in Acts 18 (O'Hare and others) or in Acts 28 (Bullinger).

2. Water baptism is not for *'this age'* since *'this age'* began in Acts 9 or Acts 13 or Acts 18 or Acts 28.

3. Bible-believing Baptists are heretics who do not follow Pauline teaching (1 Tim 1v16).

4. Since Paul did not *command* anyone to be baptized, it is *unscriptural*.

5. Since Paul was not *'sent to baptize,'* water baptism is Pre-Pauline (1 Cor 1).

6. The *'one baptism'* of Ephesians 4 automatically cancels water baptism.

'In The Body Or Out Of The Body?' - As we have demonstrated before (see The Transition Periods) the Bible does not 'chop up' as neatly as the Hypers would have you to believe. They want the so-called 'Dispensation of the Grace of God' to begin with Paul so they can seemingly get away from the different plan of salvation found in Acts 2v38. Note Sadler's flawed comment... The early chapters of Acts are merely a continuation of the earthly ministry of Christ to Israel. . . We must ask, who of the Acts 2 persuasion, preaches Acts 2v38 as the terms of salvation today?

Well, who of the 'mid Acts' position (following Paul) preaches Acts 19v6 as the terms of receiving the Holy Ghost? Biblical facts show four different 'plans of salvation' (or 'ways to get the Holy Ghost') in the Book of Acts before and after Paul's conversion (see Acts 2, 8, 16, 19). All four 'plans of salvation' fall under *one* dispensation. **Hypers confuse the dispensing of truth with the revelation of truth during the transition from Jew to Gentile (see Romans 11) in Acts.**

The beginning of the Body of Christ is easy to determine when the Bible is taken at face value, instead of the understanding of men (i.e. Paul being 'revealed' the mystery). The way for the spiritual Body of Christ was made at Calvary (Eph 2v14-16), even though it 'hinged' upon the glorification and ascension of His physical body. While it found full manifestation on the day of Pentecost, it did not necessarily begin there, and certainly did not begin after Pentecost. Ruckman... The *'one body'* did not begin with Paul at all. The verse (v16) says that the reconciliation of Jew and Gentile (see 'the mystery' given in 3v4-6) began at Calvary: 'in the one body by the cross.'

Read the following verses - Eph 2v14-16, John 16v7, John 7v39, John 17v21, Luke 24v49, Acts 1v4-5, 1 Cor 12v13 - The fact that believers were 'added to the church' (Acts 2v47), and also 'added to the Lord' (Acts 5v14) before Paul's conversion, indicate that **the body existed prior to Paul**. [Stam does *not* comment on Acts 5v14 in his commentary, nor does Sadler in his booklet The Historical Beginning of the Church] Additionally, 1 Cor 12v13 proves that Paul was preaching the mystery of the body before Acts 18. Other verses that prove conclusively that the Body of Christ was present before Paul are Rom 16v7, Gal 1v13, Acts 9v5. Romans 16v7 is so clear that Hyper-dispensationalists must make a difference between being 'in Christ,' and 'in the body of Christ.' Joel Finck writes in The Berean Searchlight - 'Being 'in Christ' is not necessarily the same as being 'in the body' of Christ.' **This is a grave inaccuracy**. Paul said that the Corinthians were 'in Christ' (1 Cor 1v30) and also that they were 'the body of Christ.' 1 Cor 12v27 Now ye are the Body of Christ, and members in particular. Gal 1v13 and Acts 9v5 confirm that the Body of Christ was on the earth as 'the church.' Otherwise, how could Paul (as an unsaved man) persecute Jesus when He was at the right hand of God? Hypers assume that the body of Christ could not exist until it was revealed to Paul. **What they do not understand, is that revelation of a truth has nothing to do with the reality of the particular truth**. For instance, the death of Jesus was an atonement for individual sinners, even though it was not revealed as such until Acts 8. Paul never said the Body of Christ began with him, he only said that the 'mystery' of it was 'revealed' to him (Eph 3v3+4). **What Hypers eventually do is invent another 'body'** (one before Acts 9) called the 'Kingdom Church.' Those in the 'Kingdom Church' would include Peter, James and John. Since Peter, James and John were baptized by the Spirit in Acts 2 (which would place them in the body), **Hypers are forced to 'teach two or three baptisms of the Spirit.'**

Hypers fail to associate John 17v21 ('that they also may be one IN US') with the promise of Luke 24v49 and Acts 1v4+5 (which see). While Baker admits the apostles were baptized with the Holy Spirit, he denies that it placed them in the 'body of believers, as described in 1 Corinthians 12v13.'

Furthermore, Hypers must get around the fact that Peter was writing to those 'in Christ' (1 Pet 3v16, 5v14), thus proving he was in the Body. Finck alleges that Peter uses the phrase 'in a redemptive sense rather than the dispensational sense of being in the body of Christ.' He does this to discount Peter's epistles for Church Age doctrine.

Hypers must also ignore plain references to other Jews (remember Paul was a Jew) living during Paul's time that were said to be a part of the 'one body.'

Rom 12v5 So we, being many, **are one body in Christ**, and every one members one of another. Finck comments: 'Paul is not saying in Rom 12v5 that every believer living at that time was a member of the Body of Christ.' **Hypers invent a special class of 'body mystery believers' converted under Paul.** According to their system Romans 12v5 might read this way: *'So, those Gentiles who were converted after my conversion and revelation of the mystery, are one body, which is different than the kingdom body of Jewish believers who received a different Gospel by Peter to the circumcision.'* They fail to remember that Peter's Gentile converts, were saved just like Paul's converts (see Acts 10).

'One Baptism' - Their attempt to prove the Body of Christ is not in Acts 2 is not their only impairment. They insist: 'water baptism ends' in Acts 28 with the rejection of the Gospel from Israel. They assert... 'Paul, the apostle of the Gentiles, the teacher of the Church, never once commands us to be baptized with water?' They answer the question, 'Should I be baptized?' While many pastors would say 'yes,' the Apostle Paul says 'no.' Water baptism was once a part of God's program for His people Israel, but it is not a part of God's program for His people today, the Body of Christ.

Although Paul never answered that question in his writings, Hypers emphatically answer 'in his name.' Paul answered with his works (he was baptized, and he baptized others). They lump baptism in with circumcision (Jewish), miracles (sign to the Jews), healing, and tongues. They think the reason Paul was 'thankful' that he did not baptize any more converts (other than Crispus and Gaius) was because he was *not* to do any more baptisms. They believe Eph 4v4+5 cancels out any water baptism for this age.

Hung up to dry… Below are the Bible answers to this anti-baptism (dry-cleaning) fixation:

Answer One

The commission in Matthew 28 is *not* distinctly Jewish, or the word 'nations' would not have been used. [All the confusion over the different 'commissions' overlooks the fact that Paul is the only apostle that fulfilled the 'Tribulation commission' of Mark 16v16-18 (all except drinking the poison).]

Answer Two

The mode of baptism in Matt 28 is *not* the same as Acts 2v38. All three names of the Godhead are used in Matt 28 while only the name of 'Jesus Christ' is used in Acts 2.

Answer Three

All three names (plural) are said to be a 'name' (singular). This is interesting, because in Acts 10v48 Gentiles are baptized by Peter, not in the name of Jesus Christ, but in the 'name (singular) of the Lord' – 'Father, Son, and Holy Ghost.'

Answer Four

Church history testifies to the fact of Believers baptism (immersion) after conversion. Hypers believe that the truth was missing all these years, and was finally revealed and 'recovered.'

Answer Five

Paul was baptized, and we are to follow Paul. To this contention, Hypers may respond, 'Paul was circumcised too, but we should not get circumcised.' This comparison is not justifiable. For, Paul was circumcised as a Jew, but baptized as a believer in Jesus Christ. Baptism was something *new converts* did. Paul was a new convert, placed into the 'one body,' and was baptized as a 'new creature,' not a Jew or Gentile. As Ruckman states, 'Paul *commanded no one* to attend church, pass out tracts, proselyte Baptists who are already saved, or argue about water baptism.'

Answer Six

Furthermore, Peter, James, and John were all baptized, and so was Jesus Christ. Hypers claim that Christ's baptism was his priestly 'anointing.' They go to 'the Greek' and are thereby confused with 'washing' and 'baptism.' Jesus was not anointed as a priest on earth. His earthly ministry was that of a prophet (John 1v25, 4v19, 6v14, 7v40, Deut 18v18). The priestly role of Jesus Christ took place after He died and rose again. See Heb 2v17, 3v1, 4v14.

Answer Seven

Paul baptized his own converts, *after* Acts 9. The meaning of 1 Cor 1v17 is clear if one adheres to the context. **A verse without a context is useless.** Christ did not send *anyone* just to baptize, but to preach.

Answer Eight

Just because the phrase 'one baptism' is used, does not annul water baptism. If it did, Paul would not have baptized anyone, and would have *commanded* believers *not* to be baptized in water.

The context again clears up any misunderstanding. Notice the framework is unity: 'one another,' (v2); 'unity of the Spirit' (v3) and seven 'ones' in the passage (v4-6). Paul is saying that there is only one 'saving baptism.' This would match Rom 6v3, Gal 3v27, Col 2v12, 1 Cor 12v13 and Matt 3v11. That must be the correct 'interpretation,' since we know there are *many* 'lords,' *many* 'faiths' and *many* 'spirits:'

1 Cor 8v5-6, Mark 3v11

Confession of Sin... As alluded to earlier, Hypers sever the word of God up into such thin slices, that *only* Paul's epistles (and maybe only his prison epistles) are allowed for Church Age doctrine. Once that presupposition is taken, Peter, James, and John are not allowed in the Body of Christ, although they are 'IN Christ' (1 Pet 3v16, 5v14). To them, Peter's epistles cannot contain *any* Church Age doctrine, nor can 1 John through Jude.

CHRISTIAN SOLDIER'S BATTLE NOTES

This brings us to an important question: Should a Christian confess his sins to God for forgiveness according to 1 John 1v9? While the Hypers do not believe in sinless perfection (like some Holiness groups), they do, however, preclude a Christian confessing his sins, distorts the Grace of God, and fail to understand the 'standing and state' of the believer. Hyper Ken Lawson, says that 1 John 1v9 'has caused untold harm and detriment to the people of God.' He thinks a Christian should not feel guilty about his sins (after salvation) since 'God wishes for us to enjoy the gift of salvation.' He claims that God will not 'continue to show him [the believer] the cold shoulder' if he 'fails to confess wrongdoing.' So, Hypers do not believe a Christian's fellowship with Jesus Christ is based on their personal, holy walk. Lawson's arguments against the 'Father, son, relationship' understanding of 1 John 1 are as follows...

It is based on a performance system of conditional blessing, and shifted my gaze away from Christ and His grace to my own faithfulness (or usually failure) to confess.

Repentance, and confession of sin (both of which Hypers snub) are *clearly* a part of the believer's fellowship with God the Father, in every dispensation. Peter had to confess his love to Jesus Christ, before he could be restored (John 21), and we are not any better than him. Who (but Hypers) would think that sin was not acknowledged (Ps 51v3) with Peter's three confessions in John 21?

Over and over again, fellowship (not salvation) is predicated upon repentance – the stem of confession. **Hypers do *not* believe in *repentance*.** Note the following verses:

Lev 5v5 And it shall be, when he shall be guilty in one of these things, that he shall confess that he hath sinned in that thing - Isa 64v6-7, Prov 28v13, Num 5v7, Lev 26v40, Neh 1v6, Ps 32v5, Ps 38v18, Josh 7v19, Dan 9v4, Hos 5v15, 2 Sam 12v13, Isa 6v5, Matt 3v6, 1 Cor 11v31, Acts 19v18 - The last two references are during the 'dispensation of the mystery.' How do you 'judge' yourself without confessing and repenting of your sins? Answer - you cannot, and some do not, therefore, they fall under the chastening hand of Almighty God according to Hebrews 12 (which Hypers disregard for the Church Age).

The real Berean who 'rightly' divides, (instead of 'wrongly shredding the word') will notice that the people who confess in Acts 19 do so under Paul's preaching. If they confessed publicly to men, you *know* they had to confess to God. In fact Paul attributed God's presence to himself while he was preaching and teaching the word - 2 Cor 2v17, 1 Thes 2v13

The next problem that Lawson has with the word of God, concerns prayer and honesty - If what I believed concerning confession was true, I was probably 'out of fellowship' much of the time, and so were most believers.

Yes, 'most believers' are 'out of fellowship' with the Lord, for only through a constant 'cleansing of ourselves' (2 Cor 7v1) through *prayer* (1 Thes 5v17) can we be 'in fellowship.' Notice Lawson's excuse: 'I had to honestly admit to myself that I found it extremely difficult to confess all my daily sins on a consistent basis.' So, since prayer and confession is 'difficult,' Hypers find scriptural alibis to disobey 1 John 1v7-9, as well as Paul's command to 'pray without ceasing.' Note also, that the verse does not stipulate confession of every sin. It simply states a fact: When you mess up, you can go to the Lord, confess, and the blood of Jesus (the basis for forgiveness) will clean you - Heb 9v14.

Lawson (as all Hypers do) reverts to Paul for a defence: Paul, the apostle of the Gentiles, is silent in all his writings on confession of sins for forgiveness, parental or otherwise.

Paul never forbad the practice either. Should we not observe the omissions as well as the commands? As pointed out earlier, Paul did *not* rebuke the Ephesians from 'confessing' (Acts 19)

ERRORS OF HYPER-DISPENSATIONALISM

when he preached. **In fact, Paul's preaching pivoted upon the message of *repentance* (which is the heart of confession) - Acts 20v21, Acts 26v20**

Going further from the truth, Lawson tries to prove 1 John 1 is not relevant to a Church Age saint, because 'A believer cannot walk in darkness any more than an unbeliever can walk in the light.' Has he failed to read the favourite book of hyper-dispensationalists – Ephesians? Eph 5v8 For ye were sometimes darkness, but now are ye light in the Lord: walk as children of light: Eph 5v11-14 - If the Lord commands us to 'walk as children of light' (Eph 5v8), then obviously there are believers who are *not* 'walking in the light.' The 'sleeper' in Eph 5v14, is *not* an unbeliever, he is a Christian. Paul often edified the believer to 'walk in the light' instead of darkness:

Rom 13v11-13, 1 Thes 5v4-8 - While it is true that positionally, every child of God is 'in the light' (IN Christ, in heavenly places), practically 1 John 1 applies along with Paul's epistles (Ephesians, Romans, and 1 Thessalonians) in a doctrinal manner to the New Testament saint. [Hypers forget that good 'sound doctrine' (1 Tim 1v10) refers not only to the revelation of the 'Pauline mystery,' but to *behaviour*. Read 1 Tim 1v9]

Some Hypers may not believe in 'sinless perfection' (like some Holiness groups) but they do believe in 'constant fellowship.' Notice Lawson again...

If any believers were living in a state of broken fellowship, it was the Corinthians.

- There were carnal divisions and contentions among them (1 Cor 1v10-13, 3v1-3).
- They were infatuated with worldly wisdom (1 Cor 1v28-2v5, 3v18-23).
- They were judging things which they should not and failing to judge things which they should (1 Cor 4v1-5, 5v6).
- They were allowing sexual immorality in the local church and were proud of it (1 Cor 5v1+2).
- They were taking each other to court before the unbelievers (1 Cor 6v1-12).
- They were visiting harlots (1 Cor 6v13-20).
- They were proud of their knowledge and causing weaker brethren to stumble (1 Cor. 8).
- They were questioning Paul's authority and apostleship (1 Cor 9v1-6).
- They were prone to idolatry by lusting after evil things (1 Cor 10).
- They had disorders at church, including making a mockery of the Lord's Supper (1 Cor 11).
- They were enamoured with the spiritual gifts but were failing to exercise them in love (1 Cor 12-14).
- They were doubting the resurrection (1 Cor 15v12-19).
- If all this was not enough, they were stingy in their contribution to the poor saints (2 Cor 8v9).

...Moreover, there is no command to confess their sins in order to receive forgiveness and restoration to fellowship. On the contrary, Paul assures them that 'God is faithful, by whom ye were called unto the fellowship of His son Jesus Christ our Lord' (1 Cor 1v9). It is a fellowship based upon God's faithfulness.

So, basically, Lawson is teaching that the immoral living Corinthians were in sweet fellowship with a holy God. Anyone who can read the letter to the Corinthians from Paul, and get that summation, would probably think the Koran contains good marital advice. Read the following verses and note how they drive at confession and repentance - 1 Cor 3v1-4, 1 Cor 3v17, 1 Cor 4v2, 1 Cor 4v6, 1 Cor 4v14, 1 Cor 4v18-20, 1 Cor 5v1-2, 1 Cor 5v6-7, 1 Cor 5v13, 1 Cor 6v5, 1 Cor 6v18, and on and on.

The very fact of their repentance (given in 2 Corinthians) stipulates confession - 2 Cor 7v9, 2 Cor 7v11, 2 Cor 12v21

Hypers teach Satan (not the Lord) burdens the believer with conviction of sin and guilt - Guilt is a killer, a killer of our joy, our peace, and our enjoyment of intimacy with God. If Satan can use guilt (which our Lord has already taken away) to use as a wedge to separate us from God, his strategy to take us as a captive in the battle is secure. . . . Our fellowship with Jesus Christ our Lord can never be broken.

They disregarded Paul's comment: 'ye sorrowed after a godly [not devily] sort' (2 Cor 7v11), and the repercussion of broken fellowship in the life of the believer – the Judgment Seat of Christ. Why the Judgment Seat of Christ, if a believer is never out of fellowship? Adam was saved by 'grace' and 'the blood of a lamb' (Gen 3v21) and he was *out of fellowship* with God. Hypers abandon the distinction ('rightly dividing' right?) between the Christian's standing and state. Scofield appositely comments: 'Positionally he [the believer] is 'perfected forever' (Heb. 10v14), but looking within, at his state, he must say, ' Not as though I had already attained, either were already perfect' (Phil. 3v12).'

This 'unfatherly grace' of Hypers culminates with a hollow answer to the problem of sin in the life of a believer ...even the most mature Christians do sin. When this happens, the first thing to remember is our complete forgiveness in Christ Jesus. This will prevent us from going on another guilt trip...

Was the 'godly sorrow' (2 Cor 7v10+11) just a 'low self-esteem' guilt trip? Or, was it true repentance and confession of sin? Lawson continues... When a Christian sins, we should agree with God's word that it is wrong (confess) and forsake the behaviour or attitude . . . So we confess our sins, not in order to receive forgiveness, but because we wish to be properly attuned to grace and to thus glorify Him who has forgiven us all trespasses.

What is all this 'behaviour,' and 'attitude' garbage? Is it Bible? 'We wish to be properly attuned?' After writing two articles with the intent of impeding the confession of sin to God, Lawson says that we should confess our sins (but not for forgiveness). Do you think the Corinthians just 'properly attuned' themselves, or did they actually *confess their sins* because they wanted restored fellowship? How could they 'repent' without confession? **A Hyper no more believes in repentance for today (Church Age) than he does Sabbath worship.** Lawson's conclusion about the doctrinal meaning of 1 John 1v9 is as shallow as a teardrop... Our key verse in 1 John 1v9 is found to be a salvation verse for Israel looking for the return of Christ to establish His earthly, Davidic, Millennial Kingdom . . . In conclusion, 1 John 1v9 is a salvation verse which fits 'hand in glove' with the Prophecy program of the Gospel of the kingdom.

If it is a salvation verse for Israel in the Tribulation, why is the word 'all' used in 1 John 1? Note: 'all sin' (v7); 'all unrighteousness' (v9). Rev 14v11 explains that there is *no remedy* (confession or otherwise) for taking the mark of the beast. A person will no more be washed from 'all sin' in the Tribulation by the confession of it, than a person *now* can be saved by the golden rule.

If 1 John 1v9 is a salvation verse for Israel in the Tribulation, why are the believers in 1 John said to be 'sons of God' awaiting the 'appearing' (not advent) of the Lord. No Tribulation saint will 'be like

ERRORS OF HYPER-DISPENSATIONALISM

him' (1 John 3) because no Tribulation saint will be a member of the Body of Christ.

'The blood of Jesus Christ' did *not* cleanse anyone during the Gospel of the kingdom message in Matthew, Mark or Luke. 1 John cannot be applied to Israel. [This brings up a difference between the 'Gospel of the kingdom' prior to the cross, and 'the Gospel of the kingdom' after the cross, preached during the Tribulation. In the Tribulation, the 'Gospel of the kingdom' will include the 'faith of Jesus' (Rev 13v10; 14v12). That is, a person must believe that Jesus Christ is not only Messiah, but the Saviour. Belief in the substitutionary atonement of Christ is crucial to a person's salvation in the Tribulation period.]

Fruits of Hyper-dispensationalism - The heresies of hyper-dispensationalists produce such 'deep Bible study,' that its adherents drown under its influences. **Their teachings are inconsistent with the Scriptures, and manufacture Christians inactive. Wining lost souls to Jesus Christ is not the 'drive' of Hypers, even though it was for the apostle Paul.** They are obsessed with stopping water baptism, and 'following Paul' nowhere. As Dr. Ruckman suitably summarizes: 'The only theme song they have is 'How dry I am, how dry I am,' and their teaching and preaching is as dry as their baptism'.

Is Jesus Standing or Sitting?

Read Acts 7v55+56, Mat 26v64 (see also Mark 16v19, Luke 22v69, Eph 1v20, Col 3v1, Heb 1v3, Heb 8v1, Heb 10v12, Heb 12v2, 1 Pet 3v22). After He went back to Heaven the Lord Jesus Christ was seated on the right hand of God, yet, here in Acts 7 we see Jesus standing. Why? It certainly wasn't because He was 'receiving Stephen's soul' into Heaven (Luke 16v22). If Jesus 'stood up' to receive every Christian that died, He would be up and down every minute of the day. He was *not* standing to receive Stephen's soul. Why is it that the 'heavens open' in Rev 4v1-3 and 19v11 in connection with the Second Coming, just as they were said to have opened at the First Coming in Mat 3v16. How does one explain the immediate calling out of the Apostle to the Gentiles in Acts 8v1, following this incident? Something happened in Acts 7, a *demarcation line* was drawn by God, which *all* POST-Tribbers haven't got a clue about! How does one explain the fact that not one single miracle ever took place in Jerusalem following this scene, although the apostles (with their SIGN-Gifts – Acts 5v12 etc.) *stayed in Jerusalem?* Interesting don't you think. God draws a line at Acts 7v60, and this line is connected with the Second Coming of His Son, the Lord Jesus Christ (Acts 7v56).

Seeing this line, the Hypers all go wild with delight at *right division* (2 Tim 2v15) and insist that the 'Body' must start *after* this time. Not one of these Hyper-Diaper-heretics is able to reconcile the date of *revelation* with the date of *origin*. This cult mentality insists that God's change of program nullifies the possibility of anything being there *before* God changed it. This is what we Bible Believers call... 'Doctrinal ERROR!'

What we have here in Acts 7 and Jesus 'standing,' is a readiness for the Second Advent that would have triggered Daniel's 'Seventieth Week,' IF the national response had been *repentance* (Acts 3v19) and an acceptance of Stephen's sermon. Remember, this is strike *three* for Israel in regard to the *rejection* of the Trinity – They rejected God the Father – 1 Sam 8v6+7, God the Son – Mat 21v37-39, and here God the Holy Spirit – Acts 7v51.

IF they had of repented and accepted Stephen's message, Deut 21v1-9 would have gone into action, the Rapture would have taken place (Ps 50v4, S of S 2v10, Isa 26v19), Judas would have come up from the pit (Acts 1v25 see comments in RRB), and the covenant between Rome and Israel would have been signed (Dan 9v27, 11v27+30).

CHRISTIAN SOLDIER'S BATTLE NOTES

The 'Body' may have remained an *unrevealed* mystery, depending upon whether or not God decided to reveal it. That it was *already* a Jew-Gentile Body is perfectly apparent from Acts 2v10 and Acts 6v1... This also means that Calvin and his bunch of heretics (All Calvinists that is...!) make a gross *error* in regard to the concept of *'eternal decrees,'* for some of them (i.e. 'eternal decrees') are *flexible* and can be *adjusted* to meet the situation, without contradicting one former decree or one former oath i.e. God has a plan A and a plan B, knowing of course what *will* happen! (*You'll blow your mind trying to figure it all out!*)

It also means all Hypers are in *error* because a Rapture *here*, would *not* have affected the 'mystery revelation' of that 'Body' (see Eph 3v15 in RRB), but the time of *revelation* hardly ever matches the time of *institution* (see Gen 2v1-3)... something that the Hyper-Diapers just can't seem to understand.

Taking verses out of context!

If you don't rightly divide the word of truth, and therefore take things out of context, you can make the Scriptures teach anything you like. As Ruckman writes... Karl Marx used Acts 2v44+45, Bill Clinton used Gal 3v28, Seventh-Day-Adventists use Mat 5v19, all unsaved liberals use 1 John 4v8 (as do all sodomites), Mohammed availed himself of Deut 20v9-14, Joshua 11v11-19, Exod 23v22-30, Mat 21v43 and Deut 17v1-7. All JW's use Ecc 9v10 and John 14v28. Every Roman Catholic uses Mat 16, 1 Cor 3v13+15, John 6v54-56 and John 21v25. All Campbellites go to Hell quoting Mark 16v16 and Acts 22v16. You see, you can teach anything from THAT BOOK! That's how cults start. That's how the Hyper-Diapers started.

Prayer in salvation...

Rom 10v9+10 - When the Bible says **For with the heart man believeth unto righteousness**, that's what it means. You go beyond the bare facts of the Gospel and make them yours *personally* so that you are totally relying on what the Lord Jesus Christ did for you to get to Heaven and out of Hell. **...and with the mouth confession is made unto salvation.** Jesus said in Mat 12v34 **...for out of the abundance of the heart the mouth speaketh**. The heart and the mouth, spiritually, are connected. You talk about the things you love. Jesus continued on in Mat 12v35 **A good man out of the good treasure of the heart bringeth forth good things**... Now, there are two things that come up at this point. The first is the place of *prayer* in salvation. It is obvious that the mere 'act' of praying *itself* saves *no one*. In Luke 18v10-14, two men go to pray at the temple, and that account ends with one man saved and the other man lost. Cornelius prayed on a regular basis (Acts 10v2), and God honoured his prayers (Acts 10v4). But Cornelius did not get saved *until* he heard Peter preach (Acts 10v34-43) and he believed on Christ (Acts 10v43-47). So prayer in and of *itself* does *not* and *cannot* save you.

Realising this, the Hyper-Diapers say that if a man *prays* to get saved (or more specifically *prays* the 'sinner's prayer'), then he is lost. The idea behind this is that 'prayer' is a 'work', and you're not saved by 'works' (Eph 2v8+9). These heretics state that all you need to do to get saved is 'assent' (*the expression of approval or agreement*) to the fact that Christ died for you and 'THANK God' for having already forgiven your sins.

Of course there are all kinds of things wrong with that **erroneous** teaching; not the least of which is *that giving thanks to God for having already saved you IS A PRAYER, therefore a 'work' in their eyes!* (See the hypocrisy?)

Prayer is prayer whether you *ask* God to save you or you *thank* God for saving you. If prayer can't save you because it is a 'work', then for 'God's sake' (as well as your own) *don't thank God for saving*

ERRORS OF HYPER-DISPENSATIONALISM

you! Otherwise, you would be mixing 'works' with your faith and then you wouldn't be saved! Capiche?

When did the Church, the Body of Christ, the Bride of Christ *start*?

Well according to the Hypers it started mid-Acts with Paul. Us Bible Believers call that a *shallow-private-cult-interpretation*. Let Scripture *speak*... 1 Cor 12v28 **And God hath set some in the church, first apostles, secondarily prophets, thirdly teachers, after that miracles, then gifts of healings, helps, governments, diversities of tongues**. Did you get that? The apostles were IN the Body of Christ *before* Paul. Oh dear Hyper-Diapers, messed your nappy again? Eph 2v16 **And that he might reconcile both unto God in one body by the cross, having slain the enmity thereby**: The Church, The Body of Christ, started *at the Cross*, not mid-Acts with Paul. Read it again... Eph 2v16 **And that he might reconcile both unto God in one body by the cross, having slain the enmity thereby**: Carry on reading... Eph 2v17-20. Eph 4v4-12 - The Body of Christ *existed before* Paul, even though it wasn't 'revealed' until Paul! Acts 8v1-3. Acts 15v4 – the apostles were IN the Body of Christ! There is *only one body of Christ!* 1 Cor 12v13. Col 1v18+24, 1 Cor 12v13, Rom 16v7, Gal 1v13 WHO persecuted the church? Paul did, because it was *in existence before Paul.* John 17v21+23 - Who is IN Christ? Eph 2v13+14+16+20, 1 Cor 12v27+28 - So the apostles were IN the church *before* Paul. Gal 3v28, Eph 5v32, Heb 9v16+17

More Hyper-Diaper claptrap.

Ruckman writes... Cornelius Stam and the 'Dry Cleaners' will tell you that the church that Paul persecuted was not the Body of Christ, and they will tell you there is no Body of Christ *until* the time of Paul. But in 1 Cor 10v32, Paul says that there are only three people in the world: Jew, Gentile, and Church. There's no 'Body' sticking out different from the 'Church!' The Body IS the Church! The Church IS the Body! In Christ, there is neither Jew nor Gentile. Right? All right, then the Church is composed of Christians. They are neither Jew nor Gentile. Outside of the Church, there is Jew and Gentile. So when he says 'church of God', he is referring to the Body of the Lord Jesus Christ. So in 1 Corinthians when he said, 'I persecuted the church of God', that told you the Body was there ***before*** Acts 9.

If a Hyper-Diaper enters your church, here are four signs to recognise them by, they believe...

1. There is no 'Body of Christ' *before* Acts 9.

2. Water baptism is *not* for 'this age' even though they were baptising up to Acts 18 – see also Acts 16v30-34

3. No deacons in the local church, although they are recommended in a Pauline epistle written *after* Acts 28 (1 Tim 3)

4. New Jerusalem is Jewish and is *not* the Bride of Christ. **She is the Father's wife, for Christ's Body is** male, not female (see how they aborted the figurative expression in Eph 4v13 to prove this)

Hyper-Dispensationalists do not preach on the street or wins souls. They do not fast and pray, and they do not build local churches. They are a cult that huddles together feeding off each other. The only growth they see is within their own cult families. They spend their entire cult-'ministries' trying to convince other Christians who have been baptized that they shouldn't have been baptized, as well as trying to convince them that the church started in Acts 9. Their other anti-Scriptural, detestable abomination before the Lord, is saying that if you *prayed* to get saved, you are lost because prayer is a 'work'.

CHRISTIAN SOLDIER'S BATTLE NOTES

Hypers destroyed by Ruckman - 1 Cor 1v13 '**Is Christ divided?**' No! '**Was Paul crucified for you?**' No! '**Or were ye baptized in the name of Paul?**' No! v14: '**I thank God that I baptized none of you, but Crispus and Gaius.**' Why? Because it's not for this dispensation? No! Why? Because there is only one baptism? No! Why? Because now that I know there is only one baptism I repent for baptizing any converts? No! '**I thank God that I baptized none of you ...Lest any should say that I had baptized in mine own name**' (v15). Now, you want to get that. Back to v14 '**I thank God that I baptized none of you...** Not because it is wrong or even because he had a different commission, but v15 '**Lest any should say that I had baptized in mine own name.**' '**And I baptized** (v16). Then he did baptize some of them. So to say, 'Well, Christ didn't send Paul to baptize,' doesn't even deal with the context. He did baptize, whether he was sent to baptize or not. So when you deal with the dry cleaning brethren- E. C. Moore, Baker, Bullinger, Stam, and Bill Sharpe, they will tell you, 'Well, the Lord didn't send Paul to baptize,' quoting v17. I wonder why they never read to you v16. Now, God didn't send me to baptize. Did you know that? I can say just what Paul said. I can go in any church in this country and 'The Lord didn't send me to baptize' but I've baptized a few folks. '**And I baptized also the household of Stephanas: besides, I know not whether I baptized any other.**' He lost track of the names. He didn't know how many he had baptized and how many he hadn't. '**For Christ sent me not to baptize but to preach the gospel** ...' (v17) The *dry cleaner* reads it this way 'Christ didn't send me under the commission of Matthew 28, but the commission of 2 Cor 5'. But of course, that is not what the verse said. The verse said '**For Christ sent me not to baptize...**' Then why did he baptize if the Lord didn't send him to baptize? In v16, he did baptize them. All right if you take v16 with the fact that he did baptize them, but the Lord sent him not to baptize, dearly beloved, the only proper interpretation you can get is the Lord didn't send him primarily to baptize, but to preach. But he did baptize a few folks while he preached. You can't get any other sense out of it than that. Any other sense is nonsense. '**For Christ sent me not to baptize**' That's true. The Lord sent him to preach. That's true. But that didn't prevent him from baptizing people. '**For Christ sent me not to baptize, but to preach the gospel...**' What the Lord sends you to do doesn't mean that you can't do other things. '**Christ sent me... to preach the gospel.**' Do you think '**preach the gospel**' is all Paul did? Was '**preach the gospel**' all Paul did in Galatians, Ephesians, Philippians, and Colossians? Paul didn't just '**preach the gospel.**' Over half the Pauline writings are not talking about the gospel at all. They deal with Christian conduct. So when it says the Lord sent him '**to preach the gospel,**' that doesn't limit his ministry to preaching the gospel and excluding baptism. These people are crazy. They can't read. '**For Christ sent me not to baptize, but to preach the gospel**' The Gospel Paul preached had two elements in it that are found in the preaching of the other apostles and the Jews. Turn to Acts 20. Let's see what Pauline preaching looks like. It is not 'dry cleaning' preaching. Paul isn't standing up there wasting all this *hot air* about the 'Body mystery' and 'the mystery of the one Body' and when did the Body start and all that tosh (just like the Hypers do). That's a scummy type of ministry, when you have got a whole New Testament to preach. With Paul's preaching, here is what is going on. The hyper-dispensationalist thinks the contents of Paul's preaching is found in 2 Cor 5v18-20, where he mentions '**the ministry of reconciliation**' and Eph 3v3-7, where the mystery of the Body is mentioned. So the hyper-dispensationalist thinks that Paul's preaching is limited to two things God showed him: the mystery of the Body of Christ and the ministry of reconciliation; therefore, Paul's ministry was simply talking about those two things. Now, if you talk about those two things, do you know what you can overlook? The Tribulation, the Rapture, the Judgment Seat of Christ, the Second Coming of Christ, and prophecy. Above all, you won't ever have to preach against anybody's sins. It is a beautiful ministry, *(and a lazy one)* because you simply preach reconciliation and then the 'one Body,' 'one Body mystery.' Never mind the baptism controversy; don't baptize them. Never mind the sins; you're reconciled. You'll just get through there high, clean, and dry, and come out smelling like a rose. If you think that is what Paul's ministry was, you know nothing about Paul's ministry (*none of the Hyper-Diapers know anything about Paul's ministry*).

ERRORS OF HYPER-DISPENSATIONALISM

Let me show you Paul's ministry. This is Paul's testimony about what kind of ministry he had. Acts 20v21 **'Testifying both to the Jews, and also to the Greeks, *repentance* toward God'** He preached the *repentance* of John the Baptist. This dispensation may not begin with John the Baptist, but John the Baptist preached something that ought to be preached in this dispensation (Acts 26v20). All right, that is what John the Baptist told them in Matthew 3 before the crucifixion. So when Paul preached, he said *'Repent*, and if you are going to repent, let's see something.' How is that for a grace dispensation? Old Paul had a little Methodist in him. Paul's ministry is certainly not limited to hot air sessions in homes about the 'mystery Body,' and the 'Body mystery' and all that stuff. He was a preacher (Acts 20v21+v25). So Paul preached *repentance*, faith, and **'the kingdom of God**.' That isn't all of it. Look at Acts 20v27, **'For I have not shunned to declare unto you all the counsel of God**.' Paul doesn't limit his preaching to **'the ministry of reconciliation'** and the Gospel. He declares **'all the counsel of God**,' everything God gave him. Everything God gave him is in Romans through Philemon. A good preacher (that is a Bible preacher not a Hyper-Diaper) will preach all the Bible at the places where it is needed, at the situations where it is called for, praying for God to give him the right verse for the right occasion in the circumstances which he finds himself. He will never limit his ministry to **'the ministry of reconciliation'** or the *mystery-of-the-one-Body-Body-mystery-dry-cleaning-one Body-mystery!* (*Smile God loves you!*) That is the work of a deluded heretic! There are many people that talk about following Paul that do not follow Paul at all. They are not the least bit 'Pauline' in their approach. *Paul was a street preacher. I don't recall Cornelius Stam (or any Hyper-Diaper) ever street-preaching!* They like their air-conditioned offices and bedrooms too much! They are a very small self-deluded arrogant cult, who haven't a clue about rightly dividing the Scriptures, or living the Christian life.

Repentance and the Hyper-Dispensationalist-cult.

Repentance is another word the Hypers just can't seem to grasp and understand for some reason. There are Christians falling over each other on YouTube and the Internet all disagreeing with the doctrine of 'Repentance'. Repentance basically means a turning from, or a change of mind, or a change of attitude about a thing. Gospel repentance is turning from sin and turning to God, and we find a great illustration of this with the apostle Paul... Acts 20v21. Yes that was Paul preaching *repentance* just like John the Baptist preached *repentance*. (See also Acts 26v20 cf. Mat 3v8, Luke 3v8) So once again, the Hyper-Dispensationalist cult fail in their understanding and knowledge of Scripture. Read Acts 11v18. Note that, 'repentance unto life'. Repentance is *not a work* in regard to salvation as the Hypers erroneously teach. God repented! (Gen 6v6, Exo 32v14 etc.) So repentance is not necessarily *a turning from sin* (as in the OT) but a change of mind. 2 Cor 7v10. **Once saved you cannot lose your salvation!** Repentance is not merely sorrow for sin as there are some people who repented in Scripture who died and went to Hell. Judas, Balaam, Saul, Pharaoh, Esau all illustrate *false* repentance. Evangelical repentance is not being sorry for what you have done, it is sorry for what *you are!* Get that! (See Peter (Luke 5v8), Job (Job 42v6) and Isaiah (Isa 6v5)) There are two kinds of repentance, one is *godly sorrow* which worketh *repentance to salvation*, the other is *worldly repentance* because you're sorry for what you've done, that worketh death. Biblical repentance is being sorry for what *you are* because you *know that you're no good*. It's not a confession of sin that marks repentance, it's turning from sin and turning unto Jesus Christ that marks repentance. That's receiving Him by faith and *not* of works. Repentance comes *before* believing - Mark 1v5, repentance comes *before* forgiveness – Luke 24v47 **(and note *all* nations *not* just Israel).** God not only can change His mind, but He can change His methods – God healed a blind man with some mud, another He touched his eyes and another He just spoke to, and one didn't get healed until he left Christ. God can do things *differently* at *different* times. You can't *box* God in. Saying that you shouldn't preach *repentance* today because *it's a work* just shows how ignorant and shallow you really are in the Scriptures. **No Gentile was ever saved by Acts**

CHRISTIAN SOLDIER'S BATTLE NOTES

2v38. If you don't differentiate the differences between Israel and the Body of Christ, the Church, you'll never understand the Scriptures. In Acts 2v38 Peter is talking about the nation of Israel *repenting* for rejecting their Messiah Jesus Christ, he's *not* preaching the Gospel of 1 Cor 15v1-4 regarding individual salvation for your sins, and the Blood atonement. Acts 17v30 **And the times of this ignorance God winked at; but now commandeth all men every where to repent**: We *should* preach repentance. When the Hyper-Diaper cult say that Jack Chick isn't saved because he preaches *repentance*, it's time for them to be 'sectioned'. Jack Chick through his Chick tracts, has probably led more souls to Jesus Christ than any other person, and I mean *millions*. To say that he isn't saved is just showing how dumb you really are. Luke 13v3 **I tell you, Nay: but, except ye repent, ye shall all likewise perish**. Luke 13v5 **I tell you, Nay: but, except ye repent, ye shall all likewise perish**. 2 Pet 3v9 **The Lord is not slack concerning his promise, as some men count slackness; but is longsuffering to us-ward, not willing that any should perish, but that all should come to repentance**. Everyone *needs* to repent and come to Christ. Jesus Christ preached *repentance*, so did John the Baptist, so did Peter, so did Paul and *so should you.* Repentance is turning *from* to *turning to*, and regarding salvation that is *not* a work. Acts 26v18.

The moment you put your faith and trust in Jesus Christ for your sins forgiven, (2 Cor 5v21) you are eternally saved (John 3v16) and placed *into* the Body of Christ, which is the church (1 Cor 12v13). By calling upon the Lord (Rom 10v13 **For whosoever shall call upon the name of the Lord shall be saved.**) in *any* dispensation, God will *hear your call*, 'cry, prayer' and He *knows your heart*, thoughts and motive, and He will respond by saving you, IF, (Rom 10v9+10 – it's all about the heart! Rom 6v17, Acts 8v22, Mat 13v15) you really desire to be saved, knowing that you are a sinner on the road to Hell. (**Note that I *didn't* say salvation was the same in every dispensation** – *there's some liars out there!*) The Lord Jesus Christ's Blood is what washes you from all your sins, and He justifies you through it (Rom 5v9), by faith (Rom 5v1). *Works* has *nothing* to do with getting saved - Read Eph 2v8+9, Titus 3v5, 2 Tim 1v9, Gal 3v21-29, Gal 5v4 etc. Hypers such as *Colic-Caldwell* would have children at the age of accountability in Hell! **Example** – Do you think that a boy of 7-10 years of age, who realises he is a sinner, and knows that he will go to Hell when he dies if he doesn't have his sins forgiven, who 'asks' the Lord Jesus Christ to save him, will be saved? *Colic-Caldwell and the Hypers* say God *won't* save him because he *asked* to be 'saved' and 'asking' is a work. Think of the millions of children all over the world who have come through Sunday school yet got saved by *asking* the Lord Jesus Christ to save them. According to the Hypers, they will all go to Hell, because if you *ask God to save you* He *won't* because 'asking' is a work. Now I kid you not ladies and gentleman, this is the mentality of the Hyper-Diaper-cult.

Now as I state all through our ministry, you're saved by grace through faith; 'works' has *nothing* to do with your salvation! 'Prayer' does *not* save you, but if you *ask* God to save you i.e. via *prayer*... He will. **Romans teaches us that we are saved by grace plus *nothing* and Galatians teaches us that we stay saved by grace plus *nothing.***

Romans 10... *not* **according to the Hypers -** In this article we shall straighten out the mess that the Hyper-Diaper cult get into with their cult teaching. Unlike the Hypers, we Bible Believers believe that you are saved once you have put your faith and trust in Jesus Christ. Hypers teach that you have to *do* some sort of 'formula' (sounds kind of 'works' to me don't you think?) They think that it's *by* 'mental assent' that you get saved and teach that if you *call upon God* to save you, He *won't*, because it's a work. (Of course that is *not* what the Scriptures teach, that's *private* interpretation - 2 Pet 1v20). Well we'll let the Lord Jesus Christ, through His word, deal with these *heretics*. We shall *rightly* divide the Scriptures (2 Tim 2v15) rather than *wrest them* (2 Pet 3v16) as the Hyper-Diapers do.

Regarding **Romans 10**, we have the middle chapter of a *three* chapter section dealing specifically

ERRORS OF HYPER-DISPENSATIONALISM

with Israel. Look at Rom 10v1 – '**Israel**', v5 '**Moses**', v19 '**Israel**', v21 '**Israel**'. Note we are in chapter 10, and the number 10 is the number of the Gentiles. Biblical Numerics makes a wonderful study and opens up a whole new world to the Scriptures. So here in Rom 10 there is no greater chapter on Gentile salvation. The 'thou' of v9 is to the Romans to whom Paul is writing. You have '**man**' in v10, as in *any individual* man. You have '**whosoever**' in v11, '**no difference between the Jew and the Greek**' in v12, '**whosoever**' in v13, '**them that are no people**' and '**a foolish nation**' (as *opposed* to the Jews who are provoked '**to jealousy by them**' in v19) Look at v20-21 '**I was made manifest unto them that asked not after me.** *But to Israel* **he saith**...' So the group that didn't ask after God was the Gentiles. Rom 10 is about how *the Gentiles get saved*, and Paul uses that as an example to the Jews he loves (v1).

Rom 10v1 **Brethren, my heart's desire and prayer to God for Israel is, that they might be saved**. Paul is burdened for Israel, his heart is heavy and he desires that all Israel turns to the Lord Jesus Christ as their Saviour, their Messiah. As Christians, our heart should be heavy and burdensome for the lost souls around us, rather than have a hard-heart which couldn't care less that souls get saved like the Hyper-Diapers. They are happy letting souls go to Hell without trying to reach them! What a Satanic cult they are.

v2 **For I bear them record that they have a zeal of God, but not according to knowledge**. The Jews are the prime example of people who are religiously zealous, they are serving God the best way *they know how*, but look at the last phrase of v2... '**but not according to knowledge**'. They may be serving God the best way they know how, they may be doing it to the best of their ability, but they are doing it *absolutely wrong*. Just like the JW's, Mormons, RC's, Muslims, Hyper-Dispensationalists, Calvinists, Post-Tribbers (aka 'Posties') Pentecostals etc. *Wrong, wrong, wrong, wrong!* Their *zeal* is misguided and they focus on all the wrong things. Now I understand that in my list above, some of them *may be saved*, and I only include them because they *major* on 'minors' e.g. '*When did the Body of Christ begin?*' But the rest of these cults and false Religions are certainly 'working' for their salvation and trying to gain self-righteousness (Luke 18v9, Luke 16v15, 1 Sam 16v7, Phil 3v9, Isa 64v6, Rom 10v3, 2 Pet 2v10+12-18 etc.) Their zeal is misguided. You either have *God's righteousness* and go to Heaven when you die, or, you have your *own righteousness* and go to Hell when you die. You don't go to Hell because you commit adultery or murder, neither stealing, lying or swearing. Moses killed a man and went to Heaven. David committed adultery and went to Heaven. Noah got drunk and went to Heaven. Peter cursed and swore and went to Heaven. A man goes to Hell because he looks God in the face and says *'I am better than you are!'* If you reject Jesus Christ as your Saviour then you think you are better than the Lord and His way of salvation (Rom 5v6+8). If Jesus Christ has completely fulfilled the righteousness of the Law (and He has, see v4), then what God offers an unsaved man is the righteousness of a *perfect man*. Any excuse an unsaved man gives for passing up the way to Heaven will be upon his own head. Christ made the way, and there is only one way, through Him. You reject Christ and you have *no hope whatsoever*. It will be the biggest mistake of your life, and will cost you *eternity* in Heaven.

v3 **For they being ignorant of God's righteousness, and going about to establish their own righteousness, have not submitted themselves unto the righteousness of God**. Here in v3 we see the key issue in the Scriptures to man's main problem, i.e. sin and self-righteousness. *How does* man remove his sin and get the righteousness he needs to please God? 99% of the world is trying to 'earn it!' *Keep the Sabbath, keep the commandments, observe the Golden Rule, live by the Sermon on the Mount, take the sacraments, get baptized, live the best you can*... and on and on it goes. Religions and cults all tell you to *work* for your salvation, for your Justification (cf. Eph 2v8+9, Titus 3v5, 2 Tim1v9, Rom 10v4, Gal 5v4, Rom 7v4, Gal 2v16, Gal 3v11+24+25 etc.) God says it's *His way*, man says it's *His wa*y. Man has *no excuse* for rejecting Christ and His righteousness.

CHRISTIAN SOLDIER'S BATTLE NOTES

If he does, he's had it. There is *only one way*, and Jesus Christ is *the* way. John 14v6. If you don't come the Lord's way, then you think you are better than Him and you know more than Him. *You are a wicked liar.* Your own works and righteousness will *never* get you to Heaven, they will only drag you down to Hell.

v4 **For Christ is the end of the law for righteousness to every one that believeth.** Christ is *the end* of *the Law* for *righteousness* to everyone that *believeth*. So a believer gets all the righteousness that was in the Law *through* Jesus Christ, because He kept the Law completely. But notice that the verse said Christ is *the end* of the Law. When Jesus Christ died on the Cross and made the blood atonement for sin, that *ended* that time of the Old Testament (Heb 9v16+17) when righteousness was attributed to a man according to how he kept the Law (Read Ezek 18).

v5 **For Moses describeth the righteousness which is of the law, That the man which doeth those things shall live by them.**

v6 **But the righteousness which is of faith speaketh on this wise, Say not in thine heart, Who shall ascend into heaven? (that is, to bring Christ down from above:)** In v5+6, Paul contrasts '**the righteousness which is of the law**' and '**the righteousness which is of faith**'. The righteousness of the Law in the Old Testament, was given to a man who *did* those things written in the Law and *lived* by them. If he sinned, the proper sacrifices had to be made for him to keep his righteousness. That is the way OT salvation worked because Jesus Christ had not yet come and fulfilled all of the Law and made a permanent sacrifice for sin. **OT and NT salvation are certainly NOT the same.** John 1v17. OT – the Law came by Moses. NT – Grace and truth came by Jesus Christ. OT – The just shall live by *his* faith (Hab 2v4). NT – The just shall live by faith (Rom 1v17, see also Gal 2v20). OT – the saints are dead in trespasses and sins. NT – the saints are born again. OT – Saints went to Abraham's Bosom. NT – Saints go to be with Christ in Heaven. In the NT, the believers are IN Christ and are spiritually circumcised. In the OT, *nobody* was IN Christ (as there was no 'Body'), Christ hadn't even showed up yet. Moreover, throughout the OT, the flesh was so connected with the *soul* that whatever defiled the *flesh* defiled the *soul* too. (See **T**he **M**inistry **Y**ears - **TMY Vol 2 issue 66 pg 7-12, also TMY Vol 2 issue 56 pg 15, and issue 62 pg 9**) The two methods of salvation have only two general commonalities: OT saints had to believe what God said and then they had to *act* on it accordingly. You have to believe what God said about Jesus Christ and then you have to *act* on that information according to the Scriptures. Other than that, there are no similarities. Your salvation is most like that *before* the Law at the time of Abraham. Abraham was saved by grace through faith. But as you see in Rom 4, even Abraham's salvation was not exactly like ours; it is only a 'type'. They're *not* the same. A lot of Christians don't get that, they don't understand that salvation is *different* in *different* dispensations. Here are a few examples of how God saved men in different dispensations...

In Gen 1+2 a man is saved by *works* alone. In those chapters, there is *no faith* involved at all. Adam and Eve are looking right at God - Heb 11v1 **Now faith is ...the evidence of things not seen.** The 'commandment' to Adam in Gen 2 was '*Don't eat off one tree and you'll be ok*'. When Adam and Eve fell, the Lord made them coats of skins. That was *grace!* It took *faith* on their part to put on the coats. So after the fall, Adam and Eve are saved by *grace through faith* – but *not* faith **IN** the Lord Jesus Christ. He was prophesied in Gen 3v15, and God showed them a type of what Christ would do, when He killed *the lamb* (Prov 27v26) and made coats of skin. But Christ was not revealed in the OT. He was *prophesied*, He was *pictured*, He *appeared* as the Angel of the Lord, but His *identity* was hidden (Prov 30v4, Dan 3v25).

From Gen 3 – Exo 20, men are saved by grace through faith, but the faith was in what God *told* each individual. E.g. Abel offered a lamb of his flock; Enoch believed God would judge the world

ERRORS OF HYPER-DISPENSATIONALISM

when Methuselah died so he walked with God; Noah believed God would send a worldwide flood and therefore built an ark. That's the message of Heb 11 (read the chapter before carrying on with this study). *Ruckman continues...* **A *work* was intrinsically connected with each person's belief in what God said.** *Works* completed what *faith* started. These Christians who say that in every dispensation it is only faith that saves and works has nothing to do with salvation, are just shallow students of the Scriptures. Read Ezek 18 for an eye opener. So salvation by grace through faith between Gen 3 – Exod 20 is *not the same* as salvation by grace through faith from Pentecost (Acts 2) to the Rapture. Faith was *not* placed **IN** Jesus Christ, and salvation was not necessarily complete upon *belief* as ours is.

In Exo 20, the Law enters, and it runs about 1,500 years to the ministry of John the Baptist (Mat 11v13, Luke 16v16). The Law is a set standard of righteousness that applies to *all* who are under it. It is a ***faith and works*** set up. Under the Law, you had to *keep* the Law. If you *didn't keep* the Law, you could lose your salvation and not get it back (as in the case of King Saul in the OT). In the OT you could lose your salvation and then *get it back again* as did Samson.

There is much confusion among Christians regarding Solomon, as to whether he was saved or not. He's not listed among the 'heroes of the faith' in Heb 11, but then again neither were others. There is also no indication that he was saved in the NT. But, according to the promise made to David in 2 Sam 7v15, God said... **my mercy shall not depart away from him, as I took it from Saul, whom I put away before thee**. But Solomon died an idolater and in rebellion to God's physical punishment for his sins – 1 Kings 11v40. Was Solomon saved?

The problem with the Law is that no one keeps it fully. When an OT saint failed to keep the Law in some point, then he was given a *blood* sacrifice to die in his place. If he *didn't* make that *blood* sacrifice or *trust in it*, then he was lost. *Ruckman continues...* There were times, in the prophets, when God was fed up with the sacrifices made by Jews because they were made by habit and *not* by faith or because they were made as a replacement for works altogether; i.e. they continued *in sin expecting* the *blood* sacrifice to make everything all right.

Under the Law it was not enough to have faith without works or to have works without faith. You had to have *both*, and you had to be in that state when you died or you wouldn't make it. The OT had no 'eternal security' for its saints, just read Ezek 18. These boys who don't believe that salvation in the OT was a faith *plus* works set up... just read Ezek 18.

The Lord always seems to have His exceptions though, and in the OT it was David. David committed *two* 'unpardonable' sins, 'adultery and murder!' No sacrifice was provided by God for either. Yet, God put away David's sins (Isa 55v3, Acts 13v34). David is the exception *not* the rule.

If you were a Jew under the Law, you would sweat out the Day of Atonement *each year*. You would be listening to those bells on the high priest's garment. If you made it through that, you would have to bring a lamb to the tabernacle every time you messed up. The next year you would do the same thing all over again. The OT saints couldn't have their sins *taken away* - Heb 10v3+4+11.

So next we come to the Gospels up to Acts 2, and this is the most difficult to define doctrinally, for Christ was here on earth while the Law was *still in effect*. It is an *intermediate period* and the most *unstable* period in the Bible. You have the 'local church', but *not* the Body of Christ; you have an organism (the vine) that is not Christ's Body. You have promises of eternal security (John 10v21-29) that don't match the Pauline epistles (Eph 5v30).

From Acts 2 to the Rapture, salvation is absolutely clear, it is *by grace through faith in* Jesus Christ and His atonement... plus *nothing, no works*. Ruckman says Acts 2 because that is the first time the baptism of the Holy Spirit occurs (Acts 1v5), and believers are placed *into the Body of Christ* by the baptism of the Holy Spirit (1 Cor 12v13).

The 6th system of salvation is during the seven year Tribulation (Jacob's Trouble). Again, it is a *faith plus works* set up! Just read the following verses... Rev 12v17 + Rev 14v12.

Finally, you have the Millennium and Eternity where you no longer have *faith* because the King is right there where you can see Him, even Hell is right where it can be clearly seen – Isa 66v24. Read Rev 22v14 – *works, works, works,* and no faith.

When those nations which survive the Tribulation stand before the King, they are judged by their works; feeding the hungry, giving drink to the thirsty, taking in strangers, clothing the naked, comforting the sick, visiting the imprisoned. Those who *did those things* enter the Millennial kingdom. Those who *don't*, go to Hell (Mat 25v31-46). Faith doesn't appear one time in the passage. If a man preaches in the Millennium, he is to be thrust through by his parents (Zech 13v3). Now what do you make of that in light of 1 Cor 1v21 + 12v28 + Rev 19v10, *if* salvation is the same in all ages?

Paul says in Heb 8v11 - No Bible prophets, No Bible preachers, No Bible teachers. Why not? Because ...**faith cometh by hearing, and hearing by the word of God**. Rom 10v17 and ...**faith is the substance of things HOPED FOR, the evidence of things not seen**. Heb 11v1. And as Paul said back in Romans 8v24... **hope that is seen is not hope: for what a man seeth, why doth he yet hope for?** There is no 'faith' required in the Millennium or Eternity.

Ruckman gives us a great golden nugget of Scriptural truth by stating that every *heresy* in this age is a *misplaced truth* of God (*Heresy is truth misplaced*) that belongs to another age. Do you want to keep the Sabbath? Then wait until the Tribulation / Jacob's Trouble, and you'll be completely Scriptural. Do you want to belong to the same 'church' as the 144,000? Then wait until Daniel's 70th Week (aka the Tribulation). Do you want to get saved by receiving the Lord Jesus Christ and stay saved by keeping the Ten Commandments? Then wait until the Tribulation. Do you want to die and go to an intermediate state that is neither Heaven nor Hell? Well that's the fifth seal of Rev 6v9... IN the Tribulation. The *heresies* taught by the JW's, Roman Catholics, Seventh Day Adventists, Charismatics etc. are 'truths' *misplaced*. They are taking Scripture for themselves that is directed to people in the OT, the Tribulation or the Millennium.

Back to Rom 10v6 **But the righteousness which is of faith speaketh on this wise, Say not in thine heart, Who shall ascend into heaven? (that is, to bring Christ down from above**:) Say not in thine heart, who shall ascend into heaven? That is what NASA has been trying to do since 1961. The actual goal of the space program is to try to prove there is no God by finding life on other planets, so the scientists can say that life evolved in different places in different ways in the universe. Going up into space is nothing but trying to prove there is no God! Think about the *billions* they have spent on this totally useless act, and what they could have spent the money on.

v6 ...**that is, to bring Christ down from above** – The word 'Christ' means 'anointed'; it is the NT version of Messiah. The Devil is called the 'anointed cherub' in Ezek 28v14. So Satan is a 'Christ' and 'Messiah' too. That is why the Scriptures distinguish 'the Lord's Christ' in Luke 2v26. It's because there is another 'Jesus', another 'Spirit' and another 'Gospel' – 2 Cor 11v4, Gal 1v8+9. The Devil, from which the Antichrist gets his power (Rev 13v2), comes down to earth out of Heaven, in the Tribulation (Rev 12v8). And of course, some day 'the Lord himself shall descend from heaven with a shout' – 1 Thes 4v16. No man can go up to Heaven and force Jesus Christ to leave His seat at the right hand of God the Father and come down to earth. So a Roman Catholic 'priest' standing at the 'altar' consecrating 'the host' is an absolute joke.

ERRORS OF HYPER-DISPENSATIONALISM

v7 Or, Who shall descend into the deep? (that is, to bring up Christ again from the dead.) In the same way, no one is going to dig in the earth and bring Christ up 'again' from the grave (Rom 6v10)... *He isn't there.* (Mat 28v6) Jesus Christ's bones shall *never* be found because Jesus Christ arose from the dead. The Lord's Christ has already come down from Heaven, and He will come again, this time with unsheathed power. But when He returns, He will come in His own time. He has already died *once for all* (Heb 10v10) and risen to give justification (Rom 4v25) and life (1 Cor 15v22).

Now, Paul is discussing 'the righteousness which is of faith'. That righteousness is by the death, burial, and resurrection of Jesus Christ (1 Cor 15v1-4). Given that, what could any man have done to make Jesus Christ do that the first time, much less repeat that sacrifice like the Catholic priest tries to do at the Mass. And of course, the answer is *nothing*. The Lord made the provision for giving you His righteousness based on His love for sinners.

v8 But what saith it? The word is nigh thee, even in thy mouth, and in thy heart: that is, the word of faith, which we preach; *Ruckman has some great comments here...* If you are going to get saved, you are going to have to believe '**the word of faith, which we preach**'. Moreover, that word isn't far off so that you have to work to get it. The Scriptures say, '**The word is nigh thee, even in thy mouth, and in thy heart.**' So if a fellow wants to know what the Lord says, he can have access to it. And if a man wants to be saved, '**the word of faith**' is right at the two places that enable him to trust Christ: the *heart* and the *mouth* cf. v9+10. God will make sure that any man who really wants to know how to be saved will get '**the word**'. But again, this is where us Bible Believers part company with the Hyper-Diapers, because if you use the 'Romans Road' to lead someone to Christ (the Hypers *never* lead souls to Christ), then v9+10+13 are the point where you tell the sinner exactly *how* to be saved. A man is saved *when* he *believes* the Gospel (1 Cor 15v1-4). In Rom 10v9+10+13, Paul explains *how* to believe the Gospel.

The first thing is to *confess* Jesus Christ. Now if you think that is a *work* you're a nut. When you 'confess' something, you admit or declare that it is so. When a man gets saved, he will confess Christ as the *only way* that he can get to Heaven. He will *confess* that Jesus Christ died for his sins. He will *confess* to God (in prayer) that he is *trusting* Christ *alone* for salvation. Many Gospel tracts quote 1 John 1v9 as part of the plan of salvation. They equate the *confession of sins* mentioned in that verse with the *repentance* that should occur when a sinner *trusts* Christ as Saviour (Acts 20v21).

Yes, a man must realise that he is a sinner and under the judgment of God. There is no way that a man can trust Christ without admitting that is so. But when a man gets saved, he doesn't need to confess every sin he has committed to *get saved*. **Repentance *before* salvation is a turning *from* a state of being.** These *nuts* that say you shouldn't repent, just don't understand what repentance is. **Before salvation you are a sinner under the wrath of God. At salvation you turn from that state of sin to receive Jesus Christ and become a son of God.** That has absolutely *nothing* to do with *any kind of works.* Acts 26v18, Acts 20v21. You are obligated to do works meet for repentance - Acts 26v20. *After* salvation you should live for Jesus Christ and show others that you have *repented* and have been *saved*

Confession of sins is different though. *After* salvation, when you sin (and *every* Christian still does), you should still repent. Now Ruckman mentions something here that the Hyper-Diapers just can't grasp... **Repentance *after* salvation is different from repentance *before* salvation.** Technically speaking, ***after*** **salvation, *if you are saved*, you are no longer a sinner, you are a saint who commits sin. There is a difference.** As a saint, you do not *repent* to receive Christ. **You are already IN Christ, and you are no longer under the wrath of God.**

CHRISTIAN SOLDIER'S BATTLE NOTES

After salvation, you turn from your sin to the service of Jesus Christ (Eph 4v25-32). But having sinned, you have also broken your fellowship with God. To restore that fellowship you must go to the Lord and tell Him exactly what you have done that was wrong, the individual acts. So you are not repenting of being IN sin, because no saved person lives IN sin, a saved person lives IN Christ! You are repenting of *committing* sin, and to do that you must *confess* it. So 1 John 1v9 has *nothing* to do with 'salvation' at all, and to use it to get a sinner to repent will only confuse him when he gets saved and finds out that he must confess his sins.

Now, before going on, let's get this matter sorted, so that it's clear. A lost man can *confess* his sins to God, or even to Jesus Christ, all he wants, and still go to Hell. Judas did (Mat 27v3-5), Balaam did (Num 22v34), Pharaoh did (Exod 10v16+17). Every one of them confessed that he was a sinner and confessed his sin, and every one of them ended up in Hell after he did it. Confession of sins isn't salvation. (*This is where the Hyper-Diapers get all screwed up, especially in regard to 'prayer'*). Confessing your sins won't save you. Anything short of a man turning to Jesus Christ for salvation and confessing Him as Lord and Saviour is *not* salvation. Confessing your sins maybe 'half-way' but it still falls short. (Mr Hyper-Diaper please note the apostrophes on half-way before kicking all your dollies out of the pram!)

v9 **That if thou shalt confess with thy mouth the Lord Jesus, and shalt believe in thine heart that God hath raised him from the dead, thou shalt be saved**. Confessing your *sins* has nothing to do with it. The next thing to getting saved is to *believe in thine heart that God hath raised Him from the dead*. The resurrection makes the atonement *efficacious* (effective) to a sinner. The resurrection makes the atonement effective to us – it brings a change in our lives. If all Christ did was to die for sin, then you could not apply the atonement to yourself. Paul said... **And if Christ be not raised, your faith is vain; ye are yet in your sins**. 1 Cor 15v17. Without the resurrection, the best you could hope for would be Abraham's Bosom in the centre of the earth. You could never make it to Heaven. If Jesus Christ hadn't risen from the dead, then He would have been like any other *man* (Rom 1v4). If Jesus Christ had not risen from the dead, then you could not be justified completely before God (Rom 4v25). Without the resurrection, you could lose whatever salvation you had gotten (Acts 13v34). If there was no resurrection, then you have no *new man* (Rom 6v4), you could not be born again.

So there are no *'ifs, ands or buts'* about it. If a man confesses Jesus Christ with his mouth and *believes in the resurrection* of Jesus Christ *in his heart*, the promise is **'thou shalt be saved'**. That is *how* you believe the Gospel. That is all there is to it. Hyper-Diapers and Calvinists make it too complicated that they get the Gospel so screwed up in their own tiny minds. But how do you believe in your heart? What is heart belief? Look at v10... **For with the heart man believeth unto righteousness; and with the mouth confession is made unto salvation**. How can you tell that you are believing with your heart and not with your head? You can tell that you're believing with your heart when you *rely* on a thing; you *trust* it; you *lean* on it. *That* is 'heart belief'. When a child calls out to the Lord Jesus Christ to save him from his sins, he is trusting in the Lord Jesus implicitly, and relying *totally* on Him for his salvation. The actual *prayer* didn't save him, Jesus Christ did. He asked the Lord to save Him and the Lord heard his prayer and answered his call.

I can 'intellectually assent' to the fact that my car will get me to my next appointment, *but I don't believe it in my heart until I get into my car and drive*. A man can agree that all the facts of the Gospel are so, he can repeat with complete sincerity the Apostle's Creed every Sunday, and he will still wind up in Hell. Belief of the head is *knowing about* Christ (e.g. the Hyper-Diapers); belief of the heart is *trusting* IN Christ (Bible Believers). *See the difference?* I *trust* Christ with **all of my heart**. John Davis is 100% depending on, relying on, and trusting IN Jesus Christ to keep me out of Hell. Hyper-Diapers 'mental-assent-gospel' will lead him to Hell.

ERRORS OF HYPER-DISPENSATIONALISM

The question for the sinner is this... '*What are you relying on to keep you out of Hell?*' Hyper-Diapers just tell you to 'believe' in Jesus just like the JW's, RC's, Mormons etc. even the Devil 'believes' in Jesus. I'm not believing with my head, but my heart; I'm trusting in Jesus Christ for my salvation. Have you appropriated the sacrifice of the Lord Jesus Christ for yourself? The heart and the mouth, spiritually, are connected (Mat 12v34). You 'talk' about things you love (Mat 12v35).

Let me reiterate what has already been said about prayer in salvation - It is obvious that the mere 'act' of praying itself saves no one. In Luke 18v10-14, two men go to pray at the temple, and that account ends with one man saved and the other lost. Cornelius prayed on a regular basis (Acts 10v2), and God honoured his prayers (Acts 10v4). But Cornelius did not get saved until he heard Peter preach (Acts 10v34-43) and he believed on Christ (Acts 10v43-47). So prayer in and of *itself* doesn't save a man.

This *new* Hyper-Diaper-cult says that if a man 'prays' to get saved (or more specifically, prays the 'sinners prayer'), then he is *lost* because prayer is a 'work'. So instead, all a man need do is 'assent' to the fact that Christ died for him and thank God for having already forgiven his sins... *which no child would understand I hasten to add. Children don't get saved under the Hyper-Diaper system of 'works-assent' and 'understanding', hence why they are not soul-winners and couldn't lead a soul to Christ if their lives depended upon it.*

Now there are all kinds of things wrong with the Hypers 'assent-Gospel', not the least of which is that *giving of thanks* to God for having already saved you *is a prayer ('work' according to them).*

Now boys and girls, 'prayer' is a 'prayer' whether you *ask* God to save you or you *thank* God for saving you. If 'prayer' can't save you because it's a 'work', then for the Lord's sake (as well as your own) *don't thank God for saving you!* You would be mixing 'works' with your faith, so you wouldn't be saved! (Eph 2v8+9)

This is the kind of nonsense that is being taught by Hyper-mid-Acts-dispensationalists today (e.g. Ed-Pfenny and Colic-Caldwell etc.) As Ruckman says... Hypers are only interested in 'retreads' rather saving souls, that's why *none of them* win souls (Colic-Caldwell, Ed-Pfenny etc.) All these heretics do is confuse weak sheep. They just cast doubt in the mind of a weak Christian's faith, as to whether he is saved or not.

Now let's have a look at this matter not only from a Scriptural point of view, but from a practical one as well. There is nothing in the Scriptures (including here in Rom 10v9+10+13) that says you *have* to pray to get saved. There is no evidence that the Ethiopian eunuch prayed to get saved, even though he *did* 'confess' with *his* mouth (Acts 8v37). As far as we know Cornelius and his household did not pray to get saved (Acts 10v43-47). At the same time though, you can't say it is wrong to pray to get saved, although the Hypers do.

If *any* sinner prays, expressing the **belief he has in his heart on the Lord Jesus Christ and His death, burial, and resurrection**, do you really think the Lord is going to reject 'an act of faith' IN Jesus Christ, expressed through prayer, after He said '...him that cometh to me I will in no wise cast out' (John 6v37)? Not according to John Wesley, Peter Ruckman, Larkin, Sunday and a billion others, but God will reject you according to the Hyper-Diapers.

If prayer is a form of *calling upon the name of the Lord* (and it certainly is), then if a man confesses his faith IN Jesus Christ to God *in prayer* then he is saved. He might not have to do it just that way, but if he does, he *isn't* 'working' his way to Heaven. After all, it isn't the 'prayer' that saves him anyway, it is the Lord Jesus Christ that saves him. Jesus Christ saves the sinner when he places his faith and trust IN Him, and the same Lord who told the sinner to believe, also told him to *confess*

CHRISTIAN SOLDIER'S BATTLE NOTES

Him with the mouth and call upon His name. You can do both *'in prayer'* (Rom 10v13). It's that simple. Ruckman goes on... 'Practically speaking, it is good for a sinner to pray when he gets saved. Nobody alive remembers when he was born physically, but most people have a birth certificate that tells them *where* they were born and *when* they were born. When a man *prays* to get saved, that gives him a tangible time to which he can point and say... 'That's the time and place where I placed my faith IN Jesus Christ and was saved'. It can strengthen the Christian's assurance'.

The 2nd thing that comes up is what if a man doesn't confess Christ when he gets saved? What you have here is a general rule. The verse is constructed in a way similar to Mark 16v16 **He that believeth and is baptized shall be saved; but he that believeth not shall be damned**. Obviously in *that* passage, salvation is conditioned on belief, *not* belief *plus* baptism. But, if a man is saved by belief in the Gospel (Mark 16v15), *then as a general rule*, he will be baptized. (Not according to the Hypers though). The exceptions to that doesn't overthrow the rule, they *prove* the rule. Generally speaking, when a man receives Christ into his heart, it will come forth *out of his mouth.* (Luke 6v45)

In John 12v42, there is a bunch of 'chief rulers' that believed on Christ, '**but because of the Pharisees they did not confess him, lest they should be put out of the synagogue**'. When Jesus Christ addressed these men in John 12v44-50, He addressed their belief, *not* their lack of confession. He made it very clear that it was their *belief* that saved them – John 12v44-46. Were they cowards? Yes! Did they love the wrong thing? Yes! Were they lost? No! Joseph of Arimathea was among that group, and eventually he came forward and *confessed* Jesus Christ – John 19v38. Nicodemus was in that group, and he came out for Jesus Christ too (John 19v39). In fact, in Acts 6v7, we discover that a *great* company of the priests were obedient to the faith.

So generally speaking, a saved man *will confess* Jesus Christ to others. I did. As soon as I was saved, I couldn't stop *confessing* Jesus Christ to others, including my own family, who took it very badly. I just couldn't stop talking about Jesus Christ. But as already discussed, there is no 'set way' (e.g. like 'prayer') that you do it. When a baby gets hungry he cries to let someone know. When a sinner makes up his mind that he needs to get saved, he will call upon the name of the Lord. At some point in the future, that saved sinner will *confess* the Lord Jesus Christ. (Mat 10v32 as an example).

v11 **For the scripture saith, Whosoever believeth on him shall not be ashamed**. Are you ashamed of the Lord Jesus Christ? Do you miss opportunities to testify and confess Jesus Christ to folks because you're ashamed? If you truly get saved, you really love the Lord, you won't stop talking about Him and you will not be ashamed. The Lord puts us all in many different situations so that we can testify of Him, let's make every one of them count, asking the Lord to give us the strength and boldness to do so. Ps 40v3, Ps 71v15-18, Eph 6v19 etc.

v12 **For there is no difference between the Jew and the Greek: for the same Lord over all is rich unto all that call upon him**. This verse, v12, *defines* the 'whosoever' of v13. 'Whosoever' does *not* mean 'the elect', it means whatever Jew or Gentile that called upon the name of the Lord shall be saved.

v13 **For whosoever shall call upon the name of the Lord shall be saved**. Gentiles included!

v14 **How then shall they call on him in whom they have not believed? and how shall they believe in him of whom they have not heard? and how shall they hear without a preacher? 15 And how shall they preach, except they be sent? as it is written, How beautiful are the feet of them that preach the gospel of peace, and bring glad tidings of good things!** Hypers don't preach the Gospel. *Why?* Because they don't know or understand what the Gospel is. They think that you have to somehow *mystically* 'mental ascend' for salvation, rather than *call upon the name of the Lord.* When God sends the Gospel out, He sends it by preachers. The word 'apostle' means one that is *sent*. The original 12 apostles were sent out to preach (Mat 10v7) Paul was sent to preach the Gospel (1 Cor 1v17) Paul said '**it pleased God by the foolishness of preaching to save them that believe.**' Now when it comes to preaching the Gospel, it is *not* limited to an 'ordained' minister, standing behind the pulpit. 'Preaching' the Gospel is simply telling someone the Gospel message of 1 Cor 15v1-4, and that is the *obligation* of *every* Christian.

Look at Phil 1v12-17 – Notice in that passage that you have two groups that 'preach Christ' (v16), and nobody in the passage is a pastor, a Sunday School teacher, a missionary, an apostle, a deacon etc. They are simply 'brethren' that 'speak the word without fear' (v14) One group is not even doing it for the right reason (v15+16), and Paul still calls it preaching. So that means *every* Christian should 'preach' the Gospel to someone in some way.

Whenever the Gospel is preached, some people reject it while others believe it. Those who believe the Gospel '*call upon the name of the Lord*' (v13) for salvation. Rom 10v15 is a quote taken from Isa 52v7 and Nahum 1v15. Of course, it is another example of Paul taking verses that, 'doctrinally' are targeted at the Second Advent and the beginning of the Millennium, and applying them to the Church Age. Notice again the ***dual application***.

All three Scriptures (Isa 52v7, Nahum 1v15, and Rom 10v15) all speak of 'peace'. In Nahum 1v15, that peace is the temporary peace after 2 Kings 19, where God delivers Judah out of the hand of Sennacherib, and the Jews are to keep the vows and feasts which they promised to God if He would deliver them. Isa 52v7 speaks of permanent peace which the Lord sends when Jesus reigns as King in Jerusalem in the Millennium. Rom 10v15 is speaking of the *spiritual* peace that the Lord gives to those who believe the Gospel.

Back to v15 – the Lord says that the Gospel of peace is a part of the Christians armour... 'Your feet shod with the preparation of the Gospel of peace' (Eph 6v15). We as Christians should be ready to go anywhere, at any time, to preach the Gospel to any one. Ruckman continues... Any Christian who is *not* actively engaged in some way to win the lost to Christ is a *heretic*, despite what he may profess. He is *not* fighting the 'good fight' as he should. Hypers don't preach the Gospel, they just attack Christians continually, telling them that they're not saved because they prayed to the Lord asking Him to forgive them, *and that is a work*. Every Christian should be able to *deliver* the Gospel when an opportunity arises. You should be able to 'preach' it in any situation if given half a chance, but can you? The Hypers can't, the Calvinists can't, but what about you? What kind of a witness are you for Jesus Christ? When was the last time you *preached* the Gospel?

v16 **But they have not all obeyed the gospel. For Esaias saith, Lord, who hath believed our report?** This is another quote from Isaiah 53v1. Like we said previously, not everyone obeys the Gospel, in fact most, reject it sadly. Note here that 'obeying the Gospel' is equated with 'believing the Gospel.' It's believing the report God gave of His Son and *trusting only in Him* for salvation.

v17 **So then faith cometh by hearing, and hearing by the word of God**. The more of the word of God a person hears, the more he is able to understand and receive what God says. It is so important to get the word of God out to sinners, whether it's by street preaching, CDs and DVDs, tracting, one-on-one reading the Scriptures to someone, but *get the word of God out!* Every Christian reading this ought to saturate the area where he lives with tracts. Sow the seed of the word of God *everywhere*. Everyone has a certain amount of faith and light within him, to receive the Gospel (Rom 12v10), yet most reject their conscience leading them to the truth, and therefore they are 'educated' *out* of believing in God. Schools are educating children *out* of believing in God by teaching them evolution. The word of God is key to increasing your faith, therefore we all ought to be reading the Scriptures daily and meditating upon them. If you choose to listen to what God is saying to you and act upon it, the Lord will give you more. If you choose to ignore or reject what God has said, the Lord will *take away* the truth that you have.

v18 **But I say, Have they not heard? Yes verily, their sound went into all the earth, and their words unto the ends of the world**. *But what about the heathen?* This question comes up a lot in conversations. Here in v18 Paul says that the heathen *have heard*, which implies that they have had a *preacher*. He then quotes Ps 19v4 to prove that the Gospel has been preached to them. Ruckman goes on... The antecedents of 'their' in Ps 19 are DAY and NIGHT (Ps 19v2) In this case, the preacher isn't even a human or a Christian. In Ps 19, DAY and NIGHT 'preach' to every man, woman, and child on the face of the earth! *What do they preach?* 1) There is a Creator! 2) There is a Godhead that is a Trinity (from the *three* different types of rays the sun puts out) 3) The Lord is against the world and the world goes against the Lord (the earth rotates against the movement of the sun across the sky) 4) The Lord dies (the sun sets in a red sky) 5) The Lord is resurrected (the sun comes *up* every morning) 6) The Lord is coming again (When the sun rises out of a red sky) 7) The Lord has a counterpart that reflects His light (moon) 8) The church starts out small and grows big and then falls into apostasy (the monthly cycle of the moon).

The heathen prove that they know these things because nearly all heathen worship is based on *sun* worship, with the moon goddess being the sun's consort. Many times the 'queen of heaven', the moon, has a virgin-born son. So the heathen testify against themselves.

Having dealt with the heathen, Paul then asks, '**Did not Israel know?**' (v19) And the implication again is *yes*, they *did* know. To prove this, Paul quotes Deut 32v21 and Isa 65v1+2.

v19 **But I say, Did not Israel know? First Moses saith, I will provoke you to jealousy by them that are no people, and by a foolish nation I will anger you**. In v19 Paul quotes Deut 32v21. The 'foolish nation' is obviously the Gentiles, but notice that it is *one* 'nation', not many. The reference is not merely to the Gentiles as a whole, but to *saved* Gentiles that compose the '**holy nation**' of 1 Pet 2v9. If there is any doubt about that interpretation, look at Rom 11v11. Speaking of Israel, Paul says... **I say then, Have they stumbled that they should fall? God forbid: but rather through their fall salvation is come unto the Gentiles, for to provoke them to jealousy**. Rom 11v11. God does this because of the character and empty worship given Him by the Jews. Notice back in Deut 32v20, that God describes the Jews of the New Testament as '**children in whom is no faith**.' They made the Lord jealous '**with that which is not God**' (Deut 32v12) and they made the Lord angry with things that were empty and meaningless to Him. That's the kind of stuff that was going on in the days of Christ and Paul.

Jesus said... **He that honoureth not the Son honoureth not the Father which hath sent him**. John 5v23 **Jesus answered, Ye neither know me, nor my Father: if ye had known me, ye should have known my Father also**. John 8v19 **If God were your Father, ye would love me:** John 8v42 **Ye are of your father the devil, and the lusts of your father ye will do**. John 8v44 **He that is of God heareth God's words: ye therefore hear them not, because ye are not of God**. John 8v47. These are the reasons why God was jealous and angry! In light of that, the Lord made the Jews jealous. If you want to see how little God *had to go* to make the Jews mad with jealousy, just read Luke 4v24-29 where all Jesus had to do was to state *two* Bible *facts* about God's dealing with the Gentiles in the Old Testament, and the Jews of Nazareth became so angry that they tried to murder Him.

Paul's situation was a little better. The Jews in Jerusalem were willing to listen to Paul's testimony up to the point where he said the words 'Gentiles', then they went 'ballistic' - Acts 22v21-23.

v20 **But Esaias is very bold, and saith, I was found of them that sought me not; I was made manifest unto them that asked not after me.** v21 **But to Israel he saith, All day long I have stretched forth**

my hands unto a disobedient and gainsaying people. Spiritually speaking, you can make the 'day' of v21, the lifetime of a man. God calls men early in life, the morning, to get saved. In John 21, Jesus comes to the disciples, after they had been fishing all night and caught nothing, and He feeds them in the *morning*. The Lord will seek a man to be saved during the 'noon-time' of his life, middle age. He saved the Samaritan woman, in John 4, when she came at noon to fetch water. And the Lord will save a man in the *evening* of his life like He did Nicodemus who came to Him by night, in John 3. If a man wants to get saved, the Lord is right there to save him. The problem is when a sinner is stubborn and self-willed, and clings to his own self-righteousness (Luke 18v9, Luke 16v15, 1 Sam 16v7, Phil 3v9, Isa 64v6, Rom 10v3, 2 Pet 2v10+12-18). And that brings us back to what Paul said at the beginning of the chapter. The Jews were clinging to their own self-righteousness and would not let go and receive God's righteousness. (2 Cor 5v21)

God offers His salvation to *all*... if you go to Hell because you refuse it, it will be your own fault. You either die IN your sins or you die with your sins forgiven by Jesus Christ... the choice is yours.

If you call upon the Lord to save you He will save you! If you pray asking God to save you, He will save you... no matter what the Hyper-Diapers tell you.

Another Hyper-Diaper error...

Hypers also think the Bride of Christ IS Israel *not* the church. All Hyper-Diapers get the *two wives* messed up because they *wrongly* divide the Scriptures. As Bible Believers, we just let the Scriptures speak and by rightly dividing them, we see who the two wives are and who the 'husbands' are. Ruckman has a great note on this is his RRB... Isa 54v6-8 **For the LORD hath called thee as a woman forsaken and grieved in spirit, and a wife of youth, when thou wast refused, saith thy God. For a small moment have I forsaken thee; but with great mercies will I gather thee. In a little wrath I hid my face from thee for a moment; but with everlasting kindness will I have mercy on thee, saith the LORD thy Redeemer.** The WIFE of v6-8 here is NOT the Church, the Bride of Christ (Eph 1v22+23 **And hath put all things under his feet, and gave him to be the head over all things to the church, Which is his body, the fulness of him that filleth all in all**. Compare with... Eph 5v25-32 **Husbands, love your wives, even as Christ also loved the church, and gave himself for it; That he might sanctify and cleanse it with the washing of water by the word, That he might present it to himself a glorious church, not having spot, or wrinkle, or any such thing; but that it should be holy and without blemish. So ought men to love their wives as their own bodies. He that loveth his wife loveth himself. For no man ever yet hated his own flesh; but nourisheth and cherisheth it, even as the Lord the church: For we are members of his body, of his flesh, and of his bones. For this cause shall a man leave his father and mother, and shall be joined unto his wife, and they two shall be one flesh. This is a great mystery: but I speak concerning Christ and the church.** 2 Cor 11v2 **For I am jealous over you with godly jealousy: for I have espoused you to one husband, that I may present you as a chaste virgin to Christ.**) ...it is Israel, the BRIDE of God the Father! See...Isa 54v5 **For thy Maker is thine husband; the LORD of hosts is his name; and thy Redeemer the Holy One of Israel; The God of the whole earth shall he be called**. The passage is explained in Hosea 2 (read it). Hyper-Diapers *confuse* these *two* wives and make the New Jerusalem a Jewish city when it is *not*. The New Jerusalem is **the Lamb's wife** not the Father's. (Rev 21v9 **And there came unto me one of the seven angels which had the seven vials full of the seven last plagues, and talked with me, saying, Come hither, I will shew thee the bride, the Lamb's wife. And he carried me away in the spirit to a great and high mountain, and shewed me that great city, the holy Jerusalem, descending out of heaven from God**) ...So John 14v1-3 **Let not your heart be troubled: ye believe in God, believe also in me. In my Father's house are many mansions: if it were not so, I would have told you. I go to prepare a place for you. And if I go and prepare a place for you, I will come again, and receive you unto myself; that where I am, there ye may be also.** ...

is for the Christian (Gal 4v26 **But Jerusalem which is above is free, which is the mother of us all.**) *not* the Jew. (See also Isaiah 62v5, Hosea 2v19-20. **Israel is the Bride of God the Father and the Church is the Bride of Christ**, 2 Cor 11v2, Eph 5v25-32 is plain in the light of Genesis 2v22-24. The Hypers appear to have missed both passages)

A thought on the 'sin unto death' – 1 John 5v16+17, Rom 6v16 - David committed sin with Bathsheba and was *guilty* of 'a sin unto death' – i.e. there was *no sacrifice* for the sin of adultery and murder. (See TfT! NEWS Issue 60 page 18). Yet he didn't die for his sin. God was gracious and merciful to both David and Bathsheba. 2 Sam 12v13 **And David said unto Nathan, I have sinned against the LORD. And Nathan said unto David, The LORD also hath put away thy sin; thou shalt not die**. David should have died because of the Law - Lev 20v10 **And the man that committeth adultery with another man's wife, even he that committeth adultery with his neighbour's wife, the adulterer and the adulteress shall surely be put to death**. God's *grace* saved David, something the Hyper-Diapers can't understand as it's outside of Paul and the 'Dispensation of Grace'. The Law is *not* made void under this 'Dispensation of Grace' as Paul stated in Rom 3v31 **Do we then make void the law through faith? God forbid: yea, we establish the law**. But the Law has *nothing* to do with salvation today. Stauffer in his book 'One Book Rightly Divided' says, in regard to the Hyper-Dispensationalists... 'Hyper-Dispensationalists want no law established, (they stand *against* Paul notice - Rom 3v21) desire no rules for living; and oppose any attempt to present the truth concerning application of the law to a Christian's daily walk with God. These individuals (Hyper-Diapers) consider the law to be outdated and obsolete... and their reaction to the law seems more rooted in their *hidden agenda*, than in sincere search for the truth. They desire to avoid the law's explicit guidance and convicting properties.' The Hyper-Diapers therefore ignore, change or spiritualise many of Paul's clear statements concerning the law e.g. 1 Tim 1v8 **But we know that the law is good, if a man use it lawfully**; Hyper-Diapers pass over verses like these, this is why they are very weak and shallow students of the word of God, they just can't reconcile these kind of Scriptures regarding *the law* in the Christian's daily life. This is another reason why none of them live *godly, holy lives for the Lord*, while serving Him and reaching lost sinners with the Gospel. All Hyper-Diapers do is *chop-up* the Bible and *wrongly divide it.* We are *not* to ignore *the law*, we are to *use it* as did the apostle Paul... lawfully. Hyper-Diapers are very carnal Christians, if they are saved that is, because they don't understand the place that the law has in the Christian's life. None of them know how to preach on the Law. Christians are not *under the Law*, (Rom 10v4, 7v4, Gal 5v4, 2v16, 3v11, Rom 6v14+15, Gal 3v23, 4v21, 5v18) in the same sense that Israel was under the Law. The purpose of the law has changed for the Christian. Prior to the Cross, if a man fulfilled the requirements under the law, he was temporarily righteous (1 Kings 8v32, 2 Chron 6v23, Psalm 1v5+6, Ezek 18v24 etc.) However, if he sinned and did not fulfil the necessary sacrifices, he could *die in his sins* (Ezek 18v21+24). Paul refers to this righteousness 'which is of the Law' as one's 'own righteousness!' Phil 3v9 **And be found in him, not having mine own righteousness, which is of the law, but that which is through the faith of Christ, the righteousness which is of God by faith**: You had to have the correct *faith* and the correct *works* to be saved. Israel often sought *the law of righteousness without faith.* Rom 9v31+32 **But Israel, which followed after the law of righteousness, hath not attained to the law of righteousness. Wherefore? Because they sought it not by faith, but as it were by the works of the law. For they stumbled at that stumblingstone**; But you couldn't get to Heaven this way, hence why no one did in the OT. You can only go to Heaven by applying the shed Blood of Jesus Christ, *not* an animal, and *not* by keeping the law. Gal **2v21 I do not frustrate the grace of God: for if righteousness come by the law, then Christ is dead in vain**. Read Heb 9+10 noting Heb 9v12+13. The *only* way to get to Heaven is by receiving Christ's righteousness (2 Cor 5v21); works today play *no part* in anyone's salvation, but they did before the Cross under the Law (Gal 2v16). Christ ended the Law (Rom 10v4) *for righteousness*, i.e. getting saved, but it still has a part to play in the Christians life. The Law has *nothing* to do with personal

ERRORS OF HYPER-DISPENSATIONALISM

righteousness during the Church Age. (Rom 3v10) Today the Law is used to show us our sinful condition (Gal 3v24+25). The key to the Law is to love your neighbour (Gal 5v13). The key to *fulfilling* the law is to avoid walking after the flesh. (Rom 8v4) The purpose of the law has changed. Under the OT the main purpose of the law was to affect the Jew's relationship with God. During the Church Age, the main purpose of the law is to directly impact our relationship *with others*, rather than our relationship with God. During the Church Age, men are to keep the law out of love one for another (Rom 13v8-10). As Christians we are to *use* the law *only* when it lines up with Paul's epistles – Read 1 Tim 1v8-11.

But what about ordinances under the law? Read Eph 2v13. Did Christ abolish the Law? No, He abolished 'the law of commandments contained in the ordinances.' The Law itself was not abolished. What were the ordinances that were abolished? These are Sabbath days, holy days, special meats, drinks, circumcision etc. Yet concerning the Law, Paul says we *establish* it and *use it* lawfully. Remember, concerning the Law and the Body of Christ, it has absolutely *nothing* to do with salvation. The Law hasn't ended but the ceremonial part has. Read Col 2v14-16. These OT ordinances *died* when the Lord died. We don't have to worry about what we eat anymore, or what day we worship on, or what holy days we choose to obey or not obey, as we are no longer under the Law. There are many Christians who try to get you *from* Calvary back under Mount Sinai and the Law. They are so legalistic they make the Pharisees look liberal. The Brethren, the Reformed Calvinist and the 'Holiness Club' among others, are typical of this kind of legalistic Christianity. They place heavy burdens on their members. (Mat 23v1-10). When one Christian tries to put another under these kind of burdens, e.g. what to eat, what not to eat, (1 Tim 4v1-3) when and where to worship, etc. *dump them.*

Now the Hyper-Diapers mess their nappy at this point regarding 'ordinances' i.e. water baptism and the Lord's Supper. Read 1 Cor 11v1+2. In the Book of Corinthians, Paul, who tells us to *follow him*, also points out the two ordinances that the Church (the Body of Christ) should do... water baptism, and the Lord's Supper, aka 'Breaking of Bread or Communion' *(and Christians fall out over the wording of that can you believe).* Paul's ordinances we are to *keep.* We don't have to keep Sabbath days, or eat special diets, or keep 'holy' days, but we are to participate in water baptism and the Lord's Supper. These are NT ordinances *not* OT ordinances. Hypers are KJV Bible *rejectors*, they certainly aren't Bible *believers.* Read Gal 2v4-9, also Gal 5v1-4 for some great insight regarding OT ordinances and being brought under bondage.

Another evil teaching from the Hyper-Dispensationalist-cult is their propaganda of telling the Body of Christ that *only* Paul's letters count and you are to disregard all the other Scriptures as being not applicable for today. This is what we Bible Believers call in 'the Greek'... hogwash! Just look at Paul himself blowing the Hyper-Diapers clean out of the water... Rom 15v4, 1 Cor 10v6+11. Hypers just chop up the Bible to fit in with their *heresies*. Remember 2 Tim 3v16... *All* Scripture is given for what? The church, the Body of Christ, can learn from the OT and we have countless examples and ensamples given us to prove it... but not for the Hypers, they can't rightly divide THE BOOK, hence why they are so shallow and miss out on so much. You can get much Church *application* from the OT. Just read Rom 16v25+26, this blows the Hypers to smithereens. (Scriptures of the *prophets*).

Another Hyper-Diaper error – '*When* did the church begin?' –The church which is Christ's Body (Col 1v18+24, Eph 1v22+23), He only has *one* Body (Not 'three/four' like the Hypers believe) See Rom 12v4+5, 1 Cor 12v12+13+20, Eph 2v16, Eph 4v4, Col 3v15. Only a *novice*, someone not grounded in the word of God, could believe that the Church started *after* Paul's conversion. Paul, on a number of occasions, repeatedly stated that he persecuted the Church. In other words, it was *already existing before* he was saved. But to get around this, the Hypers do what? Guess? You got it! They create *'another body'*. There is *only one* Body of Christ. This is another reason why they mess up regarding the Bride of Christ and the Father's wife, Israel. Again, if you don't *rightly* divide that Book, you'll land up teaching *error*. They just *chop up* the Scriptures to suit their heresies. They are always interpreting the Scriptures *privately* (2 Pet 1v20) Paul writes... Phil 3v6 **Concerning zeal, persecuting the church;** (existing *before* he was saved) **touching the righteousness which is in the law, blameless.** 1 Cor 15v9 **For I am the least of the apostles, that am not meet to be called an apostle, because I persecuted the church of God.** (*Before* he was saved the church was existing). Gal 1v13 **For ye have heard of my conversation in time past in the Jews' religion, how that beyond measure I persecuted the church of God, and wasted it**: (*Before* he was saved the church was there already). If the church began with Paul, how could he have persecuted it? Paul not only admitted to persecuting the church, but he also knew that he began preaching the very faith that he once persecuted. (Read Gal 1v23) There were others IN Christ *before* Paul... Note Rom 12v5 **So we, being many, are one body in Christ, and every one members one of another**. Rom 16v7 **Salute Andronicus and Junia, my kinsmen, and my fellowprisoners, who are of note among the apostles, who also were in Christ before me**. (*Before* Paul) Note also John 17v21+23 **IN Christ**. A person IN Christ is a *saved* person and a member of the Body of Christ (remember *one* Body *not* 'two') Hyper-Diapers don't get that the mystery of the Gospel involves Gentiles joining their Jewish brethren *already in the Body*. Redeemed Gentiles become fellow-heirs with the Jews, *not* the other way around. Eph 3v4-6 **Whereby, when ye read, ye may understand my knowledge in the mystery of Christ). Which in other ages was not made known unto the sons of men, as it is now revealed unto his holy apostles and prophets by the Spirit; That the Gentiles should be fellowheirs, and of the same body, and partakers of his promise in Christ by the gospel**: Read also Rom 11v13-17, Eph 2v13-20. These Scriptures *prove* that the Body of Christ *existed before* the 'Apostle to the Gentiles' was even saved. **Study to shew thyself approved unto God, a workman that needeth not to be ashamed, RIGHTLY DIVIDING the word of truth**. 2 Tim 2v15.

More Hyper-Diaper TOSH...

Have mercy upon me, O LORD; for I am weak: O LORD, heal me; for my bones are vexed. Ps 6v2. David's prayer here in v2 is answered in Jer 30v17 **For I will restore health unto thee, and I will heal thee of thy wounds, saith the LORD; because they called thee an Outcast, saying, This is Zion, whom no man seeketh after**. According to the Hyper-Diapers, once you are saved you must NOT confess any more of your future sins to the Lord. MERCY is COMPLETE at Calvary, but we are still told to ...**come boldly unto the throne of grace, that we may obtain mercy, and find grace to help in time of need**. Heb 4v16. So both Ps 6v2 & Heb 4v16 are APPLICABLE for the NT Christian. A Christian who does not plead for mercy, cleansing & forgiveness on a regular basis is out of fellowship with the Lord. You couldn't know Him personally without calling upon Him for mercy, cleansing & forgiveness on a daily basis.

You must rightly divide the Scriptures otherwise you'll never understand the Bible

Obviously the Old Testament & the New Testament are two different 'dispensations', they are NOT the same, & things are different in so many ways. Let's take just one example... diet / meat.

Adam – Gen 1v27-29 – No meat

Noah – Gen 9v1-3 – Every moving thing for meat

Moses – Lev 11v1-7 – Certain animals

ERRORS OF HYPER-DISPENSATIONALISM

Paul – Col 2v16+17, Gal 4v9-12, 1 Tim 4v1-6 – anything but no blood

In Acts 10, we see the transition where Simon Peter is taught that he should not call anything God hath cleansed 'common or unclean' Acts 10v14+15. Today we have Christians telling us what to eat & what not to eat. Some say we should still be eating the Jewish diet. If you don't rightly divide the Scriptures you'll teach all kinds of nonsense, like tongues are for today, you must keep the Sabbath, healing is the same today as it was in the apostolic time, water baptism is necessary for salvation, or, water baptism is not for today, 'prayer is a work', faith alone is the only criteria for salvation in every dispensation like Fake-Ed teaches… try that one on Adam & Eve who didn't require any faith at all in God! You see, the whole thing to understanding the Bible is to *rightly* divide the Scriptures.

Regarding the Hyper-Diapers they all get hung up on baptism, they have a neurotic obsession (**neurotic = abnormally sensitive & obsessive**) with it for some reason. The all-important thing to the Hyper-Diaper is to get rid of Baptist churches. These people are obsessed with this to the point of fanaticism. They get so obsessed with non-water that it's all they can think about, breathe, eat or sleep. They are constantly trying to get Christians to leave 'Baptist' churches (e.g. Colic-Caldwell etc.) & telling them that they were wrong in getting baptised… they're NUTS! The other thing with Hyper-Diapers is that, like all cults, they have to keep adjusting their theology (e.g. Ed-Fake-Pfenny has changed many times from his days with his god Richling until now, where 'he' is the only one right in the world) & keep adjusting their position closer & closer to the Scriptures without abandoning their position in order to save face… PRIDE! Hyper-Diapers follow men like Bullinger, J.C. O'Hare, Stam & Moore who state that only the prison epistles written by Paul after the close of the book of Acts, could be considered as doctrine for the Christian. They also state that the Body found in the book of Acts is NOT the Body of Christ mentioned in Eph 2 + 3. They then go on to say that the 'mystery body' Paul mentions in Eph 2 + 3 did NOT show up until AFTER the close of Acts 28. Both Hyper-Dispensationalism & Calvinism have their foundation in the book of Ephesians. The position changes a bit under O'Hare & he backslid from Bullinger's position because of a number of things. First of all was the very embarrassing (& very obvious) thing which was pointed out to him by some Bible Believing Baptist that 1 Cor 12 is ALREADY dealing with the 'mystery Body' & the members of the Body (1 Cor 12v13) & this epistle was written DURING the Acts period to converts to the Corinthian church. So O'Hare backslid & decided that the Body of Christ began in Acts 18. Acts 18 was dealing with the Corinthian church, & this 'saved face' for the dispensationalist temporarily because they had the 'Body of Christ' beginning in Acts 18 during the Acts period, & yet they still could dump the water baptism. The last cases they found of water baptism in the book of Acts were in Acts 18 & 19, & by dispensationally treating the passage in Acts 19 that dealt with the baptism of Apollos' converts (vs 1-7), they could say that water baptism ended in Acts 18; therefore, the Body of Christ began in Acts 18. Isn't it funny what people get all hung-up on… 'Water' of all things. Perhaps they didn't like baths when they were kids?! So alarm bells should start ringing if you come up against a Christian following men like O'Hare, Baker, Stam, Bullinger & Moore etc. Ruckman calls them 'dry-cleaners' because they hate *water* so much! This modern day cult are deluded fools who are following Satan without even knowing it. Occasionally one will enter your church & try to steal your sheep, so be very aware. The Hyper-Diapers are as bad a cult as the JW's, Mormons & Christadelphians, *worse even!*

Back to 'water'… In Acts 16 Paul baptised converts AFTER he knew about 'the Gospel of the grace of God'. It is also clear from Acts 15 that 'the Gospel of the grace of God' was known to ALL the apostles, for Simon Peter in Acts 15v11 says… **But we believe that through the grace of the Lord Jesus Christ we shall be saved, even as they**. In Acts 16, Paul does not tell him to repent & be baptized in the name of Jesus Christ for the remission of sins, but rather he tells him… **Believe on the Lord Jesus Christ, and thou shalt be saved**… This is the teaching of Ephesians & Romans. So, it is perfectly apparent that in Acts 16, even though Paul knew 'the Gospel of the grace of God', he STILL baptised the convert after getting him saved by grace through faith! Because of this Stam & Baker had to shift position from O'Hare... note Hyper-Diapers keep shifting & squirming all over the place.

Now this whack-head group of heretics teach that the Body of Christ *began* with Paul. They teach more than 'one' Body can you believe (Eli-Colic-Caldwell teaches 3 if not 4 the dumb-cluck). Stam's-ilk makes the Body of Christ from Acts 2 to Acts 9 one Body, & the Body of Christ from Acts 9 on, a *different* Body. This was very embarrassing for Stam & 'the Stammites' (Colic-Caldwell et al.) especially when a Bible Believer pointed out that some of Paul's followers were 'IN Christ' BEFORE Acts 9, BEFORE him! Rom 16v7 **Salute Andronicus and Junia, my kinsmen, and my fellowprisoners, who are of note among the apostles, <u>who also were in Christ before me</u>**. Oh dear, oh dear, oh dear! This drove them nuts so they had to change 'again', & shift their position, & squirm under the fence once more. Do you know what they come up with this time... *'You can be IN Christ without being IN Christ's Body!'* I kid you not! Moron-Moore taught this & Ruckman sacked him! The expression 'IN Christ' is a Pauline expression that deals with the 'mystery' of the Body, yet this CULT of the Hyper-Diapers couldn't allow anybody to be 'IN Christ' before Acts 9, even though PAUL SAID... 'Who were IN Christ BEFORE me!' The issue is this... **WHEN did the Body of Christ start?** Hyper-Diapers do NOT know. Whenever it was, the Hyper-Diapers MUST have it starting 'when & where' it excludes water baptism... remember their fixation about this! Unfortunately the *'Berean Searchlight's' bulb has just blown!* Let's us Bible Believers help them see again. One thing Hyper-Diapers just can't understand is 'dual application' of the Scriptures. Verses doctrinally aimed at the Tribulation (aka Daniel's 70th Week, or Jacob's Trouble), can also refer to the Church Age, e.g. Rev 12v11 – that's a good Church Age doctrine as ever you'll find one. They also go into a *tizzy* when talking about baptism. They say things like "In the Book of Acts they baptised in the name of Jesus not Father, Son & Holy Spirit, hence Matthew is out for the Hyper-Diaper". What they fail to miss, *because of their spiritual blindness*, is the fact that they baptised in the NAME (not 'names') of the Father, Son & Holy Ghost – Mat 28v19. Paul was even baptising in Acts 16 *after* he'd had the revelation of the 'mystery of the grace of God'. Ask a Hyper-Diaper WHEN this Church Age started, they just don't know. So how can the Hyper-Diaper tell you that water baptism is not for this age when he doesn't even know WHEN this age started... *they're nuts man!* It's like a man saying "All the animals couldn't get into the ark!" You ask him how big the ark was & he'll say "I don't know!" So how do you know they couldn't have all got on! Dumb as they come... just like the Hyper-Diaper crowd. If the apostle Paul knew it was wrong to baptise, don't you think he would have told us? Of course he would have! Hyper-Diapers are not serious students of the word of God, they are men followers... e.g. Stam, O'Hare, Richling etc. When Peter found out that a man didn't have to be baptised in water to receive the Holy Ghost, he told us – Acts 11v15-18. Paul would have done the same regarding baptism if it wasn't for this dispensation. Paul baptised converts, & so should we!

We've said it a number of times, but Hyper-Diapers (Stam, Bullinger, Funny-Pfenniger, Colic-Caldwell etc.) believe that a thing cannot be *revealed* until it is *present*, & that if a thing is NOT *revealed*, it is NOT *there!* This is what we Bible Believers call TOSH!

Now the reason I warn you about Hyper-Dispensationalists (aka 'Hyper-Diapers' – e.g. Stam, Bullinger, O'Hare, Richling, Zacher, Baby-Eli, Moron-Moore etc.) is because they are part of a small cult, one of which, likes to try to infiltrate churches & prey on the young in faith to get them to join this cult. That is what they do. Hyper-Diapers DON'T evangelise, witness or preach on the streets, they just sit in their bedrooms in front of their cameras & post YouTube videos trying to tell us how they are right & everyone else is wrong! Beware of this cult!

Ruckman writes... 'We Bible Believing Baptists have taught two things for many years. We have taught that the local church did not begin at Pentecost. This is perfectly clear in the passage in Mat

ERRORS OF HYPER-DISPENSATIONALISM

16 & 18, the calling out of the twelve, & in the commissioning of this local church in Mat 28 & Acts 1. This group has a roll of 120 names on it in Acts 1. It has a treasurer who died & was replaced in Acts 1 & Mat 27. It had a leader who was a spokesman for the group – Simon Peter, Acts 1 & 2. It was a local, called-out, assembly, called out & chosen by the Lord. As such, it was a Jewish church. It certainly had Jews & Gentiles in it after Pentecost. This local church became an organism. It became more than an organisation at Pentecost. It became a *living organism*, & its members were placed IN Christ by a baptism of the Holy Spirit. When Paul says… 'one Spirit… **One Lord, one faith, one baptism** (Eph 4v4+5)…' he can only refer to the same Holy Spirit & to the same baptism that put the Pentecostal disciples, Cornelius' family, the apostle Paul himself, & the Ephesians INTO the Body of Christ – 1 Cor 12v13.

The Lord can work anyway He wants to work! In the Book of Acts we have a 'minefield'… some people have to be baptised to get the Holy Spirit (Acts 2), some get the Holy Spirit BEFORE they are baptised (Acts 10), another man is born again BEFORE he is baptised in water (Acts 9), some people believe & are saved & baptised 'without' receiving the Holy Ghost (see Ruckman's notes in his RRB page 1444 on Acts 8v20 for some enlightenment!), some people get saved & get baptised & DON'T speak in tongues until hands are laid on them (Acts 19). The Body of Christ was throughout! Paul said ONE Spirit, ONE baptism, & ONE Body… not 2, 3 or 4 like the Hypers try to invent! You can't get a Body other than Christ's Body from Acts 2 to Acts 9… that would be 2 'Bodies!'

Were Peter, James & John IN the Body of Christ? This is too much for the Hyper-Diapers & they finally *soil* their diapers. If Peter, James & John were IN the Body of Christ, when did they get IN? Read John 17.

v6 **I have manifested thy name unto the men which thou gavest me out of the world** (There's Peter, James & John): **thine they were, and thou gavest them me; and they have kept thy word.** (There's Peter, James & John)

v9 **I pray for them: I pray not for the world, but for them which thou hast given me;** (There's Peter, James & John) **for they are thine.**

v10 **And all mine are thine, and thine are mine; and I am glorified in them.** (There's Peter, James & John)

v14-18 - (There's Peter, James & John)

Now watch it… v21 **That they all may be one** (Not two, ONE!); **as thou, Father, art in me, and I in thee, that they also may be one in us** (How do you get 'two' bodies & 'two' Spirit's out of that? … & how do you get Peter, James & John IN Christ yet NOT in His 'Body?' You can't! ONE Body, ONE Spirit!): **that the world may believe that thou hast sent me.**

v23 **I in them, and thou in me, that they may be made perfect in one;** They were IN the Body of Christ.

This is the difference between a Bible Believer & a Bible denying, Bible rejecting Hyper-Diaper.

Us Bible Believers BELIEVE that Jesus meant what He said & said what He meant, that He was IN Peter, James & John, & that Peter, James & John were going to be IN Him… which would take place at Pentecost. How could Christ have gotten INTO THEM 'before' then? He had NO 'Body' for them to be 'IN' at that time, & was physically sitting opposite to them! At Pentecost the Holy Spirit baptised them INTO His Body (1 Cor 12v13). He didn't come INTO them when He arose from the dead, He simply breathed upon them & said… …**Receive ye the Holy Ghost**: John 20v22. There is ONLY ONE 'baptism' that saves.

CHRISTIAN SOLDIER'S BATTLE NOTES

Now how about this verse for a Hyper-Diaper DESTROYER! Eph 2v19+20 **Now therefore ye are no more strangers and foreigners, but fellowcitizens with the saints, and of the household of God; And are built upon the <u>foundation of the apostles</u> and prophets, Jesus Christ himself being the chief corner stone;** The apostles were IN the Body of Christ & there are prophets IN the Body of Christ (Eph 4v11+12). The apostles were IN the Body of Christ therefore BEFORE Acts 9 & BEFORE Paul! These verses blew Moron-Moore's brains out, he just couldn't cope with them, neither could Stam, Bullinger, Baker or O'Hare.

Ready for another blow out boys...? Here we go... back to Eph 2v11-15 **Wherefore remember, that ye being in time past Gentiles in the flesh, who are called Uncircumcision by that which is called the Circumcision in the flesh made by hands; That at that time ye were without Christ, being aliens from the commonwealth of Israel, and strangers from the covenants of promise, having no hope, and without God in the world: But now in Christ Jesus ye who sometimes were far off are <u>made nigh by the blood of Christ</u>. For he is our peace, who hath made both one, and hath broken down the middle wall of partition between us; Having abolished in his flesh the enmity, even the law of commandments contained in ordinances; for to make in himself of twain one new man, so making peace**; Notice in v11, Paul is discussing the household of God & the habitation, the foundation of the building, & was making reference to what?... the Body of Christ! Note also, we are made nigh by what? The Blood of Christ! When was this? At the Cross!

Eph 2v16-18 **And that he might reconcile both unto God <u>in one body by the cross</u>, having slain the enmity thereby: And came and preached peace to you which were afar off, and to them that were nigh. For through him we both have access by one Spirit unto the Father.**

... & all this nonsense about *'there weren't any Gentiles in Acts 1, 2 & 3, so there couldn't be any Body here because the Body is a joint Body blah blah blah'* is just a load of old Hyper-Diaper TOSH! The fact that Gentiles didn't enter that Body until they got saved in Acts 10 & in Acts 8 (the Ethiopian eunuch) & the fact that pure Gentiles who weren't Jewish proselytes didn't get INTO that Body until Acts 13, 14, 15 & 16 does NOT amount to a hill of beans! **<u>The way was made for them to get in there when Jesus Christ died on the cross!</u>** Eph 2v16 **And that he might reconcile both unto God <u>in one body by the cross,</u> having slain the enmity thereby: And came and preached peace to you which were afar off, and to them that were nigh**. It got preached first at Jerusalem to a bunch of Jews & then to those 'afar off', the Gentiles! **For through him we both have access by one Spirit unto the Father.** Eph 2v18. Paul told you that the ONE Spirit that gave the Ephesian-Gentile-mystery-Body-people access to the Father, gave the Jewish-Pentecostal-apostles access to the Father following the crucifixion.

The Body of Christ was formed with the death of Christ on the Cross. The fact that the Body first contained JEWS ONLY means absolutely nothing! It was destined to have Jews & Gentiles in it, & this is the mystery that was revealed to Paul after Acts 9. The fact that it was revealed to Paul after Acts 8 has no bearing upon WHEN IT STARTED! The Body was there three years BEFORE Paul was saved. His kinsmen were IN Christ BEFORE he was IN Christ. He persecuted Christ in the person of the saints in Acts 7 & 8 because they were part of the Body of Christ already in existence. This Body is called 'the church of God' in Gal 1v13 & we are told in 1 Cor 10, 11 & 12 that the church of God is composed Jew & Gentile (1 Cor 12v13).

Let Ruckman sum up for us...

Take heed as to what the Hyper-Diaper-CULT teaches...

1) There is a period of time called 'The grace of God' which began in Acts 9 (Stam, Baker, Moron-Moore, Watkins, Colic-Caldwell & cult) or in Acts 18 (O'Hare etc.), or in Acts 28 (Bullinger,

ERRORS OF HYPER-DISPENSATIONALISM

Ballinger etc.)

2) Water baptism is NOT for 'this age' since 'this age' began in Acts 9, or Acts 13, or Acts 18, or Acts 28

3) Bible Believing Baptists are heretics who do not follow 'Pauline' teaching 1 Tim 1v16

4) Since Paul did not 'command' anyone to be baptised it must be unscriptural

5) Since Paul was not 'sent to baptise' water baptism is pre-Pauline – 1 Cor 1

6) The 'one baptism' of Eph 4 automatically cancels water baptism (Moron-Moore, Stam, Sharpe, Baker, Baby-Eli)

The Bible rebuke of the Hyper-Diaper-CULT...

1) The 'dispensation' of Eph 3v2 was the grace which God gave to Paul to preach (Eph 3v7, 1 Cor 3v10, Col 1v29). Grace was 'dispensed' to him. The 'grace of God' is found in EVERY period of time – Gen 6v8, Exod 33v13

2) The age of the ONE BODY & the 'church of the ONE BODY', began in Mat 27 (See Eph 2v12+16) with 12 apostles IN Christ (Rom 16v7) BEFORE Paul was saved (John 17v21+23)

3) Paul was baptised in water (Acts 9v18), & baptised some of his converts (Acts 16v33, 18v8, 1 Cor 1v14-16), even though he was an evangelist

4) Paul 'commanded no one' to attend church, pass out tracts, proselyte Baptists who are already saved, or argue about water baptism

5) He DID baptise (1 Cor 1v14-16) & only thanked God that people weren't baptised in his name (1 Cor 1v14-18). Paul was not sent by Mark 16v16-18, but he is the ONLY apostle who fulfilled that commission

6) The Corinthian converts who were baptised by ONE Spirit into ONE Body (1 Cor 12v13) were baptised in water – Acts 18v8

The Hyper-Diaper-CULT'S perverted teaching on Eph 4v5...

1) Stam, Baker, Bullinger, Moron-Moore, Baby-Eli etc. ALL take Eph 4v4+5 out of the context in which it appears (as any Campbellite will also do) & pretend that it is talking about 'water baptism' being replaced by Spirit baptism. This explains why 95% of those in any Hyper-Diaper congregation are ex-Baptists

2) The context of Eph 4v4-6 is the unity of the Body of Christ, NOT 'disunity' caused by carnal Christians who say 'I am of Christ...' (1 Cor 1v12)

3) The same baptism that put Paul INTO Christ ('WE' – 1 Cor 12v13) put Gentile believers (Corinth, Ephesus etc.) INTO Christ

4) The same baptism that put 'The Twelve Apostles' INTO Christ (Acts 1v5) put the Roman converts INTO Christ (Rom 6v1-3, Rom 16v7)

False teachings of the Hyper-Diaper-CULT...

1) Peter & Paul preached different Gospels. If they did then Peter was CURSED – Gal 1v8+9. God taught Peter the Gospel in Acts 10v43, which he publicly acknowledges in Acts 15v11, while all

are practising water baptism

2) Repentance should NOT be preached in this age. Paul preached it constantly (Acts 20v21) & asked exactly what John the Baptist asked for when he preached it (Acts 26v20). Paul did this after writing Romans 16v25+26

3) The Body could not have been at Pentecost because no one mentioned it! Neither did anyone mention the complete abolition of the Law (Levitical) or the fulfilling of the Law (Acts 13v38+39) though both (Col 2v14-16) were accomplished FACTS (Gal 3v13)

4) Mat 28v19+20 is limited to the Tribulation. Pure conjecture! (1 Tim 6v3 – written to the saints in the ONE Body). The 'all things' of Mat 28v20 does NOT include all pre-crucifixion instruction, which is apparent to anyone by comparing Mat 10v1-10 with Mat 28v19+20 & John 13-17. The Tribulation had NOT begun in A.D. 33... note 'unto the end of the world'. Then he sinned against God in not confessing it. He sinned against you in not telling you straight out in plain clear-cut commands (note 1 Thes 5 & Rom 14) not to make the same mistake. Every Christian leader in the New Testament was baptised in water & none of them repented of such an action!

Some more great info destroying the Hyper-Diaper CULT!

1) 1 Cor 12v27+28 – The church, the Body of Christ (ONE Body), started (FIRST) with Jewish apostles
2) Eph 2v16-20 – The church is built upon the foundation of the apostles (Jewish)
3) Col 1v18 – Who is the HEAD? Not Paul (Mid-Acts), but Christ! Jesus Christ started the church NOT Paul. Hyper-Diapers get so confused with their heresies & multiple 'Bodies' (Baby-Eli) that they forget/reject Christ & follow Paul instead – they have a terminal disease called 'Paulitus'
4) Eph 4v5+11+12 – 'Apostles' for edifying the Body of Christ because THEY are IN it. The Body of Christ is made up of Jew & Gentile
5) The foundational verse for the Hyper-Diapers is 1 Cor 3v10... but they stop at v10 & don't read v11 – READ IT! Jesus Christ is THE foundation NOT Paul. Paul was the 'foundation' of the 'local' church NOT the Body of Christ! Hypers can't read simple English! The foundation of the Body of Christ is Jesus Christ
6) Another proof text the Hypers use is 1 Tim 1v16 – 'me first & pattern' – But it does NOT say that Paul was FIRST IN the Body of Christ... Paul is a 'pattern' of longsuffering
7) Christians were IN Christ BEFORE Paul – Acts 8v1+3 (note the word church), Acts 15v4, Rom 1v16
8) No one knew 'what' the Body of Christ was before Paul, but it WAS before Paul, made up of Jew & Gentile
9) What was the mystery revealed to Paul? – Eph 3v1-6... Jew & Gentile IN the Body of Christ
10) ONE Body starting at the Cross (NOT Paul, Mid Acts TOSH) – Eph 2v11
11) Jews were IN Christ Gal 1v22 (Jews in 'Judea'), Gal 3v26-28
12) Jews & Gentiles are both redeemed the same way – 1 Pet 1v18+19, Luke 22v20

How to spot a Hyper-Dispensationalist a.k.a. 'Hyper-Diaper'

Here are some of the signs to look out for...

1) **Prayer is a work** – if you **ask** God to save you, He'll **send you to Hell** because you're *working* for your salvation – TOSH!
2) **Don't preach 'Repentance'** - even though their hero Paul DID – Acts 20v21
3) **Water Baptism and Communion** – are finished with today - TOSH!

ERRORS OF HYPER-DISPENSATIONALISM

4) **Eternal Security** – is found in every dispensation. You CAN lose your salvation in the OT and in the Tribulation.
5) **The Body of Christ** – started with Paul in Acts 9 – Known as 'Mid-Acts' nonsense
6) **Rom 10v9-17 is NOT the Gospel** – They don't understand dual application or the significance of Biblical numerics.
7) **Don't confess your sins AFTER you're saved** – Yes you should! I do it all the time with the Lord.
8) **They believe in a 'mental ascent' Gospel** – To get saved you have to *mentally ascend*
9) **The Body of Christ is not the Bride of Christ** – They think there is more than ONE Body
10) **Ruckman isn't saved because he *called upon* God to save him, he *asked* Jesus Christ to save him**

Now let's run a few verses to blow this CULT clear out of the water...

Gal 1v11-19 – Paul's Gospel was revealed to him by none other than Jesus Christ Himself. Look at the time Jesus spent with Paul. Paul didn't learn it from 'men'.

1 Cor 3v10 – the proof text for the Hypers, yet they stop short, read the NEXT verse! (v11) – Paul is NOT *the foundation*, Jesus Christ IS. The Body of Christ did NOT start with Paul in Acts 9.

Eph 2v16 – **the Church started AT THE CROSS**, not with Paul in Acts 9.

Col 1v18+24, Eph 1v22+23 (1 Cor 12v13, Rom 6v3, Gal 3v27) – The Body of Christ is the Church. You get baptised INTO Christ through the Spirit of God.

Gal 1v13 – the Church existed BEFORE Paul.

Col 1v20-22 – **The Church started at the Cross**, through the death of the Testator (Heb 9v16), you get in it through the shed Blood of Jesus Christ. OT saints were NOT in the Body of Christ.

Acts 8v1+3 – The Church existed BEFORE Paul.

Rom 16v7 – The Church, the Body of Christ existed BEFORE Paul.

Rom 12v4, Rom 12v5, 1 Cor 10v17, 1 Cor 12v12, 1 Cor 12v13, 1 Cor 12v20, Eph 2v16, Eph 4v4, Col 3v15 - There is only ONE Body. Some Hypers think that 'in the Lord' always means IN Christ... it certainly doesn't. Look up the term and see how many times IN THE LORD appears IN the OT and also during the Tribulation). You either RIGHTLY DIVIDE (2 Tim 2v15) or WRONGLY JOIN as the Hypers do all the time.

Eph 3v1-11 (note v6) Jew and Gentile IN ONE BODY, the SAME body, not two bodies.

Col 1v26+27, Eph 1v9+10 – Jew and Gentile in ONE Body was a mystery hidden in all other ages, it was a mystery revealed to Paul.

The apostles were IN CHRIST.

Gal 1v22 – JEWS were IN CHRIST – note churches in Judaea.

1 Cor 12v13+27+28, John 17v21-23, Eph 4v11+12 – **The apostles were IN THE BODY OF CHRIST.**

Eph 2v13-20 – ONE Body, starting AT THE CROSS, not with Paul, NOT 'Mid-Acts'.

NOTES

THE GOSPEL MESSAGE

Realise you are a sinner - **For all have sinned, and come short of the glory of God**; (Rom 3v23)

Death is a result of sin - **For the wages of sin is death; but the gift of God is eternal life through Jesus Christ our Lord.** (Rom 6v23)

You need a Saviour - **For unto you is born this day in the city of David a Saviour, which is Christ the Lord.** (Luke 2v11)

You **can't save** yourself – **For by grace are ye saved through faith; and that not of yourselves: it is the gift of God: Not of works, lest any man should boast.** (Eph 2v8+9)

Only Blood can wash away your sin – **In whom we have redemption through his blood, even the forgiveness of sins: (Col 1v14) But if we walk in the light, as he is in the light, we have fellowship one with another, and the blood of Jesus Christ his Son cleanseth us from all sin. (I John 1v7) Forasmuch as ye know that ye were not redeemed with corruptible things, as silver and gold, from your vain conversation received by tradition from your fathers; But with the precious blood of Christ, as of a lamb without blemish and without spot:** (I Pet 1v18+19)

There is only one Mediator - **For there is one God, and one mediator between God and men, the man Christ Jesus;** (I Tim 2v5)

God loved you so much - **For God so loved the world, that he gave his only begotten Son, that whosoever believeth in him should not perish, but have everlasting life.** (John 3v16)

It's all about His death, burial and resurrection - **Moreover, brethren, I declare unto you the gospel which I preached unto you, which also ye have received, and wherein ye stand; For I delivered unto you first of all that which I also received, how that Christ died for our sins according to the scriptures; And that he was buried, and that he rose again the third day according to the scriptures:** (I Cor 15v1+3+4)

Christ is the only way - **Jesus saith unto him, I am the way, the truth, and the life: no man cometh unto the Father, but by me.** (John 14v6)

So are you saved? - **And they said, Believe on the Lord Jesus Christ, and thou shalt be saved, and thy house.** (Acts 16v31)

If you die without Him... **He that believeth on him is not condemned: but he that believeth not is condemned already, because he hath not believed in the name of the only begotten Son of God.** (John 3v18) **He that believeth on the Son hath everlasting life: and he that believeth not the Son shall not see life; but the wrath of God abideth on him.** (John 3v36) **The wicked shall be turned into hell, and all the nations that forget God.** (Ps 9v17)

You have everything to gain - **But as it is written, Eye hath not seen, nor ear heard, neither have entered into the heart of man, the things which God hath prepared for them that love him.** (I Cor 2v9)

So what are you waiting for? *Get saved today!* Ask the Lord Jesus Christ to forgive you of all your sins right now and come and save you. You need to do this from your heart *not* from your head - **That if thou shalt confess with thy mouth the Lord Jesus, and shalt believe in thine heart that God hath raised him from the dead, thou shalt be saved**. (Rom 10v9)

You *cannot* get saved without the Blood of Christ

Eph 2v13 **But now in Christ Jesus ye who sometimes were far off are made nigh by the blood of Christ**.

Col 1v20 **And, having made peace through the blood of his cross, by him to reconcile all things unto himself; by him, I say, whether they be things in earth, or things in heaven**.

Heb 9v12-14 **Neither by the blood of goats and calves, but by his own blood he entered in once into the holy place, having obtained eternal redemption for us. For if the blood of bulls and of goats, and the ashes of an heifer sprinkling the unclean, sanctifieth to the purifying of the flesh: How much more shall the blood of Christ, who through the eternal Spirit offered himself without spot to God, purge your conscience from dead works to serve the living God?**

Heb 10v1 **For the law having a shadow of good things to come, and not the very image of the things, can never with those sacrifices which they offered year by year continually make the comers thereunto perfect**. Only the Blood of Jesus Christ can make you *perfect*. v4 **For it is not possible that the blood of bulls and of goats should take away sins**. Only the Blood of Jesus Christ can take away your sins. v11 **And every priest standeth daily ministering and offering oftentimes the same sacrifices, which can never take away sins**: *'works and sacrifices' can never take away your sins*. v12 **But this man, after he had offered one sacrifice for sins for ever, sat down on the right hand of God**; Jesus' sacrifice was once only and it was *perfect*, never to repeated. v14 **For by one offering he hath perfected for ever them that are sanctified**. v17 **And their sins and iniquities will I remember no more**. By applying the Blood of Christ, your sins are no longer remembered, they are forgiven and forgotten. v19 **Having therefore, brethren, boldness to enter into the holiest by the blood of Jesus**,

1 Pet 1v2 **Elect according to the foreknowledge of God the Father, through sanctification of the Spirit, unto obedience and sprinkling of the blood of Jesus Christ: Grace unto you, and peace, be multiplied**. Notice *when* you get *elected*... when the Blood of Christ is applied, that is *when* you are sanctified, and that happens *in time* not in eternity, hence, no-one is *elect* and placed into the Body of Christ *before* Gen 1v1.

1 John 1v7 **But if we walk in the light, as he is in the light, we have fellowship one with another, and the blood of Jesus Christ his Son cleanseth us from all sin**. There isn't one sin that the Blood of Christ *cannot* cleanse. No matter what you have done, the Blood of Christ can wash away all your sins... if you just put your faith and trust in the Lord.

1 Pet 1v18+19 **Forasmuch as ye know that ye were not redeemed with corruptible things, as silver and gold, from your vain conversation received by tradition from your fathers; But with the precious blood of Christ, as of a lamb without blemish and without spot**: If you are *not* redeemed with something 'corruptible' you must be redeemed with something *incorruptible*, and that is the Blood of the Lord Jesus Christ.

Acts 20v28 **Take heed therefore unto yourselves, and to all the flock, over the which the Holy Ghost hath made you overseers, to feed the church of God, which he hath purchased with his own blood**. Note it is God's Blood.

GOSPEL MESSAGE

Rom 3v24-26 **Being justified freely by his grace through the redemption that is in Christ Jesus: Whom God hath set forth to be a propitiation through faith in his blood, to declare his righteousness for the remission of sins that are past, through the forbearance of God; To declare, I say, at this time his righteousness: that he might be just, and the justifier of him which believeth in Jesus**.

Rom 5v9 **Much more then, being now justified by his blood, we shall be saved from wrath through him**. Nothing else can justify you, not water (baptism), sacraments, works, penance, tongues etc. You are saved from God's wrath by the Blood of Jesus Christ. Exo 12v13 ...**and when I see the blood, I will pass over you**... What a picture the Blood was at the Passover pointing to the Blood of Christ to come. Note also a very interesting verse in Exo 12v3 **Speak ye unto all the congregation of Israel, saying, In the tenth day of this month they shall take to them every man a lamb**... showing you that Calvin's 'Limited Atonement' is tosh and a heresy taught by Christians who can't *read* their Bibles.

When are you saved?

You are saved the moment you quit trusting your own righteousness to get you to Heaven, and start trusting the righteousness of Jesus Christ.

For he hath made him to be sin for us, who knew no sin; that we might be made the righteousness of God in him. (2 Cor 5v21)

Scriptures against *salvation by works* – Eph 2v8+9, Gal 3v21-29, Titus 3v5

Scriptures against *salvation by the Law* – Rom 10v4, Rom 7v4, Gal 5v4, Gal 2v16, Gal 3v11, John 1v7

Evangelism – getting the Gospel out to sinners.

From the moment I was saved back in 1989, I wanted to get this wonderful Gospel message out to sinners wherever I would meet them. I've been doing that now for over 27 years.

There are so many ways to get the Gospel out, e.g. street preaching, tracting, personal one on one conversations, through CDs and DVDs, film, radio, books, YouTube, the Internet, social media, schools work, literature tables down town, writing letters, cards, using advertising billboards etc. I'm sure you could come up with lots more examples, but the main thing is that every Christian ought to be reaching lost sinners with the Gospel. *Are you?* If not, make a start today. I used to preach on the streets once a week for years, in major cities such as Birmingham and Chester, among other places. Our ministry has changed somewhat over the last ten years or so. Preaching on the streets is more difficult these days, as you're up against the sodomites, Muslims and 'the Government,' all trying to cause you problems and catch you out. 'Free speech' is a joke here in England. If you are a street preacher, or thinking about it, **keep Gospel focused** and don't get drawn into discussions about sodomy, Islam or feminism etc. **Just preach the Gospel**, read the Scriptures, and ask God to give you opportunities to have conversations with those who are seeking the meaning of life. The Gospel message is ***the*** most important message the Christian can tell this dying world.

I have also noticed in these last days, that some Christian street preachers see you as an *inferior* Christian if you *don't* preach on the streets. This type of Christian is just an idiot, don't bother wasting your time with them. The Lord calls us all in different ways, and gives us different talents to fulfil his work. Just make yourself available for the Lord, asking Him to open and close doors according to His purpose (see the chapter on 'Knowing God's will for your life'). If you're good at computers, use them and technology to get the Gospel out. *Don't waste your talent!*

Every Christian ought to carry ***tracts*** on them. It's a great way of getting the Gospel out, whether you pass the tract onto another person, push it through letterboxes, leave it in phone boxes, on benches etc. Sow the seed of the word of God everywhere you go, from café's, doctor's surgeries, dentist receptions, libraries, and all public places. Be very careful when giving tracts to children, for *obvious* reasons these days. Don't stand in front of schools giving out tracts. This will only get you in trouble with the local authorities and the police. *Be wise!*

Here at **Time for Truth!** we produce high quality tracts as *cheap* as our printer can print them!

Through our website (**www.timefortruth.co.uk**), tracts, and CD sermon ministry, we receive emails and letters every week, from all around the world. It is very exciting. Our front room can look like a Post Office, with all the parcels, tracts, books, Bibles and CDs we're sending out. I love seeing parcels of literature being distributed all over the world. We are just a small ministry here in England, doing what we can, with what the Lord gives us.

Our focus hasn't changed since starting **Time for Truth!** back in 1997 ...*getting the Gospel out to sinners!*

NOTES

NOTES

A FEW TIPS THAT MAY HELP YOU...

Making notes in your Bible

Whatever happens, invest your money in a KJV (aka AV) Cambridge wide margin Bible, it's the best you can get.

http://www.timefortruth.co.uk/cambridge-bibles/

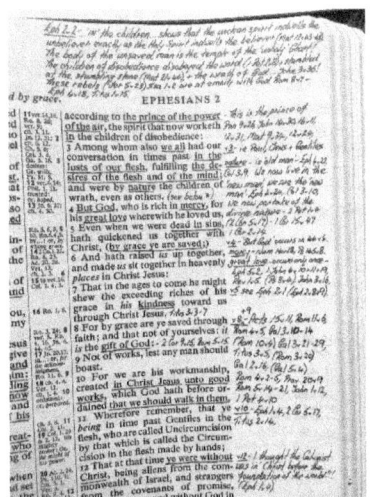

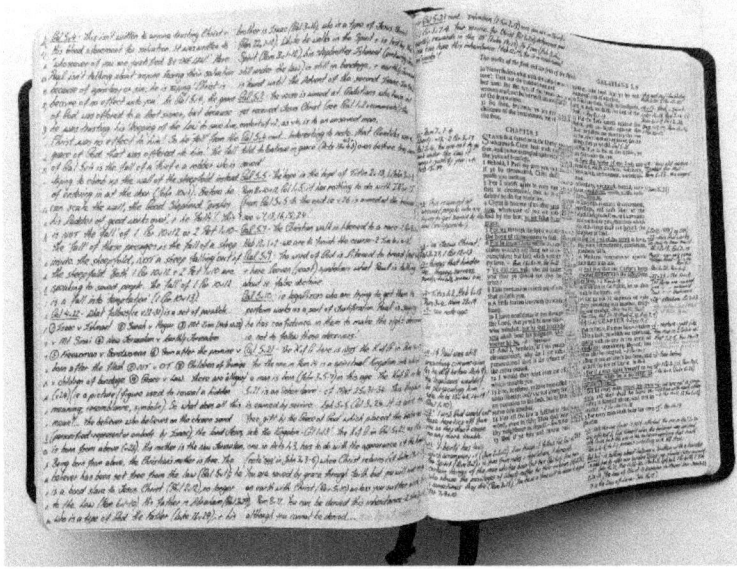

This is my own KJV Cambridge wide margin Bible

CHRISTIAN SOLDIER'S BATTLE NOTES

I try to write as many cross references next to the relevant verses as I can. With the full pages available in my Bible, I try to write as succinctly as possible. I cannot stress enough, that if you are a Christian Soldier on the frontline of ministry, a wide margin Bible is imperative. Too many Christians waste too many years without one, gathering notes elsewhere, then it suddenly hits them that they should have *started* by making notes in their Bibles. This is one of the most important pieces of advice I can pass on to you.

Need extra space?

If you're like me, you'll run out of room pretty quickly and need extra space to put your notes and cross references. I have bought a few **Leuchtturm 1917 master classic notebooks** (approx. size is 31cm x22cm). They are quite expensive, but they're the best I've found for what I need. Follow the link to view them.

https://shop.timefortruth.co.uk/tft-books.html

I put a note at the side of the relevant verse in my Bible, which says '**see <u>EN</u> pg 7**' – which means that for extra cross references and information, turn to page 7 (or whatever page number it is) in the <u>E</u>xtra <u>N</u>otes **Leuchtturm** notebook.

This is my personal **Leuchtturm** A4 ruled notebook which I use. I write on the label on the front cover the name of the book of the Bible I am studying. Here, it is **Revelation - Extra Notes (EN).**

TIPS

I use three types of pens for my Bible study notes. The first is 005 - ZIG-Millennium or Marvy UCHIDA 005. I have tried lots of different ones, but I have found these to be the best. You can purchase these via the TfT! website. I use these pens (different colours) for all the notes I write in my Bible. The ink does not bleed through the page.

http://www.timefortruth.co.uk/catalogue.php?item=37

For the notes I write in my **Leuchtturm** A4 notebook, I use an **Italix Parsons Essential** ink pen with a *medium oblique italic* nib.

http://www.mrpen.co.uk/contents/en-uk/d184.html

Postscript... To finish with, I hope this book has been a great help to you. There are going to be times in your Christian walk when you feel lonely, isolated, rejected, and feel like giving up, as the path seems so difficult (1 Sam 30v6). *You are not alone!* (Rom 11v3+4). You will get disappointed and frustrated with people, especially Christians close to you (2 Tim 4v10, Acts 15v39). There will be times when everything seems to be going wrong, no matter how hard you try (James 1v2-6). Don't worry or fret, all this is normal. These are the times when we are to draw closer to the Lord and lean on Him more than ever (Ps 73v28). The Christian life certainly isn't easy, but it's worth it. It is an *adventure*, but includes hardships, trials and temptations along the way, yet through it all, we can still find an amazing amount of peace and joy (Neh 8v10, John 14v27, John 16v33, Phil 4v7, Col 3v15). The key to living a *successful* life is to get as close to the Lord Jesus Christ as you can. *Most Christians miss that*. The closer you are to the Lord, the less you'll worry (1 John 4v18), and *worldliness* (James 4v4, 1 John 2v15-17, Mat 6v24) *and compromise* won't be such a problem (Gal 5v16).

If you can **work in a team** that is dedicated to serving the Lord, this will be a great benefit to you. *Build one if you need to!* We all *need* each other, and sharing burdens and problems together is such a blessing, rather than trying to carry them all alone. We should encourage each other on a regular basis. *What encouragement have you given recently and to whom?* When was the last time you sent a letter, an email or called someone just to encourage them along the way and ask if they needed any help? By doing this, you are serving the Lord.

When things go wrong, *and they will at times* (Gal 5v7, Heb 12v1), run to the Lord for help, guidance, comfort and protection (Ps 31v19-21+24, Prov 31v21). Get into the Scriptures, seeking the Lord through them (John 5v39).

Only He can truly satisfy (2 Cor 3v5, Ps 42). Don't *build your home* down here (John 14v1-3). Realise that soon we shall all leave this world behind, and **forever** be with the Lord. (1 Thes 4v11-18).

I do love life, but I struggle through much of it. I try to do what is right, but fail many times (Rom 7v14-25). **I want to know more of God**, *not* more *about* God, and this takes time and effort in reading the Scriptures and in prayer. Running a ministry, church and business, and all that entails, consumes much of my time.

I have also met a few amazing people in my life, that have helped and inspired me, and I am very thankful to the Lord for bringing us together, in whatever way. I have an incredible wife and two amazing best friends. I have it very good in life, all of which I thank the Lord for (James 1v17, 1 Thes 5v18).

There is much I see in today's world, and church, that I detest. I'm just 'Mr Average' struggling through life, trying to do what I can with what the Lord gives me, and allows me to do. With the Lord strengthening me, I shall continue to stand upon the truth of God's word until the Rapture.

I would also like to take this opportunity to thank all of you who pray and support the Time for Truth! ministry, we really appreciate it.

If this book has been a blessing to you, please let us know. Why not buy a copy for a friend? Please pass on our details to anyone who you think might benefit from **Time for Truth!**

If you spot any printing errors, or misquoted Scriptures in this book, please email me direct at **john@timefortruth.co.uk** – Lord willing I shall rectify them on the next print run.

NOTES

NOTES

BELOW IS A LIST OF ERRORS IN THE KING JAMES BIBLE

This page is left blank intentionally ;-)

NOTES

351 OLD TESTAMENT PROPHECIES FULFILLED IN JESUS CHRIST

I can't remember where I found this article but it is a good article proving how accurately written the Scriptures are. Only God could write the Holy Bible. Prophecy PROVES that the word of God, the Holy Bible (KJV), is indeed **the scripture of truth** Dan 10v21. No other 'holy' book dare do what the Bible does in regard to prophecy. I'm sure there are plenty more that can be added to this list.

Prophecy	Description	Fulfillment
1. Gen 3v15	Seed of a woman (virgin birth)	Gal 4v4-5, Matt 1v18
2. Gen 3v15	He will bruise Satan's head	Heb 2v14, 1 John 3v8
3. Gen 5v24	The bodily ascension to heaven illustrated	Mark 16v19
4. Gen 9v26-27	The God of Shem will be the Son of Shem	Luke 3v36
5. Gen 12v3	Seed of Abraham will bless all nations	Gal 3v8, Acts 3v25-26
6. Gen 12v7	The Promise made to Abraham's Seed	Gal 3v16
7. Gen 14v18	A priest after the order of Melchizedek	Heb 6v20
8. Gen 14v18	King of Peace and Righteousness	Heb 7v2
9. Gen 14v18	The Last Supper foreshadowed	Matt 26v26-29
10. Gen 17v19	Seed of Isaac (Gen 21v12)	Rom 9v7
11. Gen 22v8	The Lamb of God promised	John 1v29
12. Gen 22v18	As Isaac's seed, will bless all nations	Gal 3v16
13. Gen 26v2-5	The Seed of Isaac promised as the Redeemer	Heb 11v18
14. Gen 28v12	The Bridge to heaven	John 1v51
15. Gen 28v14	The Seed of Jacob	Luke 3v34
16. Gen 49v10	The time of His coming	Luke 2v1-7, Gal 4v4
17. Gen 49v10	The Seed of Judah	Luke 3v33
18. Gen 49v10	Called Shiloh or One Sent	John 17v3
19. Gen 49v10	Messiah to come before Judah lost identity	John 11v47-52
20. Gen 49v10	Unto Him shall the obedience of the people be	John 10v16
21. Exo 3v13-15	The Great "I AM"	John 4v26, 8v58
22. Exo 12v5	A Lamb without blemish	Heb 9v14, 1 Pet 1v19
23. Exo 12v13	The blood of the Lamb saves from wrath	Rom 5v8
24. Exo 12v21-27	Christ is our Passover	1 Cor 5v7
25. Exo 12v46	Not a bone of the Lamb to be broken	John 19v31-36
26. Exo 15v2	His Exaltation predicted as Jesus	Acts 7v55-56
27. Exo 15v11	His Character-Holiness	Luke 1v35, Acts 4v27
28. Exo 17v6	The Spiritual Rock of Israel	1 Cor 10v4
29. Exo 33v19	His Character-Merciful	Luke 1v72
30. Lev 1v2-9	His sacrifice a sweet smelling savor unto God	Eph 5v2
31. Lev 14v11	The leper cleansed-Sign to priesthood	Luke 5v12-14, Acts 6v7
32. Lev 16v15-17	Prefigures Christ's once-for-all death	Heb 9v7-14
33. Lev 16v27	Suffering outside the Camp	Matt 27v33, Heb 13v11-12
34. Lev 17v11	The Blood-the life of the flesh	Matt 26v28, Mark 10v45
35. Lev 17v11	It is the blood that makes atonement	Rom 3v23-24, 1 John 1v7
36. Lev 23v36-37	The Drink-offering "If any man thirst"	John 7v37
37. Num 9v12	Not a bone of Him broken	John 19v31-36
38. Num 21v9	The serpent on a pole-Christ lifted up	John 3v14-18, 12v32
39. Num 24v17	Time "I shall see him, but not now."	John 1v14, Gal 4v4
40. Deut 18v15	"This is of a truth that prophet"	John 6v14

CHRISTIAN SOLDIER'S BATTLE NOTES

41.	Deut 18v15-16	"Had ye believed Moses, ye would have believed me."	John 5v45-47
42.	Deut 18v18	Sent by the Father to speak His word	John 8v28-29
43.	Deut 18v19	Whoever will not hear must bear his sin	Acts 3v22-23
44.	Deut 21v23	Cursed is he that hangs on a tree	Gal 3v10-13
45.	Joshua 5v14-15	The Captain of our salvation	Heb 2v10
46.	Ruth 4v4-10	Christ, our kinsman, has redeemed us	Eph 1v3-7
47.	1 Sam 2v35	A Faithful Priest	Heb 2v17, 3v1-3, 6, 7v24-25
48.	1 Sam 2v10	Shall be an anointed King to the Lord	Matt 28v18, John 12v15
49.	2 Sam 7v12	David's Seed	Matt 1v1
50.	2 Sam 7v13	His Kingdom is everlasting	2 Pet 1v11
51.	2 Sam 7v14a	The Son of God	Luke 1v32, Rom 1v3-4
52.	2 Sam 7v16	David's house established forever	Luke 3v31, Rev 22v16
53.	2 Ki 2v11	The bodily ascension to heaven illustrated	Luke 24v51
54.	1 Chr 17v11	David's Seed	Matt 1v1, 9v27
55.	1 Chr 17v12-13	To reign on David's throne forever	Luke 1v32-33
56.	1 Chr 17v13	"I will be His Father, He...my Son."	Heb 1v5
57.	Job 9v32-33	Mediator between man and God	1 Tim 2v5
58.	Job 19v23-27	The Resurrection predicted	John 5v24-29
59.	Ps 2v1-3	The enmity of kings foreordained	Acts 4v25-28
60.	Ps 2v2	To own the title, Anointed (Christ)	John 1v41, Acts 2v36
61.	Ps 2v6	His Character-Holiness	John 8v46, Rev 3v7
62.	Ps 2v6	To own the title King	Matt 2v2
63.	Ps 2v7	Declared the Beloved Son	Matt 3v17, Rom 1v4
64.	Ps 2v7-8	The Crucifixion and Resurrection intimated	Acts 13v29-33
65.	Ps 2v8-9	Rule the nations with a rod of iron	Rev 2v27, 12v5, 19v15
66.	Ps 2v12	Life comes through faith in Him	John 20v31
67.	Ps 8v2	The mouths of babes perfect His praise	Matt 21v16
68.	Ps 8v5-6	His humiliation and Exaltation	Heb 2v5-9
69.	Ps 9v7-10	Judge the world in righteousness	Acts 17v31
70.	Ps 16v10	Was not to see corruption	Acts 2v31, 13v35
71.	Ps 16v9-11	Was to arise from the dead	John 20v9
72.	Ps 17v15	The resurrection predicted	Luke 24v6
73.	Ps 18v2-3	The horn of salvation	Luke 1v69-71
74.	Ps 22v1	Forsaken because of sins of others	2 Cor 5v21
75.	Ps 22v1	"My God, my God, why hast thou forsaken me?"	Matt 27v46
76.	Ps 22v2	Darkness upon Calvary for three hours	Matt 27v45
77.	Ps 22v7	They shoot out the lip and shake the head	Matt 27v39-44
78.	Ps 22v8	"He trusted on the LORD that he would deliver him"	Matt 27v43
79.	Ps 22v9-10	Born the Savior	Luke 2v7
80.	Ps 22v12-13	They seek His death	John 19v6
81.	Ps 22v14	His blood poured out when they pierced His side	John 19v34
82.	Ps 22v14-15	Suffered agony on Calvary	Mark 15v34-37
83.	Ps 22v15	He thirsted	John 19v28
84.	Ps 22v16	They pierced His hands and His feet	John 19v34-37, 20v27
85.	Ps 22v17-18	Stripped Him before the stares of men	Luke 23v34-35
86.	Ps 22v18	They parted His garments	John 19v23-24
87.	Ps 22v20-21	He committed Himself to God	Luke 23v46
88.	Ps 22v20-21	Satanic power bruising the Redeemer's heel	Heb 2v14
89.	Ps 22v22	His Resurrection declared	John 20v17
90.	Ps 22v27-28	He shall be the governor of the nations	Col 1v16
91.	Ps 22v31	"It is finished"	John 19v30, Heb 10v10-12,14,18
92.	Ps 23v1	"I am the Good Shepherd"	John 10v11, 1 Pet 2v25
93.	Ps 24v3	His Exaltation predicted	Acts 1v11, Phil 2v9
94.	Ps 30v3	His resurrection predicted	Acts 2v32
95.	Ps 31v5	"Into thy hands I commend my spirit"	Luke 23v46

OLD TESTAMENT PROPHECIES FULFILLED IN JESUS CHRIST

#	Reference	Prophecy	Fulfillment
96.	Ps 31v11	His acquaintances fled from Him	Mark 14v50
97.	Ps 31v13	They took counsel to put Him to death	Matt 27v1, John 11v53
98.	Ps 31v14-15	"He trusted in God, let Him deliver him"	Matt 27v43
99.	Ps 34v20	Not a bone of Him broken	John 19v31-36
100.	Ps 35v11	False witnesses rose up against Him	Matt 26v59
101.	Ps 35v19	He was hated without a cause	John 15v25
102.	Ps 38v11	His friends stood afar off	Luke 23v49
103.	Ps 38v12	Enemies try to entangle Him by craft	Mark 14v1, Matt 22v15
104.	Ps 38v12-13	Silent before His accusers	Matt 27v12-14
105.	Ps 38v20	He went about doing good	Acts 10v38
106.	Ps 40v2-5	The joy of His resurrection predicted	John 20v20
107.	Ps 40v6-8	His delight-the will of the Father	John 4v34, Heb 10v5-10
108.	Ps 40v9	He was to preach the Righteousness in Israel	Matt 4v17
109.	Ps 40v14	Confronted by adversaries in the Garden	John 18v4-6
110.	Ps 41v9	Betrayed by a familiar friend	John 13v18
111.	Ps 45v2	Words of Grace come from His lips	John 1v17, Luke 4v22
112.	Ps 45v6	To own the title, God or Elohim	Heb 1v8
113.	Ps 45v7	A special anointing by the Holy Spirit	Matt 3v16, Heb. 1v9
114.	Ps 45v7-8	Called the Christ (Messiah or Anointed)	Luke 2v11
115.	Ps 45v17	His name remembered forever	Eph 1v20-21, Heb. 1v8
116.	Ps 55v12-14	Betrayed by a friend, not an enemy	John 13v18
117.	Ps 55v15	Unrepentant death of the Betrayer	Matt 27v3-5, Acts 1v16-19
118.	Ps 68v18	To give gifts to men	Eph 4v7-16
119.	Ps 68v18	Ascended into Heaven	Luke 24v51
120.	Ps 69v4	Hated without a cause	John 15v25
121.	Ps 69v8	A stranger to own brethren	John 1v11, 7v5
122.	Ps 69v9	Zealous for the Lord's House	John 2v17
123.	Ps 69v14-20	Messiah's anguish of soul before crucifixion	Matt 26v36-45
124.	Ps 69v20	"My soul is exceeding sorrowful"	Matt 26v38
125.	Ps 69v21	Given vinegar in thirst	Matt 27v34
126.	Ps 69v26	The Savior given and smitten by God	John 17v4, 18v11
127.	Ps 72v10-11	Great persons were to visit Him	Matt 2v1-11
128.	Ps 72v16	The corn of wheat to fall into the Ground	John 12v24-25
129.	Ps 72v17	Belief on His name will produce offspring	John 1v12-13
130.	Ps 72v17	All nations shall be blessed by Him	Gal 3v8
131.	Ps 72v17	All nations shall call Him blessed	John 12v13, Rev 5v8-12
132.	Ps 78v1-2	He would teach in parables	Matt 13v34-35
133.	Ps 78v2b	To speak the Wisdom of God with authority	Matt 7v29
134.	Ps 80v17	The Man of God's right hand	Mark 14v61-62
135.	Ps 88	The Suffering and Reproach of Calvary	Matt 27v26-50
136.	Ps 88v8	They stood afar off and watched	Luke 23v49
137.	Ps 89v27	Firstborn	Col 1v15-18
138.	Ps 89v27	Emmanuel to be higher than earthly kings	Luke 1v32-33
139.	Ps 89v35-37	David's Seed, throne, kingdom endure forever	Luke 1v32-33
140.	Ps 89v36-37	His character-Faithfulness	Rev 1v5, 19v11
141.	Ps 90v2	He is from everlasting (Micah 5v2)	John 1v1
142.	Ps 91v11-12	Identified as Messianic, used to tempt Christ	Luke 4v10-11
143.	Ps 97v9	His Exaltation predicted	Acts 1v11, Eph 1v20
144.	Ps 100v5	His character-Goodness	Matt 19v16-17
145.	Ps 102v1-11	The Suffering and Reproach of Calvary	John 19v16-30
146.	Ps 102v25-27	Messiah is the Pre-existent Son	Heb 1v10-12
147.	Ps 109v25	Ridiculed	Matt 27v39
148.	Ps 110v1	Son of David	Matt 22v42-43
149.	Ps 110v1	To ascend to the right-hand of the Father	Mark 16v19
150.	Ps 110v1	David's son called Lord	Matt 22v44-45

CHRISTIAN SOLDIER'S BATTLE NOTES

151.	Ps 110v4	A priest after Melchizedek's order	Heb 6v20
152.	Ps 112v4	His character-Compassionate, Gracious, et al.	Matt 9v36
153.	Ps 118v17-18	Messiah's Resurrection assured	Luke 24v5-7, 1 Cor 15v20
154.	Ps 118v22-23	The rejected stone is Head of the corner	Matt 21v42-43
155.	Ps 118v26a	The Blessed One presented to Israel	Matt 21v9
156.	Ps 118v26b	To come while Temple standing	Matt 21v12-15
157.	Ps 132v11	The Seed of David (the fruit of His Body)	Luke 1v32, Act 2v30
158.	Ps 129v3	He was scourged	Matt 27v26
159.	Ps 138v1-6	The supremacy of David's Seed amazes kings	Matt 2v2-6
160.	Ps 147v3-6	The earthly ministry of Christ described	Luke 4v18
161.	Prov 1v23	He will send the Spirit of God	John 16v7
162.	Prov 8v23	Foreordained from everlasting	Rev 13v8, 1 Pet 1v19-20
163.	Song 5v16	The altogether lovely One	John 1v17
164.	Isa 2v3	He shall teach all nations	John 4v25
165.	Isa 2v4	He shall judge among the nations	John 5v22
166.	Isa 6v1	When Isaiah saw His glory	John 12v40-41
167.	Isa 6v8	The One Sent by God	John 12v38-45
168.	Isa 6v9-10	Parables fall on deaf ears	Matt 13v13-15
169.	Isa 6v9-12	Blinded to Christ and deaf to His words	Acts 28v23-29
170.	Isa 7v14	To be born of a virgin	Luke 1v35
171.	Isa 7v14	To be Emmanuel-God with us	Matt 1v18-23, 1 Tim 3v16
172.	Isa 8v8	Called Emmanuel	Matt 28v20
173.	Isa 8v14	A stone of stumbling, a Rock of offense	1 Pet 2v8
174.	Isa 9v1-2	His ministry to begin in Galilee	Matt 4v12-17
175.	Isa 9v6	A child born-Humanity	Luke 1v31
176.	Isa 9v6	A Son given-Deity	Luke 1v32, John 1v14, 1 Tim 3v16
177.	Isa 9v6	Declared to be the Son of God with power	Rom 1v3-4
178.	Isa 9v6	The Wonderful One	Luke 4v22
179.	Isa 9v6	The Counsellor	Matt 13v54
180.	Isa 9v6	The Mighty God	1 Cor 1v24, Titus 2v3
181.	Isa 9v6	The Everlasting Father	John 8v58, 10v30
182.	Isa 9v6	The Prince of Peace	John 16v33
183.	Isa 9v7	To establish an everlasting kingdom	Luke 1v32-33
184.	Isa 9v7	His Character-Just	John 5v30
185.	Isa 9v7	No end to his Government, Throne, and Peace	Luke 1v32-33
186.	Isa 11v1	Called a Nazarene-the Branch	Matt 2v23
187.	Isa 11v1	A rod out of Jesse-Son of Jesse	Luke 3v23-32
188.	Isa 11v2	Anointed One by the Spirit	Matt 3v16-17, Acts 10v38
189.	Isa 11v2	His Character-Wisdom, Knowledge, et al.	Col 2v3
190.	Isa 11v3	He would know their thoughts	Luke 6v8, John 2v25
191.	Isa 11v4	Judge in righteousness	Acts 17v31
192.	Isa 11v4	Judges with the sword of His mouth	Rev 2v16, 19v11, 15
193.	Isa 11v5	Character Righteous & Faithful	Rev 19v11
194.	Isa 11v10	The Gentiles seek Him	John 12v18-21
195.	Isa 12v2	Called Jesus	Matt 1v21
196.	Isa 22v22	The One given all authority to govern	Rev 3v7
197.	Isa 25v8	The Resurrection predicted	1 Cor 15v54
198.	Isa 26v19	His power of Resurrection predicted	Matt 27v50-54
199.	Isa 28v16	The Messiah is the precious corner stone	Acts 4v11-12
200.	Isa 28v16	The Sure Foundation	1 Cor 3v11, Matt 16v18
201.	Isa 29v13	He indicated hypocritical obedience to His Word	Matt 15v7-9
202.	Isa 29v14	The wise are confounded by the Word	1 Cor 1v18-31
203.	Isa 32v2	A Refuge-A man shall be a hiding place	Matt 23v37
204.	Isa 35v4	He will come and save you	Matt 1v21
205.	Isa 35v5-6	To have a ministry of miracles	Matt 11v2-6

OLD TESTAMENT PROPHECIES FULFILLED IN JESUS CHRIST

#	Reference	Prophecy	Fulfillment
206.	Isa 40v3-4	Preceded by forerunner	John 1v23
207.	Isa 40v9	"Behold your God, your King, the Lamb"	John 1v36, 19v14
208.	Isa 40v10	He will come to reward	Rev 22v12
209.	Isa 40v11	A shepherd-compassionate life-giver	John 10v10-18
210.	Isa 42v1-4	The Servant-as a faithful, patient redeemer	Matt 12v18-21
211.	Isa 42v2	Meek and lowly	Matt 11v28-30
212.	Isa 42v3	He brings hope for the hopeless	John 4
213.	Isa 42v4	The nations shall wait on His teachings	John 12v20-26
214.	Isa 42v6	The Light (salvation) of the Gentiles	Luke 2v32
215.	Isa 42v1-6	His is a worldwide compassion	Matt 28v19-20
216.	Isa 42v7	Blind eyes opened	John 9v25-38
217.	Isa 43v11	He is the only Saviour	Acts 4v12
218.	Isa 44v3	He will send the Spirit of God	John 16v7-13
219.	Isa 45v21-25	He is Lord and Saviour	Phil 3v20, Titus 2v13
220.	Isa 45v23	He will be the Judge	John 5v22, Rom 14v11
221.	Isa 46v9-10	Declares things not yet done	John 13v19
222.	Isa 48v12	The First and the Last	John 1v30, Rev 1v8, 17
223.	Isa 48v16-17	He came as a Teacher	John 3v2
224.	Isa 49v1	Called from the womb-His humanity	Matt 1v18
225.	Isa 49v5	A Servant from the womb	Luke 1v31, Phil 2v7
226.	Isa 49v6	He will restore Israel	Acts 3v19-21, 15v16-17
227.	Isa 49v6	He is Salvation for Israel	Luke 2v29-32
228.	Isa 49v6	He is the Light of the Gentiles	John 8v12, Acts 13v47
229.	Isa 49v6	He is Salvation unto the ends of the earth	Acts 15v7-18
230.	Isa 49v7	He is despised of the Nation	John 1v11, 8v48-49, 19v14-15
231.	Isa 50v3	Heaven is clothed in black at His humiliation	Luke 23v44-45
232.	Isa 50v4	He is a learned counsellor for the weary	Matt 7v29, 11v28-29
233.	Isa 50v5	The Servant bound willingly to obedience	Matt 26v39
234.	Isa 50v6a	"I gave my back to the smiters"	Matt 27v26
235.	Isa 50v6b	He was smitten on the cheeks	Matt 26v67
236.	Isa 50v6c	He was spat upon	Matt 27v30
237.	Isa 52v7	Published good tidings upon mountains	Matt 5v12, 15v29, 28v16
238.	Isa 52v13	The Servant Exalted	Acts 1v8-11, Eph 1v19-22, Phil 2v5-9
239.	Isa 52v14	The Servant shockingly abused	Luke 18v31-34, Matt 26v67-68
240.	Isa 52v15	Nations startled by message of the Servant	Luke 18v31-34, Matt 26v67-68
241.	Isa 52v15	His blood shed sprinkles nations	Heb 9v13-14, Rev 1v5
242.	Isa 53v1	His people would not believe Him	John 12v37-38
243.	Isa 53v2	Appearance of an ordinary man	Phil 2v6-8
244.	Isa 53v3a	Despised	Luke 4v28-29
245.	Isa 53v3b	Rejected	Matt 27v21-23
246.	Isa 53v3c	Great sorrow and grief	Matt 26v37-38, Luke 19v41, Heb 4v15
247.	Isa 53v3d	Men hide from being associated with Him	Mark 14v50-52
248.	Isa 53v4a	He would have a healing ministry	Matt 8v16-17
249.	Isa 53v4b	Thought to be cursed by God	Matt 26v66, 27v41-43
250.	Isa 53v5a	Bears penalty for mankind's iniquities	2 Cor 5v21, Heb 2v9
251.	Isa 53v5b	His sacrifice provides peace between man and God	Col 1v20
252.	Isa 53v5c	His sacrifice would heal man of sin	1 Pet 2v24
253.	Isa 53v6a	He would be the sin-bearer for all mankind	1 John 2v2, 4v10
254.	Isa 53v6b	God's will that He bear sin for all mankind	Gal 1v4
255.	Isa 53v7a	Oppressed and afflicted	Matt 27v27-31
256.	Isa 53v7b	Silent before his accusers	Matt 27v12-14
257.	Isa 53v7c	Sacrificial lamb	John 1v29, 1 Pet 1v18-19
258.	Isa 53v8a	Confined and persecuted	Matt 26v47-27v31
259.	Isa 53v8b	He would be judged	John 18v13-22
260.	Isa 53v8c	Killed	Matt 27v35

CHRISTIAN SOLDIER'S BATTLE NOTES

261.	Isa 53v8d	Dies for the sins of the world	1 John 2v2
262.	Isa 53v9a	Buried in a rich man's grave	Matt 27v57
263.	Isa 53v9b	Innocent and had done no violence	Luke 23v41, John 18v38
264.	Isa 53v9c	No deceit in his mouth	1 Pet 2v22
265.	Isa 53v10a	God's will that He die for mankind	John 18v11
266.	Isa 53v10b	An offering for sin	Matt 20v28, Gal 3v13
267.	Isa 53v10c	Resurrected and live forever	Rom 6v9
268.	Isa 53v10d	He would prosper	John 17v1-5
269.	Isa 53v11a	God fully satisfied with His suffering	John 12v27
270.	Isa 53v11b	God's servant would justify man	Rom 5v8-9, 18-19
271.	Isa 53v11c	The sin-bearer for all mankind	Heb 9v28
272.	Isa 53v12a	Exalted by God because of his sacrifice	Matt 28v18
273.	Isa 53v12b	He would give up his life to save mankind	Luke 23v46
274.	Isa 53v12c	Numbered with the transgressors	Mark 15v27-28
275.	Isa 53v12d	Sin-bearer for all mankind	1 Pet 2v24
276.	Isa 53v12e	Intercede to God in behalf of mankind	Luke 23v34, Rom 8v34
277.	Isa 55v3	Resurrected by God	Acts 13v34
278.	Isa 55v4a	A witness	John 18v37
279.	Isa 55v4b	He is a leader and commander	Heb 2v10
280.	Isa 55v5	God would glorify Him	Acts 3v13
281.	Isa 59v16a	Intercessor between man and God	Matt 10v32
282.	Isa 59v16b	He would come to provide salvation	John 6v40
283.	Isa 59v20	He would come to Zion as their Redeemer	Luke 2v38
284.	Isa 60v1-3	He would show light to the Gentiles	Acts 26v23
285.	Isa 61v1a	The Spirit of God upon him	Matt 3v16-17
286.	Isa 61v1b	The Messiah would preach the good news	Luke 4v16-21
287.	Isa 61v1c	Provide freedom from the bondage of sin	John 8v31-36
288.	Isa 61v1-2a	Proclaim a period of grace	Gal 4v4-5
289.	Jer 23v5-6	Descendant of David	Luke 3v23-31
290.	Jer 23v5-6	The Messiah would be both God and Man	John 13v13, 1 Tim 3v16
291.	Jer 31v22	Born of a virgin	Matt 1v18-20
292.	Jer 31v31	The Messiah would be the new covenant	Matt 26v28
293.	Jer 33v14-15	Descendant of David	Luke 3v23-31
294.	Ezek 34v23-24	Descendant of David	Matt 1v1
295.	Ezek 37v24-25	Descendant of David	Luke 1v31-33
296.	Dan 2v44-45	The Stone that shall break the kingdoms	Matt 21v44
297.	Dan 7v13-14a	He would ascend into heaven	Acts 1v9-11
298.	Dan 7v13-14b	Highly Exalted	Eph 1v20-22
299.	Dan 7v13-14c	His dominion would be everlasting	Luke 1v31-33
300.	Dan 9v24a	To make an end to sins	Gal 1v3-5
301.	Dan 9v24a	To make reconciliation for iniquity	Rom 5v10, 2 Cor 5v18-21
302.	Dan 9v24b	He would be holy	Luke 1v35
303.	Dan 9v25	His announcement	John 12v12-13
304.	Dan 9v26a	Cut off	Matt 16v21, 21v38-39
305.	Dan 9v26b	Die for the sins of the world	Heb 2v9
306.	Dan 9v26c	Killed before the destruction of the temple	Matt 27v50-51
307.	Dan 10v5-6	Messiah in a glorified state	Rev 1v13-16
308.	Hos 11v1	He would be called out of Egypt	Matt 2v15
309.	Hos 13v14	He would defeat death	1 Cor 15v55-57
310.	Joel 2v32	Offer salvation to all mankind	Rom 10v9-13
311.	Jonah 1v17	Death and resurrection of Christ	Matt 12v40, 16v4
312.	Mic 5v2a	Born in Bethlehem	Matt 2v1-6
313.	Mic 5v2b	Ruler in Israel	Luke 1v33
314.	Mic 5v2c	From everlasting	John 8v58
315.	Hag 2v6-9	He would visit the second Temple	Luke 2v27-32

OLD TESTAMENT PROPHECIES FULFILLED IN JESUS CHRIST

#	Reference	Prophecy	Fulfillment
316.	Hag 2v23	Descendant of Zerubbabel	Luke 2v27-32
317.	Zech 3v8	God's servant	John 17v4
318.	Zech 6v12-13	Priest and King	Heb 8v1
319.	Zech 9v9a	Greeted with rejoicing in Jerusalem	Matt 21v8-10
320.	Zech 9v9b	Beheld as King	John 12v12-13
321.	Zech 9v9c	The Messiah would be just	John 5v30
322.	Zech 9v9d	The Messiah would bring salvation	Luke 19v10
323.	Zech 9v9e	The Messiah would be humble	Matt 11v29
324.	Zech 9v9f	Presented to Jerusalem riding on a donkey	Matt 21v6-9
325.	Zech 10v4	The cornerstone	Eph 2v20
326.	Zech 11v4-6a	At His coming, Israel to have unfit leaders	Matt 23v1-4
327.	Zech 11v4-6b	Rejection causes God to remove His protection	Luke 19v41-44
328.	Zech 11v4-6c	Rejected in favour of another king	John 19v13-15
329.	Zech 11v7	Ministry to "poor," the believing remnant	Matt 9v35-36
330.	Zech 11v8a	Unbelief forces Messiah to reject them	Matt 23v33
331.	Zech 11v8b	Despised	Matt 27v20
332.	Zech 11v9	Stops ministering to those who rejected Him	Matt 13v10-11
333.	Zech 11v10-11a	Rejection causes God to remove protection	Luke 19v41-44
334.	Zech 11v10-11b	The Messiah would be God	John 14v7
335.	Zech 11v12-13a	Betrayed for thirty pieces of silver	Matt 26v14-15
336.	Zech 11v12-13b	Rejected	Matt 26v14-15
337.	Zech 11v12-13c	Thirty pieces of silver cast in the house of the Lord	Matt 27v3-5
338.	Zech 11v12-13d	The Messiah would be God	John 12v45
339.	Zech 12v10a	The Messiah's body would be pierced	John 19v34-37
340.	Zech 12v10b	The Messiah would be both God and man	John 10v30
341.	Zech 12v10c	The Messiah would be rejected	John 1v11
342.	Zech 13v7a	God's will He die for mankind	John 18v11
343.	Zech 13v7b	A violent death	Mark 14v27
344.	Zech 13v7c	Both God and man	John 14v9
345.	Zech 13v7d	Israel scattered as a result of rejecting Him	Matt 26v31-56
346.	Zech 14v4	He would return to the Mt. of Olives	Acts 1v11-12
347.	Mal 3v1a	Messenger to prepare the way for Messiah	Mark 1v1-8
348.	Mal 3v1b	Sudden appearance at the temple	Mark 11v15-16
349.	Mal 3v1c	Messenger of the new covenant	Luke 4v43
350.	Mal 4v5	Forerunner in spirit of Elijah	Matt 3v1-3, 11v10-14, 17v11-13
351.	Mal 4v6	Forerunner would turn many to righteousness	Luke 1v16-17

CHRISTIAN SOLDIER'S BATTLE NOTES

JESUS IS NOT THE FATHER!

There is a ridiculous doctrine circulating YouTube by a fringe sect / cult that teaches Jesus Christ is God the Father i.e. the Father is Jesus Christ. This is found nowhere in Scripture and is just one of those doctrines of men / devils (Mat 15v9, Mark 7v7, Col 2v22, 1 Tim 4v1, Heb 13v9). Note also that the word 'doctrines' occurs FIVE times (see chapter on **Biblical numerics**) and is never a reference to anything 'good', as it's always in the negative.

So just to clear things up, the **Godhead** aka the **'Trinity'** is a Biblical doctrine, not one that was created by Roman Catholicism as some Bible illiterates teach. Read my booklet 'Jesus Christ IS God'.

Here are a few verses proving that Jesus Christ is NOT the Father...

Heb 1v5 **For unto which of the angels said he at any time, Thou art my Son** (the Father speaking, a separate Person), **this day have I begotten thee? And again, I will be to him** (the Son, a separate Person) **a Father** (separate Person), **and he shall be to me a Son?** (a separate Person)
6 And again, when he bringeth in the firstbegotten into the world, he saith, And let all the angels of God worship him (The Son, a separate Person).
8 But unto the Son he saith (The Father speaking, a separate Person), **Thy throne, O God** (talking about the Son, a separate Person), **is for ever and ever: a sceptre of righteousness is the sceptre of thy kingdom.**
2 John 1v3 **Grace be with you, mercy, and peace, from God the Father** (a separate Person), **and from the Lord Jesus Christ, the Son** of **the Father,** (Separate Person, It says the Son **of** the Father, NOT the Son who **IS** the Father) **in truth and love.**
1 John 1v3 **That which we have seen and heard declare we unto you, that ye also may have fellowship with us: and truly our fellowship is with the Father, and with his Son Jesus Christ.** The Father is a separate Person to the Son.

Mat 24v36 **But of that day and hour knoweth no man, no, not the angels of heaven, but my Father only.** Does Jesus KNOW the 'day & hour' now? If Jesus didn't know the 'day & hour' then (but does now?), then God would have been double minded, or even 'schizophrenic' when Jesus was on earth wouldn't he, knowing but NOT knowing, because the ONE God was split? It doesn't make sense. The Godhead (aka Trinity) is ONE God but THREE 'separate' Persons... no one FULLY understands the Godhead, if they say they do, then they're LIARS. What would be the point of Jesus being the Father, why not just be Jesus? The 'oneness' doctrine of the Godhead is just another cultish lie spawn from the pit of Hell to sow confusion among believers. Jesus is NOT the Father nor the Holy Spirit, they are separate, but they are all God. It's no accident that **Godhead** (Acts 17v29, Rom 1v20, Col 2v9) appears THREE times in Scripture, & **Almighty God** (Gen 17v1, Ezek 10v5, Rev 19v15) appears THREE times in Scripture... THREE 'separate' persons but ONE God. 1 John 5v7.

Jesus Christ IS God, but Jesus Christ is NOT the Father...
1 John 3v16 **Hereby perceive we the love of God, because he** (God) **laid down his life** (God died? Jesus Christ IS God) **for us: and we ought to lay down our lives for the brethren.**
1 John 5v20 **And we know that the Son of God is come, and hath given us an understanding, that we may know him that is true, and we are in him that is true, even in his Son Jesus Christ. This is the true God, and eternal life.**
Isa 9v6 **For unto us a child is born** (the 'child' was 'born'), **unto us a son is given** (notice the son was 'given' NOT 'born' as He is from everlasting, & had NO beginning - Mic 5v2, John 1v1): **and the government shall be upon his shoulder: and his name shall be called** Wonderful, Counsellor, The

CHRISTIAN SOLDIER'S BATTLE NOTES

mighty God, The everlasting Father (Notice Jesus is CALLED the everlasting Father, it does NOT say He IS the everlasting Father), **The Prince of Peace.**

1 John 1v3 **That which we have seen and heard declare we unto you, that ye also may have fellowship with us: and truly our fellowship is with the Father, and with his Son Jesus Christ.** Jesus is NOT the Father.

2 John 1v3 **Grace be with you, mercy, and peace, from God the Father, and from the Lord Jesus Christ, the Son of the Father, in truth and love.**

The Godhead – by Jack Moorman

Although I don't agree with this guy regarding his teaching on salvation in the different dispensations (like Stauffer also) I thought I'd include his doctrinal statement regarding the Godhead aka the Trinity, which I **do** agree with…

Jack Moorman writes… God is a Trinity. He is not three gods (tritheism). Nor is He one God manifested as three personalities (modalism). He is one God, eternally existing in Three **Persons**, - Father, Son and Holy Spirit. This is a truth impossible to comprehend yet clearly taught in the Bible. These Three are identical in essence, equal in power and glory, having the same attributes and perfections, and being worthy of the same reverence, confidence and submission (Deut 6v4, Mat 28v19+20, Luke 3v22, 2 Cor 13v14, Eph 2v18, 1 John 5v7). *Jesus is NOT the Father.*

Jesus is NOT the Father!

John 5v18 **Therefore the Jews sought the more to kill him, because he not only had broken the sabbath, but said also that God was his Father** (NOT 'He was God the Father in the flesh'), **making himself equal with God.** Jesus is equal with God His Father, but Jesus is certainly NOT God the Father. It's absolutely DUMB to say He is & totally unscriptural. Note too the next few verses (v19-23)… they are **SEPARATE…** 'Persons' (NOT 'People'), it's terminology, & the cults love to play on words to 'get you' to believe what they believe. If anyone says to you that Jesus Christ IS God the Father… **dump them immediately,** switch off, never follow them again, as they will lead you astray in other doctrines too. Remember, rat poison is 95% good food, but it will still kill you. The Trinity (Godhead) was certainly NOT invented by the Roman Catholic Church… it's a Scriptural doctrine found throughout the Bible from Gen – Rev.

Jesus is NOT the Father!

Read John 8v12-16… Now look carefully at the following two verses… 17+18 **It is also written in your law, that the testimony of two men is true. I am one that bear witness of myself, and the Father that sent me beareth witness of me.** THAT'S TWO… Not 'Jesus IS the Father' that would be ONE.

Jesus is NOT the Father!

John 14v23 **Jesus answered and said unto him, If a man love me, he will keep my words: and my Father will love him, and we will come unto him, and make our abode with him.** TWO SEPARATE PERSONS.

Jesus is NOT the Father!

John 3v9-12 **Nicodemus answered and said unto him, How can these things be? Jesus answered and said unto him, Art thou a master of Israel, and knowest not these things? Verily, verily, I say unto thee, We speak that we do know, and testify that we have seen; and ye receive not our witness. If I have told you earthly things, and ye believe not, how shall ye believe, if I tell you of heavenly things?** Who is the WE? Separate Persons!

1 John 5v6-10 This is he that came by water and blood, even Jesus Christ; not by water only, but by

water and blood. And it is the Spirit that beareth witness, because the Spirit is truth. For there are three that bear record in heaven, the Father, the Word, and the Holy Ghost: and these three are one. And there are three that bear witness in earth, the Spirit, and the water, and the blood: and these three agree in one. If we receive the witness of men, the witness of God is greater: for this is the witness of God which he hath testified of his Son. He that believeth on the Son of God hath the witness in himself: he that believeth not God hath made him a liar; because he believeth not the record that God gave of his Son.

John 10v30 **I and my Father are one.** Cf. John 17v11 And **now I am no more in the world, but these are in the world, and I come to thee. Holy Father, keep through thine own name those whom thou hast given me, that they may be one, as we are.** Who is the 'WE?' ONE God, THREE 'separate' Persons.

Jesus is NOT the Father!

John 15v24 **If I had not done among them the works which none other man did, they had not had sin: but now have they both seen and hated both me and my Father.** (NOT 'me' & 'ME'... but, MY Father. NOT 'me' the 'Body' & my Father 'the Soul'). Jesus Christ is NOT the Father, they are separate 'beings'... 'Persons', yet BOTH God. The 'Jesus is the Father' crowd just want to play semantic games. Don't get sucked in.

Here's another one... John 15v26 **But when the Comforter** (the Holy Spirit who IS God – Acts 5v1-4) **is come, whom I** (Jesus Christ who IS God) **will send unto you from the Father** (the Father who IS God – John 4v24), **even the Spirit of truth** (GOD the Holy Spirit), **which proceedeth from the Father** (GOD the Father), **he** (GOD the Father) **shall testify of me** (GOD the Son): THREE God's... not so... 1 x 1 x 1 = 1. ONE God, THREE SEPARATE 'Persons'... 'Beings'... use what terminology you want Mr Semantic. NOT 'modes', NOT 'parts', NOT 'entities'. There isn't one 'person' on planet earth who can fully explain or understand the Godhead aka 'Trinity'. 1 John 5v7. If someone says they can... they are either IN a CULT, or about to form one... BEWARE! The Trinity is certainly NOT a Roman Catholic doctrine. Just because they use the phrase, or even coined it, means absolutely NOTHING. Just because the word doesn't appear in Scripture, means ABSOLUTELY NOTHING. We all use words NOT found in the Bible to try to explain what the Bible is saying.

www.ingramcontent.com/pod-product-compliance
Lightning Source LLC
Chambersburg PA
CBHW080541230426
43663CB00015B/2671